Human-Centered Service Design
for Healthcare Transformation

Mario A. Pfannstiel
Editor

Human-Centered Service Design for Healthcare Transformation

Development, Innovation, Change

 Springer

Editor
Mario A. Pfannstiel
Department of Health Management
Neu Ulm University of Applied Sciences
Neu-Ulm, Bavaria, Germany

ISBN 978-3-031-20170-7   ISBN 978-3-031-20168-4   (eBook)
https://doi.org/10.1007/978-3-031-20168-4

This Springer imprint is published by the registered company Springer Nature Switzerland AG
The registered company address is: Gewerbestrasse 11, 6330 Cham, Switzerland

Preface

Seventy-two well-respected authors and experts collaborated on this edited collection and have incorporated their knowledge and experiences into 25 chapters. Now that all of their work has been compiled, there is the opportunity to reflect on it overall and draw conclusions. One goal in publishing this book was to give order to the many different developments in the field of human-centered service design and make it more accessible to a broad public. The works included here show that a transformative process in healthcare is taking place to continually improve and optimize the healthcare system and to center it on patients' needs. The changes and interventional actions have large and small effects on individuals and groups, on organizations and society, on the culture, economy, and science. Intelligent solutions can be developed using new approaches, methods, and tools. This book covers the basic knowledge necessary for transformative processes and also offers a deeper look at essential areas of responsibility, work, research, and development. The theoretical knowledge and many practical examples presented in this book are aimed at a broad audience and encourage differentiated discussion, further development, and more concrete definitions. Among those to whom this book is addressed are physicians, nursing professionals, decision-makers at public hospitals, privately run hospital chains, and other integrated healthcare institutions. This book is also suited for acquiring and processing knowledge individually and in groups. Comprehensive expertise is required to manage current and difficult issues. Interdisciplinary expert teams with representatives from hospitals, pharmacies, health insurance funds, rehabilitation clinics, universities, and consulting firms have the potential to find and apply effective solutions. Drawing on the expertise of stakeholders in the healthcare system, it is possible to communicate, transfer, and pass on fundamental and practical knowledge and to improve it for the benefit of all.

Human-centered service design in the healthcare system focuses squarely on individuals in their entirety when designing products, services, interpersonal interactions, and processes in and between institutions (Fig. 1). One aim is to respect the individual in regard to their values, ideas, and desires and to learn what their expectations and needs are and to meet them. The individual person should be recognized and included as a partner in the process. The responses to a person's

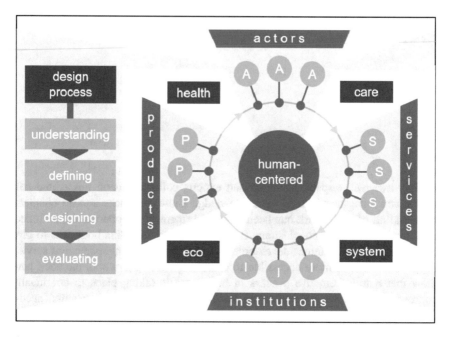

Fig. 1 Human-Centered service design for healthcare transformation. *Source* Author's own figure (2022)

requirements and changing circumstances should be more efficient, more respectful, and more transparent. The expected and the unexpected can thus be adjusted and optimized. The need to take measures in relation to the design can also be addressed. The design contributes to achieving goals and managing work tasks, but does not focus on the service provider or the provider-consumer relationship, but rather on the recipient of the services and the ecosystem surrounding the recipient. Modifying designs can have a positive influence on patients. They can improve and increase the mental and physical well-being of patients, as well as their personal development in coping with a new environment because cognitive, emotional, motivational, and sociocultural aspects are recognized and responded to. Safe, high-quality, and environmentally friendly materials in the design have an effect on a person's surroundings and on the person. Relaxation and stress reduction can be encouraged and lead to more mindfulness and less anxiety. Human-centered design can thus support patients' ability to heal in the healthcare system. It is apparent that a very special importance is given to design, because it combines objects and subjects mutually, penetrates all areas of life, and, from the patient's perspective, perfects the usefulness. Design provides the support for people to have long and healthy lives.

With increasing digitalization, patients are surrounded and influenced by credence goods that have no firmly secure basis for behavior or assessment. These tangible and intangible goods can be viewed and designed individually or as a complex whole. As this book shows, there are many approaches, strategies for action, and a wide range of perspectives to deal with this topic. Each person must undertake their own evaluation of the situation, design options, and success factors. The existing lack of focus must be used to define a framework that is not too constricted and that enables a wholistic perspective in order to include and evaluate different points of view. Interdependencies and restrictions in the presentation of points of view and situations make assumptions about norms, values, and attitudes. Mindsets, living environments, and values, such as "cost, time, and quality," must stand in a balanced relationship with each other in order to purposefully use human-centered design to transform the healthcare system. Cost pressure and capacity reduction are clear signs of a transformation in business and science and markers for the changes at the levels of structure, process, and outcome.

In the healthcare system, the patient should, as a result of centering all activities, receive high-quality treatment and care. In the course of providing this, patients are viewed as unique individuals who are dependent on help and support. Connected to centering the patient is the concentration and focus of all business and treatment processes on the patients' passage through the system. The aim is to achieve a better profitability at healthcare institutions, improve working conditions for employees who display great levels of dedication and commitment, and to improve the experience and provision of services for patients. Here, great importance is given to the relationship between the doctors and nursing staff, and the patient. Patients must be cared for, healed, accompanied, guided, and often instructed on how to handle a disease. In addition to medical treatment, the non-medical care also plays a major role, for example, if there are administrative issues such as questions about billing, problems with reimbursement or legal matters. Nevertheless, it must be taken into account that the implementation of human-centered design in the healthcare system is still inadequate. There are numerous problems and potential solutions that can be identified in the various areas. It frequently remains unclear how these areas can be interlinked to achieve high level of performance that truly places the patient at the center of healthcare.

This book succeeds in giving an overview of the topics outlined above and presenting the scientific and epistemic basics of human-centered design in a comprehensible manner. This edited work enables quick access to relevant knowledge for scholarly papers and research projects in academia and practice.

The contributions of the authors in this anthology are structured in the following fashion: contribution title, summary, introduction, main part, conclusion, bibliography, and biography. Furthermore, each author sums up his or her explanations and insights in the article for a summary at the end of the article.

I would like to thank the numerous authors of this anthology who brought a wide array of fascinating issues from practical experience and engrossing science topics into my anthology. Finally, i want to extend my warmest gratitude to the Springer Publishing AG at this point who contributed my ideas to support me in compiling the layout of this anthology and put the whole book with the chapter together.

Neu-Ulm, Germany   Mario A. Pfannstiel
2022

Contents

Bridging the Health Gap: Human-Centered Approaches to Connect Clinical and Community Care 1
Patricia Alafaireet and Philippe Diserens

The Change from Leadership to Leadershift—The Human-Centered Service Design Approach Requires New Leadership Competencies in the Health System 21
Karin Messer-Misak and Christian Lagger

Empowered Health and Social Care Staff: The Value of Human-Centred Service Design in Co-producing Transformative Change 35
Stuart G. Bailey, Karen Bell, Julie Gordon, Hans Hartung, and Zoë A. Prosser

Human-Centered Service Design and Transformative Innovation: Beginning to Understand How Innovation Culture Shifts Within the Public Health System in Western Australia 53
Sash Milne, Christopher Kueh, Stuart Medley, Neil Lynch, and Benjamin Noteboom

Enhancing Seldom Heard Perspectives in Human-centred Service Design for Health and Social Care Transformation 73
Kris Kalkman and Marikken Høiseth

Educational Challenges in Integrating Healthcare and Social Services: The Case of the University of Tartu Pärnu College in Designing a Master's Programme in Person-Centred Social Innovation 87
Ewe Alliksoo, Margrit Kärp, Heli Tooman, and Karit Jäärats

Exploring Services' patient-centredness. Design Challenges for a Future Design Agenda 109
Stefano Maffei, Massimo Bianchini, and Beatrice Villari

Human-Centered Gatekeeping: "Neyim Var?" 137
Çağdaş Erkan Akyürek, Şükrü Anıl Toygar, and Elif Erbay

Patient Autonomy and User Autonomy in the Ecology of Care 149
Miso Kim

Innovative Service Design for Global Health 167
Lesley Clack and Rachel Ellison

Formative Interventions for Healthcare Sustainability:
A Developmental Design Agenda 177
Peter Jones and Pranay Arun Kumar

Healthcare Complexity and the Role of Service Design in Complex
Healthcare Systems 197
Jürgen Faust, Birgit Mager, and Carol Massa

Zooming in and Out of Complex Systems: Exploring Frames
in Incremental Participatory Design Projects 221
Adeline Hvidsten and Frida Almqvist

Transforming Complexity: A Human-Centred Design Approach
to Engage Young People in the Philippines with Dialogues About
HIV Service Delivery 243
Christopher Kueh, Gareth Durrant, Fanke Peng, Philip Ely,
and Justin Francis Bionat

Storytelling as a Way to Design and Innovate Healthcare Services
for Children 265
Mira Alhonsuo, Jenny Siivola, Melanie Sarantou, and Satu Miettinen

The Approach of Design Sprints in Healthcare Transformation 285
Christophe Vetterli and Philipp Schmelzer

Building an Equity-Centered Design Toolkit for Engaging Patients
in Health Research Prioritization 295
Alessandra N. Bazzano and Lesley-Ann Noel

Designing a Conceptual Wayfinding Structure to Manage
Information for Human-Centered Healthcare Experience 317
Cecilia Xi Wang and Craig M. Vogel

"My Heart Jumped. Do I Have Cancer?"—Results of a Co-design
Study with Cervical Cancer Screening Participants 329
Sandra Klonteig, Jiaxin Li, and Ragnhild Halvorsrud

Not just Targets: Human Prospects in Health Services
for All—Insights from an Italian Case Study on Covid-19
Vaccination and Preventive Services 353
Gianluca Antonucci, Marco Berardi, and Andrea Ziruolo

**Telemedicine Implementation Between Innovation
and Sustainability: An Operating Model for Designing
Patient-Centered Healthcare** 375
Gabriele Palozzi and Francesco Ranalli

Integrated Care Models in Aged Care: The Role of Technology 401
Madhan Balasubramanian, Mark Brommeyer, Lucy Simmonds,
and Angie Shafei

**Exoskeletons—Human-Centred Solutions to Support Care
Workers?** 415
Riika Saurio, Satu Pekkarinen, Lea Hennala, and Helinä Melkas

Inclusive Smart Textile Design for Healthy Ageing 433
Shan Wang, Kai Yang, and Yuanyuan Yin

**Co-designing a Dementia Village: Transforming Dementia Care
Through Service Design** 449
Maria Taivalsaari Røhnebæk, Marit Engen, and Ane Bast

Editor and Contributors

About the Editor

Mario A. Pfannstiel is a researcher and lecturer in the field of hospital and healthcare management at the University of Applied Sciences Neu-Ulm. He holds a diploma from the University of Applied Sciences Nordhausen in the field of social management with the major subject finance management, an MSc degree from the Dresden International University in patient management, and an MA degree from the Technical University of Kaiserslautern and the University of Witten/Herdecke in healthcare and social facilities management. He worked as an executive assistant to the medical director at the Heart Centre Leipzig in Germany. At the University of Bayreuth, he worked as a research assistant in the Department of Strategic Management and Organization. He received his doctorate from the Faculty of Social Sciences and Economics and the Chair of Management, Professional Services, and Sport Economics at the University of Potsdam. His research includes numerous articles, journals, and books on management in the healthcare and hospital industry. Professor Pfannstiel holds lectures in Germany and abroad at regular intervals. His current research interests focus on service management, digitalization of services, service business model innovation, service design, service thinking, and innovative services. e-mail: mario.pfannstiel@hnu.de

Contributors

Akyürek Çağdaş Erkan Department of Healthcare Management, Ankara University, Keçiören/ANKARA, Turkey

Alafaireet Patricia Health Managment and Informatics, University of Missouri, Columbia, MO, United States

Alhonsuo Mira University of Lapland, Rovaniemi, Finland

Alliksoo Ewe University of Tartu Pärnu College, Pärnu, Estonia

Almqvist Frida Oslo, Norway

Antonucci Gianluca DEA—Department of Business Administration, "G. d'Annunzio" University of Chieti-Pescara, Pescara, Italy

Arun Kumar Pranay Health Systems Studio, OCAD University, Toronto, ON, Canada

Bailey Stuart G. The Glasgow School of Art, School of Design, Glasgow, Scotland, UK

Balasubramanian Madhan Health Care Management, College of Business, Government and Law, Flinders University, Adelaide, SA, Australia

Bast Ane Inland Norway University of Applied Sciences, Elverum, Norway

Bazzano Alessandra N. School of Public Health and Tropical Medicine, Tulane University, New Orleans, LA, USA

Bell Karen Development Innovation, University Hospital Crosshouse, NHS Ayrshire & Arran, Kilmarnock, Scotland, UK

Berardi Marco DEA—Department of Business Administration, "G. d'Annunzio" University of Chieti-Pescara, Pescara, Italy

Bianchini Massimo Department of Design, Politecnico di Milano, Milano, Italy

Bionat Justin Francis Mandurriao, Iloilo City, Philippines

Brommeyer Mark Health Care Management, College of Business, Government and Law, Flinders University, Adelaide, SA, Australia

Clack Lesley Department of Health Sciences, Marieb College of Health and Human Services, Florida Gulf Coast University, S. Fort Myers, FL, USA

Diserens Philippe University Hospital of Psychiatry Zurich (PUK), Zürich, Switzerland

Durrant Gareth Creative Consultant, DSIL Global, Subiaco, Perth, Western Australia, Australia

Ellison Rachel University of Louisiana at Lafayette, Lafayette, LA, USA

Ely Philip School of Design and Built Environment, Curtin University, Kent Street, Western Australia, Australia

Engen Marit Inland Norway University of Applied Sciences, Elverum, Norway

Erbay Elif Department of Healthcare Management, Ankara University, Keçiören/ANKARA, Turkey

Faust Jürgen Weinheim, Germany

Gordon Julie Emergency and Paediatric Medicine, University Hospital Crosshouse, NHS Ayrshire & Arran, Kilmarnock, Scotland, UK

Halvorsrud Ragnhild SINTEF Digital, Oslo, Norway

Hartung Hans Respiratory Medicine, University Hospital Crosshouse, NHS Ayrshire & Arran, Kilmarnock, Scotland, UK

Hennala Lea Lappeenranta-Lahti University of Technology LUT, Lahti, Finland

Hvidsten Adeline Oslo, Norway

Høiseth Marikken Department of Design, Faculty of Architecture and Design, Norwegian University of Science and Technology (NTNU), Trondheim, Norway

Jäärats Karit University of Tartu Pärnu College, Pärnu, Estonia

Jones Peter OCAD University, Toronto, ON, Canada

Kalkman Kris Department of Teacher Education, Faculty of Social and Educational Sciences, Norwegian University of Science and Technology (NTNU), Trondheim, Norway

Kärp Margrit University of Tartu Pärnu College, Pärnu, Estonia

Kim Miso College of Arts Media and Design, Northeastern University, Boston, MA, United States

Klonteig Sandra SINTEF Digital, Oslo, Norway

Kueh Christopher School of Arts and Humanities, Edith Cowan University, Joondalup, Western Australia, Australia

Lagger Christian Krankenhaus der Elisabethinen GmbH, Graz, Austria

Li Jiaxin SINTEF Digital, Oslo, Norway

Lynch Neil Office of Medical Research and Innovation, Office of the Deputy Director General, Department of Health Western Australia, East Perth, Western Australia, Australia

Maffei Stefano Department of Design, Politecnico di Milano, Milano, Italy

Mager Birgit Köln, Germany

Massa Carol Orlando, Florida, United States

Medley Stuart School of Arts and Humanities, Edith Cowan University, Joondalup, Western Australia, Australia

Melkas Helinä Lappeenranta-Lahti University of Technology LUT, Lahti, Finland

Messer-Misak Karin Fachhochschule JOANNEUM GmbH, Institut Für eHealth/Gesundheitsinformatik, Graz, Austria

Miettinen Satu University of Lapland, Rovaniemi, Finland

Milne Sash Broadwater, Western Australia, Australia

Noel Lesley-Ann College of Design, North Carolina State University, Raleigh, NC, USA

Noteboom Benjamin Office of the Executive Director, Royal Perth Bentley Group and East Metropolitan Health Service, Perth, Western Australia, Australia

Palozzi Gabriele Department of Management and Law, University Tor Vergata, Rome, Italy

Pekkarinen Satu Lappeenranta-Lahti University of Technology LUT, Lahti, Finland

Peng Fanke University of South Australia, Adelaide, South Australia, Australia

Prosser Zoë A. Social Design and Research Fellow, Innovation School, The Glasgow School of Art, Glasgow, Scotland, UK

Ranalli Francesco Department of Management and Law, University Tor Vergata, Rome, Italy

Røhnebæk Maria Taivalsaari Inland Norway University of Applied Sciences, Elverum, Norway

Sarantou Melanie University of Lapland, Rovaniemi, Finland

Saurio Riika Lappeenranta-Lahti University of Technology LUT, Lahti, Finland

Schmelzer Philipp Vetterli Roth & Partners AG, Zug, Switzerland

Shafei Angie Health Care Management, College of Business, Government and Law, Flinders University, Adelaide, SA, Australia

Siivola Jenny University of Lapland, Rovaniemi, Finland

Simmonds Lucy Health Care Management, College of Business, Government and Law, Flinders University, Adelaide, SA, Australia

Tooman Heli University of Tartu Pärnu College, Pärnu, Estonia

Toygar Şükrü Anıl Department of Healthcare Management, Tarsus University, Tarsus/MERSİN, Turkey

Vetterli Christophe Vetterli Roth & Partners AG, Zug, Switzerland

Villari Beatrice Department of Design, Politecnico di Milano, Milano, Italy

Vogel Craig M. University of Cincinnati, Cincinnati, OH, USA

Wang Cecilia Xi University of Minnesota, Minnesota, USA

Wang Shan Winchester School of Art, University of Southampton, Southampton, UK

Yang Kai Winchester School of Art, University of Southampton, Southampton, UK

Yin Yuanyuan Winchester School of Art, University of Southampton, Southampton, UK

Ziruolo Andrea DEA—Department of Business Administration, "G. d'Annunzio" University of Chieti-Pescara, Pescara, Italy

Bridging the Health Gap: Human-Centered Approaches to Connect Clinical and Community Care

Patricia Alafaireet and Philippe Diserens

ABSTRACT

Raising healthcare costs, over-burdened healthcare systems, and changing patient expectations drive the need for innovative health delivery services that bridge the gap between traditional clinical care and community level health services. This chapter outlines strategies and examples that can be used to identify health service gaps and create patient accepted, gap-spanning services, by leveraging tools, skills, and methods adapted from non-healthcare environments, including the social service arena, through service re-design that expands on health strategies developed for use in resource poor service areas and though service design strategies predicated on the development of new mid-level provider roles. Among the strategies discussed are the use of a combination of non-healthcare generated data and information with healthcare generated data/information to improve the human centeredness of health services design, the development of learning systems adapted from telehealth to meet telecollaboration needs across non-clinical health service providers, and the design of services that merge non-health sector providers into the healthcare delivery system to create high value, reimbursable services. Services so created have the potential to create reciprocal innovation in traditional healthcare delivery and, more importantly, to expand the delivery of health at the individual, local, regional, national, and global levels.

P. Alafaireet (✉)
Health Managment and Informatics, University of Missouri, 734 CS&E Building, Columbia, MO 65212, United States
e-mail: alafaireetp@umsystem.edu

P. Diserens
University Hospital of Psychiatry Zurich (PUK), Health Economics, Lenggstrasse 31, 8008 Zürich, Switzerland
e-mail: philippe.diserens@uni-bayreuth.de

1

1   Introduction—Understanding the Need for Human-Centered Design in Health

Fundamentally, improved use of Human-Centered Design (HCD) is required because half of the world's population lacks access to affordable health services (World Health Organization, 2017, 1). This percentage increases greatly when health-related social care needs are considered in the health equation (Kuluski et al., 2017, 1–11). Multimorbidity associated with health and social care needs creates complex health care needs including multiple, concurrent, chronic conditions, functional and cognitive impairments, mental health-related issues, and social vulnerability that increases the health accessibility gap (Moineddin et al., 2010, 306; Tinetti et al., 2012, 2493–2494). This complex situation has a significant impact on the lives of individuals including disruption in social participation, relationships, and societal contributions that are typically unaddressed by medical treatment plans (Abu Dabrh et al., 2015, 114–117).

For the fifty percent of individuals for whom health care is available, rising healthcare costs, over-burdened healthcare systems, and changing patient expectations drive the need for innovative health delivery services that bridge the gap between traditional medical care and community level health services. Despite a growing number of individuals presenting with complex health needs, healthcare systems continue to deliver services that focus on singular illness or services that prioritize the management of disease and symptoms over more socially orientated care (Gilmour, 2016, 23–32). Improving care for individuals with complex care needs requires the skillful integration of all aspects of health (Humphries, 2015, 856–859; Vrijhoef & Thorlby, 2016, 2493–2494). This lack of integration may be especially apparent at certain points where a combination of healthcare services and social care services are required for care delivery (Challis et al., 2014, 160–168, Hwabejire et al., 2013, 956–961). This chapter outlines several HCD strategies that support the development of gap-spanning health services. These strategies can be used to both identify health service gaps and create patient centric and patient accepted services by leveraging tools, skills, and methods adapted from non-healthcare environments, including the social service arena, through service re-design. Among the strategies discussed are cultural aspect of human-centered service design (HCSD), the use of a combination of non-healthcare generated data and information with healthcare generated data/information to improve the human centeredness of health services design, and the development of learning systems adapted to meet collaboration needs across health service providers to create high value, reimbursable services. Services so created have the potential to create reciprocal innovation in health delivery and to expand the delivery of health at the individual, local, regional, national, and global levels.

2 Role of Organizational Culture in Health Gap Creation and Gap Reduction

To improve human-centered health services design, it is important to understand the role of organizational culture as far as health gap creation and health gap reduction are concerned. There is no doubt that healthcare systems are interested in moving towards a more human-centered-based approach as systems rethink the way health care is provided and the role patients and families play in it. In the last decade, the popularity of Human-Centered Care (HCC) HCC has led to the development of several academic and quality improvement agency frameworks. Globally, healthcare systems and organizations are looking to improve health system performance through the implementation of a human-centered-based health service design (e.g., HCC model). While numerous conceptual frameworks for HCC exist, a gap remains in practical organizational culture-based guidance on HCC implementation. The conceptual framework of Santana et al. (2018, 429–440) provides a step-wise roadmap to guide healthcare systems and organizations in the provision of HCC across various healthcare sectors. One important identified structural domain includes the creation of an HCC culture across the continuum of care. The domain creating an HCC culture includes two sub-domains:

1. **The core values and philosophy of the organization:** This includes: (a) Vision and mission, (b) Patient-directed, integrating patient experience, and expertise, (c) Addressing and incorporating diversity in care, health promotion, and patient engagement, and (d) Patient and healthcare provider rights.
2. **Establishing operational definition of HCC including:** (a) Consistent operational definitions and (b) Common language around HCC.

Their framework provides an in-depth discussion on the structural pre-requisites that support the establishment of an HCC model which allows processes and outcomes to transpire. Embracing and promoting an HCC culture is essential for laying HCC foundations. Without a culture that genuinely values the patients' perspectives, alongside healthcare providers and managers, there is little impetus towards developing effective education, programs, and systems that will help foster HCC. While people can relate to the HCC concept, healthcare providers and policymakers must embark on this cultural shift in practice, and organizations must be willing to adopt and create innovative models that are conducive to providing incentives to support and practice HCC. The adoption of HCC comes with challenges and entails critical changes, particularly with regard to how care is delivered and how patients and their providers interact. However, despite the challenges, the benefits of HCC are evident and present a major opportunity for improving health outcomes. In order to improve health and health care, healthcare systems must find a way to effectively implement and measure HCC (Santana et al., 2018, 429–440).

It is important to understand the role of organizational culture in that context. HCC has a deep impact on individual behavior, performance, and employees' efforts to excellence as well as the socio-dynamics of the company. Organizational culture is a complex nonlinear integrator of any intellectual capital organization. Culture reflects the shared values, beliefs, symbols, ceremonies, and traditions in an organization. It is an intangible asset strongly related to spiritual capital, meaning it cannot be seen or touched (Ghinea & Bratianu, 2012, 257–276). Every person or employee in the organization has their own values and beliefs that work for them. Whenever someone joins any organization they must first internalize its culture and determine whether they relate to it or not (Shahzad et al., 2012, 975–985).

The contemporary business environment is challenged by the rapid change that requires continuous monitoring of organizational culture as a basis for evolving business practices and maintaining employee satisfaction as a critical market success factor. (Nayak & Barik, 2013, 47–61) Human centric factors including organizational culture factors should be analyzed carefully and their use promoted (e.g., Organization openness in managing diversity, policy of promoting innovation and change management, policy of evaluation of strategic planning, etc.) (Maithel et al., 2012, 68–74). Organizational culture is one of the important components leaders can employ to sustain performance, build ethical and moral organizations, and maintain competitive advantage. Healthcare organizations are advised to increase awareness concerning the importance of positive organizational culture and interprofessional teamwork as variables that influence human/patient-centered care. Organizational culture and quality of work life for healthcare employees lead to improved organizational effectiveness. The findings of An et al. (2011, 22–30) suggest that quality of work life is the strongest predictor of organization effectiveness.

Körner et al. (2015, 1–12) underpin the importance of investigating the characteristics and effects of working conditions more comprehensively and underpins the importance of interprofessional teamwork in healthcare organizations. To enhance interprofessional teamwork, team development interventions are recommended. Any such intervention should be tailored to the needs of the healthcare teams, and further research should evaluate these interventions to find evidence-based best practices (Körner et al., 2015, 1–12). Improving teamwork and interprofessional collaboration (IPC), through practice changes can increase clinical process efficiency and improve patient health outcomes as compared to usual care or an alternative intervention (Reeves et al., 2017, 1–40).

Let us focus on bridging organizational culture gaps through relevant structural interventions. Kuluski et al. (2017, 1–11) offer essential building blocks to address the health and social care needs of complex patient populations and how to bridge the gap between medical care and social care. They identify the persistent orientation of health systems toward acute and episodic care as the greatest challenge. But meeting the needs of people with complex care needs requires authentic and consistent relationships with providers and families and ongoing communication. Attention to non-medical factors including organizational culture, personal goals, and expectations, provides insight into care preferences and levels of engagement. Teams that recognize and support the less formalized roles of families, personal and peer support workers, are critical to the delivery of support to this population. Along with the mobilization of needed health care and social care support, this type of care delivery model can be more effectively realized with the appropriate training, incentives, and policy levels (Kuluski et al., 2017, 1–11). Due to the growing number of people living with complex care needs to be characterized by multimorbidity, mental health challenges, and social deprivation, an integration of health care and social care is required, beyond traditional healthcare services to address social determinants. Their study investigates key care components to support complex patients and their families in the community including how to best meet complex care needs in the community and how to address the barriers to delivering care to this population. The results show that meeting the needs of people with complex care needs requires careful consideration of policy levers and organizational arrangements, and of care provider's work within structures guided by rules, policies, accountability, and reporting requirements that effectively shape and often limit what is possible in their day-to-day interactions with patients, other providers, and families. Moving beyond these boundaries becomes necessary in order to meet the unique and fluctuating needs of people with complex care needs, which requires authentic and consistent relationships with providers and families and ongoing communication. Attention to non-medical factors including organizational culture, personal goals, and expectations will also provide insight into care preferences, patient needs, and levels of engagement. This type of care human-centered delivery model, along with the mobilization of needed health and social care supports should bring into practice within a system that is oriented to proactively supporting health and well-being (Kuluski et al., 2017, 1–11).

New and improved forms of human-centered patient care are crucial because healthcare organizations are currently facing major organizational and societal challenges. As a response to this shift, towards a more holistic, humanecare perspective, an increasing number of healthcare organizations acknowledge the importance of Human-Centered Design (HCD) approaches. HCD is about understanding human needs and how design can respond to these needs. Melles et al. (2021, 37–44) encourage healthcare organizations to continue to implement this much needed interprofessional collaboration in dealing with today's care challenges in the health care. The authors address in their research article three key characteristics of human-centered design, focusing on its implementation in health care:

1. Developing an understanding of people and their needs,
2. Engaging all stakeholders from early on and throughout the design process,
3. Adopting a holistic system approach by systematically addressing interactions between the micro-, meso-, and macro-levels of societal care systems, and the transition from individual interests to collective interests.

Innovative human-centered health delivery services can bridge the gap between traditional clinical care and community level health services and can lead to higher value, and more effective reimbursable services through understanding the important role of organizational culture and its potential for improvement on an employee and organizational level.

3   Gaps and Gap Creation from the Economic Perspective

As previously mentioned, the current medical care system prioritizes short episodes of care delivery, provider-driven care decisions, and rewards efficiency and cost-effectiveness in service utilization. To bridge the gap between health and social care, an integrated health and social care delivery system has to be based on strong therapeutic relationships supported by consistent care providers, time, and necessary elements to develop trust and openness to care options. Empowering patients through the choice of service, location of care, unpacking personal goals and priorities, and allowing time for this process is paramount (Kuluski et al., 2017, 1–11).

International health systems are strongly advocating for the integration of health and social care, particularly for sub-groups of patients who stand to benefit the most, including those with multimorbidity and complex care needs (Kuluski et al., 2017, 1–11). Mobilizing health and social care in the community has proved challenging because homecare services have several barriers even if they tend to be medically oriented. Supports for nursing care, physical rehabilitation, and Activities of Daily Living (ADLs) (e.g., bathing, toileting, and personal hygiene), are more likely to be publicly funded entitlements for those who meet specified eligibility criteria. On the other hand, patients may find themselves needing support from public programs that lie outside health care entirely, including workplace reintegration, obtaining or maintaining adequate and affordable housing, making home adaptations, and seeking financial support. While these types of social care services are situated outside of health care, they are inexplicitly tied to one's ability to maintain overall health. Importantly, the absence of needed social care has been linked to increased use of inappropriate medical care, which is both unnecessary and typically more expensive (Kuluski et al., 2017, 1–11).

The medical, psychological, cognitive, and social needs of older adults with serious illnesses are best met by coordinated and team-based services and support. Golden et al., (2019, 411–418) provided key principles for success in caring for persons with serious chronic disabling diseases, while lowering total costs of care. The authors highlight that services are best provided in a seamless care model anchored by integrated biopsychosocial assessments and focused on what matters to older adults and their social determinants of health; individualized care plans with shared goals; care provision and management; and quality measurement with continuous improvement. The key recommendations of their model are (1) Care models for older adults with serious illness require an integrated team of diverse professionals with a single-care plan that is built on what matters to the older adult and their family, (2) All team members for older adults with serious illness require training in aging and team collaboration, (3) Mental health services are critical, both for the older adults with serious illness and their family, (4) Effective community team communication requires an electronic communication platform that spans the system of providers and organizations with skilled technical staff, (5) Payment models for integrated care require incentives for team-based care across the continuum of services, with adequate salaries and academic loan forgiveness, are required to recruit and retain high-quality team members (Golden et al., 2019, 411–418).

Primary care practices have historically been underfunded and undervalued. Value-based payment and alternative reimbursement models that shift care from acute settings may further incentivize the provision of coordinated care rather than the volume of services. These models are a strong motivator for health systems to begin primary care re-design (PCR). Currently, systems are caught between two payment models, and therefore, a majority of health systems struggle to move their efforts beyond the pilot or implementation phase. Harvey et al. (2020, 1144–1154) interviewed 162 system executives and physician organization leaders from 24 systems to understand how health systems are facilitating PCR, examine the PCR initiatives taking place within systems, and identify barriers to this work. Leaders at all 24 health systems described initiatives to re-design the delivery of primary care, but many were in the early stages. Respondents described the use of central-ized health system resources to facilitate PCR initiatives, such as regionalized care coordinators, and integrated electronic health records. Team-based care, population management, and care coordination were the most commonly described initia-tives to transform primary care delivery. Respondents most often cited improving efficiency and enhancing clinician job satisfaction as motivating factors for team-based care. Changes in payment and risk assumption as well as community needs were commonly cited motivators for population health management and care coor-dination. Return on investment and the slower than anticipated rate in moving from fee-for-service to value-based payment were noted by multiple respondents as challenges health systems face in re-designing primary care (Harvey et al., 2020, 1144–1154).

It is a mistake to focus only on cutting costs when trying to fix the healthcare system. As Hwang and Christensen (2007, 1329–1335) emphasizes, the appro-priate solution is to encourage development of disruptive business models that can assume a greater share of the workload, not to force the old models of solution-shop medicine to twist and conform. By coupling technological advances with appropriately matched business models, disruptive innovation has brought affordability and accessibility to industries ranging from steel-making to personal finance, and it is the right prescription for the ailing the healthcare system. Even this treatment is desperately needed and long overdue, there are four main chal-lenges to new disruptive business models in health care to bridge the gap between health and social care:

1. Fragmentation of care: Carving focused facilities and user networks out of today's mixed models of healthcare delivery might indeed capture unrealized efficiencies and cost savings, but they also might fragment the delivery of care. That is why coordination of care in such a system is critical, and the importance of interoperable health information technology (IT) cannot be stressed enough.
2. Lack of a retail market: Disruptive innovation requires that a market of consumers carry proper incentives to shop for products and services that best meet their needs. It is important to recognize that the healthcare system comprises highly interdependent business models, and one cannot simply plug in a new component and expect it to work. Health Savings Accounts (HSAs) do create proper incentives for healthy behavior, but as long as the healthcare delivery system remains costly and inconvenient, customers rationally avoid spending their money on those services. Until we see business-model innovation in healthcare delivery in conjunction with HSAs, we will continue to see individuals paradoxically avoiding the healthy behavior that these vehicles were meant to encourage.
3. Regulatory barriers: Well-known battles over federal moratoria on focused specialty hospitals, state certificate-of-need (CON) policies, and restrictions on physicians' ownership of medical facilities have all involved impassioned claims by proponents of the status quo that disruptive change could jeopardize public safety for the sake of higher profits. However, these regulations unintentionally trap health care in high-cost models of care. For example, many states do not allow nurses to interpret simple test results or write basic prescriptions, leaving care delivery to be performed by physician-staffed solution shops. This makes sense for complex illnesses that require the intuition of experts, but such regulations leave no room for value-added process businesses such as nurse-staffed retail clinics that can deliver better and more cost-effective care for a growing list of conditions. Healthcare policymakers must recognize the hidden cost of supporting and renewing regulations that inhibit innovation over the long run.
4. Reimbursement: Finally, returning to our original premise that it is a mistake to focus only on cutting costs when trying to fix the healthcare system, regulators and payers often direct their attention to cutting reimbursement rates as the primary solution. However, cutting reimbursement in an attempt to force the solution-shop business models of hospitals and physician practices to somehow figure out a way to become more efficient does little to improve healthcare delivery. With lower reimbursement, hospitals and physicians struggle even more to fulfill their value propositions of providing complex, inherently expensive medical care, and they become even less inclined to hand off work to value-added process businesses (Hwang & Christensen, 2007, 1329–1335).

4 Social Determinants of Health as Enablers of Human-Centered Health Service Design

Health gaps are often latent and not directly observable in the care delivery process but the effects of the gaps are often evident in individual and population level health status (Ozkaynak et al., 2021, 1–8). Understanding these gaps requires knowledge and acceptance of the reasons these gaps form (Holden et al., 2015, 133–150). Clearer examination of the needs which form the gaps, including the need for human centric understanding of the collaboration between individual providers, the need for shared knowledge of an individual's situation, and the need for social support for individuals within the context of their community are essential to the development of systemic interventions (Ozkaynak et al., 2021, 1–8).

Since health status is shaped by the wider economic, political, and cultural context, it is reasonable to consider their intersectoral nature and seek ways to enable health gap analysis and service design that allows a similar intersectoral approach. The problem is that the wider economic, political, and cultural aspects of health are not always helpful when it comes to the design of health services for individuals. Actionable, human-centered health service design begins with understanding the social and economic realities of individuals, families, and communities and continues with understanding health behaviors, conditions present in the physical environment, and a host of other factors that are consolidated into the Social Determinants of Health (SDOH) (CSDH, 2008, 1–33). The SDOH broadly encompass economic stability, physical environment quality (e.g., housing, transportation, access to exercise and play opportunities and safety), education and literacy (language, basic and advanced educational opportunities), food and nutrition (hunger, healthy food access), community (social support, availability of social care, community engagement, discrimination, and social stress) and health care (health insurance accessibility, provider availability, access to culturally acceptable, competent care and care quality). The intersectional nature of the data that should be collected to understand the SDOH has a natural bridging effect across data collected in multiple care delivery sectors. Fundamentally, SDOH focus on determining the cause of health differentials (Blas et al., 2016, 1–52). This includes differential exposure to the physical environment (unhealthy food, toxic workplaces, poor community infrastructure), to the social environment (discrimination, unregulated marketing of unhealthy products), to differences in community and individual vulnerability (poverty, low levels of literacy, food insecurity), to differential access to health products and services (local service availability, financial barriers), differential benefits from the use of health services (biased service referral, discriminatory care, insensitive treatment), and differential consequences of illness and disability (loss of income, stigma) (Blas et al., 2016, 1–52). These differentials typically create a social gradient in health where those at the lowest end of the social gradient suffer from the worst health.

Collecting data that enables the use of SDOH in HCSD presents challenges. Services design teams need to navigate incomplete data sources, the intricacies of data retrieval in the absence of enterprise information architecture that spans health and social care, and the inconsistencies of data that is typically collected for purposes other than service design. Overcoming these challenges is a non-trivial task that presents the opportunity to humanize data collection and analysis and the services that are created based on the data. For the greatest utility as a substrate for HDC, data should be collected at the individual person level and then aggregated to form a picture of health status at the community level and further aggregated at the national and international level. Potentially useful data encompasses, psychological assets, health risk related behavior, health-related behaviors, measures of social connectedness, social status, culture and tradition, person-related factors such as citizenship, genetics, body structure and function (such as blood pressure), access to and quality of health care, patient engagement, environmental factors (such as pollution), and factors specific to a certain location, such as crime rate (Choi & Sonin, 2022, 1).

If SDOH are to be used as an effective health gap bridging solution in the development of human centric services, their use is contingent to the accurate identification of the gap itself. While the health gap is marginally recognized as being ever-present, it is most sharply apparent to care providers at junction points in the care delivery where the need for a continuum of services is readily apparent. Less apparent is the need for coordination of medical and social services as effective population health services, especially preventative services. There are multiple factors that cloud the understanding needed to effectively address health gaps including missing or siloed data, a lack of data required to believably demonstrate the social benefits accrued from addressing health gaps, and the lack of data that is needed to establish a common understanding of health across the medical and social care arenas. A human centric service model will need to address all of these factors.

5   Human-Centered Data Collection

Application of data and digital tools supports medical care and social care providers' potential to address health through awareness, adjustment, assistance, alignment, and advocacy National Academies of Sciences, Engineering, and Medicine (2019, 1–163). A plethora of data sources exist including medical claims data, data from electronic health records, census data, and data collected at the community level (National Academies of Sciences, Engineering, and Medicine, 2019, 1–163). A wide range of digital tools, including but not limited to, predicative analytics, natural language processing, geocoding, decision support systems, augmented intelligence, the Internet of Things, telehealth, and chatbots are available for application to providing health (National Academies of Sciences, Engineering, and Medicine, 2019, 1–163). However, as social care has not benefited from the influx of funding, resources, policy attention, or strategic national vision directed to digitalization of the medical sector it is generally unable to match its sophistication (National Academies of Sciences, Engineering, and Medicine, 2019, 1–163). Similarly, effective use of SDOH as a means of identifying and addressing the health gap may include improved utilization of emerging private sector solutions that aim to share medical and social care data (National Academies of Sciences, Engineering, and Medicine 2019, 1–163). Enhancement of information infrastructure, development of suitable technical and data standards, and technology architecture improvements are needed to further mature nascent efforts to ensure safe, secure data sharing (National Academies of Sciences, Engineering, and Medicine, 2019, 1–163).

Such merging or sharing of data is not without risk (National Academies of Sciences, Engineering, and Medicine, 2019, 1–163). The definition of what constitutes health care and healthcare services has been mostly driven by the cultural history of medicine making it less likely that the parameters of social care delivery are equably included in the healthcare setting (National Academies of Sciences, Engineering, and Medicine, 2019, 1–163). The lack of clarity and guidance for integrating and addressing social care with medical care may support the tendency to "medicalize" the integration of social care with medical care. Unlike social care delivery systems, medical care organizations and systems often use models of care which require the use of research methods, diagnostic codes, and technical specialization to the degree that there is added cost and complexity (National Academies of Sciences, Engineering, and Medicine, 2019, 1–163). The medical model, if extended to the merging of medical and social care data, could substantially increase the administrative costs of social care providers (National). Care and further research are needed to ensure that the integration of social care data with medical data does not increase already existing health disparities by widening the digital divide or by codifying existing bias found in medical care provision systems (National Academies of Sciences, Engineering, and Medicine, 2019, 1–163).

Data-based solutions to health gap identification and solution development also include digital linkages and communication paths between medical care and social care providers and interoperable data systems to document and assess social care needs in addition to medical care needs (National Academies of Sciences, Engineering, and Medicine, 2019, 1–163). The combination of data from sources commonly available in social care systems, including data around the SDOH, is substantially less codified and formatted compared to that commonly found in medical care. Strong support for the development of needed technical infrastructure components includes workflow re-design and refinement, the development of tailored technical assistance and support, as well as combined social/medical care data best practices (National Academies of Sciences, Engineering, and Medicine, 2019, 1–163).

Multi-source, including SDOH, data also has the potential to provide governments, legislatures, licensing boards, and professional associations with evidence to develop, expand, and standardize the scopes of practice and training available to social workers, community health workers, gerontologists, and other care workers and to create ways for reimbursement for health by public and private payers (National Academies of Sciences, Engineering, and Medicine, 2019, 1–163).

The existing body of evidence suggests that social care interventions in housing, income support, nutritional support, care coordination, and community outreach have had a positive impact on health (Taylor et al., 2016, 1–20). As such, these interventions should be of interest to policymakers and practitioners seeking to leverage social care to improve health status or reduce medical costs, but the current general lack of understanding of the direct relationship between medical and social care suggests the need for additional data and for improved use of the existing body of evidence for human centric service development (Taylor et al., 2016, 1–20). Findings and data from the current research, the majority of which was conducted with low-income populations, suggest that reducing health gaps may require linking unconventional partners to adequately address human needs (Taylor et al., 2016, 1–20).

6   Development of Learning Systems as a Human-Centered Design Approach

The adaptation and application of HCD to the learning health system framework also offer promise as an effective health gap-spanning strategy. The Learning Health System (LHS) framework strength lies in the alignment of science, informatics, and culture in such a way as to enable service improvement and innovation. In the LHS framework, best practices are preferentially embedded in the care process, patient and caregivers are active participants in the care process, and any new knowledge generated by the delivery of care is captured as a useful by-product (Institute of Medicine, 2013, 1–312; Whicher, 2017, 1–16). The LHS approach is linked to the ability of medical care providers to effectively account for and mitigate the social and economic factors that affect health, especially those which negatively affect health (Adler & Stewart, 2010, 5–23; Alderwick & Gottlieb, 2019, 407–419). These social and economic factors have profound effect on both individual and population health, but addressing these risk factors has been the province of social care providers. Thus, there is a strong case for a new type of partnership between medical and social care providers that is deliberately constructed to mitigate the negative effects of social risk factors that drive increased utilization of medical services and high health costs. Creating this type of partnership to address the social determinants of health will partially depend on creating services that address and capitalize on the differences in policy, perspective, and associated financial incentives across the two sets of care providers.

Human centric design, as part of a learning system, can play a valuable role when commonly held beliefs and perceptions are addressed. Medical care generally favors service design that is based on quantitative methods (Melles et al., 2021, 37–44). Often there is a strong preference for the results from large randomized controlled trials as foundational evidence sources for service design. HCD of relies more heavily on qualitative research approaches to establish the needed evidence base (Melles et al., 2021, 37–44). Qualitative studies and user studies with smaller sample sizes may appear, from the traditional medical perspective, to be less reliable and riskier to use when designing services (Melles et al., 2021, 37–44). Successful HCD use in the medical arena may necessitate the use of strategies to enable wider acceptance of a full range of scientific methodologies and may require a general reconsideration of what constitutes acceptable evidence thresholds (Berwick, 2008, 1182–1184). Successful HCD in medical care may require a broadening of the current mindset around the concept of what constitutes an acceptable evidence base including rethinking about the overall tendency for clinicians to be more comfortable with and trusting of design based on RCT and the resulting biases from that perspective (Berwick, 2008, 1182–1184). Other practical challenges in the medical realm exist, such as those encountered while conducting fieldwork, including how prospective service users can be acceptably involved and issues associated with responsible evidence gathering from vulnerable individuals (Groeneveld et al., 2018, 305–326). Managerial challenges, such as recognizing and accommodating differences between design research and clinical research, and clarifying the added value of design work to the stakeholder may also need to the addressed before HCD work can successfully commence (Groeneveld et al., 2018, 305–326). Consideration of time and financial restrictions will also be required (Groeneveld et al., 2018, 305–326). Broadly speaking, human centric service designers must find ways to compensate for the limited availability of medical specialists in design research. They must also consistently strive to create a safe and open research environment where they can communicate easily with healthcare providers without prejudice (Groeneveld et al., 2018, 305–326).

Practically, to effectively use HCD in a learning system context intended to reduce health gaps, designers and care providers must focus time and energy on creating and sustaining multidisciplinary collaboration. To effectively do so it is imperative that designers of human centers services focus on understanding the evidence-based mindset of clinicians and social care providers that drives the provision of care and acknowledge the associated ethical considerations. It is critical that HCD support a constructive alignment of the different perspectives across medical care and social care (Melles et al., 2021, 37–44). king forward, HCD offers a viable strategy for the development of genomics-enabled LHSs needed to provide precision medicine, allowing for LHS that combines data regarding an individuals' genomics and social risk factors to illuminate the causal pathways that lead to health disparities (West et al., 2017, 1831–1832).

7   Discussion and Conclusions

This chapter outlined human-centered service design strategies (some of which are adapted from non-healthcare environments), which can effectively support health service re-design to effectively address the global health gap. Strategies for this re-design include the combined use of multi-source date, the alignment of medical and social care, a renewed focus on organizational culture, human-centered design

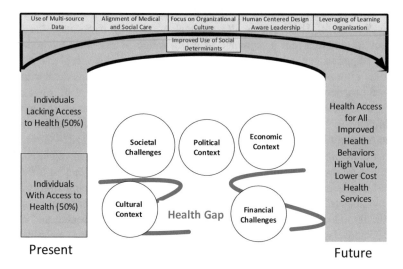

Fig. 1 Strategies for human-centered service design. *Source* Authors' own illustration (2022)

aware leaders, the leveraging of the learning organization model, and the improved use of the social determinants of health to increase access to health in the near future. (Please see Fig. 1).

Within human-centered service design, the importance of organizational leadership for interprofessional interventions, and the need for innovation in the health sector is increasingly noted in literature, but there is only limited research to guide this process (Weintraub & McKee, 2019, 138–144). Similarly, health organizations have always been expected to innovate in terms of adopting new treatments and models of care, but those who lead these organizations face many challenges. They must balance many competing responsibilities, including combining high-quality patient care with state-of-the-art research to solve patients' needs and managing highly skilled, often individualistic, professionals who, themselves, have agendas, not always aligned with those of the organization. Leaders must engage with a wide range of stakeholders, including those who pay for patient care and those who pay for research. They must manage complex partnerships, typically spanning the public and private sectors, with the complexities that this can create. There are publications proposing how healthcare leaders should be trained, but there is much less on what works, or does not, as they seek to refine their leadership styles, their relationships with their employees, and the culture of their organizations to create more human-centered services. (Weintraub & McKee, 2019, 138–144). Belias and Koustelios (2014, 451–470) suggest the key is to choose the right approach to culture change and that leadership is associated with organizational culture, primarily through the processes of articulating a vision, and to a lesser extent through the setting of high-performance expectations and providing individual support to workers. Although social systems comprising work, people, formal and informal systems, organizations are resistant to change and designed to neutralize the impact of attempts at change, culture change is necessary for creating and reinforcing organizational transformation needed to shift service creation to more human-centered interventions (Belias & Koustelios, 2014, 451–470).

Several fundamental understandings are critical to the development of services designed to address the health gap, particularity the affordability gap. First, the slow rate of affordability gap reduction may be symptomatic of inequities induced through the limited approach to understanding (and acting on) the social determinants of health (The Lancet Global Health, 2016, 1). The existing body of evidence suggests that social care interventions in housing, income support, nutritional support, care coordination, and community outreach have a positive impact on health (Taylor et al., 2016, 1–20). As such, these interventions should be of interest to policymakers and practitioners seeking to leverage social care to improve health status or reduce medical costs, but the current general lack of understanding of the direct relationship between medical and social care suggests the need for additional data and for improved use of the existing body of evidence for human-centered service development (Taylor et al., 2016, 1–20). Findings and data from the current research, the majority of which was conducted with low-income populations, suggest that reducing health gaps may require linking unconventional partners to adequately address human needs (Taylor et al., 2016, 1–20).

Human centric data is needed to effectively support understanding the ways that medical and social care services are interdependent and to address levels of mutual incomprehension which often so create deep concerns about safe provision of care, application of appropriate care standards, and information and skills transfer (Thompson, 2015, 1).

Data collected regarding the SDOH, which is inherently multi-source, can be used to help frame the financial case for addressing the health gap. Addressing the financial considerations may be especially compelling for healthcare systems and other medical providers who have embraced value-based reimbursement models, including accountable care models (Taylor et al., 2016, 1–20).

SDOH data might also be leveraged to address the "wrong pocket" issue. The wrong pocket issue occurs when an organization, industry, or market sector invests in changing care outcomes but the reward for their efforts is realized by others. The wrong pocket conundrum also reduces investments by medical care providers in non-medical factors that would improve health outcomes (Taylor et al., 2016, 1–20). Likewise, many social care interventions produce positive health outcomes, but the social care sector may receive little reward for their contribution to improving health (Taylor et al., 2016, 1–20). A medical care organization that contributes to an individual's health may not receive any social benefit from those health improvements (Taylor et al., 2016, 1–20). This disconnect in reward discourages cross-sector medical and social care collaboration even when there exists a high degree of mutual dependence and potential reward from coordinated medical and social care (Butler, 2018, 1; Taylor et al., 2016, 1–20). Data and its analysis should be available to policymakers, payers, and providers to enable them to identify and support human centric service programs and processes of care provision that can bridge the health gap (Butler, 2018, 1; Taylor et al., 2016, 1–20). Acceptance of this human-centered approach may depend on the collection and analysis of data demonstrating a positive relationship between social care investments, and improved health outcomes as well as the case for health-related investment into the non-medical sector (Butler, 2018, 1). Data is also needed to support the blending and braiding of government agency budgets to create crossover benefits and mitigate wrong pocket disincentives (Butler, 2018, 1). Data is also needed to support the development of entities dedicated to and funded for enhancing health rather than simply providing medical care or social care. Data demonstrating the full cross-sector value of investments made through and to these bodies will support the basic business model in a way that provides enhanced support for investment and spending decisions (Butler, 2018, 1).

8   Conclusion

Finally, the use of a combination of non-healthcare generated data and information with healthcare generated data/information to improve the human centeredness of health services design and the development of learning systems to meet collaboration needs across non-clinical health service providers hold promise to support the creation of high value, reimbursable health services. This chapter explored the potential to create reciprocal innovation in traditional medical care delivery and social services as a function of these gap reduction strategies, but responsibility for addressing health cannot be tied to national and international health organizations such as ministries or Non-Governmental Organizations (NGOs) as health status is shaped by the intersectoral nature of wider economic, political and cultural contexts (Leppo et al., 2013, 1–359). Arguably the very nature of these wider economic, political, and cultural contexts implies that "upstream" actions, such as policies focused on a population approach, redistributive policies, programs that address or that account for social norms and/or power relationships, efforts that address political literacy and advocacy, efforts that are place-based, participatory, or those that lead to transformative action, efforts that employ approaches that are underpinned by systems thinking and complexity management and those that employ methodological pluralism are required (McMahon, 2021, 1–8). While solutions postulated, developed, and deployed by individual health and social care entities may employ "upstream" actions, it is improbable that they have the reach to develop comprehensive solutions. What may be required is to develop solutions that bridge the gap between health care and social care that recognize and elevate the expertise held by both while acknowledging their place on the continuum of health. Solutions so created have the potential to create reciprocal innovation in health delivery and to expand the delivery of health at the individual, local, regional, national, and global levels.

References

Abu Dabrh, A. M., Gallacher, K., Boehmer, K., Hargraves, G., & Mair, F. (2015). Minimally disruptive medicine: The evidence and conceptual progress supporting a new era of healthcare. *The Journal of the Royal College of Physicians of Edinburgh, 45*(2), 114–117. https://doi.org/10.4997/JRCPE.2015.205

Adler, N. E., & Stewart, J. (2010). Health disparities across the lifespan: Meaning, methods, and mechanisms. *Annals of the New York Academy of Sciences, 1186*(2010), 5–23. https://doi.org/10.1111/j.1749-6632.2009.05337.x

Alderwick, H., & Gottlieb, L. M. (2019). Meanings and misunderstandings: A social determinants of health lexicon for health care systems. *Milbank Quarterly, 97*(2), 407–419. https://doi.org/10.1111/1468-0009

An, J. Y., Yom, Y. H., & Ruggiero, J. S. (2011). Organizational culture, quality of work life, and organizational effectiveness in Korean university hospitals. *Journal of Transcultural Nursing, 22*(1), 22–30.

Belias, D., & Koustelios, A. (2014). The impact of leaderhip and change management strategy on organizational culture. *European Scientific Journal, 10*(7), 451–470.

Berwick, D. M. (2008). The science of improvement. *JAMA, 299*(10), 1182–1184.

Blas, E., Roebbel, N., Rajan, D., & Valentine, N. (2016). Chapter 12-Intersectoral planning for health and health equity. In G. Schmets, D. Rajan, S. Kadandale (Eds.), *Strategizing national health in the 21st century: A handbook* (pp. 1–52). Geneva: World Health Organization.

Butler, S. (2018). How "Wrong Pockets" hurt health. JAMA Forum Archive. Published online August 22, 2018. A7(1). https://doi.org/10.1001/jamahealthforum.2018.0033

Challis, D., Hughs, J., Xie, C., & Jolly, D. (2014). An examination of factors influencing delayed discharge of older people from hospital. *International Journal of Geriatric Psychiatry., 29*(2), 160–168. https://doi.org/10.1002/gps.3983

Choi, E., & Sonin, J. (2022). Determinants of Health GOINVO, Retrieved from info@goinvo.com on March 1, 2022.

CSDH. (2008). Closing the gap in a generation: Health equity through action on the social determinants of health. Final Report of the Commission on Social Determinants of Health. World Health Organization, Geneva (pp. 1–33)

Ghinea, V. M., & Bratianu, C. (2012). Organizational culture modeling. *Management & Marketing Challenges for the Knowledge Society, 7*(2), 257–276.

Gilmour, H. (2016). Social participation and the health and well-being of Canadian seniors. Health Reports. 2012. Retrieved Oct 29, 2016, from http://www.statcan.gc.ca/pub/82-003-x/2012004/article/11720-eng.html

Golden, R., Emery-Tiburcio, E., Post, S., Ewald, B., & Newman, M. (2019). Connecting social, clinical, and home care services for persons with serious illness in the community. *Journal of the American Geriatrics Society, 67*(62), S412–S418. https://doi.org/10.1111/jgs.15900

Groeneveld, B. S., Dekkers, T., Boon, B., D'Olivo, P. (2018). Challenges for design researchers in healthcare. *Design for Health, 2*(2), 305–326. https://doi.org/10.1080/24735132.2018.1541699

Harvey, J. B., Vanderbrink, J., Mahmud, Y., Kitt-Lewis, E., Wolf, L., Shaw, B., Ridgley, M. S., Damberg, C. L., & Scanlon, D. P. (2020). Understanding how health systems facilitate primary care redesign. *Health Services Research, 55*(3), 1144–1154. https://doi.org/10.1111/1475-6773.13576

Holden, R. J., Schubert, C. C., Mickelson, R. S. (2015). The patient work system: An analysis of self-care performance barriers among elderly heart failure patients and their informal caregivers. *Applied Ergonomics, 47*(133), 133–150. https://doi.org/10.1016/j.apergo.2014.09.009; http://europepmc.org/abstract/MED/25479983

Humphries, R. (2015). Integrated health and social care in England-progress and prospects. *Health Policy, 119*(7), 856–859. https://doi.org/10.1016/j.healthpol.2015.04.010

Hwabejire, J. O., Kaafarani, H. M. A., Imam, A. M., Solis, C. V., Verge, J., Sullivan, N. M., DeMoya, M. A., Alam, H. B., & Velmahos, G. (2013). Excessively long hospital stays after trauma are not related to the severity of illness: Let's aim to the right target! *JAMA Surgery.,* *148*(10), 956–961. https://doi.org/10.1001/jamasurg.2013.2148

Hwang, J., & Christensen, C. M. (2007). Disruptive innovation in health care delivery: A framework for business-model innovation. *Health Affairs, 27*(5), 1329–1335. https://doi.org/10.1377/hlthaff.27.5.1329

Institute of Medicine, Smith, M., Saunders, R., Stuckhardt, L., & McGinnis, J. M. (Eds.) (2013). *Best care at lower cost: The path to continuously learning health care in America* (pp. 1–312). Washington, DC: The National Academies Press.

Körner, M., Wirtz, M. A., Bengel, J., & Göritz, A. S. (2015). Relationship of organizational culture, teamwork and job satisfaction in interprofessional teams. *BMC Health Services Research, 15*(243), 1–12.

Kuluski, K., Ho, J. W., Hans, P. K., Nelson, M., (2017). Community care for people with complex care needs: Bridging the gap between health and social care. *International Journal of Integrated Care, 17*(4):2, 1–11. https://doi.org/10.5334/ijic.2944

Leppo, K., Ollila, E., Pena, S., Wismar, M., & Cook, S., (Eds.) (2013). *Health in all policies. Seizing opportunities, implementing policies* (pp. 1–359). Helsinki, Finland: Ministry of Social Affairs and Health.

Maithel, N., Chaubey, D. S., & Gupta, D. (2012). Impact of organization culture on employee motivation and job performance. *International Journal of Research in Commerce & Management, 3*(5), 68–74.

McMahon, N. E. (2021). Framing action to reduce health inequalities: What is argued for through use of the 'upstream–downstream' metaphor? *Journal of Public Health, fdab157,* 1–8. https://doi.org/10.1093/pubmed/fdab157

Melles, M., Albayrak, A., & Goossens, R. (2021). Innovating health care: Key characteristics of human-centered design. *International Journal for Quality in Health Care: Journal of the International Society for Quality in Health Care., 33*(S1), 37–44. https://doi.org/10.1093/intqhc/mzaa127

Moineddin, R., Nie, J. Z., Wang, L., Tracy, C. S., & Upshur, R. E. G. (2010). Measuring change in health status of older adults at the population level: the transition probability model. *BMC Health Service Research, 10*(306). https://doi.org/10.1186/1472-6963-10-306.

National Academies of Sciences, Engineering, and Medicine (2019). *Integrating social care into the delivery of health care: Moving upstream to improve the Nation's Health* (pp. 1–163). Washington, DC: The National Academies Press. https://doi.org/10.17226/25467

Nayak, B., & Barik, A. (2013). Assessment of the link between organizational culture and job satisfaction (Study of an Indian public sector). *International Journal of Information, Business and Management, 5*(4), 47–61.

Ozkaynak, M., Valdez, R., Hannah, K., Woodhouse, G., & Klem, P. (2021). Understanding gaps between daily living and clinical settings in chronic disease management: Qualitative study. *Journal of Medical Internet Research, 23*(2), e17590. https://doi.org/10.2196/175901-8

Reeves, S., Pelone, F., Harrison, R., Goldman, J. & Zwarenstein, M. (2017). Interprofessional collaboration to improve professional practice and healthcare outcomes. *Cochrane Database of Systematic Reviews* (6). Art No. CD000072, 1–40.

Santana, M. J., Manalili, K., Jolley, R. J., Zelinsky, S., & Lu, M. (2018). How to practice person-centred care: A conceptual framework. *Health Expectations, 21*(2), 429–440.

Shahzad, F., Luqman, R. A., Khan, A. R., & Shabbir, L. (2012). Impact of organizational culture on organizational performance—An overview. *Interdisciplinary Journal of Contemporary Research in Business, 3*(9), 975–985.

Taylor, L. A., Tan, A. X., Coyle, C. E., Ndumele, C., Rogan, E., Canavan, M., Curry, L. A., & Bradley, E. H. (2016). Leveraging the social determinants of health: What works? *PLoS ONE, 11*(8), e0160217. https://doi.org/10.1371/journal.pone.01602171-20

The Lancet Global Health. (2016). *Bridging the global health gap.* Lancet Glob Health, Retrieved March 15, 2022, from https://www.thelancet.com/journals/langlo/article/PIIS2214-109X(16)30190-5/fulltext#articleInformation

Thompson, T. M. (2015). *We must bridge the gap between health and social care nursing.* Nursing Times, Retrieved April 15, 2022, from https://www.nursingtimes.net/opinion/we-must-bridge-the-gap-between-health-and-social-care-nursing

Tinetti, M. E., Fried, T. R., & Boyd, C. M. (2012). Designing health care for the most common chronic condition–multimorbidity. *JAMA, 307*(23), 2493–2494. https://doi.org/10.1001/jama.2012.5265

Vrijhoef, H., & Thorlby, R. (2016). *Developing care for a changing population: Supporting patients with costly, complex needs.* London, England. [Google Scholar]

Weintraub, P., & McKee, M. (2019). Leadership for innovation in healthcare: An exploration. *International Journal of Health Policy and Management, 8*(3), 138–144.

West, K. M., Blacksher, E., & Burke, W. (2017). Genomics, health disparities, and missed opportunities for the nation's research agenda. *JAMA, 317*(18), 1831–1832. https://doi.org/10.1001/jama.2017.3096

Whicher, D. (2017). National Academy of Medicine Accelerating progress toward continuous learning: A National Academy of Medicine meeting summary. Agency for Healthcare Research and Quality website. Accessed September 11, 2019, from ahrq.gov/sites/default/files/wysiwyg/professionals/systems/learning-health-systems/Learning-Health-Systems-Meeting-Summary.pdf.

World Health Organization. (2017). *World Bank and WHO: Half the world lacks access to essential health services.* Toyko: WHO press release.

Dr. Patricia Alafaireet has a broad background in biomedical informatics, health information technology, and delivery of health care in rural environments with a focus on data analytics, decision support, and enterprise information architecture. Her research and publications focus on big data use in predictive modeling, mobile health software application development, human-centered design, Accountable Health Comm-unity development, and healthcare products and services design for use in day-to-day operations. As a Co–PI, investigator or consultant on several NIH and USDA-funded grants, she has been involved in research and in projects to extend the use of informatics into regular clinical practice.

Dr. Philippe Diserens has been working in health care for over 25 years in various leading roles and functions in clinical and hospital management. Years of experience in international health systems regulation, and strategic consulting for international health service providers have enabled him to develop as a Health Economics expert for international hospital management. Dr. Philippe Diserens has been working at the Psychiatric University Hospital Zurich (Switzerland) as Vice-Director DPTS (Directorate of Nursing, Therapies and Social Work) since 2019. As the Head of Health Economics, he is managing the directorate as an independent-cooperative competence center, which helps shape the clinical business areas of the hospital with high-quality, innovative, and health-economically balanced treatment processes.

The Change from Leadership to Leadershift—The Human-Centered Service Design Approach Requires New Leadership Competencies in the Health System

Karin Messer-Misak and Christian Lagger

ABSTRACT

The human-centered design approach requires an enhanced integration of all those involved in the service process. This is particularly relevant in the health-care system, since human interaction, supported by modern IT processes, requires that the needs of the service providers and those of the patients are understood and considered holistically to enable a constantly improving itera-tive service process. Differentiated management skills are demanded to set the framework conditions in normative management, to align the planning in strate-gic management, and to design and implement the requirements in operational management. This chapter describes which new skills are required within the different management levels to achieve the best possible results in service.

1 The Challenges of Human-Centered Design of Services for Management in the Health System

Overall economic changes interact and have an impact on macro-economic sys-tems, business contexts, and their processes and interfaces where clients and health service providers come into contact. A human-centered design of services is inevitable, influences the collaboration between clients and staff in a company, and

K. Messer-Misak (✉)
Fachhochschule JOANNEUM GmbH, Institut Für eHealth/Gesundheitsinformatik, Eckerstr. 30I, 8020 Graz, Austria
e-mail: karin.messer-misak@fh-joanneum.at

C. Lagger
Krankenhaus der Elisabethinen GmbH, Graz Elisabethinergasse 14, 8020 Graz, Austria
e-mail: christian.lagger@elisabethinen.at

© The Author(s), under exclusive license to Springer Nature Switzerland AG 2023   21
M. A. Pfannstiel (ed.), *Human-Centered Service Design for Healthcare Transformation*,
https://doi.org/10.1007/978-3-031-20168-4_2

thus places new demands on management. A culture of constant change and rapid development is opposed to the desire for stability and orientation. Designing an agile and people-centered system that can provide safety and orientation between agility and stability is necessary (Freisl, 2021, 142).

1.1 Fundamental Challenges

A generational change in the workforce that is already taking place, the emerging shortage of personnel in the institutions of the health system, constantly challenges managers to optimally deploy and motivate their teams. To design the services offered as functionally as possible and to continuously adapt them to patient needs is in the foreground. Attempts to cope with the requirements by applying the usual guidelines, standards and controls are not enough. To successfully deal with the current complexity, new management patterns are required that consciously use the uncertainties and diversity.

1.2 Linking Human and Digital Interactions

The need to not only educate and empower the recipient of health services, but to actively involve them in the processes of service delivery, requires as a principle that this is useful, usable, and desirable for the client. On the part of the provider, the interfaces must be designed to be effective and efficient. Digital and human interactions are linked to provide a better service. The prerequisite for this is to understand people's needs, to look at them holistically and to design them in an iterative process. The focus is on topics such as holism, interactions, diversity, and networking.

1.3 Uncertain Conditions and Short Interaction Times

This requirement to design human-centered services, both for employees and clients, is essential for a new generation in which healthcare transformation is taking place. The challenge is obvious: as a leader, it is no longer enough to recognize trends and act in a timely manner. To consistently pursue agility and readiness for success in a shortening timeframe under uncertain conditions is the mandate. Maxwell (2019, 5) has coined the term "leadershift" for this as "the ability and willingness to make a leadership change that positively influences organizational and personal growth". Freisl (2021, 143) speaks in this context of "integrative leadership", i.e., leadership as an interaction process in which the role of the manager is understood as a system designer, innovator, and moderator.

1.4   Contradictory Demands on Management

The demands placed on management seem to be contradictory. Often the factors that seem necessary for making decisions are already obsolete or have changed. Risks are less calculable and the time available for strategic planning, gathering facts, making decisions, creating optimal conditions for implementation, and finally realizing the planned goal step by step and then reflecting on it is reduced.

"Leadershift will require you to rely on values, principles, and strategy, but will also push you to rely on innovation, to seek out options, to harness creativity" (Maxwell, 2019, 8). It is precisely this balancing act between continuity, which provides security, and the need for adaptation, which innovations require, that gives rise to the opportunities for learning and development.

In this chapter, the authors would like to show a practical reference to the current developments in service design in the health system and link these to the resulting necessities in management.

2   The Culture of Rapid Progress

The "culture of rapid progress" also demands its tribute in management: Maxwell describes concise changes in management in his book "Leadershift". Human-centered service design requires management that coordinates the social and economic actors of institutions and enables them to act on resources and create shared value (cf. Wieland et al., 2012, 12–25).

Mieke van der Bijl-Brouwer (2019, 183) defines complex social service organizations as ongoing, repetitive patterns of relationships between people. The service therefore only comes about through the interaction between the service provider and the customer and is thus immanent and heterogeneous (cf. Junginger, 2017, 38–44). Actions influence the structures and affect the actors (cf. Warg & Deetien, 2021, 2–29). One of the challenges is to act as a team. Everyone has different needs, and in management it is important to find out how the entities can optimally work together as a team. Successful organizations are not defined by one person running the company, but by each individual associated with it. The idea associated with service design that the touchpoints (Secomandi & Snelders, 2011, 20; cf. Messer-Misak, 2019, 203–205) between service organizations and their customers, including the material artifacts must be supplemented by other aspects requires an analysis of the service construct as a first step. Edvardsson and Olsson (1996, 64) divide the construct into three elements:

- The tangible or intangible, temporary or permanent outcome of the service, and how customers perceive the outcome.
- The service process that is required to deliver an outcome and actively involves the customer in the process; and
- The service prerequisites whose resources are required to deliver the service.

A holistic and interconnected system supports the staff in the organization and ideally represents a self-revitalizing system (Freisl, 2021, 145). In Fig. 1, the authors illustrate the interrelationships of a complex service organization and the management levels with their focal points and necessary management requirements.

According to Edvardsson and Olsson, the prerequisites for the development of new services must consider three components on different management levels (Edvardsson & Olsson, 1996, 64):

- At the normative level: designing a service concept that takes into account the primary and secondary needs of the clients and provides a mindset that can be lived in the core services and support services.
- At the strategic level: plan and deliver a service system that includes the work-force, the organizational elements, and the required infrastructure and considers the physical environment.
- At the operational level: defining and implementing the requirements and procedures of the service process and providing feedback for further development.

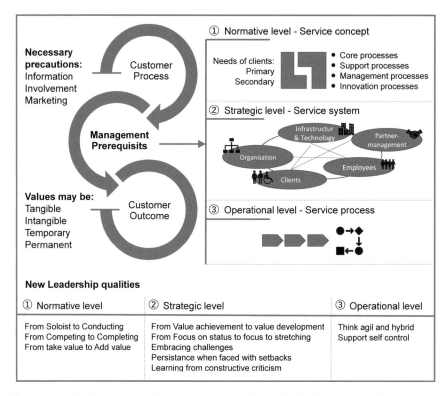

Fig. 1 Analysis of complex service organizations and the new leadership qualities. Own representation. *Source* Authors' own Illustration (2022)

The particular demands of developing, continuously maintaining, and improving a human-centered and personalized service system require new leadership patterns.

The following section describes the new demands made on management at these three levels in the health system to optimally promote further development.

2.1 Normative Level

At the normative level, goals, principles, norms, and rules of the game, which are aimed at ensuring the long-term viability and development of the organization, are defined. The building blocks are a vision, a corporate policy and constitution and the corporate culture based on them. This is where the general orientation of the company is anchored. The legal and organizational frameworks in the Austrian health system are mostly politically predetermined and leave little creative room for maneuvering with regard to a growth strategy; stabilization strategies are usually pursued.

The main pillar of normative management, responsible corporate governance, which considers corporate as well as social values, is the key to the human-centered service design approach. The special contribution lies in satisfying the needs of the reference groups, i.e., those of clients, employees, and cooperating institutions (Wördenweber, 2019, 6). The level of normative management contributes significantly to a value orientation (Zapp & Wittland, 2022, 185). The requirement here is to be efficient and flexible at the same time. This requires the use of what already exists (exploitation) as well as the exploration of what is new and is referred to as organizational ambidexterity (OReilly & Tushmann, 2008, 185; cf. Raisch et al., 2009, 685–695). Olivan (2019, 34) describes exploitation as efficiency-oriented, with costs, profit, and the fulfillment of patient needs in the foreground. In terms of corporate culture, this is characterized by low risk, stability, and high quality. This is often accompanied by rather authoritarian management styles that act in a top-down manner. Whereas in exploration, where the focus is on innovation and growth with the desire for scientific advancement, an adaptable, organic, and less routinized organizational structure is required. Behavior and culture tend to demand risk-taking, flexibility, high speed, and freedom for "experimentation". This requires a more visionary, involving leadership style. Ambidexterity can therefore only succeed if all design factors are coordinated with each other and balanced to the same extent and intensity (Fojcik, 2015, 22).

The entire service system is to be aligned in such a way that the client's involvement in the co-production of the service supports the result—thus enabling a relationship between the company and client to be established to such an extent that optimal added value is achieved.

Maxwell puts it in a nutshell: "You cannot be the same, think the same, and act the same if you hope to be successful in a world that does not remain the same" (Maxwell, 2019, 7). The goal is to connect human, digital and physical interactions to meet the needs of all stakeholders. This requires an understanding of people's needs to view the interactions holistically.

Maxwell summarizes the current requirements in management in 7 points to a framework for leadershift (cf. Maxwell, 2019, 9–18):

- Continually Learn, Unlearn, and Relearn.
- Value yesterday but live in today.
- Rely on speed, but thrive on timing.
- See the big picture as the picture keeps getting bigger.
- Live in today but think about tomorrow.
- Move forward courageously during uncertainty.
- Realize today's best will not meet tomorrow's challenges.

To promote the design approach in the health system on a normative level, it is, therefore, necessary that staff, co-partners (social insurances, referrers, cooperating healthcare institutions), and clients perceive themselves as an active part of the process, which presupposes that the primary and secondary needs of the stakeholders are known and that they are actively involved in the decision-making process. Management thus has a new role from soloist to conductor, ensuring that those involved in the service process know the way and can keep up during the process. In the past, management was often associated with leadership and speed. Leading others successfully to the goal means walking the path together at a common speed. The mindset in normative management is to move from a take value to an add value and from a thinking of competing to completing (thinks win–win, practices shared thinking, includes others).

2.2 Strategic Level

At the strategic level, the entire service system must be planned and coordinated according to the company's purpose. Human, infrastructural, material, and financial resources are to be aligned with the corporate goal. These components indirectly determine the customer potential and influence the possibilities of implementing the customer-centered service design approach. Therefore, significant preparations are already necessary in this phase, which require new management skills.

Several attempts at classifying strategy types have been developed in the literature (cf. Xaver & Haas, 2016, 178–179). The authors refer to the classifications of Xaver and Haas (2016, 179) and pick out only those strategy approaches for which new specific requirements arise for management in the health system. Depending on the question, we can distinguish between requirements for the organizational scope concerning the corporate strategy/business strategy and the functional strategy. In the hospital association, the strategies within the framework of the degree of autonomy also play a role, which primarily have an impact on the infrastructure. Here it must be considered to what extent cooperation and integration strategies can be implemented. Regarding the scope for the functions, the new requirements for the performance potentials with the focus on the personnel strategy, partner management, and the infrastructure/technology strategies can be particularly emphasized in the health system. These performance potentials contribute directly to value creation and thus to the success of the company.

2.2.1 Strategies in the Organizational Scope

Achieving excellence in all areas is our goal. Often it is not possible to achieve this status in all areas at the same time. Therefore, it makes sense to strive for and implement excellence in the essential sub-areas (view vital thing). Maxwell (c.f. 2019, 46–50) recommends to promote a culture focused on growth and not goals "promoting a culture focused on growth not goals". Our current management techniques (SWOT analysis, business performance scorecards, etc.) aim to formulate goals, plan implementation measures for them, and implement them on budget and on time. The difference to the growth-oriented culture lies primarily in the following aspects of a new approach (Maxwell, 2019, 47). Cooperation strategies can be based on

- Values Development (vs. Values Achievement),
- Focuses on Stretching (vs. Focus on Status),
- Honors Serving (vs. Honors Privilege),
- Target is growth (vs. Target is arrival).

In this context, strategies relating to independence are of particular importance: synergy effects based on cooperation between two or more companies can usually be achieved within the framework of risk and cost sharing due to the use of shared infrastructure or services (e.g., joint purchasing) (Xaver & Haas, 2016, 188). Little attention has been paid to date to possible synergy effects due to a transfer of competence.

This expanded approach in management (Maxwell, 2019, 49–50) requires a shift toward a growth mindset, in which the following qualities are particularly required:

- Believes intelligence can be developed (vs. is static),
- Embraces challenges (vs. avoiding them),
- Persists when faced with setbacks (vs. giving up easily),
- Sees effort as a path to mastery,
- Learns from constructive criticism,
- Finds lessons and inspiration in the success of others,
- Reaches higher levels of achievement.

2.2.2 Strategies in the performance processes

In the center of performance potentials, the performance process with the following components is particularly relevant (cf. Xaver & Haas, 2016, 512–513):

Human Resources Strategy

Personnel, as the bearers of all core competencies, play a special role in the health-care system. Creating differentiation and loyalty by optimally shaping the needs of the staff in interdisciplinary work with each other and toward the patient requires special new competencies. For this, it is necessary to understand the interactions between all parties involved, to uncover problem areas and identify opportunities (possibly through a customer journey map), and to focus on these.

Partner Management

The more complex the system, the more extensive the communication chan-nels, dependencies, and decision-making. Systems are capable of development if they can perceive changes in the environment and react effectively to the changes (Xaver & Haas, 2016, 255). In the healthcare system, the structure and maintenance between the individual suppliers, service providers, upstream and downstream healthcare institutions, and the organizational/governmental bodies play an essential role. On the one hand, the availability of materials and services required for the provision of services is pursued, considering the spread of the procurement risk, but also the increase of flexibility, the reduction of procurement-relevant costs, and the protection of the environment are taken into account (cf. Xaver & Haas, 2016, 517–518).

Infrastructure and Technology Strategy

In addition to the factors mentioned above, technology and the necessary infras-tructure are another potential that has a significant influence on the treatment process and thus also on the provision of client-centered services. This should be designed in an innovation-friendly and future-oriented way. One of the formulated fields of action to implement a strategy for research, technology, and innovation for the year 2030 is (Bundeskanzleramt, 2020, 2) to expand the technology infras-tructure and to ensure accessibility, as well as to develop and promote human resources. The considerations are based on a clear awareness of efficiency and increased output.

In his book "Leadershift", Maxwell (2019) describes the necessary prerequisites that are particularly relevant for the level of strategic management:

The hitherto management-oriented approach refers to the setting of "achievable but motivated" targets. Large goals are achieved step by step by breaking them down into smaller targets and thus remain manageable. Maxwell describes the change of new requirements in leader-shifts as "growth in everything to growth in a few vital things" (Maxwell, 2019, 44) as well as "growth with a timeline ver-sus growth without a finish line" (Maxwell, 2019, 46). This requires the ability to embrace change, the intention to learn every day and to reflect on what is learned (Maxwell, 2019, 51), and the passion to learn relative to the fear of making mis-takes (Maxwell, 2019, 52). The ability to react before others react and to do more than others. Maxwell describes the process of people management as a process of "pleasing people to challenging people" (cf. Maxwell, 2019, 81–101). For this, he contrasts two sides that need to be balanced to move people from "I like being on the team" to "I need to produce for the team" (Maxwell, 2019, 100).

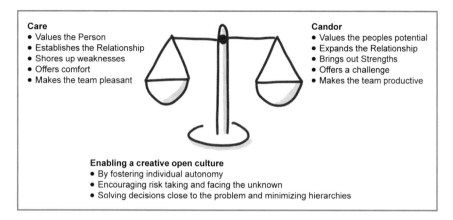

Care
- Values the Person
- Establishes the Relationship
- Shores up weaknesses
- Offers comfort
- Makes the team pleasant

Candor
- Values the peoples potential
- Expands the Relationship
- Brings out Strengths
- Offers a challenge
- Makes the team productive

Enabling a creative open culture
- By fostering individual autonomy
- Encouraging risk taking and facing the unknown
- Solving decisions close to the problem and minimizing hierarchies

Fig. 2 Balance between care and candor. *Source* Maxwell (2019, 101, modified Illustration)

Two aspects are particularly important here: Care and Candor, both of which must be nurtured and implemented in equal measure to realize the described strategic processes in the sense of a customer-oriented service organization. Figure 2 shows the individual aspects to achieve a balance.

2.3   Operational Level

Sooner or later, institutions in the health system will be faced with the challenge of digital transformation, which will not only have an impact on previous strategies and organizational forms, but also on the expectations of management in operational implementation. Strategies are implemented and feedback on the needs and interests of the individual stakeholders is required from the operational management level. Partnerships need to be fostered to create an environment conducive to innovation.

Conventional linear thinking, which is still prevalent in the health system, is now being extended by networked thinking. The provision of surgical services should be efficient. The length of stay in the inpatient sector has been reduced in recent years, not least because of improved treatment options and changes in the remuneration system, but also because all processes have been better coordinated and reformed with methods (cf. Kraft, 2016, 9–25) such as lean management, CIP (continual improvement process), TQM (Total Quality Management). Through the possibilities of systematic procedures, optimization and measurement, free potentials were identified, which were reflected in cost reductions and/or the avoidance of redundant activities.

What remains open is the desire for sustainability and an improved use of technical aids. It must be analyzed which processes are suitable for digitalization and which benefits arise from this for the clients as well as for the staff. To handle these changes in a purely project-based way does not go far enough. These processes require cross-departmental cooperation with the transparent allocation of tasks and responsibilities. A purely efficiency-driven functional orientation is not enough; the processes must be carefully planned and monitored by management and require extended implementation capabilities.

The company Index Research analyzed 203,000 job advertisements from 22 print media and 35 job boards for six months in 2021 on behalf of the StepStone company in order to filter out which skills are mainly required (cf. von Leidl & Drucker, 2022): Independent and autonomous work was demanded in job advertisements for "young professionals" as well as for managers with many years of experience in about one in three advertisements, which implies that new solutions can be proposed and thus actively contribute to the success and further development of the company. In second place was the willingness to take responsibility. Making decisions and then reliably implementing them was required in more than 26% of the job advertisements analyzed.

The ability to work in a team is becoming more and more important; especially with contact restrictions and home office activities, a constructive exchange of ideas, in which one's own suggestions are made and respectful treatment of each other is relevant. Closely related to this is the ability to communicate, i.e., how messages are conveyed within the team, to clients, company partners, and managers.

Flexibility to adapt to new demands or unforeseen situations was mentioned in more than 37,700 job advertisements, ahead of resilience and stress resistance. Figure 3 shows the skills that are currently most in demand in job advertisements.

In summary, it can be stated at the level of operational management that the change in values, the shortage of human capital, increased interdisciplinary thinking/networking and cooperation and the demand for direct active involvement of the patient in the service process require enhanced skills. The ability can be summarized as agile and hybrid leadership. In other words, the ability to take responsibility and support staff in their self-direction with the requirement to maintain an overview and immediate reflection under a high degree of flexibility.

Due to current changes in work situations, the skills of hybrid leadership are required in addition to the known classical competences. These are characterized by the promotion of cooperation in the team, which works partly in the office and partly at home; this requires strong communication skills as well as moderation skills to lead online meetings efficiently. At the same time, a sensitivity for recognizing excessive demands and hidden conflict potential.

3   Conclusion

Managers must deal with the future more than other professions. In the health system, mainly medical/therapeutic/nursing, social, political, technological, ecological, legal, and economic factors are at work, which must be coordinated with each other so that a smooth effective operation is guaranteed. We find ourselves

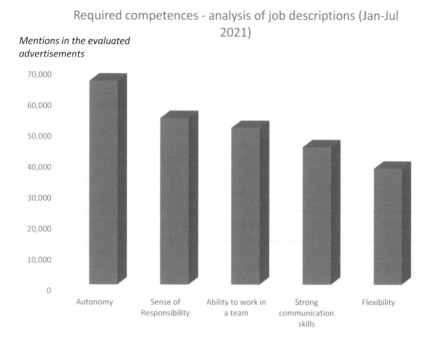

Fig. 3 Required competences—analysis of job descriptions. Source: (von Leidl & Drucker, 2022) Author's own illustration

in a radically and rapidly changing business world again. This is accompanied by a change in values that brings about new approaches in the service sector, digitalization complements this process and poses several challenges—this requires a shift in leadership or enhanced management skills.

Depending on the management level at which one operates, skills are required that enable the concept of human-centered service design to be successfully implemented. In normative management, these are above all the ability to recognize that today's approaches cannot solve tomorrow's challenges and how we can create a mindset to be able to deal with uncertainties and changing requirements quickly and creatively. Strategic management requires appropriate flexibility in organization, staff deployment, use of infrastructure and technologies, and the joy of change implemented with appropriate continuity. In operational management, hybrid and agile action is required.

References

Bundeskanzleramt. (2020). Strategie der Bundesregierung für Forschung, Technologie und Innovation (FTI) 2030 und FTI-Pakt 2021–23, Bundesregierung der Republik Österreich, Wien. Retrieved May 10, from https://www.bundeskanzleramt.gv.at/themen/forschungskoord ination_fti.html

Edvardsson, B., & Olsson, J. (1996). Key concepts for new service development. *The Service Industries Journal, 16*(2), 140–164.

Fojcik, T. M. (2015). *Ambidextrie und Unternehmenserfolg bei einem diskontinuierlichen Wandel - Eine empirische Analyse unter besonderer Berücksichtigung der Anpassung und Veränderung von Organisationsarchitekturen im Zeitablauf*. Dissertation. Universität Duisburg-Essen 2014: Springer (Strategisches Kompetenz-Management). Essen.

Freisl, J. (2021). Neue Führungsmuster für die VUKA-Welt. In: Moll, A. & Khayati, S. (Eds.), *Excellence-Handbuch. Grundlagen und Anwendung des EFQM Modells 2020* (pp. 142–148). Kissing: WEKA Media GmbH & Co KG.

Junginger, S. (2017). *Services as key to effective government, in transforming public services by design: Re-Orienting policies*. London, UK: Routledge.

Kraft, T. (2016). *Lean Management im Krankenhaus. Konzept und praxisorientierte Handlungsempfehlungen. Vom Versorgungsauftrag zum Management von Krankenhäusern*. Wiesbaden: Springer Gabler.

Maxwell John, C. (2019). *Leadershift. The 11 essential changes every leader must embrace*. HaperCollins Leadership (Ed.). Hamburg.

Messer-Misak, K. (2019). Vom Lean Management zur Reorganisation. Der Einfluss der Lean-Hospital-Philosophie auf Dienstleistungs- und Prozessinnovationen. In: M. A. Pfannstiel, K. Kassel, & C. Rasche (Eds.), *Innovationen und Innovationsmanagement im Gesundheitswesen. Technologie, Produkte und Dienstleistungen voranbringen* (pp. 203–205). Wiesbaden: Springer Gabler.

Olivan, P. (2019). *Methode zur organisatorischen Gestaltung radikaler Technologieentwicklungen unter Berücksichtigung der Ambidextrie*. Stuttgart: Fraunhofer Verlag. https://doi.org/10.18419/opus-10639

O'Reilly, C. A., III., & Tushman, M. L. (2008). Ambidexterity as a dynamic capability: Resolving the innovator's dilemma. *Research in Organizational Behavior, 28*, 185–206. https://doi.org/10.1016/j.riob.2008.06.002,pp.185-206

Raisch, S., Birkinshaw, J., Probst, G., & Tushman, M. (2009). Organizational ambidexterity: Balancing exploitation and exploration for sustained performance. *Organization Science, 20*(4), 685–695.

Secomandi, F., & Snelders, D. (2011). The object of service design published by Massachusetts Institute of Technology Press (MIT Press). *Design Issues, 27*(3), 20–34.

van der Bijl-Brouwer, M. (2019). Faculty of transdisciplinary innovation, University of Technology Sydney, Australia. Designing for social infrastructures in complex service systems: A human-centered and social systems perspective on service design. Publishing services by Elsevier B.V., Amsterdam.

von Leidl, S., Drucker, C. (2022). StepStone-Jobreport 2022. Studie. Stellenmarktentwicklung nach Branchen, Insights in Kandidat*innenmentalität & Ausblicke auf die Zukunft des Bewerbens. *index Internet und Mediaforschung GmbH*. Fa. Index Research im *Auftrag von StepStone, Wien*. Accessed May 11, 2022, from https://www.stepstone.at/e-recruiting/studien/.

Warg, M., & Deetjen, U. (2021). Human Centered Service Design (HCSD): Why HCSD Needs a Multi-level Architectural View. In: C. Leitner, W. Ganz, D. Satterfield, & C. Bassano (Eds.), *Advances in the human side of service engineering. AHFE 2021. Lecture notes in networks and systems* (Vol. 266). Cham: Springer. https://doi.org/10.1007/978-3-030-80840-2_29.

Wieland, H., Polese, F., Vargo, S. L., & Lusch, R. F. (2012). Toward a service (eco) systems. Perspective on value creation. *International Journal of Service Science, Management, Engineering, and Technology. (IJSSMET), 3*, 12–25. https://doi.org/10.4018/jssmet.2012070102.

Wördenweber, M. (2019). Normatives Management und konstitutive Entscheidungen. BoD – Books on Demand, Norderstedt.

Xaver, B. F., & Haas, J. (2016). *Strategisches management, 8* (pp. 178–179). UVK Verlagsgesellschaft mbH Konstanz.

Zapp, W., & Wittland, M. (2022). Health Care- und Krankenhaus-Management. Normatives Management und strategische Entwicklung. Werteorientierung als Grundlage betriebswirtschaftlichen Handelns, Verlag Kohlhammer, Stuttgart.

Mag. Dr. Karin Messer-Misak has been the managing director of Personal Care in Austria since 2004 and has many years of professional experience in managerial positions in international IT companies and a university clinic. She is an author and reviewer for relevant literature in the health system and lectures at universities and technical colleges. She is responsible for the MBA "Health Care and Hospital Management" and the course "Managers in the Health System" at the Medical University in Graz and active as a lecturer at the Karl-Franzens-University as well as the University of Applied Sciences Joanneum (management in the healthcare system, strategic IT-management, project- and quality management).

MMag. Dr. Christian Lagger MBA Born 1967 in Paternion/Carinthia; married; four children; studies in theology, philosophy, business administration MMag. Dr., MBA, in Salzburg, Innsbruck, Graz, Vienna; since 2010 Managing Director at the Elisabethinen (a.o. die elisabethinen graz gmbh; Krankenhaus der Elisabethinen GmbH; Elisabethinen Graz-Linz-Wien Service und Management GmbH); since 2016 spokesperson for the Elisabethinen Austria; chairman and member of several supervisory bodies, committees and associations; lecturer at FH Joanneum and Karl-Franzens-University Graz (management theory, leadership/strategic thinking, organizational culture); author of articles on leadership and health system issues (management, economics, ethics). Corporate and executive consultant. Since September 2021 President of the International Research Centre for Social and Ethical Issues in Salzburg and since November 2021 President of Ordensspitäler Austria.

Empowered Health and Social Care Staff: The Value of Human-Centred Service Design in Co-producing Transformative Change

Stuart G. Bailey, Karen Bell, Julie Gordon, Hans Hartung, and Zoë A. Prosser

ABSTRACT

Empowered staff can make meaningful change. Empowerment involves recognising the potential that lies within staff and providing them with the time and space to reflect, be creative, action change and ultimately thrive both as individuals and as team members. The authors will discuss the value of utilising human-centred service design in co-producing transformative change with empowered staff and 'extreme teams' within a complex health and social care system traditionally viewed as a linear machine system. They will question the value of the predominance of visualising a linear machine system model in twenty-first-century health care and explore the importance of delivering

S. G. Bailey (✉)
The Glasgow School of Art, School of Design, 164 Renfrew Street, Glasgow, Scotland G3 6RF, UK
e-mail: S.Bailey@gsa.ac.uk

K. Bell
Development Innovation, University Hospital Crosshouse, NHS Ayrshire & Arran, Kilmarnock, Scotland KA2 0BE, UK
e-mail: Karen.Bell2@aapct.scot.nhs.uk

J. Gordon
Emergency and Paediatric Medicine, University Hospital Crosshouse, NHS Ayrshire & Arran, Kilmarnock, Scotland KA2 0BE, UK
e-mail: Julie.Gordon@aapct.scot.nhs.uk

H. Hartung
Respiratory Medicine, University Hospital Crosshouse, NHS Ayrshire & Arran, Kilmarnock, Scotland KA2 0BE, UK
e-mail: Hans.Hartung@aapct.scot.nhs.uk

Z. A. Prosser
Social Design and Research Fellow, Innovation School, The Glasgow School of Art, 24 Hill Street, Glasgow, Scotland G3 6RN, UK
e-mail: Z.Prosser@gsa.ac.uk

M. A. Pfannstiel (ed.), *Human-Centered Service Design for Healthcare Transformation*,
https://doi.org/10.1007/978-3-031-20168-4_3

change through the lens of health and social care as an ecosystem of people and interconnected relationships. The value of human-centred service design will be illustrated with case studies from the authors' work, which involve collaborations between undergraduate students from the Innovation School at The Glasgow School of Art and a local National Health Service (NHS) health board, NHS Ayrshire and Arran (NHS A&A), both pre-pandemic and within the pandemic response. As health and social care services move out of the emergency response to the remobilisation phase with a focus on recover, restore and renew, opportunities for consolidating pandemic changes and initiating further systems change arise. The authors will reflect on the use of human-centred service design as an enabler of transformation to new models of care that recognise the importance of empowered and valued staff owning and driving journeys of possibilities.

1   Introduction

In Service Design Empowering Innovative Communities within Health care (Bailey et al., 2019) we reported on the impact of a collaboration between Glasgow School of Art and National Health Service Ayrshire and Arran (NHS A&A). The focus of that report was on the impact of service design tools on service outcomes and the role that human-centric service design plays in analysing and diagnosing the complex processes involved in delivering patient care. Since 2019, the collaboration has continued to develop, new service areas have engaged with the process and in 2020 and 2021 projects were undertaken entirely on a virtual basis. Although a virtual delivery model presented some constraints to the process, namely, a reduction in ad hoc opportunistic interactions between staff and students and more difficulty in engaging with staff who do not use digital platforms routinely in their day-to-day work, other benefits materialised that will be expanded upon later in this chapter.

In 2020 the project focussed on the Caring for Ayrshire Ambition:

'that care shall be delivered as close to home as possible, supported by a network of community services with safe, effective and timely access to high quality specialist services for those whose needs cannot be met in the community'. Caring for Ayrshire Ambition of NHS A&A (2019, n.d.).

The project focused on the integration of distributed health and social systems at the neighbourhood level. In the last 3 years, health and social care service delivery has been impacted and dominated by the response to the pandemic, and it is recognised that COVID-19 has negatively impacted the mental health of the population (Mental Health Foundation Scotland, COVID Response Programme). The staff within health and social care were not only required to deal with the pandemic on a professional level but also to reflect and cope with the impact on themselves, family members, friends and colleagues. Consequently, the focus for the latest project was staff wellbeing.

Staff wellbeing during the delivery of care during the pandemic was brought sharply to the general public and government's attention leading to public demonstrations of appreciation through initiatives such as 'Clap for Heroes' and 'Meals for the NHS'. Meanwhile, at the front-line, clinical and non-clinical staff were working tirelessly with limited resources and growing patient numbers to deliver appropriate care. Much of this work required the rapid reconfiguration of services, staff redeployment, embedding of new equipment and digital technology which required staff training within the overarching pressures of minimising infection risk and control in an environment that was changing daily. It was during this period of intense activity that insights into organisational practices and the effect on staff wellbeing were identified by staff as they initiated and experienced changes in working practices to deal with the treatment of patients with COVID-19. General feelings of being 'cogs in a machine' as a result of a linear, controlled, top-down organisational structure were replaced for a period during the pandemic with a more flexible, autonomous, self-organising style to respond to the rapidly changing demands of delivering care and treatment to patients. With time to reflect on this period, the evolving structures and interconnected relationships resembled more an open ecosystem than the closed, linear system experienced before and since the pandemic. We will consider these reflections and insights within the context of recent discussions within service science and service design research.

2   Human-Centred Service Design Experiences Throughout the Pandemic

Having explored and engaged with human-centred service design methods through collaborative projects for several years (since 2014), the authors now recognise that it is engaging with a human-centred service design process that provides the long-term benefits, rather than focussing solely on the delivery of project outcomes. As such, the scope of the projects presented as case studies involved undergraduate students who embraced co-design processes with health and social care stakeholders via their partnership with NHS A&A and delivered experimental, speculative design proposals to define and describe problems in service delivery. Value was derived from process reflections, learnings and capacity building instead of outcome implementation and has provided services with materials to continue the reflections and conversations to drive change following the end of the student projects.

The projects discussed in our previous article (Bailey et al., 2019, 137–153) focused on the human-centred design of patient service experiences and utilised collaborative design methods that were both in-person and on-site. Subsequent projects have adopted remote and hybrid engagement methods as a necessary response to the constraints of COVID-19. In previous projects, engagement with staff was limited to specific physical locations within the service and time frames. The move to a virtual platform expanded projects so that engagement could happen 24 h a day 7 days per week. The virtual platform provided staff with the opportunity to engage at a time that suited them and facilitated engagement with partner organisations and diverse stakeholders beyond clinical staff.

In 2020, the project operated entirely through distributed communication, with service design project teams utilising digital collaborative platforms to conduct research, development and co-design activities with a focus on designing speculative human-centred service experiences for the future of blended health care. Notionally this applied both to the blending of physical and digital service delivery models and the introduction of new roles within complex and place-based multi-stakeholder service delivery, such as the relationships between health and social care providers, pharmacies and third-sector organisations. In 2021, project teams built upon the previous year's methodology by developing distributed engagement methods into hybrid forms, for example by using digital technology to communicate with groups of staff members in situ (on-site). This offered a deeply personal and honest reflection of the experiences of staff, which allowed the teams to design speculative service experiences that would improve staff wellbeing.

The scope of each project has evolved, both in relation to their design methodologies and thematic areas of focus, by building upon the learnings of the previous and responding to changing health and social care contexts. These incremental changes alongside the barriers presented by COVID-19, have resulted in increased innovation of design research and co-design methods and as a result, an increase in both the quantity and diversity of stakeholder engagement. The ability to communicate and analyse human experiences throughout the phenomenon of the health pandemic has directed designers increasingly to look inward, at the complex structures and relationships that form the foundations of health and social care services.

In this section, we present three key findings from an analysis of the projects, which outlines new perspectives about the role of human-centred service design for transformative change within the system of health and social care post-pandemic. We discuss the human-centred service design methods demonstrated within the projects as drivers for change, away from traditional linear machine models towards an open and co-created ecosystem. We also discuss new initiatives and approaches that have emerged within NHS A&A during this period as system concepts that function as key change mechanisms. These include the establishment of extreme teams, the recognition of working in a VUCA context (volatile, uncertain, complex and ambiguous), collaborative decision-making with clinical and non-clinical staff, and the role of staff wellbeing initiatives to sustain agency and co-creation. The diagram below, Fig. 1, presents the project findings within a framework adapted from Sangiorgi et al. (2017, 61), which outlines the service design levels and system concepts involved in transitioning towards service ecosystems. Further analysis of the framework and its application within the context of health and social care systems transformation is discussed in Sect. 3.

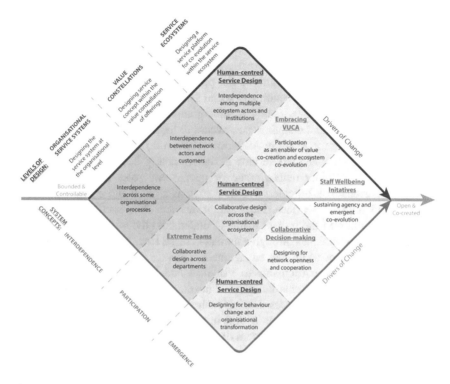

Fig. 1 Presenting drivers of change from within a framework that references Sangiorgi et al. (2017, Table 4.2, 61), 'Service design levels and related system concepts'. *Source* Author 's own figure (2022)

2.1   Distributed Engagement Methods Enhance Human-Centred System-wide Perspectives

The need to conduct primary research and co-design activities remotely during the pandemic increased the quantity and diversity of project participants in terms of their roles and experiences. While digital engagement excludes those without access and therefore cannot be adopted exclusively, it can be said that distributed and hybrid human-centred engagement methods within the projects increased opportunities for new voices to be heard and multi-stakeholder collaborations. During remote co-design workshops, for example, clinical and non-clinical NHS staff, third and voluntary sector workers and people with lived experiences from different locations were brought together. Common pre-pandemic barriers, such as physical distribution, travel and time constraints and general motivation to engage, were cited as reasons that prevented these ways of working from taking place in the past. The introduction of distributed and hybrid engagement mitigated these barriers and consequently, the majority of these stakeholders were engaging with service design activities and each other's roles for the first time.

This insight is not novel, it has been shared across service design within the public sector (McAra et al., 2021, 30). However, what this has enabled within the current projects, is a more holistic and system-wide perspective of health and social care services, beyond the initial experiences of NHS staff and patients directly involved in service delivery. Many of the project outcomes in 2020 focused on the integration of distributed health and social systems at the neighbourhood level, such as the role of charities, family members and neighbours in identifying the health needs of others and enabling their access to localised services reflecting the organisation's Caring for Ayrshire Ambition (2019, n.d.).

Engaging in human-centred service design remotely has allowed the project teams to involve a wider demographic of people and roles rapidly, and bring physically distributed stakeholders together, such as clinical and non-clinical staff, specialist and national services, local authorities and third-sector organisations. As such it has allowed the project teams to understand the wider systems around patient and staff experiences through a human-centred lens. In response, the design students' development of remote engagement methods (Fig. 2.) adopted creative activities that allowed participants to visualise and position themselves within these complex human systems iteratively and do so collaboratively with people of different roles and experiences. During such activities, both design students and diverse participants reflected upon a shift in perspective, away from a linear top-down machine model, towards a system of human connections that is dynamic and interconnected.

Fig. 2 Images of hybrid (physical and digital) co-design methods being tested and iterated by GSA students Bethany Lloyd, Eve McNeil, Gabriella Morris, Greta Cozza and Thomas O'Brien. *Source* Lloyd et al. (2020). Unpublished internal report, Future of Healthcare, Product Design year 3, Glasgow School of Art. Published with kind permission

2.2   Staff Wellbeing as an Area of Focus is Required to Support Empowerment and Engagement in Collaborative Decision-making

The lived experiences of staff shared throughout the 2020 project identified intimate struggles with wellbeing and welfare due to the pressures of the early-stage health pandemic (Gordon, 2020, n.d.).

'We already knew that many of our staff have experienced stress over the years affecting their wellbeing. We wanted to ensure that staff wellbeing was addressed across the organisation, and that we worked in partnership with our staff to ensure wellbeing initiatives were what staff wanted and needed. The pandemic crisis highlighted the need for staff support. Health and social care workers felt vulnerable as they faced an increased risk to their own health and life by coming to work. A strong sense of urgency and purpose enabled rapid developments to enhance staff support and wellbeing during these challenging times. Barriers were removed. Permission, trust and opportunity to just "do what you think is right" from the senior management team and the Medical Director encouraged us to do just that. There were no committees, delays, endless paperwork and bureaucracy. Staff felt empowered to come together to make huge changes in a very short period of time. There was a level of excitement, camaraderie and absence of hierarchy in our working together for the greater good of our colleagues and patients'. (Julie Gordon, Consultant in Emergency and Paediatric Medicine University Hospital Crosshouse, NHS Ayrshire and Arran).

In 2021, the project adopted a focus of involving clinical and non-clinical health and social care staff within the design of health and wellbeing spaces and initiatives across Ayrshire and Arran. Distributed and hybrid methods of engagement and co-design were continuously tested and developed across nine project teams addressing three different locations and three themes: spaces for health and wellbeing; distributed staff support structures; and cultures and connections of wellbeing. In doing so, they were able to deliver a variety of speculative project outcomes that stimulated further discussion about the long-term role of health and wellbeing initiatives beyond the pandemic recovery.

'Staff wellbeing isn't a new concept, however, it wasn't seen as part of NHS core business prior to the pandemic. Organisations had staff wellbeing initiatives but often these were short lived, relied on endowment or charity funding and didn't form part of the fabric of the organisation. Although done with the best intentions these initiatives were often introduced without prior engagement of staff. Early in the pandemic evidence emerged from China and Italy that getting the basics right in the Maslow hierarchy of needs was a good place to start when addressing the wellbeing needs of our staff as well as early staff support This formed the basis of our NHSAA staff wellbeing suites and staff support services'. (Julie Gordon, Consultant in Emergency and Paediatric Medicine University Hospital Crosshouse, NHS Ayrshire and Arran).

From 2020 to 2021 and in parallel with the projects, staff members who were already involved in Medical Peer Support and Wellbeing informally linked with key stakeholders within the organisation including Quality Improvement, Public Health, Occupational Health, Medical Director, Health and Safety, Catering, Estates, Hotel Services, Staff Care, Clinical Psychology and Psychiatry. Designated staff wellbeing areas were assigned at acute sites and a dedicated team of Medical Peer Support, Clinical Psychology, Staff Care and Psychiatrists were based in these areas. These areas provided a safe space for staff in the heart of the hospitals where their basic needs were met with access to utilities such as food and drinks, toilets and beds as well as access to many other wellbeing initiatives based on feedback from the staff themselves, for example, quiet areas, recreation and mindfulness support. Staff could also directly access support for their psychological and emotional wellbeing with onsite medical peer support, staff care, psychologists and psychiatry all providing a range of support from basic psychological first aid to therapy-based sessions.

'The spaces and services made staff members feel appreciated and valued. It helped several employees to stay in their jobs, overcome tough moments and unanimously staff were in favour of the wellbeing facilities continuing permanently'. (Hans Hartung, Consultant in Respiratory Medicine, NHS Ayrshire and Arran).

Distributed and hybrid research and co-design methods during the 2021 project allowed an increased number and diversity of staff to engage in conversations about the future of health and wellbeing support towards creating a vision of post-pandemic care for everyone involved in health and social care service delivery.

2.3   Service Design Supports a Human-Centred System of Health and Care that Empowers and Engages Staff in Distributed Decision-making

The collective effort of creating a wellbeing and support service for NHS staff at the start of the pandemic was significantly accelerated by the assembly of an 'extreme team' (Cameron et al, 2020, n.d.).

'As already outlined COVID-19 provided the opportunity for a Staff Wellbeing Extreme Team at NHS Ayrshire and Arran. The team recognised the importance of staff wellbeing as a key principle of patient safety. Amplified by the pandemic, the issue of staff wellbeing in health and social care had come to the forefront. Supported by senior management, a diverse group of professionals came together spontaneously with a sense of purpose and urgency to set up staff welclbeing and support services and dedicated wellbeing spaces at the three hospital sites. Frequent and effective communication between team members, absence of hierarchy, a sense of camaraderie, a high degree of autonomy and linkage with key stake holders made possible a cohesive, non- bureaucratic and rapid approach to the development of a service which was greatly appreciated by staff members across the organisation'. (Julie Gordon, Consultant in Emergency and Paediatric Medicine University Hospital Crosshouse, NHS Ayrshire and Arran).

Alongside the need to address the welfare of staff, this period of emergency response revealed emerging new ways of working beyond just remote and distributed methods. During the pandemic, unlike any other situation experienced by staff, services and patient pathways during this time required agility and responsiveness to the continuous changing clinical knowledge, information, guidance and service capacity. Key to this was the unacknowledged acceptance of working in a VUCA (Volatility, Uncertainty, Complexity and Ambiguity) driven environment. VUCA, a concept first introduced into its curriculum by the U.S Army War College in the late 1980s and is now widely used in discussions about leadership in organisations and reflects the experiences that staff found themselves in during the pandemic (Johansen & Euchner, 2015, n.d.). The urgency and pace required staff to engage in multi-layer decision-making by bypassing previously bureaucratic, rigid processes and silo boundaries. The organisation had pre-pandemic committed to utilising the methodology of Extreme Teams (Edmondson & Harvey, 2017, n.d.; Edmondson, 2019, n.d.) to underpin its approach of Caring for Ayrshire. Early in the pandemic it was recognised that Extreme Teaming could be utilised as a part of the organisation's pandemic response.

'NHS Ayrshire and Arran promotes the concept of extreme teams which was first introduced by Amy Edmondson. Extreme teaming breaks down silos between teams enabling the emergence of new knowledge in the face of complex problems in a volatile, uncertain, complex and ambiguous environment (VUCA). Such a dynamic cross-boundary team of a range of diverse professionals assembles in a non-hierarchical manner around a meaningful vision quite often on a temporary basis. The agile and non-hierarchical nature of an extreme team allows for frequent course corrections and fast learning in a psychologically safe environment. Commitment by senior leadership gives the confidence to take necessary risks and challenge the status quo to meet the objective'. (Hans Hartung, Consultant in Respiratory Medicine, NHS Ayrshire and Arran).

The spirit of the extreme team enabled spaces for human connection, light touch support, easy access to formal support, testing of new ideas and safe conversations. Appreciation of the emotional impact and the human and relational dimension of work in health and social care especially during the pandemic and irrespective of organisational priorities, processes and silos made staff feel valued and listened to. Regular formal and informal feedback, enhanced by the presence and co-design methods of the student projects, empowered a climate of co-creation and the emergence of the future trajectory for staff wellbeing. An ecosystem of collaboration across many boundaries arose around the ubiquitous issue of staff wellbeing raising an awareness of the interdependence and interconnectedness on such fundamental issues in a complex system as health and social care.

'The initiative by the extreme team ultimately resulted in the implementation of a fully funded wellbeing and support service for NHS Ayrshire and Arran staff members. What would have taken a long time to achieve under usual conditions was accomplished in the space of a few days to weeks by the connective, integrative, flexible and adaptable nature of the extreme team. For all members of the extreme team the experience was energising and positive. Connection with a collective purpose seemed to 'move mountains' forging a sense of meaningful progress'. (Hans Hartung, Consultant in Respiratory Medicine, NHS Ayrshire and Arran).

Student engagement with diverse stakeholders involved in and impacted by the Extreme Team shaped their project deliverables towards the long-term empowerment of staff. Often projects delivered methods and strategies for involving staff in distributed service decision-making while recognising the need for staff wellbeing to sustain their engagement in the wider human-centred system. Three project lenses were used by the students to explore the connections between staff wellbeing, empowerment and participation within wider system decision-making: 'self'—individual human experiences; 'organisational'—the structures of organisations and services that create human experiences; and 'system'—the wider context that influences organisations, services and the underlying beliefs and values that shape human experiences (Meadows, 2008, n.d.).

While the students have contributed service and co-design methods and increased the engagement of staff within distributed decision-making throughout NHS A&A developments, their pedagogical experiences have equally been shaped by the contributions of the health and social care staff through their participation. A wider learning environment has been created around the innovation of service design approaches for health and social care. This environment has evolved in response to immediate real-world challenges and has identified a need for new perspectives about the structure of health and social care systems and a role for collaborative human-centred service design to support staff wellbeing, empowerment and participation in system-wide decision-making.

3   Linear Closed to Open Ecosystem

In this chapter, the authors discuss how clinical and non-clinical staff often feel as if they are working in a 'machine', experienced as top-down linear command and control thinking. This experience is not limited to NHS Scotland with many physicians in the US similarly feeling 'like "cogs in the wheel" of austere corporations that care more about productivity and finances than compassion or quality' (Shanafelt et al., 2021, 641). The relaxation of control and restrictions during the COVID-19 pandemic showed that when staff experienced more autonomy and empowerment they were enabled to work in more flexible and collaborative ways, achieving amazing results within noticeably short periods of time. Experienced by NHS Ayrshire and Arran staff through the utilisation of Extreme Teams, this non-hierarchical, multi-professional approach has more in common with an open, collaborative, 'living' ecosystem than a closed, bounded, linear machine-like system. If a linear, top-down management style is endemic within the health service, then how might human-centred service design support the creation of a healthcare ecosystem?

To transform a service organisation from a closed, bounded linear system to one that is an open, living ecosystem we might consider a human-centred service design approach that considers the organisation as a living and complex adaptive system (van der Bijl-Bower, 2017, 187). How teams self-organise in line with projects, demonstrating emergent, self-organising behaviours are similar to the dynamics and behaviours of 'dissipative structures' within complex living systems.

'The understanding of living structures as open systems provided an important new perspective, but it did not solve the puzzle of the coexistence of structure and change, of order and dissipation, until Ilya Prigogine and Stengers (1984, n.d.) formulated his theory of dissipative structures' (Capra, 1996, 174).

In the case of extreme teams, we might infer that the human-centred service design processes applied are what generates the dynamics within the system, resulting in the behaviours observed. By identifying where and how design acts at the points of instability 'where order emerges spontaneously and complexity unfolds' (Ibid, 185) and considering where design interventions provide the information, resources and energy to create stability (Irwin, 2011, n.d.), we might understand how to generate more sustainable change towards organisations of co-evolved ecosystems.

The projects and experiences discussed here in this chapter reflect recent discussions within the field of service science. Service science researchers are turning to the human-centred design approach of service design, identifying that 'in order to effectively understand and design for complex human-centred service systems, a service design approach supports professionals to integrate multidisciplinary knowledge in practice' (Sangiorgi et al., 2019, 176). This multidisciplinary collaboration and human-centred approach parallels the experiences of the NHS Ayrshire and Arran Staff Wellbeing Extreme Teams as discussed earlier in Sect. 2.

If we map the human-centred service design initiatives discussed in Sect. 2 and as illustrated in Fig. 1 above, onto levels of design and system concepts (Sangiorgi et al., 2017, 61) we can identify design interventions as drivers of change that can action change to move the system from one point of stability to another, which moves the system from closed and linear to an open, adaptive and co-evolved ecosystem, as illustrated in Fig. 3. If the energy applied by the design intervention is not sustained, then the system slips back to the previous point of stability, as experienced by clinical staff and non-clinical staff post-pandemic when the system returned to previous practices. Implementing a human-centred service design approach can help us to identify, visualise and understand the dynamics of new service models. Helping us identify the core principles of not only how the new model works but how to move from the existing state to a new preferable one. This avoids falling foul of Rossi's Iron Law of evaluation (Perla et al., 2015, 2), which argues that 'as a new model is implemented widely across a broad range of settings, the effect will tend towards zero'. (Ibid 2015, 2).

Engaging with a service design process provides the means to simplify and understand complex systems and interactions; sharing tacit as well as explicit information, collectively identifying problems and opportunities that facilitate collaborative sensemaking and decision-making. And thereby facilitating a human-centred approach to transformative service system innovation (Bailey et al., 2019,

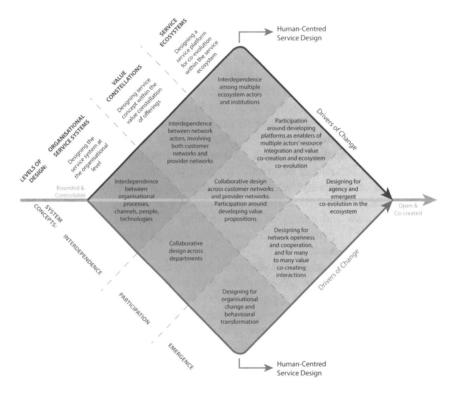

Fig. 3 From controlled, linear, machine-like service systems to open, adaptive co-evolved ecosystems. Referencing Sangiorgi et al. (2017, Table 4.2, 61). 'Service design levels and related system concepts'. *Source* Author 's own figure (2022)

140–142). The idea of the health service as an ecosystem rather than as a linear, machine-like system suggests adopting a service ecosystem design approach as discussed by Sangiorgi et al. (2017, 58–61) and Vink et al. (2021, 168–182). With reference to the characteristics of an open versus closed organisation (Foster, 2014, 17–30) and recognising organisations as complex, living and ecosystem, Fig. 3 visualises the impact of applying increasingly more complex levels of strategic design practices for increasingly open system concepts. By illustrating the continuum from a closed, interdependent system to an emergent and co-evolved, ecosystem in this way, we can begin to identify where change is facilitated through the agency of design.

Human-centred service design practices within an organisation help us navigate complexity by identifying and visualising patterns and connections to achieve a level of simplicity that can be easily understood and shared; to identify 'the "drivers of simplicity" that help us navigate the complexity to elicit simplicity' (Ng, 2019, xvi). The very nature of a living organisation of people, from a range of disciplines and backgrounds each with different agendas, makes it increasingly difficult to manage any focussed transformation, or innovation, within the service system with the traditional management styles (Bailey, 2012, 36–40; van der Bijl-Bower, 2017, 186; Jones, 2013, 17–19). However, as we have seen in the projects discussed in this chapter, a human-centred service design approach to collaborative exploration can define problems and support navigating co-evolved solutions, while importantly also reflecting the relationships experienced within a service. Therefore, recognising the human elements within the service system.

4 Conclusion

"Huge variety exists in the way primary, secondary and social care is structured and governed, so it has proved difficult to identify sensible interventions that have consistent relevance and impact across the board. The NHS is itself far from a homogenous unified organisation but rather a federated ecosystem where complex tribal and status dynamics continue to exist. Given the clear benefits of cross-boundary teamwork and collaborative behaviours, everything should be done to encourage greater parity of esteem, conditions and influence between sectors and, within secondary care, a re-balancing of the focus on acute trusts to the benefit of their community, mental health and ambulance trust counterparts. The vast majority of health and care delivery never touches the acute sector, and it is in the interests of all to keep it that way, so more equitable representation and empowerment must be a key enabler to enhanced collaboration. Equally, the more that can be done to instil locally a culture of teamwork, understanding and shared objectives across the primary, secondary and social care communities, the better will be the nation's public health outcomes.

'To those of our recommendations which require time and resource to implement, I predict a partially understandable reaction that the current pressures on the system preclude investment beyond the urgent. My response is that a well-led, motivated, valued, collaborative, inclusive, resilient workforce is "the" key to better patient and health and care outcomes and that investment in people must sit alongside other operational and political priorities. To do anything else risks inexorable decline' (Department of Health and Social and Social Care, 2022. Foreward by Sir Gordon Messenger).

This quote is from the Department of Health and Social Care independent review of the role of leadership for a collaborative and inclusive future across health and social care delivery post-pandemic. It is an eloquent summary of the situation facing the NHS in the UK and identifies that the issues facing the NHS will not be robustly resolved unless the challenges facing the workforce are addressed. NHS organisations have the growing problem of staff retention, an ageing workforce and reducing numbers of new staff. If an NHS organisation is to retain and attract staff, then it needs to build its reputation as an exemplar employer. Having a focus on staff wellbeing is key but the work undertaken by the authors suggests another element worth considering.

The authors now recognise that the collaboration is providing benefits beyond individual service changes to include the localised impact on staff engagement and power to influence change within services. The challenge now is to spread that impact so that it results in systemic change while identifying and addressing systemic barriers. The recent project collaborations in 2020 and 2021 provided opportunities to scale the work across health and partner services and staff groups, although it must be noted that the project still has the constraint of limited engagement with staff who are not using digital platforms on a regular basis. This limitation is a concern not only for these individual projects but also for an organisation when embedding the use of digital platforms for workflow transformation to ensure that staff groups are not marginalised and disenfranchised by the tools utilised.

The scope of each project has evolved, both in relation to their design methodologies and thematic areas of focus, by building upon the learnings of the previous and responding to changing health and social care contexts. These incremental changes alongside the barriers presented by COVID-19 have resulted in increased innovation of design research and co-design methods and as a result, an increase in both the quantity and diversity of stakeholder engagement. The ability to communicate and analyse human experiences throughout the phenomena of the health pandemic has directed designers increasingly to look inward, at the complex structures and relationships that form the foundations of health and social care services. Human-centred service design in this context has been demonstrated to support the engagement and empowerment of diverse staff to understand the experiences of different roles, position themselves in a wider human ecosystem and participate in distributed decision-making about service development. However, this bottom-up approach is met by top-down management structure barriers. The tension between perspectives of health and social care delivery as a linear machine model versus a human-centred, dynamic ecosystem continues to prevail. More work is required to address the adequate resourcing of staff wellbeing and empowerment and the enablement of distributed decision-making from a top-down perspective. With this comes a need for senior management structures to recognise staff not as numerical resources but as actors in an ecosystem, each with expertise drawn from lived experience that can inform effective distributed decision-making.

'A supportive system enables staff to do their job well. Being able to connect with our main purpose to help people when they are at their most vulnerable generates a sense of professional fulfilment. Feeling fulfilled in work and co-producing better outcomes with patients is directly connected to staff wellbeing' (Hans Hartung, Consultant in Respiratory Medicine, NHS Ayrshire and Arran).

In parallel to the system-wide barriers discussed, future generations of service design practitioners are becoming increasingly equipped to operate within complex human-centred systems through their participation in partnership projects such as the ones presented in this article. Their experiences of live health and wellbeing contexts and collaborative design activities with patients and staff across organisations are providing more opportunities to innovate design and pedagogical practices. This symbiotic benefit to all those involved in the projects is intended to create future opportunities to address these problems at scale through the diffusion of human-centred design skills, such as health and social care staff's increased capacity for designerly ways of thinking, design students' abilities to collaboratively innovate with diverse staff in complex environments and teaching staff's ability to evolve curriculum.

New models and roles are beginning to arise, as demonstrated by design internships and placements within NHS Ayrshire and Arran and there is an intention for these to inform similar opportunities for clinical and non-clinical health and social care staff. Proximity and partnerships between diverse people with different expertise and experiences have demonstrated an untapped potential to empower staff across a system that is truly human-driven, which we seek to further investigate in future projects.

References

Bailey, S. G. (2012). Embedding service design: The long and the short of it. ServDes.2012 conference, Co-creating Services, 8th-10th February 2012, Espoo, Finland. In *Proceedings of 3rd Service Design and Service Innovation conference, ServDes.2012. Linköping Electronic Conference Proceedings* (vol. 67, pp. 31–41). Linköping, Sweden: Linköping University Electronic Press.

Bailey, S. G., Bell, K., & Hartung, H. (2019). Service design empowering innovative communities within healthcare. In M. A. Pfannstiel & C. Rasche (Eds.), *Service design and service thinking in healthcare and hospital management; Theory, concepts, practice* (pp. 137–153). Cham: Springer Nature.

Cameron, M., Gordon, J., Hartung, H., MacAskill, C., Mulhern, S., & Wilson, I. (2020) *NHS Ayrshire & Arran staff wellbeing extreme team.* Retrieved July 3, 2022, from https://ihub.scot/improvement-programmes/scottish-patient-safety-programme-spsp/world-patient-safety-day-2020/inspiring-initiatives/can-a-wellbeing-extreme-team-promote-patient-safety-from-nhs-ayrshire-arran/.

Capra, F. (1996). *The web of life: A new synthesis of mind and matter.* Flamingo. 1997 imprint of HarperCollins, London.

Department of Health & Social Care. (2022). *Leadership for a collaborative and inclusive future. The UK Government: Independent Report.* Retrieved July 3, 2022, from https://www.gov.uk/government/publications/health-and-social-care-review-leadership-for-a-collaborative-and-inclusive-future/leadership-for-a-collaborative-and-inclusive-future.

Edmondson, A. C. (2019). *The fearless organisation: Creating psychological safety in the workplace for learning, innovation and growth.* Hoboken, New Jersey: Wiley & Sons Inc.

Edmondson, A. C., & Harvey, J.-F. (2017). *Extreme teaming: Lessons in complex, cross-sector leadership.* Bingley: Emerald Publishing Limited.

Foster, P. A. (2014). *The open organization: A new era of leadership and organizational development.* Surrey: Gower.

Gordon, J. (2020). *Staff Wellbeing during the coronavirus (COVID-19) pandemic,* Retrieved 3 July 2022, from https://www.nhsaaa.net/news/latest-news/staff-wellbeing-during-the-coronavirus-COVID-19-pandemic/.

Irwin, T. (2011). *Living systems theory: Relevance to design,* Retrieved July 3, 2022, from https://www.academia.edu/6076107/Living_Systems_Theory_Relevance_to_Design.

Jones, P. H. (2013). *Design for care: Innovating healthcare experience.* New York: Rosenfeld Media LLC.

Johansen, B., & Euchner, J. (2015). Navigating the VUCA world. *Research-Technology Management, 56* (1), 10–15.

Lloyd, B., McNeil, E., Morris, G., Cozza, G., O'Brien, T. (2020). Future of Healthcare. Unpublished internal report in the Product Design Year 3 Health & Wellbeing course, The Glasgow School of Art.

McAra, M., Broadley, C., Simms, H., Prosser, Z., & Teal, G. (2021). *Designing distributed community participation. Project report*. Glasgow: GSA RADAR.

Meadows, D. (2008). *Thinking in systems: A primer*. London: Chelsea Green Publishing.

Mental Health Foundation Scotland (2022). *COVID response programme*. Retrieved July 3, 2022, from https://www.mentalhealth.org.uk/our-work/programmes/covid-response-programme.

Ng, I. (2019). Foreword by Irene Ng. In P. P. Maglio, C. A. Kieliszewski, J. C. Spohrer, K. Lyons, L. Patrício, & Y. Sawatani (Eds.), *Handbook of service science* (vol. II, pp. xv–xviii). Cham: Springer Nature Switzerland AG.

NHS Ayrshire & Arran. (2019). *Caring for Ayrshire*, Retrieved July 3, 2022, from https://www.nhs aaa.net/caring-for-ayrshire.

Perla, R. J., Cohen, A. M., Parry, G. (2015). *Health care reform and the trap of the "Iron Law," health affairs blog technical report*, Retrieved July 3, 2022, from https://www.researchgate.net/publication/275343173.

Prigogine, I., & Stengers, I. (1984). *Order out of chaos*. New York: Bantam.

Sangiorgi, D., Patrício, L., & Fisk, R. (2017). Designing for interdependence, participation, and emergence in complex systems. In D. Sangiorgi & A. Prendiville (Eds.), *Designing for service: Key issues and new directions* (pp. 49–64). London: Bloomsbury.

Sangiorgi, D., Lima, F., Patrício, L., Joly, M. P., & Favini, C. (2019). A human-centred, multidisciplinary, and transformative approach to service science: A service design perspective. In P. P. Maglio, C. A. Kieliszewski, J. C. Spohrer, K. Lyons, L. Patrício, & Y. Sawatani (Eds.), *Handbook of service science* (vol. II, pp. 147–181). Switzerland: Springer Nature Switzerland AG.

Shanafelt, T., Trockel, M., Rodriguez, A., & Logan, D. (2021). Wellness-centered leadership: Equipping health care leaders to cultivate physician well-being and professional fulfillment. *Academic Medicine, 96*(5), 641–651.

van der Bijl-Bower, M. (2017). Designing for social infrastructures in complex service systems: A human-centered and social systems perspective on service design. *She Ji, the Journal of Design, Economics, and Innovation, 3*(3), 183–197.

Vink, J., Koskela-Huotari, K., Tronvoll, B., Edvardsson, B., & Wetter-Edman, K. (2021). Service ecosystem design: Propositions, process model, and future research agenda. *Journal of Service Research, 24*(2), 168–186.

Stuart G Bailey's research and writings have contributed to service design and service thinking within an organisational context with conference papers presented at ServDes2010 & 2012 and EAD2013, and co-authored the chapter 'Designing vs Designers' in Designing for Service, recently published by Bloomsbury. His research considers complementary areas within service design: the investigation of how organisations engage with design thinking to innovate services; and the roles and contributions of non-design-trained service designers in relation to those who are design-trained. Stuart's work investigates how service design and service thinking are embedded within and disseminated throughout an organisation.

Dr. Karen Bell manages the research portfolio of clinical and non-clinical trial activity as well as being Innovation Lead at University Hospital Crosshouse. Karen's research interests include normative alcohol usage and ageing and have established a generic research nurse team to support commercial and non-commercial trial activity. Karen also works with Scottish Health Innovations Ltd (SHIL) to develop and commercialise new innovative healthcare solutions. As an active member of NHS Research Scotland, Karen is always keen to establish collaborations with academic research partners.

Dr. Julie Gordon works part time as an ED consultant and part time as clinical wellbeing lead at NHS Ayrshire and Arran. Julie has always been passionate about staff wellbeing and along with her colleagues set up medical peer support in NHSAA in 2018, Since the beginning of the COVID pandemic she has become joint clinical wellbeing lead as well as the wellbeing champion for the NHS board looking at ways in which to best support staff. With evidence emerging from China/Italy she designed and set up staff wellbeing suites in the acute hospitals.

Dr. Hans Hartung, MD, MRCP, works as a consultant in respiratory and general medicine at the University Hospital Crosshouse. Hans has a longstanding interest in person-centred and collaborative care. He was the clinical lead of the national Co-Creating Health Project (2007–2015) funded by the Health Foundation which piloted partnership working in health care. As a Health Foundation fellow, Hans spent a year at the Institute for Health Care Improvement (IHI) in Boston in 2013/14. During the year he gained a deeper understanding of the importance of healthcare staff feeling enabled in order to engage in service redesign.

Zoë A. Prosser has led projects with the local authority and NHS partners across the UK, delivering design-led service and system transformation within health and social care. Notably 'Your Voice, Your Way' (Service Design in Government, 2021) which co-designed social care systems change with care experienced young people. Her research investigates the role of social and co-design to support access to participation within public decision-making, service and systems design.

Human-Centered Service Design and Transformative Innovation: Beginning to Understand How Innovation Culture Shifts Within the Public Health System in Western Australia

Sash Milne, Christopher Kueh, Stuart Medley, Neil Lynch, and Benjamin Noteboom

ABSTRACT

The cultivation of innovation culture in any public healthcare system is complex, requiring a thorough understanding and reframing of evolving transformation at every level. While human-centered service design is important, the organizational culture and systems that create a foundation for service delivery require specific research. It is especially important to understand the foundations for the development of strategies that enable system-wide culture transformation. This chapter provides a comprehensive mapping of the innovation

S. Milne (✉)
367 Bussell Highway, Broadwater, Western Australia 6280, Australia
e-mail: amine@our.ecu.edu.au

C. Kueh · S. Medley
School of Arts and Humanities, Edith Cowan University, 2 Bradford Street, Mount Lawley, Joondalup, Western Australia 6050, Australia
e-mail: c.kueh@ecu.edu.au

S. Medley
e-mail: s.medley@ecu.edu.au

N. Lynch
Office of Medical Research and Innovation, Office of the Deputy Director General, Department of Health Western Australia, Ground Floor, C Block, 189 Royal Street, East Perth, Western Australia 6004, Australia
e-mail: Neil.Lynch@health.wa.gov.au

B. Noteboom
Office of the Executive Director, Royal Perth Bentley Group and East Metropolitan Health Service, Level 3, A Block, Wellington Street, Perth, Western Australia 6000, Australia
e-mail: ben.noteboom@health.wa.gov.au

M. A. Pfannstiel (ed.), *Human-Centered Service Design for Healthcare Transformation*,
https://doi.org/10.1007/978-3-031-20168-4_4

initiatives and leadership across the public healthcare system in Western Australia. In-depth design-led conversations were held with stakeholders, healthcare leaders, and innovators, at all stages of their innovation development, to map system complexity and explore factors that could contribute to the development of transformative innovation.

1 Introduction

This chapter discusses a design-led research project, conducted to support the Department of Health in Western Australia to understand the complexities of transforming the organizational and systemic culture within health service delivery. This research project reflects on the transformation in organizational culture within a complex system. Through interviews with 14 WA Health leaders and representatives, we have collected non-identifiable data and narratives about their experiences of what common enablers and barriers exist to the development of innovation. We found that innovation culture within a complex organizational and systemic setting is agile and is constantly shifting. Leadership in teams and organizations and the structure of the healthcare system are found to be key factors that shape the direction of shifts in innovation culture. The following sections will first explore the innovation space in the light of human-centered service design in health care. This will lead to the discussion of our research and findings. A research model is then drawn as the conclusion and proposed way forward.

2 Innovation Culture and Human-Centered Service Design

This chapter sees that innovation in service provision is an outcome of the way an organizations culture is supporting its employees. This section explores the fundamental discussions on innovation culture in relevance to healthcare service provision and human-centered design. This sets the foundation for our research into the innovation culture within healthcare organizations and systems.

2.1 Innovation Culture

Organizational culture refers to the set of shared beliefs, values, assumptions, and rituals that are often unspoken but make up the foundation of the ways that individuals and groups function within any particular organization (Bendak et al., 2020, pp. 1–17; Chen et al., 2018, pp. 1–18; Dobni, 2008, pp. 539–559; Maguire, 2001, pp. 587–634). Berry (2019, pp. 798–792) defines the culture of an organization by how the individuals within the organization behave on a daily basis, arguing that a culture that is aspired to needs to be both role-modeled and nurtured daily.

Similarly, Johnson et al. (2016, pp. 265–288) describe the culture of the organization as its personality and explore the impact that this personality has on both the organization's performance and the well-being of the people who work within the organization. In a health context, organizational culture is critical. Literature shows the link between culture and outcomes for both staff and patients as a critical consideration for any healthcare organization (Johnson et al., 2016, pp. 265–288).

There are numerous studies that investigate the impact of culture on the organization and the sustainability of the business, but fewer have been conducted to investigate the culture of an organization and the impact this has on the capacity for innovation to thrive. Exploring the link between organizational culture and innovation is somewhat new territory for modern research and needs to start with an understanding of innovation as a mindset, and how this can lead to the development of an innovation culture. Kahn (2018, pp. 453–460) defines an innovation mindset as one of the three ways innovation presents itself within an organization, alongside process and outcome. The innovative mindset has been defined by Samet and Smith (2016, p. 5) as "optimistic because it comes from a core belief that the future can be better than the present and that there is always a better way of doing something." It is this mindset that sits at the core of an innovation culture, a mindset that comes from the belief that there is a better way. Seminal contributions have been made by Dobni (2008, pp. 539–559) and Sadegh Sharifirad and Ataei (2012, pp. 497–517) to better understand how an innovation culture could be cultivated, nurtured, and sustained within an organization. Dobni (2008, pp. 539–559) suggests that building a culture of innovation would require an organization to provide both the environment and infrastructure necessary to nurture an innovative mindset within the employees, creating space for exploring innovative processes and practices.

When considering the impact that a culture of innovation has on an organization, researchers like Martinidis (2017, p. 640) have argued that innovation is "inherently a human endeavor that succeeds when people with experience, skills, and capabilities come together" and have urged organizations and scholars to look more closely at how the human factors that create the culture of an organization also impact the organization's capacity for innovation.

2.2 Innovation Culture in Global Health

Healthcare service providers operate in high emotion situations alongside patients and complex situations (Berry, 2019, p. 79). According to leading researchers, creating a culture of innovation within the health context is not only desirable, but has also become an imperative for the continued evolution, and success of the healthcare industry as a whole (Berry, 2019, pp. 78–92; Thakur, 2012, pp. 562–569; Samet & Smith, 2016, pp. 3–15; Pillay & Morris, 2016, pp. 393–410; Lorusso et al., 2021, pp. 16–29; Marjanovic et al., 2018, p. 10; Lister et al., 2017, pp. 1–9).

Understanding the challenges that the healthcare industry faces, and establishing a case for change, has been the focus of a large body of research to date. Samet and Smith (2016, pp. 3–15) argue that health care must evolve to meet the changing needs of the consumer market and respond faster to the rapid changes that are already happening in healthcare delivery around the globe. Mende (2019, pp. 121–131) recommends healthcare organizations to start considering their cultural readiness for innovation, while Berry (2019, p. 78) argues that forward-thinking healthcare organizations already have a culture of innovation where they see that consistency in pursuing innovation as the most vital task to develop inclusive healthcare services.

Berry (2019, pp. 78–92) explores the positive outcomes of a culture of innovation in the health sector and includes increased performance, retention of talent, reduction of waste, competitive advantage, and flexibility to respond to complexity, change, and new technology. The key elements of innovation culture were highlighted by Moussa et al. (2018, p. 6) in their review of the current literature and included "shared visions, leadership and the organizational propensity to innovate," concluding the primary factor in the development of a health organizations innovation culture was a strategic commitment to an intent to innovate across every level of the organization. A series of recent studies indicate that a culture of innovation in health care may not only have a direct positive impact on the development of innovative products and services but also have a direct, positive impact on the health and well-being of staff and overall institutional and organizational effectiveness (Johnson et al., 2016, pp. 265–288).

It is a challenge to cultivate an innovation culture across the health service provision sector. A study conducted by Lombardi et al. (2018, pp. 1–7) investigates academic healthcare organizations with an aim to better understand dynamic innovation capabilities, including attitudes, processes, structures, and policies. research aimed to create a conceptual framework that could facilitate an innovative environment within health care. However, Lombardi et al. assert that even the most capable healthcare organizations may not have the systematic support required "to produce high-impact healthcare innovations on an accelerated basis," (Lombardi et al. 2018, p. 5). Innovation is not intended to be a replacement for high-functioning public health practices, but for a culture of innovation to thrive within a public health environment, the environment must have some tolerance for risk and failure, where good failure can be seen as an accelerator for the learning process (Lister et al., 2017, pp. 1–9). The current culture and environment of the public sector have a governance structure that has a low tolerance for risk-taking, putting it at odds with a culture of innovation (Brown & Osborne, 2013, pp. 186–208). In addition, researchers suggest that the complexity of the healthcare environment not only makes innovation essential for future development but also makes innovation culture development uniquely challenging due to hierarchy, low tolerance for both risk and failure, emotionally high-stakes environment, and other organizational cultural factors that are currently present across the system (see Berry, 2019, pp. 78–92; Moussa et al., 2018, pp. 1–12).

There is little doubt that transforming an organizational culture is challenging (Johnson et al., 2016, 256) and is often a long-term project (Bendak et al., 2020, pp. 1–17; Johnson et al., 2016, pp. 265–288). Public health organizations are beginning to recognize that it may be essential for long-term sustainability and effectiveness (Bendak et al., 2020, pp. 1–17; Berry, 2019, pp. 78–92; Samet & Smith, 2016, pp. 3–15), and the consequences of not doing so could be "devastating for the organization's effectiveness and individual employee well-being" (Johnson et al., 2016, p. 256). Moussa et al. (2018, pp. 1–12) state the key barriers to innovation culture in the organization are poor communication, lack of resourcing, workplace politics, and suggest that while creativity and innovation lead to a change in organizations it is the role of the leader which is essential to cultivating and sustaining innovation processes long term.

Innovation culture in healthcare service provision is especially critical when services are required to shift from improvement to transformation. Sangiorgi (2011, p. 31) sees that transformation through service design takes place at a paradigmatic level. According to her, "… projects that improve service interactions and touchpoints (service interaction design) or that help redefine service values, norms or philosophy (service interventions), don't necessarily have a transformational impact" (Sangiorgi, 2011, p. 31). This statement draws attention to the difference between service design that focuses on producing touchpoints and that which aims at achieving transformation in the community or organization.

Despite the pressure from the global health system to innovate, there is limited research on how innovation culture might impact the innovation capabilities of healthcare teams working in Western Australia. Our research project aims to better understand the innovation culture in healthcare service provision teams and how they do (or do not) sustain a culture of innovation.

2.3 Human-Centered Design (HCD)

The intersection of human-centered design (HCD) and health service provision has gained considerable interest in recent years as countries grapple with the challenge of change and innovation within the healthcare sector (see Lorusso et al., 2021, pp. 16–29; Donetto et al., 2015, pp. 227–248; DeSalvo et al., 2017, pp. 1–9; Bazzano et al., 2017, pp. 1–24; Roberts et al., 2016, pp. 11–14; Stola, 2018, pp. 28–33). Public sector organizations and systems have recently recognized that the traditional siloed work environments are no longer best suited for the development and operation of public service, and are looking to design new ways to approach evolving social problems in innovative ways (Hyvärinen et al., 2015, pp. 249–268; DeSalvo et al., 2016, pp. 621–622), by better understanding and coordinating complex networks (Van Der Bijl-Brouwe, 2017, pp. 2151–2152; Pillay & Morris, 2016, pp. 393–410). A design-led approach, therefore, provides an innovative platform for health service provision sectors to lead change, rather than merely reacting to change (Roberts et al., 2016, p. 13).

HCD provides the public sector with new ways of working and thinking that are well suited to "combat health inequalities and issues rooted in social determinants of health," (Abookire et al., 2020, p. 2) and create an opportunity for healthcare systems to innovate in delivering services that cut across organizations, political, geographical and sectoral boundaries," (Stola, 2018, p. 28). Bazzano et al. (2017, p. 2) emphasize that the approach to innovation that HCD advocates for are well suited to the complex issues of population health "which is both a social need and a social problem" (2), and Donetto et al. (2015, pp. 227–248) challenge the public health sector to consider the impact of design and social sciences perspectives and tools, stating that "these can bring theoretical insight to a change intervention aimed at addressing very practical concerns" (Donetto et al., 2015, p. 228).

In the early 2000s, the Design Council was commissioned to lead design projects to explore the roles of design in improving the lives of people with chronic diseases (Cottom & Leadbeater, 2004, pp. 5–36). The project identified that the health services at the time did not adequately address the management of chronic diseases, especially the broader lifestyle issues of the people impacted. Through exploratory design projects, the Council reported that a people-based co-design model is a sustainable way forward for the community (see Cottom & Leadbeater, 2004, pp. 15–23). The design council continues to lead healthcare innovation through human-centered design. Lately, the council engaged in projects that range from designing "informal care" services that involve families and communities, to using HCD to develop services and products that enable people to make better healthcare services (see The Design Council, n.d.). The value and contribution of design to health care have been clear as human experiences are being taken more seriously and healthcare systems are becoming more complex. Jones (2013, p. 76) advocates for the importance of building empathy, and reframing healthcare challenges based on stakeholders' needs. In his book Design for Care: Innovating Healthcare Experience, Jones (2013, pp. 271–296) emphasizes the need to have service and information design to function as a voice for patients and other stakeholders. This approach clearly illustrates that the role of design is not just about delivering visually appealing outcomes, but that design has the capability of shifting the way the healthcare sector approaches human needs, which leads to sustainable innovation.

However, bringing together HCD and the public health sector has not been without its challenges. In fact, many researchers have called attention to the tension between the evidence-based research that is typical of public health and the more ambiguous, flexible nature of HCD (Bazzano et al., 2017, pp. 1–24). Hyvärinen et al. recognize that the generative and collaborative nature of HCD practices is very foreign to public service organizations, especially those that have "expert-oriented, hierarchical and 'siloed' ways of working" (Hyvärinen et al., 2015, p. 2453). This tension between new practice and traditional practice will undoubtedly require "critical approaches to both organizational processes and design practice" (Donetto et al., 2015, p. 243). Bazzano continues this discussion by asserting that "an inherent tension exists between the way research is undertaken in design versus in the health sector… many of the central tenets of design thinking research, like iteration, tolerance for ambiguity, pivots and rapid prototyping, are inherently at odds with some prevailing processes in health and biomedicine" (Bazzano et al., 2017, p. 14). Additionally, Björgvinsson et al. (2010, 46–48) note that the design environment often unearths challenges that have no easy solution, and problems to which there is no right or wrong answer, creating ambiguity that may cause tension in a public health environment. Roberts et al. address these challenges in their research, without shying away from the skepticism and frustration that is often experienced at the intersection of public health and design, stating that the frustration is "linked to the scale and pace of change and innovation within the current health system (and) [stem] not from a lack of vision, effort or even resources; rather it arises from attempts to remake a healthcare model never designed to do the things now being asked of it" (Roberts et al., 2016, p. 13).

This tension and challenge, from a design perspective, creates a fertile ground for opportunity. With many case studies available that show the potential for transformation that HCD practice offers to health, it is not surprising that much of the literature has called out for more research in this space including cross-disciplinary research to better understand the potential of design practices and the impact on patient care (Donetto et al., 2015, p. 13).

3   Research Methods

The potential for design and transformation to come together and impact the culture in a large, complex system like public health is as immense as it is complex. Where there is complexity and wicked problems, there is a great opportunity for impact through design. It is also true, however, that a rigorous human-centered design process is hard to realize within a traditionally structured hierarchical system. It has been important to hold this tension carefully and at the forefront throughout the research process to ensure the project recognizes that there are barriers to design within the process itself and ensure as a team of researchers that we are able to continually reflect on and respond to these challenges as part of the opportunity space.

The tension between the generative nature of human-centered design research and more traditional healthcare research creates a fertile ground of opportunity for our research project. The views of relevant healthcare professionals on the impact of workplace culture on innovation can provide a practical understanding of the current system experience. The HCD approach values multiple voices and diverse experiences, each interaction designed to provide the participants with an opportunity to explore their current experiences and to design ideal future state experiences.

The research approach we took was a series of semi-structured interviews that were conducted through an online video platform. The interviews were designed specifically to explore individual experiences of innovation culture within the WA public health system. Design-led research interview techniques were employed to guide participants through an hour-long interview, focusing first on what people experience as both barriers and enablers to innovation and innovation culture. We then explored the current perception of the systemic value and success of innovation and the culture that supports it. The questions were designed to be open-ended and were never leading, allowing for the participant to help guide the discussion, sharing their own opinions and experiences in a way that was meaningful to them. Participants were asked about their personal views on the definition of an innovation culture and then expanded to their observation of such culture, or the lack of it, in the current healthcare provision sector in Western Australia. The goal of the interview was to be explorative, building upon the participant's ideas and leaving space for new ideas and meaning to emerge.

To ensure adequate representation of individuals with diverse experience of leading innovation and/or innovation engagement in the sector we intentionally targeted individuals who are innovation leaders within WA Health; are curious and trying to innovate with varied success; and those who are just beginning to engage in innovative practices. It is important to work with people who have diverse experiences of innovation across the system to gain the breadth and depth required to understand the current state of an innovation culture.

The information from the first 14 interviews was transcribed, coded, and synthesized to unearth common themes and insights and to develop a set of preliminary findings, from which we have developed visual maps that will be used in future phases of the research project to illustrate how culture currently moves through the complex system.

4   Visualizing Insights

The HCD approach allowed us to better understand stakeholder needs and experiences, and to develop preliminary findings, needs, and insights about the culture and experience of culture within the wider public health system. In the process of unpacking and synthesizing the data collected from the first 14 interviews conducted, a series of key insights began to emerge that allowed us to scope meaningful and actionable problem statements.

The original goal of this research was to create an ecosystem map to explore the complexity of the current innovation ecosystem, but as we began to uncover the insights it became clear this was a limiting approach. The qualitative data spoke directly to each participant's experience of culture within the system; how it allowed innovation to thrive or how it presented barriers. It was in the space between individual and system, where the action and reaction of the cultural system that underpins the entire complex system of public health, where we discovered key insights. We focus then not on where, or what, innovation is occurring, but instead, what impact systemic culture has on the ability for a culture of innovation to thrive.

We coded quotes and insights from the interviews to establish fundamentals to visualize the ecosystem of innovation (see Table 1).

The coding and analysis revealed the key enablers and barriers that contribute to the cultivation of an innovation culture in healthcare organizations and systems. This led us to key insights that are both based on the understanding that there is no single culture in a complex system, but instead many pockets of different cultures

Table 1 Coding and insights from interview data. *Source* Author's own Table

Code/Themes	Representative quotes	Insights
Definition of innovation and innovation culture	• "I think when we talk about innovative culture or innovation culture, we're really talking about those sort of subtle mindset shifts in the way that people think about and change and then enact behaviour change in small ways … When everybody starts thinking slightly differently, but it's taking a small step that can actually change the culture of an organization quite significantly" • "… innovation culture doesn't necessarily come from having all the toys and all the tools and things like that. It's much more about the culture of the people and the culture of the organization itself" • "But when you have this culture that sits underneath the risk aversion and fear of failure … we're strapped for time and we don't have enough money and we have too much to do, it's very hard"	• Change and innovation is driven by passionate individuals (with supportive leaders) • Improvement needs to come before innovation—and collaboration • Culture and the mindsets that underpin it play a big role in moving innovation forward (or setting it back)

(continued)

that are dependent on many different factors, actors, and events. This is true in the complex system of public health in Western Australia; many different organizational and team cultures exist, often dependent on the individuals that make up that smaller section of the ecosystem. A theme emerged that there is a power-driven culture within the system as a whole. Interestingly, we found that there were two key findings to be considered from this tension between the system, and team or organizational culture. Firstly, there are very different barriers and enablers to a culture of innovation depending on where one focuses within a system. An individual's enablers of innovation are very different from those that exist at a systemic level. Secondly, culture tends to move in one direction (top-down) in terms of its impact and capacity for transformation and systemic change.

Table 1 (continued)

Code/Themes	Representative quotes	Insights
Opportunity for change	• "… you need a really strong leadership. Have to be really clear about what innovation means to them. And why they want to innovate? And what are the principles that support innovation? And I would say that we probably don't have a united view on any of that" • "That would look like a system that encouraged collaboration. Had a clear view of why it would innovate. And I don't think that [currently it's] clear … and by clear I mean internally and externally, like a vision and a purpose" • "I guess that's all about leadership, really … If you don't have the right people above you or working beside you, innovation wouldn't work"	• Leadership is key to long term change and barrier removal
Enabler	• "We need collaborative forums" • "… there must be some kind of passion or commitment there … to actually then take that frustration and turn it into an idea" • "… most people I'm meeting [in] health are not driven by financial benefit. They are driven by patient impacts"	• Time is essential to allow people to innovate • Individual drives and passions have an important role in innovation culture. However, this needs to be recognized and nurtured by the organization and system

(continued)

4.1 Mapping the Data

To better communicate what we learned about the complexity of systemic culture we have built visual maps to explore these concepts and to support the research into its next generative design phase. The use of visualization in any design-led research is fundamental, because according to Kernbach and Svetina Nabergoj (2018, p. 362) "it helps us to share and communicate ideas, [creates] common understanding, speeds up [the] process for more and faster innovation cycles, and enables insights leading to action." In our project, it is critical to use

Table 1 (continued)

Code/Themes	Representative quotes	Insights
Barrier	• "Barriers have become more complicated and our best players don't work together in the system—they work in competition—we are the biggest risk to ourselves" • "We aren't underfunded—we are too slow/not agile" • "You know people do tend to work in silos, and you don't often get the interactions you need with other people to help generate ideas" • "Yeah, exactly that. Yeah, yeah exactly it's blame rather than learning" • "… the competitiveness and the resentment, I guess, but it is when people and teams haven't been able to get their priorities met but they say other things happening which from their perspective you know wouldn't be a priority"	• People work in silos, they are reactive, not proactive—there is no commitment to a future vision • Research and innovation are not prioritised by the system Culture of blaming others
State of the current system	• "We really want you to put your ideas in but we're not going to give you any time to actually spend on working on that innovation … you've got to do it on top of your job and for most people around frontline workers that it's just not possible" • "Teams change all the time"	• The system is too complex—it is burdensome and does not understand innovation • Organizations and system lack structure that supports innovation

visual tools to communicate the complexity of a wicked problem that is impacting a wide and complex system.

The very act of visualizing insights has a cognitive and social function in collaboration and communication that is key to building the foundation on which the second phase of the research will be built, where the aim is to co-design a response to the current cultural challenges alongside healthcare teams and professionals.

4.2   Key Enablers and Barriers to the Development of a Culture of Innovation

The initial objective of our research was set to develop a traditional ecosystem map that joins nodes (often represented as players, actors, teams, or institutions) to other nodes in a system to visually tell a story about interdependent projects and collaborations. However, the data we collected was telling a different story. We found that it was not the information on nodes that was important; rather it was the experience and events that connect nodes that have an impact on organizational culture. While it is important to understand how teams interact with each other, we are beginning to make sense of how culture moves and evolves through the system.

Figure 1 presents a visual mapping of the ecosystem of innovation in the healthcare sector, based on our research findings. Figure 1 shows that there are four zones where barriers and enablers presented themselves:

Fig. 1 Innovation culture map. *Source* Author's own figure

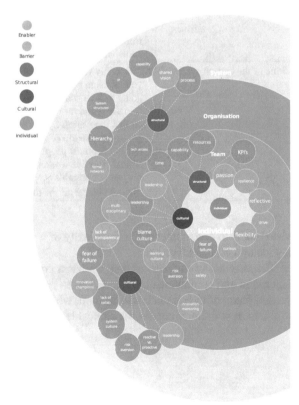

- **Individual level:** An individual player brings along their passion, enthusiasm, and curiosity, or lack of, into any team culture and is especially key in developing a culture of innovation and curiosity. Their involvement and drive to innovate could be influenced by the culture and structure of the team, organization, and system.
- **Team level:** A team of individuals starts to form cultural and structural impacts on innovation. For example, a team with a clear "top-down" leadership structure could encourage or prevent innovation from growing strong innovative leadership from a team leader could cultivate an innovation culture in the longer term but risk-averse leadership could be a barrier instead.
- **Organizational/Institutional level:** An organization is made of various teams. Innovation management at an organizational level, therefore, determines the environment for teams and individuals to innovate, or not.
- **System level:** Different healthcare organizations are governed by the healthcare system. Policy design at the systemic level could have an impact on how organizations view innovation and therefore directly impact innovation culture.

Within these layers, we found that there are four key elements that shaped the ecosystem of innovation culture:

- **Barriers:** Traditional hierarchy, structural complexity, and attitudes toward change were the primary barriers and they all sit within the control sphere of the system. For teams who had a different or more traditional structure, the biggest barrier could have been the leader. However, one team could also be experienced as a barrier by another team.
- **Enablers:** This refers to individuals, teams, activities, and leadership that would support innovation. For teams who had innovative leaders, leadership was a core enabler to the development and sustainment of an innovation culture. This was the case both at the team level and also at the institutional level.
- **Structure:** The structure of a team or an organization has a direct impact on how key players function and interact with each other. Our research found that a complex hierarchical structure would have more controls that might be barriers to nurture innovative efforts while a "flat" structure would be a better platform to have a shared vision of innovation.
- **Culture:** This refers to the rapport, relationships, and sense of belonging that shape how individuals function in a team, organization, and system. Our research found that a team or organizational culture is not static—it could be shifted intentionally or without being noticed. We refer to this as the "movement" of culture. A team or an organization could intentionally shift its culture by implementing change management. At times, a team or an organizational culture could move with outside factors such as trends, economy, and shifts in social constructs. This unintentional cultural shift in teams and organizations might not be noticed unless there is an ongoing reflective practice in place.

Barriers and enablers were found to be different depending on which players were interacting with each other and the level of the system where the interaction was occurring. Exploring barriers and enablers within the overarching ecosystem in this way highlights the different opportunities to leverage change, where those opportunities exist, and potentially, whose role it is to implement change. In an innovation ecosystem, there could be more barriers than enablers to the development of an innovation culture.

We also found that risk appetite could be a factor impacting innovation culture. Each of the 14 people interviewed spoke about the current culture of public health and rated it on a scale of one to 10 based on the system's willingness to nurture and develop a culture of innovation. The highest score was five out of 10, the lowest was two out of ten. All participants referenced risk aversion and fear as primary cultural barriers that were directly at odds with the development of a culture of innovation. In addition to this, participants also referenced a perception of blame, especially when innovation fails or something goes wrong. The perception of a lack of resourcing and a negative discourse about the system were also mentioned as key factors that damaged the system's capacity to develop a culture that encouraged innovation.

Mapping the barriers and enablers to innovation culture only captured part of the findings from the interviews. The layers and elements of an innovation ecosystem are intertwined, where changes in one would lead other aspects to shift. This was clearly emphasized when one of the participants explained:

> I think when we talk about [innovation] culture or innovation culture, we're really talking about those sort of subtle mindset shifts in the way that people think about and change and then enact behaviour change in small ways. And some of those kinds of small ways. When everybody starts thinking slightly differently, but it's taking a small step to the left that can actually change the culture of an organization quite significantly.

Innovation culture, and the different organizational cultures that it comes up against are therefore dynamic experiences of individuals moving throughout a system, not something static and immovable. This led us to start to consider how culture, especially innovation culture currently moves through a complex, traditional system like public health.

4.3   How Culture Shifts Within a Complex System

With a focus on innovation culture development, we were able to highlight moments where innovation culture was present and when it faced barriers to being sustained. However, underneath this was the traditional system that public health is built. To gain a deep understanding of the elements of a culture of innovation within the health context, we needed to gain a better understanding of how those who are trying to implement innovation and nurture a culture of innovation experience the overarching systemic culture so we explored this experience with the participants.

When analyzing the movement of culture and how it creates an impact on other parts of the system, we can learn about the potential points to leverage the system, influence change, and ultimately support transformation. This observation shows that while it appears static from the outside, the relationships between actors and barriers within a system are actually continually evolving. Figure 2 illustrates our findings that suggest innovation efforts often start with individuals' passion and drive. Collectively, these efforts could form an innovation culture at a team level. However, such culture could shift, or diminish, as it moves through barriers at the organizational and systemic levels. These barriers could be approval processes and a lack of recognition of the innovative effort that is driven by rigid organizational and systemic structures that do not support innovation. These movements are key to understanding how the system will respond to change. Designers and design researchers need to know what is relevant at these junctures and what actors can do to influence change at a system level. It is therefore important to engage iterative research methods, such as cyclical co-design, to cultivate rapport and collaborative effort among team members that would result in transformative implications within the system.

An HCD approach allowed us to frame the ecosystem from stakeholders' perspectives. The four zones as depicted in Fig. 1 show that there is a systemic

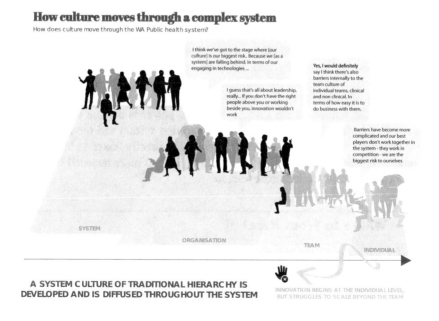

Fig. 2 How culture moves through a complex system. *Source* Author's own figure

relationship between the actors, events, and environments. This calls for a systemic approach to understand the ecosystem that would support an innovation culture. We, therefore, applied a system thinking lens to consider how transformation could happen within a system that appears to be static and full of barriers. Systems thinking as a lens provides us with "a context for seeing wholes. It is a framework for seeing interrelationships rather than things, for seeing patterns of change rather than static snapshots" (Senge, 1990). Looking through this lens can allow us to see a system as dynamic, with the possibility for change, even when they first appear to be full of barriers that are unable to be traversed. A large, complex system contains a diversity of actors, cultures, and competing motivations that are often contradictory (Conway et al., 2017, 14).

A systemic lens allows us to realize that elements within the system shift according to the dynamics in the relationships between teams and individuals. These shifts would cause the organizational culture to "move." The movement of culture and the tension that exists between innovation culture and the traditional culture of the public health system is not static, it is in fact changing constantly depending on the people that enact the cultures. However, our research data shows that innovation culture appears to thrive at both individual and team levels, where it is more protected from the rigid boundaries and structures of the organization and the system. We found that a culture of innovation struggles to thrive outside of the team environment, as the organization and the system are led by traditional cultures that are afraid of risk and failure.

While many traditional public systems prefer to approach complex issues through rational processing and negotiation, in the case of a wicked problem, an exploratory and collaborative learning approach offers more opportunity for transformation (Shaminee, 2018, p. 69). The sources of power that a public system is built upon are traditionally at odds with the kind of mindset, structures, and coalitions that allow for innovation and design to thrive (Shaminee, 2018, p. 116). This is proven to be true within the public system of health in Western Australia, as interviewees often spoke of the tension that was felt between localized or team culture and the culture of the system. Systemic power is a force to be reckoned with. It is, traditionally, what creates the underlying system and the language that the system uses when talking about itself; power is directly linked to hierarchy, but a complex healthcare service provision system presents more nuanced than simply being described as a hierarchical structure.

5   Where to From Here?

Our research finds that organizational culture and systems have a direct impact on how healthcare service provision could embrace an HCD approach. The complexity of cultivating human-centered innovation culture is as important as the design of human-centered service in health care. Figure 3 illustrates a research model that seeks to relate design research to produce human-centered service design and human-centered innovation culture. Human-centered service design projects are

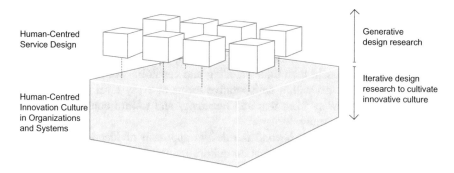

Fig. 3 Research approaches in human-centered service design and human-centered innovation culture. *Source* Author's own figure

represented as white boxes that are supported by the foundation of innovation culture in organizations and systems. Both service design and innovation culture require equal attention in applying HCD approaches. We propose design research directions for human-centered service design and innovation culture as

- **Generative design research in Human-Centered Service Design:** This research direction involves designers working collaboratively with stakeholders to identify and reframe service problems, and to co-create possibilities that would lead to service innovation.
- **Iterative design research in innovation culture:** This research direction encourages cyclical co-design approaches to build empathy and rapport, which would cultivate innovation culture in organizations and systems. As we have identified that culture within a system would move and shift, it is important that design research in this area needs to be iterative and focuses on generating meaningful discursive dialogs as outcomes.

We encourage future design-led research into human-centered innovation culture to focus on the transformation of barriers and enablers that stem from the individual, team, organizational, and systemic needs. The relationships between these elements and actors are key to the movement of innovation culture.

6   Conclusion

This chapter draws attention to innovation culture being the "back end" function of Human-Centered Service Design in health care. As we move forward into understanding how best to leverage players and relationships within the system for change, and ways to implement innovation that encourages cultural transformation, we must simultaneously combine our learnings with a breaking down of the behavior, culture, and structures that have kept the current culture alive (Shaminee, 2018,

p. 37). Using a design-led research approach to interrogate the development of culture within a complex system provides a new lens to understand transformation. Operationalizing transformation in organizational and systemic culture to allow innovation to flourish will likely pose many complex challenges that need new and thoughtful approaches: an understanding and capability for innovative thinking; collaborative teams within collaborative teams at every level of the system; a shift in language away from fear and negativity and toward courage, learning, innovation, and opportunity.

There is a need to look beyond the design approach of ideation and imagination. The cultivation of an innovation culture requires a deep understanding of systemic changes, complexity of process, and policy and regulatory frameworks. HCD approaches in these areas will help to build empathy and iterate organizational and systemic transformation that will eventually support the innovation culture to thrive.

We acknowledge that there are challenges larger than the scope of this research project. Innovation culture is agile and constantly shifting through teams, organizations, and systems. We believe that this observation is relevant to many public systems within the context of Western Australia and well beyond. We hope that this research inspires others to continue to explore the complexity of systems and how to leverage transformation within them through a lens of culture and design.

References

Abookire, S., Plover, C., Frasso, R., & Ku, B. (2020). Health design thinking: An innovative approach in public health to defining problems and finding solutions. *Frontiers in Public Health, 8,* 459–459. https://doi.org/10.3389/fpubh.2020.00459

Bazzano, A. N., Martin, J., Hicks, E., Faughnan, M., & Murphy, L. (2017). Human-centred design in global health: A scoping review of applications and contexts. *PLoS ONE, 12*(11), e0186744. https://doi.org/10.1371/journal.pone.0186744

Bendak, S., Shikhli, A. M., & Abdel-Razek, R. H. (2020). How changing organizational culture can enhance innovation: Development of the innovative culture enhancement framework. *Cogent Business & Management, 7*(1), 1712125, 1–17. https://doi.org/10.1080/23311975.2020.171 2125.

Berry, L. L. (2019). Service innovation is urgent in healthcare. *AMS Review: Official Publication of the Academy of Marketing Science, 9*(1–2), 78–92. https://doi.org/10.1007/s13162-019-001 35-x

Björgvinsson, E., Ehn, P., & Hillgren, P. A. (2010). Participatory design and" democratizing innovation". In *Proceedings of the 11th biennial participatory design conference*, Sydney, 29 Nov–3 Dec 2010, (pp. 41–50).

Brown, L., & Osborne, S. P. (2013). Risk and innovation. *Public Management Review, 15*(2), 186–208. https://doi.org/10.1080/14719037.2012.707681

Chen, Z., Huang, S., Liu, C., Min, M., & Zhou, L. (2018). Fit between organizational culture and innovation strategy: Implications for innovation performance. *Sustainability, 10*(10), 3378. https://doi.org/10.3390/su10103378

Conway, R., Masters, J., & Thorold, J. (2017). From design thinking to systems change. In *How to invest in innovation for social impact*. London: RSA Action and Research Centre (pp. 3–30)

Cottam, H., & Leadbeater, C. (2004). *RED paper 01: health—co-creating services*. London: The Design Council.

DeSalvo, K. B., O'Carroll, P. W., Koo, D., Auerbach, J. M., & Monroe, J. A. (2016). Public health 3.0: Time for an upgrade. *American Journal of Public Health, 106*(4), 621.

DeSalvo, K. B., Wang, Y. C., Harris, A., Auerbach, J., Koo, D., & O'Carroll, P. (2017). Public health 3.0: A call to action for public health to meet the challenges of the 21st century. *Preventing Chronic Disease, 14*(E78), 1–9. https://doi.org/10.5888/pcd14.170017.

Donetto, S., Pierri, P., Tsianakas, V., & Robert, G. (2015). Experience-based co-design and health-care improvement: Realizing participatory design in the public sector. *The Design Journal, 18*(2), 227–248. https://doi.org/10.2752/175630615x14212498964312

Dobni, C. B. (2008). Measuring innovation culture in organizations. *European Journal of Innovation Management, 11*(4), 539–559. https://doi.org/10.1108/14601060810911156

Hyvärinen, J., Lee, J. J., & Mattelmäki, T. (2015). Fragile liaisons: Challenges in cross-organizational service networks and the role of design. *The Design Journal, 18*(2), 249–268.

Johnson, A., Nguyen, H., Groth, M., & Wang, K. (2016). Time to change: A review of organizational culture change in health care organizations. *Journal of Organizational Effectiveness, 3*(3), 265–288. https://doi.org/10.1108/JOEPP-06-2016-0040

Jones, P. H. (2013). *Design for care: Innovating healthcare experience.* New York: Rosenfeld.

Kahn, K. B. (2018). Understanding innovation. *Business Horizons, 61*(3), 453–460. https://doi.org/10.1016/j.bushor.2018.01.011

Kernbach, S., & Svetina Nabergoj, A. (2018). Visual design thinking: Understanding the role of knowledge visualization in the design thinking process. In *2018 22nd international conference information visualisation (IV), Fisciano, Italy* (pp. 362–367). https://doi.org/10.1109/iV.2018.00068.

Lister, C., Payne, H., Hanson, C. L., Barnes, M. D., Davis, S. F., & Manwaring, T. (2017). The public health innovation model: Merging private sector processes with public health strengths. *Frontiers in Public Health, 5*(192), 1–9. https://doi.org/10.3389/fpubh.2017.00192

Lombardi, M. M., Spratling, R. G., Pan, W., & Shapiro, S. E. (2018). Measuring organizational capacity to accelerate health care innovation in academic health centers. *Quality Management in Health Care, 27*(1), 1–7.

Lorusso, L., Lee, J. H., & Worden, E. A. (2021). Design thinking for healthcare: Transliterating the creative problem-solving method into architectural practice. *HERD: Health Environments Research & Design Journal, 14*(2), 16–29. https://doi.org/10.1177/1937586721994228.

Maguire, M. (2001). Methods to support human-centred design. *International Journal of Human-Computer Studies, 55*(4), 587–634. https://doi.org/10.1006/ijhc.2001.0503

Martinidis, G. (2017). The importance of man within the system: Defining and measuring the human factor in innovation, A review. *Journal of the Knowledge Economy, 8*(2), 638–652. https://doi.org/10.1007/s13132-016-0406-4

Marjanovic, S., Sim, M., Dubow, T., Corbett, J., Harte, E., Parks, S., Miani, C., Chataway, J., & Ling, T. (2018). Innovation as a driver of quality and productivity in UK healthcare: Creating and connecting receptive places—Emerging insights. *Rand Health Quarterly, 7*(4), 1.

Mende, M. (2019). The innovation imperative in healthcare: An interview and commentary. *AMS Review, 9*(1–2), 121–131. https://doi.org/10.1007/s13162-019-00140-0

Moussa, M., McMurray, A., & Muenjohn, N. (2018). Innovation in public sector organizations. *Cogent Business & Management, 5*(1), 1475047. https://doi.org/10.1080/23311975.2018.1475047

Pillay, R., & Morris, M. H. (2016). Changing healthcare by changing the education of its leaders: An innovation competence model. *The Journal of Health Administration Education, 33*(3), 393–410.

Roberts, J. P., Fisher, T. R., Trowbridgec, M. J., & Bent, C. (2016). A design thinking framework for healthcare management and innovation. *Healthcare, 4*(1), 11–14. https://doi.org/10.1016/j.hjdsi.2015.12.002

Sadegh Sharifirad, M., & Ataei, V. (2012). Organizational culture and innovation culture: Exploring the relationships between constructs. *Leadership & Organization Development Journal, 33*(5), 494–517. https://doi.org/10.1108/01437731211241274

Samet, K. A., & Smith, M. S. (2016). Thinking differently: Catalyzing innovation in healthcare and beyond. *Frontiers of Health Services Management, 33*(2), 3–15.

Sangiorgi, D. (2011). Transformative services and transformation design. *International Journal of Design, 5*(2), 29–40.

Senge, P. M. (1990). *The fifth discipline: The art and practice of the learning organization.* New York: Currency Doubleday.

Shaminee, A. (2018). *Designing with-in public organizations: Building bridges between public sector innovators and designers* (pp. 1–206). Amsterdam: BIS Pubilshers.

Stola, K. (2018). User experience and design thinking as a global trend in healthcare. *Journal of Medical Science, 87*(1), 28–33. https://doi.org/10.20883/jms.2018.281.

Thakur, R., Hsu, S. H. Y., & Fontenot, G. (2012). Innovation in healthcare: Issues and future trends. *Journal of Business Research, 65*(4), 562–569. https://doi.org/10.1016/j.jbusres.2011.02.022

The Design Council. (n.d.). Design for care: Reinventing care for the 21st century. Retrieved July 15, 2022, from https://www.designcouncil.org.uk/what-we-do/social-innovation/design-care.

Van Der Bijl-Brouwer, M., & Dorst, K. (2017). Advancing the strategic impact of human-centred design. *Design Studies, 53*(C), 1–23. https://doi.org/10.1016/j.destud.2017.06.003.

Sash Milne is a Ph.D. candidate, practicing service designer and design strategist. Sash is currently working on her Ph.D. with a focus on using human-centered design to explore innovation culture in the Western Australian Public Health system. Her research and professional practice explore design ability to work alongside private and public enterprise, and the complex social systems that shape public life to understand and reframe challenging social problems to ultimately impact public system reform in Australia and beyond.

Christopher Kueh is a design educator/researcher, practicing information designer and design strategist. He is currently a Senior Lecturer in Strategic Design at Edith Cowan University, Western Australia. His research and practice involve helping organizations to cultivate design abilities and to understand complexities through design.

Stuart Medley is an Associate Professor of Design at Edith Cowan University. He makes comics and visual prototypes for service design to improve social impact. He is a co-founder and Chair of the Perth Comic Arts Festival. Stuart has worked as a professional illustrator and graphic designer for 20 years.

Neil Lynch is the Lead for the Innovation stream of the Western Australian Government's Future Health Research and Innovation Fund. This fund supports a number of innovation funding programs and works to encourage and facilitate clinical innovation in the Health Service Providers of the WA health system.

Benjamin Noteboom is a physiotherapist and experienced public health service manager. His current role is focused on developing and implementing strategies to improve leadership capacity and capability throughout the Western Australia public health system, with emphasis on continuous improvement, innovation, and design, and how these elements converge to ensuring a fit-for-purpose, future-ready health system.

Enhancing Seldom Heard Perspectives in Human-centred Service Design for Health and Social Care Transformation

Kris Kalkman and Marikken Høiseth

ABSTRACT

Human-centred service design is committed to considering the experiences of those affected by existing or future services. This consideration is a meaningful yet overwhelming responsibility. Critical service designers are not only equipped with a rich toolbox, including participatory principles, methods, tools and research ethics, but also committed to transgressing social and cultural norms through critical theory. However, the intention to reflect all people's experiences is often hard to realize. In this article, we present an exploration of intersectionality as a framework that can enable the enhancement of seldom-heard perspectives in human-centred service design for health and social care transformation.

1 Introduction: Experiences That Have Left a Lasting Impression

Farah is a 14-year-old girl who moved from a Middle Eastern country to a small town in Norway with her mother early in her childhood. Due to a congenital disorder, Farah has been in a wheelchair all her life. Farah used to play football but has stopped. She talks about how there is a lot of homework in middle school and how she also wants to spend time with

K. Kalkman (✉)
Department of Teacher Education, Faculty of Social and Educational Sciences, Norwegian University of Science and Technology (NTNU), Mailing Address: Gunnerus Gate 1, 7012 Trondheim, Norway
e-mail: kris.kalkman@ntnu.no

M. Høiseth
Department of Design, Faculty of Architecture and Design, Norwegian University of Science and Technology (NTNU), Kolbjørn Hejes Vei 2B, 7034 Trondheim, Norway
e-mail: marikken.hoiseth@ntnu.no

73

her friends, so she does not have time to participate in all her leisure activities. At the same time, from Farah's recollection, it becomes apparent that there is no opportunity for people using wheelchairs to be part of football training because the indoor halls are not being used, and the artificial turf outside is difficult to manage for wheelchair users. Besides that, she says that she has heard that using a wheelchair on the turf is not allowed because the field gets damaged. In addition, Farah explains that having a disability like hers is associated with low social status in her mother country. At the same time, despite the challenges she faces, Farah's biggest dream is to become a medical doctor so she can return to her native country to help children with various disabilities and contribute to making them feel equally valuable as any other child.

Over the course of the various participatory projects that we have been working with separately (though in collaboration with others), experiences like Farah's (note) (The example is based on free recall of the second author. The source of the example belongs to the project 'Participation and Quality', which is managed by the Norwegian National Advisory Unit on Disabilities in Children & Youth, in collaboration with SINTEF Digital, Health Research and several Norwegian municipalities. The project is supported by The Research Council of Norway Grant number 296365.) make a lasting impression. The reason for this is that the everyday lived experiences of people like Farah challenge us, as researchers and fellow human beings, to push forward to find informed ways to design for change through disrupting or transgressing social and cultural norms (Bardzell et al., 2012). This entails a continuous exploration of epistemological questions related to the significance of marginalized groups' lived experiences and the role that critical theory can play in achieving disruption and provocation for change. While we come from different fields of research, being researchers in human-centred design and diversity education, we both observe how social injustice unfolds through various services and systems. Over time, we have become critically aware of how people experience various forms of discrimination. Therefore, we have become knowledgeable about how experiences with discrimination are closely linked to people's intersecting social identities. Experiences with discrimination are seldom singular in nature. Prejudices are propelled through a subjective intolerance to people's age, (dis)ability, gender, sexual orientation, religion, race and/or ethnicity, nationality and/or language. If people act upon their prejudices, causing others to experience a breach in their human rights, discrimination occurs. For example, research into the intersection of racism, immigration and health reveals how racism as a structural force causes institutional discrimination without requiring individuals' active support (Song, 2020). As such, human-centred service designers should investigate not only how people experience ways of discrimination and oppression but also how the intersection of social identities produces and reproduces social and economic inequities along racial and ethnic lines on a systemic level (Viruell-Fuentes et al., 2012). Consequently, racism becomes a thrust for developing a host of social and emotional disorders and diseases, intersecting with other forms of oppression and marginalization that influence immigrants' health (Viruell-Fuentes et al., 2012). As such, if lived experiences such as Farah's are to be investigated, then the epistemology and methodology used by social healthcare design researchers should encompass and reflect both the severity of marginalization's influence on individuals' well-being and the impact that intolerance, prejudice, discrimination, and racism may have on caregivers and the surrounding community. In this article, we take a particular interest in how health and social care services are pervasive and crucial in human life and well-being. We will draw on critical theory, as this field has a long-standing tradition in head-on research aimed at investigating matters of how race, class, and gender inform each other and can lead to subordination and social inequity (Collins et al., 2021). Our motivation for this article is to explore how Farah's experiences can be understood through a critical framework that can enhance seldom-heard perspectives in intersectional social healthcare design research. We discuss how critical and reflexive thinking are vital parts of a service designer's tools for promoting social justice, enabling engagement in co-designing health and social care transformation. We hope to contribute by broadening the fields of human-centred design and social healthcare services. The structure of this article is as follows. Following this introduction, we first look at some central concepts connected to marginalization and seldom-heard perspectives. Next, we consider how human-centred service design coincides with transformational aims, specifically within a health and social care context. Then, we explore how intersectionality can be used to study healthcare encounters, with Farah's experiences as an illustrative example. Finally, we present some concluding remarks.

2 Minority Perspectives and Oppressed Groups

Minority groups are diverse, and at times, people may find it quite challenging to understand who is or is not a minority. They are not alone. The UN's Special Rapporteur on minority issues underscores in its report to the General Assembly of the UN (2019, p. 18) that a conceptual framing is needed 'to clarify what constitutes a minority based on the history and formulation of the main provisions of the United Nations on minorities in order to avoid the inconsistencies, uncertainties, and even contradictions that currently exist within and between United Nations entities, as well as with many States Members of the United Nations'. Leaving in place a situation with no common understanding as to who is a minority is not an option, since it is potentially harmful to minorities by contributing to doubts as to who can claim protective rights in relation to their culture, religion or language. This has led to a rather anarchic situation, as one can see from some of the responses by United Nations entities, which have adopted widely diverging, inconsistent and at times even contradictory and restrictive stances as to who is considered a minority.

A clarification that since has been adopted by the UN (United Nations Human Rights Office of the High Commissioner) explains that one of the main objective criteria for determining whether a group is a minority in a state is a numerical one. A minority in the territory of a state means it is not the majority. Objectively, that means that an ethnic, religious or linguistic group makes up less than half the population of a country.

This clarification makes it clear that the definition of a minority is directly related to a person or group's right to claim protective rights in relation to their culture, religion or language. Meyers (1984) traced the process by which the term 'minority group' came to be used as a general term for all groups subjected to various forms of prejudice and discrimination. He underscored that the conceptual limitations and ambiguity of the term 'minority groups' has been shaped by political factors (both domestic and international) and encompasses a contestable theory of prejudice and discrimination (related to people and groups' culture, religion or language). Meyers proposed that the term should rather be investigated from the vantage point that 'minority' is an ideological formulation, its definition excluding other marginalized groups. He suggested that the term 'oppressed groups' is more encompassing and fitting for all those experiencing marginalization (Meyers, 1984). Meyer's take is of interest. If human-centred designers in health and social care are to fully understand how people's 'deviation' from the norm occurs through the intersecting of their social identities (linked to their ethnicity, race, gender, sexual identity, religion, language, culture, disability and age), then critical healthcare researchers need to address matters related to how oppressed groups' belonging to specific social categories propel social inequality in power and vulnerability to political influence. Critical social studies have a main goal to explore the intersection of social dimensions and how discrimination occurs because of the intersection itself (Corus & Saatcioglu, 2015). This entails that critical healthcare researchers need to find ways to engage with marginalized groups, even though—at times—these may be hard to reach, or more aptly, seldom heard.

3   From Hard-to-Reach Groups to Seldom-Heard Groups

Drewett and O'Reilly reflect on the concepts of 'hard-to-reach', 'seldom heard' and 'vulnerability', all of which are closely related to marginalization and point at imminent challenges (Drewett & O'Reilly, 2021). 'Hard-to-reach' has been a commonly used term to denote a range of challenges in getting access to certain groups, from practical barriers such as gatekeepers and communication to more marginalized or vulnerable populations, people with low social status or stigmatized groups. The concept of 'seldom heard' is a more novel conceptualization that does not place responsibility within populations but rather on counterparts in the form of researchers, systems and services. Children (especially children within commonly marginalized positions such as Farah) can also be positioned as a seldom-heard group particularly prone to *be* placed in vulnerable situations. These groups are generally under-represented within health promotion activities (Liljas et al., 2019) and healthcare research.

When researching seldom-heard and/or hard-to-reach groups, the ethical requirements for approval of a study and its methodology should be subject to thorough investigation before its start (Gombert, et al., 2016). This may be 'because vulnerable groups may tend to agree to studies more readily; for example, due to lack of self-confidence, trust in the work of institutions, certain incentives such as monetary vouchers or dyslexia; and the researcher ought to be aware of how these factors may influence the relationship with the participant' (Gombert et al., 2016 p. 584). This makes it even more important that critical social healthcare researchers are fully committed to partaking in the development of a research methodology that allows seldom-heard and/or hard-to-reach groups to voice their experiences with marginalization and ways to analyse how discrimination and marginalization cannot be analysed in isolation; they do not exist in a vacuum (Turan et al., 2019).

Turan et al. (2019) calls for a better understanding of how intersecting forms of stigma are a common reality point out the need for instruments and methods that are better at characterizing the mechanisms and effects of intersectional stigma in relation to various health conditions. We go a step further and underscore the need for further development of the field of social healthcare design by embracing a critical social theory that enables investigation of how race, class and gender inform each other and can lead to subordination and social inequity (Collins et al., 2021).

4   Human-Centred Service Design and the Transformation Paradigm

Service encounters exist and unfold as service providers interact with service users. However, from a human-centred design perspective, the term 'user' brings noteworthy challenges in implying a certain passivity both in the role of people and the matter around which the interaction takes place. Whereas the industrial era created a distance between the phases of design production and use, services are not pre-defined entities that lend themselves to be used by a user in comparison to a stand-alone object (Kvelland & Høiseth, 2016). Instead, services are continuously co-produced by the people involved (King & Mager, 2009; Sangiorgi, 2011). Services are dynamic and ongoing processes, shaped and reshaped by the people participating in the encounters. This has been recognized to imply new challenges for designers 'entering the fields of organisational studies and social change with little background knowledge of their respective theories and principles' (Sangiorgi, 2011, p. 29).

Stakeholder participation is a key component of human-centred service design. It can lead to improved creative processes and innovation, a closer fit between the service offer and users' needs, and improved service experiences and higher satisfaction (Bowen et al., 2013; Steen et al., 2011). It is increasingly common and expected that end users, employees and others who are potential producers of a service are invited as active participators in co-creative processes. In this way, people who will engage in service production can find suitable solutions together. Different perspectives can bring out a variety of needs and experiences that form the basis for human-centred service development.

However, beyond these more traditional measures of benefits, services and participatory service design have increasingly been understood as 'engines for wider societal transformations' (Bowen et al., 2013, p. 231), with an affinity towards creative communities, social innovation, public services, 'collaborative services', the open-source paradigm, collaborative modes of service delivery and users' continuous participation in service design and delivery (Sangiorgi, 2011). A prerequisite for realizing this envisioned transformative role of services is to transform behaviours and deep-rooted cultural models significantly in organizations and citizens. According to Sangiorgi (2011, p. 31), achieving transformational impact calls for 'uncovering and questioning, via design inquiries, core assumptions and organizational worldviews'. We argue that part of this transformation is about accommodation for enhancing views of groups who are seldom heard. Improved diversity in co-creative processes is considered a strength not only because novel solutions may emerge but also to prevent heightened inequalities in healthcare (Chauhan et al., 2021).

Public health and social care services are intended to be potentially suitable for all citizens. All citizens have bodies and health and will need various health services to varying degrees throughout the course of life. Identifying health and social care services as experiential and co-created, Corus and Saatcioglu (2015) argue that factors such as ineffective service encounters with providers, complexities of healthcare settings or lack of knowledge underpinning effective healthcare decisions may create disadvantaged positions. Youth with minority backgrounds may experience discrimination in a variety of ways, prohibiting real opportunities for co-creation and participation. Identifying ways in which service encounters are organized to invite, silence or exclude perspectives of young citizens like Farah is an important prerequisite to fight social inequalities.

5   Intersectional Social Healthcare Design Research

Health and social care exchanges involve significant barriers to collaboration between users and providers in terms of power gaps and complexity connected to navigation within certain service settings (Corus & Saatcioglu, 2015). Health and social care represent contexts in which associated services connect directly to well-being (Anderson et al., 2013). Restricted access to services and discrimination in receiving services often result in deep gaps between minority groups and majority groups, leading to maintenance and deterioration of social inequalities spanning all service eco-levels, from micro to macro; hence, throughout one-on-one interactions, healthcare-related experiences and knowledge as well as health and social care policies in which connected service encounters are shaped and negotiated (Anderson et al., 2013; Corus & Saatcioglu, 2015).

Crocker (2021) calls for intersectional healthcare design research. Crocker emphasizes that patient (user) experience research has predominantly been done in Western contexts without adjusting for cultural and demographic variation. She states that this leaves designers 'to apply contextually specific and demographically neutral research to a wide range of healthcare systems, cultural contexts, and demographic conditions' (Crocker, 2021, p. 273). Crocker underscores that healthcare design research conducted in a variety of sociocultural conditions could help to ensure (social) healthcare facilities are designed to best suit their users' sociodemographic needs and support the health system's wider public health ambitions. Health inequalities within and between nations are well known, and while the systems and structures that inform these inequalities are complex, it is likely that design can play a role in ensuring these inequalities are not exacerbated by the environments in which care is provided. In other words, while healthcare designers may not be able to affect the geographies of inequality outside health facilities, they should endeavour to impact those within.

In line with Crocker, Collins et al. (2021 p. 691) argue that when it comes to searching for critical analyses of sociocultural norms, 'subordinated groups require tools that go beyond simple critique. Critical analysis does not only criticize, but it also references ideas and practices that are essential, needed, or critical for something to happen'. The extensive social interaction that typically characterizes encounters between service users and providers makes them highly suitable for studying aspects of marginalization through intersectionality (Corus et al., 2015).

6   Intersectionality to Study Healthcare Encounters

Following Corus and Saatcioglu (2015), we suggest that intersectionality offers a holistic look at the co-created nature of services and for designing fair, tailored services to improve consumer and societal well-being. For the purpose of this article, we have adopted their guidelines, as these are understood to be highly beneficial for further developing an intersectional approach to healthcare services. These guidelines consist of five recommendations, summarized as follows. First, the exploration starts by questioning how an intersectional approach can enrich transformative service researchers' perspectives. The aim is to better understand how multiple identity axes might disadvantage already marginalized individuals/groups to become even further marginalized. Second, when committing to intersectionality, researchers should investigate how oppressed groups experience a multiplicity of marginalization. Yet, researchers should also be adamant in paying attention to how forms of marginalization play out within marginalized groups and simultaneously be cognizant that privilege may reveal itself in other domains. Third, the field of intersectionality is broad, and researchers should make informed choices surrounding what theoretical perspectives are appropriate for their study. Corus and Saatcioglu (2015) present three main perspectives (intracategorical, intercategorical and anticategorical). Due to the limitations of this article, we have chosen to include an anticategorical perspective, as it demands further investigation of the history of a particular form of discrimination, its locality in a specific political and cultural context, and how it may relate to discrimination experiences of other marginalized groups. This entails being conscious of the fact that various experiences of health problems and healthcare issues often cannot be fitted under one primary identity category (gender, sexuality, ethnicity, race, class, etc.).

Researchers must then be aware of how marginalization, discrimination and racism are shaped by and within a larger sociocultural context. This takes us to the fourth recommendation, developing an understanding of how power operates at multiple levels and how power relations shift in time and place due to, for example, 'conflicts in terms of power, knowledge, and social status' (Lee et al., 1999 cited in Corus & Saatcioglu, 2015, p. 424). Finally, a researcher is required to determine and discuss the practicality of any political implications that come from an intersectional analysis. This fifth and final recommendation propels the social justice dimension of intersectionality. Groups that are socially excluded tend to be more reliant on public services, and as such, are more vulnerable to policy changes. Emphasizing marginalized groups' experiences demands an ethical stance that entails creating waves, illuminating how 'traditionally used categorization of social groups (e.g., class, income, health)' are not independent of each other (Corus & Saatcioglu, 2015, p. 424). Rather than focusing on a singular category, experiences should be studied as the products of intertwined social identities; they intersect, collaborate with and accommodate people's everyday experiences of marginalization within healthcare services.

7   Exploring Farah's Experiences Through an Intersectional Lens

In the following, we will take a closer look at Farah's experiences, following the framework of Corus and Saatcioglu (2015). We present an explorative outline of how intersectionality can enhance seldom-heard perspectives in critical human-centred service design for healthcare transformation.

7.1   Recommendation 1: Assess the Relevance of the Intersectionality Paradigm for the Study

From Farah's experiences, we gain insight into the multiple social categories or dimensions to which she expresses belonging. Farah presents as a young girl from a family with an immigrant background. She has a visible disability and is confined to a wheelchair. She lives with her mother, who is a single parent. Being an Arab-speaking family, it is most likely her family is Muslim. They have settled in a small rural Norwegian town. Farah makes it clear that she is aware of how her congenital disorder keeps her from particular social activities with friends in her community and how it is regarded as prohibiting upward social mobility within her mother country. From an intersectionality perspective, the aim is to seek a better understanding of how for Farah, these multiple identity axes may cause discrimination and impact her opportunities to achieve equity.

Norway commits to guaranteeing quality of life and opportunities for children and youth with disabilities or chronic diseases on an equal footing with the rest of the population (Helsedirektoratet, 2015). Norwegian politics on this matter are based on the United Nations Convention on the Rights of the Child (CRC), stating that all children and youth have a right to care, development, learning and participation in society, including the right to live a full life under conditions that ensure their dignity and promote respect for the individual's life, integrity and human dignity (UN, 1989). Children have the right to leisure and to partake in activities. As such, universal design should contribute to make environments, information and services available to all people. In accordance with the Centre for Excellence in Universal Design (CEUD) (2020), there are seven principles of universal design. Principles 5, 6 and 7 are interpreted and briefly described in the following (not in chronological order). Architectural and service design should enable efficient, comfortable use with minimum fatigue. The space should provide for approach, reach, manipulation and use regardless of a person's body size, posture, or mobility. Designed solutions should minimize hazards and adverse consequences of accidental or unintended actions (CEUD, 2020). Concerning these recommendations for universal design, Farah's experiences illuminate how people using a wheelchair do not have the opportunity to play football as they 1) must make great efforts to partake in football training and 2) that a wheelchair may damage the turf, increasing the possibility of accidental or unintended actions. Her reasoning why partaking in football is not possible may relate more to decisions about not using the indoor halls than to having too much homework. Together with Farah's reflections on the low social status of disabilities in her homeland, some suitable questions from an intersectional lens are as follows:

- How might Farah's multiple identity axes further hurt her opportunities to participate in society?
- How do Farah's multiple identity axes connect to her own and societal well-being?
- How might multiple identity axes of service providers and service values hurt Farah's opportunities to participate in society?
- How do multiple identity axes of service providers and service values connect to the well-being of Farah and society?

Further uniting an intersectional lens combined with human-centred service design:

- How can service encounters be organized to invite and incorporate seldom heard perspectives of young citizens?
- How can services be sensitive to multiple identity axes and seldom heard perspectives in service exchanges and across service domains?
- How may enhanced understandings of relationships between intersecting social categories and discrimination influence how service designers facilitate co-creation processes?

7.2   Recommendation 2: Determine Population of Interest and Identify Axes

Based on Farah's presentation of herself and how she perceives wheelchair users as subject to disability-based discrimination in organized football, populations of interest include youth with and without lived experiences of disabilities, football clubs and the rest of the sports sector, families with and without non-traditional structures with lived experiences of disabilities and immigrant backgrounds, public health service providers, school and educational service providers and policy-makers. Relevant identity axes to be considered when studying marginalization in our context include age, disability, gender, race, language, class and family organization. Some relevant questions in extension of this include the following:

- How do identity axes intersect and connect to form and uphold social inequalities?
- How might discrimination occur as a result of their intersection?
- How do specific layers intersect to echo forms of marginalization or privileges of young citizens regarding their access to participation and connected well-being?
- Are there subgroups that might have been overlooked?
- How can service co-design be applied to transform 'seldom heard' into 'clearly heard'?
- Recommendation 3: Determine what type of intersectionality is appropriate for the study

7.3   Recommendation 3: Determine What Type of Intersectionality is Appropriate for the Study

An anticategorical perspective helps to shed light on discrimination from a historical viewpoint, with specific political and cultural contexts that may interconnect with other marginalized groups' discrimination experiences. Instead of categories, the unit of anticategorical analysis corresponds to sociohistorical processes and discourses (Mehrotra, 2010). For example, such a perspective would encourage joined investigation into:

- Mutual historical origins of history of disability internationally and in Nordic countries.
- History of the oppressed, e.g., social history, gender history and minority history.
- Processes of 'othering' and experiences of 'otherness' across time, place and space.
- Political disability movement paralleling feminist movements and gender studies.

- Diversity policies, minorities, sports practices and communication.
- Disability, youth sports and ableism.
- Football studies, gender, race, disability and feminism.
- Childhood studies/geographies, multiple social inequalities and identities in diverse sociospatial contexts.
- Minority perspectives in co-production and co-design processes for healthcare transformation.

7.4   Recommendation 4: Establish the Impact of Power Dynamics at the Interpersonal and Structural Levels

Questions surrounding interpersonal power dynamics across societal levels could be:

- Which social factors were significant in Farah's process of quitting football?
- How have Farah's experiences from football shaped her ideas of equity and power?
- How would the football community be able to hold on to Farah as an equal member of the football club?
- How might Farah's continued participation in the football club influence the interest of other potential members?
- How will underlying feelings and experiences connected to her football interest impact Farah's future service encounters?
- How are attitudes towards gender, sexuality, race, disability and intersectionality rooted, practiced, and challenged in dominant football discourses?
- How are attitudes towards gender, sexuality, race, disability and intersectionality rooted, practiced and challenged in local football discourses?
- How are attitudes towards gender, sexuality, race, disability and intersectionality rooted, practiced and challenged in local political, cultural, and healthcare contexts?

7.5   Recommendation 5: Determine and Discuss Practical and Policy Implications of Intersectional Analyses

Following the framework thus far has led to the identification of several questions that tap into the shaping of experiences, identities and service interactions in various ways. Addressing and acting upon such questions will contribute to create ripples. To ensure these ripples trigger targeted action on practical and policy levels requires that researchers and designers:

- Clarify multiple types of stakeholder and leadership engagement, roles and responsibilities regarding the enhancement of minority perspectives for promoting social justice in services.
- Pay attention to implementation issues and policy perspectives from the very outset of planning and preparing projects or initiatives and throughout conducting and refining activities.
- Deliberately seek to identify and recruit diverse participants.
- Apply a service design framework that supports transformation towards minority-sensitive service exchanges through adapted principles, methods and tools.

8   Conclusion

In this article, we have presented an explorative approach to how human-centred service design can strengthen its commitment to design for social justice, considering the experiences of those affected by existing or future services. When designing with seldom heard groups, critical theory may serve as an explorative lens for constructing epistemological questions related to the significance of marginalized groups' lived experiences and the role that, for example, intersectionality can play in disruption and provocation for change. When researching marginalization (of individuals or groups), critical healthcare researchers' consideration of co-creating ways to voice people's experiences becomes not only meaningful but also a social responsibility. Service designers are equipped with a rich toolbox, including participatory principles, methods, tools and research ethics. At the same time, inspired by the critical paradigm, we recognize that an increasing number of health and social care researchers and designers have become committed to promoting people's experiences with marginalization and oppression, aiming to contribute to social transgression and challenge societies' cultural norms. Fundamental insights into designing questions for research were gained through listening to and learning from Farah's experiences. Furthermore, we are aware that to design for social justice, we are required to check our own privileges. An essential question then becomes whether we are the right people to speak on certain issues. For example, when continuing to develop participatory principles, methods, tools and research ethics, who will participate in this work and whose stories and experiences serve for change? The field of design has changed significantly over the last couple of decades, including new challenges for those who want to research and design for social change but may have little insight into the field of critical theory and its principles. Simultaneously, social researchers may likewise have limited insight into what the field of human-centred design may offer in relation to developing transformative change intended to enhance people's quality of life. Therefore, we call for transdisciplinary research efforts. This means that seldom-heard groups, researchers and designers from various disciplines find ways to collaborate in developing new conceptual, theoretical, methodological and translational aims that integrate and move beyond discipline-specific methodologies to address lived experiences. Our intention with this article has been to present approaches that encompass and reflect the intersectional and social experiences of all people. Farah's experiences were explored through questions rather than answers, exhibiting how questions prompted by an intersectional framework can enable researchers and designers to enhance those experiences and perspectives of seldom-heard individuals and groups within human-centred service design for health and social care transformation.

References

Anderson, L., Ostrom, A. L., Corus, C., Fisk, R. P., Gallan, A. S., Giraldo, M., Mende, M., Mulder, M., Rayburn, S. W., Rosenbaum, M. S., Shirahada, K., & Williams, J. D. (2013). Transformative service research: An agenda for the future. *Journal of Business Research, 66*(8), 1203–1210.

Bardzell, S., Bardzell, J., Forlizzi, J., Zimmerman, J., & Antanitis, J. (2012). Critical design and critical theory: The challenge of designing for provocation. In *Proceedings of the designing interactive systems conference* (pp. 288–297). Association for Computing Machinery (ACM), Newcastle Upon Tyne, 11–15 June 2012.

Bowen, S., McSeveny, K., Lockley, E., Wolstenholme, D., Cobb, M., & Dearden, A. (2013). How was it for you? Experiences of participatory design in the UK health service. *CoDesign, 9*(4), 230–246.

Centre for Excellence in Universal Design (CEUD). (2020). Retrieved June 30, 2022, from https://universaldesign.ie/what-is-universal-design/the-7-principles/.

Chauhan, A., Leefe, J., Shé, É. N., & Harrison, R. (2021). Optimising co-design with ethnic minority consumers. *International Journal for Equity in Health, 20*(1), 1–6.

Collins, P. H., da Silva, E. C. G., Ergun, E., Furseth, I., Bond, K. D., & Martínez-Palacios, J. (2021). Intersectionality as critical social theory: Intersectionality as critical social theory, Patricia Hill Collins, Duke University Press, 2019. *Contemporary political theory, 20*(3), 690–725. https://doi.org/10.1057/s41296-021-00490-0.

Corus, C., & Saatcioglu, B. (2015). An intersectionality framework for transformative services research. *The Service Industries Journal, 35*(7–8), 415–429. https://doi.org/10.1080/02642069.2015.1015522.

Crocker, S. (2021). A call for intersectional healthcare design research. *HERD: Health Environments Research & Design Journal, 14*(1), 273–277. https://doi.org/10.1177/1937586720964729.

Drewett, A., & O'Reilly, M. (2021). Examining the value of using naturally occurring data to facilitate qualitative health research with 'seldom heard' 'vulnerable' groups: A research note on inpatient care. *Qualitative Research.* 0(0), 1–11. https://doi.org/10.1177/14687941211039971.

Gombert, K., Douglas, F., McArdle, K., & Carlisle, S. (2016). Reflections on ethical dilemmas in working with so-called 'vulnerable' and 'hard-to-reach' groups: Experiences from the Foodways and Futures project. *Educational Action Research, 24*(4), 583–597. https://doi.org/10.1080/09650792.2015.1106958.

Helsedirektoratet. (2015). *Barn og unge med habiliteringsbehov. Samarbeid mellom helse- og omsorgssektoren og utdanningssektoren om barn og unge som trenger samordnet bistand*. Retrieved June 30, 2022, from https://www.helsebiblioteket.no/retningslinjer/barn-og-unge/barn-og-unge-med-habiliteringsbehov?lenkedetaljer=vis.

King, O., & Mager, B. (2009). Methods and processes of service design. *Touchpoint, 1*(1), 20–28.

Kvelland, L. M., & Høiseth, M. (2016). Is the 'user' term adequate? A design anthropology perspective on design for social welfare services. In *DS 85–1: Proceedings of NordDesign 2016* (pp. 247−257). The Design Society, Trondheim, August 10–12, 2016.

Liljas, A. E. M., Walters, K., Jovicic, A., Iliffe, S., Manthorpe, J., Goodman, C., & Kharicha, K. (2019). Engaging 'hard to reach' groups in health promotion: The views of older people and professionals from a qualitative study in England. *BMC Public Health, 19*(1), 629−629. https://doi.org/10.1186/s12889-019-6911-1.

Mehrotra, G. (2010). Toward a continuum of intersectionality theorizing for feminist social work scholarship. *Affilia, 25*(4), 417–430.

Meyers, B. (1984). Minority group: An ideological formulation. *Social problems (Berkeley, Calif.), 32*(1), 1−15. https://doi.org/10.1525/sp.1984.32.1.03a00010.

Sangiorgi, D. (2011). Transformative services and transformation design. *International Journal of Design, 5*(2), 29−40.

Song, M. (2020). Rethinking minority status and 'visibility.' *Comparative Migration Studies, 8*(1), 5. https://doi.org/10.1186/s40878-019-0162-2

Steen, M., Manschot, M., & De Koning, N. (2011). Benefits of co-design in service design projects. *International Journal of Design, 5*(2), 53−60.

Turan, J. M., Elafros, M. A., Logie, C. H., Banik, S., Turan, B., Crockett, K. B., Pescosolido, B., & Murray, S. M. (2019). Challenges and opportunities in examining and addressing intersectional stigma and health. *BMC Medicine, 17*(1), 7−7. https://doi.org/10.1186/s12916-018-1246-9.

UN. (1989). United Nations convention on the rights of the child. Retrieved June 30, 2022, from http://www.jus.uio.no/english/services/library/treaties/02/2-05/rights-child.xml.

UN General Assembly. (2019). *Effective promotion of the declaration on the rights of persons belonging to national or ethnic, religious and linguistic minorities, report of the special rapporteur on minority issues. A/74/160.* Retrieved June 30, 2022, from https://undocs.org/A/74/160.

United Nations Human Rights Office of the High Commissioner. Retrieved June 30, 2022, from https://www.ohchr.org/en/special-procedures/sr-minority-issues/concept-minority-mandate-definition.

Viruell-Fuentes, E. A., Miranda, P. Y., & Abdulrahim, S. (2012). More than culture: Structural racism, intersectionality theory, and immigrant health. *Social Science & Medicine, 75*(12), 2099–2106. https://doi.org/10.1016/j.socscimed.2011.12.037.

Kris Kalkman (Ph.D. in social work) is an associate professor in diversity education at the Department of Teacher Education, NTNU, contributing with research and teaching experience on transformative learning through interventions aimed at improving migrant and ethnic minority students' success in teacher education. His overarching research interests are on structural inequity, subordination and social (in)justice and how they form marginalized children and youths' experiences in formal and informal settings.

Marikken Høiseth (Ph.D. in human-centred design) is an associate professor in the Department of Design at the Norwegian University of Science and Technology (NTNU), where she teaches courses in design and supervises master students and Ph.D. candidates. She also holds a minor position at SINTEF Digital, Department of Health Research. Her research interests lie in the intersection of human-centred design, healthcare design, design with and for children, meaning-making processes, social semiotics and co-design.

Educational Challenges in Integrating Healthcare and Social Services: The Case of the University of Tartu Pärnu College in Designing a Master's Programme in Person-Centred Social Innovation

Ewe Alliksoo, Margrit Kärp, Heli Tooman, and Karit Jäärats

ABSTRACT

To provide people with consistent healthcare services and the best social support, a variety of factors are important, in particular a human-centred and holistic approach, as well as the need to reduce duplication of data collection and improve collaboration between different areas of healthcare and the social welfare system. However, encouraging people to participate actively in preventive health activities is equally important. Primary services are often not delivered on time and ultimately, more expensive services are consumed—in terms of both the money and time of patients and therapeutic resources. The reason is believed to lie in service providers focusing mainly on standardized services, thus leaving more sophisticated, as well as the issues that need to be combined between several parties, to be decided and organized by individuals. To change mindsets and behaviour patterns from a disease- or problem-oriented approach to a person-centred approach, it is essential to modify and offer comprehensive services to patients. However, there is still little research and few examples on how to educate and train professionals with new skills and knowledge. To facilitate that change, the University of Tartu Pärnu College has developed a new master's programme with the purpose of preparing

E. Alliksoo · M. Kärp (✉) · H. Tooman · K. Jäärats
University of Tartu Pärnu College, Ringi 35, 80012 Pärnu, Estonia
e-mail: margrit.karp@ut.ee

E. Alliksoo
e-mail: ewe.alliksoo@ut.ee

H. Tooman
e-mail: heli.tooman@ut.ee

K. Jäärats
e-mail: karit.jaarats@ut.ee

© The Author(s), under exclusive license to Springer Nature Switzerland AG 2023   87
M. A. Pfannstiel (ed.), *Human-Centered Service Design for Healthcare Transformation*,
https://doi.org/10.1007/978-3-031-20168-4_6

and educating professionals, including case managers, in the social service sector. These are people who understand the principles of human-centred service design, comprehend the significance of collaboration between different specialities, fields and levels of decision-making, and who use contemporary ways of involving different parties in holistic service design. This chapter will provide an overview about decoding the human-centred healthcare and social welfare services, the need for educated social work professionals and about the development process of the master's programme 'Person-Centred Social Innovation' at the University of Tartu Pärnu College, which incorporated the principles of service design throughout the whole development process of the curriculum, including practical examples.

1   Introduction

The development of human-centred services is a major challenge for both the health and social care system. Consistent treatment and the provision of the best social support are necessary in the human-centred treatment process; no less important are the reduction of duplication and the improvement of cooperation between different fields of the social and healthcare system, as well as consistent support for the patient in coping with chronic diseases.

There is no single definition for person-centred care. Terms such as patient-centred, human-centred, user-centred, etc., are used as synonyms for describing the way of thinking and doing things which sees people, who use health and social services, as equal partners in planning, developing and monitoring care to ensure that it meets their needs (Health Innovation Network, 2022, n.d.). In the person-centred approach, single persons and families are put at the heart of decisions and are seen as key experts working along with professionals to get the best outcome, while human-centred is more used in general terms. Therefore, the term person-centred is used in this chapter to emphasize each individual person.

The World Health Organization (WHO)'s strategy (WHO, 2013, n.d.) envisages the development of a comprehensive and high-quality healthcare system instead of the existing hospital-based, fragmented and disease-based model. To complete a goal of this strategy—'harnessing the potential contribution of traditional medicine to health, wellness and people-centred health care' (WHO, 2013, p. 11), and to assess its achievement through a performance indicator—'to build the knowledge base for active management through appropriate national policies' (WHO, 2013, p. 58)—the preparation of professionals with relevant knowledge and human-centred thinking is crucial.

The above refers to the great need for organizational and societal change and the development of innovative and improved health and social care services, which is the reason why more and more healthcare organizations are already recognizing the importance of a human-centred approach to service design (SD) (Melles et al., 2021, p. 43).

It is expected by citizens and politicians that the system of public support services reduces social risks and provides effective solutions. Increasing the efficiency of support systems requires changes in the system itself, including educating social work professionals, as well as changes in the forms and methods of operation. The healthcare system is transforming and shifting from treatment-based and centralized care models to more health-centred, community-based and co-produced service models using design methodologies (Freire and Sangiorgi, 2010, p. 3). Ensuring the safety and quality of care for the service users requires multidisciplinary teams, complex work processes, different regulations and the increasing involvement of customers in the development of such services, and therefore human-centred design is considered to be a suitable methodology for producing such systemic and human-based solutions (Melles, 2020, p. 42).

Practice has shown that the training of treatment teams and individual practitioners depend significantly on the application of a person-centred mindset in the delivery of care, as well as on their ability to work together to influence and reinforce people-centredness (Hardy, 2013, p. 1103). The problem, however, is the lack of educated and skilled staff who are able to design personalized health and social services.

This chapter explains the need for educated social work professionals with person-centred design skills that are necessary for the healthcare and social welfare system transformation. The chapter also provides an insight into the process of creating a master's degree programme for social field professionals, including case managers, at the University of Tartu Pärnu College. Graduates of this programme will have a high level of design thinking competence and be able to contribute to the design, development and advancement of integrated solutions for Estonian health and social care systems through human-centred design skills.

In the process of developing the new master's degree programme at Pärnu College, the SD methodology was used, from noticing and recognizing the need, defining the problem and collecting data to involving all parties and finally, creating a study programme. This approach to curriculum development has helped to design a customer-oriented educational programme that aims to incorporate design thinking into social case managers' genetic code. Moreover, in addition to acquiring knowledge and skills in design thinking, students will get to experience the curriculum created according to the principles of SD.

2   Decoding the Human-Centred Healthcare and Social Welfare Services.

The social sector is frequently criticized for developing and providing services that only service providers consider necessary and for ignoring and failing to specify the needs of actual service users, making it difficult for those in need to obtain comprehensive solutions that alleviate their condition, improve their health and give them access to vital services without overspending their own resources or those of the health and social care system (Zimmer, 2021, n.d.). The solution is seen in human-centred design—an empathic approach to problem-solving (Brown, 2008, p. 86), which puts the person at the centre of the development process, brings users' wants, pain points and preferences at the forefront and enables designing and implementing appropriate health interventions for service users, physicians and various stakeholders (Fischer et al., 2021, p. 1041; Landry, 2020, n.d.).

In line with a holistic approach to personal health, the service user experience is seen as one of the key challenges and opportunities facing health managers (Managed Healthcare Executive, 2019, n.d.). The process of changing the mindset and behaviour from an illness/problem-oriented approach to a person-centred service provider requires professionals with new skills and knowledge. Moreover, without a person-centred approach and without knowing the principles of SD, cooperation between different agencies and service providers is difficult, if not impossible.

The development and delivery of person-centred services also depend significantly on how treatment teams and different practitioners are trained and educated and able to work together to develop and embed person-centredness (Hardy, 2015, p. 521). In the case of the person-centred approach, it is important to look at each case individually, and therefore the ability to manage cases is also necessary. Case management is defined as a strategy aimed at increasing the accessibility to the resources that are necessary for individuals' lives and for the functioning of society, promoting their involvement and reducing the need for services (Hall et al., 2002, p. 133). Case management is like a bridge between different services that are not combined and may or may not overlap, so it requires the coordination of services, as well as smooth cooperation and collaboration with different stakeholders, to serve the client consistently and continuously (Bunger, 2010, p. 392, p. 397).

The importance of an inclusive and personal approach is growing, as is the importance of necessary skills, including the ability to notice and understand the client's behaviour, cope with unexpected situations and communicate with the client in a language he or she understands. One of the foundations of the person-centred approach is an understanding of functioning—not only a definition of a disability but also an assessment of a person's ability to cope with physical, mental and environmental interactions.

There is still little research and hardly any examples on how to prepare professionals who can understand the principles of design thinking, use SD tools and design person-centred healthcare services. One possible solution for transforming the healthcare and social system is seen in educating case managers for managing the complete range of services in a way that meets the customers' needs in the most efficient way.

3   Service Design in the Service of Curriculum Development

Service design is an evolving interdisciplinary and practical approach that combines different methods and tools from various disciplines. SD principles have been applied for problem-solving and solution creation in multiple businesses. Curriculum design and development can be seen as services as well, provided by the curriculum development team to adult learners with various needs and levels of experience (Scoresby et al., 2018, p. 1).

Just like every customer has different needs and expectations, each educational institution is different, and there is no specific model or framework for creating a curriculum that fully meets the needs of each learner. The implementation of six principles of SD—human-centred, collaborative, iterative, sequential, real and holistic (Stickdorn et al., 2018, p. 27)—in developing a curriculum enables to effectively customize a high-quality, learner-centred and competency-based learning experience for students so that they can meet the demands of the labour market and be competitive (Scoresby et al., 2018, p. 1).

Although different options are practised, generally, a distinction is made between the four stages of the SD process—exploration, creation, reflection and implementation (Stickdorn et al., 2018, p. 87); however, due to the fact that SD is not a direct process, there is constant jumping forth and back between these stages, sometimes even to the very beginning. Similar to this four-stage process is the double diamond model, which enables exploring an issue more widely or deeply (divergent thinking) and then taking focused action (convergent thinking). The model starts with the initial challenge or problem statement to the left, moves through a definition of the problem to be addressed in the centre and ends with the solution to the right (The Double Diamond, 2022, n.d). The practical use of this model in curriculum development is illustrated in Fig. 6.

The use of SD methodology in curriculum development is considered to be highly relevant, although some SD methods may be more appropriate in curriculum development (e.g., persona, interview mind map) than others (e.g., role play and mood board), while some methods (e.g., service blueprint and journey map) are suitable at several stages of the SD process (Mihhailova & Tooman, 2012, p. 37). In addition to SD, the collaboration of both teachers and the entire development team is crucial in creating a curriculum, as it has a positive impact on teachers' professional development as well as on curriculum implementation and innovation (Voogt et al., 2016, p. 137).

In the process of curriculum design and development in higher education institutions, development teams may face the situation where different understandings between academic and pedagogical approaches hinder collaboration. In this case, the application of the basic principles of SD—human-centredness and collaboration, as well as a competent and strong leader of the development team may be a proper solution (Burrell et al., 2015, p. 753, p. 755, p. 765).

Seeing students as customers for whom learning services are created, SD can also be considered a suitable methodology in the education system along with conventional curriculum development approaches and imminent administrative regulations. Therefore, it can be said that SD offers suitable tools and techniques for curriculum development, as the focus is on the person (student, as well as the lecturer) whose needs have to be considered in developing the curriculum as a holistic learning service. Throughout the SD process, several tools can be used, which vary depending on the university, the national education system and its requirements, the curriculum target group, teachers' experiences and the curriculum development team and its leader.

4   Development Needs of the Workforce of the Estonian Healthcare and Social Welfare System

Cooperation between different areas of the health and social welfare system, supporting the person in promoting a healthy lifestyle, dealing with chronic diseases, valuing person-centred treatment and reducing service duplication in the health and social care system should form a holistic combination of health support services to ensure consistent treatment and the best social assistance (Puis et al., 2021, p. 10–11). In Estonia, the provision of healthcare and social services is rather fragmented, and the person-centred approach involving different service providers is not applied. The use of resources is largely inefficient due to the lack of collaboration and communication between various service providers, and therefore the quality and outcome of treatment may suffer (Puis et al., 2021, pp. 10–11).

Collaboration between primary care and specialist care in the Estonian social welfare system is insufficient, leading people to spend unnecessary time in unreasonable queues, and, in turn, wasting the system resources. Service users fail to reach the necessary services in time, which eventually means later consumption of a more expensive service. The flow of information between equal-level service providers is often interrupted and cooperation between different services is incidental, based primarily on direct contacts between professionals (Kurowski et al., 2015, pp. 11–12).

One subgoal of the Estonian National Health Strategy 2020–2030 (National Health Strategy, 2021, p. 15) is person-centred healthcare (Fig. 1). This is derived from the WHO's strategy (WHO, 2013, p. 43), which envisages the development of a comprehensive and high-quality healthcare system instead of the existing hospital-based, fragmented and disease-based model. According to the National Health Strategy, people-centred healthcare is broader than patient-centred healthcare—in addition to treatment, person-centred healthcare focuses on prevention, community health and well-being and its role is to influence health policy and services, among other objectives (National Health Strategy, 2021, p. 30).

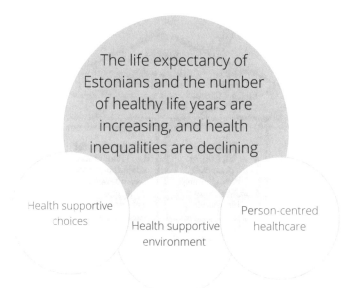

Fig. 1 The structure of the Estonian National Health Strategy 2020–2030. *Source* Estonian National Health Strategy (2021), p. 15, modified by authors

Achieving person-centred healthcare requires an approach that carefully considers the needs of each individual, carer, family and community, and shapes the individual's way of thinking and acting, giving them the knowledge, skills and resources to take responsibility for their own health. This approach considers service users an equal partner for healthcare and social care providers, giving them necessary training and guidance. Integrated health services and people-centred service systems are expected to raise the quality, availability and satisfaction of both service providers and recipients, as well as to control rising health costs. (National Health Strategy, 2021, p. 5).

Four solution paths for achieving person-centred healthcare are proposed in the strategy (National Health Strategy, 2021, p. 32), two of which are directly linked to the provision of education (two middle paths in Fig. 2) increasing the knowledge of professionals in the social and healthcare system.

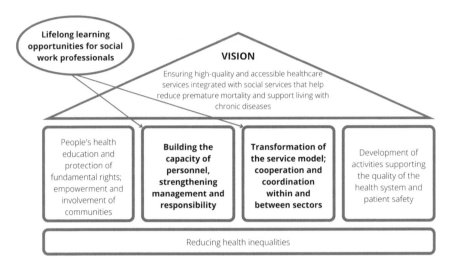

Fig. 2 Solutions for moving towards the desired result in person-centred healthcare. *Source* Estonian National Health Strategy (2021), p. 32 modified by authors

The key to a strong health system is a sufficient number of competent and self-directed professionals who are dedicated, qualified and motivated to develop person-centred and high-quality healthcare. To ensure this, it is important to value the lifelong learning of employees and encourage and support their self-development in every way (National Health Strategy, 2021, p. 35). This is where higher education institutions can contribute to the development of public health through the provision of lifelong learning opportunities.

The presence of and increase in capable and professional managers in the healthcare system who are willing and able to comprehensively reshape service models is essential. Systemic changes require planning, proper financing and the delivery of efficient, high-quality and functioning healthcare services, as well as prioritizing primary care and community services (National Health Strategy, 2021, p. 35). All the solution paths for achieving person-centred healthcare (Fig. 2) have priorities set by the National Health Strategy which require active engagement. For the two middle solution paths, the following are the priorities directly associated with the provision of education:

– Valuation of lifelong learning of healthcare workers and implementation of versatile self-development measures, adjustment of the study and practice opportunities according to the development of the health system.
– Development and implementation of coordinated and person-centred service models to ensure the availability of high-quality services throughout the life cycle, regardless of whether the service is needed at home, in a healthcare or welfare institution.

– Development and implementation of innovative, person-supporting services and solutions in parallel to the development of personal medicine and person-centred and user-friendly health information system.

Organization of better information exchange between primary care, hospital, social and work areas to ensure more effective treatment coordination in both healthcare systems. (National Health Strategy, 2021, p. 36) Designing person-centred services in the social welfare system requires people with SD skills in the system. Future trends that inevitably include the declining working-age population and the increasing number of elderlies, chronically ill and people struggling, increase the need for social workers with multifunctional skills, and a more flexible and integrated approach to service delivery, to provide excellent and people-centred care that ensures the best possible quality of life (National Health Strategy, 2021, p. 35). Social work professionals have realized that existing systems and practices are not sustainable and therefore, improving the old system is not adequate while maintaining the existing way of thinking, and that radical new solutions are needed to bring about a systemic change (Pärna, 2016, p. 31). According to the Estonian labour demand and forecasting system OSKA, 3,200 people are employed in the social field of public administration in Estonia, and the expected employment growth is about 20% in the nearest 10 years (Pihl & Krusell, 2020, p. 83). The OSKA report especially highlights the growing need for social welfare, employment and healthcare service designers and providers (Pihl & Krusell, 2020, p. 36, p. 77).

It is fairly common that specific knowledge and skills are mostly acquired through supplementary courses, and the more courses an employee has completed, the more multifunctional he or she becomes, but according to experts, graduates of the master's level meet the requirements of today's demanding social work even better (Jõers-Türn & Leoma, 2016, p. 58). The collaboration of social work professionals with specialists in related fields, such as family doctors, teachers, police officers, nurses, etc., as well as with researchers is also becoming more relevant and a greater potential is seen in involving different stakeholders (Jõers-Türn & Leoma, 2016, p. 58).

The ideal future employee is seen having a so-called T-shaped competence—with in-depth knowledge of at least one field and the ability to understand and connect different disciplines and the people involved in them. The key skills include the ability to adapt to the rapidly changing working environment and tasks, to work effectively in teams and networks, the analytical skills to understand, solve and make decisions and the ability to design services. In addition to mastering the profession, the future employee is expected to have a significantly better mastery of 'soft skills', such as communication skills, perceptions of and adaptability to different cultures. The importance of diversity, trans-disciplinarity, innovation and inspiration are also emphasized. All of these keywords point to the expectation of a modern approach to interdisciplinary learning. (Pärna, 2016, pp. 45–46).

Based on the above data and the evaluation of practitioners, the need emerged for a new master's level curriculum that would allow the social welfare and healthcare system to be transformed through the provision of new knowledge. By transferring the need of the social system for person-centred design to the education system, the challenge was to use the SD methodology in the development of the corresponding master's curriculum, in order to shape the SD mindset of students by experiencing the learning process.

5   Designing the Future of the Social Welfare System Through the Development of a New Person-Centred Master's Programme

The first signals that indicated the need for a new master's curriculum came from bachelor graduates and other social workers in the local area over several years. More strategic knowledge and skills to develop the social system as a whole, especially the design of human-centred services, were asked, and the opportunity to continue studies in the same educational institution was requested.

As a result, in January 2020, various interested parties from state institutions, social sciences faculty members, visiting lecturers and alumni were convened to discuss the need and possibilities for creating a new master's curriculum. During the brainstorming and analysing the existing data at that moment, the need for an innovative curriculum was confirmed. It was decided to start developing a new master's curriculum that would prepare professionals with diverse knowledge and skills for improving person-centred social services.

The Curriculum Statute of the University of Tartu (Tartu Ülikool, 2016, pp. 5–6, Ülikool, 2022, n.d.) stipulates that the development of the curriculum begins with the preparation of a preliminary application by the initiating academic unit. The preliminary application must include justification for opening the curriculum, analysis of the target group and labour market, description of resources, list of cooperation partners, brief description of the curriculum and comparison of the curriculum with existing curricula of the University of Tartu and other Estonian higher education institutions.

Based on the fact that SD is applicable in every field of activity and considering the learner as a customer for whom an educational service is designed, and based on previous successful experience in using SD at the University of Tartu Pärnu College to create a curriculum (Mihhailova & Tooman, 2012, n.d.), the curriculum development project team decided to use the SD methodology, specifically the double diamond model and various tools leading to solutions, when designing the curriculum.

The double diamond model reflects the four-stage SD process (Stickdorn et al., 2018, p. 87), which explores an issue more widely or deeply (divergent thinking) and then takes focused action (convergent thinking). It starts with the initial challenge or problem statement to the left, moves through a definition of the problem to be addressed in the centre and ends with the solution to the right (The Double Diamond, 2022, n.d.). The four stages of the design process in the double diamond model—discover, define, develop and deliver—were covered according to the model, aiming to create a curriculum based on the needs and wishes of the potential learner, which would allow to create a substantial change in the social welfare system through SD skills, systematic thinking and a holistic approach (Table 1).

Table 1 Curriculum development process stages and used tools at the University of Tartu Pärnu College.* Descriptions of all SD methods/tools discussed in this chapter can be found at: http://www.servicedesigntools.org/repository (Service Design Tools)

Curriculum development process stage	Methods, tools and activities used in curriculum development*
Discover Exploring the external environment and trends, understanding the issue	• Brainstorming • Trends analysis • Internet research: social field curricula in Estonia and Europe • Internet research: labor market demand and skills • Interviews with researchers of social sciences and with practitioners: expert and focus group interviews • Persona • Empathy map
Define Processing and aggregation of collected information	• Interviews with social welfare practitioners • Brainstorming • Issue cards
Develop Creating scenarios for the curriculum, verifying and iterating various approaches	• Prototype creation and verification • Interviews with social welfare practitioners
Deliver Designing the curriculum, aligning the topics and study modules, identifying and defining resources, administrative management	• Business model canvas • Value proposition canvas • Negotiations with academics • Stakeholders' recommendations

Source Authors' own illustration (2022)

In the discovery stage, various SD tools were used, such as the individual and focus group interview, brainstorming, empathy map, persona and survey. The forecast of OSKA's labour demand and monitoring, various analyses of the research company Praxis, statistical data of the Estonian Unemployment Insurance Fund and future forecasts of the labour market and economy, as well as several international curricula, were examined in this stage. Various meetings and discussions with experts in the social welfare field took place, as well as regular weekly teamwork meetings, initiated by the project manager. The existing curricula in Estonian higher education institutions were thoroughly examined and a comparative analysis was compiled. In addition, the level 7 occupational qualification standard of a social worker was examined. As a result of the analysis, individual points of contact with existing curricula could be identified.

In addition to and based on desk research, a survey was conducted by the University of Tartu Pärnu College in the period of June–August 2020 with the aim of determining the level of education and interest of people working in the social field in their prospective studies at the second level of higher education. The sample of the survey consisted of specialists from the local government, the Unemployment Insurance Fund, the Social Insurance Board, rehabilitation service providers and others, also people working in the social and health sectors.

The survey was answered by 288 professionals active in the social welfare or healthcare sector. Of the 153 respondents with an applied higher education or a bachelor's degree, 54% of who responded to the survey, wanted to continue their studies at the master's level, while 51 respondents or 62% had already decided in favour of master's studies in the social field. The respondents were asked about their willingness and readiness for master's studies to assess the relevancy of the topics covered, and new ideas on new topics were collected which experts proposed but were not suggested in the survey (see Fig. 3).

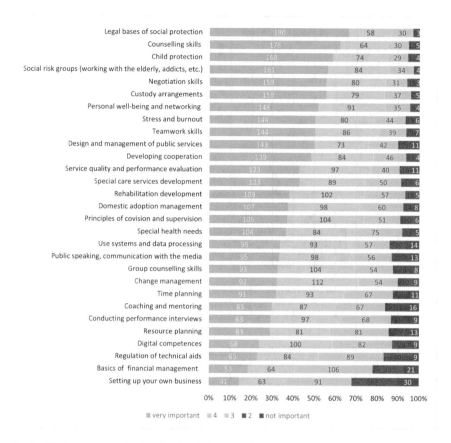

Fig. 3 The importance of topics that should be covered by a master's programme in social welfare according to professionals. *Source* Author's own illustration (2021)

The results of the study confirmed that the estimated target group is very interested in master's studies, moreover—new input was obtained on the topics that should be covered by the studies. Many of the specialists who participated in the survey showed willingness for further collaboration in curriculum development as well as in teaching specific topics and provided their contacts.

Special SD workshops were conducted at the regular summer seminar of Pärnu College in August 2020 for creating personas and empathy maps for potential students of the master's programme collectively. Four teams each created two personas and empathy maps and introduced them to the whole group (Figs. 4 and 5), from which the two most likely candidates for the master's programme were selected.

Fig. 4 Collective creation of personas and empathy maps at the workshop of Pärnu College summer seminar moderated by Ewe Alliksoo, project manager of the curriculum development team and one of the authors of this chapter. *Source* Author's own illustration (2022)

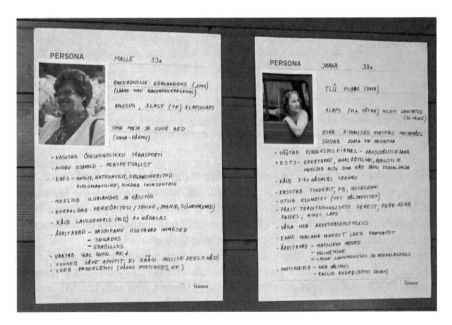

Fig. 5 Collectively created personas and empathy maps at the workshop of Pärnu College summer seminar. *Source* Author's own illustration (2021)

Based on the personas created collaboratively in the workshop, people similar to the persona, who participated in the survey and indicated their willingness to co-create the curriculum, were contacted. Four individual interviews were conducted at this stage of the process. Candidates suitable for individual interviews were found in Pärnu region, and all contacted candidates gave their consent to be interviewed.

In order to enhance the role of Pärnu College as a regional college, two focus group interviews were conducted with social and healthcare specialists in addition to the individual interviews. These focus group interviews covered five bordering counties, in addition to Pärnu County, to get a wider picture and map the areas of potential students.

The define stage included the analysis and synthesis of the data collected in the form of a brainstorming session in various smaller workshops. The topics relevant to the curriculum and their interrelations were identified. The focus of the curriculum was set, considering the areas of teaching and responsibility of universities and the need for a person-centred approach to the development of social services. Based on the desk research, survey, interviews and various workshops and discussions, the topics in which interest was revealed, and a short description of the curriculum could be compiled. The short description of the curriculum set out the objectives of the curriculum, the learning outcomes and a brief description of the curriculum content.

One important decision was made in the define stage—after a brainstorming session and various discussions, the curriculum was named 'Person-Centred Social Innovation', with the aim of providing learners with in-depth evidence-based knowledge to design human-centred social services and support their professional development. The use of social innovation in the curriculum title allows innovation to be integrated into social work. In the social field, innovation primarily means creating new practices and policies that improve the quality, efficiency and accessibility of existing services or designing new services based on specific needs (Social Services Europe, 2012, p. 5).

The preliminary application for opening the curriculum was submitted to the Council of Pärnu College; after approval, the preliminary application was forwarded to the Council of the University of Tartu at the Faculty of Social Sciences. The whole process took one year (from March 2020 to March 2021). After getting the approval from the Council of the University of Tartu at the Faculty of Social Sciences, March 1, 2021, may be considered as the point in the double diamond model, where it was proved that the correct problem would be solved.

In the development stage, the building of the curriculum structure continued (including modules, the volume and placement of practical training in the curriculum, the volume and role of the dissertation, etc.), agreeing on the objectives of the modules, learning outcomes and assessment methods and general teaching and assessment methods. At this stage, several meetings were held with the representatives of stakeholders, for example, from the Social Insurance Board, Ministry of Social Affairs, Estonian Unemployment Insurance Fund, Estonian Social Work

Association, Department of Family Medicine of the University of Tartu and others. Valuable suggestions and comments were received from each meeting regarding both the addition and omission of courses.

The design process of the master's programme as a whole is depicted in Fig. 6. In general, one and a half years of the curriculum design process was active and efficient, with a few challenges and failures; however, the whole process remained on schedule despite exceptional global events, such as the pandemic and the war in Ukraine.

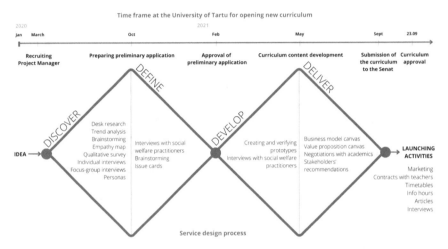

Fig. 6 The timeline of the service design process of the curriculum design. *Source* Authors' own illustration (2022)

The final 3 months of determined work and thorough negotiations with potential lecturers culminated in the completion of the curriculum structure (Table 2). With the objective to deliver the curriculum to the higher education market, it was submitted to the University Council for approval, including the financial calculation, stakeholder assessments and a comparison of learning outcomes in line with the Standard of Higher Education (Kõrgharidusstandard, 2019, appendix 1, point 3.1), and arguments for launching the curriculum. The University Council approved the curriculum on October 29, 2021.

Table 2 Structure of the 'Person-Centred Social Innovation' master's programme

Person-Centred Social Innovation	
The total volume of the curriculum 120 ECTS	**ECTS**
1st Study Module. People and Society	**22**
Entrepreneurship and Social Innovation	4
Social and Health Policy	4
Human Rights	5
Personal Wellness	5
Human Behaviour and Multicultural Environment	4
2nd Study Module. Preservation and Development of Human Resources	**22**
Social and Occupational Rehabilitation	6
Environmental and Occupational Health	4
Gerontology	4
Common Diseases	4
Social Psychiatry	4
3rd Study Module. Development and Integration of Person-Centred Services	**22**
Self-Management	6
Development of Public Services in Healthcare and Welfare Sector	6
Service Design	5
Regional Policy and Collaboration Network Management	5
4. Elective courses or international learning experience	**15**
5. Practical training	**6**
6. Research Methodology (incl. Master's Thesis 20 ECTS)	**29**
7. Optional courses	**4**

Source Authors' own illustration (2022)

Estonian Higher Education Act (2019, §3) stipulates that the curriculum approved by the University Senate is sent further for registration to the Ministry of Education and Research, which finally approves the new curriculum and registers it in the Estonian education information system. The master's programme 'Person-Centred Social Innovation' is ready to welcome new master's students in the academic year 2022/2023.

As stated and experienced, the SD process never ends, and the purposeful activities to follow the trends and needs of the social welfare sector and labour market, the expectations and needs of the students and so on will definitely continue after the launch of the curriculum.

6   Discussion

The service design methodology enables processes to be carried out in a logical sequence. During the entire curriculum development process, it was also necessary to adhere to the time frame established by the University of Tartu. This sometimes hindered the development process, as the project team was able to operate faster than the time frame allowed in some stages, so certain necessary decisions were on hold. An important component that had to be followed was keeping the curriculum within the scope of the teaching response prescribed for the University of Tartu.

Several disputes were held over the differences between practical, academic and pedagogical approaches, which taught team members to discuss, argue and find the best compromises. At times, the teams experienced fragmentation and unwillingness to give up their vision of the curriculum and the content of the courses. However, different workshops and SD tools eventually made it possible to come up with a purposeful, learner-focused curriculum. In retrospect, it can be said that after certain activities, besides the appointed project team members student representatives should have been involved in the validation of the results, as well.

The development of the curriculum brought together a large number of people from different organizations in the social welfare sector. All parties interpreted the curriculum from their point of view, which can be considered both positive and negative. The rich selection of topics and viewpoints can be deemed positive, but at the same time, it also made it difficult to make choices. Nevertheless, this led the project team to thoroughly shape the focus of the curriculum.

One of the bottlenecks in this design process was seen in prototyping the curriculum and making adjustments based on it. Although the preparatory work was done very thoroughly, the prototyping will essentially only start with the arrival of the first students. In the case of the curriculum, the continuity of the entire curriculum design process is more important than prototyping—iterative and continuous updating, improvements according to the social system demands and needs, adjusting courses of the changing types of learners, monitoring trends, adapting the curriculum accordingly, etc. The question of how to effectively use prototyping in the curriculum design process thus remained unanswered.

During the final stage of the curriculum development, a new study about the future vision for labour and skills needs in social welfare in Estonia was published, which confirmed the necessity of the courses planned in the curriculum. While OSKA's survey from 2016 (Jõers-Türn & Leoma, 2016, pp. 48–49) identified four broader groups of competencies with a growing need: communication skills, community work skills, special skills related to client work and special skills in the field (e.g., service design and quality management), the latest survey of social welfare highlighted all these knowledge and skills as very important, too (Pihl & Krusell, 2021, p. 60). As a new trend, the latest study (Pihl & Krusell, 2021, pp. 49–50) shows that the growing need for legal competencies at the specialists' level has come to the fore, which was also confirmed by the survey conducted from the development of this curriculum.

7   Conclusion

With the creation of the master 's degree programme 'Person-Centred Social Innovation', Pärnu College achieved the set goal—to offer master 's level studies necessary for the systemic transformation of the social welfare field in order to train professionals with the skills entailed in the person-centred approach. The entire curriculum development process provided the project team with invaluable experience and confirmed the importance of teamwork, the necessity of a strong project manager and project management skills throughout the process.

According to the curriculum development project manager, various elements of the SD methodology can be used very effectively in the curriculum development process. In conclusion, it may be said that SD enables an in-depth understanding of the needs of both the sector and the learners. This case of the curriculum design provided evidence of how many different parties exist with different interests and needs. Taking all these into account in creating a comprehensive curriculum was largely possible thanks to using the SD methodology.

Acknowledgements The authors would like to thank all the parties that contributed to collaborating in the course of the curriculum design process, including the professionals from the Social Insurance Board, Ministry of Social Affairs, Estonian Unemployment Insurance Fund, Estonian Social Work Association and the Department of Family Medicine of the University of Tartu, for providing great support, constructive criticism and help in developing the new master's curriculum.

References

Alliksoo, E. (2022). Magistriõppekava Inimesekeskne sotsiaalne innovatsioon. (Master's programme Person-centred social innovation). *Sotsiaaltöö*, 2/2022, 90–92. Retrieved June 30, 2022, from https://www.tai.ee/et/sotsiaaltoo/magistrioppekava-inimesekeskne-sotsiaalne-innovatsioon

Brown, T. (2008). Design thinking. *Harvard Business Review, 86*(6), 84–92, 141. Retrieved June 30, 2022, from https://pubmed.ncbi.nlm.nih.gov/18605031/

Bunger, A. (2010). Defining service coordination: A social work perspective. *Journal of Social Service Research, 36*(5), 385–401. https://doi.org/10.1080/01488376.2010.510931

Burrell, A., Cavanagh, M., Young, S., & Carter, H. (2015). Team-based curriculum design as an agent of change. *Teaching in Higher Education, 20*(8), 753–766. https://doi.org/10.1080/135 62517.2015.1085856

Fischer, M., Safaeinili, N., Haverfield, M. C., Brown-Johnson, C. G., Zionts, D., & Zulman, D. M. (2021). Approach to human-centered, evidence-driven adaptive design (AHEAD) for health care interventions: A proposed framework. *Journal of General Internal Medicine, 36*(4), 1041–1048. https://doi.org/10.1007/s11606-020-06451-4

Freire, K., & Sangiorgi, D. (2010). Service design and healthcare innovation: from consumption to co-production to co-creation. In Conference paper: Second Nordic Conference on Service Design and Service Innovation at Linköping. Linköping, Sweden: ServDes, the Service Design and Innovation conference (pp. 1–11). https://servdes.org/pdf/2010/freire-sangiorgi.pdf

Hall, J. A., Carswell, C., Walsh, E., Huber, D. L., & Jampoler, J. S. (2002). Iowa case management: Innovative social casework. *Social Work, 47*, 132–141. https://doi.org/10.1093/sw/47.2.132

Hardy, S., Jackson, C., Webster, J., & Manley, K. (2013). Educating advanced level practice within complex health care workplace environments through transformational practice development. *Nurse Education Today, 33*, 1099–1103. https://doi.org/10.1016/j.nedt.2013.01.021

Hardy, S. (2015). Perspectives: Is health and social care person centred? Hello, my name is not enough. *Journal of Research in Nursing, 20*(6), 517–522. https://doi.org/10.1177/174498711 5601516

Health Innovation Network. (2022). What is person-centred care and why is it important? Retrieved June 30, 2022, from https://healthinnovationnetwork.com/system/ckeditor_assets/attachments/ 41/what_is_person-centred_care_and_why_is_it_important.pdf

Higher Education Act. (2019). *Riigi Teataja I*, 19.03.2019, 12; *Riigi Teataja I*, 16.06.2020, 9. Retrieved June 30, 2022, from https://www.riigiteataja.ee/en/eli/525062020001/consolide

Jõers-Türn, K., & Leoma, R. (2016). Tulevikuvaade tööjõu- ja oskuste vajadusele: sotsiaaltöö valdkond. Rakendusuuring. (Future vision for labor and skills needs: the field of social work. Applied research.) SA Kutsekoda. Retrieved June 30, 2022, from https://oska.kutsekoda.ee/wp-content/uploads/2016/04/Sotsiaaltoo_OSKA_tervik_veeb.pdf

Kurowski, C., Chandra, A., Finkel, E., & Plötz, M. (2015). Ravi terviklik käsitlus ja osapoolte koostöö Eesti tervishoiusüsteemis: kokkuvõttev aruanne. (A holistic approach to treatment and co-operation between the parties in the Estonian health care system: a summary report.) Tallinn: Eesti Haigekassa, Maailmapank. Retrieved June 30, 2022, from https://rahvatervis.ut.ee/han dle/1/6046

Kõrgharidusstandard (Standard of Higher Education). (2019). Riigi Teataja I 2019, 62; Riigi Teataja I, 12.07.2019, 17. Retrieved June 30, 2022, from https://www.riigiteataja.ee/akt/112072 019017

Landry, L. (2020). What is human-centered design? *Harvard Business School*, Retrieved June 30, 2022, from https://online.hbs.edu/blog/post/what-is-human-centered-design

Managed Healthcare Executive. (2019). The biggest issues facing healthcare today. Retrieved June 30, 2022, from https://www.managedhealthcareexecutive.com/view/biggest-issues-facing-hea lthcare-today

Melles, M., Albayrak, A., & Goossens, R. (2021) Innovating health care: Key characteristics of human-centered design. *International Journal for Quality in Health Care, 33*(Suppl.133/1), 37–44. https://doi.org/10.1093/intqhc/mzaa127

Mihhailova, G., & Tooman, H. (2012). Using service design process and methods for service design curriculum development. Service Imperatives in the New Economy. Localization and Globalization. In *Conference Proceedings. Abstracts.: The 3rd International Research Symposium in Service Management (IRSSM-3)*. Ed. Kandampully, Jay; Wang, Yonggui (pp. 36–37). China, Beijing: University of International Business and Economics (UIBE), Beijing, China. Retrieved June 30, 2022, from http://bs.uibe.edu.cn/irssm3/download/IRSSM3%20C onference%20Proceedings.pdf

Pihl, K., & Krusell, S. (2020). Tulevikuvaade tööjõu- ja oskuste vajadusele: avalik haldus. Rakendusuuring. (Perspectives on labour and skills needs: public administration. Applied research.) SA Kutsekoda. Retrieved June 30, 2022, from https://oska.kutsekoda.ee/wp-content/uploads/2017/10/Uuringuaruanne_AH__2611_veebi.pdf

Pihl, K., & Krusell, S. (2021). *Tulevikuvaade tööjõu- ja oskuste vajadusele: sotsiaaltöö. Uuringu lühiaruanne.* (Future vision for labor and skills needs: social work. Short report of the study.) Tallinn: SA Kutsekoda. Retrieved June 30, 2022, from https://oska.kutsekoda.ee/wp-content/uploads/2017/01/OSKA_sotsiaaltoo_uuringuaruanne_terviktekst_2021.pdf

Puis, L., Anier, A., Oras, K., Kull, M., & Tampere, P. (2021). *Paikkondlik tervisetoetuse teenus järjepideva ravi ning parima sotsiaalse toetuse tagamiseks. Projekti lõppraport.* (Local health support service to ensure consistent treatment and the best social support. Project report.) Viljandi: Viljandi Haigla. Retrieved June 30, 2022, from https://paik.vmh.ee/#first

Pärna, O. (2016) *Töö ja oskused 2025. Ülevaade olulisematest trendidest ja nende mõjust Eesti tööturule. (Work and skills 2025. An overview of the most important trends and their impact on the Estonian labor market.)* Tallinn: Sihtasutus Kutsekoda. Retrieved June 30, 2022, from https://oska.kutsekoda.ee/wp-content/uploads/2016/04/Tulevikutrendid-1.pdf

Rahvastiku tervise arengukava 2020–2030 (National Health Strategy 2020–2030). (2021). Ministry of Social Affairs. Retrieved June 30, 2022, from https://www.sm.ee/rahvastiku-tervise-arengu kava-2020-2030

Scoresby, J., Tkatchov, M., Hugus, E., & Marshall, H. (2018). Applying service design in competency-based curriculum development. *The Journal of Competency-Based Education, 3*(3), e01171. https://doi.org/10.1002/cbe2.1171

Social services Europe. (2012). *Social innovation: The role of social service providers.* Retrieved June 30, 2022, from https://www.feantsa.org/download/social_services_europe_062 012_briefing_on_social_innovation4668816150820211891.pdf

Stickdorn, M., Hormess, M. E., Lawrence, A., & Schneider, J. (2018). *This is service design doing: Applying service design thinking in the real world.* Amsterdam, The Netherlands: O'Reilly Media Inc.

Tartu Ülikool. (2016). *Õppekava statuut (Curriculum Statute).* [Unpublished internal document]

Tartu Ülikool. (2022). *Õppekava avamise voodiagramm. (Flow-chart for opening the curriculum).* Retrieved June 30, 2022, from https://siseveeb.ut.ee/sites/default/files/siseveebi_failid/dokume ndid/%C3%95ppet%C3%B6%C3%B6/%C3%95ppekavad/%C3%95ppekava%20avamine. png

The Double Diamond. (2022). A universally accepted depiction of the design process. *Design council.* Retrieved June 30, 2022, from https://www.designcouncil.org.uk/our-work/news-opi nion/double-diamond-universally-accepted-depiction-design-process/

Voogt, J. M., Pieters, J. M., & Handelzalts, A. (2016). Teacher collaboration in curriculum design teams: Effects, mechanisms, and conditions. *Educational Research and Evaluation, 22*(3–4), 121–140. https://doi.org/10.1080/13803611.2016.1247725

WHO. (2013). Traditional medicine strategy 2014–2023. World Health Organization (WHO, Ed.). Retrieved June 30, 2022, from https://www.who.int/publications/i/item/9789241506096

Zimmer, K. (2021). *Increasing human-centered design in the social sector.* The Forbes. Retrieved June 30, 2022, from https://www.forbes.com/sites/forbesnonprofitcouncil/2021/06/04/increa sing-human-centered-design-in-the-social-sector/

Ewe Alliksoo is Project and Programme Director at the University of Tartu, Pärnu College. Areas of teaching and research include rehabilitation, holistic well-being, and a person-centred approach. She has conducted several successful public procurement projects and is the Programme Director of the master's degree programme in Person-Centred Social Innovation at Pärnu College.

Margrit Kärp (corresponding author) is Junior Lecturer in Spa Management at the University of Tartu Pärnu College. Areas of teaching and research include holistic wellness, active aging, and spa management. In addition to conducting studies, the launch of a new bachelor's curriculum in tourism and the development of study courses are ongoing, as well as participation in the development of new study modules in several international projects.

Heli Tooman is Associate Professor Emeritus of Tourism Management at the University of Tartu Pärnu College. Her fields of study, research and guidance cover tourism and service economy, service philosophy, service culture, hospitality, quality management and health and wellness. She has written numerous articles and textbooks, is a member of the editorial board of several scientific and professional journals, participates in the activities of international organisations and conferences and research and development projects as an expert. She is a member of the Patients' Council of Pärnu Hospital.

Karit Jäärats is Junior Lecturer in English Language at the University of Tartu Pärnu College. She has the competence as an Academic Affairs Specialist and experience in curriculum administration. Her area of teaching is academic and business English, specialising in translation and terminology development.

Exploring Services' patient-centredness. Design Challenges for a Future Design Agenda

Stefano Maffei, Massimo Bianchini, and Beatrice Villari

ABSTRACT

The healthcare system had important transformations, shifting from a public sphere to a wider ecosystem in which private, public and community services are intertwined. Furthermore, social, environmental and technological challenges have an impact at micro- and macro-levels, challenging health professionals, organisations, and institutions to foster innovation. New solutions and scenarios are emerging in response to the emergent healthcare and well-being challenges which include a wider range of collaborative processes aimed at making systems more citizen-centric. The discussion on person-centred does not find a univocal definition and the possible outcomes of the collaborative process are manifold. These concern the typology of artefacts such as service touchpoints, software or technological components that support the service delivery as well as the collaborative tools and practices that support the solution development. This chapter proposes a way to approach the study of the patient-centred services through a systemic lens and describes three exemplar cases developed in Italy. The cases contribute to outline how patient-centredness concerns experimental solutions, deployable on existing service layers, deriving from a multi-stakeholder agency, using digitalisation to expand relationships between individuals, organisations and territories, generating knowledge and

S. Maffei (✉) · M. Bianchini · B. Villari
Department of Design, Politecnico di Milano, Building B7, Campus Bovisa Via Durando 10, 20158 Milano, Italy
e-mail: stefano.maffei@polimi.it

M. Bianchini
e-mail: massimo.bianchini@polimi.it

B. Villari
e-mail: beatrice.villari@polimi.it

culture in the care system beyond the solution. Based on a systemic perspective characterising patient-centred services, some reflections on future service design research issues are outlined.

1   Patient-Centred Innovation and Services in the Healthcare Ecosystem

The healthcare system has experienced vast changes in the last decade, through the transformation of the public service offering into a more complex environment in which the public, private and personal spheres are clearly intertwined with challenging social, environmental and technological changes. Prevention, care and well-being have been stressed by the impact of demographic changes/ageing dynamics with an increase in the population affected by chronic diseases (World Health Organization, 2016); it has been coupled with a welfare state reform and transition generated by the automatisation and digitisation processes, and by nationwide budget cuts that have not always rapidly been received by public institutions and policymakers.

The adaptation to this always-changing scenario together with the inability to predict emergencies risks on a global scale—think of the pandemic effect—led to a growing awareness of the importance of product–service systems innovation on the one hand, and of the central role of the patients (and their supporting networks) on the other. New solutions and scenarios are emerging in response to these emergent healthcare and care challenges which include, for example, better use of monitoring data, social justice and inclusion as a consequence of better and fair accessibility to services or participated community initiatives for the improvement of health commons through collaborative processes aimed at making systems more citizen-centric.

Technology has always played a significant role in fostering transformations in products–service systems focused on patient-centric needs (Hermes et al., 2020), for example, by adopting artificial intelligence and supporting e-health systems. At the same time, patients are more informed and aware of the impact of medical treatments, and more interested in the concept of well-being (Francis, 2010). Furthermore, people are much more aware of their purchasing power (Røtnes & Staalesen, 2009), and, therefore, of the ability to orient the market towards more sustainable, more accessible solutions, closer to the real needs of consumers. Healthcare systems can though be considered as a testbed for cross-disciplinary and cultural collaborations and collective solutions. This interconnected ecosystem, therefore, not only includes health professionals, institutions and organisations but also made up of non-professionals who are increasingly acquiring an important role in the processes of prevention, treatment and care follow-up and chronicisation. The new protagonists of this innovation process are common people, caregivers, family members, patients' associations and all those formal and informal networks of competencies and experiences that contribute to innovation (for example, makers and startuppers). It also implies for professionals the need to adopt more open and collaborative approaches, to offer new care services and more generally well-being services (Anderson et al., 2013).

In this renewed innovation scenario, patients are much more aware of their role and become active agents of transformation through sometimes spontaneous co-design and co-creation processes, as well as promoters and implementers of the final solutions together with coalitions of partners and stakeholders.

This chapter is precisely focused on these emerging practices, inquiring about the people-driven ones in which the end-users design, create or implement care solutions (Maffei et al, 2022). It describes a new class of (products and) service solutions that become an extension/complement of the traditional healthcare system where the level of information, transparency, personalisation and collaboration increase (Swan, 2009) also overcoming the fragmentation of the therapeutic journey (NESTA, 2018).

If we explore the discussion on person-centred solutions, we will find rich literature, both in the medical and design fields. But we will not find a univocal definition of what is meant by 'patient-centred' ['… the term 'patient-centred' may too narrowly focus on the patient–provider interaction within the individual (clinical) consultation and insufficiently take account of the social context within which people live and that influences disease trajectories and care choice' (Hobbs, 2009; Starfield, 2011)] nor of what is meant by 'patient-driven'. The relevant distinction between solutions and processes might be derived from the nature of the patient's role: it depends on the increasing degree of decision-making power or the ability to act within initiatives in which the patient (or the caregiving system) proposes, enables and implements solutions. In general, the two roles seem to be considered almost overlapping. If we shift this discussion from the service design, implementation and delivery processes to the medical product design and manufacturing the distinction will appear clearer (considering the examples like the monitoring devices or the prostheses designed and/or produced by the patients themselves). Nevertheless, it can be said that these concepts refer to a renewed role of individuals and communities within the prevention, cure and care journeys through consistent empowerment of their participatory role within the innovation processes.

The patient is central to the healthcare system (OECD Health Ministerial Meeting, 2017; World Health Organisation, 2016) even though there is not a defined strategy—in terms of policies and their implementation, nor at the operational level—that clearly describes the implication of user-centred, patient-centred, person-centred or family-centred approaches in product–service solutions development. These approaches range from improving the quality of service in the delivery phase to different forms of people involvement in design, implementation or evaluation processes, to imagine long-term systemic changes (Nolte et al., 2020).

Nolte et al. (2020) propose a framework for describing the person-centredness concept: they identify three main user roles in which the person is the centre of the healthcare system. They describe them as choice, voice and co-production.

The choice considers the patient as a consumer, the voice includes participation in the decision-making process and co-production implies active participation in a collaborative process of service delivery. These distinctions describe, for example, the different strategies that individuals follow to find the right health provider (choice), the possibilities they have to participate in the delivery of the solutions (voice) and the power people have in co-design, plan and co-delivery the appropriate treatment (co-production).

The definition given by the World Health Organisation (2016, p. 2) considers people-centred care as 'an approach to care that consciously adopts individuals', carers', families' and communities' perspectives as participants in, and beneficiaries of, trusted health systems that are organised around the comprehensive needs of people rather than individual diseases, and respects social preferences. People-centred care also requires that patients have the education and support they need to make decisions and participate in their own care and that carers are able to attain maximal function within a supportive working environment. People-centred care is broader than patient and person-centred care, encompassing not only clinical encounters, but also including attention to the health of people in their communities and their crucial role in shaping health policy and health services'.

If we interpret it through the lens of design culture and expertise, this definition prompts us to think about the needs of an enlarged community in which the end-user is one of the underrepresented but key elements of the system. It also opens a discussion about the relevance of knowledge sharing and mutual learning processes and about the access and exchange of data and information sources: the ways in which interactions between people, organisations and institutions are performed are necessary to guarantee transparency, integrity, responsiveness, accountability and equality (OECD, 2019).

The growing demand for care is accompanied by a growing demand for participation, and NESTA (2018) identifies different patients' innovation strategies supporting: behavioural changes to prevent chronic diseases, self-management and monitoring; supporting the autonomy of people with disabilities; enabling the creation of new spaces and places centred on the users' needs; fostering new relationships between doctors and patients, and improving the services accessibility and communities mutual support. These innovations, while embracing a broad spectrum of interventions, are characterised by a common collaborative approach between the different ecosystem's participants. It is what NESTA defines as 'Collaborative Health' (NESTA, 2018), meaning a strategic approach capable of creating value through the contribution of the various players in the care system, such as doctors, operators, patients, families and communities. Similarly, Horne et al. (2013) outline a People Powered Health approach in which prevention and treatment are driven and supported by a wider community of actors and infrastructures, expanding the care journey within the home or workplace contexts.

2 Leveraging Service Design in the Patient-Centred Scenario

The design and delivery of healthcare services are increasingly centred on the person, and thus the role of designers and service designers can be expanded and strengthened (Wildevuur & Simonse, 2017) by exploring new forms of value co-creation from an ecosystemic perspective. The evolution of the service design discipline has shifted towards the inclusion of the systemic perspective, which requires the integration of the multiscale processes complexities and the evaluation of the extensive and deep interconnections within contextual practices (Patrício et al., 2018; Sangiorgi, 2009; Wetter-Edman et al., 2014).

The holistic experiences of the people are the focus of service system design. This perspective positions service design in the context of complex systems in which designers work in networked structures that cannot be fully controlled, but enabled or steered (Mager et al., 2022).

From this angle, Vink et al. (2020) propose a service ecosystem perspective that emphasises how value is based upon a long-term intentionality of change driven by a co-created multi-stakeholder conversation. This theoretical vision overcomes a simplistic vision of service design as a simple functionalist discipline and considers design interventions as a complex orchestrated intervention path that integrates organisational, relational and strategic relationships and tangible and intangible artefacts at the micro and macro scales. If, for example, health organisations need to change the care delivery process and the connected patients' relationship processes (Ekman et al., 2011), the involved professionals need to add new and not only technical skills but also rely on the capacity to manage the complexity of the interactions with the voices and the values of those involved in the system challenged. At the same time, patients and the care and prevention communities must reflect and empower their active role, negotiating services that are consistent with their expectations and an appropriate hack/adaptation of the existing healthcare solutions' system and technological/operational environment.

The integration of these multi-level barriers and opportunities generates, a reflection on what are the repercussions that people-driven models might create and how service design might evolve to include complexity (Vink et al., 2020) in the overall process of co-creation, co-design and co-production and in connection with the measurement of the social, economic and environmental impacts (Foglieni et al., 2018). Furthermore, designing services through an ecosystemic vision might imply that phenomenic observation does not occur exclusively through the lens of the end-users but through the recognition of all the actors' agencies involved in a collective design process (Vink et al., 2020).

Service design is considered a transformative approach for innovating complex systems (Sangiorgi et al., 2017); it can reduce the gap between healthcare beneficiaries and professionals, entailing a more interactive collaboration within the stakeholders' system balancing individuals and organisational needs, social well-being and solutions' viability (Patricio et al., 2020).

Mager et al. (2022) describe some overlaps between people-centred care and service design concerning the patients' role as experts and their decision power; underlining the importance of the various healthcare interactions people have in their life; focusing on people's needs and considering health as co-created. Therefore, we are interested in exploring patient innovation as related to complex systems, referring to a set of products-services, and processes generated by end-users (patients or caregivers) that involve a plurality of agencies, coalitions made of individuals, groups and communities that could be considered as independent innovators (Maffei et al., 2022). Patient-centredness is then approached in terms of system thinking (Jones, 2020) which means considering the patient experience and journeys as embedded in a multi-actor process characterised by a multitude of service providers and communities that co-create value within the service systems (Wetter-Edman et al., 2014).

Adopting this perspective, therefore, implies imagining the predictable and unpredictable elements of the design journey, the transformations of decision-making processes as well as the power balance between experts and laypersons, and a renovated patient's role understood as the fulcrum of a large and complex system of relationships and connections changing over time.

The cases outlined in the following paragraphs (focused on the Italian context) describe different examples of patient-centred care services. It is an explorative observation of existing people-centred experiments and solutions. And it is also an ongoing inquiry about how (service) designers might contribute to the development and dissemination of this approach, on the opportunities and limits of the actual service design processes, tools and capabilities.

3   Exploring Patient-Centred Practices in Care Service Ecosystems

Exploring patient-centredness requires a holistic approach: mapping practices, solutions, actors and their relationships systems needs observing the patient's role and adopting a systemic vision of caregiving roles. Caregiving practices and processes establish a direct relationship between a patient considered as a human being and involve concern and diligence, focus and zeal and emotional and physical engagement. The human-to-human interaction has progressively become more complex, regulated and disintermediated, helped and intertwined with an augmented supportive galaxy of digital services and artefacts. This more-than-human transition gains even more relevance considering the rapid development and spread of digital platforms, sometimes powered by AI/machine-based computation. For instance, the recent COVID-19 pandemic represents a turning point in considering the relevance of digital solutions within a new set of practices and norms generated in an unprecedented situation.

Analysing emerging practices in the healthcare sector is useful to show how patient-centredness works in real contexts, highlight the critical innovation points in the service solutions, and how patients participate in these processes. Parallelly, analysing the patient's involvement in producing new solutions is useful for revising or creating new service journeys.

We identify three criteria that help us select some interesting and exemplary cases for mapping the emerging scene of patient-centred services.

The first criterion filters the kind of solution we explore: It helps to map the different artefacts' typology according to their artefactual structure and technological dimension as well as their relation with the innovation processes in which patients, caregivers and care systems were involved.

The primary artefacts' typologies mapped are:

- tangible artefacts such as products, devices, equipment and physical touchpoints necessary to deliver or develop the service;
- intangible artefacts such as software, applications or parts of digital/computational technologies that enable the service functions/performance and/or make it usable;
- knowledge artefacts such as the processes and tools that contribute to raising awareness or enabling the patient's role in care processes by stimulating participation.

The second criterion maps the actors' coalitions involved in the structured system behind the solution (product–service journey). It considers, for example, the presence of a network, an alliance or an agreement between stakeholders involved in co-creation and co-design actions.

The third criterion concerns the patient's role in the service solution's design, development or implementation, described as a series of phases: engagement, co-creation, co-design and co-production.

The three criteria link to the identification of relevant aspects characterising a patient-centric solution:

- complexity of the solution provided to the patient (design, technological, organisational-operational, financial, etc.);
- community composition and dimension that is activated to implement that solution;
- patient's involvement in the solution's development process, i.e. how much his contribution is relevant in elaborating and evolving the solution over time.

Applying these criteria makes it possible to more accurately identify care solutions that reveal a potential (even if not explicit) in terms of systemic innovation, which is relevant for developing or infrastructure patient-centricity regardless of the scale of intervention at which they operate.

This basic set of criteria has been used to explore the service ecosystem within the territorial context of the Lombardy region, with a particular focus on Milan and its metropolitan area. The map was developed in 2022 and focused on 25 cases related to healthcare projects, initiatives and product–service systems solutions.

This initiative builds upon and reinforces the results of the previous research Make-ToCare (2017–2019) on Italy's patient innovation ecosystems, mainly focused on products and devices belonging to the tangible artefacts category. The research highlighted the role of Milan and Lombardy as the densest and most innovative care environments, populated by solutions (especially products and technological devices) in which the role of the patients is evident.

3.1 Exemplar Cases of Patient-Centredness Within Milan's and Lombardy's Care Service Ecosystems

The overall research collected 25 cases (The cases' informations were retrieved through a desk research using online resources such as websites, reports and academic articles). the majority of them are located in Milan urban area 5 out of them belong to tangible artefacts, 11 can be considered intangible artefacts, 14 are knowledge artefacts and 5 out of them consider two categories. In 9 out of 25 cases, we might find an explicit and well-identifiable relationship with the patient. In the other, 16 out of 25 the relationship is mapped but not evident or clearly described in depth. Twenty out of 25 cases deal with user participation, mainly concerning the engagement phase. Eight out of 25 cases testify a higher degree of involvement dealing with co-creation and co-design activities (co-production in one case).

The actors' systems that activate and provide services are heterogeneous: hospitals, third-sector organisations, universities and research centres, large pharma companies, med-tech and e-health start-ups, fab labs and makerspaces. In two-thirds of the mapped service cases (17 out of 25), services are developed by actors' coalitions through large alliances or partnerships. To highlight the characteristic patient-centredness we present three cases describing emergent perspectives in patient-centricity (Table 1).

3.2 The Tech Lab and the Caregiving System of Spazio Vita Niguarda Onlus

Artefacts' typology. Tech Lab (See https://spaziovitaniguarda.it/progetto/techlab-nuovo-ramo-dimpresa-dedicato-alle-nuove-tecnologie-per-la-fragilita) is a Laboratory developed by Spazio Vita Niguarda Onlus, a cooperative set up in 2013 by two voluntary associations that have been active for years within the Niguarda hospital in Milan. The associations develop socio-integrative protocols integrating the clinical-rehabilitation pathway of patients with spinal cord injury with interventions aimed at improving their social inclusion. Tech Lab is an incubator of ideas, services, training, workshops and activities in the field of technological innovation applied to a disability, for patients with spinal cord injuries. It is a member of the Associazione Nazionale Centri Ausili (See https://www.centriausili.it. Since 1996, GLIC has brought together public and private organisations operating in

Table 1 The mapped cases. *Source* Politecnico di Milano

nr	Case name	Artefacts' typology	Actors' coalitions	Patients' role
01	Prometeo (2022; Astrazeneca; www.cariplofactory.it)	Knowledge artefact: action that supports healthcare professionals to co-design solutions for and with patients	Astrazeneca (large pharma company), Cariplo Factory (Innovation hub); Federated Innovation @Mind (urban innovation district)	Engagement and Co-design
02	Doc 24 (2021; International Care Company; www.doc24.it)	Intangible artefact: on-demand telemedicine service that allows people to talk to a doctor from smartphones and tablets through the app	Design Group Italia (design innovation agency); International Care Company—ICC (SME)	Counselling and Engagement
03	Take Care (2021; Spazio Vita Niguarda Onlus; www.spaziovitaniguarda.it/progetto/take-care-of-disability-il-covid-non-ci-ferma)	Intangible artefact: web app telemedicine, easily usable by patients to identify their essential needs and receive targeted answers through OnLine interventions, at home or at the Spazio Vita Niguarda centre	Spazio Vita Niguarda Onlus (social enterprise); Fondazione Banca del Monte di Lombardia (foundation); Apple Academy—Università Federico II di Napoli (educational institution). Collaboration with the regional health system (Lombardy Region)	Counselling and Engagement
04	Workability (2020; Spazio Vita Niguarda Onlus; www.spaziovitaniguarda.it/progetto/workability-la-disabilita-sul-lavoro-diventa-strategica)	Knowledge artefact: job placement service for people with disabilities in enterprises	Spazio Vita Niguarda Onlus (social enterprise); BBraun (leading multinational provider of health products and services)	Engagement and Consultancy

(continued)

Table 1 (continued)

nr	Case name	Artefacts' typology	Actors' coalitions	Patients' role
05	Bridge (2017; Spazio Vita Niguarda Onlus; www.spaziovitaniguarda.it/progetto/bridge-un-ponte-tra-ospedale-e-territorio)	Intangible artefact: Based on a bio-psycho-social approach, the service works on a model of experimental accompaniment that is integrated and attentive to the care, home and work needs of persons with motor disabilities and their families	Spazio Vita Niguarda Onlus (social enterprise); ATS Milano Città Metropolitana (local health authority); Ospedale Niguarda (hospital); Università Bocconi and SDA Bocconi (university)	Engagement and Consultancy
06	Tech Lab (2020, Spazio Vita Niguarda Onlus; www.spaziovitaniguarda.it/techlab)	Knowledge artefact, Tangible artefact, and Intangible artefact: hub of technological innovation for the development of home automation solutions and customised aids for people with disabilities	Spazio Vita Niguarda Onlus (social enterprise); Fondazione Banca del Monte di Lombardia (foundation); Apple Academy–Università Federico II di Napoli (educational institution); BASF (chemical and plastics manufacturing company); Municipality of Milan (public administration); Fondazione Cariplo (foundation); Fondazione ASPHI Onlus (care foundation); Informatici Senza Frontiere (association for social advancement); Kodaly (n.a.); Ospedale Niguarda (public hospital); Città Metropolitana di Milano (public administration)	Engagement, Co-Creation, and Co-Design

(continued)

Table 1 (continued)

nr	Case name	Artefacts' typology	Actors' coalitions	Patients' role
07	Fondo Nazionale per il supporto psicologico COVID-19 (2020: Soleterre: www.soleterre. org/fondo-nazionale-supporto-psicologico-cov id19)	Knowledge artefact: A team of psychologists from the Soleterre Foundation supports people who have suffered psychological consequences as a result of COVID-19. The service provides initial psychological assistance by videoconference with the subsequent activation of a professional in the area where the patient lives	Fondazione Soleterre Onlus (foundation); Fondazione Progetto Arca ONLUS (foundation); La Cordata s.c.s. (association); Caritas Cittadina San Donato (association); La Pulce Battaglie Associazione (association); Associazione EMotion–Emozioni in Movimento (association); Centro Polispecialistico per il bambino l'adolescente, l'adulto e la famiglia, Comunità della Salute, Istituto Comprensivo di Corso Cavour (Pavia), Cooperativa Sociale KORE Onlus (social enterprise); Centro Diurno 'In&Out' (social enterprise);Associazione Pieghe (association); Cooperativa Sociale Solco Prossimo (social enterprise); Cooperativa Sociale Solco Salute (social enterprise); Centro MeME, Associazione Culturale Idee di Salute (association); Centro Psicologia Clinica Regina Pacis (care centre); Oltrefrontiere (association); Istituto Comprensivo Statale Giardini (public school). In collaboration with: Sapienza Università di Roma, (Dipartimento di Psicologia Dinamica e Clinica, university), Università degli Studi di Pavia (Dipartimento di Scienze del Sistema Nervoso e del Comportamento, university); IRCCS Policlinico San Matteo di Pavia (hospital), Ordine degli Psicologi della Lombardia (psychologists professional association)	Counseling, and Engagement

(continued)

Table 1 (continued)

nr	Case name	Artefacts' typology	Actors' coalitions	Patients' role
08	Recovery Net (2020; Welfare in Azione; www.recoverynet.it)	Knowledge artefact: network of social and healthcare companies, social cooperatives, universities, family members' and users' associations that creates actions in the areas of Brescia and Mantua dedicated to people with mental disorders	ASST Spedali Civili di Brescia (hospital); ASST Mantova Ospedale Carlo Poma (hospital); Politecnico di Milano (university); Università degli Studi di Milano Bicocca (university); Università Cattolica del Sacro Cuore di Milano (university); La Rondine (social enterprise); Teatro 19 (organisations involved in theatre production, organisation and training); Il Chiaro del Bosco Onlus (cultural association); Sol.co Mantova (consortium of social cooperatives); Alba onlus (patient association); Oltre la siepe (volunteers association). Iniziative supported by Fondazione Cariplo - Progetto Welfare in Azione (foundation)	Counselling, Engagement,
09	Smart4Alzheimer (2020; Genera Onlus; www.generaonlus.it/servizi/smart4-alzheimer)	Knowledge artefact: continuous care support service for families and caregivers of people with Alzheimer's	Genera Onlus (social enterprise)	Consulting and Engagement
10	Alzheimer Lab (2019; Fondazione Sacra Famiglia; www.sacrafamiglia.org/alzheimer-lab-accanto-agli-anziani-fragili)	Intangible artefact and Knowledge artefact: A social channel with video tutorials dedicated to the psychological well-being and cognitive and physical stimulation of Alzheimer's patients. The Foundation's professionals offer suggestions and help for a correct approach in the daily care of the person suffering from this condition. Fondazione Sacra Famiglia set up a virtual psychological support desk dedicated to family members and people caring for the elderly at home	Fondazione Sacra Famiglia (foundation); Fondazione Comunità di Milano (foundation)	Consulting, Engagement and Co-production

(continued)

Table 1 (continued)

nr	Case name	Artefacts' typology	Actors' coalitions	Patients' role
11	TOP! Together to Play and Say Eye (2019; Fondazione TOG; www.fondazionetog.org/blog/con-gli-occhi-si-puo_top-sayeye-tecnologia-eyetracking-per-riabilitare)	Intangible artefact: Two eye-tracking system-based tools for the treatment and rehabilitation of children with severe neurological disorders	Fondazione TOG (foundation), Open Dot (Fab Lab); Dot Dot Dot (design studio); WeAreMuesli (game design studio); Fondazione Mondino–Istituto Neurologico Nazionale a carattere scientifico (hospital); Perceptual computing and Human Sensing Lab–Università degli Studi di Milano (university)	Co-Designing
12	Personalised care products: Voice Instruments, La Mia Scarpa DIY (with Vibram), La Bici di Ognuno, Saddle Up, Pimpy Car, Fisio Rabbit, Doccetta, Pupazzi Autoprodotti, Glifo. (2017; Fondazione TOG and Open Dot; https://fondazionetog.org/blog/)	Tangible artefact: personalised prosthesis, device, toy and tool series co-designed with patients and developed through the use of digital fabrication technologies and the collaboration of specialists and companies	Fondazione Tog (foundation); Open Dot (Fab Lab)	Co-creation and Co-design
13	Progetto CCF–Cronici Complessi Fragili (2022; Vidas; www.vidas.it/nuovo-progetto-cronici-complessi-fragili)	Intangible artefact: project of a home-based network of social and health professionals for the recovery of patients discharged from the General Medicine ward of the San Raffaele Hospital in Milan. The service combines 24-h telephone assistance, telemedicine (with kit) and teleconsultation	Vidas (voluntary association); Ospedale San Raffaele di Milano (hospital)	Counselling and Engagement

(continued)

Table 1 (continued)

nr	Case name	Artefacts' typology	Actors' coalitions	Patients' role
14	Existo (2019; Existo; www.existo.tech)	Tangible artefact: product–service system for personalised prosthesis and wearable robotic devices	Existo (start-up); E-Novia (tech incubator). Cooperation with 10 neuro-rehabilitation centres in hospitals and nursing homes nationwide, where it is possible to receive specialised support and try Existo	Engagement
15	Patient Health Engagement (2018; Engage Minds Hub; https://engagemindshub.com/patient-health-engagement/)	Knowledge artefact: knowledge hub for patients and their associations to improve the impact of their advocacy initiatives. Research activities include evaluation and promotion of patient engagement; participatory co-design of health services; development of patient support programmes; design, support and evaluation of patient advocacy actions	Engage Minds Hub–Università Cattolica del Sacro Cuore di Milano (consumer, food and health engagement university research centre). The scientific committee of Engage Minds Hub includes healthcare scholars, patient associations and policymakers at national and European levels	Consultancy and Engagement

(continued)

Table 1 (continued)

nr	Case name	Artefacts' typology	Actors' coalitions	Patients' role
16	Therapy Adherence Patient Engagement (https://engagemindshub.com/project/verso-una-migliore-aderenza-in-asma-attraverso-la-promozione-del-patient-engagement/)	Knowledge artefact. Research project to i) explore at national and international levels which are the psychological and emotional factors that, in asthma, impact on experience and therapeutic adherence and which are the most effective interventions to support it; ii) evaluate the levels of therapeutic adherence of Italian patients with asthma, also identifying patients with poor control, also in light of the covid19 situation	Chiesi (pharma company); Engage Minds Hub–Università Cattolica del Sacro Cuore Università Cattolica del Sacro Cuore di Milano (consumer, food and health engagement university research centre–university); Federasma (volunteers organisation); Fondazione Cariplo (foundation); Respiriamo Assieme (association)	Engagement
17	Peer Education in Asthma (https://engagemin dshub.com/project/respiriamo-insieme/)	Knowledge artefact: research that active involved young people with severe asthma for better management of the disease and quality of life by activating a peer education path through social media	Engage Minds Hub–Università Cattolica del Sacro Cuore Università Cattolica del Sacro Cuore di Milano (consumer, food and health engagement university research centre–university); Novartis (pharma company); Respiriamo Assieme (association)	Engagement
18	WeCare (https://engagemindshub.com/project/wecare/)	Knowledge artefact: research project aimed at exploring the point of view of patients with IBD and RHEUMATIC DISEASES and identifying their criteria for evaluating the quality of the assistance services received. In addition, the research aims to compare the perspectives of patients and their doctors on the criteria for evaluating services along the care path	Abbvie (pharma company), Amici Onlus (association); Anmar (patient association); Engage Minds Hub–Università Cattolica del Sacro Cuore Università Cattolica del Sacro Cuore di Milano (consumer, food and health engagement university research centre–university)	Consulting

(continued)

Table 1 (continued)

nr	Case name	Artefacts' typology	Actors' coalitions	Patients' role
19	Place4Carers (https://engagemindshub.com/project/place4carers/)	Knowledge artefact: Place4Carers is a community-based participatory research project, coordinated by the EngageMinds HUB, aimed at co-generating, developing and implementing a new social and community service for family carers of senior citizens in the remote rural area of Valle Camonica	Engage Minds Hub–Università Cattolica del Sacro Cuore Università Cattolica del Sacro Cuore di Milano (consumer, food and health engagement university research centre–university); Fondazione Cariplo (foundation), NTNU–Norwegian University of Science and Technology (university); Need Institute (research foundation); Politenico di Milano (university)	Co-Designing
20	Umanizzazione, Innovazione e Partecipazione (https://www.cittadinanzattivalombardia.com/progetti/progetto-sanita/)	Knowledge artefact: Cittadinanzattiva in Lombardy has developed an experimental survey with the IRCCS Istituto Ortopedico Galeazzi, which has made itself available to collaborate in order to have citizens assess its services and present the results in a public and transparent manner	Cittadinanz.Attiva Lombardia (civic association); IRCCS Istituto Ortopedico Galeazzi (hospital)	Engagement
21	Open Care–Open Rampette (2015–2017; www.opencare.cc)	Tangible artefact and Intangible artefact: Open Rampette (2017, by WeMake and City of Milan) is a social impact project developed to gather on the same path Milanese citizens, municipality and shop owners to identify a tangible solution to the stagnating issue of accessibility in public spaces by people that require the use of a wheelchair	University of Bordeaux France (coordinator, university); Edgeryders (innovation agency); WeMake (Fab Lab); Stockholm School of Economics (university); SCImPULSE Foundation (foundation); City of Milan (public administration)	Engagement and Co-Designing

(continued)

Table 1 (continued)

nr	Case name	Artefacts' typology	Actors' coalitions	Patients' role
22	Diario Elettronico degli Attacchi (2017; AAEE Onlus; http://www.angioedemaereditario.org/)	Intangible artefact: Cloud-R HAE Electronic diary of attacks is an app that allows people with angioedema to privately share data on the appearance of symptoms with their doctors in order to get immediate support. Through the app patients contribute to clinical research by creating a database accessible to the doctors of the 20 specialised angioedema centres in Italy. Active from 2017 to today, the app has collected about 1000 users	AAEE Onlus (association) supported by ITACA–Italian Network of Hereditary and Acquired Angioedema (association), HAEI International (association hereditary angioedema); Fondazione Telethon (foundation)	Consultancy and Engagement
23	Piazza Grace and Grace Lab (2017; Genera Onlus; https://generaonlus.it/servizi/piazza-grace-villaggio-alzheimer)	Tangible artefact and Intangible artefact: Piazza Grace is the first Alzheimer's Village in the metropolitan city of Milan conceived with therapeutic habitats. Grace Lab was born with the aim of designing and experimenting environments and tools for therapeutic habitats for the treatment of Alzheimer's Syndrome	Genera Onlus (social enterprise); Fondazione Housing Sociale (foundation), Lab_i_r_int–Politecnico di Milano (university), Noon Care (start-up)	Engagement

(continued)

Table 1 (continued)

nr	Case name	Artefacts' typology	Actors' coalitions	Patients' role
24	Hackability@Milano (2015: Hackability; http://www.hackability.it/hackabilitymilano/)	Tangible artefact and Intangible artefact: Hackability@Milano, is a co-design platform created to bring together the world of making and design with the needs of people with disabilities in Milan. Hackability@Milano is a working group that brings together the skills of designers, makers and digital artisans with the needs and creativity of people with disabilities	Hackability (association); LUISS Lab Milan (innovation hub)	Co-Design
25	Mirrorable (2014; FighttheStroke; www.fighthestroke.org)	Intangible artefact: interactive platform that enables a model of rehabilitation therapy at home. The platform welcomes young people with Infantile Cerebral Palsy and their families in a new rehabilitation model, based on design, science and technology	Fight the Stroke (patient association), supported and endorsed by experts, associations and organisations	Engagement and Co-Design

the national territory providing consultancy and support services in the field of electronic and computer aids. The centres participating in the GLIC share their knowledge in order to develop tools and proposals for the real development of the whole AT sector in the face of increasing expectations and service demands of people with disabilities.) (GLIC network). A multidisciplinary team (The team consists of a social worker, psychologist, occupational therapist, architect, assistive technology technician and assistive technology designer.) operates within the Lab implementing a set of service solutions, designing tools and organising initiatives to improve the quality and autonomy of people with disabilities. Within the Tech Lab, there is a service to evaluate and identify computer aids and software for communication and the use of these devices in the home, social, school and work environments. The Lab is equipped with digital fabrication machines (similar to a Fab Lab) to materialise personalised aids for the different daily life needs of people with disabilities. Another service concerns the design of integrated assisted living systems and consultancy to companies and organisations for adapting the workstations. The last service organises training initiatives for operators and citizens, to make them aware of the potential offered by technology in improving the daily domestic and working autonomy of people with disabilities.

Actors' Coalitions. It is interesting to frame the creation of the Tech Lab within the development of the entire service ecosystem designed and developed by the Spazio Vita Niguarda Onlus with the network of stakeholders progressively involved. Spazio Vita Niguarda is supported by hospitals, municipalities, universities, bank foundations, hi-tech companies, companies specialising in healthcare supplies and voluntary associations. The social enterprise managed the construction of a multi-purpose centre at the Niguarda Hospital in Milan (the result of a fundraising campaign) and subsequently developed psycho-social support and workshop activities aimed at in-patients and people with motor disabilities in the area. Spazio Vita Niguarda started to develop services accredited by the Municipality of Milan to assist its users and increase their mobility. Together with Niguarda Hospital and with the contribution of the Lombardy Region, the non-profit organisation has developed Bridge, a service that experimented with a multidisciplinary model of care assistance for people with severe motor disabilities. In 2018, Bridge became a stable service Take Care, implemented in 2021 with Apple Academy Napoli, represents its evolution. Spazio Vita Niguarda implemented the preparatory workshop activities for the Tech Lab, increasing the number of users and family members using the non-profit organisation's services. Thanks to another project (Housing), Spazio Vita rents an accessible flat close to the hospital for independent living projects and accommodation for patients' families. Prior to the opening of the Tech Lab, other services are implemented: a service for training young people with disabilities to increase their individual autonomy (Servizio di Formazione all'Autonomia); work placements through the creation of a Branch B of the cooperative; and the acquisition of a home care service (Assistenza Domiciliare Integrata). The increase in activities and the pandemic stimulated both the physical expansion of the centre and the digitisation of services.

Patients' role. The history of Spazio Vita Niguarda shows a progression in the development of the service ecosystem that corresponds to evolution in considering the patient's needs in terms of autonomy and mobility (from 'cure' to 'care'). The first services, developed in collaboration with patients' and caregivers' associations, made it possible to create spaces equipped (also technologically) with mobility and reception services enabling users to carry out personalised activities (e.g. work). These services constitute the basic infrastructure on which more advanced services such as the TechLab have been developed, probably the most advanced in terms of patient-centredness. Tech Lab combines the knowledge gained in personal care with the use of enabling spaces and technologies to collaborate with patients in the development of personalised aids, in the configuration of living and working environments adapted to them and in the formation of a culture of care and assistance that allows them to better relate to each other.

3.3   Piazza Grace and Grace Lab by Genera Onlus

Artefacts' typology. Piazza Grace (See https://generaonlus.it/servizi/piazza-grace-villaggio-alzheimer/) is the first Alzheimer's Village in the Metropolitan City of Milan. It is developed within the Sustainable Village of Figino (near Milan), a 'dementia friendly village' that enables children, young people and the elderly to coexist to create an integrated intergenerational community. Piazza Grace is a project developed by Genera Onlus, a social cooperative that has been working in Milan and the hinterland for over 20 years in the design and development of educational, social welfare and social health services and also deals with reception, cohousing and social housing. The Alzheimer Village is an experimental housing project designed for patients facing this condition, their families and carers. The project is made up of the square, the Centro Diurno Integrato (the Care Centre) and 15 flats for the people hosted in the Village and people that have access to temporary social housing services. The Centro Diurno Integrato, located at the heart of the Village, offers space and support to the guests. In addition, the person's well-being for us passes through beauty, which is necessary to rediscover the pleasure of living. Six flats, each of which can accommodate two residents, equipped with a kitchen, bathroom and disabled access and sleeping area, are fully furnished with personal furniture. The six flats overlook a large communal kitchen, an important sharing space that allows for the organisation of social moments. Other nine flats accommodate the elderly and/or families in temporary social residencies. The housing mix is designed to encourage the sociability of people with Alzheimer's disease, who can live their daily lives in contact with the community living in the village. The living spaces are conceived as continuous therapeutic habitats, there are no architectural barriers, and paths are facilitated by orientation systems that encourage recognition of indoor and outdoor spaces. The guests of Piazza Grace can move freely in the indoor and outdoor spaces thanks to a series of wearables (named Tag Ble) that can integrate buttons for emergency calls or accelerometers capable of detecting the wearer's activities or possible falls.

Actors' coalitions. Piazza Grace is the result of integrated design work by various professionals and stakeholders. Nine of the fifteen temporary social residences are supported by the City of Milan. The Tag Ble wearables were developed thanks to the collaboration between Genera and the Milanese start-up Noon Care. In 2018, the creation of Grace Lab, a research laboratory combining the design teams of Genera and Lab.I.R.Int, a research group of the Department of Design—Politecnico di Milano specialising in interior design (Biamonti, 2018). Grace Lab was created to design and experiment with environments and tools for therapeutic habitats thanks to an interdisciplinary team of researchers, designers, operators and caregivers. Within the Lab, prototypes of products, environmental solutions and services are developed and tested in Grace environments.

Patients' role. The care and support services at Piazza Grace focus on designing solutions that meet the safety and inclusiveness needs of Alzheimer Village residents. The service touchpoints are designed to integrate non-invasively into the therapeutic habitats, which in turn are designed to be customisable. Piazza Grace's patient-centred approach is developed in two complementary directions: on the one hand, it works to include the patient in the village community; on the other hand, it works on the village community to tune it to the patients' living needs. Given the degenerative nature of Alzheimer's, the involvement of patients in the creation of therapeutic habitats is complex and requires multidisciplinary expertise in the fields of social services, social housing and interior design. Grace Lab, in synergy with Piazza Grace, can implement services based on integrated and inclusive processes of research, design, experimentation, testing and deployment of the solutions.

3.4   Alzheimer Lab by Fondazione Sacra Famiglia

Artefacts' typology. Alzheimer Lab (See https://www.sacrafamiglia.org/alzheimer lab/) is a service implemented by Fondazione Sacra Famiglia to support people affected by Dementia and Alzheimer's and their family caregivers. The initiative, created during the pandemics, concerns the creation of a dedicated social media channel with more than 100 videos where people find relevant information they need to assist their loved ones. Weekly lessons, remotely executable at home, that explain rehabilitation exercises have been divided into three areas: (i) adapted physical activities to counter functional decline in people with Alzheimer's and dementia; (ii) stimulation of different cognitive skills and functions and increasing multitasking skills through play; and (iii) support provided by a psychologist from the Care Centre to caregivers who are managing a family member with dementia at home.

Actors' Coalitions. Fondazione Sacra Famiglia is a non-profit organisation that since 1896 has been accompanying, caring for and assisting frail children, adults and the elderly, people with mental and physical disabilities, with developmental and behavioural disorders such as autism and non-self-sufficient people suffering from neurodegenerative or chronic diseases. The Foundation has developed a chain of outpatient, home and residential social and health services, accredited by the regional health system, which aim to provide a customised response to the needs of thousands of fragile families and people in Lombardy. To this end, the Foundation has over 1,500 beds and employs almost two thousand collaborators including doctors, social workers, therapists, nurses, educators, social workers, psychologists and management staff. In addition to the collaborators, there are around 1,000 volunteers. The Alzheimer Lab has been implemented involving specialised resources of Fondazione Sacra Famiglia and financially supported by Fondazione di Comunità Milano.

Patients' role. Alzheimer Lab is an interesting example of a sudden change in the provision of care services by an organisation with more than 20 sites spread across Lombardy and the neighbouring regions. COVID made it necessary to design with information content that could be easily conveyed to a population of family caregivers by providing them with both guidance to support patients at home and the possibility of psychological support to cope with the stress of living with Alzheimer's patients in an emergency condition. It is an example of resilient patient-centred service ecosystems enabled by digital transformation. The level of design and technological complexity of the solution is not in itself innovative. What is interesting is how the social channel managed to enable, train (and speed up) a form of distributed co-production of a support and assistance service for patients (pinpointing that this was done in an emergency context and, perhaps, by modifying existing protocols).

4   Conclusions: Implications and Challenges for a Patient-Centred Service Design

We are enquiring an emergent scenario in which the role of the patients and their support communities is becoming relevant for designing new cure and care service offerings. It is an emerging bottom-up agency that could progressively enter the traditional top-down project approach, linked to an outdated idea of science as the unique competent part of society able to address collective challenges and issues. Patient's (and caregiving systems) inclusion and role changes the traditional interplay in the healthcare and care organisation and processes. Patient innovation (Bogers et al., 2010; Von Hippel, 2009) has paved the way for putting patient-centredness (PC) as a cornerstone for developing open, inclusive and collaborative design practices that might use co-creation, co-design and co-production strategies. One of the conditions is exactly the systemic connection effect that links needs, competences and agencies of the actors that surround the patients: the enlarged caregiving system becomes the real influencer of the design process. As Kim et al. state (Kim et al., 2022):'Contemporarily, innovation within healthcare ecosystems also means measuring and analysing the impact of the innovation led by patients, caregivers, and caregiving systems (Zejnilović et al., 2016; Gambardella et al., 2016). Furthermore, it often means a holistic understanding of all the relationships which rule the connections between transformation mechanisms and bottom-up innovations (Keinz et al., 2012; Trott et al., 2013). As a result, a new role for design arises, to integrate and align the different actors' perspectives while co-creating value (Pereno & Eriksson, 2020; Sangiorgi et al., 2020; Vink et al., 2021). Here, design is the result of the activity of new creative profiles (i.e., citizens, makers and ultimately patients) who alter the politics of the system of production, emphasising the importance of co-design and co-creative approach in the design of healthcare services, products, and ecosystems (Maffei et al., 2022).' (Kim et al., 2022; p.4).

From the case analysis, it emerges the importance of designing services in a more systemic way, balancing human-centricity and pervasiveness of technology for innovating the culture of care. This means going beyond the current design processes, recognising that the patients' needs are (only) one of the resources of a wider community, entailing for example support communities, organisations, researchers and health professionals. The performative and functionalistic logic in designing services need to be further discussed from the theoretical and practical perspectives.

In practice, it means reconsidering the service design processes often linked to the dominant design thinking approach, in favour of a system-oriented design vision that considers a rich set of cultural, cognitive, organisational and techno-logical artefacts characterising complex actors' and coalitions' relationships with reciprocal learning and distributed agency in care ecosystems.

This reflection focuses on a concept: innovative healthcare and care services that follow patient-centredness logic are less and less concerned about the design of individual processes and the achievement of specific performances and will increasingly deal with complex assemblages of existing multilayered, multiscale, multiagent and multidomain processes which need as a main ingredient a reasoning about systemic integration, often enabled by a digital environment, between many different product–service systems.

These complex services will maintain an obvious focus on a specific pro-cess and performance, but will already include a multiagent perspective, working stratigraphically from the granular product–service solution to the final integration within the care services ecosystem. Diversely, the more traditional design-thinking-like patient innovation will maintain its predominant granular characterisation often missing the opportunity of developing a systemic scale.

The three selected exemplary cases—Tech Lab and the caregiving system of Spazio Vita Niguarda Onlus, Piazza Grace and Grace Lab of Genera Onlus, Alzheimer Lab of Fondazione Sacra Famiglia - reveal how patient-centred ser-vices might evolve using the pre-existing layers of ecosystemic infrastructures, services, technologies, relationships and knowledge.

They have specific common characteristics:

- they are close-to-the-patient because they combine tangible, intangible and knowledge artefacts to implement innovative forms of physical and virtual proximity with the patient;

- they are everyday-driven because they engage people to integrate care services into patients' daily lives, their living spaces and relationship systems;
- they are experimental because they inspire the infrastructure of laboratories (fab labs, living labs, virtual labs, etc.) to design, prototype, test and distribute services that increase patient involvement through enabling technologies.

We learned three lessons from this initial inquiry of the cases. First of all, the centrality of the patient means designing services with/for the patient and its system: the (service) designer must not only be concerned with listening, interpreting and transforming the users' needs by linking them to a participatory process. Nevertheless, it must understand how to relate the patient's needs and participation to the system of technologies, relationships and organisations that influence the creation of the tangible and intangible artefacts and knowledge that constitute the service solution.

The second important take-out is that patient-centredness is community-driven (and not only individual) and context-based: healthcare product–service system solutions are enabled by tangible, intangible and knowledge artefacts representing different patient-centredness' languages and contexts. Similarly, community experience/expertise in orchestrating the design and production of patient-centred solutions are relevant variables influencing these artefacts' maturity level. Situatedness is a specific characteristic: applying the same solution in two systems or contexts with different characteristics will inevitably generate a different outcome regarding factors such as the balance of power, social justice and environmental externalities.

Finally, patient-centredness stimulates the prototyping of innovative care and living experiences.

The cases lead to configuring home, work and care environments with laboratory characteristics. These environments present spatial and technological contexts that allow the patient to perform therapies and treatment protocols and, at the same time, to experiment more freely with care services that have a craft-like dimension (meaning that they are open to innovative experimental iterations).

If we imagine this new exploration as the start to a new way of looking at patient-centredness we have probably to search outside the simple service design culture. It's a matter of understanding the entanglement of the connections between the patient and the patient's actions, relationship, environments and artefacts. Patient-centredness is an assemblage (Müller & Schurr, 2016) in which we have to search for the connections between the vibrant matter (Bennett, 2010) and the actor–network agencies of the actants. Service design might not be considered out of the sociotechnical dynamics. It could not be a world apart in which an internalist disciplinary logic could provide explanation for this complex phenomenon. A new possibility for a wider and deeper frameworking to emerge. It's a novel philosophical contamination that needs to be done.

References

Anderson, L., Ostrom, A. L., Corus, C., Fisk, R. P., Gallan, A. S., Giraldo, M., Mende, M., Mulder, M., Rayburn, S. W., Rosenbaum, M. S., Shirahada, K., & Williams, J. D. (2013). Transformative service research: An agenda for the future. *Journal of Business Research, 66*(2013), 1203–1210.

Bennett, J. (2010). Vibrant matter. In *A political ecology of things*. Durham: Duke University Press

Biamonti, A. (2018). *Design & Alzheimer. Dalle esperienze degli Habitat Terapeutici al modello GRACE.* Franco Angeli: Serie di architettura e design. Strumenti. ISBN-10: 8891770620.

Bogers, M., Afuah, A., & Bastian, B. (2010). Users as innovators: A review, critique, and future research directions. *Journal of Management, 36*(4), 857–875. https://doi.org/10.1177/014920 6309353944

Ekman, I., Swedberg, K., Taft, C., Lindseth, A., Norberg, A., Brink, E., Carlsson, J., & Sunnerhagen, K. S. (2011). Person-centered care–ready for prime time. *European Journal of Cardiovascular Nursingm, 10*(4), 248–251. https://doi.org/10.1016/j.ejcnurse.2011.06.008

Foglieni, F., Villari, B., & Maffei, S. (2018). *Designing better services: A strategic approach from design to evaluation.* Milan: Springer Publishing.

Francis, R. (2010). Independent Inquiry into care provided by Mid Staffordshire NHS Foundation Trust January 2005–March 2009, vol. 1. Retrieved June 29, 2022, from https://assets.publis hing.service.gov.uk/government/uploads/system/uploads/attachment_data/file/279109/0375_i. pdf

Gambardella, A., Raasch, C., & Von Hippel, E. (2016). The user innovation paradigm: Impacts on markets and welfare. *Management Science, 63*(5), 1450–1468. https://doi.org/10.1287/mnsc. 2015.2393

Hermes, S., Riasanow, T., Clemons, E. K., Böhm, M., & Krcmar, H. (2020). The digital transformation of the healthcare industry: Exploring the rise of emerging platform ecosystems and their influence on the role of patients. *Business Research, 13*(3), 1033–1069.

Horne, M., Khan, H., Corrigan, P. (2013). People powered health: Health for people, by people and with people. London: NESTA. Retrieved June 27, 2022, from https://media.nesta.org.uk/ documents/health_for_people_by_people_and_with_people.pdf, http://www.oecd.org/health/ ministerial/ministerial-statement-2017.pdf

Jones, P. (2020). Systemic design: Design for complex, social, and sociotechnical systems. In G. S. Metcalf, K. Kijima, & H. Deguchi (Eds.), *Handbook of systems sciences* (pp. 787–811). Singapore: Springer Nature.

Keinz, P., Hienerth, C., & Lettl, C. (2012). Designing the organization for user innovation. *Journal of Organization Design, 1*(3), 20–36. https://doi.org/10.7146/jod.1.3.6346

Kim, M., Mages, M., Maffei, S., Ciuccarelli, P., Villari, B., Bianchini, M., Ciliotta, E. (2022). Empowering patientship: Exploring the dimensions and conceptions of patient-centredness. In *INCLUDE 2022: Unheard Voices Conference.* London.

Maffei, S., Bianchini, M., Villari, B. (2022). When the patient innovates. Emerging practices in service ecosystems. In M. A. Pfannstiel, N. Brehmer, C. Rasche (Eds.) *Service design practices for healthcare innovation, paradigms, principles, prospects* (pp. 59–76). Cham, Switzerland: Springer Nature. https://doi.org/10.1007/978-3-030-87273-1_4

Müller, M., & Schurr, C. (2016). Assemblage thinking and actor-network theory: Conjunctions, disjunctions and cross-fertilisations. *Transactions of the Institute of British Geographers, 41*(3), 217–229. https://doi.org/10.1111/tran.12117

Mager, B., Oertzen, A. S., & Vink, J. (2022). Co-creation in health services through service design. In M. A. Pfannstiel, N. Brehmer, & C. Rasche (Eds.), *Service design practices for healthcare innovation, paradigms, principles, prospects* (pp. 497–510). Springer Nature.

NESTA. (2018). La cura che cambia, Retrieved June 27, 2022, from http://wemake.cc/core/upl oads/2018/10/La-cura-che-cambia_Pratiche-e-culture-di-Salute-Collaborativa-in-Italia.pdf

Nolte, E., Merkur, S., & Anell, A. (2020). The person at the centre of health systems: An introduction. In J. North (Author), E. Nolte, S. Merkur, & A. Anell (Eds.), *Achieving person-centred health systems: evidence, strategies and challenges (European Observatory on Health Systems and Policies)* (pp. 1–18). Cambridge: Cambridge University Press. https://doi.org/10.1017/978 1108855464.004

OECD. (2019). *Government at a glance 2019.* Paris: OECD Publishing. https://doi.org/10.1787/8ccf5c38-en

OECD Health Ministerial Meeting. (2017). The next generation of health reforms. Retrieved June 27, 2022, from http://www.oecd.org/health/ministerial/ministerial-statement-2017.pdf

Patrício, L., Gustafsson, A., & Fisk, R. (2018). Upframing service design and innovation for research impact. *Journal of Service Research, 21*(1), 3–16.

Patrício, L., Sangiorgi, D., Mahr, D., Čaić, M., Kalantari, S., & Sundar, S. (2020). Leveraging service design for healthcare transformation: Toward people-centered, integrated, and technology-enabled healthcare systems. *Journal of Service Management, 31*(5), 889–909. https://doi.org/10.1108/josm-11-2019-0332

Pereno, A., & Eriksson, D. (2020). A multi-stakeholder perspective on sustainable healthcare: From 2030 onwards. *Futures, 122*(9), 1–21. https://doi.org/10.1016/j.futures.2020.102605

Røtnes, R., & Staalesen, P. D. (2009). New methods for user driven innovation in the health care sector Report, Nordic Innovation Centre project. Retrieved June 29, 2022, from https://www.diva-portal.org/smash/get/diva2:707163/FULLTEXT01.pdf

Sangiorgi, D. (2009). *Building up a framework for service design research.* Paper presented at the 8th European Academy of Design Conference, (pp. 415–420), The Robert Gordon University, Scotland: Aberdeen.

Sangiorgi, D., Lucchi, F., & Carrera, M. (2020). Recovery-net: A multilevel and collaborative approach to mental healthcare transformation, In: A. Battisti, M. Marecca & E. Iorio (Eds.) *AIMETA 2019: Urban health* (pp. 189–200). Cham, Switzerland: Springer International Publishing. https://doi.org/10.1007/978-3-030-49446-9_13

Sangiorgi, D., Patrıcio, L., & Fisk, R. P. (2017). Designing for interdependence, participation andemergence in complex service systems. In D. Sangiorgi & A. Prediville (Eds.), *Designing for service: Key issues and new directions* (pp. 49–64). Bloomsbury Academic.

Swan, M. (2009). Emerging patient-driven health care models: An examination of health social networks, consumer personalized medicine and quantified self-tracking. *International Journal of Environmental Research and Public Health, 6*(2), 492–525.

Trott, P., Van Der Duin, P., & Hartmann, D. (2013). Users as innovators? *Exploring the Limitations of User-Driven Innovation, Prometheus, 31*(2), 125–138. https://doi.org/10.1080/08109028.2013.818790

Vink, J., Koskela-Huotari, K., Tronvoll, B., Edvardsson, B., & Wetter-Edman, K. (2020). Service ecosystem design: Propositions, process model, and future research agenda. *Journal of Service Research, 24*(2), 168–186. https://doi.org/10.1177/1094670520952537

Vink, J., Koskela-Huotari, K., Tronvoll, B., Edvardsson, B., & Wetter-Edman, K. (2021). Service ecosystem design: Propositions, process model, and future research agenda. *Journal of Service Research, 24*(2), 168–186. https://doi.org/10.1177/1094670520952537

Von Hippel, E. (2009). Democratizing innovation: The evolving phenomenon of user innovation. *International Journal of Innovation Science, 1*(1), 29–40. https://doi.org/10.1260/175722209787951224

Wetter-Edman, K., Sangiorgi, D., Edvardsson, B., Holmlid, S., Grönroos, C., & Mattelmäki, T. (2014). Design for value co-creation: Exploring synergies between design for service and service logic. *Service Science, 6*(2), 106–121.

Wildevuur, S. E., & Simonse, L. W. L. (2017). Could health learn from design? Design? *For Health, 1*(1), 59–64. https://doi.org/10.1080/245735132.2017.1295707

World Health Assembly. (2016). Framework on integrated, people-centred health services: report by the Secretariat. A69/39. World Health Organization. Retrieved June 27, 2022, from https://apps.who.int/iris/handle/10665/252698

World Health Organization. (2016). Framework on integrated, people-centred health services. Report by the Secretariat. Retrieved June 27, 2022, from https://apps.who.int/gb/ebwha/pdf_files/WHA69/A69_39-en.pdf?ua=1&ua=1

Zejnilović, L., Oliveira, P., & Canhão, H. (2016). Innovations by and for patients, and their place in the future health care system. In H. Albach, H. Meffert, A. Pinkwart, R. Reichwald & W. von Eiff (Eds.) Boundaryless hospital (pp. 341–357). Berlin: Springer Verlag. https://doi.org/10.1007/978-3-662-49012-9_1

Stefano Maffei Architect, Ph.D. in Design, is Full Professor at the Department of Design, Director of Polifactory, the makerspace-FabLab of Politecnico di Milano and Director of Service Design and Design for Food Masters and Service Innovation Academy at Poli.design Politecnico di Milano. His current research and work interests focus on new production–distribution models, service design innovation and design for policy approaches.

Massimo Bianchini Designer, Ph.D. in Design is an Associate Professor at the Department of Design and Lab Manager at Polifactory, the makerspace-FabLab of Politecnico di Milano. His research interests include open design and distributed production, urban manufacturing, user-driven and patient innovation, indie innovation and circular innovation.

Beatrice Villari Designer, Ph.D. in Design is Associate Professor at the Department of Design, Co-Director of Service Design and Design for food Masters and Service Innovation Academy at Poli.design, Politecnico di Milano. Her current research and work interests focus on service design and design for policy.

Human-Centered Gatekeeping: "Neyim Var?"

Çağdaş Erkan Akyürek, Şükrü Anıl Toygar, and Elif Erbay

ABSTRACT

Information asymmetry, which is physician-oriented, unilateral domination of information, is the main characteristic of healthcare services and the main justification for clinical autonomy. A person who needs healthcare can only express his/her complaints and symptoms. Therefore, the decision to initiate the care process and determine the limitations of care is under the authority and responsibility of the healthcare professional. This causes information asymmetry by excluding the patient from the responsibility during the healthcare processes. Thus, "gatekeeping" is an important way of controlling patient traffic in the healthcare system. According to the Health Transformation Program which characterizes the Turkish Health System for the last 20 years, anyone can directly apply to any healthcare facility without using a referral chain from primary care to tertiary care although the referral chain system has been defined as a main component of the program. Because of a populistic reason which was rendered as a barrier in the front of the accessibility of the care for patients, a referral chain system has never been implemented in an administrative context for Turkish citizens. In other words, the efficiency and effectiveness of the health system were sacrificed to avoid bureaucratic barriers for the care for citizens. "Neyim Var?", which can be translated into English as "What do I

Ç. E. Akyürek (✉) · E. Erbay
Department of Healthcare Management, Ankara University, Fatih Caddesi No:197/A,
06290 Keçiören/ANKARA, Turkey
e-mail: ceakyurek@ankara.edu.tr

E. Erbay
e-mail: Elif.Erbay@ankara.edu.tr

Ş. A. Toygar
Department of Healthcare Management, Tarsus University, Takbaş Mahallesi Kartaltepe Sokak,
33400 Tarsus/MERSİN, Turkey
e-mail: saniltoygar@tarsus.edu.tr

137

have?", is an artificial intelligence-based technology that was developed by the Ministry of Health, and it has become a popular application among citizens. Anyone can log in to the system by using their own e-government code and then enter their own complaints and symptoms. The system directs the patient to the appropriate healthcare facility and clinic according to the predetermined clinical algorithms. The patient can easily arrange an appointment by the integration between "Neyim Var?" and "Central Hospital Appointment System". This text asserts that the "Neyim Var?" system can serve as an e-gatekeeper and provide some recommendations to initiate an administrative referral chain without exposing patients to bureaucratic barriers.

1   Introduction

Traditionally, an ordinary trade has two sides: buyer and seller. Although the buyer is not at the same level of knowledge as the seller, he/she generally has the level of knowledge to participate in the decision-making process in a way that protects his/her own interests during that purchase. As a result, the buyer also gives the "work order", that is, he/she has the level of information to determine which product/service and how much to buy. When it comes to healthcare, the context is completely different.

The most distinctive feature that distinguishes the provision of health services from the traditional economic exchange is the "information asymmetry" arising from professional knowledge, which indisputably puts the service provider in a superior position to the consumer of the service. In the face of the patient who is only obliged to convey his/her complaints, which health service will be provided at what intensity is within the authority and responsibility of the health service professional, that is, the work order is given by the service provider, not the consumer when it comes to health services.

However, the presence of information asymmetry does not eliminate the necessity for the recognition of patient autonomy. Patient autonomy, on the other hand, requires increasing patient participation rather than decision-making processes that are completely under the control of the physician and the patient to have a say in the selection of the medically appropriate treatment plan (Macklin, 1993, 213). Underlying the correct functioning of patient autonomy is the strengthening of the patient as required. Patient empowerment or empowered patients is a concept that makes its effects more and more felt in the healthcare industry and in some cases has become an important challenge for service delivery. Thanks to widespread internet access and media use as the benefits of the digital age, patients now apply to health institutions with a certain idea in their minds. Empowered patients want to actively participate in the decision-making processes within the scope of health services to be offered to them and their families (Akyürek & Kalaycı, 2019, 251). While correctly empowered patients can make significant contributions to the treatment processes and the effectiveness of health services by being more willing to follow the requirements of the process, on the contrary, patients equipped with false information can be more prejudiced and unsatisfied with their treatment processes.

Although the concepts of patient autonomy and empowerment arguably come to the fore day by day, it does not have the opportunity to balance the situation resulting from information asymmetry between healthcare providers and patients. How far a patient who establishes the first connection with the health system can progress within the system is again subject to the decisions of health professionals. Depending on the patient's condition, its inclusion from the right point in the system and its progress as required are direct determinants of the effectiveness and efficiency of the system and therefore its social costs.

At this critical point, the most traditional, most discussed but most effective mechanism used is gatekeeping. In fact, the practice, which aims to ensure that each patient is included in the system from the right point and receives as much service as necessary and leaves the authority in this regard to the physicians working in primary care, is criticized in many liberal countries in terms of restricting the individual freedoms of patients. It is not a popular practice especially in the eyes of citizens in terms of increasing bureaucracy, causing delays in service, and creating crowd lines in the healthcare systems where the referral chain is applied.

In fact, the Referral Chain application, which is one of the basic components of the Health Transformation Program that has shaped the last 20 years of the Turkish Health System, such as General Health Insurance, Family Medicine, Quality, and Accreditation, has not been implemented completely on populist grounds. The inability of the referral chain system to work has paved the way for patients to be included in the health system without any bureaucratic obstacles.

At first glance, it showed its true face due to the burden it created on the system after the decision not to implement the referral chain and therefore the gatekeeping applications, which received positive reactions with the comfort it created by the patients. Many ways have been tried to implement the Gatekeeping application in a human-oriented and value-creating way. "Neyim Var?", an artificial intelligence application that works with algorithms created based on common symptoms is an application that can direct patients to connect with the health system without dwelling on bureaucratic processes before they apply to health institutions.

2   What is "Neyim Var?"

People have always sought to find the answers to their health-related issues on their own and have made independent decisions about whether and when to seek medical advice. In order to better understand their symptoms and those of their loved ones, many people have now included the internet in their personal health toolkits. The purpose of this study was not to assess the impact of the internet on healthcare. Instead, it assesses the extent of this digital transformation, not the outcome (Fox & Duggan, 2013, n.d.).

The provision of the service (diagnosis-treatment) and the evaluation of the post-service output (discharge with healing and/or applying for complete well-being or additional treatment methods) are primarily carried out by the service provider (physician) in healthcare services, which makes them different from other types of services in that the consumer (patient) remains passive throughout the process (Toygar, 2018). The main logic of the application is to ensure that users have preliminary information about the symptoms they have shown before applying to a health center. Thus, it is aimed to create a virtual referral chain in a sense by ensuring that users are directed to the right clinic in line with the symptoms they have.

According to the Ministry of Health (MoH), approximately 2 million people are examined every day in Turkey, and 6 percent of them apply to an inappropriate department (Neyim Var, 2021, n.d.). The application, which will make the service delivery more efficient by reducing the number of applications made to the inappropriate department, is an artificial intelligence-supported platform that makes possible diagnostic suggestions according to the complaints of the users and tries to direct the users to the most appropriate clinic. Citizens can log into the application, which was developed and implemented by the MoH, with e-Nabız or e-Government accounts (https://neyimvar.gov.tr/).

After users log in to the application, they can specify what their complaints are in different ways. Presenting complaints can be submitted by writing in the text box with autocomplete feature or by selecting ready-made texts related to the relevant parts and symptoms in the body. In addition, the body part where the complaint is made can be selected through the three-dimensional human model (Fig. 1).

After the first step, the user is asked more specific questions about the main complaints (Fig. 2).

The possible diagnosis is determined by evaluating the answers given by the user to all questions, the symptoms he/she has previously experienced, and the tests he/she has performed by artificial intelligence (Fig. 3).

The operation of the application can be examined more closely through an example. When the complaints of "sore throat" and "cough" are entered into the system, the application will ask the user to state if she/he has any of the following complaints such as: "high fever", "joint pain", "fatigue", "headache", and "nasal flow". After selecting the complaints that are thought to be related, yes/no questions are asked such as: "is there muscle pain?", "is there nasal blockage?", "is the headache spreading from the nape of the neck to the top of the head?". After these questions are answered, possible diagnoses are listed in the last stage. In this sample, for instance, possible diagnoses such as "acute pharyngitis", "acute tonsillitis", "chronic sinusitis" and "chronic rhinitis" were suggested. In addition to these diagnoses recommended by artificial intelligence, it is also recommended to the user which clinic the user should apply to (in this case, it is recommended to apply to the family medicine, ear nose, and throat or infectious diseases) (Fig. 4).

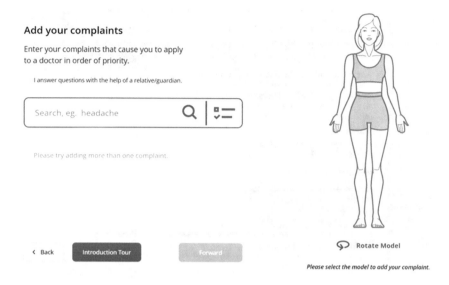

Fig. 1 The screen for adding complaints. *Source* Author's own Figure (2022)

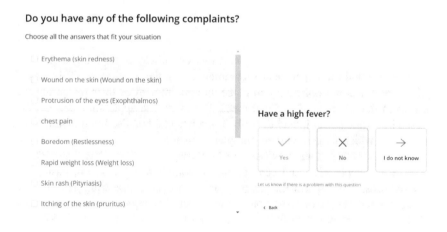

Fig. 2 An example of screen for follow-up questions related to present complaints. *Source* Author's own Figure (2022)

In the last stage of the application, the outpatient department that the user should apply to is recommended, and the user is directed to the Central Physician Appointment System (CPAS) (a system that enables people to schedule appointments with the hospitals and dentists of their choice) in order to make an appointment (Fig. 4). Thus, users can create an appointment from the relevant

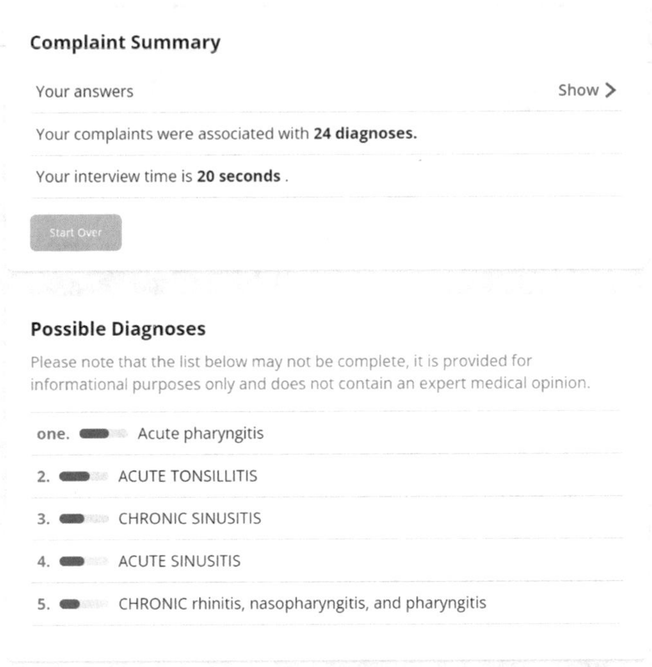

Complaint Summary

Your answers   Show >

Your complaints were associated with **24 diagnoses.**

Your interview time is **20 seconds** .

Start Over

Possible Diagnoses

Please note that the list below may not be complete, it is provided for
informational purposes only and does not contain an expert medical opinion.

one. ●●●●   Acute pharyngitis

2. ●●●●   ACUTE TONSILLITIS

3. ●●●●   CHRONIC SINUSITIS

4. ●●●●   ACUTE SINUSITIS

5. ●●●   CHRONIC rhinitis, nasopharyngitis, and pharyngitis

Fig. 3 An example of screen for complaint summary. *Source* Author's own Figure (2022)

department by connecting to CPAS with just one click, considering their possible diagnosis and the department recommended by the application. This stage is optional and it is not obligatory to make an appointment or to make an appointment from the recommended department. Therefore, the application can not only be used by patients who intend to apply to the hospital but also by individuals who want to see which diagnoses their complaints match.

Users can access their previous results through the "My Past Transactions" option in the application and can access the complaint information, past probable diagnoses, and department suggestions from each transaction. The user can also access the details of what complaints he/she has regarding each transaction and how he/she responds to the questions conveyed by the application, delete the selected transactions from the past and download the list of past transactions as a PDF.

According to the data of the MoH, "Neyim Var?" was used by 8.2 million people within 1.5 months after its implementation, more than 500 thousand people filled all their complaints and applied to physicians with the guidance of the system. MoH stated that although it is new, the application attracted great attention, that it facilitated the work of physicians, and that the data were updated and interpreted with the complaints uploaded to the system and the real diagnoses made by the physician (TRTHaber, 2021, n.d.). The Deputy Minister of Health also stated

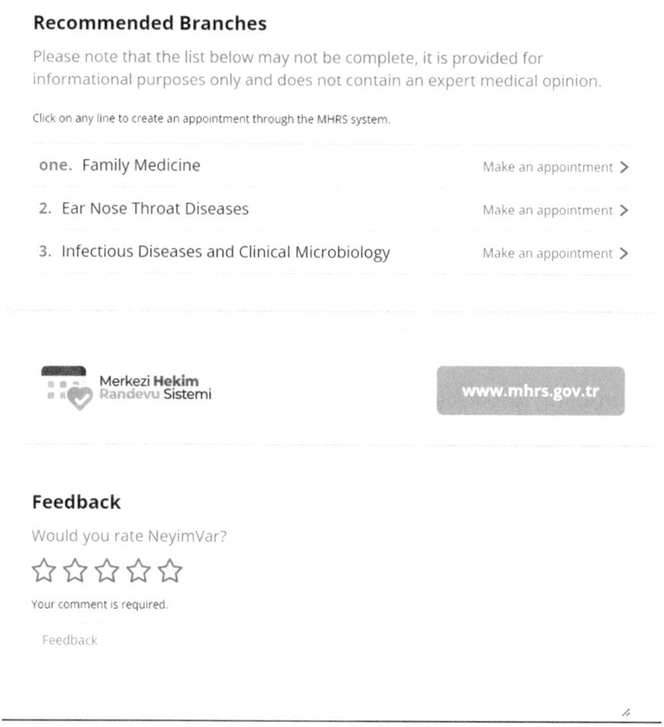

Recommended Branches

Please note that the list below may not be complete, it is provided for informational purposes only and does not contain an expert medical opinion.

Click on any line to create an appointment through the MHRS system.

one.	Family Medicine	Make an appointment >
2.	Ear Nose Throat Diseases	Make an appointment >
3.	Infectious Diseases and Clinical Microbiology	Make an appointment >

Merkezi **Hekim** Randevu Sistemi   www.mhrs.gov.tr

Feedback

Would you rate NeyimVar?

☆ ☆ ☆ ☆ ☆

Your comment is required.

Feedback

Fig. 4 An example of screen for recommended clinics. *Source* Author's own Figure (2022)

that "Neyim Var?" will yield productive results in solving problems such as individuals going to the inappropriate department, unnecessary accumulations in the secondary care, and inadequate use of the family physician, and that both costs and the burden on the health system will decrease in the long term (Anadolu Agency, 2021, n.d.).

Since the system adopts a self-learning mechanism, it is crucial to feed its algorithm with the correct data. According to the MoH officials, there were many non-patients who only used the application to test the system out of curiosity (Anadolu Agency, 2021, n.d.). In order to prevent the algorithm from being fed with incorrect data, it is asked what the purpose of the system is used at the end of each use (Fig. 5). Also as mentioned earlier, past trials can be deleted from the profile section.

In human-centered design, the focus is on human needs and how design might address them. "Neyim Var?", which can be considered an example of good practice in human-centered service design (HCD), emerges as an application that will help patients and their relatives meet their health needs faster, more accurately, and with higher quality. Since it has a self-learning system, it does not only meet the needs of patients and their relatives but also serves the purpose of facilitating the work of

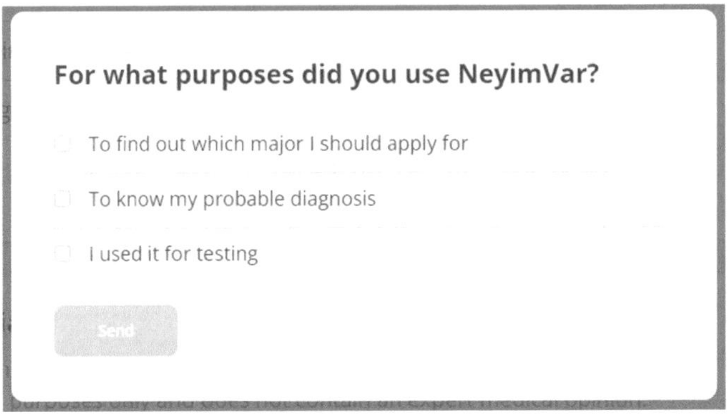

Fig. 5 The screen asking the purpose of use. *Source* Author's own Figure (2022)

physicians. For example, if there is a difference between the diagnosis suggested by the system to the patient before applying to the healthcare institution and the diagnosis made by the physician, the system carries out the self-learning process by processing these data as well. Thus, it is thought that the application, which will be covered with more patient data day by day, will help physicians to make decisions in the long run.

Although it is important to prioritize human-centered service design and attach importance to transformation and change, it is very important to integrate them with existing systems. New designs and systems developed can be successful and sustainable as long as they can be integrated with existing systems. As can be seen in the example of "Neyim Var?", the system works in integration with both the platform where electronic health records are kept (e-Pulse) and CPAS. Considering that the application is in its infancy, it is possible to say that it will become stronger in the future with the data it collects, and it will take the human-centered service delivery one step further by integrating it with different future projects.

3   Similar Applications, Potential Advantages, and Disadvantages

Applications like "Neyim Var?" with similar and identical functions are used worldwide. These programs are given below:

- Ada
- Babylon
- Buoy
- K Health
- Mediktor
- Symptomate
- WebMD

- Your.MD

The potential advantages of all the above applications can be explained as follows:

- It can reduce the burden of patients in the second and third steps by reducing unnecessary admissions.
- It could reduce waiting times.
- It could reduce the cost of treatment.
- It can increase patient satisfaction.
- It may contribute to the improvement of clinical quality.
- It may facilitate early diagnosis.
- It may reduce the negative effects of information asymmetry.
- It can make it easier for healthcare professionals to make better decisions.

It is stated that HCD applications have many advantages as well as some disadvantages. Data security concerns and the user's health problem are actually serious and may lead to the possibility of not applying to the hospital as a result of referral.

4   The Assessment of "Neyim Var?" (Conclusion)

The best available evidence is necessary to make better decisions regarding one's health and medical treatment. Unfortunately, neither well-designed observational studies nor randomized, controlled trials provide enough evidence for the majority of the decisions made today in our healthcare system. However, as powerful and sophisticated analytical tools and rich, varied digital data sources become more widely accessible for research, the research and healthcare communities now have the chance to produce the scientific evidence required to support better decisions about health and healthcare quickly and effectively (Califf et al., 2016, 2395). HCD applications can be described as an important step in this regard.

Human needs and how design might meet them are the main focus of HCD. Therefore, prior to beginning the actual development of an intervention, it is necessary to have an understanding of people, their thoughts, feelings, and behaviors as well as how they are impacted by their environment (i.e., their socio-technical system) (Melles et al., 2021, 38). We know that when individuals make decisions about their health and medical treatment without having access to enough information to make an informed decision, such decisions may be ineffective at best and harmful at worst. The only way for patients and physicians to make decisions that maximize benefits while reducing risks and, ultimately, enhance health not only at the individual level but also at the level of all communities, is when they have easy access to high-quality information. A learning health system that fully utilizes digital data to support our decision-making will be advantageous to patients, consumers, families, doctors, and society as a whole (Califf et al., 2016, 2399).

It is crucial that the HCD discipline understands doctors' evidence-based perspective and acknowledges the ethical implications of research (design) in the context of healthcare if health services are to adopt an HCD strategy. Healthcare organizations are searching for new and better ways to provide patient-centered care because of the significant organizational and social difficulties and changes they are now confronting. A growing number of health institutions are recognizing the significance of HCD techniques in response to this trend toward a more holistic, humane care perspective (Melles et al., 2021, 43).

References

Akyürek, Ç. E., & Kalaycı, E. (2019). Empowered patients as an influence of the digital age in dynamics of globalization at the crossroads of economics. In A. A. Eren & A. M. Köktaş (Eds.). Berlin: Peter Lang.

Anadolu Agency. (2021). Her 100 hastadan 6'sı yanlış doktora gidiyor. Retrieved 3 July, 2022, from https://www.aa.com.tr/tr/saglik/her-100-hastadan-6si-yanlis-doktora-gidiyor/2445330. Accessed December 22, 2021.

Califf, R. M., Robb, M. A., Bindman, A. B., Briggs, J. P., Collins, F. S., Conway, P. H., Coster, T. S., Cunningham, F. E., De Lew, N., DeSalvo, K. B., Dymek, C., Dzau, V. J., Fleurence, R. L., Frank, R. G., Gaziano, J. M., Kaufmann, P., Lauer, M., Marks, P. W., McGinnis, J. M., Richards, C., Selby, J. V., Shulkin, D. J., Shuren, J., Slavitt, A. M., Smith, S. R., Washington, B. V., White, P. J., Woodcock, J., Woodson, J., & Sherman, R. E. (2016). Transforming evidence generation to support health and health care decisions. *The New England Journal of Medicine*, *375*(24), 2395–2400. https://doi.org/10.1056/NEJMsb1610128. Retrieved July 2, 2022, from https://www.nejm.org

Fox, S., & Duggan, M. (2013). Health online 2013. Retrieved 3 July 2022, from https://www.pew research.org/internet/2013/01/15/health-online-2013/. Accessed June 30, 2022.

Macklin, R. (1993). *Enemies of patients*. Oxford: Oxford University Press.

Melles, M., Albayrak, A., & Goossens, R. (2021). Innovating health care: key characteristics of human-centered design. *International Journal for Quality in Health Care*, *33*(1), 37–44. https://doi.org/10.1093/intqhc/mzaa127.

Neyim Var. (2021). Neyim Var Portalı. Retrieved from https://neyimvar.gov.tr/. Accessed December 22, 2021.

Toygar, Ş. A. (2018). E-Sağlık Uygulamaları. *Yasama Dergisi*, *37*(2), 101–123.

TRTHaber. (2021). 'Neyim Var?' uygulamasını 1,5 ayda 8,2 milyon kişi kullandı. Retrieved July 3, 2022, from https://www.trthaber.com/haber/saglik/neyim-var-uygulamasini-15-ayda-82-mil yon-kisi-kullandi-628098.html. Accessed December 22, 2021.

Çağdaş Erkan Akyürek is an Associate Professor at Ankara University Faculty of Health Sciences, Department of Healthcare Management. He received his Ph.D. with the thesis entitled "Outsourcing in Heatlh Care System: Evaluation of Outsourcing Practices at T.R. Ministry of Health Hospitals" from Hacettepe University. His academic interest areas include Decision Making in Health Care, Health Policy and Planning, Strategic Management in Health Care, and Operations Management. He also gives lectures in his academic interest areas both in graduate and postgraduate programs.

Şükrü Anıl Toygar is an Associate Professor at Tarsus University, Faculty of Applied Sciences, Healthcare Management Department. He received his Ph.D. in Healthcare Management at Gazi

University. His research publications cover numerous areas of policy analysis, occupational health and disease, health policy, and health technologies. He gives lectures on nursing management, health policy, health technologies, and management. His articles have been published in both national and international journals.

Elif Erbay is a Research Assistant at Ankara University Faculty of Health Sciences, Department of Healthcare Management. She holds a master's degree in Healthcare Management. Her research interests include quantitative decision-making in healthcare, healthcare policy, and social media management in healthcare. She is currently working on her Ph.D. thesis titled "Forecasting the Demand for 112 Emergency Health Services and Selecting the Location of Ambulance Station: The Ankara Sample."

Patient Autonomy and User Autonomy in the Ecology of Care

Miso Kim

ABSTRACT

Patient autonomy is the foundational moral principle of healthcare. In this chapter, I review how autonomy has been conceptualized in the medical field and compare that with understandings of autonomy discussed in design. I argue that patient autonomy in healthcare has mainly been understood as negative freedom—independence from the interference of others, especially medical paternalism. Therefore, patient autonomy has been conceptualized as decision-making and has been applied to practice as a procedural means to cure rather than an end in itself. In contrast, user autonomy in design highlights positive freedom—the elevated state of one's ability to govern one's own life according to an internal will. Therefore, autonomy in design has been construed more broadly as a concept that encompasses thoughts, decisions, and actions, and has been seen as an end in itself. The collaboration of healthcare professionals and designers allows for productive opportunities to holistically support patients and their caregivers, as this collaboration brings together autonomy as means and autonomy as ends. I conclude the chapter by proposing that the study of autonomy as a guiding principle is essential in expanding healthcare service design to consider diverse agents.

M. Kim (✉)
College of Arts Media and Design, Northeastern University, 239 Ryder Hall, 360 Huntington Ave., Boston, MA 02115, United States
e-mail: m.kim@northeastern.edu

© The Author(s), under exclusive license to Springer Nature Switzerland AG 2023
M. A. Pfannstiel (ed.), *Human-Centered Service Design for Healthcare Transformation*,
https://doi.org/10.1007/978-3-031-20168-4_9

149

1   Introduction

Plato's Phaedrus begins with a symbolic setting: Socrates and Phaedrus walk outside the Athenian Wall into the wilderness to search for a suitable place for their conversation. They choose a holy place known as the location where Boreas, the God of the North Wind, carried the Athenian girl Orithyia away. Plato explains that in reality, Orithyia must have fallen from a cliff, pushed by a strong wind. Here, Plato is retelling the myth in order to reposition it as an allegory to foreshadow his later discussion about the flight and fall of the soul. In order to do this, he also adds a divine character, Pharmacia, as the playmate of Orithyia. Pharmacia is a nymph who is known to have the power to transform well water into poison or medicine, as her name, "pharmacy," indicates.

In other words, Plato is introducing the problem of a soul (Orithyia) that was experiencing a transformation, potentially related to health, as indicated by the allegory of Pharmacia, but ended up "falling" due to a conflict between inner will and external force. The significance of this story is that it introduces the most fundamental principle in medical ethics—autonomy. The rest of the Phaedrus is a discussion about the soul, a rather antique yet holistic interpretation of what constitutes a person's humanity. When the "horse" of action and the "horse" of passion are balanced via the driving factor of human reason, the "chariot" of the soul is liberated from the external necessity of the material world, represented by gravity, and gains autonomy.

Almost 2500 years have passed since Plato presumably composed the Phaedrus and described autonomy as the flight of free will toward the ethical ideal. Many more interpretations of autonomy have since been proposed, such as Rousseau's citizen self-governance (1762/2018, n.d.), Kant's self-imposed universal moral law (1785/1998, n.d.), and Nietzsche (1883/2008, n.d.)'s mastery, which balances self-love and self-respect. Psychological studies, such as self-determination theory (Deci & Ryan, 2008, pp. 182–185) and locus of control (Rotter, 1966, pp. 1–28), reveal that autonomy is essential for well-being, providing the utilitarian foundation for the importance of autonomy in healthcare. Today, healthcare is one of the areas in which research on the concept of autonomy is most active. Autonomy is one of the four pillars of medical ethics (Beauchamp & Childress, 1979, pp. 60–62) and is broadly accepted as a central value in Western medicine (Varelius, 2006, p. 377). Scholars like Jennings (2016, p. 11) even argue that autonomy is the sole foundational concept in the contemporary development of bioethics.

As the collaborative opportunities among designers and healthcare professionals increase, designers need to understand autonomy as a key moral principle of medical ethics and embed it in the services they create. Medicine is transformative, as previously indicated in the allegory of Pharmacia, and so too is service design (Karpen et al., 2017, p. 391; Kim, 2021, pp. 89–90; Sangiorgi, 2011, pp. 29–40). Patients and users shape and are shaped by the practices and processes that constitute these respective fields. Therefore, nurturing autonomy is important for enhancing patient experience in healthcare service design; furthermore, exploring a human-centered perspective in design can enhance a patient-centered approach in healthcare. However, there is a dearth of research that reviews the definitions and dimensions of patient autonomy for designers.

In this chapter, I aim to examine the concept of autonomy in healthcare and design, highlighting the importance of autonomy as a grounding principle that can integrate multidisciplinary collaboration in healthcare service design. I present autonomy's central role in medical ethics, the broadly accepted principle of patient autonomy to respect patient's rights to make independent decisions, and the recent discussions on relational autonomy. I then introduce concepts of autonomy represented in design. Designers have emphasized the need to design products and services in a way that controls technology to properly nurture the autonomy of users.

2   Autonomy in Healthcare and Design

The Dictionary of Public Health defines autonomy as "free will; self-governing, ability of a person or a group to choose a course of action. Autonomy is a basic human right and is one of the principles of bioethics (Last, 2007, n.d.)." As indicated in this definition, many scholars agree that autonomy is closely related to the concept of freedom. In this respect, Berlin's (1969, pp. 118–72) conception of negative liberty/freedom and positive liberty/freedom provides a useful framework for this study, which aims to compare autonomy in healthcare and design. According to Berlin (1969, p. 121), negative freedom refers to an external state without "the source of control or interference that can determine someone to do, or be." This conception of negative freedom often serves as a basis for an understanding of autonomy as the right to make independent, uncoerced decisions as one wishes.

However, other scholars argue that not all freedom is autonomy; many philosophers suggest that autonomy includes the responsibility to use reason to self-control one's freedom in a way that aligns with universal moral law (Rousseau, 1762/2018, n.d.; Kant, 1785/1998, n.d.; Nietzsche, 1883/2008, n.d.) In other words, respect for other agents' autonomy is the precondition for one's own autonomy. For example, Kant (1785/1998) theorizes that autonomy necessarily requires treating other humans as ends, not as means. Berlin's (1969, pp. 118–72) conception of positive freedom refers to this internal autonomy—the moral ability to effectively direct one's own life according to self-imposed rules that align with community values. Therefore, autonomy as positive freedom involves not only making independent decisions but also making good decisions, leading to the capacity to carry out actions according to one's thoughts.

I propose that patient autonomy tends to result from negative freedom, as it provides a minimal condition for freedom from external coercion, while user autonomy is an outgrowth of positive freedom, as it seeks holistic support for actions, thoughts, and decision-making. Additionally, I present two perspectives on how autonomy is discussed in practice in the two fields of healthcare and design: autonomy as means and autonomy as ends. Generally speaking, patient autonomy in healthcare approaches autonomy as a procedural means to ensure a cure as the ends. In contrast, user autonomy in design assumes autonomy as the ends of services and products/services that provide care as the means.

2.1   Patient Autonomy in Healthcare

Today, patient autonomy, or personal autonomy, is broadly accepted as a fundamental principle in healthcare. The bioethical principle of respect for autonomy generally refers to healthcare professionals' obligation to provide a condition for autonomy regarding the medical intervention or treatment that they will receive (Pugh, 2020, p. 298). Specifically, autonomy generally refers to respect for or protection of individuals' self-determination (Schermer, 2002, p. 1) that is "shaped by personal preferences and choices" (Beauchamp & Childress, 1979, p. 58), as in the definition of patient autonomy as "allowing or enabling patients to make their own decisions about which healthcare interventions they will or will not receive" (Entwistle et al., 2010, p. 41). In medical practice, patient autonomy manifests itself as minimal yet concrete procedures, such as an explanation of potential risk and the magnitude of harm in regard to certain inspections, treatments, or surgeries, as well as signing forms to ensure informed consent.

Historically, recognizing patient vulnerability has been the antecedent of patients' autonomy. The Hippocratic oath, one of the first expressions of medical ethics, reveals early concerns about protecting patients' bodies and private information from abuse (Edelstein, 1943, n.d.). In the twentieth century, respect for autonomy (RFA) evolved as a response to unethical experiments during the Second World War and medical paternalism that can lead to an imbalance of power and information. The Nuremberg Code (1947), known as the foundation of bioethics, emphasized the essentiality of the informed and voluntary consent of human subjects. The Nuremberg Code, in turn, impacted the Declaration of Geneva (1948), the Physician's Oath (1948), and the Belmont Report (1978), which clarified research-related ethical principles. The first of these principles was respect for persons (RFP), which includes a requirement to protect patient autonomy. Today, autonomy has become one of the most important principles, along with benevolence, nonmaleficence, and justice, in the foundational Principles of Biomedical Ethics published in 1979 (Beauchamp & Childress, 1979, n.d.).

Shaped by this historical background, contemporary medical ethics places a strong liberal emphasis on individual rights, such as protecting privacy and self-determined choices (Tauber, 2001, pp. 299–319). Beauchamp and Childress observe that "to respect autonomous agents is to acknowledge their right to hold views, make choices, and to take actions based on their values and beliefs" (Beauchamp & Childress, 1979, p. 106). Therefore, truth-telling, informed consent, and conditions that ensure uncoerced decision-making are emphasized. Beauchamp and Childress further assert that the following four points are integral to personal autonomy: (a) being free from the controlling influence of others, (b) being free from limitations that prevent meaningful choice, (c) being free from inadequate understanding, and (d) being able to freely act in accordance with a self-chosen plan. Burkhardt and Nathaniel (2002, pp. 205–32) also assert that underpinning personal autonomy is an environment that encourages independence and freedom of choice. In light of the points raised by scholars of medical ethics, there appear to be two essential conditions for personal autonomy: those of liberty (independence from controlling influences) and those of agency (capacity for intentional action).

However, there are also downsides to this strong focus on patients' independent choice and the provision of minimal conditions to protect patients' decisions from medical paternalism. The underlying assumption is that a generally capable individual can make autonomous decisions as long as interference is removed (Mackenzie & Stoljar, 2000, n.d.). It is often presupposed that patients are rational and are well aware of what decisions are best for their well-being. This liberal, procedural, and rather narrow interpretation of autonomy based on negative freedom becomes problematic because it can miss other complicated aspects of autonomy that often pose challenges to less-represented populations and require more active interventions (Entwistle et al., 2010, pp. 741–745).

As for an alternative, recent studies highlight the importance of relational autonomy proposed by feminist theorists. Individuals are products of their social relationships, which often limit or enhance their autonomy (Friedman, 1986, pp. 26–29). Many studies in healthcare, especially nursing and gerontology literature, argue for the need to expand the concept of patient autonomy beyond atomism and decisional autonomy regarding a specific medical situation (Perkins et al., 2012, pp. 214–215; Walker, 2000, 97–111; Lindberg et al., 2014, pp. 2208–2221). A relational view of patient autonomy provides a critical examination of conditions that can reduce autonomy and sheds light on how autonomy can be shared and assisted (Mackenzie & Stoljar, 2000, n.d.), as individuals who were traditionally seen as less capable of independence can still have the capacity for autonomy with proper support (Sherwin & Winsby, 2011, pp. 182–190). This emphasis on relational autonomy calls for the need to expand and diversify these minimal, individualistic conceptions of autonomy to a more holistic ecology of care (Lindberg et al., 2014, pp. 2208–2221). Here, design can play a key role in actively mediating not only patients and healthcare professionals but also the family and personal relationships of patients, with the help of products and services.

2.2   User Autonomy in Design

The term "patient autonomy" is seldom referenced in the field of design, but there are a few recent studies that show that this topic is an emerging theme in healthcare design. Zhu et al. (2020, pp. 230–244) propose using bioethical conditions for promoting patient autonomy as principles for designing a healthcare environment that respects the autonomy of patients. Kim et al. (2022, pp. 143–164) discuss the importance of relational autonomy in older adults' healthcare and later-life transitions and propose utilizing autonomy as a key principle in service design.

Another area in which autonomy in a healthcare context has been actively studied is assistive technology. Güldenpfennig et al.'s (2019, pp. 1–14) study on people with multiple sclerosis using assistive devices shows that design plays a central role in promoting or restricting autonomy by helping users manage factors that are closely related to their sense of autonomy, such as digital technology. The mission statement of the Active and Assisted Living (AAL) program of the European Union is to extend "the time people can live in their preferred environment by increasing their autonomy, self-confidence, and mobility."

There are further studies that have researched the autonomy of users in the context of their relationship with technology. Friedman (1998, pp. 26–29) discusses the significance of users' control over technology and how technology should be designed to enhance users' lives. Littlewood (1996, pp. 427–435) proposes that the "ability (knowledge about the choices available)" and "willingness (motivation and beliefs about one's own capabilities)" of users are important factors that promote their autonomous use of technologies. Calvo et al. (2014, pp. 37–40) propose the importance of environments and tools that promote autonomy in users' everyday activities through personalized design that supports the psychological development of users. While these studies focus on human agents' use of technology as tools, recent discussions on autonomy highlight the interaction between two agents—human agents and artificial intelligence (AI). Here, the focus is on the difference between automation and autonomy of technology, and how AI can support and benefit human autonomy (De Visser et al., 2018, pp. 1409–1427; Rozenblit, 1992, pp. 1–18), which is often related to ethics for responsible AI. As healthcare is a sector where new technologies are constantly adopted and adapted, these studies on human autonomy in relation to technology acquire newfound importance in healthcare service design.

Design principles and theories are other important areas in discussions on autonomy in design. For example, Friedman (1996, n.d.) proposes user autonomy as one of the key principles in her theory of value-sensitive design. She posits that designers should perceive users as autonomous agents who can best promote their own values. Davy (2015, pp. 132–148) discusses the autonomy of vulnerable individuals as an important concept in inclusive design, in which there is a need to expand the concept of autonomy to include diverse people who deviate from the standardized images of users. Millar (2015, pp. 47–55) argues that a designed thing serves as a moral proxy in a designer–technology–user trio, as it acts on behalf of a person. He proposes that designers should pay attention to avoiding paternalism and respecting user autonomy, drawing upon the conception of human moral proxies in healthcare. Scholars in the 2014 Conference on Human Factors in Computing Systems (Calvo et al., 2014, 37–40) workshop collectively organized different conceptions of autonomy as principles in design as follows: (a) enhancing users' sense of control over technology; (b) supporting independence in users' daily lives; (c) empowering users to create their own technology, which makes them more autonomous; and (d) fostering autonomy as an overarching characteristic of psychological development.

Overall, the conceptions of user autonomy in design are different from the conceptions of patient autonomy in several aspects. User autonomy in design illuminates broader, general senses of positive freedom that coordinate one's action to align with one's belief, preferred situation, or moral value. Therefore, I argue that the conception of autonomy in design is broader than patient autonomy—it encompasses contexts such as socio-cultural situations and human connections, thought, identity, and autonomous action, which expands the relatively narrow interpretation of patient autonomy simply as decision-making. Therefore, autonomy in design is considered an end in itself—designers create products and services that are geared toward solving specific problems, but this is, in the end, to enhance the autonomy of those who use it. This self-justifying nature of user autonomy is in contrast to the procedural nature of patient autonomy.

However, I argue that patient autonomy and user autonomy are not necessarily diametrically opposed. Rather, these concepts complement each other by connecting two different opportunities of healthcare for the patient-user: the point of cure in a hospital setting, and the points of care throughout patients' lives where the patient and their family and diverse service experts manage their health. Procedural autonomy as means is more practical in the former case, while the latter case should aim for a broader sense of self-justifying autonomy as ends to position the patient's life at the center of care. By providing practical, objective, and efficient guidelines in the form of informed consent, medical professionals can ensure that they provide minimal, but concrete and essential, conditions that allow for the decisional autonomy of patients. From the patient's perspective, they have to manage their own health in their everyday lives, and medical treatment is just one aspect of living autonomously. Designers can intervene with products and services to support patient-users' autonomy in a holistic way and enhance their relational autonomy by actively connecting them with other agents of care.

3   Case Study: Designing for the Health Autonomy of Older Adults

Managing one's own health is an important aspect of autonomy and requires design intervention, as this activity needs holistic support, such as access to health information, health literacy, and proper communication among people who are important to a patient's life. To demonstrate how different conceptions of autonomy can be applied to healthcare design, I introduce a service design project titled "Designing for the Health Autonomy of Older Adults" as a case study. In this academic project, our research team interviewed 15 adults aged 65 years and older and 5 caregivers at three local senior homes (The Hearth at Olmsted Green, the Grove at Olmsted Green, and St. Helena's House in Boston) and one senior community center (Boston Centers for Youth and Families Grove Hall Senior Center) in Greater Boston Area, Massachusetts, USA, to learn about the factors that nurture or thwart seniors' health autonomy. The participants included 17 females and 3 males; 10 were African American, 3 were Caucasian, 2 were Asian, and 5 were of other races, including those who identified as mixed race. All the participants suffered from at least one chronic disease and were in need of home-based self-care.

The outcome of this research reveals that there is a need to support autonomy both as means and ends to comprehensively support older patients as they navigate their everyday lives. Our participants expressed that they wanted information to enhance their decisions in healthcare not only when they found themselves in medical treatment situations but also in other situations in which they are advocating for their health. These could include conversations about disease prevention, health insurance negotiations, and other encounters with healthcare professionals, such as making appointments (see Fig. 1). At the same time, they wanted this information personalized so that it was relevant to their everyday needs, rather than in a form of abstract knowledge that is less applicable to their specific needs and action goals. Said information could help them carry out practical tasks, which would enhance their sense of autonomy in their lives. The participants also strongly preferred plans that privilege relational autonomy by involving their family members, friends, senior-home caregivers, public service workers, and healthcare professionals, such as primary-care physicians, nurses, and pharmacists whom they trust.

According to these findings, the team initially generated a service concept that utilizes storytelling and games to move the foci of health information from topic-based nouns (e.g., broken hipbone) to scenario-based actions (e.g., what do I do

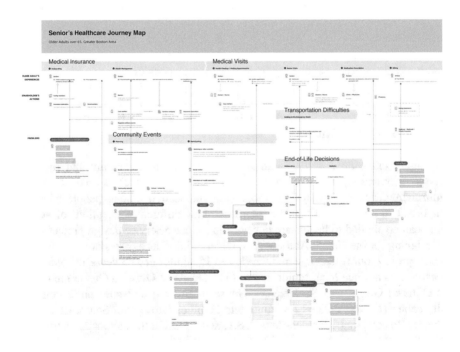

Fig. 1 Seniors' healthcare journey map. *Source* Author's own figure (2022)

if I fall and cannot stand up?) that are contextualized in seniors' everyday lives and tasks. These games included themes such as action (making appointments and visiting hospitals using mobile apps), decision (creating protocols for emergency situations), and thought (deliberating in advance on end-of-life care). However, the COVID-19 pandemic mandated that people quarantine and practice social distancing, which forced our team to shift the focus of our research to prioritizing the urgent needs of the isolated residents in local senior homes. Therefore, as the next phase of the health autonomy project, we collaborated with Middlesex Community College's nursing students to provide basic health checkups and disseminate health information to isolated older adults in our partnering organization, the Peter Sanborn Center for Senior Living in Reading, Massachusetts (see Fig. 2).

Procedural support (autonomy as means) for decisional autonomy gained key significance in this extreme situation. When conducting the research, we followed the Institutional Review Board (IRB) protocol thoroughly. The IRB approval process to ensure research participants' informed consent is one of the methods that designers have adopted from biomedical research, which systematically embeds procedural autonomy in the design process. However, the situation senior residents faced, in which they were isolated in their rooms and only a limited number of service workers had access to the senior homes, created additional challenges. A more difficult and particular factor was our participants' low technology literacy. We were unable to use virtual platforms, such as Zoom, for our research. Therefore, the assistance of senior-home workers was essential for promoting procedural autonomy. Instead of interviewing the participants in person or gathering

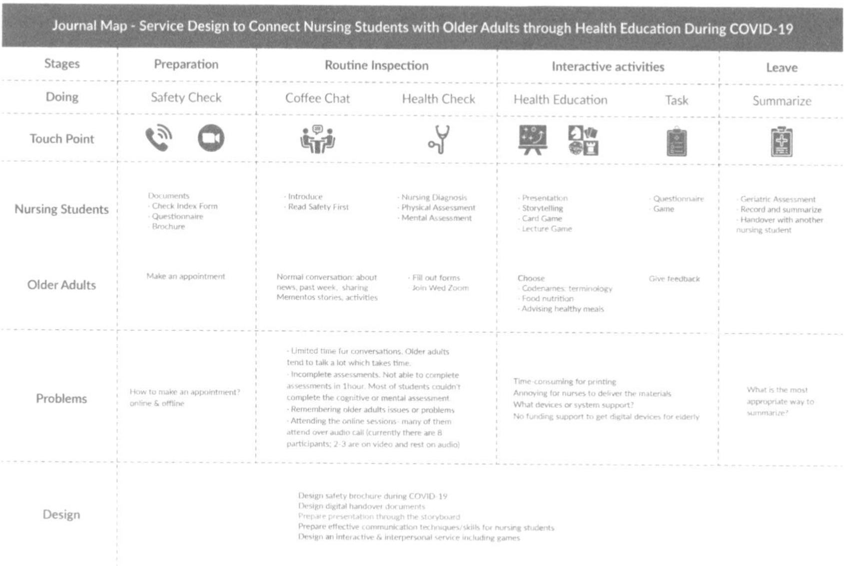

Fig. 2 Health checkup and well-being education journey map. *Source* Author's own figure (2022)

opinions in focus group sessions, we distributed multiple surveys, newsletters, and flyers via senior-home workers to ensure the participation and informed procedural autonomy of the senior residents.

As the COVID-19 situation improved, we gained permission from the management for nursing students to enter the senior homes and perform basic health checkups on senior residents who wanted the service. Therefore, the senior residents had to make a decision: whether to minimize their exposure to COVID-19 by not participating in this event or to participate in the health checkup event to alleviate the impact of not being able to visit hospitals regularly during the pandemic. In order to create an environment to optimize the residents' decisional autonomy, the team thoroughly informed them about the face-to-face meeting and health checkup protocols. We also provided the residents with details of the students' action protocols that they would be following to protect the seniors from potential exposure to the COVID-19 virus. In order to deliver all this information, we also created digital journals, information flyers, and a service blueprint that outlined the face-to-face assessment procedures. Senior-home workers also communicated with the residents to explain the procedures and conducted surveys so that the service design could reflect the opinions and preferences of the senior residents. For example, the surveys showed that the majority of senior residents preferred personalized health checkups in their rooms rather than collective outdoor events in which residents undergo checkups together. Therefore, we designed the service accordingly such that nursing students would visit residents' rooms wearing personal protective equipment.

During this process, we also intended to utilize and nurture relational autonomy. Studies show that older adults' autonomy is characterized by its emphasis on connectedness rather than independence, highlighting the importance of relational autonomy (Kim et al., 2022, pp. 143–164). Many design solutions today aim to provide services that individuals can use independently on their personal devices. However, we learned that older adults who are not familiar with technology generally gain a better sense of control when communicating with real people instead of using digital interfaces. Therefore, throughout the pandemic, senior residents' sense of relational autonomy has been significantly impacted because of their isolation from human interaction and the digitalization of services. Our research provided the conditions for senior residents to communicate frequently with senior-home staff members, as we sought to fortify our participants' procedural autonomy. Additionally, this project helped the senior residents become more connected to healthcare networks and the local community via interactions with nursing students. As a result of the increased communication, the residents' relational autonomy has also been improved.

In addition to the health checkup, we created a series of wellness lectures delivered by nursing students. The goal of this lecture series is to nurture the foundational capability for autonomous action—in this case, we interpreted autonomy as an end in itself as the outcome of this project. Each week, two nursing students selected various health-related topics and conducted hour-long lectures for 10–15 participants. These lectures were provided virtually via Zoom in order to allow for social distancing. Therefore, the team first had to increase the technology literacy of older adults. The team helped senior residents to adapt to virtual meetings by designing how-to-join flyers, troubleshooting questionnaires, guidelines for senior home-owned devices that could be rented, and information cards that the participants kept next to their phones. By improving the residents' technology literacy, we not only wanted to engage the participants in virtual lectures but also encourage them to overcome fears of new technologies and increase their action capacity by teaching them to use digital services. Contemporary healthcare services are increasingly incorporating digital technology; therefore, digital literacy education is fundamental to a patient's actional autonomy, as they can manage their own well-being and pursue healthier lives.

In addition, we designed the lectures such that senior residents were continually engaged. Thus, we drew upon research we had conducted prior to the COVID-19 pandemic regarding the creation of personalized, thematic games designed to enhance seniors' health autonomy. These games are personalized in that they account for each resident's unique needs and the particular everyday situations in which they find themselves. The design ideas that we embedded in the wellness lectures included a hybrid bingo game, conversational objects, and goodie bags with instructions and tools so that our subjects could participate in the game, as well as audio-based prompts for those who did not have a computer but were participating via phone. Our intention was to help the senior residents make direct connections between the systematic knowledge that they gain from the lectures and their resultant improved sense of actional autonomy. This improved sense of autonomy is exemplified in activities such as planning for health scenarios in advance and setting goals, thereby taking actions that contribute positively to their health.

After the partnering organization finished giving vaccines to senior residents, the management center developed the wellness education sessions into an official program offered as an ongoing series by the organization's regional wellness nurses, using our tools to facilitate conversations and activities (see Fig. 3). Additionally, we are in the process of exploring procedural autonomy by utilizing a deliberate forum (Fishkin & Luskin, 2005, n.d.) for enhancing the senior residents' autonomy as thoughts when deciding the topics and ideas of these wellness lectures. Deliberate forum is a grassroots, democratic process that enables citizens to deliberate about local issues with the support of structural processes. We will assess how collective decision-making about the topics, forms, and games comprising the lectures can serve as a self-sustainable system that supports the autonomous co-design of the lecture series by senior residents and staff members.

Fig. 3 Touchpoint materials created for the wellness session series. *Source* Author's own figure (2022)

4   Discussion

I have reviewed how autonomy has been conceptualized by healthcare and design scholars. Broadly speaking, healthcare scholars have focused on procedures that protect decisional autonomy in medical interventions, while design scholars extend the conception of autonomy to include relational and actional autonomy in broader contexts. I argue that the study of autonomy is essential in developing human-centered principles of healthcare service design, as services are coproduced by diverse people, and there is a need to consider the different aspects of these multiple agents. Multidimensional concepts of autonomy will help expand the concept of healthcare services and create opportunities for design interventions, hence broadening the horizon of possibilities that healthcare services can strive to achieve and offer. I will discuss the autonomy of multiple agents who are involved in the system of cure and care and highlight a few questions that can nurture discussions of autonomy in healthcare service design and the development of methods, tools, and projects.

4.1   Autonomy of Patients

Patients are not a single entity, as discussed in the scholarly literature about relational autonomy, and providing support to better connect people is one way that designers can provide their expertise. Scholars of healthcare service design need to include relational identity in their discussions of autonomy in addition to discussing individual identity. Moreover, they should extend their concept of an autonomous unit from an individual to their family and caregivers. Such a shift opens up the possibility of expanding the service system so that it is more inclusive and thus considers the autonomy of patients who do not express themselves in the same way that so-called standard patients would. These patients would include children, people with mental issues, or patients with other severe conditions, such as dementia or terminal cancer. The discussions of people with disabilities and chronic disease reveal that their autonomy is intensely situational. I argue that the dependency that arises due to these conditions does not necessarily diminish a patient's autonomy. Rather, dependency can supplement one's autonomy from the perspective of seeing the patient as a holistic person. How can we design a system that considers the unique needs of less-represented populations and, in so doing, arrive at a more comprehensive understanding of autonomy? How can we design systems that provide holistic support in the ecology of care as ongoing processes that benefit patients and their families throughout their lives? How can designers gradually nurture the autonomy of patients during their transition from cure (e.g., surgery) to care (e.g., continued self-care) phase so that the patient recovers their life in a holistic sense? How can designers create services to provide personalized support for the different autonomy needs of patients, which could include autonomy of thought, autonomy of action, and autonomy of decision-making?

4.2   Autonomy of Healthcare Workers

The principle of respecting patient autonomy in medical ethics has evolved to protect the decisional rights of patients, but at the same time, it is also a procedure created to protect healthcare workers from potential conflict with patients and their families. Doctors are only a small part of the diverse community of experts and laborers who support healthcare systems, and issues associated with a lack of protocols and burnout of healthcare workers have surfaced during the pandemic. How can we create a system that can better support the autonomy of these workers and also protect their decisional rights? How can services and products help these workers so that they can carry out actions that reflect the decisions of patients and their families? Additionally, in practice, there are continued efforts by healthcare workers to support patients so that they can make "correct" decisions. How can services and products nudge patients and their family members so that they can make the best decisions while keeping the efficiency of autonomy grounded in the concept of negative freedom?

4.3   Autonomy of Designers

One thing that differentiates the field of design from fine art may be that designers must consider the unique needs of various agents when designing, especially those of users. However, there have been more discussions that suggest designers do have authority over the design process and about how the autonomy of designers influences the value manifested in products and services. Designers can learn from the history of medical ethics, as the relationship between the autonomy of designers and the autonomy of users recalls discussions about medical paternalism and the autonomy of patients. For example, when considering medical paternalism and patient's rights, designers can examine the array of healthcare design products and services on a spectrum. At one end, there are products and services that strongly reflect the intention of the designer and limit the autonomy of users. At the other end, there are products and services that ask so much of users that users become confused. How can we balance the autonomy of designers, users, and clients when making design decisions and determining the intended usage of healthcare products and services? How can we create more concrete methods, models, and tools that can help designers to consider the autonomy needs of multiple agents when designing and thus strive for balanced autonomy in healthcare design research and processes? What can design learn from healthcare in terms of respect for autonomy? For example, as there is already an emphasis on autonomy as ends in the field of design, designers should learn from healthcare experts' concept of autonomy as means. In so doing, designers can more concretely develop systematized procedures in the creation, usage, and evaluation of healthcare services and products from the perspective of autonomy.

4.4   Autonomy of Technology

Technology is a new agent in healthcare ecology, which is one reason why design is gaining critical importance in healthcare. Many people share the expectation that fast-evolving technology will soon obtain its own autonomy. In the near future, highly autonomous machines and intelligences will manage social systems, even without the intervention of human agents. Although these technologies may not entirely usurp human agents, this situation begs the question: What is the role of designers in a society where technology will gain autonomy when there is no proper support for people's autonomy? This question is especially applicable to healthcare where patient autonomy is crucial. In this respect, it is essential to develop the ethics and guidelines of healthcare design, especially in relation to evolving technology. I would argue that the concept of autonomy based on positive freedom is synonymous with the philosophical tradition of moral autonomy (autonomy of thought), which is closely tied not only to individual identity but also to the moral value of certain societies. Design materializes these thoughts and helps users to reflect them in their decisions and actions in a way that can be justifiable to all stakeholders. In this sense, design is a moral process, especially when designers create healthcare-related products and services that directly impact people's lives and well-being. Therefore, designers need to pay ethical attention to the design of healthcare services and products when incorporating technology, which will be another key agent.

5 Conclusion

In this chapter, I have introduced the diverse conceptions of autonomy discussed in both healthcare and design. This study contributes to these two fields by providing a grounding principle of autonomy for the collaboration between healthcare and design. I propose that there is a need to expand the burgeoning discussion of autonomy in healthcare design and provide a more comprehensive understanding of autonomy that considers autonomy as both means and ends. The discussion on autonomy provides a framework for healthcare service designers to develop methods and tools that highlight the importance of autonomy in design processes. The study of autonomy as a human-centered principle of healthcare design provides a new lens for scholars who study medical and design ethics. I hope this chapter will provide the opportunity for the design community to discuss autonomy beyond the control of interface to a broader service-level consideration and a self-justifying value of design that supports people's everyday lives.

References

Beauchamp, T. L., & Childress, J. F. (1979). *Principles of biomedical ethics.* New York, Oxford: Oxford University Press.

Berlin, I. (1969). Two concepts of liberty. In I. Berlin (Eds.), *Four essays on liberty* (pp. 118–172). London, UK: Oxford University Press.

Burkhardt, M. A., & Nathaniel, A. K. (2002). Practice issues related to patient self-determination. In N. Y. Albany (Ed.), *Ethics & issues in contemporary nursing* (pp. 205–232). Albany, NY: Delmar Thomson Learning Inc.

Calvo, R. A., Peters, D., Johnson, D. & Rogers, Y. (2014). Autonomy in technology design, In *ACM CHI 2014 extended abstracts on human factors in computing systems* (pp. 37–40).

Davy, L. (2015). Philosophical inclusive design: Intellectual disability and the limits of individual autonomy in moral and political theory. *Hypatia, 30*(1), 132–148.

Deci, E. L., & Ryan, R. M. (2008). Self-determination theory: A macrotheory of human motivation, development, and health. *Canadian Psychology/psychologie Canadienne, 49*(3), 182–185.

De Visser, E. J., Pak, R., & Shaw, T. H. (2018). From automation to autonomy: The importance of trust repair in human–machine interaction. *Ergonomics, 61*(10), 1409–1427.

Edelstein, L. (1943). *The hippocratic oath: Text, translation and interpretation.* Baltimore, MD: The Johns Hopkins Press.

Entwistle, V. A., Carter, S. M., Cribb, A., & McCaffery, K. (2010). Supporting patient autonomy: The importance of clinician-patient relationships. *Journal of General Internal Medicine, 25*(7), 741–745.

Fishkin, J. S., & Luskin, R. C. (2005). Experimenting with a democratic ideal: Deliberative polling and public opinion. *Acta Politica, 40*(3), 284–298.

Friedman, B. (1996). Value-sensitive design, *Interactions, 3*(6), 16–23.

Friedman, B. (1998). User autonomy: Who should control what and when? A CHI 96 workshop. *ACM SIGCHI Bulletin, 30*(1), 26–29.

Friedman, M. A. (1986). Autonomy and the split-level self. *The Southern Journal of Philosophy, 24*(1), 19–35.

Güldenpfennig, F., Mayer, P., Panek, P. & Fitzpatrick, G. (2019). An autonomy-perspective on the design of assistive technology experiences of people with multiple sclerosis. In *The ACM CHI conference on human factors in computing systems*, Glasgow, UK (pp. 1–14), 4–9 May.

Jennings, B. (2016). Reconceptualizing autonomy: A relational turn in bioethics. *Hastings Center Report, 46*(3), 11–16.

Kant, I. (1785/1998). *Groundwork for the metaphysics of morals* (M. Gregor, Trans.). Cambridge, UK: Cambridge University Press.

Karpen, I. O., Gemser, G., & Calabretta, G. (2017). A multilevel consideration of service design conditions: Towards a portfolio of organisational capabilities, interactive practices and individual abilities. *Journal of Service Theory and Practice, 27*(2), 384–407.

Kim, M. (2021). A study of dignity as a principle of service design. *International Journal of Design, 15*(3), 87–100.

Kim, M., Ramdin, V., Pozzar, R., Fombelle, P., Zhou, X., Zhang, Y., & Jiang, M. (2022). Healthy aging adviser: Designing a service to support the life transitions and autonomy of older adults. *The Design Journal, 25*(2), 143–164.

Last, J. M. (2007). *A dictionary of public health.* Oxford, UK: Oxford University Press.

Nietzsche, F. (1883/2008). *Thus spoke Zarathustra: A book for everyone and nobody.* Oxford, UK: Oxford University Press.

Lindberg, C., Fagerström, C., Sivberg, B., & Willman, A. (2014). Concept analysis: Patient autonomy in a caring context. *Journal of Advanced Nursing, 70*(10), 2208–2221.

Littlewood, W. (1996). Autonomy: An anatomy and a framework. *System, 24*(4), 427–435.

Mackenzie, C., & Stoljar, N. (Eds.). (2000). *Relational autonomy: Feminist perspectives on autonomy, agency, and the social self.* Oxford, UK: Oxford University Press.

Millar, J. (2015). Technology as moral proxy: Autonomy and paternalism by design. *IEEE Technology and Society Magazine, 34*(2), 47–55.

Perkins, M. M., Ball, M. M., Whittington, F. J., & Hollingsworth, C. (2012). Relational autonomy in assisted living: A focus on diverse care settings for older adults. *Journal of Aging Studies, 26*(2), 214–225.

Plato, P. (1995). Translated by A. Nehamas and P. Woodruff. Indianapolis, IN: Hackett.

Pugh, J. (2020). *Autonomy, rationality, and contemporary bioethics.* Oxford, UK: Oxford University Press.

Rotter, J. B. (1966). Generalized expectancies for internal versus external control of reinforcement. *Psychological Monographs: General and Applied, 80*(1), 1–28.

Rousseau, J. J. (1762/2018). *The social contract and other later political writings.* Cambridge, UK: Cambridge University Press.

Rozenblit, J. W. (1992). Design for autonomy: An overview, *Applied Artificial Intelligence an International Journal. 6*(1), 1–18.

Sangiorgi, D. (2011). Transformative services and transformation design. *International Journal of Design, 5*(2), 29–40.

Schermer, M. (2002). *The different faces of autonomy: Patient autonomy in ethical theory and hospital practice* (Vol. 13). Berlin, Germany: Springer Science & Business Media.

Sherwin, S., & Winsby, M. (2011). A relational perspective on autonomy for older adults residing in nursing homes. *Health Expectations, 14*(2), 182–190.

Tauber, A. I. (2001). Historical and philosophical reflections on patient autonomy. *Health Care Analysis, 9*(3), 299–319.

Varelius, J. (2006). The value of autonomy in medical ethics. *Medicine, Health Care and Philosophy, 9*(3), 377–388.

Walker, M. U. (2000). Getting out of line: Alternatives to life as, *Mother time: Women, aging, and ethics* (pp. 97–111).

Zhu, L., Zhang, S. & Lu, Z. (2020). Respect for autonomy: Seeking the roles of healthcare design from the principle of biomedical ethics, *HERD: Health Environments Research & Design Journal, 13*(3), 230–244.

Dr. Miso Kim, Ph.D., is an assistant professor in the Department of Arts + Design at Northeastern University. She is the founding co-director of the Healthcare and Wellness Design Lab, and the design director of the NuLawLab, an interdisciplinary laboratory of legal design. She studies service design through humanist frameworks. Specifically, she is interested in enhancing dignity, autonomy, and participation in service. She has worked on more than seven projects in collaboration with local senior homes and organizations to enhance the autonomy of older adults. She holds a Ph.D. in Design, an M.Des in Interaction Design, and an M.Des in Information Design from the School of Design at Carnegie Mellon University. She also holds a B.S. in Architecture from Sungkyunkwan University. Prior to joining Northeastern, she worked as a Senior User Experience Designer at Cisco Systems in Silicon Valley. She is the co-editor of the upcoming book, Legal Design: Dignifying People in Legal Systems.

Innovative Service Design for Global Health

Lesley Clack and Rachel Ellison

ABSTRACT

Innovative service design has become popular in recent years, particularly in healthcare. Innovative service design thinking can be used to differentiate organizations from their competition and help them to compete in global markets. In order for organizations to implement innovative services designs, it is important for them to understand the challenges with service design thinking for global health, identify innovative ways of thinking about service design in healthcare on a global scale, and understand the process of implementing an innovative service design on a global scale. Frameworks such as the ExpandNet/World Health Organization Scaling-Up Strategy are important for providing a strategy for organizations to follow. For healthcare organizations to be successful in the current market faced with rapid advancement of technology and globalization, innovative service design is essential.

1   Introduction

Innovative service design is an inventive application centered around design thinking methods that coincide with the development of services (Eberling, 2019, n.d.). These services are existing services that can be improved or completely new services that are created. Innovative service design has become popular over the past few years with the focus on improving customer experiences. The popularity in

L. Clack (✉)
Department of Health Sciences, Marieb College of Health and Human Services, Florida Gulf Coast University, 10501 FGCU Blvd., S. Fort Myers, FL 33965, USA
e-mail: lclack@fgcu.edu

R. Ellison
University of Louisiana at Lafayette, 104 E University Dr. Lafayette, Lafayette, LA 70504, USA

growth stems from the need to include a human perspective, one that is designed around customers and their experiences (Panwar & Kahn, 2021, p. 25).

Customers want to be heard and met with respect when receiving goods and services, especially when they are paying for them. Customers have very high expectations when receiving services. They tend to want an inspiring experience (Eberling, 2019, n.d.). Recent studies have shown that organizations believe they provide "above-average" customer service experiences. Data from those studies show that only 8% of customers share that view (Eberling, 2019, n.d.). There is a clear gap in the way organizations view customer service and the way customers view what exceptional customer service is.

Innovative service design thinking can be used to differentiate organizations from the competition and gain loyal customers. The process of using design thinking methods to garner competition and gain loyal customers may take different approaches to succeed. Some of the approaches include:

- Research: Using research methods to understand employees and customers ' expectations.
- Ideation: Using creative and human-centered focused ideas.
- Prototyping: Testing new ideas before implementation (Eberling, 2019, n.d.; Panwar & Kahn, 2021, p. 30).

Innovative service design and design thinking methods are used to foster relationships among organizations and customers and are essential to improve the overall customer service experience. These approaches have been implemented in many industries and have resulted in successful outcomes.

The health industry has always been in the forefront when it comes to customer experiences. The health industry depends on positive customer service experiences to enhance customer loyalty and to establish a value-creating culture where customers' needs are met (Berry, 2019, p. 80). Global health and healthcare in general embark upon the methods and ideologies of innovative service design and implement the approaches where necessary. Global health is defined as improving health and achieving health equity for all people worldwide, and the shift from an innovative design standpoint is now on individual health and not on health care (Chauhan et al., 2021, p. 286).

Our global society was pushed to the brink during the pandemic that began in early 2020. There was not only much success with global health response but also lessons and areas of improvement that need to be addressed. People and their well-being were impacted by the pandemic. Innovative service design has the potential to shape and provide solutions for global health initiatives.

After reading this chapter, you will be able to:

- Understand the challenges with service design thinking for global health.
- Identify innovative ways of thinking about service design in healthcare on a global scale.

- Understand the process of implementing an innovative service design on a global scale.
- Examine the World Health Organization (WHO)'s Scaling-Up Strategy and explore its use in innovative service design for global health.

2 Challenges for Service Design Thinking

There can be barriers and challenges when introducing service design thinking to an industry, field of work, or even a group of individuals that are hearing about it for the first time. Service design thinking is a practical way to improve existing services or design new ones to meet the needs and demands of customers in practically any field (Ash, 2017, n.d.). Service design thinking, particularly service business model innovation, is especially important in today's value-driven healthcare environment (Clack, 2017).

Innovation in health care is mostly driven by the need for smarter and better solutions for customers (Ash, 2017, n.d.). This can cause challenges on many levels. Utilizing service design thinking on a global scale can take time and buy-in from many involved parties, stakeholders, customers, and healthcare leaders. It is best to approach the challenges with confidence and a plan.

Challenges and barriers:

- Regulatory and governance standards.
- Resistance to change.
- Siloed mentality.
- Lack of buy-in.
- Time and pressure.
- Short-term thinking (Ash, 2017, n.d.).

As mentioned earlier in the chapter, global health has been in the forefront since the emergence of the COVID-19 pandemic. Since then, providing customer-centered care has taken a much-needed front seat in conversations to improve the design of customer service and care. The challenges listed above are not new and will continue to evolve over time. "Over the last decade we, as practitioners of design of global health, have been encouraged by the increasing changes in the field, to promote empathy, equity and inclusion" (Chauhan et al., 2021, p. 290). A transformation in language is a simple example of a design change. For example, changing the word "patient" to "customer" is more inclusive (Chauhan et al., 2021, p. 285). On a small scale, this seems simple, but, on a global scale, it is a challenging endeavor.

To address challenges on a global scale it is beneficial to first define the challenge, the range of stakeholders, the users, and customers (Chauhan et al., 2021, p. 286). It will be necessary to understand the challenge from a customer's point of view. Get their feedback and ideas. Communication is a boundless tool used in service design thinking (Ash, 2017, n.d,).

Globally, service design thinking has already made an impact in healthcare. The advancement in technology has improved patient care immensely. Mobile health and telehealth have made it possible for a large portion of people in the world to have access to health services (Ash, 2017, n.d.). There were challenges and still are many barriers in innovation and technology to allow for more access and equity for all people worldwide. From the challenges of service design thinking thus far, the lessons learned are to keep the big picture in mind and strive to provide the best customer-centered experience (Chauhan et al., 2021, p. 292).

3   Innovative Ways of Thinking

The emphasis on innovation promises the acceleration of growth in specific areas relating to customer experiences (Clack & Ellison, 2019, p. 86). Thinking innovatively, especially in the realm of healthcare and global health, the mind tends to think of technological advancements and customer-centered care. This thinking, service design thinking, is currently being used in the areas of information technology, digital assets, medical devices, patient experiences, and the hospital environment (Lee, 2017, p. 181). The consideration of the customer's experience is a top priority. In healthcare, the only way to know what the customer has experienced and to improve the design of services is to understand the customers' requirements (Lee, 2017, p. 182).

Service design has been accepted as human-centered and a co-creative process (Korper et al., 2020, p. 305). In healthcare, to establish co-creativeness and innovation, organizations use different methods and approaches. One element that is constant in all methods is ensuring value is provided in all services. Healthcare organizations constantly seek ways to provide services in a way that customers value (Clack & Ellison, 2019, p. 89).

When a customer engages during a care service, he/she provides insightful and innovative ideas and feedback. This provides the healthcare organization a new perspective that can lead to innovative ideas on how to better provide value and a customer-centered experience. When a hospital or healthcare organization focuses on the customer's experience, it examines the experience through the customer's own eyes throughout the entire journey, before and after the services were performed (Lee, 2017, p. 183). To achieve co-creation and value, the customer is actively participating in the service delivery process which will create a better customer-centered experience. This, in turn, will heighten the apparent value for customers (Lee, 2017, p. 183). For organizations to be successful at co-creating and enhancing value several things can be done:

- Co-produce value together by participating in the care service process.
- Communicate to support customer's own health needs.

- Customers provide health conditions then medical staff suggest medical diagnosis/potential value.
- Interaction and exchange of information between customer and provider is more fluid.
- Integration of resources using technology is user-friendly and efficient (Lee, 2017, p. 184).

Actively being involved in creating an innovative, customer-centered experience is essential to improve value and quality in healthcare.

The speed of innovation needs to improve in order to understand the global health crisis that needs to be addressed. On a global scale, design has increasingly gained recognition as a valuable approach to respond better to customers' needs and wants and to drive innovation (Mishra & Sandhu, 2021, p. 199). There are three beneficial advantages to innovative design in global health.

1. Framing. This approach identifies the problem and keeps the customer and community 's perspective at the center. The designers conduct research early on with the stakeholders in the community to determine the best approach for the specific ecosystem. This ensures the community, and their needs are met.
2. Intention. Innovative service design intends to create space to solve problems the right way. This part of the process is intended to test ideas, many times and early on to ensure it is designed the right way with correct priorities, the needs and wants of the community and its customers.
3. Collaboration. Innovative design brings customers and communities together for a common purpose. Multidisciplinary teams working together define the true value of design. This type of work can contribute to more sustainable outcomes and equity in the global health efforts (Mishra & Sandhu, 2021, p. 199).

The purpose of global health is to improve health and achieve health equity for all people worldwide. How can innovative design advance equity for all? Inequities that exist in healthcare systems exist globally (Mishra & Sandhu, 2021, p. 199). By designing innovative healthcare systems that frame community collaboration, where policies are built on shared interests, and creating a space for collaborating equitable outcomes in the community, equity for all can be achieved.

4   Implementation of Innovative Service Design

Similar to design thinking, service design is typically divided into exploration, concept development, prototyping, and implementation (Korper et al., 2020, p. 305). As is true with many processes in organizations, implementation is one of the most difficult steps. Some experts have stated that organizations should shift from a perspective focused on the implementation of innovative tools and should instead place more priority on the service design process (Shaw et al., 2018, p. 2). Taking it

Table 1 Challenges in global service innovation (Parida et al., 2015, p. 38)

Challenges in global service innovation
Lack of understanding of heterogenous global markets, conditions, and requirements
Dispersed, disorganized skills and competencies across regional units
Inability to understand and address the unique operational needs of global customers
Scattered, disconnected IT systems in regional units
Inability to deliver new services quickly to meet regional market requirements
Variation among regional units in offerings, sales, and delivery capacity
Lack of collaboration between siloed teams across global regions
Lack of specified global-regional integrator roles
Inability to join forces with external partners in global markets

a step further, other research has suggested that service design should be integrated into organizational practices and processes (Yu & Sangiorgi, 2017, p. 46).

Like many other industries, healthcare has no shortage of innovative service offerings. Leaders in organizations are faced with deciding on which innovations to implement (Victorino et al., 2005, p. 556). Organizations have to balance their decisions on whether organizations, provide a competitive advantage, enhance service differentiation, or provide a financial benefit (Victorino et al., 2005, p. 556). Organizations are being driven by global competition to implement innovative service offerings.

Innovative service design on a global scale presents organizations with significant challenges such as the diversity of customer segments and the differences in laws and market conditions (Parida et al., 2015, p. 37). Challenges in global service innovation are displayed in Table 1. In order for organizations to be successful in global service innovation, they should develop global customer insights, integrate global knowledge, create global service offerings, and build a global digitalization capability (Parida et al., 2015, p. 38).

5   Service Design and Global Health

With increasing pressures from technology and globalization, innovative service design has become key to economic and social development (Patricio et al., 2017, p. 3). Countries across the world have a growing capacity for innovation. To maximize the potential of service design innovation in global health, organizations need to search for technological solutions exemplified by global public–private product development partnerships and focus on systemic solutions exemplified by health policy and systems research (Gardner et al., 2007, p. 1052). The adoption of innovative technologies has become increasingly important in the wake of the COVID-19 global health pandemic. Implementation of technologies can provide organizations with a competitive advantage and a means for survival (Akpan et al., 2020, p. 608).

The process of expanding the use of innovative health interventions is referred to as scaling up (Mangham & Hanson, 2010, p. 85). Scaling-up has been defined as "deliberate efforts to increase the impact of successfully tested health innovations so as to benefit more people and to foster policy and programme development on a lasting basis," and the scaling-up strategy refers to "the plans and actions necessary to fully establish the innovation in policies, programmes and service delivery" (ExpandNet/World Health Organization, 2010, p. 2). ExpandNet and the World Health Organization created a framework for scaling up (Table 2).

There are four key principles that should guide all aspects of analysis, planning, and decision-making when moving through the nine-step process of scaling up. The first is systems thinking which refers to "being aware that the expansion and institutionalization of innovations occurs in a complex network of interactions and influences, which should be taken into account in order to ensure scaling-up success" (ExpandNet/WHO, 2010, p. 5). The second principle is a focus on sustainability. The third principle is enhancing scalability. The fourth principle is respect for human rights, equity, and gender perspectives (ExpandNet/WHO, 2010, p. 5).

There are several types of scaling up. Diversification/functional scaling up expands program breadth by adding additional services. Political scaling up expands political support by building a supportive network. Organizational/institutional scaling up builds strategic alliances with other organizations and develops the technical and management capacity needed to sustain program efforts and support sustainability (World Health Organization, 2016, p. 5).

Table 2 Conceptual scaling up framework (ExpandNet/World Health Organization, 2010, p. 5)

World health organization scaling up framework	
Step 1	Planning actions to increase the scalability of the innovation
Step 2	Increasing the capacity of the resource team to support scaling up
Step 3	Assessing the environment and planning actions to increase the potential for scaling-up success
Step 4	Increasing the capacity of the resource team to support scaling up
Step 5	Making strategic choices to support vertical scaling up (institutionalization)
Step 6	Making strategic choices to support horizontal scaling up (expansion/replication)
Step 7	Determining the role of diversification
Step 8	Planning actions to address spontaneous scaling up
Step 9	Finalizing the scaling-up strategy and identifying next steps

6 Conclusion

For organizations to remain viable in the current healthcare environment, innovative service design is essential for success. Organizations must understand the challenges of innovation and learn how to scale up and adopt innovative interventions in order to be able to compete with rapidly advancing technology and the globalization of healthcare.

References

Akpan, I. J., Soopramanien, D., & Kwak, D. (2020). Cutting-edge technologies for small business and innovation in the era of COVID-19 global health pandemic. *Journal of Small Business & Entrepreneurship, 33*(6), 607–617. https://doi.org/10.1080/08276331.2020.1799294

Ash, S. (2017). Designing for global health challenges. *Prototypr.* Retrieved July 3, 2022, from https://blog.prototypr.io/designing-for-global-health-challenges-89b181eb1e96.

Berry, L. (2019). Service innovation is urgent in healthcare. *Journal of Academy of Marketing Science, 9*(2), 78–92. https://doi.org/10.1007/s13162-019-00135-x

Chauhan, A., Donaldson, K., Santos, A., & Ngigi, M. (2021). What's next in design for global health? How design and global health must adapt for a preferable future. *Global Health: Science and Practice, 9*(2), 283–294. Retrieved July 3, 2022, from https://www.ghspjournal.org/content/9/Supplement_2/S283.

Clack, L. A. (2017). Strategies with service business model innovation. In: M. A. Pfannstiel & C. Rasche (Eds.), *Service design and service thinking in healthcare and hospital management. Theory, Concepts, Practice,* (pp. 85–92) Cham: Springer Nature.

Clack, L. A., & Ellison, R. L. (2019). Innovation in service design thinking. In: M. A. Pfannstiel & C. Rasche (Eds.), *Service business model innovation in healthcare and hospital management: Models, strategies, tools* (pp. 21–30). Cham: Springer Nature. https://doi.org/10.1007/978-3-030-00749-2_6.

Eberling, J. (2019). Service design innovation and why it is gaining importance. *Lead Innovation.* Retrieved July 3, 2022, from https://www.lead-innovation.com/english-blog/service-design-innovation, Retrieved July 3, 2022, from https://jdt.ut.ac.ir/article_82244.html.

ExpandNet, World Health Organization. (2010). *Nine steps for developing a scaling-up strategy.* Geneva, Switzerland: WHO Press.

Gardner, C. A., Acharya, T., & Yach, D. (2007). Technological and social innovation: A unifying new paradigm for global health. *Health Affairs, 26*(4), 1052–1061. https://doi.org/10.1377/hlthaff.26.4.1052

Korper, A. K., Patrício, L., Holmlid, S., & Witell, L. (2020). Service design as an innovation approach in technology startups: A longitudinal multiple case study. *Creativity and Innovative Management, 29*(2), 303–323. https://doi.org/10.1111/caim.12383

Lee, D. (2017). A model for designing healthcare service based on the patient experience. *International Journal of Healthcare Management, 12*(3), 180–188. https://doi.org/10.1080/20479700.2017.1359956

Mangham, L. J., & Hanson, K. (2010). Scaling up in international health: What are the key issues? *Health Policy and Planning, 25*(2), 85–96. https://doi.org/10.1093/heapol/czp066

Mishra, P., & Sandhu, S. (2021). Design is an essential medicine. *Global Health: Science and Practice, 9*(2), 198–208. https://doi.org/10.9745/GHSP-D-21-0033

Panwar, K., & Kahn, K. (2021). Integrating design thinking in service design process: A conceptual review. *Journal of Design Thinking, 2*(1), 23–36.

Parida, V., Sjodin, D. R., Lenka, S., & Wincent, J. (2015). Developing global service innovation capabilities: How global manufacturers address the challenges of market heterogeneity. *Research-Technology Management, 58*(5), 35–44. https://doi.org/10.5437/08956308X5805360

Patricio, L., Gustafsson, A., & Fisk, R. (2017). Upframing service design and innovation for research impact. *Journal of Service Research, 21*(1), 3–16. https://doi.org/10.1177/109467051 7746780.

Shaw, J., Agarwal, P., Desveaux, L., Palma, D.C., Stamenova, V., Jamieson, T., Yang, R., Bhatia, R.S., & Battacharyya, O. (2018). Beyond "implementation": Digital health innovation and service design. *NPJ Digital Medicine, 48*(1), 1–5.

Victorino, L., Verma, R., Plaschka, G., & Dev, C. (2005). Service innovation and customer choices in the hospitality industry. *Managing Service Quality: An International Journal, 15*(6), 555–576.

World Health Organization. (2016). *Scaling up projects and initiatives for better health: From concepts to practice.* Geneva, Switzerland: WHO Press.

Yu, E., & Sangiorgi, D. (2017). Service design as an approach to implement the value cocreation perspective in new service development. *Journal of Service Research, 21*(1), 46–58. https://doi.org/10.1177/1094670517709356.

Dr. Lesley Clack is an Associate Professor and Chair of the Department of Health Sciences at Florida Gulf Coast University in Fort Myers, FL. She teaches undergraduate and graduate courses in healthcare administration and specializes in the areas of Organizational Behavior and Strategic Management. She has a Doctor of Science degree in Health Systems Management from Tulane University, a Master of Science degree in Counseling Psychology from the University of West Alabama, and a Bachelor of Science degree in Biological Science from the University of Georgia. She has 10+ years of teaching experience, in addition to clinical and administrative experience in healthcare.

Dr. Rachel Ellison is an Associate Professor at the University of Louisiana at Lafayette. She teaches undergraduate courses in the Health Services Administration program and specializes in Health Policy, Health Care Leadership, and Health Care Finance. She has a Doctor of Philosophy degree from Capella University in Health and Human Services, a Master of Science degree in Health Care Management from Kaplan University, and a Bachelor of Science degree in Health Care Systems Administration from Ferris State University. She has 10 years of teaching experience, in addition to administrative experience in healthcare.

Formative Interventions for Healthcare Sustainability: A Developmental Design Agenda

Peter Jones and Pranay Arun Kumar

ABSTRACT

This chapter proposes a developmental design approach to build a long-term design research agenda to study and advise healthcare services towards meeting sustainability challenges. The study involved the application of systemic design tools in a participatory design workshop to create a formative understanding of the stakeholders, contexts and systemic interventions towards sustainability of healthcare systems. Healthcare services draw on vast logistics systems, generating waste streams and redundant uses, with a significant sustainability impact. Analysing the complex functions of any regional healthcare system reveals material flows and proscribed service interactions that reinforce continuing breaches of preferred sustainability levels. These flows are largely due to institutional arrangements defined far upstream of use and disposal. Yet, the actions and choices of healthcare consumers are becoming larger factors to consider in the overall environmental impact of healthcare systems. Patient-centred healthcare shifts a significant share of the responsibility of health outcomes on the consumer, including waste generated through home healthcare which is typically routed through municipal waste streams. Whether policies, healthcare services, or individual patient choices—nearly all actions in the healthcare system trigger actions with sustainability impacts. Healthcare's complex systems are difficult to navigate individually, especially for non-experts. Although constant strides are being made towards making healthcare systems more sustainable, their complexity makes it difficult to verify the efficacy of interventions within the system and across the interconnected network of stakeholders and sub-systems.

P. Jones (✉)
OCAD University, 100 McCaul St., Toronto, ON M5V 1V3, Canada
e-mail: pjones@ocadu.ca

P. Arun Kumar
Health Systems Studio, OCAD University, 100 McCaul St., Toronto, ON M5V 1V3, Canada

177

1   Introduction

Healthcare services are the source of significant unsustainable environmental threats. The increasing impacts of energy and material use, global supply chains and toxic waste streams of healthcare systems contribute to massive environmental impacts, including non-recyclable landfill waste, toxic chemical and plastics waste in land and water flows, and greenhouse gas emissions (Eckelman & Sherman, 2016). With an increasing demand for healthcare services from both modernizing and ageing populations worldwide, a vicious cycle of healthcare for individual patients at the cost of the health of entire populations is observed, causing moral and ethical tensions in the operation of health systems and the provision of health-related services in a responsible manner (MacNeill et al., 2021).

Recent events of the COVID-19 pandemic, increasing natural disasters around the world and an acknowledgement of climate change as a global challenge have escalated the conversations among healthcare policy-makers towards mitigating the environmental impacts of the healthcare industry (Ossebaard & Lachman, 2021). These conversations are translating to research on reducing emissions of healthcare systems, adopting less wasteful practices and finding a balance between economic and environmental sustainability (Sherman et al., 2020). Although these initiatives are encouraging and necessary for the transition to sustainable healthcare, they are predominantly piecemeal studies that are simplifying a complex problem (Arun Kumar, 2020, 2021; Arun Kumar & Wang, 2021; Kumar & Wang, 2019). It is unclear whether the individual initiatives are contributing meaningfully towards mitigating the impact on climate change, or are generating new problems which may be further degrading our environment, such as the practice of 'greenwashing' that give public relations cover to policies that continue to exacerbate environmental degradation.

A complex systems approach is useful in creating a holistic understanding of healthcare system problems (Sturmberg, 2020) and visualizing complex causes and effects across various networks of elements. A systems visualization, such as a synthesis map (Jones & Bowes, 2017), enables the participants to foresee the effects of probable interventions on the entire system, to take a more informed approach towards solution finding and resolution. This study used systemic design tools to engage participants with diverse backgrounds and interests to tackle a complex issue, visualizing their unique perspectives while inter-linking these perspectives to create a holistic understanding (Jones & Van Ael, 2022). In this case, the design study engaged diverse participants to discern how individual actions within sub-systems affects healthcare systems to envision intervention for high-leverage sustainable practices.

The study illustrates a systemic design approach to unveil the complexities in healthcare sustainability interventions. A participatory design workshop was conducted with design experts in healthcare and sustainability at a symposium using three different systemic design tools to map the stakeholders involved, the context of healthcare sustainability and potential leverage points for intervening in such complex systems. The workshop produced five representations that visualize the actors of the system, the context in which they operate, and the areas of intervention towards reducing the environmental impact of these systems.

The Systemic Design Toolkit, designed by Namahn and developed by Jones and Van Ael (2022), is a set of system modelling canvases designed for participatory workshops to engage participants from diverse backgrounds to address complex problems. The toolkit brings together the powers of systems thinking, human-centred design and service design approaches to support engagement with wicked problems, complex system interventions and development of higher level policy and practice across industries. Although the toolkit comprises over 40 canvases for a seven-stage methodology, this study was carried out in a condensed format, using three canvases, while developing a rich understanding of the system as well as potential interventions towards healthcare sustainability.

2   Design Agenda for Healthcare Sustainability

We recommend an incremental, developmental approach to making interventions in high-complexity contexts (Flach, 2012), within a long-term agenda towards stronger sustainability in consumer health and institutional healthcare. This early stage study reports on outcomes from a design workshop and content analysis, with continuing artefact development and literature analysis. In this exploratory phase of the study, we framed the workshop generative activities on defining actors, contexts and interventions to address critical environmental sustainability issues, such as consumer waste flows and sustainable product development and procurement. However, the participants in the workshop activities were not involved in follow-on analyses.

We find two contexts to account for a significant proportion of sustainability decisions accessible to service design: the patient as a consumer of healthcare services and the healthcare institutions as systems of healthcare provision. There are contexts in the total healthcare systems other than the individual patient and the hospital-level system, such as health policy, equipment suppliers and human-centred systemic design. But these two areas—the patient and hospital institution—widely differ in volume of material flows, types of waste, hazardous materials and single-use products. The consumer, patient, clinician and the hospital can all be seen as actors within a whole healthcare system for the purposes of sustainability transformation.

Healthcare sustainability has been approached from several perspectives, all of which are necessary to consider in a systemic view of healthcare. Pereno and Eriksson (2020) used a similar approach to explore the landscape of healthcare sustainability across multiple national and system contexts. Also acknowledging the significant complexity in this domain, they defined a variety of primary actor groups recruited for collaborative foresight approach, including health industries, health providers, managing authorities, universities and research centres, clusters, non-governmental organisations and healthcare networks, and professional consortia.

This study is structured to serve the aims of descriptive and normative research, using design action research to facilitate a series of learning cycles. The workshop and following activities establish the context to promote a longer term design agenda as a systems-change programme. We consider the agenda-formation process as a necessary stage of developmental design, and recommend a series of inquiries, learning cycles, and artefact cocreation and publication.

Based on the Warfield model of scientific programme development (Jones, 2018) a series of design engagements proceeds from the Lab (internal model development) to Studio (workshop cocreation of content) to the Arena (co-development within the healthcare industry), returning to the Lab for theory development, in a full developmental cycle of research. Tightly scoped research can contribute to the developmental design process, but in formative stages of agenda formation, an exploratory, interpretive research disposition is helpful, to err on the side of a comprehensive sweep of prevalent ideas in complex sustainability.

2.1   Towards Developmental Design

Design interventions and design research encounters can be considered as socially constructive performances that produce objects of design (Pedersen, 2007). These objects are produced by the participants in a given, defined design process and can be assumed to evolve with the project. The objects are the result of reflections on development of the knowledge attained towards and in the process of making the object, thus being outcomes of multiple tacit and explicit knowledge bases. One of the goals of the overall programme is to then relate these objects to the public and open dialogue for external input, particularly from those affected by the objects, in more of a reflective learning process rather than prototype testing.

The precedent of developmental evaluation was envisioned by Patton (1994) as an effective defining process for agenda formation. Developmental evaluation uses an action-research-oriented reflection cycle to make progress towards long-term goals through cooperative evaluation of interventions, as processes towards these goals (Patton, 1994). Patton has further developed the evaluation methodology in Principles-Focussed Evaluation (Patton, 2018) for complex social change programmes, and more recently as applied to global systemic problems such as climate change in the planetary Blue Marble Evaluation (Patton, 2021).

The developmental approach is intentionally incremental, following insights from learning from each step to the next towards long-term impact, i.e., from learning in event one (systemic design workshop) that drives event two (deeper analysis and publication), then event three (synthesis map) and so on.

Design practices customarily orient towards improvements in effective delivery, as implementation is a known weakness in design practice. We might note that in instructional design, an adjacent concept is found in the proposals for formative design (Frick & Reigeluth, 1999), but this has also not been applied towards longer term constantly progressing design or research agendas.

There appears to be no direct analogy or equivalent in design methodology. It is different than iterative evaluation cycles, or learning journeys, because those practices are not 'forward intervening' to change their subject domain, as in design. We do not conceive of developmental design as iterative construction towards an optimized outcome, but as an expansion of learning that builds an open agenda of proposed interventions that can be developed and tested, even independently from our proposed platform. Developmental evaluation does provide support for constructing research agendas, in terms of defining new problems of interest and possible interventions and outcomes.

The beginning and end of a designed artefact are open and not limited to the project. Design is related to user appropriation and hence the process must be open to appropriation as well (Krippendorff, 2005). This appropriation is reflective in nature and any change occurring to the context affects the relationship between the artefact and the user. The reflective practice of practitioner fields such as management and design, as described by Schön (2017), suggests that a key action of reflection in and on practice involves the evaluation of effectiveness of action, echoing the values of developmental evaluation. Furthermore, the use of research for the improvement of practice and this cyclic process of reflection in and on practice creates a base for the focus on developmental design as a method of reflection *through* practice. This aspect of reflection through practice, as in Research through Design, (Jonas, 2007) is not typical in evaluation, and is an important component of developmental design—the design of artefacts as a reflective practice towards the long-term research, development and intervention in complex systems.

3   Methods and Approach

A two-hour workshop was conducted with 19 participants and two facilitators via remote facilitation, as an accepted workshop in the 10th Relating Systems Thinking and Design Symposium (Jones & Arun Kumar, 2021). The workshop was facilitated by the authors, involving brief topical presentations via a Zoom conference call and the participants used systemic design tools displayed as image files on the Miro online whiteboard platform. The Zoom call and the chat log were recorded and the outcome from the workshop was recorded and analysed ex post.

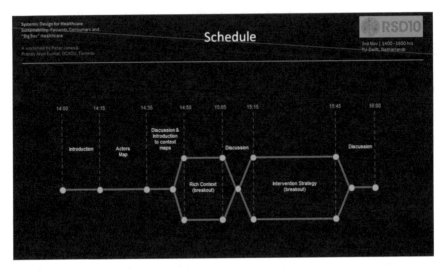

Fig. 1 Workshop schedule and structure. *Source* Author's own figure (2022)

The workshop was conducted in three phases (Fig. 1) using three systemic design tools to frame the actors of the problem (Actors map), to frame the context of the problem (Rich Context map) and to explore solution areas within this defined system (Intervention Strategy).

Before engaging participants in the mapping exercise, the facilitators provided a brief introduction to the workshop, the context of healthcare sustainability being addressed, and the use and relevance of systemic design tools for this workshop. Each phase involved an introduction to the tool as well as to the method of using the tool, followed by facilitating participants to use the tools effectively and concluded with a guided discussion on the mapping experience as well as answering queries from participants on the tools and processes.

The first phase, the identification and mapping of actors and stakeholders using the Actors map, was conducted with the entire group participating together on the same map image. The remaining two phases were conducted by organizing participants into two groups, one focussing on the patient as a consumer of healthcare services and the other on healthcare systems as service providers. The objective of breaking the team into two groups was to enable participants to have a more focussed approach towards context and intervention identification within either the micro-perspective of the individual's agency in complex problem-solving or the macro-perspective of the systemic and institutional agency. Participants were asked to choose from the two groups they preferred, depending on their interests.

For each of the three phases, the participants used electronic sticky notes to add elements on the maps, and then linked the elements with each other and defined these relationships between elements. Participants were also free to change their sticky notes and change their positions if they felt there was a more appropriate position, based on discussions with the facilitators and other participants.

The methodology described above had four objectives: 1. to introduce the participants to systemic design tools as methods to engage with complex problems; 2. to allow the participants to leverage diverse academic and professional backgrounds and contribute to rich dialogue with nuanced perspectives towards a problem that was elusive but palpable; 3. to identify points of intervention within healthcare and health systems for influence and impact and 4. to progress from tangible and infrastructural issues towards identifying and elucidating the moral and ethical tensions in healthcare sustainability.

4 Analysis and Findings

We report on three classes of findings of interest for the discussion. The findings from the data generated by participants were analysed as content relevant to informing both expected or near-term sustainability practices. The use of a rapid system analysis method was perceived as valuable and effective for the purpose of collective learning and design. The workshop process yielded effective interaction from a self-selected group of participants that suggests the utility of the interactive design tool-driven process.

The participants of the workshop had diverse professional backgrounds including expertise in systemic design, service design, clinical medicine, mental health, sustainability, product management, industrial design, design education and other related fields. Most, if not all of the participants were new to the use and application of systemic design tools, even though many were designers and could relate to the explanations of the tools provided by the facilitators. The participants could be classified primarily as 'tourists' according to the Design Journeys (Jones & Van Ael, 2022) methodology, i.e. interested novices to systemic design with ideas to contribute. The workshop generally served as an introduction to systemic design tools for most participants as well.

A total of five maps were generated over the period of two hours through the workshop (Figs. 2, 3, 4, 5 and 6). Participants were told to use sticky notes of a single colour on a map, to ensure that their contribution to the mapping process was identifiable, even though the annotations were anonymous. The high number of notes and diversity in colours used indicated engaged participation in the workshop.

4.1   Actors Map

The Actors map (Fig. 2) was used as the first tool to identify the ranges of stakeholders (actors and actants) associated with the system as identified by the participants. These actors ranged from individuals such as patients and caregivers, to institutions and organizations such as ministries of health and universities. These candidates were positioned on the Actors map depending on the participants' perceived understanding of the knowledge the actor possessed of healthcare sustainability and their ability to influence decision-making within the system. Within the 15 minutes provided for this exercise, the participants managed to identify stakeholders in all four quadrants of the map at various levels of power and influence. The participants were also able to create links between stakeholders where a suitable relationship was identified, even though they were not able to flesh out the relationships between the stakeholders within the allotted time.

Fig. 2 Actors map produced from the workshop. *Source* Author's own figure (2022)

4.2   Rich Context Maps

The second phase of the workshop involved developing the *Rich Context map*. This tool is used to define the sociocultural and business contexts of a complex situation. The Rich Context served two purposes in the workshop, to collect responses associated with the contextual categories to define system features and to be able to compare sustainability issues between the patient and healthcare system contexts. The Rich Context identifies long-term trends in a system (e.g., ageing and longer lifespans), the current practices in healthcare systems (e.g., self-care based on online resources before consulting clinicians) and niche innovations which are influencing changes in the system (e.g., bio-plastics for medical equipment). The relationship between the trends, practices and innovations provided a clearer understanding of the context in which the system was being studied. In this case, the set of participants divided themselves into two groups, one focussing on the consumers of healthcare (Fig. 3), and the other on service providers of healthcare as agents of healthcare sustainability (Fig. 4).

The Systemic Design Toolkit suggested the participants could conduct secondary research to identify the trends and practices before attempting the *Rich Context map* (Jones & Van Ael, 2022). However, in this study, participants had to draw on their expertise on the subject to suggest the trends, practices and innovations. In the *patient-centred rich context* (Fig. 3), we could see a dense contribution in *long-term trends* and *current practices* within the culture and practices quadrants, while the *emerging niche initiatives* area showed very few contributions. Within the *current practices* ring, the participants seemed to indicate a low relevance of economic structures to the ensuing long-term trends, with a relatively low contribution of annotations to the *economic structures* quadrant. The niche initiatives suggested by the participants indicated stronger correlations with culture and routine behaviour than with institutional or economic structures.

In the *healthcare services-centred rich context* (Fig. 4), there was a dense contribution to *long-term trends* supported by perceived current practices in the prevalent economic structures and routine behaviours of these organizations. The few niche initiatives identified also link primarily to culture and routine behavioural practices.

The Actors and the Rich Context maps helped frame the system within which this study operated. The framing of this system involved identifying the stakeholders and their influence and power in the system, as well as the long-term trends, current economic, institutional, cultural and behavioural practices and new innovations disrupting the system. These two phases of the study provided a frame of reference to identify suitable interventions towards making healthcare systems sustainable.

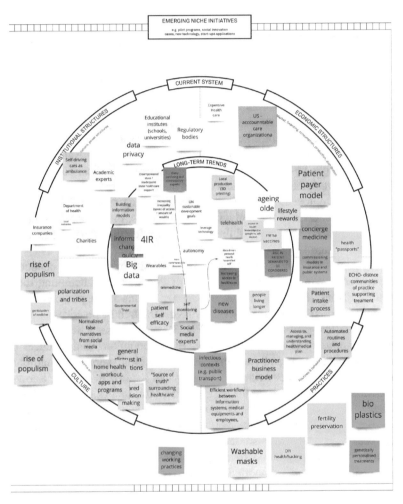

Fig. 3 Rich Context map, patients as consumers in healthcare sustainability. *Source* Author's figure (2022)

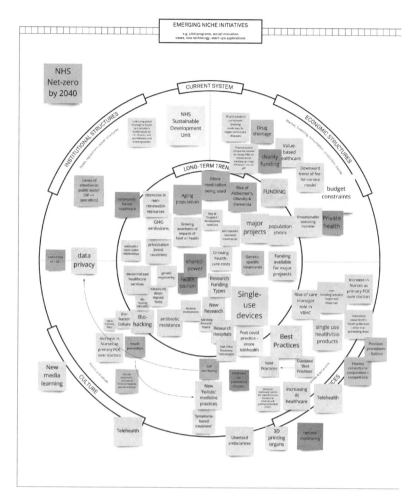

Fig. 4 Rich Context map, healthcare system sustainability issues. *Source* Author's figure (2022)

4.3 Intervention Strategy Maps

The third exercise of the workshop involved the *Intervention Strategy tool*, designed to elicit leverage points for change towards desired outcomes (in this case, sustainable healthcare). Participants stayed with their previous teams, focussing either on patient-centred interventions or on healthcare system interventions. Two maps were developed as mentioned above (Figs. 5 and 6). While the first two phases framed the system for its context and stakeholders, this phase focussed on identifying suitable interventions to navigate the context towards sustainability innovations in both domains.

In both the intervention maps, a seemingly uniform contribution can be observed across the 12 leverage points and many links between the elements have

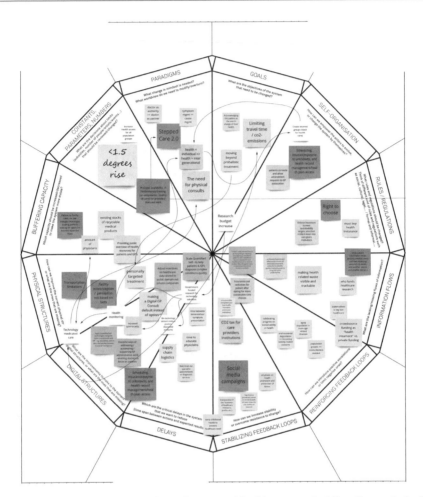

Fig. 5 Intervention Strategy map for patient-centred healthcare sustainability. *Source* Author's figure (2022)

also been created. As a first assessment of potential intervention strategies, the participation in this exercise indicated many leverage points identified which could be further explored and developed as individual projects. While the intervention strategies identified were discussed within each mapping group as well as with the workshop participants as a whole, the strategies were not reviewed and edited from a thematic perspective, as suggested by Jones and Van Ael (2022). Furthermore, the ideas were not elaborated upon or distinctly defined, and were left open to interpretation and abstract in some cases.

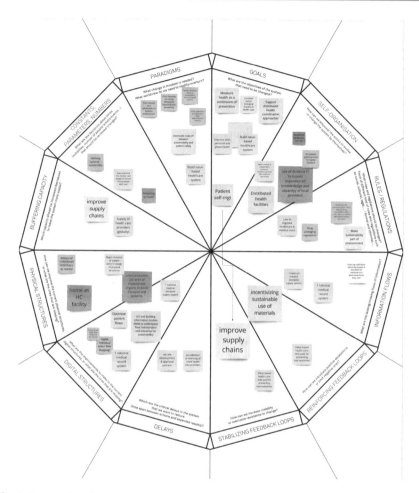

Fig. 6 Intervention Strategy map, healthcare system sustainability issues. *Source* Author's figure (2022)

5   Discussion

The use of systemic design tools for complex problem interventions gives stakeholders and designers structured approaches towards high-level problem-solving. Yet the use of these methods and the process of designing system interventions have various factors to consider for maximum efficacy. In this section, we discuss some of the factors that influenced the output from the workshop conducted, and the relevance of these factors for future participatory design workshops using systemic design tools.

5.1   Cognitive Factors in Participation

It is important to note that the expected lack of experience in using systemic design tools served two different purposes in this study. Firstly, the lack of prior knowledge of the tools allowed diverse interpretations of the mapping process, with participants using their own justifications and reasoning for placing elements in the map. The prior knowledge of such tools tends to promote the intuitive formation of strategy among users which limits their ideas and the openness to method-use approaches, whereas a lack of such intimation allows a more playful and exploratory approach, eliciting a broader range of ideas, which is a valuable outcome of using the systemic design tools. However, the lack of experience also left some participants apprehensive of contributing freely to the mapping process. This was observed through regular inquiries in the chat and during discussion periods of the workshop, when participants would verify the most appropriate position for a certain annotation with the facilitators and how they could justify their meaning by location before placing the label in position. Some participants were also left questioning the relevance and value of their ideas to the maps, which limited their contributions. There was a lack of comfort in the ambiguity and diversity of ideas for some participants.

Each of the maps represented a first iteration of mapping for the workshop and was designed to be completed in 15–20 minutes to accommodate for the duration of a two-hour workshop. The aim of the exercise was to explore the breadth of ideas and cross-pollinate diverse perspectives on the system across disciplines and areas of interest to compare and explore the salient issues in healthcare sustainability. This study should not be confused with a clear identification of system boundaries or solution sets, and rather should be observed for the rich discourse provided through the maps, which can be a resource for more targeted navigation towards future solutions for healthcare sustainability.

5.2   Ecological Factors for System Mapping

The first iteration of the maps helped provide the widest diversity in ideas and perspectives on the system, and acted as a sounding board for exploration of relationships between elements and their value in intervening in the system. If the context of this study was that of a structured project working towards interventions in a predefined system, this exercise could be continued through multiple iterations, resolving the focus of the project and elaborating the nuances of the network of elements and the relationships between the elements to arrive at suitable solutions that may responsibly disrupt the system with a granular understanding of the effects of the disruption across the system.

However, the maps generated in this study have a wider use as triggers for researchers, practitioners and policy-makers developing projects on healthcare sustainability. As part of the developmental design approach described earlier, the findings from the workshop will be translated to a synthesis map, which would serve as a design artefact for further reflection and progression towards co-design of systemic interventions with stakeholders (from studio to the arena and back to the lab). The authors subsequently presented the synthesis map and research agenda to the subsequent RSD11 symposium, in 2022.

5.3   Domain Knowledge Factors

This study serves as one of the first holistic explorations of the nuances of making healthcare systems sustainable. Most studies on this subject by the scientific community have typically relied so far on hypothesis testing, generating specific evidence towards defining the problem or a specific solution, which has been the modus operandi in scientific research (MacNeill et al., 2020; Sherman et al., 2019). This deductive reasoning model leaves little room for exploratory, complexity or visual approaches to the discovery of saliency and critical patterns in complex systems. By visualizing the complexity of the systems involved, new opportunities can be unearthed through collaborative mapping, such as with the tools used in this study, to provide multi-level, multi-perspectival insights into complex problem contexts (Jones & Bowes, 2017). This study reflects not only the complexity of the problem at hand, but also the diverse perspectives generated by an interdisciplinary set of participants towards a common goal, one that is difficult to structure and theorize purely through mathematical modelling. Although with enough data, these systems can also be modelled with clear quantitative results, at this stage the system is yet to be comprehensively defined for further analysis, towards which this study provides one piece of the puzzle.

The placement of the annotations within each map and the overall density of contributions in various sections of each map can be attributed to various factors. In the Actors map (Fig. 2), all participants were contributing simultaneously and had no restrictions on how to contribute. The predominant contributions of actors with a perceived higher knowledge of the system and varying levels of power or influence in the system (top-right and bottom-right quadrants) could be a reflection of the background and expertise the participants brought to the exercise.

In the two Rich Context maps and the two Intervention Strategy maps however (Figs. 3, 4, 5 and 6), there were other factors at play. Firstly, the participants were asked to pick between the patient-centred map or the healthcare-services-oriented map, and the number of participants on each map were not equal. The quantity of annotations on each map may be a reflection of the number of participants, the knowledge of the system possessed by the participants and the interest to participate (which may vary with interest and fatigue of individual participants). In the Rich Context maps (Figs. 3 and 4), participants were asked to start by identifying major trends (inner circle) in the landscape, then to define current practices in the dominant regime (middle ring) and end with emerging niche initiatives (outer canvas), as suggested by Multi-Level Perspective theory (Geels, 2005) and in the tool itself (Jones & Van Ael, 2022). The time periods for each of these three sections were not strictly monitored and the lower contributions to niche initiatives could be partly attributed to a smaller time devoted to this section, or a lack of knowledge of actual innovations in the four quadrants (Institutional, Economic, Cultural, Social). The low contributions in some cases could also be attributed to taking time to learn a new tool and use it, as discussed earlier.

The diagrams provided above have been left in their original state as produced by the participants in the workshop, to indicate the process and original outcomes. Further work has since been done to refine the maps, and present them as a cohesive exploration of stakeholders, contexts and intervention strategies for healthcare sustainability, potentially as a synthesis map with relevant literature and bibliographic sources for future reference. The maps and their diverse perspectives offer a window of opportunity for exploration of ideas towards healthcare sustainability at various scales and contexts.

6   Conclusion

The value of this project as a developmental approach is to promote a design agenda for healthcare sustainability at the industry level. Developmental design uses a series of interventions and analyses to develop a continuing discourse with the intention of finding and engaging with stakeholders, who will be discovered over a period of time as feedback and priorities are returned into formative development of a design agenda. Like developmental evaluation, the long-term nature of complex system projects requires a staged series of analyses and artefacts that are all aligned towards a long-term outcome. It can be seen as a mode of designing within systemic design.

The impacts of environmental degradation and climate change are creating normative business and service challenges for the healthcare industry. The intensification of public health demands, as witnessed during the COVID-19 pandemic emergency measures produced billions of single-use non-biodegradable masks and syringes. These challenges require new approaches to understand and frame problem contexts, as well as our proposals for effective intervention. This study analyses and proposes interventions in healthcare systems from a macro-perspective (healthcare service systems) and a micro-perspective (the role of patient-consumers) as potential agents of change. The study illustrates the opportunities for developing new research and intervention avenues through a participatory design workshop involving design experts in healthcare and sustainability, and the role of systemic design tools in visualizing complexities of systemic problems. The study is part of a long-term project to engage with the problem of healthcare sustainability in a climate-conscious world through developmental design to elicit innovation across system and service levels in healthcare.

Acknowledgements We would like to thank the RSD10 Symposium organizers for providing us with a platform to conduct the workshop on systemic design for healthcare sustainability and use the contents of the workshop for this publication. We would also like to thank the participants of the workshop for their enthusiastic participation and contribution to the workshop activities.

References

Arun Kumar, P. (2020). *EcoDesign for medical devices: Barriers and opportunities to eco-effective design of medical devices*, M.Phil. Thesis, Royal College of Art (Ed.), London. Retrieved July 26, 2022, from https://researchonline.rca.ac.uk/4467/

Arun Kumar, P. (2021). Regulating environmental impact of medical devices in the United Kingdom—A scoping review. *Prosthesis, 3*(4), 370–387. https://doi.org/10.3390/prosthesis3040033

Arun Kumar, P., & Wang, S. J. (2021). The design intervention: Opportunities to reduce procedural-caused healthcare waste under the Industry 4.0 context—A scoping review. In A. Brooks, E. I. Brooks, & D. Jonathan (Eds.), *Interactivity and game creation, ArtsIT 2020. Lecture Notes of the Institute for Computer Sciences, Social InformartsIT 2020. Lecture Notes of the Institute for Computer Sciences, Social Informatics and Telecommunications Engineering* (Vol. 367, pp. 446–460). Cham: Springer Nature. https://doi.org/10.1007/978-3-030-73426-8_27

Eckelman, M. J., & Sherman, J. (2016). Environmental impacts of the U.S. health care system and effects on public health. *PLoS ONE, 11*(6), e0157014. https://doi.org/10.1371/journal.pone.0157014

Flach, J. M. (2012). Complexity: Learning to muddle through. *Cognition, Technology & Work, 14*(3), 187–197. https://doi.org/10.1007/s10111-011-0201-8

Frick, T. W., & Reigeluth, C. M. (1999). Formative research: A methodology for creating and improving design theories. In C. M. Reigeluth (Ed.), *Instructional design theories and models: A new paradigm of instructional theory* (pp. 633–652). New York: Routledge.

Geels, F. W. (2005). Processes and patterns in transitions and system innovations: Refining the co-evolutionary multi-level perspective. *Technological Forecasting and Social Change, 72*(6), 681–696. https://doi.org/10.1016/j.techfore.2004.08.014

Jonas, W. (2007). Research through design through research: A cybernetic model of designing design foundations. *Kybernetes, 36*(9/10), 1362–1380. https://doi.org/10.1108/03684920710827355

Jones, P. & Arun Kumar, P. (2021). Systemic design for healthcare sustainability: Patients, consumers and "big box" healthcare (workshop). In *Proceedings of the 10th Relating Systems Thinking and Design Symposium (RSD10)*, October 13–16, TU Delft, Delft, Holland.

Jones, P., & Bowes, J. (2017). Rendering systems visible for design: Synthesis maps as constructivist design narratives. *She Ji: The Journal of Design, Economics, and Innovation, 3*(3), 229–248. https://doi.org/10.1016/j.sheji.2017.12.001

Jones, P., & Van Ael, K. (2022). *Design journeys through complex systems*. Amsterdam: BIS Publishers.

Krippendorff, K. (2005). *The semantic turn: A new foundation for design*. Boca Raton: CRC Press.

Kumar, P. A., & Wang, S. J. (2019). Encouraging DfE in design education to promote sustainable medical product design. *Designing Sustainability for All, 4*(1), 1354–1359. Retrieved November 2, 2022, from https://lensconference3.org/index.php/program/posters/item/79-encouraging-dfe-in-design-education-to-promote-sustainable-medical-product-design

MacNeill, A. J., Hopf, H., Khanuja, A., Alizamir, S., Bilec, M., Eckelman, M. J., Hernandez, L., McGain, F., Simonsen, K., Thiel, C., Young, S., Lagasse, R., & Sherman, J. D. (2020). Transforming the medical device industry: Road map to a circular economy: Study examines a medical device industry transformation. *Health Affairs, 39*(12), 2088–2097. https://doi.org/10.1377/hlthaff.2020.01118

MacNeill, A. J., McGain, F., & Sherman, J. D. (2021). Planetary health care: A framework for sustainable health systems. *The Lancet Planetary Health, 5*(2), e66–e68. https://doi.org/10.1016/S2542-5196(21)00005-X

Ossebaard, H. C., & Lachman, P. (2021). Climate change, environmental sustainability and health care quality. *International Journal for Quality in Health Care, 33*(1), mzaa036. https://doi.org/10.1093/intqhc/mzaa036.

Patton, M. Q. (1994). Developmental evaluation. *Evaluation Practice, 15*(3), 311–319. https://doi.org/10.1177/109821409401500312

Patton, M. Q. (2018). *Principles-focused evaluation: The Guide.* New York: Guilford Press.

Patton, M. Q. (2021). Blue marble evaluation perspective: How evaluations help solve global crises. In R. D. van den Berg, C. Magro, & M.-H. Adrien (Eds.), *Transformational evaluation for the global crises of our times* (pp. 19–36). International Development Evaluation Association Exeter, UK.

Pedersen, J. (2007). *Protocols of research and design*, Ph.D. Thesis, IT University of Copenhagen (Ed.). Copenhagen. Retrieved July 26, 2022, from http://dasts.dk/wp-content/uploads/2007/11/protocols-of-resarch-and-design.pdf

Pereno, A., & Eriksson, D. (2020). A multi-stakeholder perspective on sustainable healthcare: From 2030 onwards. *Futures, 122*, 102605. https://doi.org/10.1016/j.futures.2020.102605

Schön, D. A. (2017). *The reflective practitioner.* London: Routledge. https://doi.org/10.4324/9781315237473

Sherman, J. D., MacNeill, A., & Thiel, C. (2019). Reducing pollution from the health care industry. *JAMA, 322*(11), 1043. https://doi.org/10.1001/jama.2019.10823

Sherman, J. D., Thiel, C., MacNeill, A., Eckelman, M. J., Dubrow, R., Hopf, H., Lagasse, R., Bialowitz, J., Costello, A., Forbes, M., Stancliffe, R., Anastas, P., Anderko, L., Baratz, M., Barna, S., Bhatnagar, U., Burnham, J., Cai, Y., Cassels-Brown, A., Cimprich, A. F. P., Cole, H., Coronado-Garcia, L., Duane, B., Grisotti, G., Hartwell, A., Kumar, V., Kurth, A., Leapman, M., Morris, D. S., Overcash, M., Parvatker, A. G., Pencheon, D., Pollard, A., Robaire, B., Rockne, K., Sadler, B. L., Schenk, B., Sethi, T., Sussman, L. S., Thompson, J., Twomey, J. M., Vermund, S. H., Vukelich, D., Wasim, N, Wilson, D., Young, S. B., Zimmerman, J., & Bilec, M. M. (2020). The Green Print: Advancement of environmental sustainability in healthcare. *Resources, Conservation and Recycling, 161*, 104882. https://doi.org/10.1016/j.resconrec.2020.104882

Sturmberg, J. P. (2020). Systems design for health system reform. In G.S. Metcalf, K. Kijima, & H. Deguchi (Eds.), *Handbook of systems sciences.* Tokyo: Springer Japan. https://doi.org/10.1007/978-981-13-0370-8_56-1

Dr. Peter Jones Ph.D., is an Associate Professor at OCAD University, Toronto in the Design for Health and Strategic Foresight and Innovation and M.Des programmes. He is a co-founder of the Systemic Design Association and its conference series, the RSD Symposia, and conducts research and designs tools for complex social systems design. He is the founder of multiple systems-change programmes, from communities of practice to economic transformation initiatives and applied research labs, including the Strategic Innovation Lab and Flourishing Enterprise Institute. For nearly 20 years, he has led the design of 'tools for thinking', decision support and information services for professional work practices through mixed-methods design and engaged fieldwork. He has authored four books and numerous articles, developing systemic design methodology and design research into healthcare systems, new economics and sustainability as flourishing.

Pranay Arun Kumar M. Phil, is a Designer and Researcher based in New Delhi, India. He graduated with a Bachelor's degree in Product Design from the National Institute of Design, Ahmedabad in India and a Master's degree in Design Research from the Royal College of Art, London in the United Kingdom. He has been working as an independent design and research consultant in the field of accessible, affordable and sustainable healthcare and medical devices. He is a recipient of two International Design Awards, has developed medical devices with numerous small and medium enterprises in India, and supported research and development projects through mentorship and design services for organizations including IIT Delhi, AIIMS Delhi, ICRC, WHO and the University of Oxford. He is a Visiting Faculty at OCAD University in Toronto, Canada and at the National Institute of Design in Ahmedabad, India.

Healthcare Complexity and the Role of Service Design in Complex Healthcare Systems

Jürgen Faust, Birgit Mager, and Carol Massa

ABSTRACT

There is a continuous change in healthcare experiential and operational challenges that require a shift to a collaborative approach which fosters the new ways utilizing methods and requires expanding perspectives. Therefore, service design within the healthcare sector gets increasingly important. It increases the need for understanding complexity, since healthcare systems and subsystems can always be called complex. Traditionally, service design and complexity has been framed by a wicked problem approach which has been a great description of complexity situations and the need for adapting to wicked problems when designing. Therefore, this article starts with a recommendation of five mindsets in service design before it explores the value of service design drawing from interdisciplinary knowledge when unraveling healthcare systems. An interdisciplinary exploration of complex systems, considering the various thinking schools, adds fundamentally to the framework to understand emergency departments within hospitals and healthcare systems and shows what service design can contribute to such healthcare systems. The second part of the paper follows a research and design process, looking at a healthcare system using service design to improve the emergency department experience. Because of the deadline, the description of this application comprehends the intelligence and design phase, showing how complexity can be handled by carefully designing, enacting, and testing the mindsets presented. It shows that in complex systems

J. Faust (✉)
Steingasse 8, 69469 Weinheim, Germany
e-mail: Jurgen.faust@mobile-university.de

B. Mager
Mülheimer Freiheit 56, 51063 Köln, Germany
e-mail: mager@service-design.de

C. Massa
4008 Maguire Blvd, Apt 5113, 32803 Orlando, Florida, United States

like healthcare and emergency departments, service design practice needs to be done with time and care, since systems and subsystems react and present interdependencies that need to be intentionally designed.

1 Service Design and Complexity

Healthcare systems are shifting from a centralized and authoritative approach toward a decentralized and collaborative approach, which favors partnerships and co-creation (Cottam & Leadbeater, 2004, pp. 94–98). The involvement of both patients and service providers in the development, implementation, and execution of healthcare initiatives lies at the heart of service design (Mager et al., 2017, pp. 6–10). The key philosophy is that people need to participate in the design of the healthcare products, services, and systems that affect them.

1.1 What is Service Design?

So, what exactly is service design? Service design choreographs the people, technologies, and processes within a complex service system to co-create value for the relevant stakeholders. The term "choreography" indicates the need for a perfectly formed, even artful, interplay between the different actors, technologies, and systems, and, of course, an interplay between efficiency and elegance.

Service design uses a specific process, user- and process-focused methodologies, and a particular way of visualizing, thus reducing the fear of complexity by making it all more accessible. Above all, service design requires a mindset that is focused on designing improvements and innovations in a continuous way. Service design broadens the perspective on the user journey: where does the health system start, and where does it end? It reframes problems, aiming to achieve better answers by asking better questions.

Service design works within complex systems by engaging with the networked structures of dynamic subsystems (Weisser et al., 2018, p. 39), which cannot be controlled but only influenced and steered. This work with living systems requires co-creation with users, providers, and experts during all phases of the design and delivery of services.

The following five "mindsets" can guide the application of service design within a complex system such as the healthcare system (Mager & de Leon, 2022, pp. 492–494).

Mindset 1: Exploration is the key to success. The basis for successful innovation is continuous, in-depth, qualitative and quantitative exploration of user needs, user experiences, competitors, employee perspectives, and technology analysis, together with constant engagement with a changing societal value architecture.

Mindset 2: Successful innovation must break through boundaries. The experiences that users have with services should not be structured by departmental boundaries nor by the channels through which the services are provided. The user journey must be designed holistically, through interdisciplinary co-creative ways of working, and this process must be established by default.

Mindset 3: Using interdisciplinary co-creative service design methods, alternative concepts are developed from a variety of ideas and then evaluated and translated into relevant business models. In the early phase of this development, the boundaries must not be drawn too tightly. This mindset is an invitation to think the unthinkable, to wish for what is not yet feasible, and to dream about things that do not yet exist.

Mindset 4: Prototypical and iterative ways of working save time and money and yield better results. In service design-driven projects, prototypes are used throughout the process, continuously tested in all versions—from low to high fidelity—with users and stakeholders, and iteratively refined. This saves time and money and leads to the identification of the best options.

Mindset 5: Employee satisfaction is directly correlated with user satisfaction. Using the analogy of a stage, employees are considered the actors, on the front stage, whose responsibility is to obtain applause from the users in the audience. The actors must be secure in their roles and be motivated and supported by props and the backstage processes. Technologies are nothing but tools that serve the people. A great employee experience will enable a hospital to attract and retain top talent.

1.2   The Impact of Service Design in the Healthcare Sector

Service design enables strategic change to happen and policies to be created that will ensure a better future. It drives the design of improvements and innovations that seek the best for both users and providers. It does this in collaboration and co-creation with relevant stakeholders (Mager et al., 2022, n.d.). In 2017, the Service Design Network published a qualitative study that highlighted five key impact areas for service design in the health sector: organizational change, cultural change, patient engagement, education and capacity building, and policy-making (Mager et al., 2017, p. 8). The study pointed out that more than 170 organizations globally were active in 680 projects focused on healthcare service design, with 40% of those projects already being implemented and scaled. A key focus in these service design projects was the engagement of stakeholders in the process, including in the design of new service offerings and their implementation. The importance of moving beyond tokenistic stakeholder engagement in this space was acknowledged. In particular, this work highlighted the benefits of service design, building on an ongoing tradition of support from peers and expert users in healthcare. This

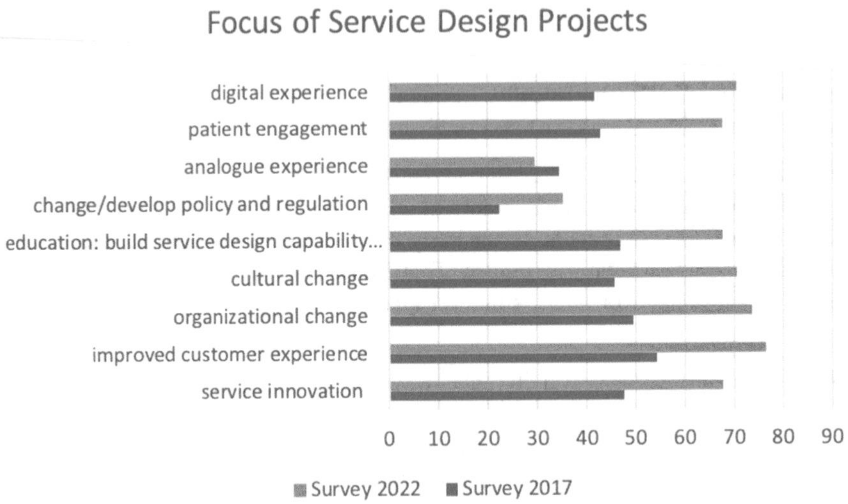

Focus of Service Design Projects

Fig. 1   Focus of service design projects. *Source* Mager (2022)

highlights the need to deepen the understanding of the importance and benefits of meaningful co-creation in healthcare service design.

A new unpublished qualitative study on the impact of service design in the health sector, conducted in 2022 by Birgit Mager, shows that service design projects are often focused on several objectives at the same time, and that service design for digital experiences is growing in importance, whereas design for analogue experiences is losing impetus (see Fig. 1).

Hundred percent of the participants agreed that service design helps to unravel complexity in interdisciplinary teams. The responses included a statement that interdisciplinary research is a means for making the complex more accessible by creating a shared understanding of the system and of the objectives of any change project. The participants also pointed out that a multitude of methods are used within the service design process: ecosystem maps, stakeholder maps, visual representation of stakeholders, visualization of patterns, journey maps, blueprints, storyboarding, prototyping, and video prototyping—to name just a few.

One particular contribution of service design, which is highlighted in this article, is dealing with the complexity within the healthcare system. In the next chapter, we look more deeply into the challenges that healthcare organizations face due to their complexity, especially in relation to their emergency departments.

2   Complexity in Healthcare Organizations, Especially in Emergency Departments

The following sections explore complexity concepts within the context of service design, looking from a traditional perspective, the wicked problem approach, which is common in design, but as well by using complex system theory to search and develop a service design approach handling the complexity of emergency departments.

2.1   Approaching Complexity Through Service Design

During the first generation of service design, there was a tendency to refer to Rittel and Webber's 1973 concept of "wicked problems" when explaining why conventional scientific approaches had failed to solve the problems of pluralistic urban societies (Zellner & Campbell, 2015, p. 457). From the conceptual perspective, the description of wicked problems helped greatly to qualify the complexity of the environment, but it lacked both the vision and the methodology for tackling the wicked problems and for moving beyond the concept into action.

It is therefore interesting to look further into research that considers complex systems, as this has now enlarged the scientific base for working in complex environments. Zellner and Campbell (2015, p. 452) re-evaluated wicked problems by considering them from a complex system perspective and came to the following conclusion: wicked problems focus on characterizing the problems and their structures. In contrast, complex system thinking focuses on modeling representations of organized complexity (Jacobs, 1961, p. 14), which, while characterizing the nature of the wicked problems, include interventions that engage with those complex systems. The goal of systems thinking is to explore potential solutions. Complex systems thinking thus illuminates wicked problems by identifying the crucial actors and intervention points for system-wide transformation in a diverse, adaptive, multi-agent world (Campbell & Zellner, 2020, p. 1654).

The intersection of wicked problems and complex systems is, especially for service design, a rich ground in which to understand possibilities and explore potential solutions. We find ourselves at this intersection when evaluating the complexity of the emergency department.

The situation in the emergency room, the onboarding place in hospitals, is recognized to be extremely complex. In recent decades, many authors have drawn attention to the complexity of the emergency department (ED), with a focus on providing solutions by engaging with the complexity (e.g., Ahmad et al., 2015, p. 361; Franklin et al., 2011, p. 469; Woods et al., 2008, p. 26).

Mäurer (2018, p. 3) describes the situation in his introduction to his book, Nightmare Emergency Room (Albtraum Notaufnahme), as follows:

> Crowded waiting areas, patients and relatives complaining loudly, overworked staff. On the one hand, there are real emergencies that require fast and expert clinical care, and on the other hand, there are "perceived emergencies", usually in greater numbers, that certainly do not require the care structure of a hospital.

> All of this contributes to considerable frustration on the part of both healthcare professionals and patients, and this frustration is being released with increasing frequency. For patients

and relatives in the form of inadequate behaviour, and for healthcare professionals by questioning our care system, which not infrequently leads to uncertainty, especially among our junior staff (Mäurer, 2018, p. 3).

In mechanical systems, boundaries are fixed and well defined, but in complex systems, the boundaries are fuzzy (Plsek & Greenhalgh, 2001, p. 625). We frequently do not know where the systems start and end. For instance, the emergency department is a part of a bigger entity, the hospital. When looking at such complex adaptive systems, the agents are seen to be acting on rules, internalized rules, that cannot be understood from the outside. Many of these internalized rules are not common between organizations and agents, for instance, between medical specialists. These agents adapt to different situations, they adjust to a particular situation, and therefore the systems are adaptive, and they co-evolve (Plsek & Greenhalgh, 2001, p. 625). Because these systems interact, there will be tensions between them, for instance, the ED will interact with various clinical systems, between which there is competition, cooperation, and politics. In systems as complex as the healthcare system, subsystems, such as the ED, will be nonlinear in function; for example, the unpredictability of patient flows over time is inherent. However, through observation and given enough time, we are able to identify and analyze patterns. In the Science of Complexity, these are called attractors. Another important aspect of these complex systems is that they will organize themselves on the basis of certain rules that they give to themselves. There is no central agent who tells everybody what needs to be done. There would be no time to follow instructions if there was a sudden patient overflow in the ED. A degree of uncertainty is inherent in the system, and it inevitably results in self-organization (Plsek & Greenhalgh, 2001, p. 627).

2.2   Complexity as a Framework

Complexity is a difficult term, since the use of the term will change depending on the context and on the literature we choose to follow. Complexity may involve a collection of nonlinear interacting parts; it may be a study on how "wholes" emerge from parts, a study of systems whose descriptions are not appreciably shorter than the systems themselves, or it may refer to a philosophy, a set of tools, a set of methodologies, or a worldview. In relation to design, complexity usually refers to "wicked" problems (Richardson, 2006, p. 211).

Therefore, one possibility is to take reality as complex, since the phenomena we try to capture are the result of nonlinear complex processes that feed back on each other. It is no surprise that the Science of Complexity points to the limits of a scientific understanding of complexity, which means that if the universe is a complex system, or a whole, then a philosophy of reality must be complex as well. Richardson (2006, p. 191) proposes that we look first into different schools of thought to get an understanding of different ways in which we can approach complexity, and that this might also shed light on how service designers should frame the complexity discourse.

The first school of thought, associated with physics, is the classical reductionist approach, based on the assumption that the world is nonlinear, and therefore complexity can be handled only by the use of computer simulation, in the form of bottom-up, agent-based modeling (Richardson, 2006, p. 191). The reductionist approach frames Complexity Science as follows:

Premise 1: There are simple sets of mathematical rules which, when followed by a computer, give rise to extremely complicated patterns.

Premise 2: The world contains many extremely complicated patterns.

The conclusion here is that, with the help of powerful computers, scientists can identify these fundamental rules (Richardson, 2006, p. 192). Some authors have warned against this assumption, since they conclude that the "verification and validation of numerical models of natural systems is impossible" (Oreskes et al., 1994, p. 642). However, simulations of emergency department complexity have been conducted and researched for decades. An early paper, by Hannan et al. (1974, p. 382), describes the application of a FORTRAN simulation model, simulating the influence of new patient demands, administrative decisions, and the impact of new policies. According to the reductionist approach, computer simulation can be used to model and handle emergency department complexity.

The second school of thought is the metaphorical school. In organizational science, a theory of organization has been developed that is based on metaphors. Terminologies such as connectivity, edge of chaos, far from equilibrium, dissipative structures, emergence, epistatic coupling, and co-evolving landscapes are used to describe the complexity inherent in sociotechnical organizations (Richardson, 2006, p. 192). The belief underlying this approach is that the social world is intrinsically different from the material world. This means that theories that have been developed through the examination of natural systems are not directly applicable to social systems. Metaphorical approaches to complexity can also be grounded through criticism, not perfectly, but acceptably. The school of complexity that uncritically imports ideas and perspective via the mechanism of metaphors from a diverse range of disciplines can be called the metaphorical school. It represents the greatest source of creative models, which constitutes quite a challenge, since we know that creativity alone is not sufficient to create excellence in design. The first two schools of thought can therefore be seen as extremes: the metaphorical and the reductionist schools lie at either end of the spectrum, metaphorically speaking.

The third school of thought is the critical pluralist school, which lies midway between the first two and connects them. The critical pluralist school of complexity focuses more on what cannot be explained than on what can be explained. It focuses on the limits. It refers to a particular model rather than referencing some models over others. Furthermore, it ends in some relativism, where anything goes, and this school emphasizes open-mindedness and humility (Richardson, 2006,

p. 192). All possible perspectives are helpful in shedding light on complexity, but not every perspective is equally valid. Complexity thinking is the art of maintaining a tension between pretending that one knows something and knowing nothing for sure.

2.3   What is a Complex System?

Richardson (2006, n.d.) defines a complex system as an observable phenomenon, which is the result of intricate, nonlinear causal processes between parts, often unseen. At a deep, fundamental level, the universe is well described as a complex system where everything observed emerges from that fundamental substrate. Thus, everything is the result of nonlinear (complex) processes.

Anything that can be examined in detail should not inevitably be treated as complex. This also means that if we look for perfect answers, a theoretical impossibility will appear.

Richardson provides the following definition:

A complex system is composed of a large number of non-linearly interacting non-decomposable elements. The interactivity must be such that the system cannot be reduced to two or more distinct systems and must contain a sufficiently complex interactive mixture of causal loops to allow the system to display the behaviours of such systems (Richardson, 2006, p. 195).

Cilliers (1999, pp. 3–4) describes complex systems in the following way:

1. Complex systems consist of a large number of elements.
2. A large number of elements are necessary, but not sufficient.
3. Their interaction is fairly rich.
4. The interactions themselves have a number of important characteristics. First, the interactions are nonlinear.
5. The interactions usually have a fairly short range.
6. There are loops in the interactions.
7. Complex systems are usually open systems.
8. Complex systems operate under conditions far from equilibrium.
9. Complex systems have a history.
10. Each element in the system is ignorant of the behavior of the system as a whole; it responds only to information that is available to it locally.

If we add the notion of subsystems within systems, the complexity outlined here is very much in line with the description of complexity in healthcare systems by Plsek and Greenhalgh (2001, p. 628). How can this exploration help to design services in the emergency department, and how can it help to frame systems design in healthcare? By exploring and understanding these conditions and their environment, we will be helping to non-function blindly. Knowing the context will bring a steep increase in intelligent understanding, which will create the basis for informed service design.

2.4   Boundaries in Complex Systems

If we take the outline of complexity seriously, we recognize that there are no real boundaries in complex systems, and that the very concept of boundaries is inappropriate in a complex system (Richardson, 2004, n.d.). But how do we retrieve knowledge if there are no boundaries, since knowledge needs differentiation, and to be differentiated, form has boundaries?

From the complexity perspective, it would seem that there is an outcome, because we can "observe" resident and relatively stable structures and patterns emerging. There is a distribution indicating boundary stability, even if there is no evidence of such boundaries (Richardson, 2006, n.d.). Such a framing does not contradict the framing that involves form and knowledge, since structures and patterns are only recognizable due to their characteristic form (see Fig. 2).

A presentation, such as the above, has no empirical or theoretical basis, but it describes a possibility. At one end of the spectrum, there are boundaries/structures/patterns, such that we can say that they are real and absolute. On the left side of the figure, we can see how the scientific community has been able, intersubjectively, to converge upon some agreed principles that may actually be tested through experimentation. From this, we retrieve quasi-objective knowledge. Therefore, in certain circumstances, reductionism appears perfectly valid. But it is still approximate—a route to an understanding of complex systems. At the other

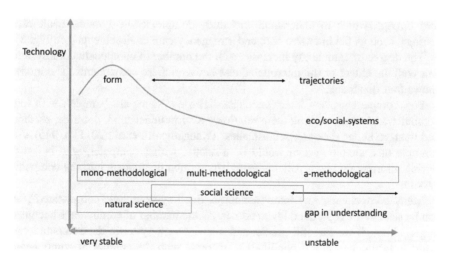

Fig. 2 Boundary stability, systems, methods, and knowledge. *Source* own presentation, adapted from Richardson (2006, p. 213)

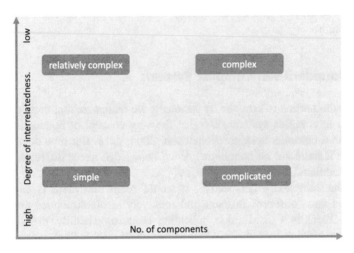

Fig. 3 The range of complexity depending on number of and degree of interrelatedness between components. *Source* Kannampallil et al. (2011, n.d.)

end of the stability spectrum is essentially "noise", which persists in being unrecognizable and non-analyzable. Within the mid-region of the spectrum, we find both, although boundary recognition and allocation here is not a trivial task. However, "in accepting the complex systems, we are committed to be critical of how we use the notion since it affects our understanding of such systems and influences the way in which we deal with them" (Cilliers, 2001, p. 142).

What does this mean for the designing of healthcare services and for the designing of ED services in particular? Kannampallil et al. (2011) propose a theoretical lens through which to understand and study complexity in dynamic healthcare settings, such as the intensive care and emergency care environments (see Fig. 3).

The degree of complexity increases with the number of components in a system and with the extent of the interrelatedness between these components. The model shows four quadrants:

Few components, low interrelatedness. "These systems are 'simple', with low computational costs, making them relatively easy to understand, describe, predict, and manage under various circumstances" (Kannampallil et al., 2011, p. 945). An example of a simple system would be a doctor, with a computer, who is transferring information about patients from handwritten documents into the computer system.

Many components, low interrelatedness. Such systems are "complicated", as can be seen in the right hand lower corner. As the number of components becomes larger, although we can still predict and manage such systems, the computational effort is far greater, and it continues to increase with the number of components and the variables. Such a system might be an EMR system used by all the staff in a clinic, including the physicians, nurses, pharmacists, and administrators. Here, they all act within the system, but in the specific role assigned to them within it (Kannampallil et al., 2011, p. 945).

Few components, high interrelatedness. As Kannampallil et al., (2011, p. 945) state, such systems are "relatively complex", and if they are computed, the effort is high. The number of components is small, but the interrelatedness is high. An example might be a critical care unit, or the ED, where only a few members of the team are called because the trauma situation requires a specialist. Research shows that the divergence in performance can be high in this situation (due to errors and deviations from protocol) (Shetty et al., 2009, p. 28).

Many components, high interrelatedness. These are the most "complex" systems, and here the computational efforts are very high. Kannampallil et al., (2011, p. 945) give as an example of multiple critical care teams attending to traumas following a mass casualty event, who have to deal with multiple patients with different conditions, and within a significantly changed work environment (e.g., where trauma protocols come into play).

2.5   Service Design: Handling Complexity in Practice

The framework just presented poses a challenging task, since the complexity of a system will change according to the perspective and the research questions applied. Systems may appear quite different if the granularity changes in relation to the angle adopted by the researcher. Therefore, one research question may require greater complexity than another. The research question can be answered from a general perspective, or the complexity may be divided into smaller functioning units and the relationship between them considered (Simon, 1991, p. 470).

However, the components of a complex system must be identified (the limit being what is known), the number of relationships, their uniqueness, and strength have to be determined, since the degree of interrelatedness will affect the functioning of the system. Tight or weak relatedness between components will affect their behavior in a complex system. The probability, the correlation, or the direction between components will all affect the functioning of the system and therefore cannot be ignored. Disregarding interrelationships between components may have a greater or lesser impact on the functioning of the system, depending on how strongly linked the behavior is. Kannampallil et al. (2011, p. 945) give the ED as an example, and they describe the difference between patient-related information and information about bed management and availability.

The analysis of the system and the description of the interrelatedness of its components are extremely important and need to be considered in any context where the components of a system are interrelated and cannot be separated (Weaver, 1991, p. 5). Weaver describes such systems as disorganized complex systems. For example, the patient flow in the ED on particular days is less predictable than the patient flow over a longer time period, for which patient arrival rate can be presented and described statistically. It is important that we are conscious about disorganized complexity and search for appropriate variables to be considered when describing it.

3 Applying the Framework to Reimagine an Emergency Department Visit Experience

This third chapter of the paper presents the application of the service design framework to a complex healthcare system. It illustrates how service design has helped unravel complexity and promote market differentiation in an ongoing development of the emergency services in a healthcare system in Central Florida, in the United States. When this article was submitted for publication, the project described was still ongoing, and we are therefore only able to present preliminary findings on the reimagining and enhancing of the ED services.

As in all human-centered service design work, the design process is based on a creative problem-solving approach applicable to all human activities. The process will be framed by Simon's description of the design process as comprising intelligence, design, and choice (Simon, 1977, n.d.).

Another consideration is that, as far as we know, within a complex system, the intelligence process is never finished, since the knowledge gained can be retrieved and increased at all stages of the project. Within this context, we accept a pragmatic approach, knowing that the paper presented will always be a fragment, even during the descriptive phase of collecting what is known about emergency departments and their complex service systems.

3.1 The Given ED Service Design System Circumstances

To illustrate the conditions of this project, there is a need to collect and systematically summarize what is known and what is a given in relation to the resources for this project:

1. In recent decades, EDs have come to be considered the front door for emergency care. Although it is hard to predict how consumers/patients will choose which emergency department to go to, that visit will become the baseline of their hospital experience and thereafter affect their choice to utilize one health system over another. As a result, the ED plays an increasing role in relation to marketing activities for hospitals and healthcare systems. It can become a brand reference, and the visit experience can become a key opportunity for differentiating service designs.

2. As discussed, healthcare services are designed around highly complex systemic structures to deliver the most basic need—to ensure that people can live their best lives. Around the world, observable healthcare systems (both public and private) attempt to improve their current processes, their operations, and how they deliver human-centric healthcare experiences. Changes made in this

highly complex environment can mean the difference between life and death. A more radical position holds that the ED experience should make a positive contribution from the moment the patient arrives, and that it should provide what the patients care most about (Güse & Schuster, 2016, p. 175). Thus far, we could hypothesize that there is a worldwide competition, a global dialogue on learning and adaptation, concerned with how best to design and manage ED services.

3. As the relationship between consumers and service providers becomes increasingly complex and interconnected, being able to recognize, deconstruct, and re-imagine complex service interactions becomes the new norm.

4. Due to ongoing changes in the competitive landscape in Central Florida, and the evolution of consumer expectations, top-down leadership identified an opportunity to re-imagine their emergency department visit experience. The assignment focused on prototyping a reimagined service experience for an ED visit and was similar to opportunities that have arisen in European countries.

5. To re-imagine an emergency department experience requires a systemic approach, where the sum of the parts is greater than the whole. Key stakeholders from the Florida health system agreed to break down the larger system into smaller parts: including the arrival and the departure experiences. This made it possible to identify key driving forces and existing relationships that can be researched and reimagined.

6. A further condition imposed on the task was the decision to engage an internal innovation team, consisting of researchers, service designers, and strategic thinkers. This team would be responsible for designing innovative approaches for the largest division of Central Florida's healthcare system.

7. The time scale of the project was decided on the basis of budget constraints and intent, which dictated speed-to-market.

8. The selection of emergency departments to be used in the study and to learn from was based on market share volume, key target audience, and the competitive landscape. The subsequent selection of facilities was approved by the top administration.

9. A stakeholder committee and a group of subject matter experts were formed, and they were included in the overall team that reported on the structure of the project.

10. The project focused on including an outside-in perspective (human-centric design) from consumers/patients who experience the service. Leveraged by service design methods, the healthcare organization was able to make impactful decisions affecting the patient ED visit experience and designs for change.

Attempting to put these conditions into a visual display highlights the complexity of the project, even before touching on the internal system components and the relationships that make up the actual service experience of an ED visit. The visual below (see Fig. 4) describes the outer circumstances that affect the conditions to be considered when designing an ED system. Such a system is considered an open

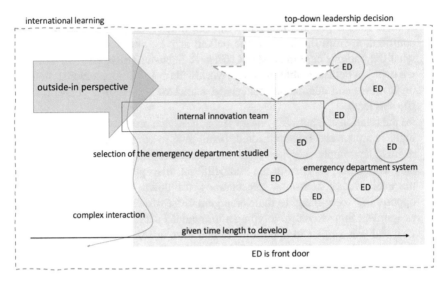

Fig. 4 Outer circumstances impacting ED system design. *Source* Author's own figure (2022)

system (Cilliers, 1999, p. 4), and as such, it has an ongoing exchange of social, technological, and procedural knowledge and expertise.

By identifying the current ED system conditions and the external forces that influence the way in which it operates, the internal innovation team employed their service design skills in tackling the challenge of how to re-imagine and create a consumer-driven experience within the highly complex operational system.

3.2   Application of the Service Design Model

The Central Florida healthcare organization mentioned in this article has a centralized Innovation team responsible for bringing their innovation to the market. It is important to highlight that the innovation mindset needed for performing this innovative work in this organization is based on Theory U from Scharmer (2009, p. 44). Scharmer (2009, p. 40) refers to an open mind, an open heart, and an open will, as the prerequisites for initiating change and growth when dealing with the complexity of today's world. As a result, the design model, created by the team's executive leader, was based on three key pillars: Empathy Research (immersive research methods, such as applied ethnography, which uncovers unmet needs among consumers, employees, and the organization), Co-creation (cross-functional groups come together to solve organizational and local challenges through creative problem-solving exercises), and Iterative Prototyping (the creation of prototype(s) for key ideas/concepts to enable quick and cost-effective iterations of possible solutions based on the consumer/employee/organization feedback). The design process usually ends with a hand-over to a local operational team, which eventually pilot

Table 1 Three phases of the process. *Source* Author's own table (2022)

Phases	1. Intelligence	2. Design	3. Choice/Selection
Approach	Frame and collect current-state data	Brainstorm ideas and prototype concepts	Develop people, process, platform/tech requirements for small-scale pilot
Service Design Methods	• Shadowing and interviews • Focus groups • Emergency medical • Staff interviews • Operational interviews • Subject matter expert's interviews	• Cross-disciplinary ideation sessions • Concept development • Evaluative research • Bodystorming sessions	• Testing sessions • Capability assessment • Pilot design manual/playbook

concepts on a small scale, learn from it, and incorporate the learnings to accommodate local and national needs. At the end of the process, the Innovation team plays a strategic partner role to ensure that unmet needs and design intent are still being met as the solutions are implemented and scaled (see Table 1).

The innovation team started the design process with scoping research, and they continued to be involved until they had prepared an operational team for a pilot. The team started by assessing the current state, re-framing the problem, and defining their research strategy—the intelligence phase (Simon, 1977, p. 19). The main objective at this point was to understand how the ED works, and to identify key experiential and operational opportunities from the moment the consumer decides where to go, until the moment they conclude their ED visit. To accomplish this, five research work streams were established: focus groups, with target demographics; ethnographic studies (shadowing and interviewing staff); EMS interviews; key operational interviews with team members; and expert interviews with ED practitioners around the world. Some of the core questions that were initially driving the research were as follows:

• How much is known about the consumer/patient journey when coming to an emergency department?
• What driving forces are active when someone is in pain?
• What is the patient's experience from arrival until discharge?
• What are the key moments in the consumer/patient's journey through an emergency department visit?

The team believed that by looking across the five streams, the learnings could potentially be shared across regions, facilities, and departments. Having intelligent data available could lead to improvements in the current service.

Documenting how ED throughput works can be an overwhelming task, since the system shows signs of anticipatory qualities: it plans to cope with possibilities (e.g., patient overflow) and adapts like a biological life system (Plsek, 1997,

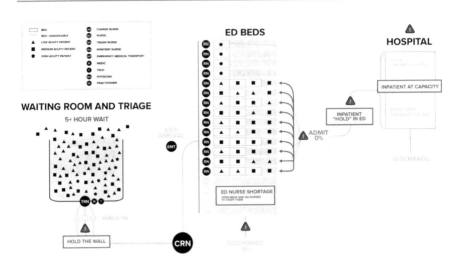

Fig. 5 Representation of the emergency department throughput. *Source* Patrick O'Connor and Carol Massa (2022)

p. 627). It works as a living complex entity that is dependent on other parts of a healthcare system. To solve these communication challenges, the Innovation team leveraged the service design to demonstrate how the system units work and their core interdependency. In this way, both top-down and bottom-up team members had a shared understanding of the operational effort required to deliver the service experience (see Fig. 5).

In addition, once the research was conducted and the key insights identified, the Innovation team produced a current-state journey map, to be used as an alignment tool, and they created a frame of reference for stakeholders, staff, and team members to visualize the typical key stages of the patient experience, combined with the operational steps of the clinical team supporting the visit—from arrival until discharge/admission. This map served as the baseline for the co-creation phase and helped to identify areas of opportunities, and high and low points in the interaction between consumer/patient and operations.

After that, the Innovation team moved from the intelligence phase to the design phase (Simon, 1977, p. 19). Following key mindsets 2 and 3, as mentioned above, for applying service design within a complex system like healthcare (Mager & de Leon, 2022, pp. 492–494), the current-state journey map was used during cross-functional team brainstorming exercises to generate ideas and potential pathways, or courses of action, that could potentially deliver a high level of value exchange between consumer/patient, operators, and organization (see Fig. 6).

This map became the source of truth for the innovation work. However, to prioritize and solidify which concepts would have a high level of desirability, feedback sessions were held with real consumers to collect their reactions and to identify gaps in the current selection of ideas/concepts.

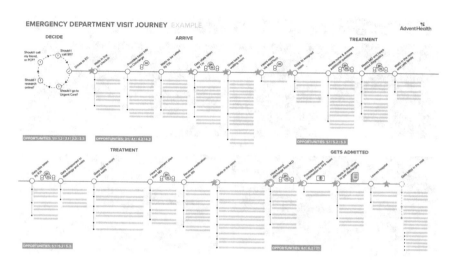

Fig. 6 Current-state journey map of a typical ED visit. *Source* Author's own figure (2022)

After the feedback sessions, concepts were refined, but due to the complexity and speed in the emergency department, it was important to consider the concepts as a system. As a result, the iterative prototyping (Sanders & Stappers, 2015, p. 6; Blomkvist, 2014, pp. 24–25) phase was utilized to bring the ideas to life in a way that the organization had not been exposed to before.

To break down innovation barriers and to save time and money (Mager & de Leon, 2022, pp. 492–494), during this next phase of design, the Innovation team designed prototypes that created the illusion of a finished product. In this way, the interdisciplinary teams were able to quickly learn and gain valuable insights before spending significant resources. It was important to emphasize to key stakeholders that the reimagined experience can be brought to life in a variety of fidelities. Although these may not look or behave anything like the final outcomes, they do provide a space for problem-solving, experimentation, and learning from bringing a cross-disciplinary team together.

With this in mind, the innovation team decided to iterate the concepts by using a bodystorming exercise (Erwin, 2014, p. 157) as the main prototyping technique. This technique allowed teams to mock-up conceptual ideas, using non-existent technology, and to interact with frontline care team members in an experiential environment. During week-long prototype sessions, designers and non-designers (people not trained in design) were creatively co-designing and working together through the prototype process (Sanders & Stappers, 2008, pp. 5–7). With the performing arts being used as a reference for the team during the bodystorming sessions, actors were invited to play out key scenarios and pressure-test the generated concepts, iterating on them "live" and identifying gaps in the processes, training, and tools needed to deliver on the vision. The non-designers in these sessions were the actors, frontliners, nurse leaders, and managers. They all

Fig. 7 Images 1–4. Bodystorming session photos. *Source* Author's own figure (2022)

came together to act out scenes from key moments of the reimagined experience. Redesigning an emergency department visit requires seamless integration between people, roles, responsibilities, tools, training, process, and technology. As a result, these experts created a shared vision for an ideal ED visit experience in a "safe physical" space (see Fig. 7).

The outcomes of the week-long session facilitated by the Innovation team concluded the design phase of the project. A set of requirements was being generated, which would form what would ultimately become the pilot version (a part) of the systemic reimagined ED visit (the whole). By documenting these requirements, the Innovation team started to build a landscape for the implementation work. However, the biggest challenge in breaking down such a complex journey is that the parts may not add up to the whole. To ease the transition from the parts to the whole, the Innovation team decided to elevate the level of fidelity of the prototypes, and they conducted one in a semi-live, controlled testing environment.

In addition, certain design activities required making decisions and establishing criteria before moving forward, which is why key stakeholders from the established reporting structure were involved in the process. They suggested using a facility in the north of Florida, which potentially would benefit from the concepts being designed. In going through the choice phase (Simon, 1977, p. 19), the Innovation team followed the recommendation of the committee and engaged with the local leadership of the chosen facility.

An important note: the semi-live testing was carefully designed to allow the team to go "undercover" and to be part of the care team without compromising patient care and clinical regulations, such as the EMTALA (Emergency Medical Treatment and Labour Act, which ensures public access to emergency services regardless of their ability to pay), and the HIPAA (Health Insurance Portability and Accountability Act, which is the standard that addresses the use and disclosure of individuals' health information—known as "protected health information"—by entities subject to the Privacy Rule).

If this semi-live test generated positive results, it would encourage leaders to visualize the potential impact of these concepts not only for the pilot but also for the reimagined ED visit experience. This testing was dependent on the Innovation team and key facility members being comfortable making non-clinical mistakes and practising rapid adaptive learning. Internal communication was key to creating an environment of trust and a no-judgement zone.

The emergency department is a highly sensitive place in which to work (due to patient care and the possible violation of healthcare policies); this makes the environment vulnerable and unstable, just as is observed in a complex adaptive system.

The innovation team spent an entire month trying out different variables and combinations of key elements of the service experience. Although some digital tools were not available, some "workarounds" were prototyped at a low-fidelity level. However, the team was still able to learn from that, create protocols, and collect baseline information to guide future developments of new processes and new roles that would play important roles in the reimagined service experience.

Overall, it was highly valuable for the Innovation team to go "undercover" and become part of the system where they were able to test, learn, and adopt new ways of designing conditions for reimagining Emergency Department visits.

At the time when this article was sent to print, the case study was still happening, and a play book was being developed to inform the pilot team how to run the experience on a smaller scale. The final results of this testing were not available at the time of writing; however, learnings were already being collected and shared as the Innovation team conducted the semi-live testing sessions and had open feedback sessions with the operational team, where key learnings were shared and identified to help with implementation and scale.

The first learnings gleaned from the ED service design system development:

1. The scoping of a complex project, such as that for the emergency department, can benefit from additional references to systems thinking, chaos theory, and complexity theories to help understand what approaches can be beneficial in an unstable environment in order to avoid unintended consequences that could potentially break the system. In this case, "breaking" the healthcare experience would have a highly negative impact on the patient's care and must be prevented.

2. When designing to re-imagine experiences that require the integration of people, systems, tools, and technology, ensure that sufficient time for testing and learning across different facilities and demographics is incorporated. Avoid speeding up the process by moving too quickly from ideas to piloting and implementation. When working with complex systems and the current state of experience, it is important to take time to test and to learn how the system reacts to different combinations and varying "intensity" levels of intervention.

3. Finally, as we recognized when the Innovation team went undercover and became a variable in the current system, we had learned to identify the weak touchpoints or lack of capabilities in the ones who do serve and will serve in the new interactions. Moving from a current-state system, where the components seem to be in some sort of balanced state, to a new/reimagined future state needs to be carefully designed, simulated, conceptualized, and communicated, down to the last detail.

As the insights in the project show, further research is needed to simulate a small-scale representation of the reimagined experience before a pilot phase can be considered.

4   Conclusion

As our research shows, the complexity of the challenges in emergency departments creates a huge opportunity for service design and needs further research and re-framing. However, as we already know, there will be no final description of a situation, since systems adapt and change, even during observation.

Service design can bring real value if it draws from interdisciplinary knowledge when unraveling the ecosystems within ecosystems. This observation is much in line with a recent study (Sun et al., 2022, p. 7), which provides the key finding that a shift toward a transdisciplinary approach in service design may have a significant impact in solving complex and wicked problems.

The application of service design methods often brings to the surface the inter-dependence of system entities. Therefore, in complex systems, service design practice needs to be done with time and care, since systems and subsystems react and present interdependencies that need to be recognized and documented.

The service design practice is vital when advancing services and preventing system collapses. At the beginning of this article, the attitude needed was described in terms of mindset. It is impossible to control a complex service system (Weisser et al., 2018, p. 39), but it can be influenced and manipulated. As secondary research shows, the metaphorical approach (Richardson, 2006, p. 192) can be quite successful when service design teams leverage such approaches. Why should we not also test a reductionist approach, using DES (discrete event simulation) systems to model patient flow (Ahmad et al., 2015, p. 360–362; Duguay & Chetouane, 2007, pp. 311–320; Komashie & Mousavi, 2005, pp. 2681–2685), since logistic complexity, which is also a part of ED complexity, can be modeled, presented, estimated, and tested? Subsystems, such as the Emergency Department, may be less complex, but they are not necessarily simple and tend to be rather complicated. It contains many components, and there is a high interrelatedness between the system parts, the computational effort of modeling everything might be too high. However, it would certainly help to first test the impact of what we are designing. By breaking down systems into more comprehensive parts, keeping in mind that there may be huge issues in doing so, the design team should be able to explore and experiment while minimizing the risk. It is not only a challenge to present such systems in an adequate format; it is an even bigger challenge to influence and manipulate service design systems in the ED. For such tasks, the five mindsets, outlined early in this article, are strongly recommended.

References

Ahmad, N., Ghani, N. A., Kamil, A. A., & Tahar, R. M. (2015). Modelling the complexity of emergency department operations using hybrid simulation. *International Journal of Simulation and Process Modelling, 10*(4), 360–371.

Blomkvist, J. (2014). *Representing future situations of service: Prototyping in service design.* Linköping Studies in Arts and Science, Dissertation No. 618. Linköping, Sweden: Linköping University Electronic Press.

Campbell, S. D., & Zellner, M. (2020). Wicked problems, foolish decisions: Promoting sustainability through urban governance in a complex world. *Vanderbilt Law Review, 73*, 1643.

Cilliers, P. (1999). 'Complexity and postmodernism. Understanding complex systems'. Reply to David Spurrett. *South African Journal of Philosophy*, *18*(2), 275–278.

Cilliers, P. (2001). Boundaries, hierarchies and networks in complex systems. *International Journal of Innovation Management, 5*(02), 135–147.

Cottam, H., & Leadbeater, C. (2004). *RED paper 01: Health: Co-creating services.* London, United Kingdom: Design Council.

Duguay, C., & Chetouane, F. (2007). Modelling and improving emergency department systems using discrete event simulation. *SIMULATION, 83*(4), 311–320.

Erwin, K. (2014). *Communicating the new: Methods to shape and accelerate innovation.* Hoboken, NJ: Wiley Pub.

Franklin, A., Liu, Y., Li, Z., Nguyen, V., Johnson, T.R., Robinson, D., Okafor, N., King, B., Patel, V.L., & Zhang, J., (2011) Opportunistic decision making and complexity in emergency care. *Journal of Biomedical Informatics, 44*(3), 469–476.

Güse, C., & Schuster, S. (2016). Kundenorientierte Dienstleistungsprozesse für alte Menschen in der Notaufnahme. In *Dienstleistungsmanagement im Krankenhaus* (pp. 173–202). Wiesbaden: Springer Gabler.

Hannan, E. L., Giglio, R. J., & Sadowski, R. S. (1974). A simulation analysis of a hospital emergency department. In *Proceedings of the 7th conference on winter simulation*, Washington DC, January 14–16, 1974 (Vol. 1, pp. 379–388).

Jacobs, J. (1961). *The death and life of great American cities.* New York: Random House.

Kannampallil, T. G., Schauer, G. F., Cohen, T., & Patel, V. L. (2011). Considering complexity in healthcare systems. *Journal of Biomedical Informatics, 44*(6), 943–947.

Komashie, A., & Mousavi, A. (2005). Modelling emergency departments using discrete event simulation techniques. In *Proceedings of the winter simulation conference*, Sunday, December 4–7, 2005, Orlando, FL. (pp. 2681–2685). Institute of Electrical and Electronics Engineers (IEEE).

Mager, B., & de Leon, N. (2022). Service design-innovation for complex systems. In B. Edvardsson & B. Tronvoll (Eds.), *The Palgrave handbook of service management* (pp. 483–496). Cham: Cologne, Germany: Springer Nature.

Mager, B., Haynes, A., Ferguson, C., Sangiorgi, D., Gullberg, G., & Jones, M. (2017). Impact and future perspectives. In B. Mager (Ed.), *Service design impact report: Health sector*. Cologne, Germany: Service Design Network (pp. 94–98).

Mager, B., Oertzen, A.-S., & Vink, J. (2022). Co-creation in health services through service design. In M. A. Pfannstiel, N. Brehmer, & C. Rasche, *Service design practices for healthcare innovation. Paradigms, principles, prospects.* (pp. 497–510). Cham: Springer Nature.

Mäurer, M. (2018). Springer Medizin. Albtraum Notaufnahme. *Der Neurologe & Psychiater, 19*(2), 3–3.

Oreskes, N., Shrader-Frechette, K., & Belitz, K. (1994). Verification, validation, and confirmation of numerical models in the earth sciences. *Science, 263*(5147), 641–646.

Plsek, P. E. (1997). Systematic design of healthcare processes. *Quality in Health Care, 6*(1), 40.

Plsek, P. E., & Greenhalgh, T. (2001). The challenge of complexity in health care. *British Medical Journal (BMJ), 323*(7313), 625–628.

Richardson, K. (2004). The problematization of existence: Towards a philosophy of complexity. *Nonlinear Dynamics, Psychology, and Life Sciences, 8*(1), 17–40.

Richardson, K. A. (2006). Complex systems thinking and its implications for policy analysis. In G. Morcol (Ed.), Handbook of decision making (pp. 189–221). https://doi.org/10.1016/s0000-0000(00)00000-0.

Sanders, E., & Stappers, P. (2008). Co-creation and the new landscapes of design. *Co-Design, 4*(1), 5–18. https://doi.org/10.1080/15710880701875068

Scharmer, C. O. (2009). *Theory U: Leading from the future as it emerges.* San Francisco, CA: Berrett-Koehler Pub.

Shetty, P., Cohen, T., Patel, B., & Patel, V. L. (2009). The cognitive basis of effective team performance: Features of failure and success in simulated cardiac resuscitation. In *AMIA annual symposium proceedings* (Vol. 2009, p. 599). American Medical Informatics Association (AMIA). November 14, 2009–November 18, 2009, Hilton San Francisco & Towers, San Francisco, CA.

Simon, H. A. (1977). *New science of management decision.* Reading, PA: Prentice Hall.

Simon, H. A. (1991). The architecture of complexity. In *Facets of systems science* (pp. 457–476). Boston, MA: Springer.

Sun, Q., Phoebe, J., & Ziwei, L. (2022). Service design practice and its future relevance. In *The 23rd DMI: Academic design management conference proceedings* (pp. 21–34). DMI.

Weaver, W. (1991). Science and complexity. In *Facets of systems science* (pp. 449–456). Boston, MA: Springer Publishing.

Weisser, T., Jonas, W., & Mager, B. (2018). Successfully implementing service design projects. *Touchpoint, 10*(1), 34–40.

Woods, R. A., Lee, R., Ospina, M. B., Blitz, S., Lari, H., Bullard, M. J., & Rowe, B. H. (2008). Consultation outcomes in the emergency department: Exploring rates and complexity. *Canadian Journal of Emergency Medicine, 10*(1), 25–31.

Zellner, M., & Campbell, S. D. (2015). Planning for deep-rooted problems: What can we learn from aligning complex systems and wicked problems? *Planning Theory & Practice, 16*(4), 457–478.

Jurgen Faust is Professor and Program Director of Design Management MA as well as UX & Service Design MA at SRH Mobile University, Germany. He holds his Ph.D. from the University of Plymouth, GB. He worked as Professor and Dean in four countries, the United States, Mexico, Italy, and Germany. Between 2013 and 2020 he served as the President of Macromedia University, Munich. His research and his publications focus on design theory and theory design, researching the changing artifact in design and management.

Birgit Mager is Co-Founder and President of the International Service Design Network, publisher of Touchpoint, the international Journal of Service Design. Since 1995 Birgit Mager holds the first ever professorship on "Service Design" at the University of Applied Sciences Cologne, Germany and since then has developed the field of Service Design constantly in theory, methodology, and in practice. Her numerous lectures, her publications, and her projects have strongly supported the implementation of a new understanding of the economical, ecological, and social function of design in the domain of services.

Carol Massa is a Multi-disciplinary Designer with 10 years of experience across many fields of design including visual design, branding, and strategic design. Through recent years, she has worked as a Consultant and a Mentor for Fortune 500 companies, helping teams work through complexity and overcome business challenges to deliver meaningful solutions through a service design approach. Today, she is a Design Manager at AdventHealth Central Florida Division, helping the organization design for healthcare service experiences. She is SDN Accredited and teaches at SDN Academy on strategic design with people across the world.

Zooming in and Out of Complex Systems: Exploring Frames in Incremental Participatory Design Projects

Adeline Hvidsten and Frida Almqvist

ABSTRACT

Designers are increasingly working with wicked problems in complex systems, which defy simple solutions. Such problems require flexible problem-solving approaches, and it has been suggested that designers and other change-makers can draw flexible boundaries around them. This chapter explores the concept of framing through a case of incremental participatory design in the complex system of Norwegian health care. We apply an analytical approach which zooms in and out across time and space, finding that for incremental design, participants work within frames which have shifted over time. However, some participants are more aware of and have more frame-defining and re-framing power than others. We also find that when zooming out, time is an important aspect. When trailing the relationships between components within the frames to components outside, current frames are invisibly and powerfully determined by current and past developments as well as future possibilities. When dealing with outdated frames, participants can re-frame in order to give new attention and momentum to the design endeavor, enrolling new actors that might facilitate implementation. However, it is vital to remember that re-framing tends to result in compromise, meaning that while some actors are included, others are not—and not all participants have the same framing capacity.

A. Hvidsten (✉)
Skogvollveien 16c, 0580 Oslo, Norway
e-mail: adeline.hvidsten@kristiania.no

F. Almqvist
Galgeberg 3g, Oslo, Norway
e-mail: frida@halogen.no

1 Introduction

This chapter explores the concept of framing incremental participatory design in complex systems, presenting a case from Norwegian health care. Health care is an example of a complex system: a combination of many different types of components, where their relationships are just as important, or even more, than the attributes of the components themselves (Norman & Stappers, 2015a). Problems that emerge in complex systems are a certain type of wicked problem, networked, continuously mutating problems which cannot be fully framed, understood or solved by one discipline alone (Jones, 2014; Rittel & Webber, 1973). These systems are resilient and keep operating even though most of them have one or many fundamental flaws, this also makes them very difficult to transform. For human-oriented approaches such as participatory design, invisible but powerfully structuring components such as regulatory, economic, cultural and organizational aspects constrain and limit the impact of innovation. Dealing with these characteristics, many scholars call for making incremental changes and small-step innovations that together push the system towards transformation over time.

Incremental design efforts bring forth many interesting topics. The first is the attention that needs to be given to the aspect of time and temporality. Incremental design means that design is never finished, and that any design effort is part of a "chain" of previous and future interventions. The second is the acknowledgement that designers might be restricted in their efforts, due to the nature of design projects, and the limited scale and scope of their tools (Jones, 2014; Jones & van Patter, 2009). Third, when time passes, the world changes. Incremental design requires framing the design problem, which influences who and what is included in the process—and who "falls out of the current frame"—as well as the attention given which influences for example funding and the ability to enroll other disciplines and change-makers (Jones, 2014, p. 114). While designers update and change frames, the frame will also be skewed by the passing of time, by the influence of the involved participants, and the fact that any attempt to frame and solve a wicked problem by definition will also change the problem itself (Rittel & Webber, 1973). Acknowledging the relational aspect of systems, components within the current frame will by definition also stretch beyond it, in time and space.

In the next section of the chapter, we give a brief overview of complex systems and some perspectives dedicated to understanding and transforming these problems and systems through Human-Centered Design (HCD). We focus on particular on the notion of incremental change and the concept of framing, before we present the suggested analytical framework of zooming in and out as a way to explore accountabilities across time and space.

Later, we present the case from Norwegian health care. E-messaging between Norwegian hospitals and municipalities were implemented in the period of 2013–2014 after a 15-year public process. Users quickly found multiple issues in their daily work lives such as missing and buried information, arguing between organizations and problems with coordinating the admittance and discharge of patients to hospital. The chapter presents findings from facilitating and following an incrementally focused re-design project initiated by "the Hospital" in 2014, resulting in the implementation of keywords in e-messaging in 2017.

Lastly, we discuss how zooming in and out sheds light on the invisible but powerfully structuring components which might influence the implementation of incremental design, and how the notion of framing and re-framing emphasizes the power of some stakeholders to mobilize and align with such components. We underline the power that lies in framing efforts, and how these are related to events happening "elsewhere" in time and space.

2 Systemic Human-Centered Design: Eating the Whale One Bite at a Time

Human-Centered Design (HCD) has the potential to transform health care by emphasizing the needs and experiences of real people (Malmberg et al., 2019, p. 2). In this chapter, we understand it as an umbrella term for overlapping literatures such as co-design and participatory design. Participatory design (PD), focus on involving end-users in the design process, and has two main propositions: the right of users to be directly included (moral), and the usefulness of their expert perspective in the design process (pragmatic) (Carroll & Rosson, 2007). Co-design can be defined as designers and non-designers working together in a design process, expanding the notion of the user to multiple stakeholders (Sanders & Stappers, 2008). Such a democratic approach to design and innovation has been highlighted and prioritized in past and current Norwegian public legislation and regulation (Almqvist, 2020; Ministry of Health & Care Services, 2014).

Health care is an example of a complex societal system with many interconnected components whose interaction constitutes, and are critical for, the behavior of the overall system. Even though most such systems are imperfect, as they have one or many fundamental flaws, they are "amazingly robust", (Norman & Stappers, 2015a, p. 93). Complex systems survive long-term by growing and transforming slowly in the absence of a major disruption/disaster. Due to their resilience and complexity, facilitating the transformative change of, and implementing smaller changes within (Rodrigues & Vink, 2016, p. 1), such systems are difficult.

Further, the subject matter of design, especially in complex systems, is indeterminate and wicked (Buchanan, 1992; Jones, 2014). The notion of wicked problems in design was made popular by Horst Rittel, defining 10 attributes of wicked problems (Rittel & Webber, 1973), and they are often described as:

A class of social system problems which are ill-formulated, where the information is confusing, where there are many clients and decision makers with conflicting values, and where the ramifications in the whole system are thoroughly confusing. (Churchman, 1967, p. 141)

Partly due to these dynamics, there is a history of failed implementations in health care, and HCD comes with a danger for naivete; believing that all human-centered design will work per se, without seeing the need for larger changes in the organization in question (Deserti & Rizzo, 2014; Rodrigues & Vink, 2016). In health care, some of "the biggest barriers to implementation can be found in the social, political and economic frameworks"—a project can find the seemingly optimal solution based on the needs of the people involved, but still struggle with actual implementation (Myerson, 2015, p. 101). This calls for examining the larger system that design initiatives are part of, and especially implementation: "when political, economic, cultural, organizational, and structural problems overwhelm all else" (Norman & Stappers, 2015b, p. 83).

As such, we need to understand the relationships between what traditionally have been seen as the "top down" and the "bottom-up". Co-design following participatory design propositions are "bottom-up" design processes with participants who have the right to influence their own lives. However, there often require the support "top down" from organizations, industries and governments in order to actually make change happen (Manzini, 2014a, 2014b).

Jones (2014, p. 102) suggests that a socio-technical system (socio-technical systems can be written with and without the hyphen. We use the concept with the hyphen here, as it signals the approach to the social and the technical as ontologically separate entities) approach can show the whole-system ecology of services, which becomes the target of design. This is a complex systems perspective that sees social and technical components of systems as independent entities that are intertwined in reciprocal influencing relationships (Cozza, 2021, p. 181) There are differing interpretations on how designers might target socio-technical systems as an object of design. Baek et al. (2015, pp. 63–67) aim for a virtuous cycle between the social and technical components. They argue that designers can intervene in the technical system to re-enforce the social system. Other scholars such as Junginger (2017, p. 168) criticize an over-focus on technological innovation, and Norman and Stappers (2015a, p. 90) believe the answer "lies in the way that human-centered design treats the human part of systems".

Jones (2014, p. 102) postulates four layers of practice in socio-technical systems, where "each level constrains the social and work practices in the adjacent lower level within a range circumscribed by economics, practice, and professional norms":

1. Human layer: Bottom layer where needs emerge and technological interaction is applied (the user, the patient, the customer)
2. Work unit/activity layer: Determined by top layers
3. Industry and Organization layers: Top layers forming long-term contexts, practices, roles and skills in the system. Faces historical constraints such as policy and barriers to organizational change. Supervising processes.

Jones (2014, p. 103) further highlights that while the needs and experiences of actual humans exist at the bottom layer, service systems are often directed towards goals at the highest-level context of systems:

Table 1 Two approaches to the increasing complexity of the subject matter of contemporary design. *Source* Author's own Table (2022)

Buchanan's (1992; 2001) four orders of design	Jones and van Patter's (2009) four (highly connected) dimensions of design
1. Graphic symbols 2. Physical objects 3. Services, interactions and strategic planning 4. Systems, environments and organizations	*Design 1.0:* Designing artefacts and communication (e.g., traditional design) *Design 2.0:* Designing products and services for value creation and interaction (e.g., service design) *Design 3.0:* Designing organizational transformation (e.g., work practices, structures, strategy) *Design 4.0:* Designing societal transformation (e.g., policy, social systems)

Electronic health records systems are not procured for patient needs, or to enhance the work practices of a given activity. They primarily meet organizational objectives for reporting, information control, and operational economics. In the US, these systems have been encouraged by extraordinary financial incentives established by government policy (Industry layer), which essentially drive their procurement and deployment.

Baek et al. (2015, p. 77) argues that there might be an inherent dichotomy between user-centered and system-oriented design, as the needs of humans in the system sometimes are in direct contrast to the needs and intentions of the system itself. Design scholars have tried to synthesize how the domain of design ranges from artefacts and symbols to complex systems, where complexity increases as we move from the first to the last. Table 1 gives an overview of the categorizations by Buchanan, and Jones and van Patter.

Systems in practice cannot be approached by methods and toolkits such as Human-Centered design in its design studio-form, as there can be mismatches between the scale and scope of design methods and practice and the systemic issues (Jones, 2014; Jones & van Patter, 2009). In order to transform sociotechnical systems, designers must scale up their interventions from artefacts, communications, products and services to organizational and social transformation.

Design can pose a flexible and intuitive orientation towards wicked systemic problems, instead of a traditional analytic and procedural approach (Jones, 2014). In this chapter, vi focuses on the concept of boundary framing or re-positioning in design processes, and the potential of incremental design.

2.1   Re-positioning Problems and Solutions

Wicked problems are ill-formulated problems that do not have clear boundaries and accountabilities, and that change over time. The wickedness of design problems requires those working with design to "discoverer or invent a particular subject out of the problems and issues of specific circumstances" because even the most detailed brief is only one possible definition of a problem—that will most likely be subjected to re-positioning by designers (Buchanan, 1992, p. 16).

One suggestion of how designers can deal with wicked and systemic problems is through setting and re-negotiating frames and boundaries for design, to discover the subject matter for design in a given context (Buchanan, 1992; Dorst, 2015b). Buchanan (1992, p. 8) presents the idea of placements; fluid and flexible boundaries around specific situations. By setting temporary boundaries designers form and test hypotheses, updating and moving them as they learn throughout the process as part of creative invention. Placements can be considered a useful heuristic for furthering the field of design, moving from designing the symbolic and physical to the complex environment as described in the section above. However, the concept can also be considered the core of design practice, the ability to re-position an iniquity and discover new relationships: He argues that designers should be regarded as masters in the exploration of the doctrine of placements (Buchanan, 1992, p. 14).

Similarly, Dorst (2015a, p. 23) sees how professional designers work with frames and has the ability to re-frame a problem "if they suspect the design solution is inadequate". Framing and re-framing also means that the designer has the ability to redefine both the problem and the solution at the same time, and that they sometimes have the freedom to step away from initial paradoxical problem definitions (Dorst, 2015b; Paton & Dorst, 2011). Participants in a project might go into it with different framing of projects, and not be aware of how frames can change as part of the process (Paton & Dorst, 2011, p. 575) Frame creation as a professional design practice means artificially broadening the frame to understand the networked nature of problems, exploring histories, paradoxes and stakeholders to understand needs and values (Dorst, 2015a, p. 26). While this has been growing out of professional design practice, Dorst (2015a) believes that it can now be seen as a more general problem-solving approach that can be used by more stakeholders—propelling designers into more complex endeavors.

The power of professional designers, and other co-designers implicated in the process, to set, create and negotiate boundaries, frames and placements can be seen as a type of power of influence. Boundaries set engage some actors, while excluding others, influencing components such as attention given to issues and financing (Jones, 2014, p. 114). For example, during design synthesis (moving from lots of insights towards solutions), designers "must decide that one piece of data is more important than another", what is relevant for the current problem-solving context as well as forge connections between (often previously unrelated elements) (Kolko, 2010, p. 21). Especially as designers have expert power, partly power in designing the project, and to a large degree to define access, roles and rules for the process as well as the potential solution (Goodwill et al., 2021). Further, there are some issues which might occur in framing and re-framing, such as becoming locked into a mental model where their frame becomes limiting (Buchanan, 1992), and fixation, "a bias towards the known, the attachment to a previous idea or course of action" (Jones, 2014, p. 113).

2.2   The Challenge of Incremental Design

As designers engage with systemic problems, there is not one obvious best way forward. Understanding the invisible, intangible, emergent nature of systems and services, and the unpredictability of human action, Systemic Design approaches suggest continuous evaluation, adaption, dialogue, iteration and multiple actions over time (Jones, 2014). Designer's main function become creating conditions for actions to happen, relationships to form and systems to self-organize (Baek et al., 2018; Jones, 2014). Dealing with systemic issues might be best attempted by spreading solutions on different "nodes" and focusing on developing "local initiatives in which those directly affected—that is, those who know the problem best and from close up—are directly involved" (Manzini, 2016, p. 57). Such incremental solutions might not make radically better outcomes, but push the system slowly into the right direction, as larger changes are difficult due to the resilience and interdependence of systems; designing for the real world entails compromise (Norman & Stappers, 2015a, p. 94). For example, Gleason and Bohn (2019) highlighted the effect of small-step designing to make changes that might seem as mundane or routine—but have a positive impact on patients' experience of services and their health outcomes. Moore and Buchanan (2013, pp. 11–16) similarly call for "sweating the small stuff" short-term, in addition to long-term large-scale projects.

In this chapter, we focus on the role of frames and the influence of invisible but powerful for determining the nature of higher-level systems comments such as attention and financing on re-framing of incremental participatory design. In the next section, we suggest how an analytical framework that consists of zooming in and out through selective repositioning might help us understand the potentially conflicting components in larger-systems and the consequences of framing.

2.3   Zooming In and Out: Accountabilities Across Time and Space

From a socio-technical perspective, the higher-level layers are subject to long-term slow change, and these layers have a big influence on organizations and the humans in lower-levels (Jones, 2014, p. 103). As such, systemic approaches require both micro/macro and short/long-term understanding:

> things like supply chains, standards that serve multiple stakeholders in different situations, legal constraints, decision making groups, scheduling issues, and long-term productivity often are large, complex processes in themselves, with time frames measured in hours, days, and even years (Norman & Stappers, 2015a, p. 89).

Dorst (2015a, 2015b) believes that the ability to expand the frame through for example focusing on the history, is important for the practice of re-framing. In this section, we propose the analytical approach inspired by Nicolini's (2009) notion of zooming in and out. This does not necessarily mean zooming in for more granularity, or out for the bigger picture, but also switching theoretical lenses to for example understand how phenomena can be both locally constituted and distributed over space and time (Nicolini, 2009). The idea is that adopting certain lenses brings some things to the fore and backgrounding others; without one lens being superior. For example, Hungnes and Hvidsten (2017) explored the case of Aker Health Arena in Oslo, relating the physical and organizational challenges happening in the arena to the larger political context in the Oslo area. Gorli et al. (2018) studied how the translation of a local hospital space was influenced by the larger idea of patient-centeredness.

Nicolini (2009, p. 1393) applies four different lenses to show how they provide different accounts and understanding of his data: one of them is the methodological and theoretical toolkit found in the Sociology of translation when zooming out. This has also been suggested by Kimbell and Blomberg (2017, p. 89), as sociomaterial approaches to designing for services might bring to the fore "the specific cultural, economic and political practices and institutions that co-articulate service". The sociology of translation has a rich tradition of understanding how and why change happens over time, as part of a historical effort by multiple actors. This allows us to explore design in-the-making, not just ready-made-design, and avoid after the fact "blind" explanations (Akrich, 1992, p. 207; Akrich et al., 2002, p. 190). Nicolini (2009, p. 1410) was inspired by how the approach might explain how, in his study, the local accomplishment of telemedicine was actually influenced and influencing "by events and practices taking place elsewhere". In this chapter, we apply the concept of translation (Nicolini draws mainly on other concepts such as mediators and generalizers. However, it is outside the scope of this paper to go into a detailed discussion of the multiple tools and concepts found in the sociology of translation.) to explore the mobilization of policy and economic aspects co-framing incremental participatory design in practice.

Somewhat simplified, we can apply the concept of translation to understand power: how some actors end up speaking and acting on the behalf of others. Change, design and innovation, happens through multiple translations over time. For example, when a problem is identified there are always multiple interpretations of what the problem really is, and as such what solutions might be relevant. Over time, some of the implicated actors convince other actors to "join" their perspective; mobilizing and enrolling them and speaking and acting on their behalf. What first appears as a complex network of controversy begins to appear like a single node in a network. Tracing associations back in time might show how some actors enrolled others and translated networks and ended up being powerful actors today. In the sociology of translation, actors refer to both humans and non-humans, granted they are the source of the translation/action (Latour, 1996, p. 373). As such, it is a post-human sociomaterial lens. While a socio-technical perspective sees humans and technology (and other non-humans) as ontologically separate entities and often focuses on their separate attributes, a post-human lens rather focuses only on the emergent effects and relationships between actors. As such, in this perspective, we can temporarily collapse the layers presented by Jones (2014, p. 103) and seeing only actors and their relationships over time.

In this chapter, we zoom in on frames in local human-oriented incremental design and zoom out on their dependency on economic and political decisions made elsewhere (sometimes travelling both in time and space). The next part of the chapter presents our methods and will give an overview of the lenses applied in our efforts of zooming in and out by re-positioning our conceptual lens.

3   Methods

The research material presented in this chapter is part of the first author's PhD-project, generated in the time period of 2014–2017. The case for this part of the project was a human-centered participatory re-design initiative to improve electronic coordination between hospitals and municipal health care services in Norway. It was inspired by different approaches for collaborative intervention, especially the research traditions of action research and participatory design (Greenwood & Levin, 2007; Simonsen & Robertson, 2013).

Research material was generated through participatory observation of work practices, workshops and work groups, semi-structured interviews and document analysis. The overall PhD-project had 146 respondents, 48 semi-structured interviews and approximately 250 h of observation. 31 public policy documents were also analyzed in order to trail connections by zooming out (Nicolini, 2009). The re-design part project consisted of two inter-organizational workshops facilitated by researchers and three work groups facilitated by an administrative ward at "the Hospital" (see Fig. 1). Being a part of a larger project, it was also very much informed by the overall data collection. Short follow up interviews were also conducted in 2017 after implementation.

Workshops and work were conducted with participants from both "the Hospital" a large Norwegian hospital and from two large municipalities within its catchment area ("Hillside" and the two city districts from "Central"). In the workshops, researchers functioned as facilitators and orchestrators.

Semi-structured interviews, workshops and workgroups were recorded and transcribed in full and supplemented with written notes. Notes, observation notes and transcriptions were coded into categories using the software NVivo. It was also

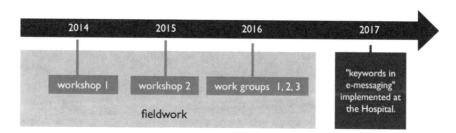

Fig. 1 An overview of the re-design project in time. *Source* Hvidsten (2019), p. 86

used for document analysis, exploring the historical development of electronic coordination and e-messaging through public policy (Akrich, 1992, pp. 221–222; Akrich et al., 2002; Nicolini, 2009). Following an abductive approach, we moved between research material, theory and existing studies, testing out frames for zooming in and out (much in the same way a designer would).

In the next part of the chapter, we present the case of incrementally re-designing e-messages at the Hospital and municipalities in its catchment area.

4   Findings: Local Re-design Related to E-messaging in Norwegian Health Care

This part of the chapter presents the experiences of participatory re-design of a standardized e-messaging module in an incremental collective design effort. The module was designed to facilitate the coordination of information between hospital wards and municipal health care services upon the hospitalization, treatment and release of patients. It was integrated into the Electronic Patient Journal (EPJ) system of both organizations, was developed through national innovation projects since 2004, and implemented at the Hospital and the municipalities in its catchment area in 2013. Figure 2 shows the flow of e-messages between EPJ systems, where municipal messages are denoted M and Hospital messages denoted H.

After the implementation of the module in 2013–2014, wards and administrative functions at hospitals and municipalities all over Norway were experiencing challenges with the new e-messaging module. The two organizations (hospital and municipal services) were now continuously messaging each other, and critical information flowed across geographical and professional boundaries. However, there were few, or no, guidelines in the interface. This meant that, for example,

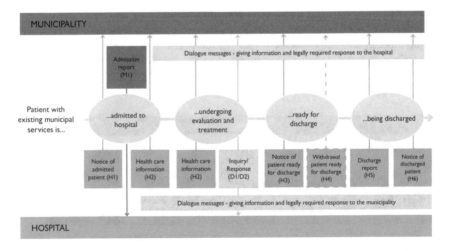

Fig. 2 E-messaging between hospital and municipal services. *Source* Hvidsten (2019, p. 165)

nurses at the Hospital did not know what kind of information nurses in the municipality needed. This led to multiple requests and responses back and forth, each containing a fragment of the full picture. These long strings of messages were troubling for both the nurses, as well administrators at the Hospital and municipalities, seeing important information "buried" in the multiplicity of messages and other, more irrelevant information. This took time to form the nurse's schedules, could delay the discharge of patients and even threaten the safety of their care. The messages were also, at times, a catalysator for the underlying issues of cooperation and coordination between the two organizations. While trained nurses were sending the messages between both organizations, their priorities for—and perspectives on—the right treatment for patients differed dramatically. This led to quarrels, stigmatizing those in "the other" organization and attempts to cheat the formalized processes for decision making. The situation was more complex than simply that of e-messaging.

For some time, the Hospital and municipalities Central (represented by city districts 1 and 2) and Hillside had been unsuccessfully reporting local issues to Supplier H and M. A shift in the political wind from the exchange of (messaging) to the access to information (universal and shared EPJ) in 2012 had made e-messaging passé (see blue field, Fig. 3) (Ministry of Health & Care Services, 2012). Suppliers quickly moved on to more profitable pursuits (However, it had taken 15 years from the first suggestion of e-messaging in 1997, to their implementation in 2013. Today (2022), ten years after the suggestion of an all access EPJ, it has still not been realized. As such, there is still no real alternative to e-messaging.), and attention towards the module disappeared. Figure 3 below shows the national and local innovation projects, strategy documents and white papers that contributed to the development of IT-architecture, legislation, organization and the technical solution of e-messaging module, implemented in 2013. Efforts were fueled by a 2008 Coordination Reform (Ministry of Health & Care Services, 2008) (dark green field, Fig. 3), highlighting e-messaging key for solving issues of fragmented and uncoordinated services, currently putting patients at risk, giving legislation and re-organization a final push towards the realization of the project which had been in the pipeline for many years.

After the e-messages were implemented in practice, they were suddenly "stuck" in coordinative practices between the Hospital and the municipal services. The development of legislation meant that nurses were obliged by law to use it for exchanging information, as well as coordinating efforts as patients were admitted and released from the hospital. A set of nationally developed standards formed the foundation of every e-messaging module for every EPJ in Norway, and these could not be changed without national effort. In 2014, one project to update standards had already failed due to conflicts between users and national organs of health care. Further, updates had to happen simultaneously for all EPJs (there could be as many as 10–15 in one region) to not lose any critical patient information carried. This was not plausible, much due to costs, safety and other practical concerns.

However, as they had been closely involved with the implementation in the first place (The Hospital had taken a lot of responsibility for the implementation of

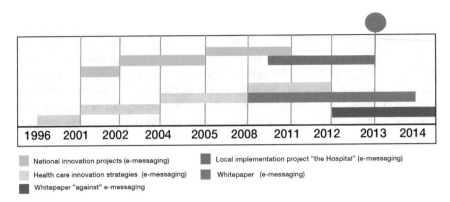

■ National innovation projects (e-messaging)   ■ Local implementation project "the Hospital" (e-messaging)

■ Health care innovation strategies (e-messaging)   ■ Whitepaper (e-messaging)

■ Whitepaper "against" e-messaging

Fig. 3 The historical development of e-messaging. *Source* Authors own figure based on Hvidsten (2019, p. 113)

e-messages in their region, and they had worked closely to involve the municipalities.), administrators at the Hospital asked the project researchers to help with a local re-design project. The project did not have resources outside time the used by researchers and was acknowledged as an incremental design effort. The formal mandate from the Hospital was to explore possibilities of adjusting e-messaging practice locally. Hospital administrators were especially interested in the idea of a technical solution in the interface itself. Three existing "workarounds" for the module that were currently employed at one of the wards, as well as two by other hospitals were set at the starting point for the project. This problem influences the municipal health care services in their daily work lives, and they were also contacted for involvement. Like the Hospital, they were very much interested in any re-design initiative concerning the module, especially a technical solution in their own EPJ.

Suppliers were at this point mainly tasked with monitoring and correcting minor issues. They were contacted as both organizations wanted to explore technical opportunities within e-messages. While the new policy climate made it difficult to change national standards, suppliers H and M acknowledged that "there is a huge potential for improvement in the messages" (Consultant, Supplier M) and that "the messages are very flexible, there are lot of opportunities" (Consultant, Supplier H). Here, they meant locally in the EPJ of the Hospital and municipalities. However, programming for EPJ-based solutions would require funding which the project did not have.

The re-design project was designed as a participatory project where both participants from the municipalities and hospital were considered equal experts on their own needs and experiences. Two participatory workshops were held at the hospital with participants from both organizations, facilitated by researchers. Further, local workgroups at the hospital elaborated on the solution suggested in workshops and overseeing its implementation in 2017.

4.1   Workshops and Fieldwork

The first workshop was focused around exploring coordination between the Hospital and municipalities in its catchment area and evaluating some "workarounds" as was the mandate set by the Hospital. The aim was collectively defined as "patients should experience the transitions between municipal and hospital health care as positive and coordinated" after a collective discussion and understanding of how the current situation was hurting patients (For example, how they experienced confusion over who made decisions about their treatment, long hospitalizations as the hospital and municipalities were not able to agree on treatment, specifications of medication and equipment buried in dialogue and many more.). The first workshop was preceded by qualitative fieldwork, focusing on the issues experienced by individual nurses as well as their needs and suggestions related to e-messaging and coordinative practice. An administrator at the Hospital saw it as such: "[e]-messaging is a tool to transfer information; what information the municipality needs and what the hospital needs is not something that the e-messaging itself should solve". Asking them to question the status quo was surprising for many nurses in both the Hospital and municipal services, as no one had ever asked about their experiences. Exploring the potential, several ideas emerged from stakeholders. For example, another smaller hospital had pooled its resources to designate a coordination nurse, responsible for coordinating efforts across organizations. Another suggestion was secondment, where nurses from each organization could work a few days in the other organization to better understand their practices as information needs. Further, it was suggested to create films depicting the daily work lives of the other organization, or how they should consider using the phone more. Some of the more innovative ideas focused on the distribution of responsibility between them, the content of the messages, and working on their timing in relation to each other's schedules and other interdependencies.

A summary of the fieldwork was presented in the first workshop, where participants were from both the Hospital and municipalities within its catchment area, some had been previously interviewed, and others not. In the first part, participants used post-its and a simple patient journey to communicate where they currently had issues or lacked information, and what their information needs were. Post-its were then used to formulate insights, questions, pinpointing issues with coordination and collaboration, existing service delivery and learning about interdependencies and ways of working in the different organizations.

The Hospital administration had wanted concrete suggestions for improvement of the e-messaging system as outputs of the project. As part of field work, researchers had explored the existing workarounds suggested in the project mandate. In the workshop, participants discussed the most technically feasible: (1) Hospital IPLOS, and the use of a (2) pocket sized check-list as messaging heuristics found on one of the wards at the Hospital, and (3) key words in the interface. These become anchor points for the rest of the discussion, and by the end of the workshop, a combination of keywords and paper lists were suggested as the best way to move forward for the next workshop. The discussion changed from over-arching and open in the first part of the workshop, to focused and detailed in the second part, discussing on the level of individual key words.

In closing, it was suggested that Hospital IPLOS was not wanted, that checklists might be useful but could also just become "another list/paper notice" (they were everywhere, "even the toilet!" said one participant), but that key words in the inter-face were interesting for both organizations. Both key words in e-messages and a paper list were to be examined in further field work and dialogue with suppliers H and M. Fieldwork revealed that any paper-based tool should to be coupled with keywords, which was explored and confirmed in the second workshop. Develop-ing key words for the municipal Admission Report (A1, Fig. 2) and the hospital Health Care Information (H2, Fig. 2) messages became the focus. The paper list could reduce the number of key words in the EPJ and be adjusted across wards and units with different specializations (e.g., the orthopedic ward could have lists than the geriatric ward), while the EPJ keywords could be similar for all.

At this point in the process, the realities of the system the nurses worked began emerging. In the first workshop, an administrator from the hospital that had not been involved with the national pilot was a participant. In the second workshop, two administrators from the hospital who initiated the re-design project attended. They had also been closely involved in the national e-messaging project and the local pilot. In the discussion of what information to include, one of the participants printed different documents for inspiration, which was used in discussing infor-mation needs. However, the administrators also steered the conversation towards technically plausible outcomes, being experts on the system. As everyone in the room knew that e-messaging in its current form was not always fulfilling the needs of nurses, most had developed their own "forbidden" practices and workarounds to make it work for them. It was important that these were discussed, as they rep-resented nurses' needs and experiences. However, when sharing these "forbidden" practices, attending nurses would look at administrators and make half-jokes about "cursing in church" or how administrators might not approve of what they were about to hear, before or after they would make a statement. The outcomes of the second workshop were a sketch of key words to implement in the e-messages, as well as a flexible paper check-list that could be adapted to the specializa-tion of different wards at the Hospital and Municipal services. Figure 4 shows how the keywords in the H2 message (left) would look together with paper lists specification (right).

The next section explores what happened when parts of the suggested solution were realized in practice.

4.2   Workgroups and Implementation

At this point in the re-design initiative, ideas from the workshops and fieldwork had to be validated and explored in terms of technical and practical feasibility. Here, funding was a critical issue in terms of realizing the technical part of the solution.

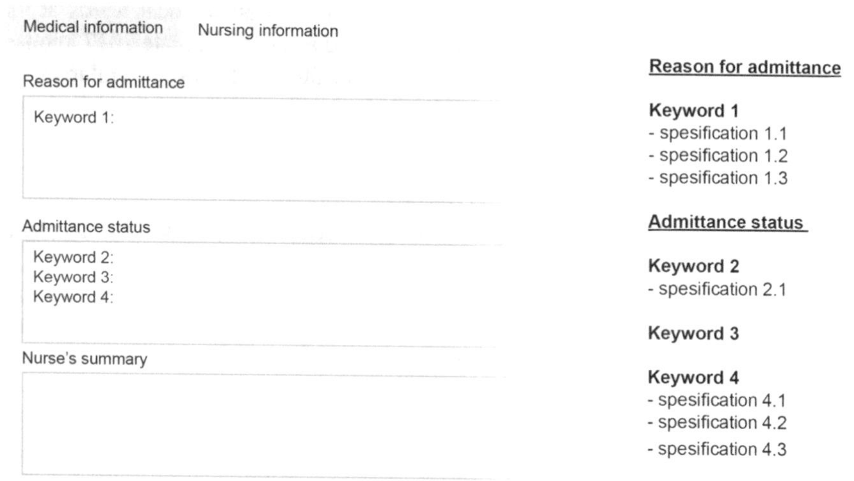

Medical information   Nursing information

Reason for admittance   **Reason for admittance**

| Keyword 1: | **Keyword 1**
| | - spesification 1.1
| | - spesification 1.2
| | - spesification 1.3

Admittance status   **Admittance status**

| Keyword 2:
| Keyword 3:   **Keyword 2**
| Keyword 4:   - spesification 2.1

                                                              Keyword 3

Nurse's summary

                                                              Keyword 4
                                                              - spesification 4.1
                                                              - spesification 4.2
                                                              - spesification 4.3

Fig. 4 Keywords in e-messaging interface in the hospital, with spesifications for paper list. *Source* Hvidsten (2019, p. 232)

In the Hospital, Supplier H was currently developing a new version of the EPJ, and they saw the development of keywords in e-messages as a way of piloting parts of the update:"I think that these [keywords] are something that will be very interesting for the next generation [of the EPJ]" (Developer, Supplier H). The key words could be seen as an experiment for finding words and terms that both nurses in the hospital and in the hospital found meaningful and useful. This was something that all parties regarded as interesting. For their EPJ, the solution could be turned on for the entire hospital using a simple fix. Further, the project could be included in an ongoing initiative at the Hospital to re-evaluate routines for the discharge of patients. The same approach was attempted with Supplier M. They were also working on a larger project related to the EPJ at the time. Meanwhile, Supplier M could not find a way to integrate key words in their messages without larger and expensive changes to the system. They suggested another workaround; however, this was not followed up by administrators at the Municipalities, and hence the municipal side of the solution dwindled away.

The Hospital organized three work group-sessions where nurses from municipalities were tasked with creating the key words (being the receivers of this information). The paper list-aspect of the proposed solution disappeared from the project, which now focused solely on the technical part of the solution. However, they ran into another issue. Even though the changes to the EPJ were small, all local adjustments had to be regionally approved. While the administrators were afraid this would delay or stop the process, it was quickly approved. One administrator expressed that: "I had described the whole situation, and, yes, I think there actually are many who are interested in this". The regional authority had recognized the potential for other users of e-messages.

The key words in e-messaging were implemented at all medical wards at the Hospital in the spring of 2017 and were considered a success. In late 2017 another national update to the e-messaging standards had failed. However, similar initiatives to key words have since being initiated at other hospitals and municipalities, and even regionally, based on the learnings from the Hospital.

5   Discussion: Framing in Incremental Participatory Design

Here, we outline some lessons for human-oriented incremental design in complex systems, based on the findings presented in the previous section. Similarly to Jones (2014, p. 103) and Baek et al. (2015, p. 77) we find the existence of contradictions between the needs of humans and the needs and purposes of systems. For example, the need for accountability on a systems-level trumped the need to update the e-messaging system in order to make it user-friendly for people trying to deliver good quality care for patients. While the system even worked as a catalyst to some of the fundamental flaws that exist in the Norwegian health care system—such as the issue of not working well together across disciplines—this was not enough for the system itself to break down. For, at the same time, the system was indeed increasing safety and accountability at a higher level. The system keeps operating even in the face of fundamental flaws (Norman & Stappers, 2015a, p. 93). In the next section, we dive into the concept of frames in the local incremental design project.

While administrators at the Hospital (and party the municipal services) started the project with a mandate that was focused mainly on technological solutions to the messaging module in the EPJs, the project began by participations in negotiating the frame; understanding that the e-messages cannot solve the bigger issue of information requirements. The frame was widened to understand the larger context (Dorst, 2015a)—could the issues they experienced be solved by other means? Sharing their experiences from other situations, participants suggested new frames and placements for the problem; secondment, distribution of responsivity, informative films etc. However, the strict mandate from the Hospital was manifested through the agenda of the workshops, which evaluated and discussed the concrete suggestions included in it. In the second workshop, administrators from the hospital actively steered and "policed" the conversation with language and artefacts. The workgroups manifested the re-negotiation of the frame for the initiative, where municipal nurses become informants, not developers of their own solution. Bear in mind that at this point in the process, the municipal solution had disappeared. As such, we see that the Hospital had the power to re-frame the project, and even push the frame back when participants tried to leave it. This highlights the importance of not seeing framing and re-framing as a neutral and straight forward action only used by designers, especially in situations of Human-Centered Design. It also emphasizes the political nature of framing, for when the framing shifts someone will most likely fall out of the frame.

This case is difficult to fully explain by only zooming in on the local framing efforts by researchers, participants and administrators implicated in the re-design project. In a systemic approach, the relationships between components become just as, or even more, important as the components themselves. However, it is impossible to capture all relationships within one frame. As such, some relationships must per definition stretch outside of it. These relationships can be trailed across time and space (Nicolini, 2009). Time is an important aspect in regard to framing, since participants can enter design situations within a certain frame—not always being fully aware of that the frame itself often changes over time (Paton & Dorst, 2011, p. 575). Further, wicked systemic issues change over time and in response to interventions (Rittel & Webber, 1973), making the frames used in the past outdated.

The re-design project did not have the same conditions for design as the national e-messaging project and the local implementation project. As time passed, the frames had become outdated. For example, lack of funding had made some of the previous components in the system into powerful and non-negotiable nodes. While the e-messaging project could be seen as transforming of parts of the system through sequential processes of translation empowering e-messages, re-designing became an incremental change initiative with vastly different frame-options.

In this project we found that the frame(s) for incremental design were strongly determined by events happening elsewhere in time and space; in this chapter, we focus on the past and the future. The project participants tried to expand the frame of the project, aiming to open up conversations about their needs and the possible futures of communication in the Norwegian health care system. Meanwhile, administrators at the Hospital mobilized the powerful agency of the e-messaging module with its standards, legislations and distribution of responsibility. The agency of the 15-year long process of developing these components was hard to protest against. As other participants found that the administrators represented this power, their suggestions were subdued in the second workshop, and the focus became the possibilities within this adjusted frame. As such, the process experienced the issue of "fixation", where powerful stakeholders were biased towards a technical solution, narrowing the frame in this part of the process (Jones, 2014, pp. 112–113).

Framing could also be directed at the future, which we found as an important aspect for securing implementation. Re-framing a problem can shift the attention given, and the following allocation of funds and other resources such as financing (Jones, 2014, p. 112). In this case, key words in e-messaging were framed from being an incremental improvement for e-messaging, to a pilot for the new version of the hospital's EPJ system. Indeed, we can see this as a translation, where keywords were now acting on behalf of the next generation of hospital EPJs. This new framing mobilized the network around this actor, and as such funding, attention and momentum. Similarly, administrators convinced the regional health authority that this was interesting for other hospitals in the region, in terms of future projects. However, in the "old" framing of e-messaging, the municipal solution gradually disappeared. As such, local human-centered design projects, based on the needs and experiences of real people, can become tokenistic (Morrison & Dearden, 2013) due to shifting frames. This means that people might not get a real say or actual influence in change processes that can alter their reality. Indeed, framing will exclude some while including others (Jones, 2014, p. 112). The Hospital could still continue their co-design project with input from the municipal services, whose conditions for participation had changed.

This paper explores how stakeholders as participants in Human-Centered Design processes have different capacities to frame and re-frame incremental design projects, related to mobilizing (and being enrolled by) actors from the past and the potential of the future. While designers might partly have power in designing the project and defining access, roles and norms for the process, as well as the potential solution (Goodwill et al., 2021), we also find an array of other powerful human and non-human stakeholders. In line with other researchers, we find that there are powerful but invisible influences that shape design for humans in complex systems. We argue that by exploring them from the perspective of sociology of translation we collapse the hierarchies, and this allows us to explore the temporality of components (not ready-made-design); and some of the way "specific cultural, economic and political practices and institutions that co-articulate [designing for] service" and complex systems" (Kimbell & Blomberg, 2017, p. 89).

6   Conclusion

In this case, a small-step solution was implemented for improving the systemic issue of lack of coordination in Norwegian health care. The solution was merely a part of the initially suggested solution. Its incremental nature allowed the development of a feasible and practical solution for nurses at the hospital. The process in itself did not follow the democratic principles of human-oriented design all the way through. Meanwhile, it ended up improving the conditions of e-messaging for the involved actors, and it became an inspiration for similar initiatives on a national basis.

In this chapter, we experimented with the analytical approach of zooming in and out inspired by Nicolini (2009) to explore the dynamics of time and framing incremental design. We found that the concept of framing plays an important role in participatory incremental design in complex systems, but it is difficult to explain what happens in the present without zooming out on the larger context. Moreover, we found it important to be able to discard an outdated frame and re-frame projects and situations in order to implement solutions in practice. However, not all stakeholders in participatory processes have the same capacity to frame and re-frame projects, problems and situations. From a democratic point of view, we argue that it is also vital to consider who defines the frames, and the people this affects—who are included, and who are excluded?

References

Akrich, M. (1992). The description of technical objects. In J. Law & W. E. Bijker (Eds.), *Shaping technology/building society. Studies in sociotechnocal change* (pp. 205–224). Cambridge, MA: MIT Press.

Akrich, M., Callon, M., & Latour, B. (2002). The key to success in innovation part I: The art of interessement. *International Journal of Innovation Management, 6*(02), 187–206. https://doi.org/10.1142/S1363919602000550

Almqvist, F. (2020). *Service design in the later phases. Exploring user insights, handovers and service design roadmapping in the transiition from service concept to implemented service.* (Ph.D. Dissertation), The Oslo School of Architecture and Design (Ed.), Oslo.

Baek, J. S., Meroni, A., & Manzini, E. (2015). A socio-technical approach to design for community resilience: A framework for analysis and design goal forming. *Design Studies, 40*(2015), 60–84. https://doi.org/10.1016/j.destud.2015.06.004

Baek, J. S., Kim, S., Pahk, Y., & Manzini, E. (2018). A sociotechnical framework for the design of collaborative services. *Design Studies, 55*(2018), 54–78. https://doi.org/10.1016/j.destud.2017.01.001

Buchanan, R. (1992). Wicked problems in design thinking. *Design Issues, 8*(2), 5–21. https://doi.org/10.2307/1511637

Carroll, J. M., & Rosson, M. B. (2007). Participatory design in community informatics. *Design Studies, 28*(2007), 243–261. https://doi.org/10.1016/j.destud.2007.02.007

Churchman, C. W. (1967). Guest editorial: Wicked problems. *Management Science, 14*(4), B141–B142.

Cozza, M. (2021). *Key concepts in science and technology studies.* Lund, Sweden: Studentlitteratur AB.

Deserti, A., & Rizzo, F. (2014). Design and organizational change in the public sector. *Design Management Journal, 9*(1), 85–97. https://doi.org/10.1111/dmj.12013

Dorst, K. (2015a). Frame creation and design in the expanded field. *She Ji: THe Journal of Design, Economics, and Innovation, 1*(1), 22–33. https://doi.org/10.1016/j.sheji.2015.07.003

Dorst, K. (2015b). *Frame innovation: Create new thinking by design.* Cambridge, Mass: MIT Press.

Gleason, B., & Bohn, J. (2019). Using small step service design thinking to create and implement services that improve patient care. In M. A. Pfannstiel & C. Rasche (Eds.), *Service design and service thinking in healthcare and hospitalmanagement. Theory, concepts, practice.* Cham: Springer Nature.

Goodwill, M., Bijl-Brouwer, M. V. D., R., & Bendor. (2021). Beyond good intentions: Towards a power literacy framework for service designers. *International Journal of Design, 15*(3), 45–59.

Gorli, M., Mengis, J., & Liberati, E. G. (2018). A new space for patients—How space enters innovation translation processes. In T. Hoholm, A. La Rocca, & M. Aanestad (Eds.), *Controversies in health care innovation.Service, technology and organization* (pp. 21–52). Oslo: Palgrave Macmillan.

Greenwood, D. J., & Levin, M. (2007). *Introduction to action research* (2nd ed.). Thousand Oaks, CA: Sage.

Hungnes, T., & Hvidsten, A. H. (2017). A controversy of interpretation: Emergent agencies in repurposing Aker Local Hospital. In T. Hoholm, A. La Rocca, & M. Aanestad (Eds.), *Controversies in health care innovation.service, technology and organization* (pp. 185–214). Oslo: Palgrave Macmillan.

Hvidsten, A. (2019). *The role of incompleteness in co-designing collaborative service delivery. A case study of electronic coordination in Norwegian health care.* (Ph.D. dissertation), BI Nowegian Business School (Ed.). Oslo: Palgrave Macmillan.

Jones, P. H. (2014). Systemic design principles for complex social systems. In G. Metcalf (Ed.), *Social systems and design. Translational systems sciences* (Vol. 1, pp. 91–128). Tokyo: Springer Publishing.

Jones, P. H., & van Patter, G. K. (2009). *Design 1.0, 2.0, 3.0, 4.0: The rise of visual sensemaking*. New York: NextDesign Leadership Institute (Ed.).

Junginger, S. (2017). *Transforming public services by design: Re-orienting policies, organizations and services around people*. London, England: Routledge.

Kimbell, L., & Blomberg, J. (2017). The object of service design. In D. Sangiorgi & A. Prendiville (Eds.), *Designing for service. Key issues and new directions* (pp. 81–92). London: Bloomsbury Academic.

Kolko, J. (2010). Abductive thinking and sensemaking: The drivers of design synthesis. *Design Issues, 26*(1), 15–28. https://doi.org/10.1162/desi.2010.26.1.15

Latour, B. (1996). On actor-network theory: A few clarifications. *Soziale Welt, 47*(4), 369–381.

Malmberg, L., Rodrigues, V., Lännerström, L., Wetter-Edman, K., Vink, J., & Holmlid, S. (2019). Service design as a transformational driver toward person-centered care in healthcare. In M. A. Pfannstiel & C. Rasche (Eds.), *Service design and service thinking in healthcare and hospital management. Theory, concepts, practice*. Cham: Springer Nature.

Manzini, E. (2014a). Design and policies for collaborative services. In C. Bason (Ed.), *Design for policy* (pp. 103–112). Surrey, UK: Gower Publishing Limited.

Manzini, E. (2014b). Making things happen: Social innovation and design. *Design Issues, 30*(1), 57–66. https://doi.org/10.1162/DESI_a_00248

Manzini, E. (2016). Design culture and dialogic design. *Design Issues, 32*(1), 52–59.

Ministry of Health and Care Services. (2008). Samhandlingsreformen: Rett behandling—på rett sted—til rett tid. (St.meld. nr. 47 (2008–2009)) [The Coordination Reform: Right treatment—in the right place—at the right time. (St.meld. nr. 47 (2008–2009)]. Oslo: Ministry of Health and Care Services.

Ministry of Health and Care Services. (2012). Én innbygger—én journal. Digitale tjenester i helse- og omsorgssektoren (Meld.st. nr. 9 (2012–2013)) [One Citizen—one Journal. Digital services in the health and care sector (Meld.st. nr. 47 (2012–2013)]. Oslo: Ministry of Health and Care Services.

Ministry of Health and Care Services. (2014). HelseOmsorg21: Et kunnskapssystem for bedre folkehelse: Nasjonal forskning- og innovasjonsstrategi for bedre folkehelse [Helseomsorg21: A knowledge system for better public health: National research and innovation strategy for health and care]. Oslo: Ministry of Health and Care Services (Ed.).

Moore, C., & Buchanan, D. A. (2013). Sweat the small stuff: A case study of small-scale change processes and consequences in acute care. *Health Services Management Research, 26*(1), 9–17.

Morrison, C., & Dearden, A. (2013). Beyond tokenistic participation: Using representational arte-facts to enable meaningful public participation in health service design. *Health Policy, 112*(3), 179–186.

Myerson, J. (2015). Small modular steps versus giant creative leaps (Commentary on Norman and Stappers). *She Ji: THe Journal of Design, Economics, and Innovation, 1*(2), 99–101. https://doi.org/10.1016/j.sheji.2016.01.002

Nicolini, D. (2009). Zooming in and out: Studying practices by switching theoretical lenses and trailing connections. *Organization Studies, 30*(12), 1391–1418. https://doi.org/10.1177/017084 0609349875

Norman, D. A., & Stappers, P. J. (2015a). DesignX: Complex sociotechnical systems. *She Ji: THe Journal of Design, Economics, and Innovation, 1*(2), 83–106. https://doi.org/10.1016/j.sheji.2016.01.002

Norman, D. A., & Stappers, P. J. (2015b). DesignX: For complex sociotechnical problems, design is not limited to one person, one phase, or one solution. *She Ji: THe Journal of Design, Economics, and Innovation, 1*(2), 15–16. https://doi.org/10.1016/j.sheji.2016.01.002

Paton, B., & Dorst, K. (2011). Briefing and reframing: A situated practice. *Design Studies, 32*(6), 573–587. https://doi.org/10.1016/j.destud.2011.07.002

Rittel, H. W., & Webber, M. M. (1973). Dilemmas in a general theory of planning. *Policy Sciences, 4*(2), 155–169.

Rodrigues, V., & Vink, J. (2016). Shaking up the status quo in healthcare: Designing amid conflicting enacted social structures. In *Paper presented at the relating systems thinking and design (RSD5) 2016 Symposium*, October 14–15, 2016, OCAD University, Toronto, Canada.

Sanders, E., & Stappers, P. (2008). Co-creation and the new landscapes of design. *CoDesign, 4*(1), 5–18.

Simonsen, J., & Robertson, T. (Eds.). (2013). *Routledge international handbook of participatory design*. New York: Routledge.

Adeline Hvidsten is a design researcher and head of the bachelor programme in Service Design at Kristiania University College in Oslo, Norway. She holds a Ph.D. from BI Norwegian Business School related to service design and innovation in health and care services. Her research is focused on topics such as power dynamics, politics, materiality and gamification in the context of designing for service and systems.

Frida Almqvist holds a Ph.D. in service design from the Oslo School of Architecture and Design in Norway. In her research she has looked into service design handovers and practical approaches that help bridging the gap between conceptualization and implementation in service development processes. She is currently working in the Norwegian design consultancy Halogen.

Transforming Complexity: A Human-Centred Design Approach to Engage Young People in the Philippines with Dialogues About HIV Service Delivery

Christopher Kueh, Gareth Durrant, Fanke Peng, Philip Ely, and Justin Francis Bionat

ABSTRACT

Positive transformation in HIV and STI-related service delivery is complex as it involves emotional and cultural considerations. The project discussed in this chapter shows the importance of human-centred design (HCD) processes in encouraging young people to think, reflect, and visually map service delivery networks. The project involved interviews with service providers, while engaging young people in conversations and visual mapping exercises. Being the first initiative of its nature and context, the holistic view of the complex service

C. Kueh (✉)
School of Arts and Humanities, Edith Cowan University, 2 Bradford Street, Mount Lawley, Western Australia 6050, Australia
e-mail: c.kueh@ecu.edu.au

G. Durrant
Creative Consultant, DSIL Global, 179 Thomas Street, Subiaco, Perth 6008, Western Australia, Australia
e-mail: gareth@disilglobal.com

F. Peng
University of South Australia, K4-29 Kaurna Building, City West Campus, Adelaide, South Australia 5000, Australia
e-mail: Fanke.Peng@unisa.edu.au

P. Ely
School of Design and Built Environment, Curtin University, Kent Street, Western Australia 6102, Australia
e-mail: philip.ely@curtin.edu.au

J. F. Bionat
Blk. 5, Lot 2, Imperial Homes 5 Subdivision, Guzman St., 5000 Mandurriao, Iloilo City, Philippines
e-mail: justinfrancis.bionat@wvsu.edu.ph

M. A. Pfannstiel (ed.), *Human-Centered Service Design for Healthcare Transformation*,
https://doi.org/10.1007/978-3-031-20168-4_14

system provides a platform for meaningful dialogues that could generate transformative pathways in the ways young people navigate the health system. The outcome is different from big data approaches, geo-spatial mapping, and administrative taxonomies, as the HCD approach generates richness in the storytelling of complex social systems where young people were enabled to discuss their environment and sketch those health systems out.

1   Introduction

The Philippines has one of the fastest-growing HIV epidemics in the world and the fastest in the Asia/Pacific region (Department of Health: Republic of the Philippines, 2021, 1–2). Originally considered an HIV epidemic among female sex workers, the country responded to epidemic shifts toward men who have sex with men (MSM) and people who inject drugs, by increasing community engagement that is centred on civil society leadership (Department of Health: Disease Prevention & Control Bureau, 2021, 5–6).

Young Key Populations (YKP) is a broad term representing young MSM, young transgender people, young people who inject drugs, and young sex workers. Young Key Populations (YKP) represent an alarming majority of new HIV infections, and whilst this term used in public health designates communities at higher risk of HIV exposure appears at first a rather homogenous delineation, for designers of new services this marker represents very specific unique behaviors and lived experiences; experiences that change over time and are shared to varying degrees across cohorts.

The objective of the project discussed in this chapter was to map the nationwide service delivery network for YKP services, develop a holistic view of the service delivery landscape, explore the impact of current interventions, and develop and strengthen care pathways for YKP across the HIV and Sexual and Reproductive Health (SRH) continuums of care. Coming from a healthcare design context, we raise the question: how can we put the lived experiences of these young people at the center of inquiries to help design innovations in health services in ways that directly benefit?

The scope of this project was beyond simple service improvements. It aimed to develop more holistic service delivery and social innovation while acknowledging the heterogeneous networks they interact with to meet their needs. The project explored the main challenge of aligning young people's individual agency and choice so that the health and wellbeing system reflects their view of themselves, their worldviews and—most importantly—their needs. This approach required an understanding of how young populations are navigating current service systems in ways that reflect their situated context and how such a system may be designed to augment people's lived experiences. The fresh perspectives explored during this project provided the service authority with insights into possible service transformations.

Our project reveals the importance of thinking beyond the quantitative in designing health systems (e.g., data points such as usage, bottlenecks, and interactions). Instead, we explore how the use of methods such as storytelling of interactions with complex social systems empowers young people to discuss their environment and make visible the health systems, paving the way for alternative realities to emerge. These discursive methods encouraged transformation in the shift of young people's perspectives about, and relationships with, healthcare services.

2 From Human-Centred Design and Service Transformation

Human-Centred Design (HCD) is a design discipline that aims to understand human needs to tackle social and human problems (van der Bijl-Brouwer & Dorst, 2017, 18–19; Giacomin 2015, 608–614; Holeman & Kane 2019, 495–500). It is argued that practice in HCD is different from other traditional design practices as far as HCD emphasizes people's interaction with products, services and systems, rather than traditional design practice's focus on the designer's self-expression through design outcomes (Giacomin 2015, 610). Recently, however, there are calls to rethink the development of HCD practice: for example, the ubiquitous use of design models and 'how-to' toolkits has been seen to reduce the degree of criticality required in design (Baker & Moukhliss, 2019, 307) and the need to understand the value and role of HCD in public section innovation and transformation (van der Bijl-Brouwer, 2016, 2151–2152).

To effectively discuss HCD to drive transformation in healthcare, it is important to understand the contemporary shift of HCD from 'solution-focused' to a dialogical (Kueh et al., 2022, 128–129) and process-driven practice. HCD has its root in ergonomics and technology with an emphasis on the users' needs in the production of objects and systems (Giacomin 2015, 608). During the development and evolution of HCD, practitioners combined product-improvement perspectives with those of understanding people's emotional, cognitive, and cultural needs (Bijl-Brouwer & Dorst, 2017, 2–6). Whilst business and technological imperatives place great emphasis on improvements in the production process (for the creation of new technologies and ways of doing), designers in HCD have argued for a deeper consideration of human understanding in cultural and social settings. In the early years of development in HCD, Krippendorff (2004, 48) stated:

Human-centredness takes seriously the premise that human understanding and behavior goes hand-in-glove; that what artifacts are is inseparably linked to how their users perceive them, can imagine interfacing with them, use them and talk about their stake in them with others. Human-centred design is concerned less with assuring that artifacts work as intended (by their producers, designers, or other cultural authorities) than with enabling many individual or cultural conceptions to unfold into uninterrupted interfaces with technology.

The importance of emphasizing people's interaction is echoed by Gasson (2003, 29–30) who stated the difference between user-centred and human-centred approaches: user-centred approaches focus on technology and production of solution, whilst human-centred approaches circle around experience and systemic inquiry. Design should therefore be a dialectic between organizational problem inquiry and the implementation of human-centred strategies (Gasson, 2003, 29). This early body of knowledge in HCD demonstrates the need to focus on interaction (and the relations between technologies, systems, people and social and cultural norms) rather than merely on the production of artifacts.

Contemporary application of HCD has shifted its focus to the development and measurement of design 'tools' and techniques to interact, build empathy and stimulate people to understand their needs and experiences in products, services and systems (Giacomin 2015, 610). Design practice requires a far more critical and reflexive approach, which is conversational and dialogical between 'users' (people) and service providers, especially in projects with complex contexts (Kueh et al., 2022, 116–119). By way of example, Holeman and Kane (2019, 491) emphasize that HCD practice in health needs to include the following:

- meaningful participation of people who will engage with, and be affected by, new systems in their daily lives.
- supporting transformative efforts in collaboration and improving people's skills, rather than focusing on technological advancement purely to increase efficiency or managerial control.
- genuine and holistic concern for the community and people's life experiences.

Our project fully embraced the expansion of HCD from technology- and method-based practice to the holistic engagement of the community in meaningful conversations.

Service Transformation and Complexity

Designers have a huge responsibility when they engage in service transformation projects. This is especially critical when vulnerable communities are involved. A challenge facing transformational design is that the quality and effectiveness of such interventions are hard to evaluate in the short term and within traditional design parameters (Sangiorgi, 2011, 31). According to Sangiorgi (2011, 29),

... service design has recently been considering services less as design objects and more as means for societal transformation. The intrinsic element of co-production of services in transformation design necessitates the concomitant development of staff, the public and the organization.

HCD approaches in the transformation design of 'intangible' services are critical, especially with the increasing complexity of the 21st Century; services are embedded in human (social, cultural, political, economic), biological, environmental and technical systems that are in a constant state of flux. The discourse surrounding the transformative nature of design, therefore, requires an understanding of this complexity. Taking a more systemic approach, Jones (2013, 23–28) and

Jones and VanPatter (2009, 2–12), have recognized that there are four levels of design approach aligned with the levels of emergent complexity in problems, thus:

- **Design 1.0 Traditional 'form-giving' design:** This design approach focuses on creating design solutions in the form of websites, logos, and posters. This deals mainly with a discrete problem that can be solved with an obvious solution.
- **Design 2.0 Service and product design:** This design approach seeks to explore complicated problems associated with human experiences, through products and services. Designers often seek collaboration with stakeholders to explore possibilities in innovating experiences.
- **Design 3.0 [Organizational] transformation design:** Common in complex organizational challenges, designers engage in activities such as co-design of change processes for organizations and business systems. Challenges that are facing designers here are bounded by systems and strategies. This level of design, therefore, focuses on complex problems, which require designers to understand complexity before resorting to ideation and solution-generation.
- **Design 4.0 Social transformation:** This design approach focuses on wicked problems that are ill-defined and difficult to be solved. Designers functioning at this level do not seek a 'solution' to tackle a 'problem'. Design activities include iteration of prototyping interventions, observing their impact on the community, and reframing the design problem. Projects commonly seen in this phase are often social challenges that are difficult to be defined.

Design 3.0 and 4.0, therefore, provide designers with the appropriate mindset for approaching complex and wicked problems with iterative processes that reframe challenges. This is a perspective shared earlier by Burns et al., (2006, 20–22) who explained that to tackle overly complex and wicked challenges, the following features of design practice were required:

- defining and redefining the brief, as designers engage before the definition of the brief and participate in the formulation of the right problem to tackle;
- collaborating between disciplines, as the complexity of contemporary challenges requires multidisciplinary efforts;
- employing participatory design techniques, as users and front-line workers can bring in their ideas, expertise and knowledge; 4) building capacity and not dependency, as transformation projects aim to leave the capacities and skills for ongoing change;
- designing beyond traditional solutions, as designers focus on changing behaviors (and not only forms) and need to tackle issues with a more holistic perspective;
- creating fundamental change, as projects can initiate a lasting transformation process, leaving a vision and champions to continue the work.

Jonas et al. (2016, 14–15) further explain transformation design being an attitude toward designing, which involves seeing design as a holistic approach without misconceiving itself as a savior of the world; transdisciplinary without pretending to know things better; provocative without reducing itself to an experience-provider or animator; and normative without wanting to impose norms from the outside. We see that the contribution of design to the development of transformative services may be best served through the adoption of these attitudes, especially in the idea of design as a platform to generate and provoke discursive conversations about the future. The discursive and speculative nature of design is a critical feature that requires more attention.

Design for transformation, therefore, needs to involve design as a discursive conversation platform to critic policy and systems, and an imaginative and speculative driver to visualize the ideal situation for a transformed community. This echoes von Anshelm's (2016, 23–32) call for transformation design to start with dreaming and imagination.

3   Human-Centred Service Design and Transformation in HIV and STI-Related Service Delivery

HIV among young people presents complex challenges in the Philippines. Young Key Populations (YKP) represent an alarming majority of new HIV infections. Most new infections in the Philippines are occurring among MSM and specifically young transgender women specifically (Department of Health: Epidemiology Bureau, 2021, 3). Positive transformation in HIV and STI-related service delivery is sorely needed.

Compounded by the lack of insights about YKP's lived experience, limited access to consistent HIV/STI services and prevention and awareness-raising information that targets young people is adding to the complexity of providing effective services to young people with HIV. There is a lack of research (and data) on hidden and hard-to-reach young, key populations and an inadequacy of laws to fully protect these key populations from stigma and discrimination.

Fortunately, The Philippines has established policies and strategies for future holistic design and transformation. For example, The Philippines Health Sector HIV Strategic Plan 2020–2022 pays special attention to YKPs aged 15–24 years, as does the 6th AIDS Medium Term Plan (AMTP) for 2017–2022. These strategic documents are aligned with the Global Sustainable Development Goals (SDGs) and the global target to end the HIV and AIDS epidemic by 2030 (Department of Health: Disease Prevention & Control Bureau, 2021, 6).

The Philippines has also prioritized Service Delivery Networks (SDN) as a path to health transformation. An SDN is defined as a "network of organizations that provides (or makes arrangements to provide) equitable, comprehensive, integrated, and continuous good quality health services to a defined population, with minimum duplications and inefficiencies" (Department of Health cited in Concha, 2019, 1). SDNs are a way to encourage health facilities and Community Based-Organizations (CBOs) to work together within a network or a system, but they are not panaceas. Formal, responsive, functional, and active service delivery networks for YKPs are difficult to build and sustain. Significant investment and infrastructure are needed to ensure the efficient implementation of the service delivery network.

Beyond explicit targets and service delivery activities, there is a noted willingness to engage young key populations. During the 2019 high-level meeting presentation of the National HIV Joint Programs Review in the Philippines, the Department of Health (DoH) Undersecretary Myrna Cabotaje stated that "[w]e need to change: let us ask our clients or the end-users to think for themselves. Perhaps we should change the way we are doing things. Let us not decide for them. Let the youth decide for themselves" (cited in Philippine Department of Health: National AIDS & STI Prevention Control Program, 2019, 103). However, there are limited studies that tangibly deepen the understanding of designing for human factors beyond formal needs assessments— studies that should explore complex emotional and cultural considerations needed for transformative solutions in HIV and STI-related service delivery for these high-risk groups in the Philippines (UNICEF East Asia and Pacific Regional Office and the Interagency Task Team on Young Key Populations 2019, 16).

One of the largest CBOs and service providers in the Philippines for this key population–LoveYourself Inc, ran two studies in 2020 looking into how lockdown and geographical factors influenced sexual practices and how key population-responsive online programming might be provided as an innovative solution to prevention (Rozul et al., 2021, n.d.). However, neither of these initiatives engaged young people directly in the service design dialogue. In addition, USAID-supported work used HCD to develop prototype solutions with young people in the Philippines, yet this focus was on unintended teenage pregnancy and adolescent reproductive health, not HIV (John Hopkins Center for Communication Programs, 2020, 5–7).

Framework and Methodologies: HCD processes to encourage young people to think, reflect, and visually map service delivery networks.

In 2021, as part of a Global Fund technical assistance project working alongside the Australasian Society for HIV, Viral Hepatitis and Sexual Health Medicine (ASHM), consultants Gareth Durrant from DSIL Global and Justin Bionat (Current Executive Director of Youth Voices Count) sought to explicitly adopt Human-Centred (HCD) processes to engage young people in the Philippines to think, reflect, and create visual maps of local service delivery networks. Youth Voices Count (YVC) is a regional network of young lesbian, gay, bisexual, transgender, queer and intersex individuals in Asia–Pacific.

This project applied an HCD approach because data-based mapping or geospatial directories do not make distinctions in terms of how friendly these health services are for young people; nor do they reflect the interplay or service delivery pathway from a youth (individual) perspective. These data-led approaches are privileged by policymakers and service providers, for they (appear) to be empirically sound and unarguably persuasive. However, Polaine, Lovlie and Reason (2013,

38–40) draw the distinction between 'truth' and 'insights': quantitative research produces objective data that provides a seemingly 'truthful' picture of a situation while qualitative research generates insights of people's needs informed by in-depth stories and lived experience. In the context of our project, data-based mapping generates a statistical overview of young people accessing services but might not be able to inform meaningful service transformation. Insights formed by stories and lived experience would provide opportunities for designers to better understand the gaps in our understanding of human interaction with multiple systems and services, beyond the knowledge gleaned from an analysis of data sets.

Human-Centred Design (HCD) approaches aimed to engage young people, service delivery users, providers, and key stakeholders to map service delivery pathways in their specific context. This ensures capture of the interplay between access points of services within the service delivery landscape. These approaches placed young people at the centre of a problem-solving process that works through an understanding of the human factors and contextual challenges in developing sustainable solutions for health. The following are three key pillars of the design approach applied in the project:

- Include young people in the mapping and service design: meaningful and documented participation of people who are indeed service delivery users or implementers or otherwise be affected by the appropriateness of the services for young people.
- Ensure service delivery points and networks for YKP in the Philippines are not only mapped but fully activated: Supporting cooperative activity within the health system making service design pathways and their value visible beyond a linear referral pathway for HIV prevention and treatment.
- Considering YKP as holistic agents: concern for the whole young person and their life experiences, reframing purely service delivery issues in relation to the broader human context of youth and their lives.

These three pillars were inspired by Holeman and Kane's (2019, 489) HCD direction of being holistic and inclusive of people's lived experiences and stories. Our three pillars emphasized that mapping research is not just about understanding young people's relationships with, and perspectives on, sex.

We partnered with a local youth organization that had extensive networks and was trusted by the community. We actively recruited youth voices from often underrepresented and marginalized sub-populations.

Guided by the three pillars and principles of engagement, this project employed the following methods:

1. Co-design workshops to engage young people in conversations and visual mapping: The first co-design workshop was led by Gareth Durrant in English, which served as a template for subsequent co-design sessions, whilst the second was led by Justin Francis Bionat and another youth representative in both of native Tagalog and English. Such an approach allowed local partners to build their own competency and capacity for co-design, without exorbitant external resources. These co-design workshops saw participants engaged in mapping activities to develop rich narratives and pictures depicting the current situation in the three major regions in the Philippines: Luzon, Visayas and Mindanao.

There were 37 participants across the two co-design workshops. Advocacy groups, Civil Society Organizations (CSOs) or Non-Government Organizations (NGOs) registered with the Securities and Exchange Commission were well represented. So too were youth-led community organizations, university-based organizations and support groups for PLHIV or LGBTIQ + . The youngest attendee was 19 years old, and participants over the age of 24 were often leaders of service delivery organizations fundamental to YKP service delivery in the Philippines.

The co-design workshops aimed to achieve the following:

- Live prototyping and role-play of various stakeholders' perspectives to gain insights into how dynamics within the landscape play out. This combined 'eco-ductions' of the service delivery landscape they were most familiar with as well as physically sketching the landscape and annotating diagrams before sharing together. Ecoductions are a portmanteau of the ecosystem and introduction to the ecosystem in which participants live or know well.
- Develop clarity on the essentials of good YKP service delivery. Participants were asked to describe their 'non-negotiables' for good service delivery for YKP. These were clustered using an Availability, Accessibility, Acceptability, and Quality framework developed by Youth Voices (see Youth Voices County, n.d.).
- Seek feedback on the rapid stakeholder mapping to confirm characteristics of who is in the system and their respective service functions. Participants were also asked to identify five actors, players, institutions, clinic networks, or community organizations that they believed the national system could not do without.
- Map additional positive forces ('enablers') and negative forces ('inhibitors') that contribute to the current conditions. Participants were then asked to role-play as the institutions, clinic networks, or community organizations that were on their 'Dream Team' - those who specifically would have the power to change the way young key populations engage with service delivery.

2. Interviews: Semi-structured interviews with service providers were designed to explore connections and networks, policy and legal environment, community's perception and their aspirations for the landscape. Questions were designed around eliciting dynamic and future-focused responses. For example, when asked to describe 'What connections exist currently in the YKP/LGBTI service delivery landscape?' interviewees were prompted to go beyond listing organizations and touchpoints and instead name the people they are currently working with and those they would like to include in the future.

The objective was to understand how local service providers might already be expanding and strengthening service pathways; what their perception was of how YKP think and feel about the youth service delivery locally; the service providers' place in it and the service ecosystem. Additionally, service providers were asked to reflect on what could be achieved in 5–10 years that would constitute a major step forward toward service delivery for young key populations locally.

The interviewees were presented with prototypes from the earlier co-design workshops, and service providers were asked to describe what they saw, reflecting on what was missing or unclear based on their own perspectives. It is important to note here that service providers themselves did not map out possible future service provision: this was conducted by the young key populations and service providers then situated themselves within this construction.

3. Future probing: The project concluded with a final youth-focused co-design session asking the question "What does an AIDS-free future look like for YKP and how do we get there?" This was to explore YKP's perspective on the future of services.

These methods ensured that comprehensive and rich assessments of the general state of service delivery pathways and programming can be articulated by young people, even when these dynamic landscapes were in a state of flux.

4   Mapping, Insights and Storytelling

In the first phase of the co-design workshop, participants mapped how key elements of YKP programs interacted relationally within the service and life ecosystem in the form of 'ecoductions'. An example of a rich landscape as described by a YKP from Taguig City is presented below.

> "I see the effort of the whole ecosystem to design the service delivery to make it more "user-friendly". Young Key Populations in Taguig City can access HIV screenings through two public HIV treatment hubs in the City, the Taguig Social Hygiene Clinic and Taguig City Drop-in Center. Staff from the government treatment hubs also do house-to-house CBS (Community Based HIV Screening) through appointments via Social media (Twitter, FB and Grindr). There is also a TGW [Transgender Women] focused private/NGO treatment hub called Lily by LoveYourself along the border of Taguig and Sucat, Parañaque City. HIV AIDS Support House (HASH) a CBO, also have CBS volunteers in the area, doing CBS via personal appointments or in Queer Saunas/Bathhouses within the metro. Pre-pandemic, Taguig hubs also did on-ground events like beauty pageants for TGW which incorporated into the contest testing drives, ie the candidate who encouraged the highest number of people to get tested at the venue scored more points. The Red Whistle also did HIV testing campaigns at state universities like Taguig City University and University of Makati pre-covid." Participant, Taguig City, 25 years old

Individual mapping occurred when participants were asked to draw a map of the service delivery pathways in their specific context and explain the interplay between access points of services within the service delivery landscape (see Fig. 1).

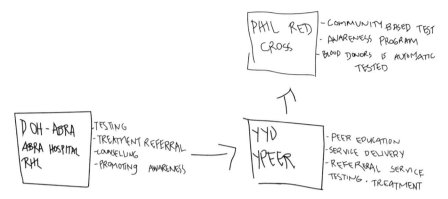

Fig. 1 Participant (from Province of Abra, 19 years old) showing 'ecoduction' map. *Source* Authors ' own illustration (2022)

Analysis and synthesis of these participant-drawn pathways identified common themes and understanding of pathways. Our aim was to approximate how YKP might engage with Prevention, Testing and Treatment within the current environment as well as attempt to display the more complex interplay of services described by participants. We conducted this analysis in partnership with Youth Voices Count who was able to help us interpret participant contributions (see Figs. 2, 3 and 4).

When mapped, we identified three key service delivery pathways: (1), a community-based screening and prevention pathway and/or (2), a direct-to-public-facility pathway (Fig. 2) and (3), minor paths which involve other youth-led

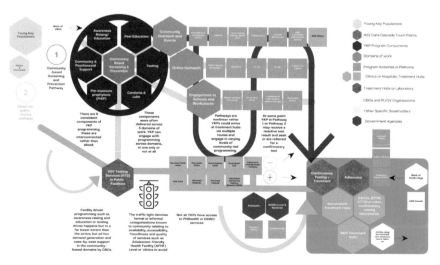

Fig. 2 Synthesis of participant mapping, depicting Pathway 1 & 2. *Source* Author's own illustration (2022)

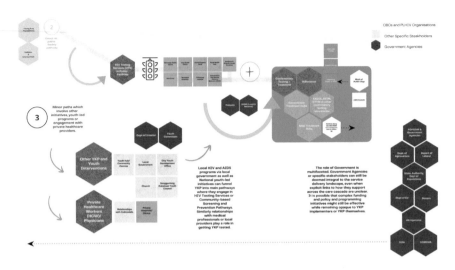

Fig. 3 Depicting Pathway 3. *Source* Author's own illustration (2022)

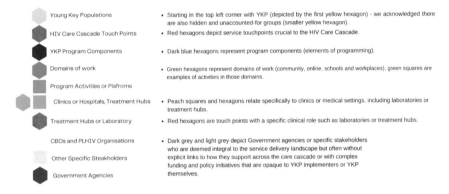

Fig. 4 Map Key. *Source* Author's own illustration (2022)

initiatives or engagement with private healthcare providers (Fig. 3). These were often non-linear pathways, insofar as YKPs could arrive at treatment hubs via multiple routes and engage in varying levels of community-led programming. These mappings, therefore, portray the complexity involved in the transformative effort through services. Each of these synthesized pathways is described in more detail below.

1. Community-based Screening and Prevention Pathway: Within community-based screening and prevention programming and services there were 6 consistent components: Awareness Raising and Education, Peer education, Testing, Community and Psychosocial support, PrEP and Condoms & Lube. These components were often delivered across 3 domains: 1. Community Outreach and Events 2. Online Outreach 3. Engagement at Schools and Workplaces. The primary role of CBOs in this space is to engage in prevention activities and generate demand for HIV testing services. CBOs describe themselves consistently as playing an enabling role in channelling YKP towards engaging with health facilities and providers for HIV testing services or testing in a community setting. However, they also describe themselves as equally important in ensuring treatment starts, adherence is maintained and supporting YKP navigate health facilities and providers within the province or city-wide health systems. This is ad-hoc rather than coordinated with low-resourced CBOs essentially using a scatter approach to demand generation and case-by-case support as required. Community-led YKP programming is essentially a pathway that starts with multi-touchpoint outreach and education which then pivots to support patient advocacy once a test is reactive. There were limited explicit referral support pathways to ensure YKPs move from the Community Based Screening & Prevention space to Confirmatory Testing and Treatment.

2. Direct-to-public-facility Pathway: YKPs were also depicted as moving along a direct-to-public-facility pathway. This was either by choice, preferring to engage with provincial hospitals or treatment hubs directly, or first attending a Barangay Health Facility, City Health Office, Social Hygiene Clinic or Rural Health Unit. The more interconnected the environment with efforts across CBOs and online and face-to-face, and the more streamlined activities were between local, municipal and provincial levels of government and facilities, the wider the safety net for YKPs.

3. Other Minor Pathways: HIV and AIDS programs via local government as well as National youth-led initiatives can funnel YKP into main pathways where they engage in HIV Testing Services or Community- based Screening and Prevention Pathways. Similarly, relationships with medical professionals or local providers play a role in getting YKP tested and engaged with the HIV care cascade. Specific Local Government Units, Local AIDS councils and Sangguniang Kabataan Councils were broadly described as 'hit or miss' in the landscape. With some contexts being active and others not. Even when described as active it was unclear what exactly the pathway might have been from initiatives on the ground to testing services and beyond. This was the same for private healthcare providers. Sometimes pharmacies and private clinics were mapped as options for YKP to access services often with the caveat that these were more expensive and rarer.

Direct feedback was sought from community members on the mapping prototypes as well as part of the 1:1 interviews with key stakeholders. Edits were made to reflect feedback. There were several iterations. The third and final engagement was conducted to present recommendations, further explore 'probable, plausible and possible design futures for services delivery with Young Key Populations' as well as capture additional tangible examples of solutions. An activity was conducted with conceptual links to eco-philosopher Joanna Macy's (2006, n.d.) work in "Work that Reconnects" (WTR) which seeks to have groups play out (either through dialogue or movement) complex problems and situate those problems at different moments in time. It is also inspired by Kueh et al., (2022, 128–129), in which design is to be implemented as a platform to generate discursive and speculative dialogues with the broader communities.

4.1 Complicated Stories

Implementers of facilities and CBOs running HIV programs targeting young people, other stakeholders, and target users of YKP programming and services all had clear ideas about what their local SDN looks like. Across the two co-design workshops and interviews, when asked to describe or map programs and facilities, participants were able to identify distinct starting points for where to obtain information and services for YKP and the next steps in the pathway along the prevention, testing and treatment continuum.

The stories collected from co-design workshops with YKPs, and the broader YKP-led mapping suggest that YKPs navigate pathways differently depending on region and availability of services, avoiding, or utilizing different service touch-points based on perceived quality and their individual needs. Some YKPs avoid government clinics in lieu of community testing, whilst others will travel across provinces or municipalities to attend clinics outside their local area to ensure confidentiality.

When YKPs were depicted or described as moving along a direct-to-public-facility pathway, this was often annotated to highlight issues relating to availability, accessibility, friendliness, and quality of services. Maps and descriptions were often non-linear to depict choice. For example, Fig. 5 shows the annotations depicting YKP being hesitant to engage with hospitals because of stigma and discrimination, the lack of service availability, and presented unflattering depictions of local AIDS councils.

There are two major opportunities that emerged from the data collected. Firstly, YKP were not passive service users but fully realized curators of their own service experience (choosing when, who and from which point to engage). Secondly, YKP finds ways to navigate the service delivery pathways despite disruptions and the informal nature of service provision. The mapping also suggests informal community monitoring exists (although it is decentralized) and at the very least community knowledge around HIV care-related issues for YKP can be made available to service users and stakeholders for quality improvement purposes.

Participants were able to describe both shortfalls, and non-negotiables, as well as what an ideal service delivery landscape would look like. Young people felt that more collaboration between entities was desirable to improve services. CBOs wanted to work in partnership with each other (with schools, workplaces, and grassroots level facilities) and saw the proliferation of safe spaces that share the workload for community-based screening CBS and HIV services (supported and funded by the government) as critical to the future development.

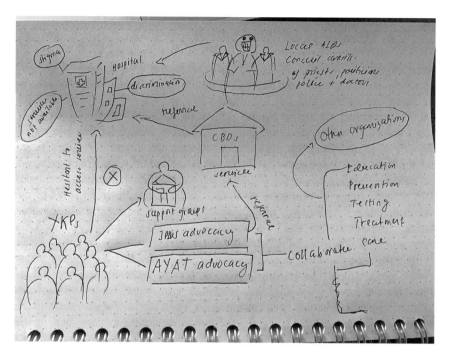

Fig. 5 A participant from Ilocos Norte, 23 years old, visualized the complexity involved in accessing health services. *Source* Author's own illustration (2022)

Participants were asked to describe their non-negotiables for good service delivery for YKP. For YKPs who participated in our co-design workshops, accessibility was expressed across a spectrum of affordability (free, low cost, affordability), as well as increased options for online consultations, over-the-phone conversations, a wider array of testing options, ship-to-home features, and home services. This included ideas about reaching beyond urban areas and a sense of proactively reaching out to the communities and target population via online platforms and campaigns. For young key populations who participated in our co-design workshops, acceptability was expressed across a spectrum of confidentiality (must guarantee 100% confidentiality, anonymity, and privacy would be respected). Participants described acceptable service delivery as flexible, responsive, adaptable, sensitive, accommodating, and inclusive. There were also themes of evidence-based healthcare services to those who need them, providing care that responds to individual preferences or language needs and timeliness.

4.2 From Stories to Transformation: Complexities in Knowledge and World Views

Being the first initiative of its nature and context, the holistic view of complex service systems provides a platform for meaningful dialogues that can generate transformative pathways in the ways that young people navigate the health system. However, such dialogues require a direct engagement with young people (in their local environment) and engaging in discussion around (in this case) sexuality. By such an interaction, researchers can understand young people's formal and informal knowledge about HIV and, more importantly, their worldviews in this context. Relating this to the notion of Design 1.0, 2.0, 3.0 and 4.0 (see Jones, 2013, 23–25; Jones & VanPatter, 2009, 2–12), the transformative impact of this project lies with the discovery of complexity in Design 3.0 (organizational structure of service provision and its system) and Design 4.0 (young people's social construction of a 'real world' where HIV is a norm).

By engaging with young people in processes of co-design and dialogue, we can provide greater clarity [improved fidelity] of service pathways and experiences, allowing us to identify not only user-perceived gaps in service, but also reframe such services from a human need's perspective. Their worldview was made visible in the form of amalgamated mapping of the various pathways and experiences and then became the common canvas from which to seek feedback from service providers. Their ideas not only shaped the design and delivery of services but effectively 'housed' those discussions.

Workshops with young people also revealed that leadership by - and the centering of - YKP within ecologies of tangible power, and fundamental shifts within Filipino social norms were the two most important topics that emerged from the discussions: YKP's ability to be able to shape policy and draft ordinances was a key theme; taboos and conversations around freeing young people from conservative restraints within the family were considered a necessary first step towards this AIDS-free future.

Active community-based monitoring of providers by young people could curtail poor-performing service delivery points or inform better strategies. However, designing a healthcare system that makes sense for young people's sexuality is difficult in low resources settings and particularly difficult in countries with strong religious institutional resistance to such work.

Unsurprisingly, young people approached the complexity of the HIV service system as a dynamic, non-linear environment that can be navigated by their own choice and agency despite barriers. For example, clinic proximity was not a barrier because, paradoxically, the closer the clinic the more likely you would be spotted; a clinic further away can ensure anonymity whilst also providing access to sex-on-premise venues such as saunas. Further, a public park within cycling distance was a youth-friendly venue for a rapid test and far more appropriate than a well-resourced brick-and-mortar clinic.

4.3   Transformation from Young People's Perspectives

The use of co-design workshops, virtual collaboration and social media has provided transformative methods to connect with youth. Indeed, our methods mirror how young people experience services themselves, where any initial physical contact is preceded by multiple service delivery touchpoints online. It poses the question: what might tangible transformation look like if service designers used digital or online-only environments, not as mere 'channels' for communication, but considered such environments as the sine qua non of all interactions and communication? What would virtual models of service delivery look like? Young people were already imagining this possible future:

> "The pandemic has taught us some valuable "new ways" of doing things. Accessibility is key, plus confidentiality of course. A robust logistic and supply-chain system will solve the problem re: antiretroviral (ARV) dispensing and test kits distribution. Zoom counseling or over the phone counseling will also make the service more accessible" Participant, Cebu City.

For example, one social media user from Mandaluyong City has 144 K followers and offers HIV testing from his home garage. By comparison, Love Yourself has just over 40 K followers despite being both the most resourced player in the sector and is widely known for its digital outreach efforts. The number of followers is not the only metric to determine influence, but it is worth noting this gulf in the number of followers, warranting further research into where (and how) young people create their identities and how relevant physical space is in terms of HIV services for this YKP. Whilst the research did not initially explore this phenomenon, such insights nevertheless reveal the benefits of taking human-centred design approaches to service development. By further investigation of online behaviors, technologies, and practices and, in relation to sexual health and wellbeing—we can understand how sexual relations are mediated by alternative, non-mainstream forms of communication and use these to help shape future communication and service provision. These insights have transformed our understanding of the way the community sees the problem, reframing the design problem towards asking how could young peoples' lived experiences online create opportunities for health services to align and evolve?

5   Discussion: Towards Transforming Complexity Through Human-Centred Services

In this chapter we have explored how engaging directly with multiple stakeholders can drive incremental transformation. Such work reveals the following key characteristics of transformative design:

- Complex healthcare service environment requires holistic perspectives, where researchers should construct a deep understanding of all stakeholders' needs.

To do so, it is vital to consider research participants as research partners. It is an approach that differs from 'data mining' strategies as it provides a discursive platform for real human insight.

- It is important to rethink and reinvent the roles of 'researchers'. To be able to access insights from complex community settings, researchers should involve community members who have already built a rapport with other key stakeholders. For example, having participants interview other participants could generate insights and stories that external researchers might not be able to access
- Being participant-friendly requires more than a welcoming environment and communication. The application of certain design research methods needs to be agile and sensitive enough to the situated conversations and dialogues with those present (Simonsen et al., 2014, 10).
- In dealing with complexity, there is a tendency for clients, stakeholders, and design teams to focus on specific touch points or target populations. However, the advantages of design-led approaches to innovation are the systemic worldviews that the designer can adopt in looking at 'the bigger picture'(Cross, 2007, 99–100; Dorst, 2015, 1–9). This is not to neglect micro-levels of human concern, but to embark on a constant process of simultaneous convergence and divergence (Goldschmidt, 2016, 115–122); looking at the 'detail' and the wider systems view (Drew, 2021, n.d.).

Reflecting our project findings on the complexity design levels discussed by Jones and VanPatter (2009, 23–25), we see that Design 4.0 and Design 3.0 are underlying complexities that are foundational to Design 2.0 and Design 1.0 (see Fig. 6). We present our reflections on Human-Centred Service Design for Complex Healthcare Transformation as a model illustrated in Fig. 6. We posit that by starting with complexity (Design 4.0), we can move towards a better understanding of emerging problems and solutions which—over the duration of projects—slowly focus on discrete (manageable) problems (Design 1.0). In this model, discrete problems in Design 1.0 can be easily measured through the evaluation process. Design 2.0 involves slightly more complicated (but not intractable) problems that involve designers engaging with people's actions and experiences.

At Design 3.0 Knowledge Transformation level, reflective practice plays an important role in encouraging dialogue for transformation. Here, the notion of project partners instead of end-users is critical to respectful and ethical co-design. In our case, we noticed that engaging youth as project partners instead of users, whilst intentionally approaching key stakeholders later in the design process, allowed us to develop youth-centred prototypes which shifted power and agency away from service providers and towards the very people that need these services. Centering young people's own knowledge production changes how others work with the design outputs, they are forced into youth-driven dialogue. Understanding the complexity of healthcare services for HIV is one thing but understanding the complexity of healthcare services from a youth perspective is transformational.

Design 4.0 involves wicked problems that are made of social and cultural challenges that are often emergent across generations. Transformation at this level calls

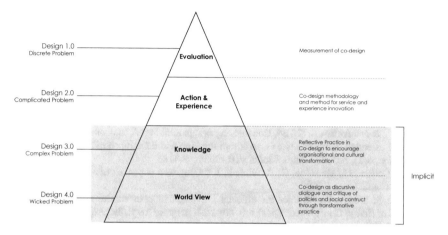

Fig. 6 Human-centred service design for complex healthcare transformation model. *Source* Author's own illustration (2022)

for a shift in a particular society's worldview. By creating reflexive and speculative worlds/maps/narratives where young people were free and empowered to express themselves, we were able to recognize the biases and prejudices in communities and wider society.

6   Conclusion

The Philippines remains a conservative political and religious society. Health design in this context ironically seems to distance itself from notions of sexuality, preferring instead an instrumentalist preoccupation with service design networks and coordination. We acknowledge, therefore, that our mapping and references to where sexual encounters occur were limited in our co-design workshop, meaning that mapping and context around sex behaviors of YKP were not well understood. Sexual behavior is crucial to our understanding of the decision-making and motivations of end-users of sexual health services. However, our integrated approach has helped to inform investment where it counts and has highlighted inadequate or underperforming service delivery and ineffective community-based monitoring strategies.

This chapter demonstrates that the transformation through service design takes place in a highly complex social and cultural paradigm. The mapping of stakeholders' lived experiences is not to be treated as 'data collection' but is a stories-gathering process that could reveal insights that lead to transformation. We concluded that the very effort of centering youth perspectives through the HCD process has a transformative effect on the design context. Young Key Populations are the experts in their own service delivery experience and the landscape. A designer's posture is simply to provide space for those insights to emerge and radical adoption of youth worldviews. More HCD-led research is therefore needed into the sex lives of young key populations and what motivates them to engage, avoid or disengage from current service delivery networks.

References

Baker, F. W., & Moukhliss, S. (2019). Concretising design thinking: A content analysis of systematic and extended literature reviews on design thinking and human-centred design. *Review of Education, 8*(1), 305–333. https://doi.org/10.1002/rev3.3186

Burns, C., Cottam, H., Vanstone, C., & Winhall, J. (2006). Red paper 02: transformation design. Design Council (pp. 1–33).

Concha, A. S. (2019). Wishlist for the efficient implementation of service delivery networks. *Journal of Health Care Services, 5*(1),1–3. http://n2t.net/ark:/76951/jhcs9rq3t2

Cross, N. (2007). *Designerly ways of knowing*. Birkhauser.

Department of Health: Epidemiology Bureau. (2021). HIV/AIDS and ART registry of the philippines (HARP) epidemic trends of HIV/AIDS in The Philippines, Jan 1984-Mar 2021. Retrieved May 26, 2022, from https://doh.gov.ph/sites/default/files/statistics/EB_HARP_March_AIDS reg2021.pdf

Department of Health: Republic of the Philippines. (2021). A briefer on the Philippine HIV estimates 2020. Retrieved June 1, 2022, from https://doh.gov.ph/publications/non-serials/a-briefer-philippine-hiv-estimates-2020

Department of Health: Disease Prevention and Control Bureau, 2021 Department of Health: Disease Prevention and Control Bureau. (2021). *Philippine health sector HIV strategic plan 2020–2022*. Milan: Department of Health

Dorst, K. (2015). *Frame innovation: Create new thinking by design*. Cambridge: MIT Press.

Drew, C. (2021). Developing our new systemic design framework. Retrieved May 20, 2022, from https://medium.com/design-council/developing-our-new-systemic-design-framework-e0f 74fe118f7

Gasson, S. (2003). Human-centered vs. User-centered approaches to information system design. *The Journal of Information Technology Theory and Application (JITTA), 5*(2), 29–46.

Giacomin, J. (2015). What is human centred design. *The Design Journal, 17*(4):606–623. https://doi.org/10.2752/175630614X14056185480186

Goldschmidt, G. (2016). Linkographic evidence for concurrent divergent and convergent thinking in creative design. *Creativity Research Journal, 28*(2), 115–122. https://doi.org/10.1080/104 00419.2016.1162497

Holeman, I., & Kane, D. (2019). Human-centred design for global health equity. *Information Technology for Development, 26*(3), 477–505. https://doi.org/10.1080/02681102.2019.1667289

John Hopkins Center for Communication Programs. (2020). *Technical report on USAID's reach-health's human-centered design activity with teens and those who influence them: Improved health for underserved Filipinos (Family planning and maternal and neonatal health innovations and capacity building platforms)*. Baltimore, John Hopkins Center for Communication Programs.

Jones, P. H. (2013). *Design for care: Innovating healthcare experience*. Brooklyn: Rosenfeld.

Jones, P. H., & VanPatter, G. K. (2009). Design 1.0, 2.0, 3.0, 4.0: The rise of visual sensemaking. New York: NextDesign Leadership Institute.

Jonas, W., Zerwas, S., & von Anshelm, K. (Eds.). (2016). *Transformation design: Perspectives on a new design attitude*. Basel: Birkhauser.

Krippendorff, K. (2004). Intrinsic motivation and human-centred design. *Theoretical Issues in Ergonomics Design, 5*(1), 43–72. https://doi.org/10.1080/1463922031000086717

Kueh, C., Peng, F., Ely, P., & Durrant, G. (2022). A speculation for the future of service design in healthcare: Looking through the lens of a speculative service design framework. In M. A.

Pfannstiel, N. Brehmer & C. Rasche (Eds.), *Service design practices for healthcare innovation: Paradigms, principles, prospects* (pp. 115–131). Cham: Springer International Publishing. https://doi.org/10.1007/978-3-030-87273-1_6

Macy, J. (2006). *The work that reconnects*. Gabriola Island: New Society Publishers.

Ngoc, H. N., Lasa, G., & Iriarte, I. (2022). Human-centred design in industry 4.0: Case study review and opportunities for future research. *Journal of Intelligent Manufacturing, 33*, 35–76. https://doi.org/10.1007/s10845-021-01796-x

Parker, S., & Parker, S. (Eds.). (2007). *Unlocking innovation: Why citizens hold the key to public service reform*. London: Demos.

Philippine Department of Health: National AIDS and STI Prevention Control Program. (2019). *Final report: National HIV Joint Program Review*. Manila: Department of Health.

Polaine, A., Lovlie, L., & Reason, B. (2013). *Service design: From insight to implementation*. Brooklyn: Rosenfeld Media.

Rozul, C. D., Domingo, R., Corciege, J. O., Bagasol Jr, E., Ruanto, J. D., & Pagtakhan, R. (2021). *Safer sexual health awareness, attitudes and practices among HIV key populations in the early months of the COVID-19 pandemic in the Philippines IAS 2021*. Retrieved May 28, 2022, from https://theprogramme.ias2021.org/Abstract/Abstract/1266

Sangiorgi, D. (2011). Transformative services and transformation design. *International Journal of Design, 5*(2), 29–40.

Simonsen, J., Svabo, C., Strandvad, S. M., Samson, K., Hertzum, M., & Ole Erik Hansen. (2014). Situated methods in design. In J. Simonsen, C. Svabo, S. M. Strandvad, K. Samson, M. Hertzum & Ole Erik Hansen (Eds.), *Situated design methods* (pp. 1–21). Cambridge, MA & London, England: MIT Press.

UNICEF East Asia and Pacific Regional Office and the Interagency Task Team on Young Key Populations. (2019). *Looking out for adolescents and youth from key populations: Formative assessment on the needs of adolescents and youth at risk of HIV (Case Studies from Indonesia, the Philippines, Thailand and Vietnam)*. Retrieved May 25, 2022, from https://www.unicef.org/eap/media/4446/file/Looking%20out%20for%20adolescents%20and%20youth%20from%20key%20populations.pdf

Van der Bijl-Brouwer, M. (2016). The challenges of human-centred design in public sector innovation contex. In *DRS 2016 International Conference: Future-Focus Thinking*. Brigthon.

Van der Bijl-Brouwer, M., & Dorst, K. (2017). Advancing the strategic impact of human-centred design. *Design Studies, 53*(C), 1–23.

von Anshelm, K. (2016). Transformation design starts with people dreaming: Designers and theatre makers design utopias for major transformation. An Essay. In W. Jonas, S. Zerwas & K. V. Anshelm (Eds.), *Transformation design: Perspectgives on a new design attitude* (101–113). Basel: Birkhauser.

Youth Voices Count. (n.d.). *Jumping Hurdles: Access to HIV health services for young men who have sex with men and young transgender persons in Asia and the Pacific*. Retrieved June 1, 2022, from https://www.apcom.org/wp-content/uploads/2015/09/jumping_hurdles_-_discussion_paper.pdf

Christopher Kueh is a design educator/researcher, practicing service designer and design strategist. He is currently a Senior Lecturer in Strategic Design at Edith Cowan University, Western Australia. His research and practice involve helping organizations to cultivate design abilities and to understand complexities through design.

Gareth Durrant MPH is a public health practitioner turned designer. Gareth brings a wealth of field experience in design and health innovation having worked across Asia, the Pacific and Australia in medical and humanitarian emergency sector. He blends research and practice in his current role as a Creative Consultant with DSIL Global (Designing for Social Innovation and Leadership).

Fanke Peng is an Associate Professor in Design, at UniSA Creative, University of South Australia. Her research focuses on design and health, cross-cultural design pedagogy, and service design for sustainability and social impact. She has worked on a range of interdisciplinary projects that were funded Australian Council for the Arts, UK research councils (AHRC, ESRC, EPSRC, TSB), the Museum of Australian Democracy, the Australian Department of Foreign Affairs and Trade Fund. Recent publications include Cross Cultural Design for Healthy Ageing (co-edited book 2020), and Service Design Thinking for Social Good (co-authored journal article 2020).

Philip Ely is Senior Lecturer at Curtin University where he is course director of the Master of Design. Philip is a design practitioner, educator, theorist and entrepreneur with over 20 years in industry. He founded The State of Design research network across Western Australia's five universities, exploring the impact and value of design in the region. In 2015, he was voted one of Britain's top business advisors by Enterprise Nation. Philip has served as a peer reviewer for the both the Australian and UK research councils and recently published work on the design value helix in the Design Management Journal and on differential design in the journal Design & Culture.

Justin Francis Bionat is the executive director of Youth Voices Count (YVC), a regional network for young people in the Asia-Pacific region. He holds a Master of Arts in Human Rights and Democratisation from Mahidol University, Thailand. His thesis utilized queer theory to discuss the access to sexual health care of gay, bisexual and MSM identities in Cambodia. He advocates for health human rights for sexual and gender minorities, especially LGBTIQ persons, in all aspects of his work. He is presently a lecturer at West Visayas State University and Colegio del Sagrado Corazon de Jesus, Philippines teaching the social sciences.

Storytelling as a Way to Design and Innovate Healthcare Services for Children

Mira Alhonsuo, Jenny Siivola, Melanie Sarantou⊙, and Satu Miettinen⊙

ABSTRACT

First starting in 2019, large construction projects are underway at Lapland Central Hospital, the northernmost hospital offering both primary healthcare and specialist care in Finnish Lapland. As a service provider, the hospital also covers healthcare services for children. One ongoing integration is focusing on children's hospital services by providing psychiatry as an integral part of somatic care. The children's hospital offers opportunities for innovative and creative approaches to explore storytelling as a way to innovate healthcare services with children. This study explores fiction-based research practices and how they can be adapted as a visual service journey mapping tool, which is a commonly used method in service design. This chapter discusses how children can be involved in planning hospital services through creative storytelling, how service design can be used to produce imaginative materials and analysing the data produced during creative design processes. As an outcome, a fiction-based storytelling method and visual service journey mapping tool will be presented as the result of using the materials of the children's service design process in hospital settings in Finland.

M. Alhonsuo (✉) · J. Siivola · M. Sarantou · S. Miettinen
University of Lapland, PL 122, 96101 Rovaniemi, Finland
e-mail: mira.alhonsuo@ulapland.fi

J. Siivola
e-mail: jsiivola@ulapland.fi

M. Sarantou
e-mail: melanie.sarantou@ulapland.fi

S. Miettinen
e-mail: satu.miettinen@ulapland.fi

1   Introduction

Healthcare and design have a long history together (e.g., Rowe et al., 2020, p. 328); increasingly, these two areas have been applied together in patient involvement and co-design approaches (Nesta, 2013, p. 6). The focus has not only been on the different service experiences of healthcare service processes, such as patient–doctor interactions, but also on hospital environments and interiors. In recent years, designers working in healthcare have been increasingly starting to recognise the importance of how taking emotional needs into account helps create healing spaces so that care becomes more than just a cure (Bogaert, 2021, p. 355; DuBose et al., 2016, p. 43). For example, sound can be emotionally satisfying and expressive (Bogaert, 2021, p. 360; Austin, 2016, p. 19), and music especially helps children relax, diminish their pain and reduce their anxiety (Austin, 2016, p. 21).

Patients' experiences are influenced by emotional experiential issues, which, in turn, affect clinical outcomes (Rickert, 2014, n.d.). Emotions dominate our decision making, command attention and affect memory by minimising some memories while amplifying others (Van Gorp & Adams, 2012, p. 4–6). Also, patients face different variations of emotions during their visits to hospitals (Alhonsuo & Colley, 2019, p. 725); hence, it is important to consider a holistic service experience, understand what people really feel and how the service could be designed better. Also, embracing an emotional connection strategy across the organisation would help not only to have more satisfied customers, but also to have a more satisfied staff (Magids et al., 2015, p. 4). This can have a major impact on a holistic service journey, patient satisfaction and healing in hospitals. However, to design emotional experiences, we need to understand what triggers certain emotions (Singh, 2014, p. 27, p. 31).

One of the fundamental values of service design is co-creating services with service end users and understanding what people really want, what their needs and desires are and how they experience service from the beginning to the end. However, children are still a marginalised group in development processes (Hargreaves & Viner, 2012, p. 661), and they often depend on adults, who may be in power-dominant and decision making positions (Hansen, 2017, p. 1). The role of children in the design process has changed tremendously in the participatory design field (Read & Markopoulos, 2013, p. 3), even though it has been criticised that involving children in open-ended and future-oriented work and analysing the creative contributions by children is not easy (Mechelen et al., 2017, p. 770). Previous studies have addressed how tools, such as Play-Doh, Lego blocks or crayons, can stimulate play to facilitate interaction and communication when interacting with children (e.g., Rygh & Clatworthy, 2019, p. 99), but another approach could be the use of stories and storytelling.

For children, stories are a playful way to build imagination skills, but also to deal with other issues such as trauma (Killick & Boffey, 2012, p. v, p. 2). Storytelling empathises with both speaking and listening, which are simple to do, engage children and help children learn about feelings (Killick & Boffey, 2012, p. 2). Thus, stories play an important role in helping understand what people have experienced (Bate & Robert, 2007, p. 58) or how they would like to experience something. In addition, we can hear stories everywhere in our lives. Fairy tales, everyday situations, movies and even commercials are built around stories. The service design field introduces many design methods that are based on stories or storytelling; these methods aim to emphasise people's perspectives and understand their experiences and emotions throughout the service journey. In this chapter, children are placed at the centre of the study and are seen as valuable actors in the development process of the new children's hospital, which integrates psychiatry and somatic care.

Lapland Central Hospital is located in Rovaniemi and is the northernmost hospital offering both primary healthcare and specialist care in Finnish Lapland. Lapland region is divided into 21 municipalities, and the ongoing reform is restructuring the healthcare, social welfare, and rescue services. In the future, the wellbeing services counties will be responsible for ensuring that people receive the health, social and rescue services they need. In Lapland, long distances, a low population density, and different weather conditions challenge healthcare services, but at the same time the reform enables new initiatives to be considered.

New and co-creative methods for developing a human-centred healthcare service are needed to understand the needs of different stakeholders. Thus, this chapter discusses how children can be involved in hospital planning through creative storytelling and how service design can be used to interpret imaginative materials. These two research questions are answered through a storytelling template sent to families with children. The aim is to utilise the data as a part of the new Lapland Central Hospital construction process, more specifically in the children's hospital, which will integrate somatic care and psychiatry. The construction project started in 2019 and is scheduled to be completed in 2028.

Following fiction-based research guidelines (Leavy, 2017, p. 199), the storytelling template used in the current research made it possible to either share lived experiences or create a dream healthcare service through imagination. In this chapter, the stories from 14 responses from children between 3 and 13 years old were received over a period of three weeks and were analysed using a service journey mapping tool, a core method in the service design field. Borrowing from futures research approaches (Finn & Wylie, 2021, p. 1; Jarva, 2014, p. 5; Sools, 2020, p. 451 the results of the study highlight that the stories built on imagination brought forth commonalities related to feelings, senses, spatial awareness and interpersonal interactions, for example, patient–doctor or patient–nurse interactions. Although most of the ideas were simplistic and ineffective to implement in hospitals, space was created for futuristic innovations.

First, this chapter introduces the background of the theories based on designing healthcare services with children and storytelling as an approach to understanding their wishes and lived experiences. Second, the storytelling method, along with its art-based and fiction-based research approaches, are described and analysed. At the end of the chapter, the findings of the method and results are discussed.

2   Theoretical Background

In the following subchapters, relevant theories for the study are introduced, starting with healthcare service design with children before zooming into stories and what kind of role they play in design methods. In addition, the definitions and backgrounds of designing for emotions are described to bring more meaningful insights to the topic.

2.1   Designing Healthcare Services with Children

Service design is a multidisciplinary practice (Blomkvist et al., 2010, p. 308), that represents a creative, iterative and human-centred approach to creating new services, in which different disciplines contribute to service innovation through design-based tools and methods (e.g., Patrício & Fisk, 2013, p. 195). Service design drives transformation (Patrício et al., 2018, p. 12) and "is playing an increasingly prominent role in supporting change and innovation within the healthcare sector, particularly in relation to catalyzing co-creation." (Mager et al., 2022, p. 507). One of the fundamental values of service design is co-creating services with the end users of services. According to Read and Markopoulos (2013, p. 3), the role of children in the design process has changed tremendously in the participatory design field. Service designers seek to understand what people really want, what their needs or desires are and how they experience the service from the beginning to the end of the service experience. Designers aim to visualise a holistic picture of a service, and to reach that point, a service designer must find ways to connect with different users of the service and understand how experiences, needs and desires can be gathered from them.

Healthcare and design have a long history together (e.g., Rowe et al., 2020, p. 328), which has increasingly applied patient involvement and co-design approaches (Nesta, 2013, p. 6). Healthcare is personal and universal, and "extremely technical" (Jones, 2013, p. xv), which includes many different system types. It is a universally used service that has an impact on economies and quality of life (Berry & Bendapudi, 2007, p. 111) and in which the interactions among various stakeholders are relied upon (Bowen et al., 2013, p. 230). In addition, healthcare is a continuously changing environment. In Finland, ongoing social and healthcare reforms and several hospital construction projects offer new opportunities to develop healthcare services and systems through design methods with relevant stakeholders.

According to Mager (2017, p. 10), one of the impacts of healthcare-related service design is stakeholder engagement. As service users, patients represent a large body of different user groups of all ages, genders and backgrounds. In addition, patients can face different variations of emotions, such as fear, trauma, frustration or happiness during their stay in the hospital (Alhonsuo & Colley, 2019, p. 725). In many services, children represent a specific user group, who are often dependent on adults with more power in decision making and what is the child's best interest

(Hansen, 2017, p. 1). In the development process of improving patients' services, children and young people under the age of 16 can still be seen as marginalised (Hargreaves & Viner, 2012, p. 661). However, according to the report by Ian Kennedy (2010, p. 45), children and young people should be at the centre of the services and involved in shaping them. Child-centred design connects service design, children's rights and a child-centred approach, where children are seen as valuable actors in the development process (Kalliomeri et al., p. 8). Involving children in open-ended and future-oriented work and analysing the creative contributions by children is not easy (Mechelen et al., 2017, p. 770). However, research has been done, for example, on how tools should stimulate play to facilitate interaction and communication when interacting with children, highlighting that Play-Doh, Lego blocks, or crayons to draw with are useful tools for this purpose (Rygh & Clatworthy, 2019, p. 99).

2.2 Why Stories Matter

Patients' experiences are important to consider when developing healthcare services because they are influenced by emotional experiential issues, in turn affecting clinical outcomes (Rickert, 2014, n.d.). In addition, Neuhoff et al., (2022, p. 523) argue that story-centred co-creative methods create relationships that are characterised by empathy, sensitivity and trust; in their study, this led to safe, authentic and informal design environments. Narrations play an important role in helping to understand what people have experienced (Bate & Robert, 2007, p. 58) or how would they like to experience something. As Goodwin notes, 'Healthcare experiences that we share with family and others are typically presented as a story because it is as a story that we are able to create a sense of the connections between the events and the feelings that together form the memories and meanings of what occurred' (2020, p. 57).

Storytelling is an essential approach in design, and it is an integral part of many methods of service design. Service journeys, service prototyping and various walkthrough methods, along with other methods, include a story that highlights people's perspectives. For children, stories are a playful way to build imagination skills, but they are also a way to deal with other issues such as trauma (Killick & Boffey, 2012, p. v, p. 2). Stories can be seen as a way to create a dream world or describe a lived experience that can be better told through a story. Storytelling empathises with both speaking and listening, which are simple to do and help in engaging children and learn about feelings (Killick & Boffey, 2012, p. 2). Stories can be told anywhere; hence, it is an easy method for approaching children. The story can be told during a car ride, while waiting for a bus or even as a bedtime story. However, the role of the storyteller is also relevant. It matters how the story is experienced so that the relationship with the child, the motivation for the story and the freedom for creativity and imagination are maintained.

2.3 Designing for Emotions

Emotion is the biggest influence in the everyday lives of a human beings; it domi-
nates our decision making, commands attention and affects memory by minimising
some memories while amplifying others (Van Gorp & Adams, 2012, p. 4–6). Emotions are always about something— one cannot simply be afraid; one is afraid of
something. This means that if we want to design an emotional experience, we
need to understand what triggers certain emotions (Singh, 2014, p. 27, p. 31).
Magids et al.'s (2015, p. 4) research across hundreds of brands shows that it
is possible to measure and target the feelings that drive customers' behaviour;
in addition, customers themselves may not be aware of these emotional motivators. A person-centred perspective in designing healing environments seeks a
better understanding of what people see and feel in these spaces. On this, Bogaert
states, 'Hospital administrators, designers and architects will need to work with
the patient groups, patients, families, and healthcare workers to design appropriate person-centred methodologies in order to capture how these spaces are lived
emotionally' (2021, p. 362). To reach this understanding, approaches for gathering
in-depth experiences of different people are needed. Thus, the storytelling template in this chapter is presented as a way to study the emotions and feelings of
individuals.

In recent years, designers working in healthcare have increasingly been starting to recognise the importance of how taking emotional needs into account helps
create healing spaces so that care becomes more than just a cure (Bogaert, 2021,
p. 355; DuBose et al., 2016, p. 43). Hospitals cannot be seen as places for enjoying
or spending time for fun. However, embracing an emotional connection strategy
across the organisation would help not only to have more satisfied customers, but
also in having a more satisfied staff (Magids et al., 2015, p. 11). This means
that emotional experiences should be considered in the patient's service journey.
Research in emotional design has shown that properly used sound can be emotionally satisfying and expressive (Bogaert, 2021, p. 360; Austin, 2016, p. 19),
and music especially helps children relax, diminish their pain and reduce their
anxiety (Austin, 2016, p. 21). Bogaert (2021, p. 360) concludes that auditory privacy in hospitals has been largely understudied, but it has been shown that too
much silence in hospital environments increases vulnerability, while the 'gentle
hum' of people doing things reduces isolation. Designing an overall soundscape
in hospitals helps minimise abrasive sounds, and it is also a relatively inexpensive and simple way to make the environment more welcoming (Bogaert, 2021,
p. 360). Light and colour also impact our emotional experiences in the hospital.
Natural light or the right kind of artificial light can create an emotionally soothing
environment (Bogaert, 2021, p. 360), and colours in the blue range are considered
to have a calming effect (Van Gorp & Adams, 2012, p. 155). In the storytelling
template, these different elements have been considered.

Bogaert (2021, p. 356) argues that Gaston Bachelard's phenomenology of
homely and emotionally secure spaces can be extended even to a hospital environment. Especially small, nest-like corners or familiar and 'home-like' objects give

patients some feeling of privacy and security, which will help reduce their anxiety about the hospital experience. A person can spend quite some time in the hospital waiting rooms, either waiting for an appointment or for updates about a loved one's condition. Making these spaces more hybrid—a place where one can find intimacy and security but also allow movement and interaction—reduces negative emotions (stress, anxiety and fear; Bogaert, 2021, p. 358). Although the environment cannot cause actual healing, it can facilitate engagement in emotions that support healing by inducing emotional responses, such as happiness, joy and relaxation. Studies show that home-like environments reduce patients' distress and that positive emotions are the outcome of providing views of nature and natural light in hospitals (DuBose et al., 2016, p. 48; Bogaert, 2021, p. 359–360). When walking into the hospital, it should feel calm, safe and respectful rather than institutional.

3 Storytelling Through Imagination

This subchapter introduces the methodological approach for the present study, starting from the values of qualitative art-based research before zooming into a fiction-based research and storytelling template. It visually introduces the method created for the study and how the narrations have been analysed in the visual service journey mapping tool.

3.1 Fiction-Based Research

Human experiences, subjectivity, multiple meanings and depth of understanding are the values of qualitative research (Rogers, 2014, p. 1). Diving in deeper, arts-based research (ABR) is an approach that offers a practice-based, creative, holistic and engaged way to look at the world under study and in which values emerge from an aesthetic understanding, evocation and provocation, enabling participants to be highly individualistic (Leavy, 2017, p. 191). ABR includes genres such as short stories, poetry, theatrical scripts and visual arts, which have similarities with service design tools and methods, such as service journeys and role playing. An approach to combine storytelling, imagination, creativity and service design is fiction-based research (FBR).

The chosen approach of the chapter has similarities with narrative research, where stories produced by research participants can be spoken life stories, photographic self-portraits or day-by-day journals (Squire et al., 2014, p. 8). However, FBR is an ABR design approach with unique capabilities for creating engaging and evocating research and that can be used to portray the complexity of lived experiences (Leavy, 2017, p. 199). Using fiction as a design practice offers opportunities for the writer to simulate the environment, sounds, sights and even smells of reality in a virtual way (Leavy, 2013, p. 53). This can captivate readers' imaginations, which, in the current study, arises from the imaginary and fictive words of children. According to Bate and Robert, 'Words are the vessels or messengers of meaning and experience' (2007, p. 39), forming stories and anecdotes from past to present. By collecting these words, a storytelling template has been created for the children.

'Stories are sacred, as is the space created through the sharing of stories. When we share our stories, they come to life through the telling; however, the story has a life of its own and that life is given through the spirit of the story and the storyteller' (Lewis, 2011, p. 507). Stories are ubiquitous fictional novels, such as fairy tales (Polkinghorne, 2007, p. 471), which consist of a beginning, middle and end (Polkinghorne, 1988, p. 145). Hence, a story also structures the service journey mapping, where people's experiences are visualised as a timeline. As a narrative research approach, telling stories gives voice to the voiceless and traditionally marginalised, hence providing a less exploitative research method (Hendry, 2007, p. 489; Lewis, 2011, p. 506).

3.2   'Once upon a Time...'

As Leavy (2017, p. 199) states, FBR can be stories, novellas and novels. For the current study, the story has been partly written to help children use their imagination in the specific context: children's healthcare services. The story begins the night before the hospital trip and continues the morning of the following day. The story goes step by step inside the hospital, building from the service moments of the service journey and considering, among other things, service touchpoints and emotions.

'Imaginative narratives' (Finn & Wylie, 2021, p. 7) and storytelling methods have been widely used in research approaches to reimagine personal futures with the aim of transforming lived realities (Finn & Wylie, 2021, p. 1; Jarva, 2014, p. 5; Sools, 2020, p. 451). Various methods have been developed to assist research participants in imagining ideal spaces (Pereira et al., 2018, p. 1), for example. Using storytelling in future studies (Jarva, 2014, p. 5) is based on the idea that stories should be more useful and purposeful in assisting individuals and communities to shape their realities and build common understandings (Finn & Wiley, 2021, p. 10). Temporal, spatial and cultural realities can be reinterpreted through imaginative storytelling, through which hopes, wishes, needs and feelings can be expressed to identify the solutions and possibilities for the future. These approaches to storytelling have been used in service design and policy-making processes (Sarantou et al., 2021, p. 133).

The story for the present study has been created as a storytelling template format, providing both online and paper-based versions. Surveys are one of the common approaches used to gather patients' experiences in healthcare services (Rickert, 2014, n.d.). However, challenges are highlighted in ensuring that the data are understood and acted upon throughout the healthcare organisation (Kumah et al., 2017, p. 24), for which further use of the data as part of the visualisation of the service journey has been investigated. In service design processes, the data are often utilised later in the design process or during the next phases.

This means, for example, that survey data or data from the template can be presented, supplemented and deepened in the co-creation workshops with relevant stakeholders.

Before publishing the template, it was tested with three children, ensuring the story was logical and the open fields were easy to understand. In total, 14 responses from children between 3 and 13 years old were received over a period of three weeks. The template were conducted completely anonymously, and only age was asked in the background data. Based on this, it was difficult to identify how many children reflected on their lived experiences in healthcare services. The template was opened 452 times, and the response rate for replies was 100%, which means that those who started filling out the template finalised it without withdrawing. The template was shared through social media channels and with acquaintances and relatives. The story was written in Finnish, and for this chapter, it has been translated into English (see Fig. 1).

3.2.1 'Continue the Sentence…' Exercise

At the end of the storytelling template, six focused questions were asked based on more concrete ideas for the hospital design. The aim was to clearly understand what kind of colour, shape, fairy tale, animal, landscape and sounds would be the most welcoming in the hospital. This was done by asking the respondent to continue the following sentences (see Fig. 2).

3.3 Visual Service Journey Mapping

The service journey is a service design method that visualises the process of service and the experience of a person in a timeline, helping find gaps and explore potential service solutions (Stickdorn et al., 2018, p. 44). It consists of service moments that represent the main sequenced phases in the service journey. In the template, each open question represented a service moment, highlighting more detailed questions about feelings and different senses, such as hearing.

The template data were analysed and evaluated through visual service journey mapping on the Miro board, which is an online whiteboard for visual collaboration. The visualisation enabled us to see the children's multiple views and how they would like to experience the healthcare services in Lapland Central Hospital. In addition, the written responses were visualised: each comment received an image, icon, emoji or colour to represent the response. This enabled the use of the data later in co-creative workshops with relevant stakeholders, such as children, their parents and healthcare professionals. Visuality helps in understanding the data without having the skills to read it.

Storytelling template

It's a spring evening, and you've just curled up on your bed under your own blanket. Tomorrow is your hospital trip ahead, and you have been waiting for a while. Thinking about a hospital trip makes you feel _____,
and you hope you get a good night's sleep now.

You close your eyes and decide to imagine what a hospital trip would be as welcoming as possible. What kind of hospital would it be then, what would it look, sound and smell like in there, what would happen there and who are working there?

You will soon fall asleep and begin to see a dream where this, the most welcoming hospital you can imagine, manifests before your eyes. In your dream, you will be accompanied on a hospital trip by _____. You walk across the hospital yard together. The weather is _____, and you are looking at _____. You will soon be at the hospital's front door, which is _____.

As you step inside the hospital lobby, first you pay attention to _____. You are greeted by _____. You will be happy when the walls in the hospital lobby are _____ and there are _____ on them.

You admire the ceiling and floors of the lobby because you could not have believed that the hospital could look like this. Later, you describe what you saw by saying: _____ _____

In the lobby, you are greeted with a smile by the employee. Before you go looking for a place where you can sit down, you stop to listen. You relax when you find out that as a background noise, you hear _____. You are looking for a suitable waiting place for yourself, and you found it. The seat you selected is located at _____. You chose it because _____. You are excited to find that you can spend time waiting for your doctor by _____.

In no time, the doctor calls you. The doctor is _____. You get up and walk towards the doctor's examination room. At the door, you greet each other, and the doctor keeps the door open for you as you step inside. You are entering a room that is _____, and there is _____. Although the situation makes you a little nervous, you calm down when you notice _____

A visit to the doctor takes a moment, and before you leave the room, you get to take a _____ with you.

Afterwards, you memorise your hospital trip. In particular, you remember _____ and _____.

You wake up from your sleep. What a lively dream it was! Before you continue your day with other things, you can tell us more about what would make you as comfortable as possible in the hospital: _____ _____ _____

Fig. 1 The storytelling template. *Source* Author's own illustration (2022)

4 Findings

In the following section, the main categories and results from the storytelling template are highlighted. As a part of the written results, some of the visualisations of the data are illustrated as an example.

If the hospital was as welcoming as possible and this was shown as a colour, it would be _____.

If the most welcoming hospital was a shape, it would be _____.

If the most welcoming hospital possible was a fairy tale, it would be _____.

If the hospital as welcoming as possible was an animal, it would be _____.

If a hospital as welcoming as possible was a landscape, it would be _____.

If the hospital as welcoming as possible was sound, it would be _____.

Fig. 2 'Continue the sentence…' exercise. *Source* Author's own illustration (2022)

4.1   Commonality of the Stories

There were either differences or similarities between the different responses. For example, the state of emotion 'How do you feel about a hospital trip' caused apprehension for seven respondents, while two found the experience only caused a little apprehension. Individual responses included 'bad and shy' and scary. Also, the weather was described as sunny in 11 out of the 14 answers, and the rest of the weather conditions were good and windy. Another common topic was art in the hospital. The art and paintings were seen in many service moments, such as on the walls of the hospital lobby and in the doctor's room. Figure 3 illustrates the commonalities in three service moments in a service journey mapping.

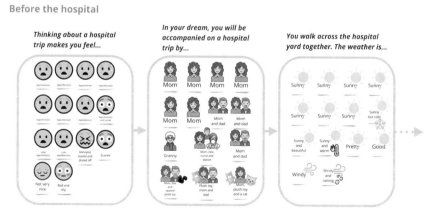

Fig. 3 First three service moments from the visual service journey mapping. *Source* Author's own illustration (2022)

The major differences in the responses were for the question, 'You enter the hospital lobby in your sleep, you pay attention first …'. Answers differentiated from 'Camera surveillance', 'To plants', 'To the multitude of people', 'Waiting room benches', 'To the brightness of the space and yet the colourful walls', 'For caregivers walking in the hallways', 'For an elderly person in a wheelchair' and 'To the reindeer'.

4.2   Nature-Based Environment and Animals

Many of the responses contained nature and the senses associated with nature. Nature-themed images, landscapes or colours were desired on the hospital's surfaces, such as walls, floors and ceilings. In the storytelling template, the hospital walls were reflected 'as a nature' and 'night sky' and where you can see 'pictures of giraffe', 'funny animals' and 'the northern lights'. In addition, various forests were imagined, such as a Christmas tree forest and palm landscape, in addition to the ordinary forest. Nature and animals came up with many responses related to different senses, such as hearing. The children imagined voices from nature and, for example, 'the chirping of birds'.

One of the main highlighted elements was the water, which was heard both as the babbling of a creek and as a concrete aquarium in the waiting room of the hospital. The walls were also painted in a water colour style, and the colour of the turquoise water came up in several responses. This resonates with the study by Van Gorp and Adams (2012, p. 155), where blue colours are shown to have a calming effect. As Bogaert (2021, p. 360) and Austin (2016, p. 19) address, the properly used sound can be emotionally satisfying and expressive, and especially with children, music helps to relax, diminish pain and reduce anxiety (Austin, 2016, p. 21). Hence, it is important to listen to children's wishes about the sounds in the hospital environment. Figure 4 visualises the collage of nature-based elements in the data. The visualisation will be used later in the workshop.

4.3   Home-Like Environments

'The roof was low and the floor soft. There were not too many bright lights or resonant rooms anywhere' (quote from a participant in a template). Home-like spaces and objects were presented in many of the responses. In the waiting room, there should be 'plants', 'toys', 'bean bags', 'soft sofas' and a private corner, which was described to be 'dim' and 'peaceful'. The ideal walls would be colourful (pink, green and turquoise were prominent replies), 'wallpapered' and with art hung or painted on them. In the background, some of the children would like to hear music, radio channels or their 'mother's own voice', and they would like to spend time by 'making art', 'reading Donald Duck', 'watching TV' and 'playing'. Most of the replies showed a desire to strip the stereotypical institutionality away from the hospital environment, instead preferring the home-like elements. As Bogaert (2021,

Fig. 4 Nature-based elements from the responses. Source: Author's own illustration (2022)

p. 356) argues, small, nest-like corners or 'home-like' objects give patients a feeling of privacy and security; this was also well seen in the replies. In Fig. 5, objects of home-like environments are mapped as a visual collage. The visualisation will be used later in the workshop.

Fig. 5 Collage about home-like objects and things from the responses. Source: Author's own illustration (2022)

4.4   Innovating Through Stories

The storytelling template with the imagination of children was a great way to innovate services of how to make the experiences more fun or relaxed. One child replied that in the hospital, 'There are rainbows on the roof and walls. Pink colour, too. The floor had "footprints" and a "jumping grid"'. In addition, a slide was desired for the playful waiting area. The doctor's treatment room was described as a playroom, 'where is a dog', 'all kind of toys', and 'that the doctor's had a teddy bear who was also undergoing operations/examinations'. Teddy bears and other flush toys were mentioned in other questions, too. Four children replied that they would get small toy lizards when they left the doctor's room. However, none of the ideas required a huge effort to implement, which reflects the fact that small changes can make the 'service more enjoyable'.

4.5   Challenges in Responding

Overall, 14 respondents were received over the three-week period, even though the template was opened more than 450 times. The study period was first extended from two weeks to three weeks because many responses were received because of allowing more time. The reason for this could be, based on our assumptions, that filling the template with a child needs a proper place and time. When a parent received a template for the first time and if the timing was not good at that moment, filling it out may be forgotten. Also, it may be that parents are just stretched for time and don't have a chance to fill the template with their children. The link to the template was shared mostly through social media. It may have gotten lost with other social media updates, and after this, it may have been difficult to find it again. An active reminder of the template could have prompted more replies. Also here, the responsibility to complete the template rested on the parents when the template was shared in social media channels, such as Facebook and LinkedIn.

Another way to get more replies to a template could have been to share a paper version of it in the hospital waiting room. The parents and children could have filled it out while waiting. In this case, the hospital as a physical environment could have either limited the respondents' imagination or prompted some concrete development ideas. No paper-based template was conducted, however. The reason for this was that we thought the online version of the template was an easy and quick way to reach a wide range of respondents and a variety of replies.

However, the comments from the parents who did reply to the template with their child were positive. The method was seen as an inspiring and nice activity together with the child. One parent wrote, 'The boy did well. It took a little over 10 min [to answer the template] and then a few minutes to read the whole story again so he could listen to and correct any more answers he wanted (only one point he wanted to fix). He said it was nice to answer such a survey'. The parent continued, 'This is certainly also influenced by how the interviewer, that is, the reader of the story, experiences and how well the child is motivated to listen to the story, empathises and is excited to take it forward through their own imagination'. The children who tested the survey before it was published said, 'This was fun and easy! Took me only eight minutes, and thinking about it like a dream made me REALLY think what would be nice and new'.

5   Discussion

This chapter has sought to answer the following questions: How can children be involved in hospital planning through creative storytelling, and how can service design be used to interpret imaginative materials? In this section, the research questions are answered and discussed.

5.1   Children-Centred Involvement Through Creative Storytelling

One of the impacts of healthcare-related service design is stakeholder involvement (Mager, 2017, p. 10), and while designing healthcare services for children, the children should be at the centre of the services and involved as valuable and active actors in the design process (Kalliomeri et al., 2020, p. 8; Kennedy, 2010, p. 45). However, there are some barriers to engaging with children in designing. Not only do adults have the power in decision making and what is in the child's best interest in terms of services (Hansen, 2017, p. 1), but they also have the decision whether to participate or not in developing healthcare services with children. As addressed in the current study, the online template did not reach as many replies as expected, even though the comments about the template from several parents were very positive. From this point of view, the channels and formats may need some rethinking. An online option works, but it might need reminders or should be more easily accessible. It was noteworthy that it was important to give enough time to respond. Finding the right moment to go through the story may not be possible on the same day.

It has also not been possible to observe storytelling between a child and parent while completing the template, nor how empathy, sensitivity and trust have been created (Neuhoff et al., 2022, p. 523) because the template was answered by a child with the help of an adult. The template could also be looked at more closely from the perspectives of playfulness, interaction and communication, as Rygh and Clatworthy (2019, p. 99) have studied with concrete tools, such as Play-Doh and Lego blocks. However, these playfulness approaches will be taken into account later in the research project when the template data are used in the workshops with families. In the present study, the storytelling template was used to gather an initial understanding from the children, but it would not be enough for creating a holistic picture of the children's hospital services, where psychiatry and somatic care are integrated. Thus, the storytelling template can be a starting point for data collection and further use in the co-designing workshops, were not only the children with their parents, but also healthcare representatives, are creating the services.

In recent years, designers working in healthcare have been increasingly starting to recognise the importance of how taking emotional needs into account and how this helps create healing spaces so that care becomes more than just a cure (Bogaert, 2021, p. 355; DuBose et al., 2016, p. 43). Hospitals cannot be seen as places for enjoying or spending time for fun. However, embracing an emotional connection strategy across the organisation would help not only to have more satisfied customers, but also to have a more satisfied staff (Magids et al., 2015, p. 11). This means that emotional experiences should be considered in the patient's service journey. However, through the storytelling template, several inexpensive and simple solutions regarding the sounds, music, lights and colours were presented for hospital environments, which can have a healing effect or relax the children (e.g., Austin, 2016, p. 19; Bogaert, 2021, p. 360). Through these easily implantable ideas, we can strive to take greater account of patients' emotional experiences.

5.2   Interpretating and Translating the Story Through Visualisations

When creating the template and its story, we wanted to emphasise FBR. Hence, the dreamlike story was created to enable us to dive into imaginary thinking where anything is possible. The introductory text of the storytelling template allowed the children to immerse themselves in their imagination through the world of sleep. Still, the structure of the template guided the child to keep the story more systematic, which first helped the researchers in analysing and interpreting the material and, second, better identify the feelings and senses in the data. The data emphasised many similar emotions and feelings during the service journey, and adding the emojis for the replies made the data more visible and understandable. It seemed that the storytelling template enabled us to deal with emotional experiences in a more playful way, as Killich and Boffey (2012, p. v, 2) have also argued.

While interpreting and translating the data in the visual service journey mapping, the holistic journey picture started to be perceived with many ideas. The outcomes from the stories were not only considering the interior of the hospital, but also the interactions between the service provider and end user. Finally, the visualised service journey, which was used as a compiling mapping tool for the study, was completed as a very rich set of data. The hospital environment and holistic service experience go hand in hand and cannot be separated into their own categories when it comes to hospital design. The service journey intertwines, among other things, what we (or would like to) see, hear, experience and feel. The visual service journey mapping will later be utilised in co-creative workshop sessions with children, parents and healthcare providers. Here, the role of dialogue increases as a combination of created visual service journey mapping. This can also support the analysis of creative contributions by children, which was argued to be difficult (Mechelen et al., 2017, p. 770). The service journey helps in mapping sequences and grouping of the data, where visuality enables everyone to understand it and recognise unifying ideas and innovations. Visuality is important, especially when co-designing with children who cannot yet read.

6 Conclusion

The current study was a starting point for the ongoing hospital construction project, which focuses on integrating children's hospital services by providing psychiatry as an integral part of somatic care. The construction project is a large, long-term project in which service design is partly utilised. For this chapter, only one method was introduced and described in more depth. However, the storytelling template offered viewpoints and insights for designing healthcare services with children, allowing them to participate as contributors to the healthcare service design.

The combination of the storytelling template and visual service journey mapping created a systematic continuum for the use of the material. The material from the current study will be continued in co-design workshops involving children, parents and healthcare professionals alike. The aim is to continue the research of storytelling methods and service design that seeks to design healthcare services and hospital settings. Children's thoughts are as important as any other service users; thus, storytelling is one creative, playful and inspiring way to engage a marginalised service user group. Storytelling as a creative method provides endless approaches to research that should be further investigated.

References

Alhonsuo, M., & Colley, A. (2019). Designing new hospitals–Who cares about the patients? In *MuC´19: Proceedings of Mensch und Computer 2019* (pp. 725–729). Hamburg, Germany: Association for Computing. https://doi.org/10.1145/3340764.3344898

Austin, M. L. (2016). Safe and sound: Using audio to communicate comfort, safety, and familiarity in digital media. In S. Tettegah & S. U. Noble (Eds.), *Emotions, technology and design* (pp. 19–35). Washington, DC, USA: Elsevier Inc., Howard University.

Bate, P., & Robert, G. (2007). *Bringing user experience to healthcare improvement: The concepts, methods and practices of experience-based design.* Oxford, New York: Radcliffe Publishing.

Berry, L. L., & Bendapudi, N. (2007). Health care: A fertile field for service research. *Journal of Service Research, 10*(2), 111–122.

Blomkvist, J., Holmlid, S., & Segelström, F. (2010). This is service design research: Yesterday, today and tomorrow. In M. Stickdorn & J. Schneider (Eds.), *This is service design thinking* (pp. 308–315). Amsterdam: BIS Publishers.

Bogaert, B. (2021). Moving towards person-centreed care: Valuing emotions in hospital design and architecture. *HERD: Health Environments Research & Design Journal, 15*(2), 355–364. https://doi.org/10.1177/2F19375867211062101

Bowen, S., McSeveny, K., Lockley, E., Wolstenholme, D., Cobb, M., & Dearden, A. (2013). How was it for you? Experiences of participatory design in the UK health service. *CoDesign, 9*(4), 230–246.

DuBose, J., MacAllister, L., Hadi, K., & Sakallaris, B. (2016). Exploring the concept of healing spaces. *HERD: Health Environments Research & Design Journal, 11*(1), 43–56. https://doi.org/10.1177/2F1937586716680567

Finn, E., & Wylie, R. (2021). Collaborative imagination: A methodological approach. *Futures, 132*(102788), 1–11.

Goodwin, S. (2020). *Meaningful healthcare experience design: Improving care for all generations.* New York: Productivity Press.

Hansen, A. S. (2017). *How to best communicate with and encourage children during a design process.* Retrieved June 30, 2022, from https://www.ntnu.edu/documents/139799/127914 9990/13+Article+Final_anjash_fors%C3%B8k_2017-12-07-20-11-11_Co-Design+with+Chi ldren+-+Final.pdf/b8dd19c4-d2b1-4322-a042-718e06663e13

Hargreaves, D. S., & Viner, R. M. (2012). Children's and young people's experience of the National Health Service in England: A review of national surveys 2001–2011. *Archives of Disease in Childhood, 97*(7), 661–666. https://doi.org/10.1136/archdischild-2011-300603

Hendry, P. M. (2007). The future of narrative. *Qualitative Inquiry, 13*(4), 487–498.

Jarva, V. (2014). Introduction to narrative for futures studies. *Journal of Futures Studies, 18*(3), 5–26.

Jones, P. H. (2013). *Design for care: Innovating healthcare experience.* New York: Rosenfeld Media.

Kalliomeri, R., Mettinen, K., Ohlsson, A-M., & Tulensalo, H. (2020). *Child-centreed design.* Save the Children Finland. Retrieved June 30, 2022, from https://resourcecentre.savethechildren.net/document/child-centered-design/

Kennedy, I. (2010). *Getting it right for children and young people: Overcoming cultural barriers in the NHS so as to meet their needs* [Independent report]. Retrieved June 30, 2022, from https://www.gov.uk/government/publications/getting-it-right-for-children-and-young-people-overcoming-cultural-barriers-in-the-nhs-so-as-to-meet-their-needs

Killick, S., & Boffey, M. (2012). *Building relationships through storytelling: A foster carer's guide to attachment and stories.* Fostering Network. Retrieved June 30, 2022, from https://www.thefosteringnetwork.org.uk/sites/default/files/resources/publications/building-relationships-thr ough-storytelling-31-10-12.pdf

Kumah, E., Osei-Kesse, F., & Anaba, C. (2017). Understanding and using patient experience feedback to improve health care quality: Systematic review and framework development. *Journal of Patient-Centered Research and Reviews, 4*(1), 24–31.

Leavy, P. (2013). *Fiction as research practice: Short stories, novels and novels* (1st ed.). Routledge. New York. https://doi.org/10.4324/9781315428499

Leavy, P. (2017). *Research design: Quantitative, qualitative, mixed methods, arts-based, and community-based participatory research approaches.* New York: The Guilford Press.

Lewis, P. J. (2011). Storytelling as research/research as storytelling. *Qualitative Inquiry, 17*(6), 505–510. https://doi.org/10.1177/1077800411409883

Mager, B. (2017). *Service design impact report: Healthcare sector.* Service Design Network. Retrieved June 30, 2022, from https://www.service-design-network.org/books-and-reports/ser vice-design-impact-report-health-sector-en

Mager, B., Oertzen, A. S., & Vink, J. (2022). Co-creation in health services through service design. In M. A. Pfannstiel, N. Brehmer & C. Rasche (Eds.), *Service design practices for health-care innovation* (pp. 497–510). Cham: Springer Publishing. https://doi.org/10.1007/978-3-030-87273-1_24

Magids, S., Zorfas, A., & Leemon, D. (2015). The new science of customer emotions—A better way to drive growth and profitability. *Harvard Business Review.* Retrieved June 30, 2022, from http://sproutresearch.com.au/wp-content/uploads/2015/11/HBR-The-New-Sci ence-of-Customer-Emotions.pdf

Nesta. (2013). *By us, for us: The power of co-design and co-delivery.* Retrieved June 30, 2022, from https://media.nesta.org.uk/documents/the_power_of_co-design_and_co-delivery.pdf

Neuhoff, R., Johansen, N. D., & Simeone, L. (2022). Story-centreed co-creative methods: A means for relational service design and healthcare innovation. In M. A. Pfannstiel, N. Brehmer & C. Rasche (Eds.), *Service design practices for healthcare innovation* (pp. 511–528). Cham: Springer Publishing. https://doi.org/10.1007/978-3-030-87273-1_25

Patrício, L., & Fisk, R. P. (2013). Creating new services. In R. P. Fisk, R. Russell-Bennett, & L. Harris (Eds.), *In serving customers globally* (pp. 185–207). Prahran, VIC: Tilde University Press.

Patrício, L., Gustafsson, A., & Fisk, R. P. (2018). Upframing service design and innovation for research impact. *Journal of Service Research, 21*(1), 3–16.

Pereira, L. M., Hichert, T., Hamann, M., Preiser, R., & Biggs, R. (2018). Using futures methods to create transformative spaces. *Ecology and Society, 23*(1), 1–13.

Polkinghorne, D. E. (1988). *Narrative knowing and the human sciences.* New York: State University of New York Press.

Polkinghorne, D. E. (2007). Validity issues in narrative research. *Qualitative Inquiry, 13*(4), 471–486. https://doi.org/10.1177/1077800406297670

Read, J. C., & Markopoulos, P. (2013). Child-computer interaction. *International Journal of Child-Computer Interaction, 1*(1), 2–6. https://doi.org/10.1016/j.ijcci.2012.09.001

Rickert, J. (2014). *Measuring patient satisfaction: A bridge between patient and physician perceptions of care.* Retrieved June 30, 2022, from https://doi.org/10.1377/hblog20140509.038951/full/

Rogers, R. H. (2014). Fiction strengthens research: A review of Patricia Leavy's fiction as research practice: Short stories, novellas, and novels. *The Qualitative Report, 19*(46), 1–4. https://doi.org/10.46743/2160-3715/2014.1133

Rowe, A., Knox, M., & Harvey, G. (2020). Re-thinking health through design: Collaborations in research, education and practice. *Design for Health, 4*(3), 327–344.

Rygh, K., & Clatworthy, S. (2019). The use of tangible tools as a means to support co-design during service design innovation projects in healthcare. In M. A. Pfannstiel & C. Rasche (Eds.), *Service design and service thinking in healthcare and hospital management* (pp. 77–114). Cham: Springer Publishing. https://doi.org/10.1007/978-3-030-00749-2_7

Sarantou, M., Alhonsuo, M., Gutierrez Novoa, C., & Remotti, S. (2021). Generating stakeholder workshops for policymaking. in digital environments through participatory service design. In R. Vella & M. Raykov (Eds.), *Supplement issue on socially engaged art and global challenges* (vol. 15, pp. 119–136), Malta Review of Educational Research. Retrieved June 30, 2022, from http://www.mreronline.org/wp-content/uploads/2021/12/7-MRER-15-Supplement-Melanie-Mira-CarolinaSilvia.pdf

Singh, A. (2014). *Managing emotion in design innovation.* Boca Raton: CRC Press Taylor & Francis Group.

Squire, C., Davis, M., Esin, C., Andrews, M., Harrison, B., Hydén, L., & Hydén, M. (2014). What is narrative research? Starting out. In *What is narrative research?* (The 'What Is?' Research Methods Series, pp. 1–22). New York: Bloomsbury Academic. https://doi.org/10.5040/9781472545220.ch-001

Sools, A. (2020). Back from the future: A narrative approach to study the imagination of personal futures. *International Journal of Social Research Methodology, 23*(4), 451–465.

Stickdorn, M., Hormess, M., Lawrence, A., & Schneider, J. (2018). *This is service design doing: Applying service design thinking in the real world: A practitioner's handbook.* Sebastopol: O'Reilly Media Inc.

Van Gorp, T., & Adams, E. (2012). *Design for emotion.* Amsterdam: Elsevier Morgan Kaufmann.

Van Mechelen, M., Høiseth, M., Baykal, G. E., Van Doorn, F., Vasalou, A., & Schut, A. (2017). Analyzing children's contributions and experiences in co-design activities: Synthesizing productive practices. In *Proceedings of the 2017 Conference on Interaction Design and Children* (pp. 769–772). Stanford California, USA: Association for Computing Machinery (ACM).

Mira Alhonsuo is a Postdoctoral Researcher at the University of Lapland, Finland. Her research interests include design methods, empathy and user experience, especially in the healthcare sector. Currently, she is working with cultural tourism development in a project called 'Smart Cultural Tourism as a Driver of Sustainable Development of European Regions' (SmartCulTour).

Jenny Siivola is a Service Designer at Lapland Central Hospital and has a background in media education and student counselling. Currently, she is carrying out her master's studies in service design at the University of Lapland. Her study interests are both story-based and strategic service design.

Melanie Sarantou is a Senior Researcher and Adjunct Professor at the University of Lapland, Finland. Her current research explores the role of arts in societies that exist on the margin of Europe in the European Commission project 'AMASS'.

Satu Miettinen is Professor of Service Design and Dean of the Faculty of Arts and Design at the University of Lapland, Finland. Her research interests span themes such as design methods for Arctic engagement, service design and the participatory development of services, as well as socially engaged art and design.

The Approach of Design Sprints in Healthcare Transformation

Christophe Vetterli and Philipp Schmelzer

ABSTRACT

John F. Kennedy shouted out with great motivation that they had chosen to go to the moon, not because it is easy, but because it is hard. Truly committed healthcare transformation agents foster transformation not because it is easy, but because it is hard AND necessary. Accompanying the senior physician Andrea Imhof, you will learn what the effects of design sprints are at core process transformation. Design Sprints do not need as often referred to, a sprinters attitude to transform healthcare. It is much more an interplay of a marathon-like endurance and the sprinter's energy to fulfill the nowadays requirement for transformation. Based on the approach of Design Thinking Design Sprints help to increase the resilience of solutions, raise the height of innovation and provoke team medicine, which is so much needed to address the emerging complexity of today's patients.

1 Design Sprints Are not Quick and Dirty

John F. Kennedy shouted out with great motivation that they had chosen to go to the moon, not because it is easy, but because it is hard. Truly committed healthcare transformation agents foster transformation not because it is easy, but because it is hard AND necessary. We need to reach the next "planet" in the evolution of this healthcare system, because the current one does not fit the future needs and dynamics. The transformation needs a marathon-like performance and there the

C. Vetterli (✉) · P. Schmelzer
Vetterli Roth & Partners AG, Poststrasse 30, 6300 Zug, Switzerland
e-mail: christophe.vetterli@vetterlirothpartners.com

P. Schmelzer
e-mail: philipp.schmelzer@vetterlirothpartners.com

first paradox comes in: Design Sprint sound like quick and dirty—it is not. It is probably one of the most successful and marathon-like approach to continuously foster the transformation of healthcare. The athletes who go for the long run are typically not the sprinters and vice versa. In Healthcare you will need both, because the way how the design sprints the authors are referring to, are a combination of both.

2   Never Enough Time for Transformation

They are major challenges in healthcare such as cost pressure, lack of experienced staff, digital backlog, inefficient processes with silo structures and so on. Those need to be addressed in the transformation of healthcare. One of the most crucial success factors is the engagement of staff when developing new solutions. Unfortunately, the staff which you want to have in your transformation teams, are scarce of resources and you need to provide them with real valuable time as well as a very goal-oriented procedure. And exactly here the concept of design sprints comes into action.

3   Origin of Design Sprints and Adaption to Healthcare

The term "design sprint" was originally coined by Jake Knapp, John Zeratsky and Braden Kowitz from Google Ventures (Knapp et al., 2016, pp. 21–48). In their book, they describe their structured approach to achieving the most tangible solutions possible within a standardized week using Design Thinking as an underlying approach. Each project is structured in the same way. Before the first day of the design sprint, the challenge is concretized and defined so that on Monday of the design sprint week, the goal for the sprint can be correctly selected and the challengers of the solutions can be chosen. Tuesday is all about ideation and sketching possible solutions. This divergent phase is followed by a convergent one on Wednesday, as the solutions are evaluated and the best one is then prototyped on Thursday. The finished prototype is then evaluated and tested with target customers on Friday. The learning gained in this way will be used to further develop the prototype.

   Healthcare sprints which trigger core process changes such as OR, Outpatient, inpatient processes or ED processes are typically different. Of course, there is the potential for the classical one-week design sprint however most healthcare institutions are not (yet) as agile as other industries. Therefore, it needs sometimes a little more time to adapt a few things, such as e.g., shift times (if possible) or data streams in a highly not yet digitalized environment. Due to the high level of expertise and the many interfaces in a hospital, the focus is placed more on prototyping during the sprints. Unlike Knapp, Zeratsky and Kowitz two to three double days are usually dedicated to prototyping in the design sprint in the healthcare projects. Finally, the original 5-day structure starting with a concretizing of the problem and ending with a concrete prototype is being adjusted to address the very core of healthcare transformation: overcoming silos and hierarchies, and synchronizing expertise and experience. Hence, implementation must always be considered after solution development. Therefore, the solutions are evaluated and further developed at regular intervals after the go-live in so-called-sustainable sprints.

4 The Healthcare Design Sprint

Andrea Imhof is a senior physician in pneumology and was invited to the "Design Sprint I" of the project "Process Definition Walk-in Clinic". She heard what is meant by this in the project kick-off and that she is away from daily operations for two days at a stretch. She is very curious to see whether the project structure mentioned, and its results are different from the previous project results.

It's Tuesday, 9 a.m. and the design sprint starts on time with a huddle, where the goals and risks are reviewed and synchronized together. Andrea quickly notices that there is a certain dynamic and that people are involved in the new outpatient processes, far away from the daily business. The question "What happens now when the patient has her appointment and is standing at the entrance of the building?" is open but still concrete enough for the colleagues to develop precise ideas. They work out different "prototypes" of solutions and test them several times during the day. A lively but interesting discussion ensues. Andrea had to answer her phone again and again in between, because "the hut is on fire" in the existing outpatient clinic. But she hopes that things will be better tomorrow. The day ends punctually at 4 p.m. and the results are impressive–one day and the content is already well advanced. She was finally able to prototype a future process for the error prone lung function appointments with her colleagues and show why proximity to other walk-in processes is central. Besides the excitement for tomorrow's second day of the 2-day sprint, she ponders shortly before falling asleep why the workshop was so productive today. In the other project, which is about the introduction of the digital fever curve, the project group meets every fortnight for 2 h to discuss the project status. The colleagues are less punctual, and she has the feeling that the work is less "productive". Above all, there is a lot of discussion. This is probably what the coaches meant today by "we design haptically with prototypes". Concrete "designs" of the solutions are emerging. It remains exciting and Andrea is looking forward to the next day.

Properly applied, design sprints provoke innovation, speed, and a different kind of collaboration. Prototype-based work, focused questions and fast iterations are core elements that are part of the standard procedure in design sprints, as Andrea Imhof is experiencing. Surprisingly, what the authors could observe in pursuing over 100 design sprints in healthcare, between 4 and 10 days of sprinting (mostly in 2-day blocks) are enough to create concrete realizable prototypes for e.g., a complete new ED process, integrated capacity management structure or the new design of a cardiological patient flow from ED to the cardiological ward (see Fig. 1).

Fig. 1 8 day prototype for a processs and functional design. *Source* Vetterli Roth & Partners & Lucerne Canton Hospital (2021)

5   Provoking Team Medicine via Design Sprints

Prototype-based work is the central mode in Design Sprints, which is characterized by a clear focus, little fragmentation, a needs-oriented process, constant evaluation, and intensive collaboration. The guided development process is based on the world's leading innovation approach Design Thinking and the latest findings from innovation research. This enables the design teams to prototype even better solution elements from their own experience and best practices. This results in tailor-made innovation for the current situation as well as the needs of the clients and teams on site. Throughout the course of the project, the questions of the project are developed and evaluated in several two- to three-day sprints ("prototyping"). Within these days, an interdisciplinary design team goes through several learning and development loops. Typically, a two-day problem analysis and synchronizing of each other's perspective on the problem is conducted before the sprints. This is also dedicated to establishing a common understanding of the needs to be addressed for patients and employees. For this purpose, the events on site are observed in a so-called "Gemba" and findings for the prototyping work are derived. During the first two days, situational interviews are also conducted with key persons and topic experts. This first phase of the problem analysis–Gemba–is crucial for the further course of the sprints. If the problem was misunderstood or if the focus was not on the most important needs, the team develops prototypes that miss the target. For example, Andrea discovered during these two days how important the information is when registering patients, but it never reaches her as the attending doctor. Something definitely has to change there.

In the subsequent design sprints, prototypes for the corresponding question are developed and tested in rapid succession and with a clear focus. What does the prototype with multimorbid patients look like? What requirements arise from this core process for the future IT? What is now important from a capacity management perspective for daily hospital planning? The findings from the tests are in turn used to improve the prototypes. In this way, the solutions are improved bit by bit and adapted to the needs of the patients and employees. This procedure ensures that only solutions that offer added value to employees and patients are implemented. A two-day block of the design sprint therefore pursues several iterations of prototyping and testings.

Another story, from a healthcare research-oriented environment, which underlines the appliance of several iterations within the design sprint: a healthcare research team was quickly focusing on an administrative support for Principal Investigators along the research projects. It was clear that this would be a workaround for a first generation, however, the team spent a lot of time in the design sprint concretizing this role. Finally, they come to the conclusion that if it needs to be really innovative, we have to skip that role completely. It took courage to do so and it was clear that they needed to have run through several iterations to be sure that without that role it will be a more sustainable role. If the team would not have spent a significant time and discussed it intensively upfront there wouldn't be that aligned comprehension that it has to function without that role.

The following diagram shows a typical design sprint-based innovation project (see Fig. 2).

Yet two thirds of all transformation projects fail in the implementation phase (McKinsey, 2021). There are two main reasons for this: lack of involvement of middle management and resistance of employees to the change. Both causes are taken into account by involving a large number of people (from middle management) in the development process and co-designing the prototypes with the help of the design thinking approach. The members of the design teams act as ambassadors of the solutions for all those affected and carry them into the organization. This enables and simplifies the change process. In addition, coaches help to embed the solutions sustainably in the organization.

Andrea is so enthusiastic about this methodology that she will propose it directly in the next project. The new way of project work is characterized by an unbroken focus on the problem. Above all, she appreciates that no "classical" "meetings" have to take place in order to provoke relevant results. Booking two consecutive days for a project initially sounded like too much of a use of resources. But when she compares the rapid progress of the project, the quality of the results achieved and the sustainable implementation with the otherwise fragmented project work and the resistance during implementation, the investment

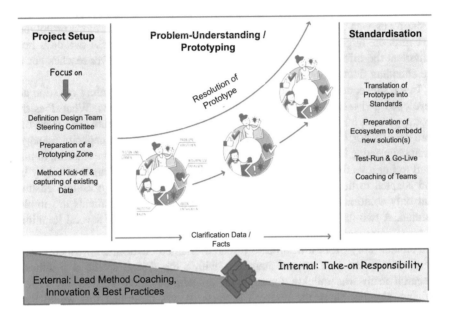

Fig. 2 Project structure via design sprints. *Source* Translated from Vetterli and Leifer (2021)

pays off. In the end, she was able to develop so actively for the first time shoulder to shoulder with her nursing colleagues. She also notices how communication has improved in day-to-day business.

6   Learnings Out of Practical Applications

The design sprint structure helps from several perspectives to foster transformation, especially in core processes.

The 7 principles for successful design sprints based on design thinking
On an operational level design sprints follow the Design Thinking approach and therefore following learnings are inherent. The most important principles of the prototype-based working method in the Design Sprints are (see Fig. 3):

Designing prototypes haptically
Is the project team once again lost in a discussion or getting nowhere in solving a problem? Then it's worth getting haptic. Take the nearest cardboard box and build something concrete out of it. The hand–eye coordination promotes creativity and you have created a first visual prototype that makes it easier to discuss the problem. Furthermore, it helps between prototyping sessions to better remember what has been discussed so far. Besides, it's fun. So, get to work on the cardboard boxes! (see Fig. 4).

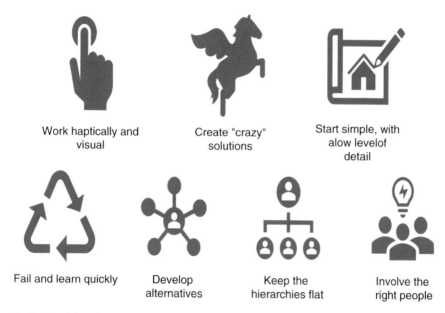

Work haptically and visual	Create "crazy" solutions	Start simple, with alow levelof detail
Fail and learn quickly	Develop alternatives	Keep the hierarchies flat	Involve the right people

Fig. 3 Principles of prototyping. *Source* adapted from Osterwalder and Pigneur (2014), pp. 78–79

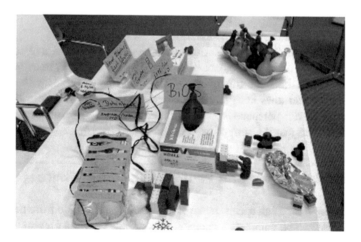

Fig. 4 Prototyping a research process at a biobank (Biobank of the Medical University Graz). *Source* Author's own Figure (2022)

Crazy ideas pay off

It has proven successful to develop so-called "dark horse" prototypes. This refers to radical solutions in which the underlying assumptions are completely rethought. While "reasonable" solutions are often close to the actual state, previously unthinkable possibilities come into play here. These thought experiments are extremely profitable for further work. According to a study by Stanford (Durão et al., 2018), 68% of fundamental innovations are based on dark horse prototypes. The Dark Horses really provoke something new! Each design Sprint should ideally integrate one Dark Horse prototyping session.

Increasing detail and resilience of the solution by frequent and fast iterations
At the beginning of the learning process, prototypes are developed with a low level of accuracy. The learning effect is greatest if you fail early and often and expose the work as soon as possible, i.e., test it in the design team or with clients. The more often the design thinking cycle is run through, the better prototypes result. Through the iterations, the solutions are further fleshed out and gained in detail. The goal is to develop prototypes in a first step that covers 80% of the occurring patient's (and employee's) volume. The leveraging of details throughout the sprint will also strengthen the resilience of the solution for the implementation path.

First Quantity–then quality
In the course of prototyping, it is important to develop many alternative solutions. According to the motto "Kill your Darling", not too much weight should be given to a single prototype or partial solution. There is a need for several different solutions throughout a design sprint. Only with several iterations with different alternatives you can start to raise the resolution of one or two promising solution systems.

Flat hierarchies and focus on the essentials
In the design sprint, it is important to keep the hierarchies low and to let each interest group have its say in a balanced way. This is the only way to avoid fruitless discussions and at the same time ensure that the design team keeps the focus on what is relevant and does not get lost in questions of detail. The best ideas occur when many different perspectives with different experience levels come together to form more than just the sum of each other.

7   Involving the Right People in the Right Space

When planning the design sprint, make sure that the right people from the relevant areas are present. The company's decision-makers must also be present so that the interests of the company as a whole are not lost sight of in the event of dissent in the group or in the case of decisions that point the way ahead. Furthermore, it is crucial to create space and time for the design team without distractions so that the provoked innovation can also emerge. This focused time benefits the entire solution in the medium and long term.

8 Conclusion–Sprinter's and Marathon runner's Attitude

As initially stated the healthcare transformation agents nowadays need a marathon spirit and the agility of a sprinter to successfully implement changes. Hence, even if the design sprint structure allows for a high target-oriented speed in development, the sustainable embedment of bigger processual and cultural changes needs resilience in the quality of the solution. This will serve to overcome the dozens of "no's", "I've already tried that 15 years ago" or the "we need a more convenient IT" to solve all the problems. Hence the sprint and its iterative nature help to raise the quality of the solution and the innovation height. The sustainable implementation however needs endurance like a marathon runner. It is a constant switching between a sprinters attitude to quickly develop another iteration of the solution and a marathon spirit of going along the complete path of invention to implementation to foster innovation. The implementation phase in healthcare will need several coaching sprints focusing on the deviations of the intended solutions, readjusting to the "harder to embed" solution (and more innovative solution) instead of taking the "easy" way. Healthcare stays one of the hardest industry to transform. However, JFK would smile.

References

Durão, L. F. C., Kelly, K., Nakano, D. N., Zancul, E., & McGinn, C. L. (2018). Divergent prototyping effect on the final design solution: The role of "dark horse" prototype in innovation projects. *Procedia Cirp, 70*(2), 265–271.

Knapp, J., Zeratsky, J., & Kowitz, B. (2016). Sprint. Solve big problems and test new ideas in just five days. In *Simon & Schuster paperbacks*. New York: Simon and Schuster.

McKinsey (Ed.). (2021). Losing from day one: Why even successful transformation fall short. McKinsey. Retrieved July 15, 2022, from https://www.mckinsey.com/business-functions/peo ple-and-organizational-performance/our-insights/how-to-beat-the-transformation-odds

Osterwalder, A., & Pigneur, Y. (2014). *Value proposition design: How to create products services customers want*. Weinheim: Wiley.

Vetterli, C., & Leifer, L. (2021). Design thinking. In A. Angerer (Ed.). New healthcare management–7 concepts for success in healthcare. Berlin: Medizinisch Wissenschaftliche Verlagsgesellschaft.

Christophe Vetterli is fostering the embedment of Design Thinking into healthcare. He graduated from the University of St. Gallen (Switzerland) with a PhD on Embedding Design Thinking and has published numerous scientific publications. During his PhD he worked closely at the intersection of science and business and collaborated with business partners as well as scientific partners from Stanford University (U.S.A.). He was a year-long partner in a healthcare consulting firm before he co-founded his own consultancy company. Vetterli Roth & Partners Ltd. focuses on the transformation of healthcare, mainly hospitals and clinics, towards patient's and further stakeholders needs. Thereby Vetterli enables the healthcare stakeholders to put patients & relatives at the core of their strategic & innovation work. The prototyping-based development of processes and solutions leads to patient-& client centric solutions. He is co-responsible for a master's degree on healthcare real estate management, gives lectures at different international leading universities and is on the board of several companies.

Philipp Schmelzer is applying his in-depth healthcare knowledge for the healthcare consultancy Vetterli Roth & Partners. He holds a master degree in Business Innovation from the University of St.Gallen (Switzerland). Philipp accompagnies healthcare institutions since many years towards their sustainable transformation, preferably in core processes such as wards, outpatient processes, emergency departments and psychiatric clinics. He earned his experiences in several university and bigger regional hospitals in the german speaking area in Europe. Lean Healthcare Management and Design Thinking serve as the base for his methodological application mix.

Building an Equity-Centered Design Toolkit for Engaging Patients in Health Research Prioritization

Alessandra N. Bazzano and Lesley-Ann Noel

ABSTRACT

In this project, an equity-centered design thinking process facilitated the engagement of people from communities underrepresented in the prioritization of health research on COVID-19 and increased the capacity for designers, researchers, and community members to work together across traditional boundaries. A partnership was formed between five patient partners and academic design and public health researchers to co-create a process and simple set of tools for health research on outcomes important to people's lived experiences. During the COVID-19 pandemic, stakeholders participated in equity-centered design thinking activities through a series of virtual design workshops and meetings. The goal of these activities was to identify new designerly ways to understand significant issues that were affecting the health and well-being of communities severely impacted by health disparities. Following the conclusion of each workshop, interviews were conducted with the participants to obtain their input on the design thinking methodologies used and the overall process of co-design, and two further usability workshops were held with health researchers to gauge their perception of the resulting design tools. Because it is human-centered, multifaceted, and can be used via remote or in-person techniques, a design approach lends itself to improving patient experience in health research and comparative effectiveness research. An equity-centered design lens is crucial for ensuring that the people most likely to be impacted by health

A. N. Bazzano (✉)
School of Public Health and Tropical Medicine, Tulane University, 1440 Canal St, Suite 1838, New Orleans, LA Mailcode 831970112, USA
e-mail: abazzano@tulane.edu

L.-A. Noel
College of Design, North Carolina State University, 50 Pullen Rd, Raleigh, NC 27607, USA
e-mail: lmnoel@ncsu.edu

disparities are included in the service design transformation of healthcare. The experience of co-designing a process and toolkit for equity-centered community engagement in health research is presented.

1   Introduction

In order to advance patient-centeredness and improve equity in health research, novel approaches are needed to overcome barriers that have kept the voices of patients from historically underrepresented communities out of the conversation. This chapter will introduce the rationale for an equity-centered design thinking approach to patient engagement, provide information on a case study, as well as share lessons learned about how the approach and resultant toolkit can be used to improve service design and health outcomes research.

1.1   The Need for Patient-Centered Engagement in Research on Health

Population-level trends for health outcomes in the twenty-first century are characterized by large disparities between groups with more resources and those with fewer, from the global scale to the local level (Global Burden of Disease 2019 Viewpoint Collaborators, 2020, pp. 1135–1159). Differences in economic opportunity, environment, access to healthcare services, and social determinants contribute to health disparities among populations. During the COVID-19 pandemic, these disparities were made more evident, as they are exacerbated through fractured health systems which rely on widely varying resources (COVID-19 Cumulative Infection Collaborators, 2022, pp. 2351–2380).

In order to improve health for all, designers and health researchers aiming to change health outcomes must work to understand the perspectives, desires, and experiences of individuals who have the fewest resources and greatest health needs. People from racial and ethnic minority communities typically experience more preventable disease and poorer health outcomes linked to structural inequalities than do people in dominant social groups—which has been deeply evident during the COVID-19 pandemic (Mackey, et al., 2021, pp. 362–373) yet they are not included in research studies as often. For example, in the United States, racism and discrimination are closely associated with worse health outcomes, yet the people most likely to be impacted by such health outcomes are often excluded or underrepresented in health research, both as participants and researchers. Unless participants from different races, ethnicities, and backgrounds are equitably involved in patient-centered outcomes research (PCOR), an important opportunity to address key health issues and thereby reduce health disparities will be missed. Stakeholders engaged in research agenda-setting must include groups that have been historically excluded or underrepresented, and doing so will contribute to improvements in health equity.

Working together with patients in order to understand their perspectives and needs is crucial to improve population health through research. Patients in patient-centered research may be broadly defined as people who have lived with and experienced an illness or injury, caregivers or family members of such people, or members of a relevant advocacy organization. The Patient-Centered Outcomes Research Institute (PCORI) defines patient engagement as "The meaningful involvement of patients, caregivers, clinicians, and other healthcare stakeholders throughout the entire research process—from planning the study, to conducting the study, and disseminating study results". (PCORI, 2022, n.d.)

PCOR and comparative effectiveness research (CER) may be conducted to identify ways to prevent and mitigate ill health, especially where research priorities and agendas can originate from authentic community needs. Patients are infrequently consulted when researchers develop funding proposals or delineate research questions, which are more often arrived at in top-down fashion from funding agencies and biomedical research organizations. Because it is human-centered, multifaceted, and can be used in a variety of ways via remote or in-person techniques, a design approach lends itself to PCOR and improving patient experience.

In the early stages of the COVID-19 pandemic, when evidence was rapidly evolving, requiring adaptation for behavior change, a potential bridge was created between design and public health, where design mindsets, skills, and processes could be applied to prioritizing COVID-19 health research, creating a unique opportunity for the intersection of these two disciplines.

By using an equity-centered design approach, we sought to understand how design methods and abilities could play a role in improving communication between public health practitioners and agencies and the public. We analyzed the design process and design research tools and methods, isolating distinct parts of the design process and several specific design tools.

Several methods were considered and a short list was created that included visual ethnographic methods, journey mapping, prototyping, futuring, and narrative methods loosely inspired by talk-aloud methods and storytelling. The team aimed to use innovative methods, even where these might be more challenging than methods commonly used by service designers. The candidate methods were prototyped in a series of public workshops delivered virtually in a university-community partnership setting before the final three methods were selected, and these are described in the next section.

The methods are influenced by other fields that influence design practice and research such as ethnography and anthropology. The selected methods and the activities of the workshops are borrowed from the ways that designers work and emphasized creativity, making, or futuring. These methods drew on the designer's creative process and aimed to use designerly ways of thinking and communicating ideas to encourage participants to share their experience of public health. Ultimately a toolkit was co-designed with patient partners to be used by design and health researchers and community members for improving equity through engagement in PCOR/CER.

2   Case Study: The GRID Toolkit

The following sections present a detailed case study on the use of an equity-centered design process. The project from which the case study originated was funded by the not-for-profit Patient-Centered Outcomes Research Institute (PCORI) Eugene Washington PCORI Engagement Award (EAIN 00,175). The purpose of the project was to develop resources to improve the engagement of all people impacted in patient-centered outcomes research and comparative effectiveness research.

2.1   Introduction to the Process

As an interdisciplinary team based at a university, we began this project by identifying and inviting a core group of patients to participate from local communities that have been underrepresented in health research and more severely impacted by the COVID-19 pandemic, specifically Black and formerly incarcerated Americans in the New Orleans metropolitan area. Louisiana was an early hotspot in the pandemic and New Orleans residents were among those most affected in the early stages, with limited access to preventive care and treatment. To accomplish the recruitment of patient partners, we reached out through existing community organizations and networks associated with the social science and behavior department of a large school of public health with a long history of research on infectious disease and epidemiology, as well as a strong history working at the community level. A group of five patient community members agreed to participate in a year-long project, conducted entirely virtually, through online meetings (for health safety), which was aimed at developing a toolkit for research prioritization around COVID-19, working together with a health researcher and a designer, as well as two program managers. One program manager was primarily responsible for liaising with patient community members and had prior experience with community-engaged work and as a patient navigator, while the other program manager had experience with academic public health research and project management. The staff from the university consisted of four team members and the five-member patient community group. Once patient community members agreed to participate, an introductory meeting was organized to get to know one another as well as to discuss the planned work.

In addition to being informed by design approaches, the project had a focus on improving equity in the relationship between health researchers and patients, so the initial meeting included facilitation by an organization consulting on diversity, equity, and inclusion. With this facilitation, the group discussed, set up, and agreed on a communication framework in order to set the stage for authentic partnership and co-design. We also introduced community partners to the design thinking approach at the first meeting—as a process, mindset, and skillset, with information on how the project framed design as an emancipatory or liberating practice with the interest of shifting power to people at the heart of a health issue. The core tenets of the communication framework and the participation of both the project team and the patient community members in all activities throughout the meeting and subsequent workshops allowed us to break down hierarchies and create a space for open dialogue and creative discussions. The project was funded by PCORI, a federal institute focused on patient-centered health outcomes in the United States, and the university team also included as a partner with experience in patient engagement projects, the Louisiana Public Health Institute (LPHI).

The patient community partners reported that they enjoyed participating in the activities and the workshops and that they found it valuable to have input into prioritization of health issues that affected them. They described many issues that were faced by their communities during the COVID-19 pandemic. A lack of faith in healthcare organizations and the government was a predominant concern and one that made it hard for participants to trust in research processes. They spoke about mixed messages from the medical establishment regarding ways to protect health during the pandemic as causing confusion and mistrust. Mental health and social isolation were also priority areas for the participants, as was the added burden of the pandemic on women for caregiving, not only for children but also for grandchildren, spouses, and other family members. The mental health of young people especially was noted as an area of concern, and its relationship to neighborhood health and violence. Access to care and the delaying of preventive health services during the pandemic also came up as an important topic and the lack of safety for essential workers who had to be exposed during their jobs at hospitals or other places where COVID-19 precautions were not strictly enforced. Finally, trust in COVID-19 vaccines among non-white communities was an important topic identified by partners, with sharing of stories about those who were hesitant as well as those who were confident to get the vaccine. An important topic was how to have concerns about the vaccine's safety addressed.

After the three patient community member workshops, health researchers identified through LPHI's networks (REACHnet/PCORnet) were invited to participate in two workshops where we presented our work so far with patient community members and described the equity-centered design activities that were becoming part of the draft toolkit. Researcher workshop participants were enthusiastic about the activities and methods of engagement and provided feedback on what would be helpful for them, such as videos demonstrating the activities, and further training on using the toolkit. They noted that they would be interested in using the toolkit with their patient partners. With this feedback, the toolkit draft was ready for final patient community partner input, which we received during a feedback meeting.

Once partners provided their comments, a final toolkit was prepared in collaboration with a graphic designer. We intentionally made the toolkit visually simple and readable, using plain language that could be understood by patient partners and health researchers alike.

Among patient engagement resources, this is the first of its kind to our knowledge to use equity-centered design as a unique contribution to patient-centered outcomes and involvement in the consideration of health research. We did not identify other resources that specifically addressed both equity and engagement in research prioritization for health that also specifically considered the needs of patients from minoritized communities using a design thinking approach. This perspective and the utility of the toolkit deliverables will be of great relevance to patients, policymakers, clinicians, funders, and other stakeholders because they will allow groups most impacted by health issues like COVID-19 and other equity-related health conditions to use their voices.

2.2   Justice and Equity-Centered Design

We wanted to use a justice-centered approach to design. To do this we surveyed existing design thinking methods with a focus on equity and social justice, such as the design justice movement (Design Justice Network, 2022, n.d.) and the equity-centered design framework by the Creative Reaction Lab (Creative Reaction Lab, 2022, n.d.). Design Justice is a growing movement in design with, at the time of writing, over 2,000 signatories to the principles on the Design justice website. The main principle is to "sustain, heal, and empower communities, as well as to seek liberation from exploitative systems" (Design Justice Network, 2022, n.d.). Guided by these principles that focus on justice, equity, agency, and collaboration were key principles in our work, where we sought to implement these principles by sharing power with participants through soliciting regular feedback on the workshop sessions and content and by ensuring that participants could actively participate at every session rather than just having to listen more passively.

Why design abilities?
Though the modern field of design may have originated in the design of artifacts to support capitalist production, such as the design of objects, visual communication such as posters, and more recently apps and other digital products, there is a growing movement to use the application of design and the key methods and mindsets outside of commercial applications. These key mindsets which can be applied to social spheres pertain to skills such as visual literacy, collaborative problem-solving, iteration, making, and future worldbuilding qualities of designers. In this project, we sought to explore how these skills could be used and mobilized by patients to describe their lived experiences and, ultimately, to create research priorities for improving health of patients and communities.

We borrowed design and studio ways of thinking for the value we felt they could bring to public health communication. Designerly ways of thinking and the design process require many ways of understanding, deep reflection on problems and solutions, as well as the ability to move swiftly between thinking and doing (Lawson & Dorst, 2009; Cross, 2011, p. 23). Shön also positioned design activities as tacit dynamic knowledge with much action and reflection (Broadfoot & Bennett, 2003, p. 1–3). The workshops recreated a virtual studio ambiance. The value of the studio is that it creates adequate conditions for knowledge, values, and ambiguity (Orr & Shreeve, 2017, p. 7). The studio is also a place of collaboration and shared experiences, while co-design activities can equitably bring together mixed communities of residents, researchers, educators, and more around a shared mission (Costanza -Chock, 2020, in Van Kampen et al. 2022, p. 10). The studio environment facilitates both private and public reflections, collective sharing, and debriefing, as studio members build relationships and establish and blur boundaries to do their creative work (Marshalsey & Lotz, 2022, pp. 1–15). Designers develop the skill of framing problems differently through a flexible thought process called design abduction, where exploring the unknown leads to innovative solutions to complex issues (Dorst, 2015, p. 49).

2.3   About the Team

Reflecting on personal identities was important to the equity-centered approach, including acknowledging the identities of the project team, composed of four people. The all-female team was led by a white New Orleanian public health researcher with design experience, a Black non-New Orleanian and non-American trained as a designer and design researcher, a Black New Orleanian community health research coordinator, and a South Asian research coordinator who recently started studying for a doctorate in public health. The multidisciplinary research team came from a school of public health and a center for design thinking and social innovation of a private university in the city of New Orleans, a historic, racially, and ethnically diverse city in the United States. The population demographics of the city make it a unique location for equity-informed design projects—23% of New Orleanians adults are living in poverty, with 39% of children living in poverty (far higher than the national average, Data Center Research, n.d., n.d.), and 60% of residents are Black and 6% Latinx(as per the US Census Bureau, Census, n.d., n.d.).

2.4   About the Participants

The community member who participated in the project are referred to by pseudonyms: Ms. C, Ms. G, Ms. D, Mr. B, and Ms. M. The participants were all Black residents of New Orleans or surrounding areas and between the ages of 30–70, with varying occupations and interests which contributed to the diversity of perspectives. Initially, a community member who was also a religious leader joined, but was subsequently unable to continue with the team, so Mr. B joined from the 2nd workshop onward. The participants were recruited through established relationships with the community health networks of the research university. None of the participants had a background in design, but Ms. C had participated in design thinking workshops and had a working relationship as a community liaison with the university on a project. The participants were compensated for their valuable time over the course of the year-long study as per the guidelines of the federal funding body sponsoring the research.

2.5 Technology

The project took place between August 2020-July 2021 at a time when social distancing was strongly encouraged. As a consequence, all of the meetings took place using video conferencing. Participants joined either via telephone or their personal computers. Virtual whiteboard apps were used for visual collaboration.

2.6 Setting the Stage

Before the three workshops, we held a preliminary meeting to set the stage and prepare participants for the type of activities in which they would be involved over the next year. The preliminary meeting aimed to introduce participants to remote collaboration via a virtual whiteboard and equity-centered design thinking. The community members were introduced to an online whiteboard with a shared poster illustrating the project mission and approach (see Fig. 1).

The first meeting opened with a moment of reflection on how many people's lives had been lost to the COVID-19 pandemic, followed by an assurance by the facilitating team of the commitment to equity and ensuring that all stakeholders' voices were publicly heard, acknowledging that the health and social care system in the United States feels broken, and that many people are left out when it comes to public health. A group specialized in equity, diversity, and inclusion for multicultural communication, Visions Inc, was invited to consult on the project and opened the workshop series with reflective activities around what equity, inclusion, and freedom from oppression mean in relation to the work. Much of the discussion in the first meeting focused on oppression and how it functions in society, as well as how structural oppression might be addressed through (re)design.

The facilitators set the stage for future discussions by establishing communication guidelines to foster authentic and open exchange and by assuring participants that it was okay to disagree with each other. Participants were invited, as they moved through the program over the next year, to reflect on their historically included and excluded identities, intent vs impact, and confidentiality, among other concepts.

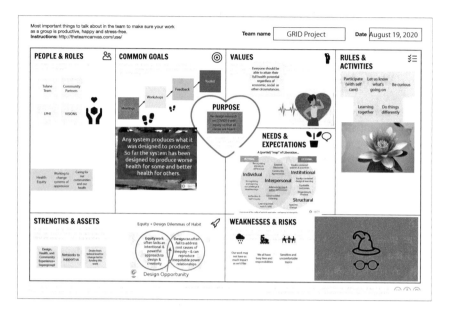

Fig. 1 Illustration of the project approach presented to participants for discussion. *Source* Author's own Figure (2022)

3   Overview of Patient-Centered Design Activities for Developing the Toolkit

Over the course of three equity-centered design thinking workshops conducted online through Zoom, we engaged in activities borrowed from the design field to co-create a toolkit that could be used by others interested in finding innovative ways to engage community members in understanding research priorities for COVID-19 and other health topics. We used online whiteboard tools to do our work together in the virtual space and also spent time building community through activities that helped us get to know one another. In each workshop, we tried out different design activities (described in more detail below) and talked with participants about their experiences doing these activities to know whether they were appropriate. All workshops included "warm-up" activities to get the creativity going, and partners discussed how COVID-19 had affected them, their families, and their communities. During workshops, we tested activities that would become part of the toolkit to be shared at the end of the project, and we also tried out different ways to prioritize or rank health topics that were most important to individuals in the group. Importantly, everyone participated in the workshop sharing and activities, including the health researchers and facilitators, to break down hierarchies and foster authentic partnerships in sharing experiences. Following the workshops, participants were interviewed to learn what they thought about the activities and suggested toolkit methods. They provided their feedback on what went well and what could be improved and gave information on how they thought the activities for the toolkit could be useful in their communities.

3.1   Workshop 1. An Introduction to Visual Ethnography

The first workshop drew on auto-ethnographic methods inviting the participants to visually document life changes during the pandemic. They were given the prompt to take a few photographs representing what had changed in and around their homes, where most people were quarantined as a result of the pandemic, and then send these to the project team via email or instant message before the meeting so that facilitators could place them on the virtual whiteboard. The photographs would be used to start or guide a conversation about the pandemic and public health.

The two-hour workshop began with a warm-up activity to build community, where the participants were asked to share something about themselves and find a way to connect empathetically with another group member who had a similar identity or interest.

The participants then shared their photographs. One photograph depicted a mask and a computer, which led to a discussion about social distancing, working remotely, and not being able to travel. This conversation on limited mobility continued around diabetes and weight gain, due to not being able to be more active. Another photograph showed a package that had taken three months to arrive at its destination due to COVID-related delays in the postal service. The person who shared the image complained about the lack of control over systems during the pandemic. She also shared an image of sanitizer by her front door. Nobody could enter her home without using hand sanitizer. This led to her sharing her gratitude for being alive since she was recovering from the coronavirus (see Fig. 2).

Two participants shared photos of boxes because they were either moving or had moved recently. One shared that at the start of the quarantining she felt trapped in her apartment which had prior to the pandemic been an exciting place since it was located in the downtown area of New Orleans. She could not go outside during the early months of the pandemic. The feeling of being trapped led her to eventually purchase a home with more space. The second participant who shared an image of boxes had also just bought a house.

Food was another recurring theme in the photographs. One person shared a photo related to online grocery delivery since she could no longer go to the store. Another participant shared a photo related to eating junk food and drinking wine. She described how being at home all the time led her to snack more and drink more—which felt like a loss of self-control. A third participant also shared a photo of snacks. She no longer had time to cook dinner for herself and her husband. They, therefore, relied on snacks instead.

One of the women shared a photo of her grandchildren, saying that she was thankful that the pandemic allowed her to spend more quality time with them. The pandemic had changed their routine; they were able to go to the previously busy

A window into our Covid experiences...

Fig. 2 Photo elicitation of images related to pandemic changes from the visual ethnography workshop. *Source* Author's own Figure (2022)

downtown area at night, which was now deserted, for the first time. They spent more time in nature when they would normally be at school and had fed the ducks at the park that week.

There was also significant discussion about the expanded workloads of women during the pandemic. Participants noticed the gender imbalance in pandemic roles. The extra housework, childcare, and office work of women. One participant also noticed that even in the research group for this project there were only women.

While the participants shared their photos, one of the facilitators made notes of the major themes that had emerged throughout the conversation on sticky notes on the virtual whiteboard. Participants jointly grouped the ideas. Some worked directly on the whiteboard, while others called out their instructions as they watched on the shared screen.

There were feelings that recurred as people shared the various images, such as not being in control and gratitude. Some other themes that emerged included coping, family (spending more or less time with them), nutrition and alcohol, mental health, entertainment or lack thereof, inaccessibility of preventive healthcare, exercise, and changes in living spaces. There was extensive conversation about how the pandemic had affected alcohol-drinking habits. Themes were noted down by

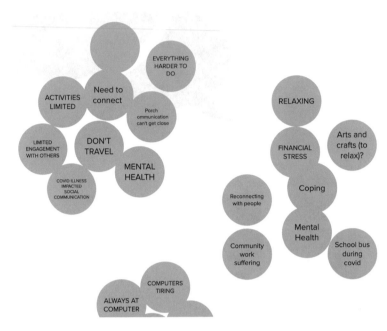

Fig. 3 Topics participants described as important to health research elicited through visual ethnography workshop. *Source* Author's own Figure (2022)

participants, and as a group, they were clustered together; see Fig. 3 for a sample of candidate themes. After twelve larger themes were organized, the participants voted on which themes or issues they thought were most pressing and should be considered for future research by the public health researchers. The clustering and voting process was used as a prototype for ranking and prioritizing health issues which were surfaced through shared sense-making and insights.

In this workshop, participants used the photographs to record changes in their environment, but also as a way of making meaning of the phenomena that they experienced collectively. In this way, the photographs also acted as a form of icebreaker to both foster the relationship between participants and to generate discussion. This activity created several points of reflection and sharing and then created an opportunity for participants to rank their key health priorities.

3.2   Workshop 2. Rapid Critical Utopian Action Research

The second workshop took place in December 2020. This workshop was based on an action research strategy called Critical Utopian Action Research. Different members joined this virtual workshop. One member had COVID and was unable to join, while a new male participant joined the group, changing the gender balance of the team.

For the warm-up activity, the participants brainstormed about how many things they could do or make with a surgical mask worn for COVID protection. The creative answers reflected the local context and included Halloween or Mardi Gras masks, a potholder, and other interesting artifacts. This activity was meant to place participants in a creative frame of mind.

3.2.1 Imagining Futures

For the workshop activity, the participants were asked to imagine they were in the future, in the year 2030. They would then go back to just before the pandemic (in 2019 and early 2020) and tell people they met how they could or should prepare for the pandemic. The aim was to use this tension between the past, present, and future to uncover the concerns of the participants.

The participants worked on a virtual whiteboard, while in the background, the theme song from the 2018 movie, The Black Panther, played, and the whiteboard was also decorated with images from the same movie, to help participants enter a futuristic frame of mind. The theme music played for two minutes while they responded to the prompt question 'We are in 2030 and COVID has been eradicated... What would you tell people back in 2019 before the pandemic so they could prepare better? This was framed as what might have been done differently, for example at the levels of individuals, organizations, governments, health services, and the exercise was nicknamed "woulda ... coulda ... shoulda ...". While the music played, they thought and filled out their responses on the virtual whiteboard. Participants who had difficulty using the platform were invited to type their thoughts in the chat. They were reminded to focus on the advice they would give to others related to public health based on what they knew nine months into the pandemic (see Fig. 4).

Some of the advice to people in the (hypothetical) pre-pandemic past included helping communities find sustainable fresh food sources, creating labor unions to

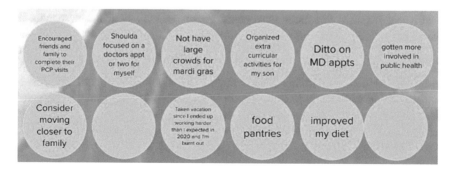

Fig. 4 An image from futuring workshop that depicts where participants thought they should have concentrated their energy before the pandemic. *Source* Author's own Figure (2022)

protect workers' rights, creating better infrastructure for the distribution of vaccines, educating the community about financial freedom, focusing on their health pre-pandemic, e.g., not canceling preventive health appointments, since they now knew they would have to wait for months to access general healthcare. Healthcare, community food resources (e.g., community gardens), and access and proximity to loved ones were major themes that emerged during the activity. Taking better care of personal health through diet, exercise, and self-care was also a recurring theme. They reflected on where they believed there had been missteps, such as in crowded indoor Mardi Gras parties and celebrations just prior lockdown in March 2020.

Ms. G brought up the need to rest in order to take care of others, noting the care burden that some experienced in the early phases of the pandemic, as they had to take care of others. Also tied to the theme of care was the need to let others know that you cared for them since you did not know when you might lose them. The pandemic made people aware of the fragility of life.

When they moved beyond personal levels and reflected on organizational or governmental levels, community partners complained that they felt "the higher-ups knew about it …before the people found out". They expressed that the government, the departments of health, and medical systems should have done more to prepare for the crisis. They felt that community gardens and food pantries needed to have been part of the early pandemic solutions. They acknowledged how politics impacted the pandemic response. Communication problems and skepticism of constantly changing information were the major themes when they focused on the governmental and organizational response. The fact that organizations were prevented from sounding the alarm early on in the pandemic for political reasons was identified as an issue in the discussions.

3.2.2 Headlines

In the second future-focused activity of the workshop, participants created future headlines based on some of the discussions arising from the themes. They created positive or negative headlines that would appear in hypothetical newspapers in the year 2030. After a short discussion about the headlines, they voted on which headline most represented issues they felt public health agencies should focus on (Table 1).

During the debrief, participants said that they really enjoyed this method, especially working with others to create the headlines. They said that they appreciated the time to connect with others (despite the isolation of the pandemic) and to reflect on the needs of their community. They enjoyed the breakout sessions and getting to know each other.

3.2.3 Workshop 3. Low-Fi Approaches for Engagement: Worksheets and Prototyping

During the first two workshops, participants had some challenges using the virtual whiteboard. Sometimes they had to join via their mobile phones. Sometimes they could not easily navigate between the virtual whiteboard and the video conference

Table 1 Future headlines created by participants, *Source* Author's own table (2022)

Rank	Headline	Votes
1	Policies made for the CDC and other organizations to be able to speak the truth	8
2	Americans' healthcare services no longer utilized—trust has declined	4
2	Due to the research for the COVID vaccines, other safe and effective vaccines were made more quickly in the future	4
4	Health organizations no longer under administrative control: independent agency to inform and educate citizens	3
5	Federally funded organizations no longer required to abide by rules	2
5	African Americans' disbelief in the vaccine because of past history and the fear of being used as guinea pigs—caused more death!	2
7	Citizens no longer trust the public healthcare system	1
7	The world has completely lost trust in vaccines and public health!	1
7	Communities on the edge! COVID causes a lack of jobs, childcare, food, and money to take care of the communities!	1

screen. In light of this, for the third workshop, it was decided to experiment with not using the virtual whiteboard, and analog approaches were tested even though the meeting was still conducted remotely via videoconferencing.

3.2.4 Opening Together

Before the workshop, participants were sent two large envelopes to their homes by ground delivery for the two different parts of the workshop. Envelope A contained worksheets, a small sticky notepad, and markers for the first half of the workshop, while envelope B contained additional materials for making and prototyping in the second half. These packages were sent several days prior to the meeting.

To create a sense of drama, participants were asked to wait to open their packages together during the workshop. This allowed them to feel together even though they were apart. They opened package A for the activities using the worksheets (see Fig. 5).

Fig. 5 Packets sent with instructions to participants' homes. *Source* Author's own Figure (2022)

The warm-up activity for this workshop required them to draw. They used sticky notes and black markers from package A. They were first asked to draw a squiggly line and then to turn this squiggle into a bird. They then compared the birds and marveled at each other's creative and artistic ability as well as reflected on how in creative and design-led approaches information can start out messy (as in a squiggle) and be turned into something meaningful (a bird).

Envelope A contained worksheets with simple, narrative activities. Ms. C. said receiving the packages and contents at her home made her feel important. The two worksheets for participants to fill out and return to the project team were titled "Three Wishes" and "A COVID Story". For the first exercise, participants were asked to think about three wishes for themselves or others during the pandemic. The purpose was to reflect on wishes or wished-for changes that could be made on an individual, social, and/or environmental level, and though the team did not know what would emerge, it was expected that these changes would be related to improving health. After opening the Three Wishes worksheet and receiving instructions, participants muted their microphones for a moment and recorded their wishes either as text or voice notes and sent it to the facilitator.

The activity spurred discussions about social interactions and networks, participants also talked about new forms of socializing, e.g., drive-by graduation or birthday parties, where party-goers stayed in their cars, as required for social distancing. Participants were concerned about social support and neighborhood crime and safety—New Orleans has consistently had a high rate of violent crime and certain neighborhoods, including those where participants lived, have been badly impacted by gun violence. Mental health was identified as a concern in general in New Orleans, including for young children. Even more than fifteen years after Hurricane Katrina, the event continues to be felt as a source of destabilization within communities. There has been for many years a lack of opportunities for young people in New Orleans. The participants said this began with Hurricane Katrina and continues today as communities suffer severe impacts from COVID. They also talked about several events that had impacted the country as a whole: storms due to climate change, elections and politics, and access to healthcare (both in terms of improvements and challenges).

Another worksheet invited the participants to write a "design-lib" similar to the game MadLibs, titled "A COVID story". For this worksheet, participants used a fill in the blanks method to help them talk about how the pandemic had impacted people in different ways. They were invited to create a story about themselves or someone they knew, using a pseudonym, and fill in the story using the prompts in the worksheet.

Ms. M. told a story about a lady called Doris, who had been separated from her family during the pandemic. She indicated that Doris' biggest issue was social isolation and anxiety or overthinking. She described Doris' loss of all the support and recreational opportunities that she had access to in the past. She also described Doris' skepticism about the pandemic, and the impact of the virus, along with her vaccine hesitancy.

Ms. C. decided to create a story about a real person Michelle, who is separated from her family. She is significantly affected by COVID due to the death of several family members. She has not been able to mourn the losses because in-person funerals have not taken place during the pandemic. Michelle felt the government could provide more information for people. Lack of trust in healthcare was an important issue in Michelle's story. As Ms. C told the story, she switched between "she" and "I", and it became clear that she drew on personal experience. Ms. C. told us that Michelle believed in old-fashioned remedies and self-healing. She believed that post-COVID, both of these would be more prevalent due to the strain the pandemic had caused for Black communities. Ms. C expressed concern that everyone will be forced to take the vaccine in the future. As she told her story, Ms. C. reminded the group that as a locally active leader, community members trusted her and came to her for home remedies. She shared that she did not have a primary care doctor, though there were some medical professionals that she trusted and that she was committed to self-treatment passed down from prior generations. She said that even her doctors knew that she didn't believe in medicine. Ms. C. shared that she did not believe the vaccine would have the same effect on everyone and was hesitant to accept it personally.

Each person spent several minutes finishing their story. Ms. M wrote about her aunt and the difficulty of working (as an essential worker) in Alabama, such as her aunt not being able to visit family while working during the lockdowns. Writing the story made her think about community conversations she had over-heard or participated in about public health, such as discussions she would have with other women of color at the hair salon regarding COVID and vaccinations. As someone with training in health and medical care, she wondered how to best address the public health concerns of people of color in her community. Mr. B. wrote a story about himself and his experience of getting COVID. The stories led to conversations about people who he and his family knew who did not want to get the vaccine. They discussed the role of the media in vaccine hesitancy, e.g., the stories about people who did not want to get vaccinated and their various reasons for being wary.

3.2.5 Making to Tell Stories

The second package in the set, envelope B included colorful materials for pro-totyping. As Ms. C. opened it, she expressed her excitement "OMG! Fun stuff! Fun stuff! Fun stuff!" The package included paper plates and clothes pins, pipe cleaners, markers, and washi tape. The facilitators gave a mini-introduction about making meaning through making, and the role of prototyping in design. They were asked to use the items in their packet to make something to help them address or balance their mental health for the next pandemic. Mental health was a recurring theme throughout the workshops, and therefore, it was chosen as the focus for this reflective prototyping activity. Prompts were given that the item could be a game, meditation tool, or anything they wanted, but they had to use the contents of the envelope to externalize and materialize some of the topics of conversation from the Three Wishes activity and A COVID Story and now make a thing. They had

Fig. 6 Prototyping together online. *Source* Author's own Figure (2022)

7 min to do this activity while music played in the background. They listened to music by Elis Marsalis and Manu Dibango, two artists who had succumbed to the coronavirus (see Fig. 6).

Mr. B. made a tribute or shrine to people who had lost their lives during the pandemic. He mentioned personal losses, people he knew, and people who he did not know such as actors and musicians. Ms. M. said she did not know what to do with the materials. Ms. C made a sanctuary or a bunker that would be underground and filled with food and medical supplies. She said that we must think about the "what if". One person made a pod-finder to help people find people who they were compatible with and could then stay with for a long quarantine period. One of the project team members got a blue plate from her kitchen and said it represented the pandemic. She cut up another patterned plate and stuck it on the blue and said it represented all the people in the pandemic. Another participant made a time travel device to transport people to their happiest childhood memories. The prototyping session borrowed from design and innovation sprint methodologies and provided a light yet reflective activity that prompted participants to share. Mr. B. closed the workshop by saying how much he enjoyed sharing personal stories with everyone.

3.2.6   The Co-Designed Toolkit

Based on our experiences from the engagement workshops, a toolkit was created to facilitate the use of design-based methods in research prioritization by other stakeholders interested in improving health outcomes, such as researchers, patient partners, service designers, and community members. A draft of the toolkit was shared with the community partners for their feedback. After revisions had been made, the toolkit was shared with health researchers who also provided feedback to gather feedback on its usability. The toolkit is available for download on the websites of PCORI and LPHI. In its current format, it is comprised of 53 cards. The toolkit explains the aims of the work. It provides background information and step-by-step descriptions of each activity, so that other facilitators can repeat these easily (see Fig. 7).

Fig. 7 A selection of cards from the toolkit that explain the methods. *Source* The authors. *Source* Author's own Figure (2022)

4   Lessons for the Future of Patient-Centered, Equity-Focused Design

We believe that activities and methods described in this chapter can make it easier for patients to discuss their health experience in different ways and that these shared experiences can inform patient-centered healthcare transformation. In all three examples, the design activity prompts (whether visual as in photographs, tactile as in prototyping, temporal as in the future scenarios, or narrative such as the story-building activities) gave the participants the chance to externalize their experiences and share with others to find important priorities. Participants sometimes switched between the third person and first person as they made up stories around the photos, objects, scenarios, etc. The participant sharing and stories included personal insights as well as insights about other people that they knew, creating space for thick, rich accounts of lived experiences that could feed into patient-centered health research and quality improvement. More commonly used methods and activities may not provide as much space for participants, particularly those from underrepresented communities, to feel comfortable and at ease in sharing. This approach may come closer to the ideal of meaningful involvement of patients, caregivers, clinicians, and other healthcare stakeholders, where people are invited into the design process, not simply consulted through a survey or interview.

As they responded to the request for prioritization of health issues related to the pandemic, the visual methods provided experience-based ways of ranking concerns and making hierarchies for issues. The virtual whiteboard facilitated this process as participants could interact without having to say something where they might feel less confident. Similarly, they could revise and change the whiteboard objects to reflect their input or ask the facilitation team to do so, providing a visual marker of their engagement and participation. For example, participants could increase the size of the circles that represented importance, or they could move the high-priority themes around on the virtual whiteboard. They could also express satisfaction or dissatisfaction through emojis.

Benefits

Some of the benefits of these methods included that they broke down the barriers between participants and researchers through shared experiences. The facilitators engaged in the same activities and responded to the same prompts that the participants did, offering personal sharing. The activities presented helped to externalize the issues so people could use the objects and images to help them articulate how they felt about the topics. The creative activities provided a reflective and democratic forum for sharing and agenda prioritization. When using the visual prioritization methods, the participants could enlarge and reduce the size of the issues on the virtual whiteboard, or they could see visually the size of the clusters of the sticky notes with their concerns. This created a very tangible form of communication about their priorities, and they could easily rank and compare the hierarchies as they discussed. This visual approach was less abstract than a word-centric (text or speech) approach which would make it easier for more people to participate in a discussion, regardless of age, language ability, and other factors.

Challenges
Since the project took place virtually, some of the methods were impacted by the available technology and familiarity of participants with using newer communications technology. At the start of the project, a technology survey allowed the team to learn about what devices participants would be using to connect and to assess whether additional supports would be helpful. As a result, the project supplied earbuds or headphones to participants who had difficulties with their audio. Participants who depended on older or slower mobile phones sometimes had difficulties accessing the video conferencing, while the virtual whiteboard also could not be accessed easily on mobile phones. There was a high learning curve for stakeholders to confidently use the virtual whiteboard. We felt we had to use the virtual whiteboard to work remotely early on in the pandemic. By the end of the program, the project team also incorporated analog methods that could be used remotely.

5   Conclusion: Future Potential

The case study presented a community-engaged, equity-centered design project aimed at creating patient engagement and health research prioritization tools. The toolkit that was created at the end of the project is publicly accessible and can be shared to support both service designers and health researchers as they work with diverse populations. The co-designed process and resulting methods created unique and novel opportunities for participants to reflect on and share their public health journeys, with a particular focus on improving health during the early period of the COVID-19 pandemic. The methods also provided engaging and embodied ways for them to examine and establish health research priorities, optimizing for patient-centered healthcare solutions. Future applications of these methods could be for improving service delivery, fostering diversity in patient engagement, and bridging public health design for innovation that addresses lived experiences of patients to improve health equity for all.

References

Broadfoot, O., & Bennett, R. (2003). Design studios: Online? Comparing traditional face-to-face design studio education with modern internet-based design studios. In *Apple University Consortium Academic and Developers Conference Proceedings* (pp. 9–21). Wollongong: Apple University Consortium Academic and Developers Conference.

Census (n.d.) Retrieved July 28, 2022, from https://www.census.gov/quickfacts/neworleanscitylouisiana

COVID-19 Cumulative Infection Collaborators. (2022). Estimating global, regional, and national daily and cumulative infections with SARS-CoV-2 through Nov 14, 2021: A statistical analysis. *Lancet, 399*(10344), 2351–2380. https://doi.org/10.1016/S0140-6736(22)00484-6

Cross, N. (2011). *Design thinking: Understanding how designers think and work*. Oxford: Berg.

Creative Reaction Lab (2022). *Our approach*. Retrieved July 28, 2022, from https://crxlab.org/our-approach

Data Center Research. (n.d.). Retrieved July 28, 2022, from https://www.datacenterresearch.org/

Design Justice Network (2022) *About us*. Retrieved July 28, 2022, from https://designjustice.org/about-us

Dorst, K. (2015). *Frame innovation: Create new thinking by design*. Cambridge, MA, USA: MIT Press.

GBD 2019 Viewpoint Collaborators. (2020). Five insights from the global burden of disease Study 2019. *Lancet, 396*(10258), 1135–1159. https://doi.org/10.1016/S0140-6736(20)31404-5

Lawson, B., & Dorst, K. (2009). *Design expertise*. Abingdon: Taylor & Francis.

Mackey, K., Ayers, C. K., Kondo, K. K., Saha, S., Advani, S. M., Young, S., Spencer, H., Rusek, M., Anderson, J., Veazie, S., Smith, M., & Kansagara, D. (2021). Racial and ethnic disparities in COVID-19-related infections, hospitalizations, and deaths: A systematic review. *Annals of Internal Medicine, 174*(3), 362–373. https://doi.org/10.7326/M20-6306

Marshalsey, L., & Lotz, N. (2022) Illuminating themes and narratives in studio through expert elicitation and collaborative autoethnography. In D. Lockton, S. Lenzi, P. Hekkert, A. Oak, J. Sádaba & P. Lloyd (Eds.), DRS2022: Bilbao. Bilbao, Spain. https://doi.org/10.21606/drs.2022.273

Patient Centered Outcomes Research Institute (PCORI). (n.d.). Retrieved July 28, 2022, from https://www.pcori.org/engagement/value-engagement

Orr, S., & Shreeve, A. (2017). *Art and design pedagogy in higher education: Knowledge, values and ambiguity in the creative curriculum*. London, England: Routledge. https://doi.org/10.4324/9781315415130

van Kampen, S., Galperin, A., Jager, K., Noel, L., & Strube, J. (2022) Where do we go from here? Rethinking the design studio after the Covid-19 pandemic. In D. Lockton, S. Lenzi, P. Hekkert, A. Oak, J. Sádaba & P. Lloyd (Eds.), DRS2022: Bilbao, Spain: Design Research Society. https://doi.org/10.21606/drs.2022.345

Alessandra N. Bazzano PhD, MPH is Associate Professor with tenure in the Department of Social, Behavioral, and Population Sciences at the Tulane University School of Public Health and Tropical Medicine, and Director of its Center of Excellence in Maternal Child Health. Dr. Bazzano applies design theory to public health and uses an interdisciplinary lens in research, teaching, and service, informed by collaborations across professional boundaries. Having previously served as Carnegie Corporation of New York Professor of Social Entrepreneurship through the Taylor Center for Social Innovation and Design Thinking, Dr. Bazzano continues to research how public health can be improved through equity-centered design thinking; teaches and mentors future health leaders; and publishes regularly in peer-reviewed journals, in addition to collaborating internationally with colleagues centering the improvement of health equity.

Lesley-Ann Noel PhD, MBA is a Trinidadian design educator based in Raleigh, North Carolina, where she is an Assistant Professor in the Dept. of Art and Design at North Carolina State University. Dr. Noel teaches courses on contemporary issues in art and design, design for social innovation, and design studies. Her research focuses on using equity-centered design methods to support design-based pathways into STEM careers, youth agency and participation, social innovation in communities, and patient-centered public health. Dr. Noel is currently creating a social-justice-centered design curriculum for youth that combines game design with Afrofuturism. In addition to her teaching and research, Dr. Noel is an active member of the Design Research Society, where she is the co-Chair of the Pluriversal Design Special Interest Group, which focuses on promoting the design research and practice of designers outside of the Global North.

Designing a Conceptual Wayfinding Structure to Manage Information for Human-Centered Healthcare Experience

Cecilia Xi Wang and Craig M. Vogel

ABSTRACT

This article traces the development of an information navigation toolkit that weaves the conceptual wayfinding structure of information management theory into the healthcare design for a holistic patient experience. Inspired by the human-centered design philosophy and design thinking, this method also draws on information management science and patient education literature. It is an embodiment of the prostate cancer patient experience supportive toolkit. Developed in response to challenges encountered in communicating research findings to multidisciplinary design teams, the Prostate Cancer patient experience supporting toolkit has been developed to redesign patients' experience and facilities in hospitals and prostate cancer department settings in the United States. We argue that this process and toolkit support information management through design synthesis and can support information management in other contexts. This paper draws on research with the support of The University of Cincinnati Barrett Cancer Center (UCCC) and LiveWell Collaborative.

1 Introduction

One of the core problems patients face is sorting through the vast amount of information they receive to make informed decisions (Hewitson et al., 2005, p. 16 X). Exploring the information management toolkit to provide patients with the

C. X. Wang (✉)
University of Minnesota, Twin Cities, Minnesota 55455, USA
e-mail: ceciw@umn.edu

C. M. Vogel
University of Cincinnati, Cincinnati, OH 45221, USA
e-mail: vogelcg@ucmail.uc.edu

correct information at the right time throughout their care journey is critical for quality patient experience (Kenney, 2012, n.d.). However, there exist many situations in which patients and health providers lack healthcare information navigation and management capabilities or support frameworks (Bose, 2003, p. 61), e.g., conceptual wayfinding structure, healthcare information management, and patient education tools. Low uptake associated with health providers' perception that information management does not apply to situations may reflect the lack of healthcare information management approaches to patients' problems.

Strategic use of healthcare information may offer one of the few promising avenues for lasting improvement. A conceptual information navigation structure may help to build an upgrade healthcare experience. To further explore this idea, we researched the prostate cancer patient population's underlying needs. Pairing various learning styles with typical profiles was another critical method for identifying information mediums best suited for communicating personally. Thus, we established a variety of decision-making preferences related to prostate cancer treatment information.

A critical insight was that patients needed better education and awareness about treatment options and possibilities to reduce anxiety and improve outcomes (Coulter et al., 1999, p. 320). The pivotal point was creating personas that could highlight decision-making's complexity at various branch points in patient journeys (Jones, 2013, n.d.). After conducting structured interviews, it was agreed that patients prefer human guidance above all but benefit from various educational tools adapted to their information managing style and personality. The team focused on three different methods to deliver educational resources to patients— an information hub website, an educational video suite, and an interactive patient journey map. Key benefits across these concepts include patient education that better informs decision making, a new personalized care journey, and scalable opportunities for future collaboration.

Targeting patients' educational needs and supporting healthcare information management and decision-making activities will lead to a more cost-efficient utilization of resources. Additionally, by designing the process of catching patients to a more personalized treatment plan, appropriate care can be delivered more human centered. This process also improves outcomes and patient satisfaction. Strategic information management in the healthcare sector can be a powerful tool for human-centered healthcare service integration. It involves a two-step process: redefining healthcare services in critical stakeholder relationships and then choosing information management tools and frameworks that capitalize on and reinforce them. This article offers a guide to help healthcare managers envision service innovations and select appropriate tools to support them. Our emphasis here is on the conceptual "front end" of this strategic planning process. We will propose two specific frameworks to help healthcare managers think about information systems in strategic terms. These frameworks are intended to supplement rather than replace more tactically oriented information planning methodologies. We begin our discussion with a hypothetical healthcare services system undergirded by conceptual wayfinding information management applications. We then look in more depth at the notion of a strategic orientation for healthcare services and review and adapt the information management tools of planning to the public environment. We conclude by applying these frameworks to other specific healthcare services examples.

2   Designing for Information Management

Information management (IM) is defined as—providing a secure, end-to-end, fully automated solution for controlling access, transmission, manipulation, and audibility of high-value information (Nerlikar, 1997, n.d.). Information management involves the processes for identifying, capturing, structuring, sharing, and applying an individual's or an organization's information to extract competitive advantage and create sources of sustainable growth (Rice & Leonardi, 2014, p. 428).

There is a clear understanding among healthcare managers and practitioners about the healthcare industry's transformation towards an information-based industry. All the stakeholders of this community create, share, and use the information to improve the healthcare service quality and reduce cost. The team includes patients and caregivers from different stages during the whole patient experience journey. A human-centered healthcare experience's success depends on how effectively and intelligently information is being used to improve the process (Kohli et al., 1999, p. 86; Jadad et al., 2000, p. 363).

Design management practitioners and theorists have agreed that any management process would involve:

- Identifying and capturing existing information.
- Creating new information.
- Transferring existing information throughout the organization.

Organizations should use information management to manage data flow and information as information management is considered to have utility in the above context. It deals inherently with the learning capacity of the human resources of an institution.

Health information management may be helpful for:

- Minimizing the procedure by sharing health information with patients.
- Better deliver care that addresses the medical and human concerns of patients.
- Suggesting more efficient utilization of providers and staff to support patient decision-making even in remote areas.
- By upgrading the process of matching patients to a more effective and personalized treatment plan, appropriate care can be delivered in a more medically and cost-efficient manner.
- Improving the quality of outcomes and patient satisfaction by reducing untimely information.

3   Designing for Human-Centered Experience

Some of the earliest writing on human-centered experience design looked to John Dewey's pragmatist philosophy of experience as a starting point for thinking about it. Shedroff (2001, p. 53) offered a designer's view of Dewey's philosophy relating examples of great design (buildings, websites, information systems) to the idea of providing the user with 'an experience' that marks out the significant interaction from the mundane and humdrum. He also used Dewey to show how all experiences grow out of previous experiences and help shape future experiences. That is, experience as a process is both continuous and cumulative.

While Shedroff's work aimed to inspire designers and get them thinking about what it means to design for experience, Forlizzi and Battarbee (2004, p. 262) used aspects of Dewey's work to develop a new model of interaction for Interaction Design. One aspect of their model is a classification of human–product interactions that owes much to Dewey. The interactions help the user form a relationship to a product or some aspect. Interaction is seen as fluent where the interaction is well-learned and automatic, cognitive where the product is present at hand and the subject of conscious reasoning, and expressive.

Forlizzi and Battarbee also distinguish three types of experience. They use the term experience to refer to the constant stream of consciousness and activity that constitutes life. An experience is a stream coalesced into a beginning, middle, and end, which can be named, discussed, and evaluated. For Forlizzi and Battarbee, co-experience is a particular category of created and shared experiences between people. This final category emphasizes the social and physical context in which people make sense of their experiences. For example, running out of fuel on a car journey can be an adventure or a disaster depending on the place and the company. Forlizzi and Battarbee also argue that although emotion and pleasure are often considered as something separable from thinking and intellect, they are, in fact, not only central parts of human activity but also the motivating force for intelligent action. Forlizzi and Battarbee's paper is a valuable starting point for understanding the role that pragmatist conceptions of human experience can offer interaction design. Supporting the perception of a significant change occurring, at about the same time as Forlizzi and Battarbee were developing their model, others also published Dewey-inspired work on the role of and potential for experience in Interaction Design. For example, Petersen et al. (2004, pp. 269–270) pointed to a growing interest in the aesthetics of interactive systems design. They used Dewey's work in developing a framework for understanding aesthetics as a complementary perspective on user-centered design.

4   Building It All Together-Prostate Cancer Patient Conceptual Wayfinding Structure Toolkit

This section is presented in four parts. First, we reflect on how the design thinking methods and co-creation activities support the multidisciplinary team building the conceptual wayfinding structure toolkit for Prostate cancer patients. In the following sections, we explore the human-centered healthcare experience based on a series of workshops and interviews with multistate holders.

4.1 Build the Conceptual Wayfinding Structural Toolkit

Patients and healthcare providers face an overwhelming amount of change when diagnosed with cancer (James et al., 2007, p. 356). The critical purpose of the project is to translate patient and clinical needs into interventions that will improve the experience for all stakeholders. After completing a 16-week design process, the team focused on three different methods to deliver educational resources to patients—an information hub website, an educational video suite, and an interactive patient journey map. Empirically understanding, groundbreaking insights, and outstanding results have been achieved by putting patients' and stakeholders' needs first.

To build the conceptual wayfinding structure toolkit for prostate cancer patients, we need a robust understanding of the holistic patient experience journey, the key stakeholders during the journey, the current situations, and the information management conceptual gaps. The team began their research by benchmarking different visual styles of journey mapping, comparing highly ranked institutions, educational tools, and existing resources from internal and external sources. The research phase determined that to reduce anxiety and improve outcomes, patients needed better education and awareness about treatment options and possibilities throughout the prostate cancer journey.

4.2 Prostate Cancer Patient Journey

The research phase's pivotal point was creating personas that could highlight the complexity of decision-making imposed by the various branch points in prostate cancer journeys. The team used patient journeys as a guide to help understand how different tools could be suitable for individuals with varying needs. By pairing various learning styles with typical patient profiles, the team was able to identify other information mediums best suited for communicating on a more personal and individual level. The team's persona represented a different age, backstory, and medical circumstance. Through this, the team was able to identify a variety of decision-making preferences related to prostate cancer diagnosis and treatment information. Advocating for the patient became the priority and inspired the subsequent ideation and refinement phases (see Fig. 1).

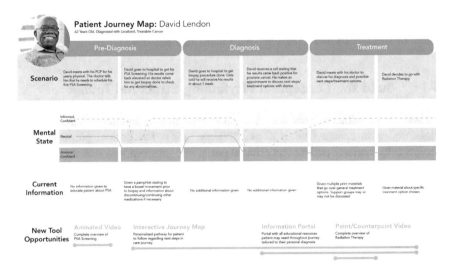

Fig. 1 Prostate cancer patient persona. *Source* Author's own figure (2022)

4.3   Co-creation for the Prostate Cancer Patient Information Management Tools

After conducted interviews during the ideation phase, it was agreed that patients prefer human guidance above all but would benefit from various educational tools that adapt to both their learning style and personality. The team then began creating educational tools to help enable and extend human support. Patients were given a deck of cards with various tools (both human, technological, and analog) and were asked to rank the tools based on how useful they would have been in their prostate cancer journeys (see Fig. 2).

The main perceptions are patients who overwhelmingly value and prefer interactions with people, and any tech that is used must be created to help enable and extend human support (see Table 1).

4.4   Stakeholder Ecosystem Analysis

Stakeholder ecosystem analysis compares their weight of influence and powers and their relationships. It helped the team identify who has the resource or ability to influence prostate cancer patient experience. Based on the team's information assemble and analysis activities, they can work more effectively together (Raum, 2018, p. 178) to address healthcare information management issues.

The team designed the stakeholder analysis matrix and organized a series of co-creation workshops to determine who influences the prostate cancer patient journey and who interacts with the patient the most. The workshops' design activities led

Fig. 2 Patient co-creation activity. *Source* Author's own Fig. (2022)

to exploring the stakeholder ecosystem that developed to support prostate cancer patient experience design (see Figs. 3 and 4).

The team listed multi-stakeholders with different roles and responsibilities during the prostate cancer patient journey. The journey was separated into four stages, including (1) pre-diagnosis, (2) diagnosis, (3) treatment, and (4) post-treatment. The information gap was identified to be the nurse navigator, and survivorship, and support groups should extend their influence into the pre-diagnosis stage.

4.5 Prostate Cancer Patient Conceptual Wayfinding Structure Toolkit

Prostate Cancer Patient Conceptual Wayfinding Structure Toolkit.

The team focused on three different methods to deliver educational resources to patients in the refinement phase—an information hub website, an educational video suite, and an interactive patient journey map. Key benefits across these concepts include (see Fig. 5).

- Patient education that better informs decision-making.
- A new personalized care journey.
- Scalable opportunities for future collaboration.

5   Conclusion

The prostate cancer patient conceptual wayfinding information management toolkit evolved in response to challenges we encountered communicating information management research to multidisciplinary teams designing for human-centered healthcare experience. This included difficulty identifying and articulating user beliefs about information management, focusing on desirable and useable solutions, and imagining innovative healthcare management solutions.

This article draws on a deep theoretical base in information management, patient education, and human-centered design thinking theory to explain how the conceptual wayfinding information management tools support design synthesis and

Table 1 Patients prefer resource and analog/digital tools

	Type	Demands
Most preferred resources and supports	Personal consultation with a doctor	To receive information about patient personal journey directly from their primary care physician or specialist
	Meet with a support group/mentor	Talk to others to hear their personal experience and
	Meet with survivorship	Meet with survivorship early on to discuss next steps and receive information about available resources
The most preferred analog and digital tools	Text/phone/email communication	Be able to communication back and forth with someone about follow-up questions, schedule appointment, and receive information in real time
	Interactive treatment Options	Be able to look at patient results from their biopsy procedure and interact with it to determine best treatment options in terms of risk, benefits, chance of recurrence, etc.
	Visualized journey map	Have a clear understanding and path for patients to follow regarding the next steps in your care journey
	Educational video & print materials	Have current information in the form of both video and print materials that pertain to each point in the patients' journey that are trusted and recommended by their specialist and primary provider

Source Author's own table (2022)

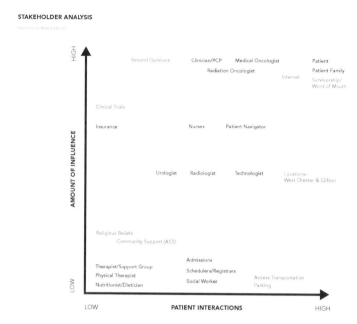

Fig. 3 Stakeholder matrix. *Source* Author's own figure (2022)

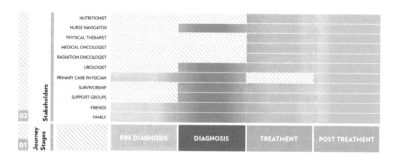

Fig. 4 Stakeholder journey. *Source* Author's own figure (2022)

value creation. The team focused on three different methods to deliver educational resources to patients in the refinement phase—an information hub website, an educational video suite, and an interactive patient journey map. Successful collaborations of this format depend on the design thinking orientation of healthcare information management and ideas revealed during the process and an ability to communicate and work with a multidisciplinary team to identify design solutions under uncertainty.

What is more, in exploring human-centered healthcare experience design, we discovered evidence of a share-decision-making heritage that underpins or reflects a series of popular design thinking tools and processes. We argue this conceptual

Fig. 5 Prostate cancer patient conceptual wayfinding structure toolkit. *Source* Author's own figure (2022)

wayfinding toolkit has application well beyond formal healthcare information management contexts, particularly in environments where changes to the healthcare world's complex situation challenge existing information structures. In summary, this method supports the work of multidisciplinary design teams working circumstances across different disciplines. It does so by helping multidisciplinary teams understand and collaborate with shared research methods and philosophies that support designing solutions for complex situations.

Acknowledgements This paper draws on research carried out by Cecilia Xi Wang and Craig M. Vogel with the support of The University of Cincinnati Barrett Cancer Center (UCCC) and LiveWell Collaborative. This paper and the research behind it would not have been possible without the exceptional support of my suppervisor and co-workers from LiveWell Collaborative, Linda Dunseath, Bain Butcher, Matt Anthony, Morgan Beatty, Munazza Aijaz. I thank the following individuals from the UCCC for their expertise and assistance throughout all aspects of our project and for their help in conducting the research, Dr. William Barrett, Dr. Timothy Struve, Michelle Kirschner, Jennifer Parkhurst, Kelly Acker, Natalie Ciulla, Alexandra Heekin.

Declaration of Interests The authors declare that they have no known competing financial interests or personal relationships that could have appeared to influence the work reported in this paper.

References

Bose, R. (2003). Knowledge management-enabled health care management systems: Capabilities, infrastructure, and decision-support. *Expert Systems with Applications, 24*(1), 59–71.

Coulter, A., Entwistle, V., & Gilbert, D. (1999). Sharing decisions with patients: Is the information good enough? *British Medical Journal (BMJ), 318*(7179), 318–322.

Forlizzi, J., & Battarbee, K. (2004). Understanding experience in interactive systems. In *Proceedings of the 5th Conference on Designing Interactive Systems: Processes, Practices, Methods, and techniques* (pp. 261–268), August 1–4, 2004. New York, US: Association for Computing Machinery.

Hewitson, P., & Austoker, J. (2005). Part 2: Patient information, informed decision-making and the psycho-social impact of prostate-specific antigen testing. *BJU International, 95*, 16–32.

Jadad, A. R., Haynes, R. B., Hunt, D., & Browman, G. P. (2000). The Internet and evidence-based decision-making: A needed synergy for efficient knowledge management in health care. *Canadian Medical Association Journal (CMAJ), 162*(3), 362–365.

James, N., Daniels, H., Rahman, R., McConkey, C., Derry, J., & Young, A. (2007). A study of information seeking by cancer patients and their carers. *Clinical Oncology, 19*(5), 356–362.

Jones, P. (2013). *Design for care: Innovating healthcare experience.* New York: Rosenfeld Media.

Kenney, C. (2012). *Transforming health care: Virginia Mason Medical Center's pursuit of the perfect patient experience.* New York: CRC Press.

Kohli, R., Tan, J. K., Piontek, F. A., Ziege, D. E., & Groot, H. (1999). Integrating cost information with health management support system: An enhanced methodology to assess health care quality drivers. *Topics in Health Information Management, 20*(1), 80–95.

Nerlikar, V. M. (1997). U.S. Patent No. 5,629,981. Washington, DC: U.S. Patent and Trademark Office.

Petersen, M. G., Iversen, O. S., Krogh, P. G., & Ludvigsen, M. (2004). Aesthetic interaction: A pragmatist's aesthetics of interactive systems. In *Proceedings of the 5th Conference on Designing Interactive Systems: Processes, Practices, Methods, and Techniques* (pp. 269–276).

Raum, S. (2018). A framework for integrating systematic stakeholder analysis in ecosystem services research: Stakeholder mapping for forest ecosystem services in the UK. *Ecosystem Services, 29*, 170–184.

Rice, R. E., & Leonardi, P. M. (2014). Information and communication technologies in organizations. In: *The SAGE handbook of organizational communication: Advances in theory, research, and methods* (pp. 425–448). USA: Sage Inc.

Shedroff, N. (2001). *Experience design 1.* Indianapolis, IN: New Riders.

Dr. Cecilia Xi Wang is a design researcher, educator, and practitioner focusing on service design, user experience design, digital media collaborative, visual communication design, interaction design, healthcare design, and multidisciplinary design research and practice. Dr. Cecilia Xi Wang's primary research interests lie in the overlap of design philosophy, user experience design, healthcare design, service design, visual communication design, and multi-disciplinary design. With the underlying of an increasingly complex and dynamic social and culture, we must rethink the value of design. The critical near-term challenge is understanding how better design thinking can help achieve an organic flow of experience in concrete situations, making such experiences more intelligent, meaningful, and sustainable. Dr. Wang is interested in discovering designers' ability to find new relationships among signs, things, actions, and thoughts take advantage of design thinking, the challenge is to reconsider and reconstruct the relationship between design research and practice. With her visual communication and user experience design and research experience, she feels well-placed to recognize how to exploit new design thinking philosophy and methods for ever more meaningful and valuable experience in concrete situations. She got her Ph.D. of design in the School of Design at Jiangnan University in June 2018. She studied communication design for her BS and MS at the Zhengzhou University of Light Industry and Jiangnan University. She is working as an assistant professor at the Graphic design department, College of Design at the University of Minnesota at present.

Craig M. Vogel is professor and the College of Design, Architecture, Art, and Planning (DAAP) at the University of Cincinnati. He has served for the past twelve years as Associate Dean of Graduate Studies and Research for the College of DAAP. He is also a professor in the School of Design with an appointment in Industrial Design, and co-founder of the Livewell Collaborative in Cincinnati and Singapore. He is a Fellow, Past President Elect and Chair of the Board of the Industrial Designers Society of America (IDSA). Vogel is co-author of the book, Creating Breakthrough Products, Financial Times, Prentice Hall, with Professor Jonathan Cagan. He is one of three authors of the book on innovation and organic growth, Design of Things to Come. During the last 25 years Professor Vogel has been a consultant to over 20 companies and advised and managed dozens of research projects and design studios collaborating with industry. He has also been a visiting scholar in China for the past two decades. Vogel is recognized as one of the most admired professors in architecture and design in the United States by Design Intelligence for 2008 and 2011. In 2015 he was recognized as one of 50 most Notable IDSA Members in the last 50 years.

"My Heart Jumped. Do I Have Cancer?"—Results of a Co-design Study with Cervical Cancer Screening Participants

Sandra Klonteig, Jiaxin Li, and Ragnhild Halvorsrud

ABSTRACT

Cervical cancer can be prevented by routinely taking cell samples from the cervix (screening). The frequency of screening is a crucial factor, and there is great potential to utilize the registry data from the cervical screening program for the benefit of both the screening participants and their doctors. However, with the constant emergence of new types of tests and guidelines, not only screening participants but also their doctors may become uncertain about what the test results mean and what follow-up procedures should be in place. The goal of this study was to explore how to present test results to participants in a way that supports optimal screening frequency without causing unnecessary worry. This chapter presents the results of co-design workshops engaging women in the target group. Through the use of personas, trigger questions, and trigger material, we explored the group's current barriers and information needs. In all, 19 paper prototypes were produced during the workshops. Through a content analysis of the workshop material, we derived user requirements for a future digital tool intended to support optimal participation in the cervical screening program. We also report on lessons learned, threats to validity, and future research.

S. Klonteig (✉) · J. Li · R. Halvorsrud
SINTEF Digital, Box 124 Blindern, N-0314 Oslo, Norway
e-mail: Sandra.klonteig@sintef.no

J. Li
e-mail: Jiaxin.Li@sintef.no

R. Halvorsrud
e-mail: Ragnhild.Halvorsrud@sintef.no

1   Introduction

Cervical cancer screening involves mass examination of a population with no symptoms. The purpose is to detect early-stage cancer before the disease spreads and, in some cases, to detect and prevent precancer from developing. Cervical cancer is a type of cancer that occurs in the cells of the cervix—the lower part of the uterus that connects to the vagina. This type of cancer can be prevented by routinely checking cell samples from the cervix to detect precancerous changes. The incidence and mortality rates of cervical cancer have dropped substantially in the female population since the Nordic countries implemented screening (Vaccarella et al., 2014, pp. 965–969). The Norwegian Cervical Cancer Screening Programme (NCCSP, hereafter referred to as "the screening program") (Cancer Registry of Norway, n.d., n.d.) is run by the Cancer Registry of Norway, targeting all women between the ages of 25 and 69. The NCCSP is responsible for managing and developing cervical cancer screening and has collected health data from almost two million women since 1992.

Historically, the screening interval for cervical cancer was every three years, following the principle of "one size fits all." However, the screening program has changed continuously in recent years due to new knowledge, technological advances, and improved methods. New and more targeted tests have been introduced, imposing changes in the recommended screening intervals. The screening program also provides personalized guidelines (algorithms) for how abnormal test results should be followed up. These guidelines are based on a combination of previous test results and a combination of different tests performed at the same time, collectively referred to as test history. With the constant emergence of new types of tests and guidelines, not only screening participants but also their primary care doctors may become uncertain as to what the test results mean and how they should be followed up. In addition, it is difficult to determine when it is time for a new test, even with normal test results.

Correct frequency of screening is a crucial factor in the prevention of cervical cancer. Every year, the screening program sends a reminder to about 450,000 women that their expected screening interval is overdue (Engesæter et al., 2020, p.12). A recent survey shows that there are approximately 200,000 women who have not taken a screening test within the past 10 years or longer, increasing their risk of undetected precancers (Anderssen, 2021, n.d.). On the other hand, 1 in 10 women takes screening tests too often (Klungsøyr et al., 2009, pp. 91–97), which may lead to overtreatment of insignificant precancers (Soper et al., 2020, pp. 3569–3590).

There is great potential to utilize the register data of the cervical screening program better and more efficiently for the benefit of both the individual participants and the healthcare system. To realize this potential, an innovation project for the public sector called "ShowMe" was initiated in 2021 with the overall goal of developing effective educational tools to support optimal participation in the cervical screening program.

1.1　Research Challenge

The right to access own health data is a statuary right for Norwegian citizens. The health service is aware that many patients have problems understanding and using the information they receive from healthcare professionals (Nutbeam, 2000, pp. 259–267). Internet searches for participants in the screening program can be particularly demanding. Participants who search the internet without guidance are faced with a jungle of information, and potential challenges are misinformation due to highly variable quality of Web information. The screening program has historical data from many years back and may contain abnormal test results that have been resolved. Accordingly, it may be challenging to convey large amounts of available data to the screening participant without creating unnecessary worries.

The main research challenge is to present test results to screening participants in a way that supports optimal screening frequency without causing unnecessary worry. A further challenge is to offer decision support to screening participants and their primary care doctors for the proper follow-up of abnormal results.

In this chapter, we report the results from co-design workshops with end-users (screening participants). The focus has been on scenarios in which women have received normal test results, reflecting 90% of the screening test results per year (Engesæter et al., 2020, p.18). However, we have also explored a situation with mild cell changes that may create concerns, although it can be resolved without treatment.

2　Background

In the following chapter we will share some knowledge about cervical cancer, and how cervical cancer screening program is practiced in Norway. Then we will move on to the challenges in cervical cancer screening program that have been discovered in other literatures.

2.1　Cervical Cancer and Cervical Cancer Screening

Virtually all cervical cancers are caused by persistent infection of carcinogenic strains of the human papillomavirus (HPV). HPV infections are common in the population and are transferred by sexual contact. There are an estimated 197 subtypes of HPV, most of them harmless. However, some subtypes correlate with a higher risk of developing precancerous lesions that can develop into cervical cancer after many years. HPV subtypes 16 and 18 have historically been found in about 70% of cervical cancers and are considered the main carcinogenic subtypes. A persistent infection with HPV-16 or 18 (or another known carcinogenic HPV subtype) is, therefore, a risk factor for developing precancerous lesions in the cells of the cervix that can potentially develop into invasive cancer (Bzhalava et al., 2015, pp. 341–344).

The goal of the screening program is to discover precancerous changes that can be treated locally before they develop into cervical cancer. The screening program involves two different types of tests: (1) the Pap test, in which cervical cells are checked for abnormalities under a microscope (cervical cytology), and (2) the HPV test, a more automated test that detects the genetic footprint of the HPV virus. The Pap test is used for women under 34 years of age, while the HPV test is used for women over 34 years of age. Until now, the sampling procedure has been the same from the screening participant's point of view, both involving a gynecological examination. In addition, the screening program is piloting self-administered HPV testing.

A typical screening pathway in Norway involves a primary care doctor or a gynecologist performing the test and communicating the results to the screening participant. After a sample of cervical cells has been collected, it is sent to a laboratory for analysis. The results are returned to the requester and the registry of the screening program. Both private and public laboratories analyze tests and communicate the results to doctors and the screening program. The screening program provides guidelines (algorithms) for how test results should be followed up. These guidelines are based on a combination of the age of the woman, previous test results, and a combination of different tests performed at the same time, collectively referred to as the test history.

What complicates the interpretation of the screening results is that there is no linear relationship between persistent HPV infection, cervical cell abnormalities, and invasive cervical cancer. HPV infection can go away spontaneously and indeed does so in most cases. Moreover, abnormal, precancerous cervical cells can revert to normal cells. The likelihood of this happening varies with age and other factors. With new types of tests and guidelines constantly emerging, not only screening participants but also their primary care doctors may become uncertain as to what the test results mean and how they should be followed up.

The public website concerning health services for Norwegian residents is known as Helsenorge.no. Here, personalized content from various healthcare providers is available (prescriptions, for example), a vaccination overview, and a summary care record with important health information. In the future, Helsenorge.no is expected to convey medical screening data to individuals. As of today, there is no integrated digital solution for communicating test results and history to screening participants.

2.2 Related Work

A recent study focusing on screening participants' awareness and needs reveals a general lack of information about the screening program, procedures, HPV, and confusion about the interpretation of the test results (Siegel, 2022, n.d.). Not only is the information itself important, but also the timing of the information.

Research has repeatedly found that increasing women´s knowledge of cervical cancer can relieve anxiety and stress and improve their willingness to participate in extra screening steps (Markovic-Denic et al., 2018, pp. 178–183; Papa et al., 2009, pp. 66–71). However, numerous research reports (Ciavattini et al., 2021, n.d.; O'Connor et al., 2014, pp. 1421–1430; Szwarc et al., 2021, pp. 453–463; Verhoeven et al., 2010, pp. 101–105) have pointed out that getting adequate information from health care personnel remains a big problem for women, leading them to look for answers online. For women who had a positive HPV test or abnormal Pap smear test, there was a large gap between the information they desired and the information they received. Specifically, they demanded more information concerning the explanation of results, the implications of results, the progression of the disease, disease management (follow-up steps and what patients can do personally to contribute to their recovery), the risks of cervical cancer, and sexual transmission of the disease. Similar findings were found in another survey with women from Spain, France, and Portugal: 80% of the participants wanted more information, especially on the consequences of the disease on emotions, family life, and partner relationships (Monsonego et al., 2011, n.d.). Marlow et al. (2020, n.d.) found that there are different information needs among women with positive HPV and those with negative HPV. Women with positive HPV were concerned about the casual and clinical aspects of cervical cancer, such as when they were infected, the cause of infection, and what they could do to treat the current infection and prevent future infection. HPV-negative women often raised questions about the purpose and procedure of HPV testing, specifically the differences between HPV tests and Pap smear tests.

Other than the lack of information, Monsonego et al. (2011, n.d.) found that around a quarter of the participants in their study had difficulty understanding the results. In a survey of 153 women who had abnormal test results, 71.4% of participants said that they felt confused over the HPV diagnosis and the different consequences caused by high-risk and low-risk HPV types (Daley et al., 2010, pp. 279–290). Many women reported that they were confused about the meaning of HPV and how they got it (McBride et al., 2021, pp. 395–429), and others did not know if positive meant good or bad. The main cause of this confusion was probably a lack of knowledge about HPV. While some participants were familiar with the term normal in the Pap test, they could not explain what the term meant, which reflects a lack of understanding of the results (Head et al., 2017, pp. 37–46).

3   Method and Approach

We used a co-design approach to gain insight into what current challenges the participating women experienced and how they envisioned the solution. Co-design, also called Participatory Design (n.d., 2022a, 2022b, 2022c, n.d.), emphasizes active involvement of all stakeholders in the design process, which includes "knowledge development, idea generation and concept development" (Dahl et al., 2014, pp. 207–216). The designer will offer tools to help and support users in creating solutions. By involving users in creating solutions together with designers, it can generate more creative solutions (Mitchell et al., 2016, pp. 205–220; Trischler et al., 2018, pp. 75–100), and can promote user acceptance and satisfaction. Therefore, we decided to conduct co-design workshops in which users were given tasks and asked to create their own solutions. Personas were used to help users address their needs and promote user involvement (Nielsen, 2011, n.d.).

3.1 Recruitment and Workshop Preparation

In this study, we used the convenience sampling (Leedy & Ormrod, 2019, p. 272) method to recruit participants. We sent out invitations with a poster through the SINTEF (Sintef is a research institute with 2000 employees. https://www.sintef.no/en/) internal email list, through our personal LinkedIn channels, and through some Facebook groups (https://www.facebook.com/groups/oslojobs/permalink/188 5890831801179/). The inclusion criteria were that women be between 25 and 69 years old and speak Norwegian. Both workshops were held physically inside a building belonging to SINTEF. Almost half of the participants were employees of SINTEF.

To facilitate the co-creation session, we created materials and two personas with sample histories (Figs. 1 and 2). Since cervical screening is a sensitive topic, we created fictional personas so that participants could refer to them instead of themselves if they did not want to disclose their own experiences. We created personas to reflect typical use cases based on background studies and consultations with clinical experts. The persona called Karen is 35 years old. She has recently moved to another municipality and cannot remember when she took her previous test. Another persona, Maria (55 years old), had a recent test that revealed mild cell changes, which should not have caused a high degree of anxiety or worry, but did because of poor communication of the test results. In addition to personas and sample histories, we also prepared example sketches in various levels of fidelity to serve as inspiration (see Fig. 3).

3.2 Workshop Procedure

The workshops were designed for a duration of two hours. Each workshop started with participants signing a consent form. The researchers then presented the screening program, the screening pathway, and current challenges. After the presentation, the researchers explained the ethical considerations of the study and set up some basic rules for the creative sessions. The participants were divided into two groups, each supported by a facilitator. The first several minutes were used to introduce the participants to each other and to discuss why they had signed up for the workshop.

The main activity in the workshop was a sketching exercise. The participants were introduced to the persona Karen and her sample history. First, they were asked to elaborate on Karen's challenges. They were given blank paper templates imitating a mobile screen (see Figs. 4 and 5) and instructed to individually draw a

"When did I actually take the previous test?"

Background

- Karen received an invitation from the Cervical Cancer Screening Program when she turned 25, and has taken a test at her primary care doctor in Trondheim every 3rd year.
- All test results have been normal so far.
- The last time she was tested, her primary care doctor recommended she take another test in 5 years instead of 3, and this confused her.
- Karen recently moved from Trondheim to Oslo and changed her primary care doctor.
- She didn´t remember when she took the previous test, and couldn´t find it on Helsenorge.no.
- Her new primary care doctor didn't know when Karen took the last test either, and recommended she take a new test "for the sake of safety."

Karen 35 years old

Pain points

- Can´t remember when she took the last test
- Confusion about when the next test should be taken - every 3rd or every 5th year?
- Doesn´t receive the test result if it´s normal

Goals

- Have access to understandable test results and test history
- Know when she should take the next test
- Overview of how data is stored and who has access

Name	Age	Date	Type of Test	Test Result
Karen	35	31/03/2022	HPV	Not Detected
Karen	34	15/04/2021	HPV	Not Detected
Karen	31	20/05/2018	Cytology	Normal
Karen	28	14/06/2015	Cytology	Normal
Karen	25	10/07/2012	Cytology	Normal

Fig. 1 Persona of Karen. *Source* Author's own figure (2022)

"What does my test result mean?"

Background

- Maria has taken pap smear test regularly for many years. Usually, she doesn´t get answers when the result was normal.
- Last year, she saw the test results and was shocked when she had mild cell changes and was HPV-positive (even though the type of HPV virus is low risk).
- She tried to google what the result meant and thought she had cancer.
- She was very worried, so she sent a message to her primary care doctor on PasientSky, her primary care doctor told her not to worry but to come back for a new test next year.
- Maria contacted a gynecologist for a "second opinion."
- One year later, she took another test and waited anxiously for the results. Since she did not hear anything, so she assumed that everything was normal.

Maria 55 years old

Pain points

- Can´t remember when she took the last test
- Doesn´t understand the test results
- Was terrified when she googled the test results
- Doesn´t have access to previous test results

Goals

- Easy to understand what the test results means and what she should do
- Know when she can get the next test result
- Have access to understandable test results and test history

Name	Age	Date	Type of Test	Test Result
Maria	55	31/03/2022	HPV	Not detected
Maria	54	15/03/2021	Cytology	Mild cell changes
Maria	54	15/03/2021	HPV	Detected, not type 16/18
Maria	47	25/05/2014	HPV	Not detected
Maria	41	20/05/2008	HPV	Not detected
Maria	34	14/06/2001	HPV	Not detected
Maria	31	10/07/1998	Cytology	Normal

Fig. 2 Persona of Maria. *Source* Author's own figure (2022)

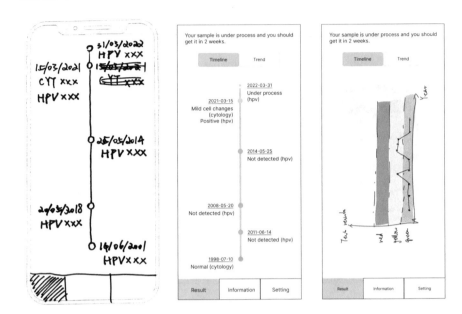

Fig. 3 Prompts and low-fidelity prototypes. *Source* Author's own figure (2022)

solution to present and visualize Karen´s sample history. When they had finished the drawings, the participants presented their ideas to the rest of the group. Each facilitator presented the summary findings of her group to the other group. After the exercise with persona Karen, we repeated it with a different persona, Maria, who had a more complicated sample history. This sketching exercise was useful in revealing what information was needed in a sample history and how it should be visualized.

Fig. 4 Simple drawings of test results sketched by participants. *Source* Author's own figure (2022)

Fig. 5 An integrated solution sketched by a participant. *Source* Author's own figure (2022)

Adjustments to the Procedures

In the first workshop, both groups showed a certain reluctance to draw, so we provided them with some prompts (see Fig. 3). After seeing the prompts, one group started to draw while the other still hesitated. Therefore, we presented the hesitant group with some low-fidelity interfaces (see Fig. 3) and asked them to provide feedback on what they liked and disliked about them. We also asked whether the participants wanted to make changes to the interfaces.

After the first workshop, three facilitators reflected on why we had received fewer creative outputs than we had expected from the participants. One possible reason they identified was that the sample history printouts had too many design details, which may have limited the participants' creativity. The same reasoning was applied to the low-fidelity interfaces. The second reason the facilitators identified was that the task of visualizing the sample history was too difficult for the participants. To increase the outcomes from the second workshop, we agreed to make some small modifications, but we kept most of the procedures identical in the second workshop to ensure the consistency necessary to generalize findings across workshops.

In the second workshop, we presented a more simplified sample history printout and did not present prompts or low-fidelity interfaces. Since sample results are highly related to sample history, and the participants were more familiar with sample results than with sample history, we asked them to visualize the sample results before designing the sample history. We gave them time to reflect alone before drawing on the papers and gave them ample encouragement. With these small modifications, we noticed big changes in the second workshop compared to the first one; the participants were more willing to draw and share their ideas.

3.3   Data Analysis

We used elements from rapid analysis, an approach that enables a time-efficient analysis compared to thematic content analysis (Gale et al., 2019, n.d.). Transcript summaries of the workshop sessions were made using spreadsheets in MS Excel following the chronology of the workshop procedure. A matrix was prepared to identify and sort themes and to connect the transcripts with the visual descriptions. The themes used were "user needs/requirements" and "exemplary quotes." Two researchers conducted the initial analysis.

In the second iteration, one researcher collated all the sorted material into a single spreadsheet. Here, material coded as "user needs/requirements" was then split into subthemes, namely, "current situation," "information needs," and "communication preferences." The main themes and subthemes were discussed among the three researchers until we reached agreement. All the themes will be presented in detail in the following results chapter.

4   Results

We conducted two workshops in May 2022 with 7 and 10 active participants, respectively. Their ages ranged from 25 to 55 years; thus, all participants were in the target group of the screening program. All but one of the participants had experience with cervical screening, meaning they had had a Pap test taken one or more times. Three of the participants informed us, unsolicited, that they had experienced test results in which abnormal cells and/or HPV virus were detected.

The procedure described in Sect. 3.2 triggered the participants' curiosity and many questions, which will be discussed in Sects. 4.1 and 4.2. During the co-design sessions, the participants created a broad range of suggestions and solutions. A total of 19 paper sketches about the visualization of the test results and sample history were produced during the workshops: 5 from the first workshop and 14 from the second. These sketches ranged from content with detailed wording (i.e., as shown in Fig. 4) to modulars, such as the integrated applications shown in Fig. 5.

In the following two sections, we will elaborate on these results, which are structured in the following categories: current problems, information needs, and user-requirements.

4.1 Current Problems

Knowledge About Screening Tests (Cytology and HPV), Algorithm, and Program

Most participants were familiar with the practice of Pap smear sampling. However, several had low awareness of being part of a cervical screening program. One participant said she had not heard about screening tests before. Another said,

> I am uncertain whether I have ever taken a screening test. I guess I have, but I have never been notified about it. I guess my primary care doctor has this under control.

Several of the participants were not familiar with the two different types of primary screening methods, namely HPV testing and cytology. Furthermore, they were not aware of abnormal cells, the various degrees of cell changes, or the causes of these changes. One participant said,

> I would never have known that cell changes potentially could disappear by themselves.

For HPV specifically, knowledge varied among the participants. During conversations, we noticed that some participants were not familiar with different HPV types and risks, or how these were involved in cervical cancer, but a few had more knowledge. We are uncertain as to why some participants had more knowledge than others; however, we saw a trend that those participants who had experienced positive HPV results had more knowledge. Additionally, some participants were familiar with the HPV virus through vaccination programs.

In general, the participants showed low awareness of the recommended screening intervals. Some of them thought they should take the test on a yearly basis; others had no knowledge of this at all. One participant said,

> "I think I have taken way too many tests. I took a test through my primary care doctor in [town], and he told me I should take the test yearly. When I came back the following year, he suddenly told me I should come back in three years. I did not understand anything." Another reported, "I have no idea when I should take the test, or that I have switched from a three- to five-year interval [participant is older than 34 years]. I thought one could check this through Helsenorge."

Only a minority of the participants knew the correct recommended interval to take the next test.

Reminders sent out from the screening program were also discussed. Some participants remembered that they had received a reminder, while others did not. One participant questioned the reminder system:

> Let's say I do not receive a reminder. How do I know if it is not time yet or if there has been a technical mistake?

Test Histories and Test Results

As described in the Background, there is currently no integrated digital solution available to access test histories. The following strategies can be used to access piecewise information related to the screening test: (1) reminders from the screening program, available from the public messaging service (DigiPost); (2) logs of previous appointments with primary care doctors, available for doctors in electronic patient journals; (3) communication logs with doctors offered through eHealth system or text messaging dialogs; (4) patient portals offered by private laboratories containing the date of screening test analysis (but not the results).

In addition to challenges related to accessing a test history, many participants reported that they did not receive test results from their doctor, and they assumed that it meant there had been nothing to worry about. However, such a passive way of receiving a normal test result, or "silent OK," often involves worries over time. Besides, maintaining consistency in result delivery is also important, as one participant said:

> The gynecologist took the test and said she would not contact me if the result was normal. She might have picked up that I was of the more nervous type. [later] I received a text message starting with, 'I have received your test results.' My heart jumped. Do I have cancer? The test results were actually normal, and I bet my gynecologist meant to be nice, but…

When they did get results, several participants experienced difficulties interpreting them, often leading to anxiety after googling the test results.

Another significant challenge mentioned by the participants was the wait time for test results. They are not sure how much time it takes to get test results, and since they don't always receive the results, it can be challenging to know when they can relax. One participant said,

> Now I have taken the test, but when will I receive the answer? We need to help the patient ´put it away´by informing about WHEN the patient can expect to receive answers.

As a solution to these types of challenges, participants suggested live updates of the screening status, similar to the tracking of packages, or simply showing the expected time for the result to be delivered.

4.2   Information Needs

During the two workshops, the need for information was a recurring topic. The amount and type of information needed varied based on the test results and individual preferences. If the test results were abnormal (as compared to normal), participants reported that their need for information would be greater. This includes explanations of the different types of tests taken (HPV and cytology), specific HPV type, what they should do next, how dangerous it is, and so on. A few participants even wanted access to the raw data. For normal results, some participants said it would be sufficient to know whether the result was normal or not and the time for the next test, while other participants wanted to have explanations for the results and general knowledge about cervical cancer screening.

General Information on HPV

Several participants requested more general information about HPV infections, different types of HPV and their associated risks of developing precancer, the difference between HPV and cytology tests, and when/why these two types of testing are combined in the screening program. One participant reflected, in hindsight, on a positive HPV result:

> If I had just known what HPV was when I received the answer [positive HPV test], I would not have been so afraid. Now that I have educated myself, I do not think it is that scary anymore.

Some participants preferred information about the detected HPV type in relation to the test result/screening history. As one participant pointed out,

> I want to know specifically which HPV type it is so I can educate myself on that particular type. I do not want to know it was not type 16/18.

One group also suggested integrating HPV vaccination status into the digital solution. Because these topics are related, it would be beneficial to have "everything in one place."

Medical Codes and Terms in the Test Results

The participants required more information on the reliability/sensitivity of the sampling method, explanations of the results (especially when medical terms were used), rationale behind the recommended follow-up, and so on. Many discussions focused on medical codes and terms. The participants preferred non-medical terms whenever possible; for instance, one participant suggested the use of "cell test" instead of "cytology." However, some participants still preferred to have the medical term and the raw data available in a deeper information layer, for instance, to ease communication with health personnel. If any medical terms were used, participants felt explanations of these terms should be provided:

> All difficult words should have a link to something explaining the meaning of that word.

For instance, why the medical code "not detected" is interpreted as a normal test result should be explained to the participants. Another example is another medical code called "invalid test." Participants requested an easy explanation of this code, especially when the invalid result was not caused by the screening participants. Participants also discussed whether it was possible to use common terms, such as "detected" and "not-detected," for both cytology and HPV results, and whether they could receive additional specification on HPV type or cell changes.

Decision Support

Several participants wanted decision support, both for normal results (to follow the recommended screening interval) and for abnormal results. For normal results, participants wanted to know when the previous test was taken and when to take the nest text (i.e., "Your next test is in 2026").

For abnormal results, one participant commented,

> "I need to know what is happening next, be informed whether the doctor will contact me, or other things that should happen. For us [screening participants], this is not obvious." Another participant said, "If the test result is not normal it has to be clearly communicated in a message what they have found, and that it requires × follow-up."

Several participants stressed that this information should also be available and accessible in the test results and test histories. One group suggested including a schedule of when future tests should be taken; the schedule could be dynamic in such a way that it could be updated if case results indicate a different time interval or changes in follow-up.

To aid decision support, participants stressed the need to know why the particular test(s) was taken, and the reasoning behind the suggested action. One participant said, "If you are going to report what [test] has been done, it is also important to inform you about *why* this has been done." Another said,

> If I was told to wait 12 months to take a new test, I would need to know if it was because [the health institution] does not have capacity, or if it is because it is really no rush. Another participant said, "I would never wait 12 months if I was told to wait 12 months with no explanation as to why. I would have booked an appointment at a private clinic immediately."

4.3   User Requirements

In general, participants agreed that they should have the right to access their test results and test history. As one participant said,

> The solution must be available so that everyone can get the test results.

Most participants were in favor of having this information available on an existing platform, which is an online portal for conveying health information (Helsenorge.no), instead of a separate application. However, one participant suggested having a separate application. This section will present further requirements for digital solutions that present test results and history.

Information Architecture

Many of the participants provided suggestions for how the information architecture of the digital solution should be designed, emphasizing that the front page should be clear and easy to understand, while more detailed information could be hidden further behind. As one person said,

> I do not want to click through several layers of information; I just want to see the test results immediately." Another person said, "The most important thing is to see the most recent test results, not the test history.

As to how to easily access additional information in the deeper layers, the participants suggested the use of information boxes, hyperlinks, notes, and FAQs. For instance, one suggested,

> We can have a symbol right next to the test results, so you can click to read more about the different degrees of abnormal cells or HPV types.

This readily available information could reduce the participants' needs to Google. In sum, information should be structured, accessible, reliable, and readily available.

Visualizations of Test History

This section will examine some of the suggested visual elements in relation to the test history, see Fig. 6. In general, many participants preferred tables over timelines. Some reasons reported were that timelines could be difficult to orient (especially when using a phone), and that the scaling of time could be confusing. In general, the participants commented that the table could provide a better overview.

Participants also suggested alternative versions, some including everything on one site, while others included menus or tabs. Some suggested having everything on one screen with the possibility of scrolling. Furthermore, they suggested the possibility of hiding the history when having many test results and the opportunity to sort according to age or date. Another discussion was whether to include one table for all screening tests or to alternatively have one each for HPV and cytology. Here, the preferences also varied.

Communication Preferences

A variety of communication preferences were reported during the workshops, ranging from how participants wanted to be notified about the results and time for the next test to the wording and tone of voice that should be used when communicating the results.

The participants mentioned that they wanted to have live chat communication with doctors and chatbots. For some purposes, they preferred to have direct consultation with humans (e.g., a doctor), while some simple, frequently asked questions could be taken care of by a non-human chatbot. If none of these were possible, several participants suggested that at least the doctors' contact information should be available in case there was a need for a call.

In addition, the participants would like to have notifications regarding test results or the time for the next test, with the flexibility to choose the preferred communication channel and an active (e.g., pull notification) or passive (e.g.,

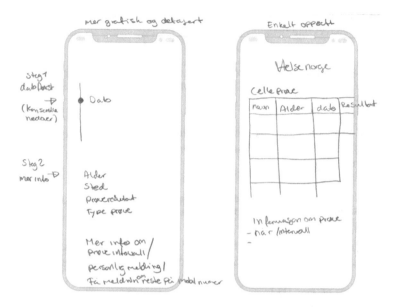

Fig. 6 Sketches by participants illustrating two different visualizations of test history. *Source* Author's own figure (2022)

push notification) communication style through personalized settings. Push notification means that the server sends a notification to the user (n.d., 2022a, 2022b, 2022c, n.d.), while pull notification means the user initiates the request for specific information (n.d., 2022a, 2022b, 2022c, n.d.). As mentioned previously, the time interval between two sample tests can be up to 5 years, which can be quite challenging for a human brain to remember. Although they might currently receive a physical or digital notification letter, some participants said they would prefer to receive a push notification (SMS or email) to remind them that it is time for the next test. One participant wanted a table showing the schedule for all upcoming tests over the next 10 years.

As for how the test results should be delivered, preferences varied based on the situation. As one participant said,

> If the test result is very serious, I want someone to call me. If it does not require immediate action, i.e., minor cell changes, a well-formulated message could be sufficient.

Despite the desire to receive test results quickly, some participants wanted an SMS notification informing them that the test results were available without revealing the results. However, for women who had difficulty accessing the digital portal to see the results, one participant suggested adding an option to "contact your primary care doctor."

Regarding tone of voice, the majority of the participants preferred an informal, personal communication style (e.g., starting with "Hello [name]") regardless of normal or abnormal results. One participant explained,

> Bad news also has to be communicated, and it would be best if bad news were delivered in a human way.

Others commented that the wording should be carefully chosen and individually adjusted. When one participant saw "don't worry, this should be ok, etc." in the example sketches we provided, she seemed offended at being told how she should *feel*. Here is her quote:

> My test result doesn't need to be so much 'don't worry, this should be ok, etc.' I just need to know what the results are and what we should do about them. If I received a message [like the one with 'don't worry' written in it] and something was actually wrong, I would be pretty annoyed.

Categorization of Test Results

There were heterogeneous opinions among the participants on how test results could be best categorized. Some preferred a simple binary "OK/not OK" or "detected/not detected," while others preferred more nuanced categories, e.g., a triage system to indicate normal results (green), a need for follow-up (yellow), and immediate follow-up (red). However, some reacted to the use of colors, claiming that a non-green color would be more frightening than clarifying. For HPV testing, some suggested indicating whether the HPV type was low, medium, or high risk. As one participant said, "'Not type 16/18' means nothing to me."

Transfer History from Tests Taken in Other Countries

Some participants had a non-Norwegian birth country and stressed the necessity of including test results from countries outside of Norway. For instance, one of them explained, "I moved to Norway and received a message saying I should take a screening test, but I had already taken the test a couple of months earlier in my home country." For these screening participants, it could be valuable to manually add history manually from tests taken in other countries to their records.

5   Discussion

The prevalence of cervical cancer in Nordic countries has declined and has become a rare disease as a result of high-quality screening programs. To support further development of the Norwegian screening program, the aim of this study was to explore the potential for improved screening experiences by giving participants access to screening data. This implies the design of a user-friendly, precise presentation of complex, longitudinal medical data and mapping preferences for decision support for end-users with various test results.

The current procedure for communicating the test results to the screening participant is highly variable. Given a normal result, many are not actively informed (silent ok) (Lindau et al., 2002, pp. 938–943). Participants in the workshop reported that this could cause unnecessary worry, and that they would prefer the opportunity to check the test results. In Britain, according to the NHSCSP guidelines, all women should receive an answer within 6 weeks after they take the test (Goldsmith et al., 2006, n.d.). Abnormal test results are communicated through phone calls, in most cases, followed by letters. Sometimes the laboratory results are sent from the physician to the women, with some variations in different countries (Monsonego et al., 2011, n.d.).

A general finding from the co-design workshops is the need for basic knowledge about cervical screening, the screening algorithm, and the HPV virus (see Table 1). These findings are in line with a number of other studies (Head et al., 2017, pp. 37–46; Monsonego et al., 2011, n.d.). Furthermore, these findings show that the need for additional knowledge changes radically when the test results are not normal. For instance, when the result is normal, a simple "thumbs up" can be sufficient, but when it is abnormal, participants want to be informed about screening methods, algorithms, risks, and other matters. These findings are also prevalent in other studies (Marlow et al., 2020, n.d.). Previous studies have indicated that additional knowledge can reduce stress and anxiety among screening participants receiving abnormal test results (Markovic-Denic et al., 2018, pp. 178–183; Papa et al., 2009, pp. 66–71).

Participants described the current situation for accessing previous test results as a fragmented service, where they must combine and integrate data from different sources to gain information about their previous results and their next due date. We identified several user requirements for a digital solution presenting test results and history from the cervical screening program (see Table 2).

Table 1 Information needs identified in the workshops

Topic	Frequently asked questions
Primary screening methods	What is the difference between cytology and HPV tests? Why/when do you combine the tests?
Screening algorithm	How long should I wait before I take the next test? Why should I take a different test after I turn 34? I have usually waited 3 years. Why should I wait 5 years now? Someone told me you should take the test every year. Why 3/5?
HPV virus and genotypes	How is HPV related to cancer? What is type 16/18, and what does it mean? Can HPV infections pass? When did the enrollment of HPV as a primary screening method begin?
Cytology	What do you mean by "abnormal cells"?
Cervical cancer	How much time does it take to develop cancer?

Table 2 User requirements identified in the study

User requirements	Explanation
Access to data and accessible tools	Everyone should be able to access their test results and test history The digital solution should be available to everyone, preferably through HealthPortal
Information architecture	Patients should be able to see the most recent test results first and also the estimated date for the next test Ability to dig deeper and get more information, including information on screening history, HPV vaccinations, and raw data
Explanation of medical terms	Medical terms should be simplified when possible (i.e., use "cell test" instead of "cytology") If a medical term is used, an explanation of that term should be available
Immediate access to information	Information must be immediately available, i.e., if cytology is mentioned, it should be easy to immediately find more information about cytology (for example, via a hyperlink in the word itself)
Reliable sources	Referral to trustworthy sources to avoid misinformation and random googling
Decision support	Information about "what is next" regardless of test results If the test results are abnormal, there is a need for more in-depth explanations and the ability to contact someone (i.e., a chatbot or the primary care doctor)
Overview of test status	The ability to see the status of the test to avoid worrying while waiting for the results (i.e., the test is currently being analyzed by the lab) Some type of reference points as to how long it takes to get results
Flexible settings for reminders and notifications	Some want a reminder of when to take the next text or when the test results will be available; others do not Communication channels vary; some prefer SMS, others prefer e-mail
Transfer history from tests taken in other countries	If you have taken a test in another country, it should be possible to add this test into the digital solution so the user can have an overview

5.1   Lessons Learned

Involving users in the development of a digital solution for access to, and presentation of screening data led us to some valuable lessons that could be of use to researchers and designers. Using personas was a good strategy. Concrete stories helped focus the discussion and overcome the "cold start" problem. The use of personas eased communication and collaboration, as participants did not need to share their own experiences. On the other hand, the personas addressed too many pain points and challenges, which could be overwhelming for the participants. Focusing on fewer challenges would probably reduce the cognitive load on the participants and give them more flexibility in the time schedule. Additionally, the proposed trigger questions for designing a solution to visualize the test history in the first workshop were too broad, which made it difficult to get started. Providing time for self-reflection before sharing in sub-groups was a success factor, as it fueled the group discussion and resulted in less dominance from the more talkative participants.

5.2   Limitations and Threats to Validity

We identified several limitations in this study. The sample in the current study was relatively small and biased toward women working at a research institute, which lacks representativeness of the general female population. Therefore, the user needs concerning improving information on the test results and providing time for the next test—for the purpose of increasing their participation and adherence to the screening program—that we found in this group of women might not apply to women of other backgrounds. Another limitation is the priming of the participants. The researchers provided participants with knowledge about cervical screening in the introduction of the workshop, which may, for instance, have stimulated curiosity and elicited the need for more information. Specifically for the co-design, the participants may have been impacted by the researchers showing examples (test histories and prompts).

6   Conclusion and Future Work

We conducted two workshops with 17 female participants in total. Using a co-design method has given us rich data material, including knowledge of the current situation and user requirements for a digital solution. Our findings indicate a need for a digital solution to provide screening participants with an overview and decision support related to their test results and history. Furthermore, our findings are in line with previous studies showing that screening participants need more basic knowledge about cervical cancer and cervical screening. A digital solution dedicated to the cervical screening program is needed and would probably support improved screening frequency, both to reduce unnecessary sampling and to prevent infrequent sampling. More research is in the pipeline to explore needs from screening participants and for doctors, including a survey to quantify and validate findings in this study, and interviews/workshops with doctors to understand their needs and challenges in communicating test results to women.

Acknowledgements We would like to express our gratitude to all the workshop participants. Special thanks also to Ameli Tropé, Linn Fenna Groeneveld, Kristin Hoel Brenden, and Jan F. Nygård at the Cancer Registry of Norway and Mona Stensrud and Ingvill Moe at the Norwegian Cancer Society for their comments on the manuscript and their fruitful collaboration throughout this project. Special thanks to Charlotte J. Haug for her contributions to the manuscript. The "ShowMe" project receives funding support from the Norwegian Research Council, grant 321081.

References

Anderssen, H. (2021, October 12). Kvinner som ikke har testet seg for livmorhalskreft på 8–10 år får tilbud om hjemmetest. Retrieved July 3, 2022, from https://www.healthtalk.no/alle-art ikler/onkologi-tilbud-om-hjemmetest-for-livmorhalskreft-til-kvinner-som-ikke-har-testet-seg-på-8-10-år/.

Bzhalava, D., Eklund, C., & Dillner, J. (2015). International standardization and classification of human papillomavirus types. *Virology, 476* n.d), 341–344. https://doi.org/10.1016/j.virol.2014. 12.028.

Cancer Registry of Norway. (n.d.). *Cervical cancer screening programme.* Retrieved July 1, 2022, from https://www.kreftregisteret.no/en/screening/cervix/org/.

Ciavattini, A., Delli Carpini, G., Giannella, L., Del Fabro, A., Banerji, V., Hall, G., Barbero, M., & Sopracordevole, F. (2021). An online survey on emotions, impact on everyday life, and educational needs of women with HPV positivity or abnormal Pap smear result. *Medicine, 100*(45), e27177. https://doi.org/10.1097/MD.0000000000027177

Dahl, Y., Linander, H., & Hanssen, G. K. (2014). Co-designing interactive tabletop solutions for active patient involvement in audiological consultations. In *Proceedings of the 8th Nordic Conference on Human-Computer Interaction: Fun, Fast, Foundational*, October 26–30, 2014, Helsinki, Finland, NordiCHI '14 (pp. 207–216). https://doi.org/10.1145/2639189.2639221

Daley, E. M., Perrin, K. M. (Kay), McDermott, R. J., Vamos, C. A., Rayko, H. L., Packing-Ebuen, J. L., Webb, C., & McFarlane, M. (2010). The psychosocial burden of HPV: A mixed-method study of knowledge, attitudes and behaviors among HPV+ women. *Journal of Health Psychology, 15*(2), 279–290. https://doi.org/10.1177/1359105309351249.

Engesæter, B., Groeneveld, L., Skare, G., & Tropé, A. (2020). *Screeningaktivitet og resultater fra Livmorhalsprogrammet Årsrapport 2020.* Retrieved July 3, 2022, from https://www.kreftregiste ret.no/globalassets/livmorhalsprogrammet/rapporter/arsrapport-lp/arsrapport2020_final.pdf.

Gale, R. C., Wu, J., Erhardt, T., Bounthavong, M., Reardon, C. M., Damschroder, L. J., & Midboe, A. M. (2019). Comparison of rapid vs in-depth qualitative analytic methods from a process evaluation of academic detailing in the Veterans Health Administration. *Implementation Science, 14*(1), 11. https://doi.org/10.1186/s13012-019-0853-y

Goldsmith, M., Bankhead, C., & Austoker, J. (2006). *Improving the quality of the written informatoin sent to woman about cervical screening.* NHSCSP. Retrieved July 3, 2022, from https://assets.publishing.service.gov.uk/government/uploads/system/uploads/attach ment_data/file/465874/nhscsp26.pdf.

Head, K. J., Imburgia, T. M., Zimet, G. D., & Shew, M. L. (2017). Women's understanding of their Pap and HPV test results: Implications for patient–provider communication. *Journal of Communication in Healthcare, 10*(1), 37–46. https://doi.org/10.1080/17538068.2017.1282085

Klungsøyr, O., Nygård, M., Skare, G., Eriksen, T., & Nygård, J. F. (2009). Validity of self-reported Pap Smear history in Norwegian women. *Journal of Medical Screening, 16*(2), 91–97. https://doi.org/10.1258/jms.2009.008087

Leedy, P. D., & Ormrod, J. E. (2019). *Practical research: Planning and design* (12th ed., p. 272). Pearson.

Lindau, S. T., Tomori, C., Lyons, T., Langseth, L., Bennett, C. L., & Garcia, P. (2002). The association of health literacy with cervical cancer prevention knowledge and health behaviors in a multiethnic cohort of women. *American Journal of Obstetrics and Gynecology, 186*(5), 938–943. https://doi.org/10.1067/mob.2002.122091

Markovic-Denic, L., Djuric, O., Maksimovic, N., Popovac, S., & Kesic, V. (2018). Effects of human papillomavirus awareness and knowledge on psychological state of women referred to cervical cancer screening. *Journal of Lower Genital Tract Disease, 22*(3), 178–183. https://doi.org/10.1097/LGT.0000000000000397

Marlow, L., Forster, A. S., McBride, E., Rockliffe, L., Kitchener, H., & Waller, J. (2020). Information needs among women taking part in primary HPV screening in England: A content analysis. *British Medical Journal Open, 10*(12), e044630. https://doi.org/10.1136/bmjopen-2020-044630

McBride, E., Tatar, O., Rosberger, Z., Rockliffe, L., Marlow, L. A. V., Moss-Morris, R., Kaur, N., Wade, K., & Waller, J. (2021). Emotional response to testing positive for human papillomavirus at cervical cancer screening: A mixed method systematic review with meta-analysis. *Health Psychology Review, 15*(3), 395–429. https://doi.org/10.1080/17437199.2020.1762106

Mitchell, V., Ross, T., May, A., Sims, R., & Parker, C. (2016). Empirical investigation of the impact of using co-design methods when generating proposals for sustainable travel solutions. *CoDesign, 12*(4), 205–220. https://doi.org/10.1080/15710882.2015.1091894

Monsonego, J., Cortés, J., Silva, D., Jorge, A., & Klein, P. (2011). Psychological impact, support and information needs for women with an abnormal Pap smear: Comparative results of a questionnaire in three European countries. *BMC Women's Health, 11*(1), 18. https://doi.org/10.1186/1472-6874-11-18

Nielsen, L. (2011). personas in co-creation and co-design. n.d., n.d.

Nutbeam, D. (2000). Health literacy as a public health goal: A challange for contemporary health education and communication strategies into the 21st century. *Health Promotion International, 15*(3), 259–267.

O'Connor, M., Costello, L., Murphy, J., Prendiville, W., Martin, C., O'Leary, J., Sharp, L., & the I. S. R. Consortium (CERVIVA). (2014). 'I don't care whether it's HPV or ABC, I just want to know if I have cancer.' Factors influencing women's emotional responses to undergoing human papillomavirus testing in routine management in cervical screening: A qualitative study. *BJOG: An International Journal of Obstetrics & Gynaecology, 121*(11), 1421–1430. https://doi.org/10.1111/1471-0528.12741.

Papa, D., Moore Simas, T. A., Reynolds, M., & Melnitsky, H. (2009). Assessing the role of education in women's knowledge and acceptance of adjunct high-risk human Papillomavirus testing for cervical cancer screening. *Journal of Lower Genital Tract Disease, 13*(2), 66–71. https://doi.org/10.1097/LGT.0b013e31818a53f0

N.d. (2022a). Participatory design. *Wikipedia.* Retrieved July 3, 2022, from https://en.wikipedia.org/w/index.php?title=Participatory_design&oldid=1081804462.

N.d. (2022b). Pull technology. *Wikipedia.* Retrieved July 3, 2022, from https://en.wikipedia.org/w/index.php?title=Pull_technology&oldid=1083662193.

N.d. (2022c). Push Technologie. *Wikipedia.* Retrieved July 3, 2022, from https://en.wikipedia.org/w/index.php?title=Push_technology&oldid=1095286228.

Siegel, L. (2022). Under Kontroll. The Oslo school of Architecture and Design (Ed.). Oslo.

Soper, B. C., Nygård, M., Abdulla, G., Meng, R., & Nygård, J. F. (2020). A hidden Markov model for population-level cervical cancer screening data. *Statistics in Medicine, 39*(25), 3569–3590. https://doi.org/10.1002/sim.8681

Szwarc, L., Sánchez Antelo, V., Paolino, M., & Arrossi, S. (2021). "I'm neither here, which would be bad, nor there, which would be good": The information needs of HPV+ women. A qualitative study based on in-depth interviews and counselling sessions in Jujuy, Argentina. *Sexual and Reproductive Health Matters, 29*(1), 453–463. https://doi.org/10.1080/26410397.2021.199 1101.

Trischler, J., Pervan, S. J., Kelly, S. J., & Scott, D. R. (2018). The value of codesign: The effect of customer involvement in service design teams. *Journal of Service Research, 21*(1), 75–100. https://doi.org/10.1177/1094670517714060

Vaccarella, S., Franceschi, S., Engholm, G., Lönnberg, S., Khan, S., & Bray, F. (2014). 50 years of screening in the Nordic countries: Quantifying the effects on cervical cancer incidence. *British Journal of Cancer, 111*(5), 965–969. https://doi.org/10.1038/bjc.2014.362

Verhoeven, V., Baay, M. F. D., Baay, P. E., Lardon, F., Van Royen, P., & Vermorken, J. B. (2010). Everything you always wanted to know about HPV (but could not ask your doctor). *Patient Education and Counseling, 81*(1), 101–105. https://doi.org/10.1016/j.pec.2009.12.006

Sandra Klonteig is a researcher at SINTEF Digital, Norway. She is part of the Department of Health Research, focusing on population health, healthcare systems, services, stakeholders, and technologies to improve health and quality of life in the population, as well as sustainable and efficient healthcare services of high quality. Klonteig has a strong interest in research on women's health, and her expertise lies in the intersection of technology in health services, psychology, and human–computer interaction. Specifically, she focuses on the triangulation of research methods to capture human experiences when interacting with health services through technology.

Jiaxin Li is a researcher at SINTEF Digital, Norway. She is part of the research group Human-Computer Interaction, specializing in the interplay between technology, humans, and society. Li's interest and expertise lie in human-centered design, participatory design, service design, and information visualization, specifically in understanding users' problems and needs and exploring solutions in various technologies.

Ragnhild Halvorsrud is a senior researcher at SINTEF Digital, Norway. She is part of the research group Human-Computer Interaction, specializing in the interplay between technology, humans, and society. Halvorsrud's expertise spans the fields of service science to the empirical investigation of human experiences and modeling of user journeys. Through several research and innovation projects, she has led the development of a modeling language for user journeys, which has been adopted by public and private service providers both nationally and internationally.

Not just Targets: Human Prospects in Health Services for All—Insights from an Italian Case Study on Covid-19 Vaccination and Preventive Services

Gianluca Antonucci, Marco Berardi, and Andrea Ziruolo

ABSTRACT

The sustainability of national health services focuses on the efficient and effective use of devoted public resources. On the one hand, new public management (NPM) theories guide public systems toward a more managerial and competitive approach. On the other, the new public governance (NPG) paradigm takes a relational service-dominant approach. Framed by this dichotomy in the literature, this chapter—based on an Italian case study on Covid-19 vaccinations and preventive services—examines which factors foster the planning and implementation of effective universal public health services. In particular, this study—through an analysis conducted in the field that incorporates semi-structured interviews and surveys with both health professionals and users—outlines effective and efficient elements which were found to be foundational, independently of whether they could be traced back to NPM or NPG frameworks. On the one hand, targets and logistics, as well as the "use" of already structured components (e.g., military forces), and downsizing, etc., appeared to be central in spinning the wheel and measuring achievements. On the other, trust in the system as well as in the personnel (from civil servants to general practitioners and health staff), and the existence of solid relations between practitioners and users, etc., were fundamental in motivating people to become vaccinated also if, in the analyzed phase, there were no obligations. In the conclusion, based on our results, we sketch some features determining a

G. Antonucci (✉) · M. Berardi · A. Ziruolo
DEA—Department of Business Administration, "G. d'Annunzio" University of Chieti-Pescara, Viale Pindaro 42, 65127 Pescara, Italy
e-mail: gianluca.antonucci@unich.it

A. Ziruolo
e-mail: andrea.ziruolo@unich.it

© The Author(s), under exclusive license to Springer Nature Switzerland AG 2023
M. A. Pfannstiel (ed.), *Human-Centered Service Design for Healthcare Transformation*,
https://doi.org/10.1007/978-3-031-20168-4_20

scheme of interrelations among the different factors that should be considered in planning effective and efficient health services for all.

1   Background and Research Aim

Nearly three years ago, cases of Covid-19 were found outside China, leading to the declaration of a pandemic by the World Health Organization (Cucinotta & Vanelli, 2020). We now know that nothing will be the same again (Caroppo et al., 2021). The shaping of the post-pandemic era depends on our capacities to reinvent the world after the crisis (Katzourakis, 2022). Overcoming Covid-19 and resetting the public sector management system is largely considered the "hardest challenge of the century" (Organization for Economic Co-operation and Development [OECD], 2021a).

Healthcare systems, especially public ones—which were asked to redesign, in a short time, their service delivery processes based on the need to reduce contact among individuals, thus disrupting the "in-hospital" paradigm of service providing—are now dealing with the request for a "new normal" able to contend with the future. This is because the importance of placing primary healthcare at the core of health systems has been demonstrated, both to manage an unexpected surge of demand and maintain continuity of care for all (OECD, 2021b). In most countries, esteem for public health services and respect for medical research are changing accordingly (Bargain & Aminjonov, 2020). The Covid-19 crisis is contributing, among other factors, by requiring a better consideration of value-based healthcare creation (Teisberg et al., 2020), necessitating the involvement of professionals, organizations, and institutions engaged in supplying services, as well as the active role of patients/users.

With this search for a new normal in public health systems, this chapter takes into account that the sustainability of national health services (NHSs) still has to focus on the efficient and effective use of devoted public resources. Nevertheless, we sustain the idea that, in the case of such a complex system, some basic elements should be considered, preventing a "simple" application of public management theories.

Looking at the major theoretical forces which have been driving public sector reforms (including public health ones) in the last decades, we have a kind of dichotomy. On the one hand, new public management (NPM) theories (Hood, 1991, 1995) guide NHSs toward a more managerial approach and a competitive basis for providing services. NPM is driven by a business equation, which treats production and consumption separately. On the other hand, the new public governance (NPG) paradigm (Osborne, 2006, 2009) takes a relational service-dominant approach. It emphasizes relationships in service delivery systems, affirming that a managerial approach cannot capture the complexity of health services, because a product-dominant basis is counter-productive in designing universal health services, especially in healthcare, where the staff represent a key component.

Framed by this dichotomy in the literature, and focusing especially on the necessity of a new normal for public health systems, this chapter—based on an Italian case study on Covid-19 vaccinations and preventive services—aims to examine which factors foster the planning and implementation of effective universal public health services. In particular, this evaluation—through an analysis conducted in the field that includes surveys and semi-structured interviews with both health professionals and users—outlines effective and efficient elements found to be foundational, independently of whether they could be traced back to NPM or NPG frameworks.

The choice of Italy as the study case has its relevance because it was the first western country to detect a case of Covid-19 and was among the most severely hit in the first two quarters of 2020 (Balmford et al., 2020). It recorded, in the first year of the pandemic, more than 90,000 deaths and over 2,500,000 illnesses (Senate of the Italian Republic, 2021), thus pushing the government to enact several restrictions on Italian citizens, with an initial severe lockdown of three months followed by a series of other restrictions. At the end of 2021 the increase in deaths—despite the greater infectivity incidence of the Alpha and then Delta variations which had arrived in the meantime (Pouwels et al., 2021)—was reduced to 50,000 in a year, and the most important change was that the pressure on health services was finally constantly decreasing (Ministero della Salute, 2022).

A significant role in this turnaround, in terms of the decrease in the incidence of acute infections, was played by the local branches of the Italian NHS (Cepiku et al., 2021). This occurred regardless of the fact that the Italian NHS System, as redefined by a constitutional law in 2001, has great disparities among the territories in terms of quality and expenses (Garattini et al., 2022).

Starting from the considerations reported above, our study intends to investigate the issue at a public policy level, overturning its logics. We sustain the thesis that a public NHS system cannot be based only on the definition of targets to be achieved—although these are fundamental in allowing for planning, monitoring, and accountability—but should also consider other factors, which, although not easily measurable, are at the base of its quality and thus its effectiveness.

This paper is structured as follows: after this introduction, the Sect. 2 depicts the theoretical framework regarding the dichotomy between NPM and NPG. The Sect. 3 describes the relevance of the case study, while the Sect. 4 illustrates the research methodology. The Sect. 5 one reports the findings, followed by the discussion of the results in the Sect. 6. The Sect. 7 provides some final remarks to conclude this chapter.

2 Theoretical Framework: Fallacies in the Definition of Targets for Public Health Service Systems

A foundational turnaround in fostering the sustainability of public services in terms of the efficient and effective use of devoted public resources can be traced to the dawn of NPM theories at the beginning of the 1990s. According to Hood (1991)—who can be considered the father of NPM—seven interrelated components are foundational in NPM: hands-on professional management, explicit standards and measures of performance, greater emphasis on output controls, the disaggregation of units in the public sector, a shift to greater competition, a stress on private sector styles of management practice, and an emphasis on greater discipline and parsimony in resource use. Later on, Pollitt (1995) described NPM as being composed of eight factors: cost cutting and transparency in resource allocation; the downsizing of bureaucratic organizations into separate agencies; decentralization through public agencies; a distinction between public services provision and purchasing; the introduction of market- and quasi-market-type mechanisms; performance management through targets, indicators, and output objectives; changes in public employment rules with management-related pay; and increasing emphasis on service quality, standard setting, and customer responsiveness.

NPM was initially regarded as an administrative philosophy for governments to be result-oriented and productive (Atreya & Armstrong, 2002). Several academics contributed to defining and drafting NPM through different points of view (e.g., Gore, 1993; OECD, 1995; Osborne & Gaebler, 1992) which, although not providing a unique common shared definition of NPM, emphasized the necessity of reforming governments to make them effective and responsive to citizen demands. Its foundational element was managerialism, that is, the application to the public sector of management rules and principles which were thought valid and effective in private businesses. This assumption was sustained by the idea that all human behaviors were dominated by self-interest, thus aiming at maximizing personal benefits (Boston et al., 1996).

All through the 1990s, NPM seemed to be the silver bullet for transforming the public sector and especially the delivery of public services. But in the same period citizens' expectations were becoming more sophisticated, thus requiring greater focus on choice and quality in the provision of public services. This was leading to a paradigmatic revolution which no longer saw the hegemony of the state in meeting expressed public needs, rather than more complex different approaches, which increasingly required the governance of multiple relationships among service providers (Osborne & Brown, 2005).

The result has been a change in the nature of public services provision which increasingly became a task no longer undertaken by a single entity, but rather by a range of organizations in what has become known as the plural state (Osborne & McLaughlin, 2002), which includes "different" organizations (from government, non-profit, and business sectors) that need to collaborate in the provision of public services, focusing their attention not on the administration of public services, but rather on their management and governance, where the governance of plural relationships has become the central task for the provision of effective public services (Kickert et al., 1997).

Inspired by the considerations reported above, public management theories viewed the development of NPG (Osborne, 2006) as an important paradigm of public services delivery. It is based on the consideration that public services should move beyond the transactional approach of NPM, taking a relational and public service-dominant approach. This service-dominant approach ought to be based on "building relationships across the public service delivery system, understanding that sustainability derives from the transformation of user knowledge and professional understanding of the public service delivery process and being predicated upon the inalienable co-production of public services with service users" (Osborne et al., 2014, p. 314). This implies a more plural and pluralist model of governance and provision, especially in welfare and health services, based on public–private networks, where citizens play a more active role as co-producers of some of the services they expect, demand, or even depend on, in their daily lives (Pestoff, 2014).

These changes are necessary, according to NPG principles, because such services cannot be driven by a business equation (as inspired by NPM), which treats production and consumption separately, assuming that the costs of the former can be reduced without affecting the latter (Osborne et al., 2014). On the contrary, in the production of public services—which are completely different from manufactured products because production and consumption are simultaneous, and also because they are intangible, heterogeneous and inseparable (Moeller, 2010)—the reduction of production costs directly affects their quality.

Although, since the mid-2000s, the NPG paradigm has highlighted some incongruences of NPM, some basic elements have nevertheless maintained their influence upon public health services planning, especially the assumption that most civil servants and front-line staff have to be incentivized by targets to achieve policy objectives (Le Grand, 1997). Indeed, setting targets has been viewed as the best way to monitor and account from the center of governments (from national to local branches) to the front lines (Kettl, 2008) because, according to managerialism and self-interest assumptions, data collection is the most effective means to "force" staff to improve performance, either by promising rewards or threatening punishments (Davies et al., 2021).

In terms of our field specifically, it is known that measuring service productivity is challenging due to its intangibility (Jääskeläinen, 2009) and management in the healthcare sector should be properly addressed (Sousa et al., 2021; Vold & Haave, 2020).

Since the beginning of the 2010s (if not before), western countries' governments have been searching for a way to improve the quality and efficiency of health systems. The strategy of this decade mainly tries to support and "modernize" the primary care sector to better engage with the rest of the healthcare system (Armitage et al., 2009). This change should be based on the unification/integration of care among sectors, continuity of chronic care for patients and families, and community-based health services (Rosen et al., 2011). But if the aim and the output are clear, the method to achieve them has not yet been determined (Nicholson et al., 2013).

It has indeed been noted that the need for these reforms, especially in countries with public NHSs, is arriving after decades during which public health systems were permeated by reforms inspired by NPM theories and principles (Cairney, 2002), whose efficacy, in a system as unique as healthcare, has not been a success (Andrews et al., 2019). In recent years, on the contrary, instead of an increase in efficiency and effectiveness, we have been witnessing a fragmentation of health services which has created a complex, rapidly changing, and often impersonal health system, which is difficult to manage for the well-being of citizens (Jackson et al., 2010).

When discussing innovation in a healthcare system, the internal and external collaborations, between hospitals and other parties, need to be specifically analyzed, investigating how the healthcare innovation environments behave and how flows within them are managed (Polónia & Gradim, 2021). In this situation it must also be noted that the demands of healthcare services in western countries are changing greatly. First, the aging of the population is increasing the number of patients with multi-pathological chronic conditions (Hajat & Stein, 2018). Second, most of the patients are, nowadays, more informed, thus leading to a rise in expectations for public healthcare systems (Parker, 2006). Moreover, there are financial pressures which require public healthcare organizations to provide greater and better services with equal (if not decreasing) resources (Gabutti et al., 2017). As a consequence, healthcare systems are destined to change. Their own sustainability in time requires outstanding levels of performance in terms of quality, and efficiency, as well as equity and appropriateness (Zaadoud et al., 2021).

All these aspects assume a particular relevance in a country like Italy, one of the countries with the most aged populations in the world and with a public NHS which must be modified accordingly (Mazzola et al., 2016). Its public NHS, as redefined by the constitutional law in 2001 (which assigned to the regions the responsibilities of health planning and management within their borders, fixed at a national level for all) has great disparities among the territories in terms of quality and expenses (Garattini et al., 2022). Nevertheless, despite these variations and problems, during the peaks of the Covid-19 pandemic, a fundamental role was played by public bodies and by the local branches of the Italian NHS (Cepiku et al., 2021). We, therefore, decided to study "how" these branches acted and especially reacted in such a unique situation. In synthesis, we used the Covid-19 period as a litmus test to analyze the relevant factors which acted, in an emergency situation, and were able to find valid solutions. Our idea is that these elements should be at the basis of the planning and implementation of the needed primary care services of the aspiring new normal.

3   Management of a Health Emergency

The Covid-19 health emergency represents the most dramatic international event since the Second World War onwards, affecting the entire global population in a silent and transversal manner. Faced with an international health emergency, Italy was the most severely hit country in the first two quarters of 2020. The impact of the pandemic on the national health system was devastating, to say the least, as several governments indicated that they were aiming to "push down" the epidemic curve. The evolution of the epidemic in Italy supports the World Health Organization's recommendation that stricter containment measures should be introduced as early as possible in the epidemic curve (Sebastiani et al., 2020).

After investigating the main efforts by the public system in the post-pandemic era, many authors have suggested Italy was the first western country to address the effects of the pandemic and quickly reacted with specific reforms and national measures (Malandrino & Demichelis, 2020). In this context, different scholars have conducted studies on the contribution of public policies to the creation of public value, including in relation to the healthcare system, municipalities, and social services (Capano et al., 2020).

According to this logic (considering that, as noted before, the Italian NHS system includes different autonomous regional authorities which act according to national indications) the management of the health services of each region had to analyze the contribution of the national policy, along with the engagement among politicians, health managers, local administrators, and citizens, in order to overcome Covid-19, based on the rationale of the "achievement of public value" (Bracci et al., 2019).

We thus decided to concentrate our analysis on one of the Italian regions, to be able to examine it in depth, considering all the different components of one location, instead of undertaking comparisons which could be misleading. We chose the Abruzzo region because it can be considered significant as it is, according to data, a median one in most of the Italian National Institute for Statistics (ISTAT) indicators. Most importantly, it was among the regions which had to change their health systems during the 2000s because it was one of those with the largest deficits in health accounts (the so-called rogue regions), and then became one of the "virtuous ones" (Consiglio Regione Abruzzo, 2011). Thus, it was an area which passed through a long period of strict control in terms of targets and objectives that had to be respected. Moreover, it has been one of the zones that were hardest hit in Italy during the spreading of the "second wave" of the pandemic (October 2020, January 2021), but also among those with a relatively small proportion of casualties considering the number of infections (Minsalute, 2021).

During the first months of the pandemic, the Abruzzo region built up (following the similar path given at national level) a special "task force," composed of medical doctors (who were mostly also academics in the fields of epidemiology and virology), politicians, and local managers, along with data analysts and engineers, to analyze the "wave of contagion" during the management of the emergency, the so-called "wise man committee" (Regione Abruzzo, 2020).

While the first months of the pandemic were considered a "punch in the face" and the NHS collapsed under the "fire of the enemy," the task force built up algorithmics to analyze the spreading of the contagion along with the ethical best practices to prevent it (Regione Abruzzo, 2020). During the second wave, the lessons learnt by the task force contributed to the operational capacity of the public administrations and materialized the production of objectively valid results for citizens.

In terms of extraordinary events not attributable to humans that will arise, such as, for example, natural disasters or pandemic events, part of the international literature underlines the key role of central governments in the management of business processes "in an emergency," highlighting how the classical paradigms of programming (Hood, 1995; Moore, 1995; Papi et al., 2018) concerning the declination in "objective indicators and targets," is overcome by the need to preserve trust between citizens and institutions (Bargain & Aminjonov, 2020).

In these scenarios, there is a need to reorganize the "public administration," both from a regulatory point of view, but above all, from an operational one, especially in the case of healthcare services, by resorting to best practices consolidated over time (Sargiacomo, 2015). The interesting although sad point, in our case, is that such an emergency as the Covid-19 pandemic had no precedents, so almost no best practices to resort to.

In this regard, many authors underline how the alignment between governance and public administration managers is one of the key elements in achieving institutional performance (Walker et al., 2013). On the other hand, "internal alignment" alone is not sufficient, as the effects of an "emergency" are also conditioned by the behavior of subjects external to the "public administration" in the strictest sense. In our specific case, this meant citizens and stakeholders who had, in the first period, respected the lockdown and then followed rules regarding the proper use of personal protective equipment, and finally agreed to being vaccinated.

In addition, the international literature emphasizes that the positive effects of policies cannot ignore the will of citizens to align themselves with the choices made by administrators, even where the alignment involves limitations to individual freedoms. These restrictions are, as shown by various authors, not always welcomed, even when they are functional to the achievement of a higher good (Battiston et al., 2020).

Having considered all of the above, we decided to investigate whether there were specificities in such a unique situation which could address the planning of the new normal in public NHS systems. We chose to examine both sides, the delivery of the public NHS on the one hand and the perspective of the recipients on the other. We chose to do this because Italian citizens, as demonstrated, in comparison to the cliché, displayed a great respect for these rules (Guaitoli & Pancrazi, 2021) as well as a high level of vaccinations, especially in 2021 (Marziano et al., 2021), thus representing a great collaboration (during the first two waves of the Covid-19 pandemic).

4   Research Design and Methodology

Aiming at investigating influencing factors, rather than targets, regarding the effectiveness of an NHS system, we undertook a case study addressing the "why" and "how" issues (Yin, 1994) of these specific public services (Osborne & Strokosch, 2013).

We present here the result of an investigation which is part of a large ongoing project focusing on changes in local public administrations, during and after the most impactful waves of Covid-19. Considering that we wanted to investigate perceptions and ideas of both health services administrators and citizens in such an emergency, we decided to conduct a survey along with semi-structured interviews when the "Alpha variant" had just become predominant in Italy, and the vaccination campaign had recently been opened to the whole population (after the priorities which had been given first to the vaccination of health personnel, and others at risk, such as police forces, school personnel, people over 70, and fragile categories).

We were interested in looking for gaps between health administrators' planning and citizens/stakeholders' perceptions, trust, and alignment. We decided to focus on the medical precincts of the Chieti-Pescara metropolitan area, where 1/3 of the whole Abruzzo population lives and which was one of the areas in Italy which were hit hardest by the Covid-19 Alpha variant.

According to our research aims, we prepared two tailored questionnaires measured by a Likert scale scored 1–5, for the two categories, dealing with the following arguments.

1. Governance and trust (Battiston et al., 2020)
2. Public sector communication (Heath et al., 2018)
3. Influence by public opinion (Faour-Klingbeil et al., 2021)
4. Respect for health protocols (Pollak et al., 2020)

For each argument, we derived items (presented in the following section with the different results obtained), considering the literature references cited above.

At the beginning of the mass vaccination, which was open to all age categories (second quarter of 2021), we submitted a survey to citizens that attended for a swab or to be vaccinated in one of the cities' hubs included in our data set. We conducted our data collection by asking people to answer our questions while waiting for their turn, within the dedicated swab and vaccination temporary structures arranged in areas usually used for exhibitions or indoor sports. We established one person for each queue to collect data on different weekly days and in varying hours to avoid any bias due to a possible greater presence of some categories during specific days and/or hours (e.g., schoolteachers had a greater presence on Saturdays mornings). We had been previously specifically authorized to submit the questionnaire by the local public body (health service or municipality, according to the different sites) which requested that we provide a negative swab before the data collection, independently of being vaccinated. We were also properly equipped to avoid any risk of contagion. The data were directly collected by our personnel to avoid any exchange of papers, pens, etc.

Although not obliged to, nearly all the present persons agreed to answer the questionnaire. The average duration, for the data collection, was around 15 min, with a maximum of 25/30 min. The longest interviews were usually with people aged over 70 who, in some cases, needed more explanations (specific control questions were asked in these cases to ensure that the interviewees had no misunderstandings).

All the collected data were then manually transcribed in electronic spreadsheets to allow for data elaboration. We initially tried to use tablets to directly collect data, but we soon found that this was not practicable. For example, we could not repeat the same question to check if the previously given answer was the same. Moreover, in some cases, when asking the control question, we used local slang terms and dialects instead of Italian.

We submitted 343 surveys to citizens who were attending for their turn, as well as 41 surveys to local administrators including the 15 members of the "wise man committee," two mayors of the municipalities of the area, and 24 civil servants. The demographics of the interviewed people, divided in the two categories, are shown in Table 1.

Table 1 Demographics

Items	Decision-makers (41)		Citizens (343)	
	Frequency	%	Frequency	%
Age				
18–30	–	–	46	13
31–44	–	–	93	27
45–59	32	78	157	46
60–79	9	22	42	12
80+	–	–	5	1
Gender				
M	40	98	205	60
F	1	2	138	40
Education				
No schooling completed	–	–	7	2
Nursery school to grade 8	–	–	117	34
High school	–	–	196	57
Bachelor's or master's degree	26	63	21	6
PhD	15	37	2	1

Source Author's own Table (2022)

While conducting the surveys, we verified the availability of respondents to add personal comments and/or impressions about the emergency that they were living. As this was possible, we deepened our investigation with a semi-structured interview, based on the same items. This operational mode allowed for ensuring data reliability through control questions and, most of all, gave us the opportunity to better comprehend the true feelings and opinions of the interviewed persons.

Considering that this further research was not for all the participants, but only for those who needed clarifications, and/or for those who voluntarily wanted to add or say something more, we were not allowed to record them. Indeed, at the beginning we had only planned to carry out the questionnaire by asking the control questions, but we discovered then that several interviewees wanted to express their opinion. We found this desire to express their views interesting. Therefore, we took appropriate notes to document the relevant information and details. The notes of those who wanted to add something as well as some derived from the necessity to clarify points during control questions were analyzed through content analysis (Bauer & Gaskell, 2000).

The research findings are reported in the next section.

5 Findings

During the period of our analysis, the emergency was still spreading, and the efficiency of the health planning measures (from lockdowns in 2020, to mass vaccination beginning in the second quarter of 2021) appeared effective. While the literature, as shown in Sect. 3, evidenced an alignment between policies and institutional performance, our findings revealed partial misalignments, as demonstrated in Table 2, which reports the synthesis elaboration of the different average values from the respective components of the four items.

First of all, it is interesting to note that both the parties had high perceptions about the "respect for health protocols." This was also confirmed by data for that period. From the third quarter of 2021, some problems would arise with the so-called "no-vax" movements, and in 2022 with those arguing for a relaxation of restrictive measures like the obligation to wear masks, but during that period the vast majority was aligned, believing that those protocols were necessary and effective. A partial misalignment was found in "governance and trust," specifically in the different perceptions about the alignment, at local level, with the national protocols, where decision-makers were sure about full respect, while citizens thought that there were distances from what was requested and what realized.

In relation to the other two items, on the contrary, there was a greater distance between the two categories. A common feature in these differences could be found in the underestimation, by decision-makers, of the role of the community, as is discussed in the next section, which reports some explanatory indications arising from the assertions given by people who agreed to discuss their views in more depth during the interview.

Table 2 Results of the surveys

Items	Decision-makers (41)	Citizens and stakeholders (343)
	Likert scale values	Likert scale values
Governance and trust	**3.73**	**3**
Local policy-making aligned with the national protocol	5	2.6
Citizens aligned with the prescriptions/restrictions	3	3.8
The protocol adopted is effective in public healthcare	3.2	2.8
Public sector communication	**5**	**3**
Institutional communication and public debate effectiveness	5	2
Relevance of "trusted" word of mouth	2.6	4.7
Alignment and respect for different prescriptions by local authorities (NHS local branches; municipalities)	5	3.8
Influence by public opinion	**1**	**3**
Any influence from social networks or media (including SMS and WhatsApp) on your opinion on the adequacy of the measures adopted	1	3.8
Any influence on your beliefs about healthcare protocols	1	2.1
Respect for health protocols	**5**	**4.8**
Self and personal respect for protocols	5	4.7
Knowledge about the disrespect of measures by others	Not relevant	5

Source Author's own Table (2022)

6 Discussion

A fundamental component has been found in trust (Battiston et al., 2020). This includes the trust and public confidence of citizens toward decision-makers, and the trust of decision- and policy-makers toward scientists and experts, as well as the hope that citizens will put aside their egos for a better collective good. It is not by chance that aspects regarding targets for measures such as budgeting and public spending were never considered by any of our interviewees. The priority was to structure a system upon "saving lives," not "budget savings." In such an emergency we observe how the conviction of the policy-makers to plan in a traditional manner changes during the imploding of the external environment. While, during the first wave, policy-makers decided to adopt extraordinary measures such as the almost total "lockdown" of the country, during the spread of the Alpha variant, decision-makers had to look to other measures, at varying levels, to counterbalance different risks, taking into consideration that another complete lockdown would have led to other deaths, not of lives but of economies. As a result, the main effort of the public policy has been "save lives" to achieve public value (Faour-Klingbeil et al., 2021).

The difference was based not so much upon trust and alignment, but rather on the way in which this was created and maintained. In particular, decision-makers underestimated the influence, upon citizens, of their peers and especially of "recognized figures" within the unique daily community life modified by the pandemic.

The decision-makers believed that they were acting in the best possible way, taking actions inspired by reliable data, within the legal framework defined at the national level. Most of their assertions highlighted aspects such as: "everything is decided collegially, we analyze objective data and act consequently"; "we give indications to mayors (In Italy, mayors have responsibility for hygiene and public health in their territories and the power to enact specific rules in case of an emergency) and they act according to our indications"; "we now run all our weekly meetings online using dedicated digital platforms, we think we are also going to use it after the pandemic." One aspect in which they demonstrated their beliefs that they were taking the best course of action was the reference, made by most of them, to the decision of December 2020. In the first week of December, the Abruzzo region declared that it was moving from the red classification to orange (According to what was decided in that period by the so-called "emergency laws," each region had to respect rules about restrictions to the free movement of citizens with a classification according to the number of infections per 1 k inhabitants: white (no restrictions), yellow, orange, red (almost a lockdown)) three days before the shift at the national level, thus allowing traditional "Christmas shopping" in the weekend comprising the bank holiday of December 8th. The assertion in this case was "we manage our data daily and we knew we had no risks in those days, while at national level they do weekly elaborations, that is why they thought we were still at risk. We took our decision upon reliable data."

While according to the decision-makers there were, in several cases, references to "citizens are following our indications because they know we are acting for their best and our decisions are taken according to reliable data," for the recipients the situation was slightly more nuanced. If it is true that several citizens declared "I am not an MD, so I must respect the protocol, to guarantee the effectiveness of the prescribed measures. I deeply trust the 'wise man committee" it is also true that in more than a few cases there were other sentiments. We collected several claims that "they limited our freedom in the attempt of decreasing the spreading of the virus, while in other countries, such as the UK and Sweden, personal wills are taken much more into account" or "I am a free citizen, and I cannot tolerate that my mayor limits my moving along with the possibility to meet relatives and friends."

Following this, the question becomes: if these citizens were not completely in agreement with the emergency rules in place, why were they queuing there? We found that the answer was in the role of the community which, in several cases, acted as a "creator" of alignment.

An initial example of this can be seen by analyzing the dealignment in the item "Influence by public opinion." First of all, we found that decision-makers clearly underestimated the relevance of the influence of peers and especially that through social media. In this sense, it must be noted that if on the one hand it is true that Covid-19 pushed toward the digital transformation of public administrations (Gabryelczyk, 2020), on the other, the general population, and young people in particular, increasingly used more social media platforms (Lee et al., 2022). But while the first aspect was viewed, by decision-makers, as a relevant one for the digitalization of health services (e.g., in several cases they reported the "dematerialization" of medical prescriptions) and for making controls and targets more measurable and effective (from the scheduling to the creation of European Union certifications), the second was essentially not considered.

On the contrary, citizens affirmed that the influence received through social media was relevant, and found, as opposed to what the decision-makers believed, the use of public digital tools was not entirely user-friendly, but effective anyway. We discovered that in most cases people located fundamental information (e.g., how to book for a swab or vaccination; which categories were already allowed to book for vaccination; where were the hubs; what were the opening hours) through exchanges of information through social media, rather than searching for institutional communications (whether or not through the web).

Moreover, while digital tools for booking and monitoring the vaccination campaign were seen as a great innovation by the decision-makers, we discovered that those targets were possible, thanks to the help of families rather than because of the effectiveness of the tools. We indeed found that, especially for people aged over 70, using different platforms to provide data and book vaccinations was not so easy. They had the best performance in measured targets of vaccinated people anyway, because every bureaucratic aspect, in most cases, was performed online through the digital platforms by sons, daughters, grandchildren, and even neighbors.

But apart from the completely different perceptions about the increased use of digital tools and their roles, the main point about the different views regarding the possibility for citizens to be influenced by public opinion, was provided by the understanding of the role of communication. According to the decision-makers' beliefs, their institutional communication was good. But most of all, for them, it was clear that they were acting in the best possible way, so citizens were understanding the situation and trusting them. On the contrary, apart from the difference in the obtained results, we found that people, as demonstrated before, were aligned. Nevertheless they also formed their own opinions, so they were not "simply" acting as they were requested to.

We found that a great role in this sense was performed by the community. Apart from the aspects regarding the help in dealing with digital platforms already reported, we discovered that the role of people able to "push" citizens toward a decision (especially that of "trusted figures") was essential. We discovered that—apart from the relevance of digital social networks noted above—in many cases the information was provided by other bodies of the community. People received information and trusted indications from the schools of their children, unions, and even churches. In several cases we noted that people who, as reported above, did not agree with the rules enacted by decision-makers, agreed to be vaccinated anyway (at that time there was no obligation) because of requests from places of work, or because they were persuaded by people they trusted, etc. But most of all a great function was fulfilled by a category not considered in any measures for targets (especially in that phase): the one of the general practitioners (GPs). The GPs were completely trusted, and they were close to their patients. Their role, according to our collected indication, was fundamental in many cases. They were not viewed as part of the NHS system which was, together with local administrators, enacting rules and restrictions. They were trusted persons.

A final element to be emphasized concerns the component "Knowledge about the disrespect of measures by others." This question was not asked of decision-makers because we found that it was not relevant for them. It was, on the contrary, specifically thought to address the difference in citizens' opinions regarding their own respect for protocols and the general respect by the whole population. All the interviewed citizens declared that they had a full respect for the rules but, on the other hand, they also claimed to know about "some other people" not respecting them. One case also discussed the role played by a citizen as part of the community: "I know that my neighbors, during the second period of partial lockdown, organized parties to celebrate her daughter's bachelor's degree [aspect confirmed by news appeared on local newspaper] so I decided to call cops to stop this dangerous disrespect of the rules."

7   Conclusion

Framed by the dichotomy in the literature between NPM and NPG, and especially looking at the necessity of a new normal for public health systems, this chapter—based on an Italian case study on Covid-19 vaccinations and preventive services—ntended to examine which factors foster the planning and implementation of effective universal public health services. In particular, this study—through an analysis conducted in the field that incorporated surveys and interviews with both health professionals and users—demonstrated some contradictions between the perceptions of decision-makers, whose beliefs are based on data provided by the achievement of targets, and those of the recipients/users, which are based on the creation of their personal convictions. Notably, we found that while there is an alignment, this is not fully based upon trust for decision-makers, but upon a belief constructed by the convincing and help of different organizations, and especially people, of the community. In this sense a great role is played by GPs.

The main emerging aspect, in our research, is the importance of trust between policy-/decision-makers and stakeholders, as suggested by part of the literature.

The alignment between decision-makers and stakeholders is the key tool for managing local public services and preserving public value (Al Ahbabi et al., 2019; Walker et al., 2013). But the point is that alignment can be seen as the result of different components, of which trust in decision-makers is only one, and sometimes the less relevant one. The greater trust is in the community, and particularly the people acting in it. In our case the role of GPs was found to be fundamental, although it was not measured by any of the targets and not even considered by the decision-makers interviewed.

In this sense, the sharing of information and knowledge (Gore & Gore, 1999) along with creative solutions emerged by seeing things in new ways and redefining problems (Sternberg et al., 1997). It has been pushed by a "smart governance" approach that, along with the pandemic, overcame the traditional manner of managing Italian local authorities.

According to our research, the new normal of public NHS systems should be inspired by this smart approach rather than being focused only on NPM theories or the NPG paradigm. On the one hand, targets, logistics, the "use" of already structured components, downsizing, etc., appear to be central in spinning the wheel and measuring achievements. On the other, trust in the system and in the personnel (from civil servants to GPs and health personnel within the community), as well as the existence of solid relations between practitioners and users, etc., are fundamental in enabling alignment.

Our results confirm that a fragmentation of health services, especially through an impersonal health system, is not effective for the well-being of citizens (Jackson et al., 2010) because alignment is produced by trust in the community and not in the service. Therefore, the new normal should be based on the unification/integration of care among sectors, through community-based health services (Rosen et al., 2011). Moreover, we saw that most of the patients are, nowadays, more informed, thus leading to a rise in expectations of public healthcare systems (Parker, 2006), but this growth of information is provided by synergies among different components, in which the role of trusted competent persons is fundamental. In our case, that of GPs was particularly relevant.

On the one hand, it is true that financial pressures require public healthcare organizations to provide more and better services with equal (if not decreasing) resources (Gabutti et al., 2017), thus requiring the sustainability of public NHS systems, as well as an outstanding level of performance in terms of quality, efficiency, as well as equity and appropriateness (Zaadoud et al., 2021). On the other hand, it is also true, according to our results, that an outstanding performance cannot be achieved "simply" though targets, but the importance of interaction with the community, and especially trust toward personnel, must be considered. It is people's trust toward these figures which means an alignment can enable the achievement of better results. In our case, the significance of GPs is in line with the research of Spandonaro et al. (2021), which found that Italian citizens quoted the relationship with GPs as the greatest strength of the Italian NHS system.

We would like to conclude by giving an example of the importance of not only considering targets, but also the level of personnel professionalism, in a delicate field such as public health.

At the beginning of our research, the regional services were free to organize their own vaccinations and there were several differences among territories. Then the organization was centralized (under the authority of military services under the command of General Figliuolo, chief of military logistics) and hubs were monitored at the regional level, providing data to the national system to check the entirety. Even the platform for booking vaccinations was established at national level (in collaboration with the Italian Post Office). All decision-makers interviewed in the second period of our investigations highlighted the effectiveness of the modified system with the definition of targets, procedures, monitoring systems, etc. Indeed, the new system allowed Italy to reach, in that period, one of the highest performances in Europe in terms of vaccinations per day (WHO, 2021).

Nevertheless, in considering the importance of targets, we must remember that everything in Europe started because the first case of a person positive for Covid-19 in the area was found in Italy, although he had never visited China or been in contact with people who had been in China in the previous weeks. This detection was possible because a doctor of the Italian NHS decided to go further than the strict respect of the limitations given by the fixed targets. She decided to "use" a swab to detect positivity to Covid-19 despite the fact that, according to the rules which were then in force, she was wasting public money using a swab (which in February 2020 were expensive and especially hard to find) for a person who had not been tested according to fixed protocols. In that moment she was at risk of a disciplinary action, but her professional personal judgment allowed for an earlier intervention and probably saved a lot of lives, and not only that of the individual who has now become known as patient No. 1.

References

Al Ahbabi, S. A., Singh, S. K., Balasubramanian, S., & Gaur, S. S. (2019). Employee perception of impact of knowledge management processes on public sector performance. *Journal of Knowledge Management, 23*(2), 351–373. https://doi.org/10.1108/JKM-08-2017-0348

Andrews, R., Beynon, M. J., & McDermott, A. (2019). Configurations of new public management reforms and the efficiency, effectiveness and equity of public healthcare systems: A fuzzy-set qualitative comparative analysis. *Public Management Review, 21*(8), 1236–1260. https://doi.org/10.1080/14719037.2018.1561927

Atreya, B., & Armstrong, A. (2002). *A review of the criticisms and the future of new public management* [Working paper]. Victoria University, Melbourne, Australia. Retrieved April 9, 2022, from https://vuir.vu.edu.au/169

Armitage, G. D., Suter, E., Oelke, N. D., & Adair, C. E. (2009). Health systems integration: State of the evidence. *International Journal of Integrated Care, 9*, e82. https://doi.org/10.5334/ijic.316

Balmford, B., Annan, J. D., Hargreaves, J. C., Altoè, M., & Bateman, I. J. (2020). Cross-country comparisons of Covid-19: Policy, politics and the price of life. *Environmental and Resource Economics, 76*(4), 525–551. https://doi.org/10.1007/s10640-020-00466-5

Bargain, O., & Aminjonov, U. (2020). Trust and compliance to public health policies in times of COVID-19. *Journal of Public Economics, 192*(104316), 104316. https://doi.org/10.1016/j.jpu beco.2020.104316

Battiston, P., Kashyap, R., & Rotondi, V. (2020). Trust in science and experts during the COVID-19 outbreak in Italy. OSF Preprints 100721. https://doi.org/10.31219/osf.io/twuhj

Bauer, M. W., & Gaskell, G. (2000). *Qualitative researching with text, image and sound.* London: Sage Publishing.

Boston, J., Martin, J., Pallot, J., & Walsh, P. (1996). *Public management: The New Zealand model.* Oxford: Oxford University Press.

Bracci, E., Papi, L., Bigoni, M., Deidda Gagliardo, E., & Bruns, H. J. (2019). Public value and public sector accounting research: A structured literature review. *Journal of Public Budgeting, Accounting & Financial Management, 31*(1), 103–136. https://doi.org/10.1108/JPBAFM-07-2018-0077

Cairney, P. (2002). New public management and the Thatcher healthcare legacy: Enough of the theory, what about the implementation? *The British Journal of Politics and International Relations, 4*(3), 375–398. https://doi.org/10.1111/1467-856X.00085

Capano, G., Howlett, M., Jarvis, D. S. L., Ramesh, M., & Goyal, N. (2020). Mobilizing policy (in)capacity to fight COVID-19: Understanding variations in state responses. *Policy and Society, 39*(3), 85–308. https://doi.org/10.1080/14494035.2020.1787628

Caroppo, E., Mazza, M., Sannella, A., Marano, G., Avallone, C., Claro, A. E., Janiri, D., Moccia, L., Janiri, L., & Sani, G. (2021). Will nothing be the same again?: Changes in lifestyle during COVID-19 pandemic and consequences on mental health. *International Journal of Environmental Research and Public Health, 18*(16). https://doi.org/10.3390/ijerph18168433

Cepiku, D., Giordano, F., Bovaird, T., & Loeffler, E. (2021). New development: Managing the Covid-19 pandemic—From a hospital-centred model of care to a community co-production approach. *Public Money and Management, 41*(1), 77–80. https://doi.org/10.1080/09540962.2020.1821445

Consiglio Regione Abruzzo. (2011). *Regione Abruzzo da 'Canaglia' a 'Virtuosa' in materia di sanità.* Retrieved June 14, 2021, from https://www.consiglio.regione.abruzzo.it/rassegna-notizie/regione-abruzzo-da-canaglia-virtuosa-materia-di-sanit%C3%A0

Cucinotta, D., & Vanelli, M. (2020). WHO declares COVID-19 a pandemic. *Acta Bio-Medica Atenei Parmensis, 91*(1), 157–160. https://doi.org/10.23750/abm.v91i1.9397

Davies, N., Atkins, G., & Sodhi, S. (2021). *Using targets to improve public services.* Institute for Government, London, UK. Retrieved June 20, 2022, from https://www.instituteforgovernment.org.uk/publications/targets-public-services

Faour-Klingbeil, D., Osaili, T. M., Al-Nabulsi, A. A., Jemni, M., & Todd, E. C. D. (2021). The public perception of food and non-food related risks of infection and trust in the risk communication during COVID-19 crisis: A study on selected countries from the Arab region. *Food Control, 121*(2021), 107617. https://doi.org/10.1016/j.foodcont.2020.107617

Gabryelczyk, R. (2020). Has COVID-19 Accelerated digital transformation? Initial lessons learned for public administrations. *Information Systems Management, 37*(4), 303–309. https://doi.org/10.1080/10580530.2020.1820633

Gabutti, I., Mascia, D., & Cicchetti, A. (2017). Exploring "patient-centered" hospitals: A systematic review to understand change. *BMC Health Services Research, 17*(1), 364. https://doi.org/10.1186/s12913-017-2306-0

Garattini, L., Badinella Martini, M., & Zanetti, M. (2022). The Italian NHS at regional level: Same in theory, different in practice. *The European Journal of Health Economics, 23*(1), 1–5. https://doi.org/10.1007/s10198-021-01322-z

Gore, A. (1993). *The Gore report on reinventing government: Creating a government that works better and costs less.* Report of the National Performance Review, Three Rivers Press, New York, USA.

Gore, C., & Gore, E. (1999). Knowledge management: The way forward. *Total Quality Management, 10*(4–5), 554–560. https://doi.org/10.1080/0954412997523

Guaitoli, G., & Pancrazi, R. (2021). Covid-19: Regional policies and local infection risk: Evidence from Italy with a modelling study. *The Lancet Regional Health—Europe, 8(2021)*, 100169. https://doi.org/10.1016/j.lanepe.2021.100169

Hajat, C., & Stein, E. (2018). The global burden of multiple chronic conditions: A narrative review. *Preventive Medicine Reports, 12*, 284–293. https://doi.org/10.1016/j.pmedr.2018.10.008

Heath, R. L., Johansen, W., Fredriksson, M., & Pallas, J. (2018). Public sector communication. In R. L. Heath, & W. Johansen (Eds.), *The international encyclopedia of strategic communication.* Hoboken, New Jersey, USA: Wiley Online Library. https://doi.org/10.1002/9781119010722.ies c0141

Hood, C. (1991). A public management for all seasons? *Public Administration, 69*(1), 3–19.

Hood, C. (1995). Contemporary public management: A new global paradigm? *Public Policy and Administration, 10*(2), 104–117.

Jääskeläinen, A. (2009). Identifying a suitable approach for measuring and managing public service productivity. *Electronic Journal of Knowledge Management, 7*(4), 447–458. https://academic-publishing.org/index.php/ejkm/article/view/865

Jackson, C. L., Nicholson, C., & McAteer, E. P. (2010). Fit for the future—A regional governance structure for a new age. *The Medical Journal of Australia, 192*(5), 284–287. https://doi.org/10.5694/j.1326-5377.2010.tb03510.x

Katzourakis, A. (2022). COVID-19: Endemic doesn't mean harmless. *Nature, 601*(2022), 485. https://doi.org/10.1038/d41586-022-00155-x

Kettl, D. (2008). Public bureaucracies. In S. Binder, R. Rhodes, & B. Rockman (Eds.), *The Oxford handbook of political institutions* (pp. 366–384). Oxford: Oxford University Press. https://doi.org/10.1093/oxfordhb/9780199548460.003.0019

Kickert, W., Klijn, E.-H., & Koppenjan, J. (1997). *Managing complex networks—Strategies for the public sector.* Thousand Oaks, Kalifornien, USA: Sage. https://doi.org/10.4135/9781446217658

Le Grand, J. (1997). Knights, knaves or pawns? Human behaviour and social policy. *Journal of Social Policy, 26*(2), 149–169. https://doi.org/10.1017/S0047279497004984

Lee, Y., Jeon, Y. J., & Kang, S. (2022). Social media use and mental health during the COVID-19 pandemic in young adults: A meta-analysis of 14 cross-sectional studies. *BMC Public Health, 22*(995), 1–8. https://doi.org/10.1186/s12889-022-13409-0

Malandrino, A., & Demichelis, E. (2020). Conflict in decision making and variation in public administration outcomes in Italy during the COVID-19 crisis. *European Policy Analysis, 6*(2), 138–146. https://doi.org/10.1002/epa2.1093

Marziano, V., Guzzetta, G., & Mammone, A. (2021). The effect of COVID-19 vaccination in Italy and perspectives for living with the virus. *Nature Communication, 12*(7272), 1–8. https://doi.org/10.1038/s41467-021-27532-w

Mazzola, P., et al. (2016). Aging in Italy: The need for new welfare strategies in an old country. *The Gerontologist, 56*(3), 383–390. https://doi.org/10.1093/geront/gnv152

Ministero della Salute. (2022). *Covid-19 Monitoraggi Covid-19 Ministero della della Salute, Roma.* Retrieved Nov 2, 2022, from https://www.salute.gov.it/portale/nuovocoronavirus/archivioMoni toraggiNuovoCoronavirus.jsp

Minsalute. (2021). *Ministero della Salute (Italian Ministry of Health)—Novel coronavirus reports.* Retrieved May 25, 2021, from https://www.salute.gov.it/portale/nuovocoronavirus/homeNuovo Coronavirus.jsp?lingua=english

Moeller, S. (2010). Characteristics of services—A new approach uncovers their value. *Journal of Services Marketing, 24*(5), 359–368.

Moore, M. (1995). *Creating public value: Strategic Management in government.* London, England: Harvard University Press.

Nicholson, C., Jackson, C., & Marley, J. (2013). A governance model for integrated primary/secondary care for the health-reforming first world—Results of a systematic review. *BMC Health Services Research, 13*(1), 528. https://doi.org/10.1186/1472-6963-13-528

Organisation for Economic Co-operation and Development. (1995). *Governance in transition: Public management reform in OECD countries.* Organisation for Economic Co-operation and Development (OECD, Ed.), Paris, Frankreich.

Organisation for Economic Co-operation and Development. (2021a). *The territorial impact of COVID-19: Managing the crisis and recovery across levels of government OECD policy responses to coronavirus (COVID-19).* Retrieved May 10, 2021a, from https://www.oecd.org/coronavirus/policy-responses/the-territorial-impact-of-covid-19-managing-the-crisis-and-rec overy-across-levels-of-government-a2c6abaf/

Organisation for Economic Co-operation and Development. (2021b). *Strengthening the frontline: How primary health care helps health systems adapt during the COVID-19 pandemic POLICY BRIEFS, OECD.* Retrieved May 20, 2022, from https://read.oecd-ilibrary.org/view/?ref=1060_1060243-snyxeld1ii&title=Strengthening-the-frontline-How-primary-health-care-helps-health-systems-adapt-during-the-COVID-19-pandemic

Osborne, S. (2006). The new public governance? *Public Management Review, 8*(30), 377–387. https://doi.org/10.1080/14719030600853022

Osborne, S. (2009). Delivering public services: Are we asking the right questions. *Public Money and Management, 29*(1), 5–7. https://doi.org/10.1080/09540960802617269

Osborne, S., & Brown, K. (2005). *Sustaining change and innovation in public service organizations.* London: Routledge.

Osborne, D., & Gaebler, T. (1992). *Reinventing government: How the entrepreneurial spirit is transforming the public sector.* New York, USA: Prentice-Hall.

Osborne, S., & McLaughlin, K. (2002). From public administration to public governance: Public management and public services in the twenty-first century. In S. Osborne (ed.), *Public management—Critical perspectives* (Vol. I, pp. 1–10). London, England: Routledge.

Osborne, S., & Strokosch, K. (2013). It takes two to tango? Understanding the co-production of public services by integrating the services management and public administration perspectives. *British Journal of Management, 24*(1), 31–47. https://doi.org/10.1111/1467-8551.12010

Osborne, S., Radnor, Z., Kinder, T., & Vidal, I. (2014). Sustainable public service organisations: A public service-dominant approach. *Society and Economy, 36*(3), 313–338.

Papi, L., Bigoni, N., Braci, E., & Deidda Galiardo, E. (2018). Measuring public value: A conceptual and applied contribution to the debate. *Public Money & Management, 38*(7), 503–510. https://doi.org/10.1080/09540962.2018.1439154

Parker, R. M. (2006). What an informed patient means for the future of healthcare. *PharmacoEconomics, 24*(2), 29–33. https://doi.org/10.2165/00019053-200624002-00004

Pestoff, V. (2014). Hybridity, coproduction, and third sector social services in Europe. *American Behavioral Scientist, 58*(11), 1412–1424. https://doi.org/10.1177/0002764214534670

Pollak, Y., Dayan, H., Shoham, R., & Berger, I. (2020). Predictors of non-adherence to public health instructions during the COVID-19 pandemic. *Psychiatry and Clinical Neurosciences, 74*(11), 602–604. https://doi.org/10.1111/pcn.13122

Pollitt, C. (1995). Justification by works or by faith? Evaluating the new public management. *Evaluation, 1*(2), 133–154.

Polónia, D. F., & Gradim, A. C. (2021). Innovation and knowledge flows in healthcare ecosystems: The Portuguese case. *Electronic Journal of Knowledge Management, 18*(3), 374–391. https://doi.org/10.34190/ejkm.18.3.2122

Pouwels, K. B., Pritchard, E., Matthews, P. C., Stoesser, N., Eyre, D. W., Vihta, K.-D., House, T., Hay, J., Bell, J. I., Newton, J. N., Farrar, J., Crook, D., Cook, D., Rourke, E., Studley, R., Peto, T. E. A., Diamond, I., & Walker, A. S. (2021). Effect of Delta variant on viral burden and vaccine effectiveness against new SARS-CoV-2 infections in the UK. *Nature Medicine, 27*(12), 2127–2135. https://doi.org/10.1038/s41591-021-01548-7

Regione Abruzzo. (2020). *Emergenza Covid19—Deliberazioni Ufficio Presidenza.* Retrieved June 12, 2021, from https://www.consiglio.regione.abruzzo.it/taxonomy/term/10880

Rosen, R., Mountford, J., Lewis, G., Lewis, R., Shand, J., & Shaw, S. (2011). *Integration in action: Four international case studies.* The Nuffield Trust (Ed.), London, England.

Sargiacomo, M. (2015). Earthquakes, exceptional government and extraordinary accounting. *Accounting, Organizations and Society, 42*(2015), 67–89. https://doi.org/10.1016/j.aos.2015.02.001

Sebastiani, G., Massa, M., & Riboli, E. (2020). Covid-19 epidemic in Italy: Evolution, projections and impact of government measures. *European Journal of Epidemiology, 35*(4), 341–345. https://doi.org/10.1007/s10654-020-00631-6

Senate of the Italian Republic. (2021). *Documentazione sull'emergenza sanitaria da COVID-19.* Retrieved May 10, 2022, from http://www.senato.it/20101?categoria=1301

Sousa, M. J., Dal Mas, F., & Da Costa, R. L. (2021). Advances in health knowledge management: New perspectives. *The Electronic Journal of Knowledge Management, 18*(3), 407–441.

Spandonaro, F., d'Angela, D., & Polistena, B. (2021). *17° Rapporto CREA Sanità, Il futuro del SSN: vision tecnocratiche e aspettative della popolazione.* Locorotondo Editore. Mesagne (BR). Italy.

Sternberg, R. J., O'Hara, L. A., & Lubart, T. I. (1997). Creativity as investment. *California Management Review, 40*(1), 8–21. https://doi.org/10.2307/41165919

Teisberg, E., Wallace, S., & O'Hara, S. (2020). Defining and implementing value-based health care: A strategic framework. *Academic Medicine: Journal of the Association of American Medical Colleges, 95*(5), 682–685. https://doi.org/10.1097/ACM.0000000000003122

Vold, T., & Haave, H. M. (2020). Relevance of adult higher education on knowledge management in the healthcare sector. *Electronic Journal of Knowledge Management, 18*(3), 236–254.

Walker, R. M., Jung, C. S., & Boyne, G. A. (2013). Marching to different drummers? The performance effects of alignment between political and managerial perceptions of performance management. *Public Administration Review, 73*(6), 833–844. https://doi.org/10.1111/puar.12131

WHO. (2021). WHO Coronavirus (COVID-19) Dashboard. World Health Organization (WHO, Ed.), Retrieved July 29, 2022, from https://covid19.who.in

Yin, R. K. (1994). *Case study research: Design and methods* (Applied Social Research Methods Series, 5 Vols.). New York. USA: Sage.

Zaadoud, B., Chbab, Y., & Chaouch, A. (2021). The performance measurement frameworks in healthcare: Scopus study. *Journal of Health Management, 23*(2), 275–293. https://doi.org/10.1177/09720634211011694

Gianluca Antonucci (M.Sc London School of Economics and Ph.D. University of Rome Tor Vergata) is assistant professor at "G. d'Annunzio" University of Chieti-Pescara, where he is tenure of the courses: "Sustainability Reporting" (master's degree in economics and management), "Management of Sports Organizations" (degree in sport sciences), and "Business Economics of the Building Sector" (degree in building construction). His research focuses on co-production, public accountability, and sports management.

Marco Berardi is a fellow researcher at Università degli studi "G. d'Annunzio," Dipartimento di Economia Aziendale, in Pescara (Italy). Marco conducts research on the creation of public value in public administrations, accounting, and reporting of local authorities. He is also a business consultant and statutory auditor and advises on public administration in anti-corruption and integrity issues.

Andrea Ziruolo is a full professor in business economics at the Università degli studi "G. d'Annunzio," Dipartimento di Economia Aziendale, in Pescara (Italy). Andrea carries out research in public administrations, accounting and reporting of local authorities. He is also a business consultant and statutory auditor. In 2019 he became a member of the board of risk management for the Italian Anticorruption Authority (ANAC).

Telemedicine Implementation Between Innovation and Sustainability: An Operating Model for Designing Patient-Centered Healthcare

Gabriele Palozzi and Francesco Ranalli

ABSTRACT

An aging population and new illnesses are contributing to increasing incidences of chronic diseases, multi-pathologies, and new syndromes. This jeopardizes the sustainability of worldwide National Healthcare Systems (NHSs), which are involved in providing high-quality healthcare under cost containment. To address this challenge, especially in the post-pandemic context, OECD countries have recognized digital technologies as a critical factor to deliver adequate care while reducing contact among individuals. Accordingly, the Italian Recovery & Resilience Plan (PNRR), as encapsulated within the Next Generation EU funds, focuses on digital health to enhance the protection of health as a fundamental public right. Within the sphere of digital transition of NHSs, coherently with the Value-Based Healthcare principles and user-centric innovation theories, telemedicine can be considered as able to increase access to healthcare and to reduce its related resource consumption. Nevertheless, despite its high potentialities, diffusion of telemedicine is struggling to gain access current practices of healthcare institutions. Notwithstanding the copious technology availability, this seems to be due to the organizational changes (operational assets, know-how, and operative processes) needed to adopt an innovation that requires a radical modification of cost and organizational structure for healthcare providers. Thus, the analysis of processes and resources involved in this modernization of healthcare supply structures is a prerequisite for its improvement and implementation. Based on the literature background (both peer-reviewed and technical reports) in the field of eHealth, this chapter wants to sketch features (actors, roles,

G. Palozzi (✉) · F. Ranalli
Department of Management and Law, University Tor Vergata, Via Columbia 2, 00133 Rome, Italy
e-mail: palozzi@economia.uniroma2.it

F. Ranalli
e-mail: ranalli@uniroma2.it

responsibilities, and flowcharts) for designing human-centered services based on telemedicine. By formalizing both an operational definition of telemedicine and designing a general model for its operation, this contribution aims to support healthcare organizations' decision-making about implementation of investment in telemedicine infrastructures by fostering awareness of management about financial and organizational issues, related to the necessary changes, connected to the intervention.

1 Background and Research Aim

Recent evolutive dynamics and scientific advancements have brought about an increase in life expectancy in Western Countries with consequences in demographic changes and related needs for citizenships. This entails different implications in terms of socio-economic policies, which involve both public and private expenditure in Pension, Healthcare, and Educational Systems with many consequences for economic growth. Particularly, an aging population contributes to increasing rates of chronic diseases, multi-pathologies, and new syndromes within OECD countries (OECD, 2019), which overcharge for health expenditure.

In the context of the high pressure toward the necessity to deliver qualitative-adequate services while containing costs, the Covid-19 outbreak has further caused worldwide NHSs to adopt new strategies to provide health care by respecting social distancing while guaranteeing continuity of care.

Moreover, the pandemic has stimulated a strong change in the healthcare demand of the population. On the one hand, as pushed by institutional communication (Kieweg et al., 2021) with the aim to convey measures against the unprecedented crisis, people have been encouraged to adopt preventive measures, such as self-isolation, avoiding public places, and face mask wearing (Wang et al., 2021; World Health Organization, 2021), requiring professional health consultations at a distance. On the other hand, the pandemic has often caused people to compulsively research health information from non-professional sources (Bick et al., 2020; Farooq et al., 2021) with the obvious consequence of several incidence of anxiety and psychological disorders (Bäuerle et al., 2020). From this standpoint, thus, the pandemic has created new issues in health care, collateral to the new pneumonia issues and its related health disorders (known as long-Covid pathologies).

Considered overall, an aging population and the pandemic have drastically changed healthcare needs for people in the last two decades; this subsequently has brought about the need for additional services aimed at accomplishing the demographic and epidemiologic changes that have occurred. These circumstances are jeopardizing the economic sustainability of worldwide healthcare systems, which are always more challenged when providing high-quality health care under expenditure containment.

In this scenario, the Italian Health System (IHS) could be considered as a particularly interesting case, given it is the only universal healthcare system still existing (Spano & Aroni, 2018). The term "universal" is meant that the IHS is accessible by anyone who lives in the national territory (including immigrants and tourists) without any direct charge to patients. With the exception of partial contributions for some specialist tests, this system is funded by the direct taxation of the population and no integrative health insurance is mandatory for accessing care in Italy.

Clearly, this universal access to Italian health care is very expensive. As a consequence, the economic sustainability of this system is particularly complex and the pressure on cost containment is more exacerbated than in other countries.

Reinforcing the Italian context, the Italian national statistical institute (Quattrociocchi et al., 2020) shows that in 2019, in Italy, people over 65 represent about 23% of the entire population. Moreover, 21.5% of people in that age bracket are non-self-sufficient (OASI Report, 2021). Between 2010 and 2017, the number of elderly people increased by 1.3 million (+11%) becoming one of the highest rates in Europe. In 2020, in Italy, those patients with at least one chronic disease accounted for 40.9% of the whole population, while chronic and multi-pathologic patients represented 20.8%. These values increase hugely if we consider only people over 75; about 83% are sick with at least one chronic disease and 65% are multi-pathologic.

In 2016, the number of non-self-sufficient elderly people was about 3 million versus 300,000 patient-beds in public hospitals (OASI Report, 2018). Of these people, 25% of over 85 s are hospitalized at least once a year, with average bed occupancy of 11 days and their repeated hospitalization rate within 12 months is about 67%. Particularly worrying is that only 16% of this over 85 population is discharged with a continuity follow-up plan in place within the territory, with the goal of monitoring the patient's health status aimed at preventing pathological relapses.

Concerning the Covid-19 crisis, the pandemic struck Italy very harshly; in the first year of the pandemic alone, Italy observed more than 75,000 deaths, while at the middle of 2021 the number of infections has exceeded 4 millions (Carosi et al., 2021). Moreover, the 2020 situation has had severe effects also in terms of economic downfall; according ISTAT (2021), the Italian economy lost 150 billion GDP in 2020, with a collapse in the gross domestic product of 8.9%, more than double the percentage of the world's GDP loss (−4.4%).

Within this constrained financial resource scenario, the demographic changes and pandemic crisis undermined the conditions for Italian welfare system sustainability, requiring a fast turnaround due to being hit by the pandemic and needing to recover in terms of economic growth (Cepiku et al., 2021).

To support the recovery, the Next Generation EU Program has attributed Italy with financial resources to stop both the health and economic crises and enhance a structured reform plan. Accordingly, Italy relies heavily on the implementation of its National Recovery and Resilience Plan (PNRR), aimed at reviving the economy and overcoming its pre-existing economic, social, and environmental fragility (PNRR, 2021).

In the healthcare landscape, the PNRR has asked the IHS to play a crucial role in accomplishing the recovery challenges. The IHS has been asked to disrupt the "in-hospital" paradigm of service provision by re-designing many service-delivery processes in order to enhance the provision of health care while reducing unnecessary contacts among individuals. An inefficient government of healthcare demand, in fact, tends to stimulate requests for emergency services when the patient is in the "acute" phase, while anticipating patients' needs by monitoring the progress of their health status. Real-time analysis of patients' health would enable clinicians to take the most informed decisions and to offer patients greater control over their own medical attention (Green & Vogt, 2016). Emergency services, on the contrary, often represent a "buffer" method to manage the contingent needs of patients, which results, therefore, in sometimes being inappropriate from the clinical point of view of long-term care. To this end, it is fundamental to place primary health care at the core of health systems, both to manage an unexpected surge in demand and to maintain continuity of care for all (OECD, 2021) toward the predictive medicine principles (Azfal et al., 2020).

Regarding Western countries, Porter (2008) affirmed that "we are trying to deliver 21st-century medicines with 19th-century organizational structures, management processes, and measurement systems" (p. 503). Worldwide modern NHSs are still too focused on the mere sum of individual specialist services provided to each patient (Porter, 2010), rather than thinking of new solutions for an integrated and holistic management of each subject's diagnostic and therapeutic pathway. Accordingly, a systematic "prospective–predictive" management of patients is, to date, still lacking; the consequences are the overcharging by NHSs with requests for emergency services for treating acute clinical episodes and the subsequent reduction of general accessibility to care.

As a consequence, pressure on cost containment together with the need to maintain high-quality standards (without compromising the possibility of access to care) are causing the necessity to "re-design" the healthcare delivery process (Dávalos et al., 2009).

In this context, digital technologies seem to be an extremely useful element in order to optimize the cost-effectiveness ratio of the healthcare provision. Accordingly, Osborne (2006) considers investments in technological innovation as the crucial element for the public system's sustainability, as levers for stimulating the delivery of high value social and welfare services to users. The author, moreover, underlines that technological advancement represents the driver that is able to improve corporate inter-organizational processes. Particularly, Health Technology (HT) is "any drug, device, medical or surgical procedure, used in the prevention, diagnosis, treatment and rehabilitation of a disease" (Banta et al., 1981); therefore, HT is any technological innovation and infrastructure that impacts, directly or indirectly, on a patient's health status and his/her management.

To this end, specifically referring to technological innovation and investment in healthcare infrastructure, the Italian PNRR intends to stimulate Italian Health System advancement by allocating:

- about €7 billion to support asset investments in Proximity Network and Telemedicine for local health care, aimed at strengthening and reorienting the Healthcare System toward a model centered on local areas and social and healthcare networks;
- about €8.6 billion to foster Healthcare Innovation, Research and Digitization for the NHS, aimed at modernizing ICT infrastructures and strengthening the healthcare system's information and digital tools.

Among the various technological opportunities in rethinking healthcare around patients' needs, it is clear that digitalization is considered by the Italian (and European) Institutions as one of the most powerful strategic levers for improving health care and increasing its accessibility, while enhancing economic sustainability.

Accordingly, digital technologies (Cavallone & Palumbo, 2020; Jung & Padman, 2015), such as big data, cloud computing, and Internet of Things (IoT), enable integration among business units, processes, routines, and capabilities (Bharadwaj et al., 2013) within the entire healthcare value chain by offering new ways to manage and deliver services (Mettler & Pinto, 2018).

In particular, defined as "the use of information and communication technology to provide health care services to individuals who are some distance from the health care provider" (Roine, 2001, p. 765), telemedicine concerns the process of acquisition, exchange, and storage of data (Tresp et al., 2016) toward remote clinical services; in this way, it contributes to filling the gap between healthcare providers' needs (i.e., reducing the workload and cost of care) and patient demands (i.e., high-quality health care, accessibility to care, personalized services, and transparency on healthcare processes) (Binci et al., 2021).

Moreover, telemedicine can be surely considered as a virtuous example of cost-effective and accessible innovation, able to combine cost containment with the qualitative improvement of services offered. Specifically, positive effects of the use of telemedicine are consolidated in the literature and the main benefits of its employment are linked to the following aspects:

(1) Increasing equity in access to high quality and specialist care (du Toit, 2017; Griffiths & Christensen, 2007; Kyle et al., 2012; Kroenke et al., 2010, Moffat & Elay, 2010; Palozzi et al., 2020a);
(2) Cost saving and better cost-effectiveness (Bergmo et al., 2015; Burri et al., 2011; Hasan & Paul, 2011; Rosenborg et al., 2012; Stensland et al., 1999; Switzer et al., 2013, Taylor et al., 2018, Yilmaz et al., 2019).

Notwithstanding these benefits, employment of telemedicine is, to date, still limited. According to Rosemberg et al. (2012), the main reason for telemedicine under-usage is attributable to the lack of a reimbursement rate that is able to remunerate a healthcare "process–service", which differs a lot from standard services delivered in person. The lack of reimbursement rates, in fact, limits the propensity of healthcare providers to invest in telemedicine infrastructures, given an unsatisfactory expected return of the investment, impoverished by the lack of potential earnings (Amatucci & Mele, 2011). To date, in Italy, the absence of a structured set of reimbursement rates for the different telemedicine services, however, is not only due to financial restrictions; it is also highly justified by the shortage of knowledge about the actual process of delivering health care remotely and about the subsequent accounting information concerning the necessary resources for running services.

Telemedicine service provision needs of a multiplicity of activities (clinical and managerial). These activities should be carried out by a wide range of actors (including co-producer patients, Cepiku & Giordano, 2014; Osborne et al., 2016; Ostrom, 1996), which relate with an articulated pathway of observation, monitoring, and management of individuals' health status. Some studies, indeed, qualitatively examine how telemedicine modifies the traditional paradigm of health care toward new co-production schemes (Osborne & Strokosch, 2013). Razkmak & Belanger (2017), for instance, discuss how telemedicine modifies the doctor-patient relationship in communication and in individual behavior. It seems to be clear, in other words, that telemedicine implementation is not only a financial issue concerning the resources required for investment in new infrastructures and technologies; it regards the comprehension of any change needed to adopt the innovation at any level of the organization.

Before the pandemic, the Italian NHS had experienced only a patchy distribution of digital health experiences (ranging from telemedicine to electronic health records and apps for dematerialized prescriptions), funded by specific and designated financial resources. The Covid-19 crisis has undoubtedly produced an acceleration toward digital technologies' adoption: the Italian Government, moved by the necessity to guarantee continuity of care by limiting waiting and physical contact (Gabbrielli et al., 2020), pushed providers to move toward telemedicine services (OASI Report, 2021) by rewarding them with the provision of remote services by a tariff calculated on the corresponding in-office medical examination.

Actually, the pandemic has introduced a reimbursement system for telemedicine in Italy; it was, however, limited only to those remote services involved with Covid-19 patients' management (and related pathologies). Accordingly, since 2021, Italian health institutions (Ministry of Health, Regional Health Sub-Systems, National Superior Institute of Health, and National Agency for Regional Healthcare Services—AGENAS) have started several researches and consultation tables aimed at understanding the standard consumption of resources for delivering a particular type of health service, which are: (i) provided remotely, (ii) as a continuous process, and (iii) involving several actors.

Nevertheless, in order to start reflecting on an adequate reimbursement rate for different clusters of telemedicine services, it is necessary to know both the resources involved in its provision and the organizational/structural changes (operating flows, know-how, etc.) that the healthcare organization should undertake in order to sustain it in order to maximize advantage from the innovation.

In particular, regarding the maximization of value created for a patient by monitoring his/her health status, it is fundamental to define a general operative scheme able to show flowcharts and interconnections related to providing a healthcare service when the patient and clinician are not in the same place simultaneously. The design of a general scheme for telemedicine services is aimed to clarify the phases (and subsequent resources) to practitioners, which is necessary to manage a telemedicine service within a healthcare organization.

Given the above, on the basis of the main literature (both scientific and technical) about telemedicine implementation, this work aims to synthetize an operational definition of telemedicine and depict a general operating model for a telemedicine service, which includes relationships between technologies, actors, roles, and responsibilities involved in remote health service provision.

This analysis is a prodromic condition to figure out the impact of the introduction of an innovative approach within a healthcare organization. This would allow management both to understand what the requested organizational change is and to make an approach with an assessment of its economic impact and the potential conditions for a positive return of the investment. Moreover, the formalization of a general operating scheme for telemedicine service provision could support public institutions in setting reimbursement tariffs, as a formalization of resources and related interconnections is necessary for running the service.

To achieve its purpose, this chapter follows this outline; after the introduction to the background and research aim, the second section reports the operational definition of telemedicine. The third section links telemedicine innovations to the sphere of the value-based healthcare principles. The fourth section presents and explains the general operating model for a telemedicine service, as an adaption of the Hub & Spoke framework. The fifth section discusses the model and the last provides some final remarks about the employment of telemedicine as an effective strategy for enhancing healthcare sustainability toward centrality of patients.

2   Institutional Definitions of Telemedicine

In Garshnek et al. (1997) opened the debate about telemedicine by recognizing that this innovation refers to a process, not a mere technology, that "shifts the paradigm of transporting the patient to the site of the expert care giver to transporting expert knowledge to the health care provider closest to the patient" (p. 38), thanks to the possibility of moving information instead of the individual.

Since that time, many definitions of telemedicine have been provided by practitioners and researchers over the last 20 years; several came from institutional entities. These institutional sources are considered, for the aim of this section, as the cornerstone for understanding telemedicine features from the perspective of its implementation within actual NHSs.

The World Health Organization introduced, in (1998), Telemedicine as "the delivery of health care services, where distance is a critical factor, by all health care professionals using information and communication technologies for the exchange of valid information for diagnosis, treatment and prevention of disease and injuries, research and evaluation, and for the continuing education of health care providers, all in the interests of advancing the health of individuals and their communities".

The European Commission (2008), through the COM (689), has asserted that "telemedicine is the provision of healthcare services, through use of ICT, in situations where the health professional and the patient (or two health professionals) are not in the same location. It involves secure transmission of medical data and information, through text, sound, images or other forms needed for the prevention, diagnosis, treatment and follow-up of patients."

Both of these definitions underline that the telemedicine concept refers to a medical act that takes place when two (or more) subjects are connected by technological infrastructures in order to exchange biomedical data. The goal of this personal connection is to trigger clinical decisions that foster patients' management aimed at improving their health status.

In the Italian context, the Health Ministry (2014), as inspired by the previous COM definition, issued guidelines about telemedicine, where it was considered as "a new healthcare delivery process, based on innovative technologies, provided when patient and professional are not physically in the same place."

Enhancing these guidelines, some abstracted insights are as follows (translated from Italian): telemedicine "is a new way to manage patients that allows guaranteed continuity of healthcare in remote areas and a better integration between hospital and district/patients." And again: "telemedicine involves the secure transmission of medical information and data in the form of texts, sounds, images or other forms necessary for the prevention, diagnosis, treatment and consequent monitoring of patients." "Telemedicine must comply with all the rights and obligations of any health act." Finally, "telemedicine services should be assimilated to any diagnostic/therapeutic healthcare service. (…) However, services provided in telemedicine do not replace the traditional personal physician–patient relationship, but they integrate it in order to potentially improve efficacy, efficiency and appropriateness."

This structured definition certainly focuses on medical acts by indicating also that telemedicine refers to any type of output (texts, sounds, images, or other) capable of supporting a clinical process (prevention, diagnosis, treatment, and subsequent control). Nevertheless, this definition submits the reader to a contradiction: firstly, it equalizes telemedicine services with any other clinical act, and then it declares that these services cannot replace the basic physician–patient relationship, but just fosters its integration.

Among these different meanings of telemedicine proposed by the Italian Health Ministry, this work considers those more oriented to the operational and clinical needs, as support for the diagnostic activities and the remote monitoring of vital signs.

Accordingly, Table 1 reports the taxonomy of health services delivered remotely, issued by the Italian Health Ministry (2020) within the activities of the Italian State—Regions Conference.

Starting from these definitions and their empirical implication, this work proposes an operational definition of telemedicine, which is the basis for the comprehension of the operating inputs necessary for running a healthcare service at distance, as explained in the following sections.

Table 1 Taxonomy of telemedicine services

Service	Definition
Tele-visit	Medical act in which the clinician remotely interacts in real time with the patient (even with the support of a care-giver)
Medical tele-consultation	Medical act in which the specialist physician interacts remotely with one or more doctors in order to support them about the treatment of a specific patient
Clinical tele-consultation	Healthcare activity in which a clinician remotely supports a/other clinician/s while delivering a health service
Tele-assistance	Healthcare activity in which a clinician remotely supports a patient/care-giver in his/her healthcare
Tele-reporting	Report remotely issued by a specialist physician on an instrumental examination undergone by the patient; the written content is transmitted via digital and telecommunication systems

Source Italian Health Ministry (2020)

Thus, by synthesizing the previous explanations, telemedicine can be defined as the provision of healthcare carried out, thanks to the use of hardware and software infrastructures, when the clinician and patient are not simultaneously in the same place. Clinical information deriving from this digital interconnection has the same features of accuracy and affordability with respect to those personally acquired. The consequent professional information exchange is suitable, per procedures and timing, to trigger a decision-making process that enables the clinician to intervene as to a patient's health status at an appropriate time, depending on the specific case.

3   Telemedicine from the Lens of Value-Based Healthcare Principles

Increasing the value around the patient should represent the primary interest for actors involved in healthcare. Beyond the cost-effective employment of available resources, actual impulses toward the sustainability of healthcare delivery should pass through the centrality of patients among the myriad of services offered.

In the last decade, Michael Porter has certainly expressed his opinion on this subject. In the two-year period 2010–2011, the author has enucleated the theories on Value-based Healthcare, according to which, in order to face the limitations of patients' choice regarding the access to care (caused by the scarcity of financial resources (Porter & Tisberg, 2006), National Healthcare Systems should have concentrated their policies on increasing the quality of services provided by re-designing toward maximizing value created for patients and users.

This approach represents an advancement of the Total Quality Management (TQM) framework (Deming, 1994) aimed to enhance performance by increasing quality. TQM theory, as well as the value-based paradigm, was based on.

- users' centricity;
- empowerment and involvement of all individuals within organizations toward service process;
- continuous quality improvement according to users' expectations;
- ongoing learning and growth in order to identify room for service improvements and new opportunities.

Thus, starting from theories on competition and strategic management (Porter, 1991, 1997), value-based logic involves a shift of the healthcare paradigm: from a concept of care based on volume and intensity of services, toward patient-centered care based on value. The goal of the value-based healthcare theory is to improving the outcome and increasing the access to treatments. According to Porter (2010), better health status improves resources' allocation by reducing, prospectively, the expensiveness of health (Porter & Teisberg, 2006). As a consequence, healthcare could become a system characterized by a competition on value (instead of volumes), which is the most potent driver of continuous improvement.

Nevertheless, in order to accomplish the value creation around the patient, the traditional concept of healthcare delivery should be reformulated. There would be the necessity of moving from an "industrial" healthcare approach based on the number of services performed, to a new approach based on patients' clinical needs (Porter, 1991, 1997) and expectations.

The patient, featured per pathology and class of severity, is the subject to whom the whole supply chain of healthcare should be referred. This means that a patient's needs should be considered as the core of healthcare: from his/her "first meeting" with the healthcare organization to his/her follow-up after the home and hospital care is received (Fig. 1).

Figure 1 shows that the traditional approach of healthcare provision (which, actually, is the driver for financing the healthcare system) is focused on the single service performed "within the walls" of a healthcare organization. On the contrary, instead, the logic of Value-Based Healthcare wants to consider the entire pathway of the patient in his/her environment, from the initial contact with the Healthcare Systems to the post-discharge control stages.

This holistic approach of "taking care of patient" certainly has positive impact on healthcare economic sustainability. In this sense, Porter (2010, p. 2477), provocatively, argues that in order to reduce healthcare costs, the best approach is often "to spend more on some service to reduce the need for others" (p. 2477). The author affirms that the only way to make a modern healthcare system economically sustainable is to "invest" in patient care by fostering managerial models able to prospectively reduce the needs for in-hospital emergency treatments (which, instead, should be exclusively dedicated to the management of unexpected and unpredictable clinical contingencies).

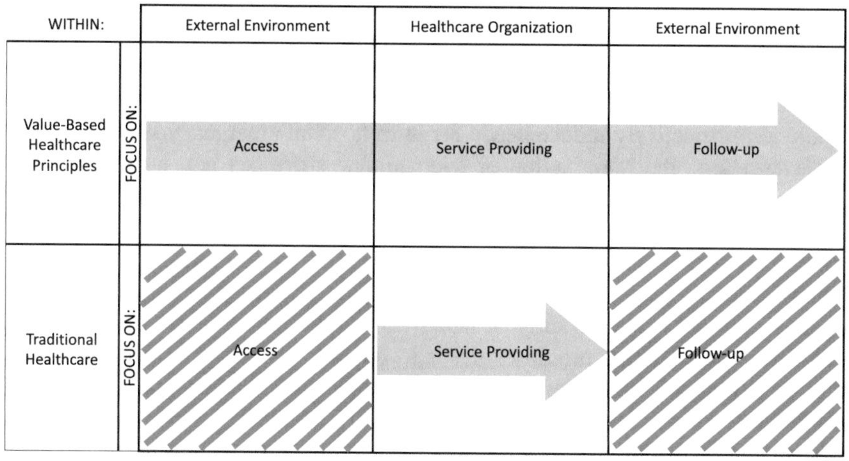

Fig. 1 Value-based healthcare vs traditional healthcare: focus on phases of healthcare delivery. *Source* Author's own figure (2022)

To this end, Kaplan and Porter (2011) discuss that the entire "healthcare supply chain" deserves to be evaluated in order to compare costs of services and benefits in terms of value created for users. In particular, the analysis of operating activities belonging to the entire healthcare pathway allows hospital managers to verify the presence of potential operational inefficiencies, whose corrections should improve cost-effectiveness ratios of the services provided. This makes them sustainable and valuable for the health system.

According to Porter (2008), from the perspective of current NHS sustainability, the change of the paradigm from "hospital-centric" healthcare to "patient-centric" seems necessary and it can no longer be postponed. This is particularly true for a "universal" and completely "free-open access" NHS, like the Italian one.

Universality and free-accessibility of the Italian Health System (IHS) have always put it at risk of insolvency; for this reason, since the early 90 s, Italian legislation has moved toward the introduction of potential corrections to the exclusive centrality of hospitals in health services (first reform of the IHS—Decrees 502/1992 and 517/1993). Although never fully implemented, this reform aimed at a more local widespread diffusion of healthcare. Its goal was a tentative reduction of in-hospital treatment costs by emphasizing the integration of the patient's entire clinical pathway with healthcare providers of his/her geographical area. As explained in the first section of this work, this pressure to improve local and home health care has been resumed by the PNRR Health Mission, which is pushing investments toward strengthening integrated management of patients within their geographical area. This PNRR strategic orientation aims at reducing necessities of (more expensive) in-hospital services by improving local and home care. Perfectly coherent with the above-described value-based healthcare principles, this approach aspires to anticipating the evolution of patients' health status by allowing hospitalization only for severe clinical conditions.

Consistent with this approach, telemedicine can certainly represent an example of operating investment in supporting provision of "outside of hospital" care that is able to prospectively reduce needs for intra-hospital emergency services.

Nevertheless, the introduction of telemedicine strategies into healthcare organizations deserves to be carefully analyzed by management. Accordingly, value created for clinicians and patients through telemedicine strategy is the result of complex dynamics and interactions between operational structures, processes, people, and technology (Bellè, 2015; Kaplan & Norton, 2001; Uphoff & Krane, 1998), together oriented toward quality of health care. As a consequence, the impact of telemedicine on internal processes needs to be carefully analyzed and forecasted, in order to assess if its implementation is coherent with strategic goals of an organization that intends to adopt the innovation and its effect on current assets, rules, and responsibilities of clinical staff involved.

4   General Operating Model for Telemedicine Implementation

As mentioned above, the telemedicine approach connects a patient with a reference clinician, whose resulting healthcare service is obtained from the information exchange between patient and health professional via digital HTs.

In this context, Hub & Spoke (H&S) models (Elrod & Fortenberry, 2017; Skorin-Kapov & Skorin-Kapov, 1995) help us to represent the overall operation of telemedicine services (Hess et al., 2005; Huddleston & Zimmermann, 2014).

The origin of the H&S structure was born in the field of transport as a framework for operational networks aimed at the logistic management of goods and passengers. Shaw (1993) and O'Kelly and Miller (1994) have based this model on two key components, which interact within the network: (i) HUB; and (ii) SPOKE.

Fotheringham and O'Kelly defined the Hub as "a type of facility located in a network in a way so as to provide a switching point for flows between other interacting nodes" (Fotheringham and O'Kelly, 1989, p. 171). The Hub is recognized as the focal point of a network as the provider of a specialist service to which spoke centers are interconnected.

Spokes, otherwise, are secondary structures within the network (by size and location), which mainly interact with the hub. Despite being poorer in terms of know-how and operative structures in comparison with hubs, spokes are widespread in the geographical area, such that they represent the point of contact for those users who cannot refer directly to the specialist hub, due to logistical reasons (Demaerschalk et al., 2009).

From the digital health standpoint, we can imagine a hub as the specialist center that provides telemedicine services to those many related spokes. This model looks like a digital "planet-satellites" system that keeps the health of individual patients (spokes) interconnected with a specialist healthcare organization (hub) within a structured network. Accordingly, the network and its interconnections are designed toward the achievement of strategic healthcare outcomes, corresponding to health needs of specific clusters of patients (e.g., chronic heart diseases), whose care is strategic for NHS sustainability (du Toit, 2017; Mueller et al., 2014).

For a telemedicine service design, while the hub centers always correspond to healthcare organizations who provide health services, spokes can be represented by:

- a single patient (possibly supported by a care-giver), equipped with the necessary technological infrastructure, who communicates directly with the HUB center (this is the case, for example, of patients with chronic pathologies enrolled in post-discharge remote follow-up);
- a professional clinician (e.g., nurse/physician working in a clinic, general practitioner (GP), or specialist doctors) who, referring to the health status of a specific patient, communicates directly with the HUB center (this is the case, for example, of a GP who needs a specialist medical tele-consultation in order to be supported in the management of a heart patient belonging to a protection program).

This HUB-SPOKE model is based on an "Input to Feedback" mechanism and it is perfectly compatible with the provision of telemedicine services. It can be represented as in Fig. 2.

On the base of literature (Black et al., 2013; Huddleston & Zimmermann, 2014) and case studies (Palozzi et al., 2017, 2018), this chapter highlights the "one to one" relationship between hub & spoke. Thus, starting from the operational definition provided at the conclusion of Sect. 2, Fig. 3 depicts a general model for telemedicine service delivery.

Let us focus on Fig. 3's contents; it shows the existence of two macro spheres of interest:

- the sphere of the patient (SPOKE);
- the sphere of the healthcare organization (HUB).

In a telemedicine service, these two subjects are usually "distant", at least for one of the following reasons:

- physical/geographical: patient (or his/her care-giver) and clinicians could not be in the same place;
- temporal: patient (or his/her care-giver) and clinician could be in the same place, but not simultaneously;

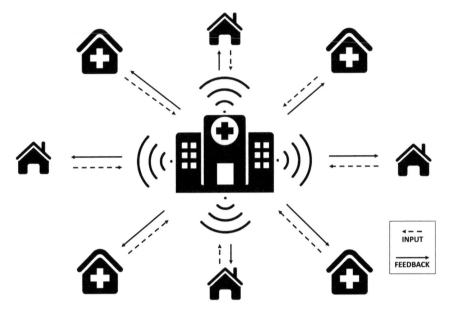

Fig. 2 Hub & Spoke model in a telemedicine network. *Source* Author's own figure (2022)

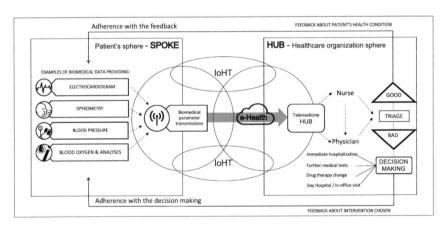

Fig. 3 General operating model for telemedicine service delivery. *Source* Author's own figure (2022)

- cultural: patient (or his/her care-giver) and clinician could not communicate using the same specialized technical-medical language.

Accordingly, telemedicine acts to reduce these distances.

Taking advantage of the innovative approach of the Internet of Health Things (IoHT) (Rghioui & Oumnad, 2018; Terry, 2016), on the basis of information exchange through digital interconnection of medical devices, patients (or their care-giver) are enabled to send professionals data about their own health status at the specialist hub center. Therefore, clinicians working for the hub center are enabled to carry out, remotely, clinical evaluations of patients' health and pathology evolution. Their clinical reaction is triggered thanks to the availability of objective biomedical data, and not on mere qualitative and perceptive sensations described verbally.

Below are the precise phases of the "input to feedback" process regarding a telemedicine service providing:

(1) In the "patient's sphere", the medical examination takes place; through the use of professional medical devices, the patient is able to detect measurements of his/her objective biomedical data (in the form of texts, sounds, images, or tracks).
(2) Medical devices, connected to an Internet network via a personal device (e.g., PC, tablet, smartphone, or PDA), sends the patient's clinical input parameters to a cloud server.
(3) The cloud server makes the patient's biomedical data available for downloading to the "sphere" of the healthcare organization.
(4) The specialist telemedicine hub center is triggered to clinical evaluations of the patient (TRIAGE) by involving medical and/or nursing staff according to its own internal operating flows.
(5) TRIAGE may have two types of results, which will have repercussions on the decision-making process and, therefore, from the operational point of view:
    - **GOOD**—Clinical evaluation gives a negative result: no anomaly is found on the patient's health status; the patient obtains feedback (report, medical opinion, call) from the telemedicine hub and continues his/her regular follow-ups (if planned).
    - **BAD**—Clinical evaluation gives a positive result: some anomalies are found on the patient's health status. On the basis of the professional information and biomedical parameters received, a clinical decision-making process on the patient management is triggered. Decisions may include:
        – indication of immediate hospitalization;
        – request for an in-office specialist visit;
        – request for further medical tests;
        – change/adjustment in drug therapy.
            The decision about clinical intervention is immediately communicated to the patient or his/her care-giver.

(6) Patient (or his/her care-giver) receives feedback from the HUB healthcare staff and s/he have to comply with the medical indications received.

In deepening the clinical evaluation phase (5), of particular interest is the organizational behavior of staff operating for the hub (both nursing and physician) when clinical data are received and TRIAGE activities are promptly carried out, in order to firstly manage the more potentially dangerous cases for patients' health, exactly as happens in Emergency Room (ER) departments.

Usually, an operational telemedicine protocol aims to give priority to the transmission containing urgencies that need to be analyzed immediately (Palozzi et al., 2017). There is a "semaphore light" priority code that requires specific reactions from the hospital staff involved in the telemedicine service. This code, as inspired from an operating ER, can be summarized as:

- **Green code**—Triage is GOOD and transmission regards routine check-ups, requiring no immediate feedback to the patient. The nurse communicates the output of the medical examination to the patient and, eventually, suggests continuing with his/her follow-up.
- **Yellow code**—Triage is quite BAD or something has changed in the patient's health status, which requires priority from nursing staff who immediately analyze the origin of the problem (eventually with the support of a physician) and give feedback to the patient.
- **Red code**—Triage is BAD and something is endangering the patient's life; this requires priority attention from nursing staff and a physician's competence is immediately requested. A prompt clinical decision has to be taken. The patient has to be immediately informed about his/her health condition and about the clinical strategies that have to be undertaken.

5   Discussions

The general operating model for telemedicine service presented in this paper shows basic interconnections between clinicians and patients in the context of a digital-health network. The aim of the model is to highlight and summarize the standard operation of telemedicine-based healthcare services, whose network design integrates and magnifies the traditional "in-office" relationship between physician and patient. For example, the telemedicine approach decreases distances between user and provider of the service by involving the former as the subject directly involved in the achievement of the health outcome resulting from the care received. Kim et al. (2020), accordingly, emphasized the appropriateness of this co-productive approach in designing health-related programs toward designing new healthcare services focused on centricity of user, as based on consumer engagement and collaborative patient-provider relationships (Anderson et al., 2018).

In the telemedicine sphere, the co-productive connection between clinician and patient is possible through communication technologies and IoHT (Terry, 2016), which make intelligible and reliable health data supplied from users to healthcare providers, as a basis for remote service delivery through patients' involvement in e-health interventions (Sankaran et al., 2018).

Nevertheless, the availability of technologies is only a technical prerequisite for telemedicine implementation. Technological advancement, in fact, gives only new operational opportunities; without the integration with people and assets already existing within the organization, however, innovation cannot be considered truly suitable and available.

In this regard, the main obstacle to widespread adoption of telemedicine regards those structural adjustments of the healthcare organization (in terms of know-how, procedures, and hardware-software infrastructures), which are necessary for "updating" the healthcare delivery system toward new patient-centric schemes. Particularly, actual telemedicine adoption can only be possible through an adequate process of organizational change (Driessen et al., 2016; Gagnon et al., 2012; Segrelles-Calvo et al., 2017) for those health providers who intend to deliver remote services. Accordingly, the process toward telemedicine adoption in an organization requires its acceptance from users, both clinicians and patients, whose intrinsic features, preferences, and expectations are critical variables for the effective implementation of the digital innovation (Binci et al., 2021).

From the operational standpoint, moreover, the choice to adopt telemedicine is concretized by making those necessary investments in HTs and integrating them within the current processes. Considering the costs of this operational change, however, may not be so easy due to the myriad of factors involved. According to Dávalos et al. (2009), an organization that aspires to become a hub in a telemedicine network has to implement resources for: (i) initial investments (implementation costs); and (ii) delivering the service to patients/spokes (operating costs) (Palozzi et al., 2020b).

Nevertheless, all these potential resources needed for implementing telemedicine services are strictly dependent on the specific clinical necessities that healthcare organizations intend to address. Resource employment represents the translation of strategic orientations related to the delocalization of healthcare (European Commission, 2004) into operational goals (Ferreira & Otley, 2009). This consists of requesting a change in how staff operate and new functional flowcharts, whose organizational impacts should be considered before any deployment of financial resources (Sampietro-Colom et al., 2015).

In this regard, the operational definition of telemedicine and the operating model proposed by this paper should sustain the investment decision in e-health infrastructures by supporting the design and the subsequent forecasting of operational changes required for implementing a specialist telemedicine hub. From the perspective of a tariff system that reimburses remote healthcare services, this lays the foundations for considering revenues corresponding to telemedicine provision, as a basis for the economic evaluation of the investment required for value-based healthcare aims.

6   Conclusion

To conclude this chapter about the operating peculiarities of telemedicine, as a strategy for patient-centered healthcare delivery, it seems useful to recap on some key steps of the work in order to highlight the main contribution for managerial purposes, both for practitioners and academia.

An aging population in Western countries (ODEC, 2019; Quattrociocchi, 2020) together with the Covid-19 outbreak (World Health Organization, 2021) have changed people's health needs, so much so that it requires NHSs to modernize their healthcare delivery models (OASI Report, 2021) by adopting new solutions for increasing accessibility to qualitative services. As a result, this change calls for "rethinking" the ways to provide healthcare services in order to enhance a greater centrality of patients toward the transition from "hospital-centered" to "human-centered" health care. This would mean a higher propensity for NHSs' "investment" in people's wellbeing and health, with the subsequent ultimate goal of a progressive reduction of emergency services and their related costs (Kaplan & Porter, 2011; Porter, 2010).

In this context, digital technologies (Cavallone & Palumbo, 2020; Terry, 2016) seem to be suitable tools in supporting healthcare provision. In line with the implementation of P4 (predictive, personalized, preventive, and participative) medicine, moreover, digital healthcare enables the design of new care pathways (Alonso et al., 2019) according to the heterogeneity of responses to therapies and the stratification of diseases (Hood & Friend, 2011). Digital innovations allow the forecasting of patients' health evolution, contributing also to avoid phenomena of over-diagnosis and overcharging of inappropriate specialist service provision (Binci et al., 2021), with the result of contributing to make health care more sustainable (Bradford et al., 2016) and better supported by management.

In particular, telemedicine guarantees effective, fair, and reliable levels of care by contributing to creating higher value for patients in the process of their care as a whole; moreover "telemedicine-based" health care is potentially able to take into consideration all the necessities required by patients (medical, social, and economic) and not only those strictly related solely to clinical conditions (Kemm et al., 2004). Accordingly, telemedicine allows for simplified access to specialist consultation via one port of call/transmission (Preston et al., 1992); this provides remote diagnosis and, when required, it might assist in managing patients locally by also reducing unnecessary transfers.

Nevertheless, the change of healthcare management and its digitalization still struggle to happen. The reasons for this inertia, more than in financial restrictions, seem to be mainly due to the necessity of upgrading operational structures of healthcare organizations toward digitalization in terms of assets, updating staff, and internal processes, which are the factors that would be consequently repaid by the reimbursement system.

Accordingly, in the Italian landscape, the PNRR Mission 6 acts to stimulate the advancement of the healthcare system toward enhancing accessibility of services and patients' new needs. The PNRR represents an unprecedented opportunity for

Italy to implement an ambitious health investment plan across the country, which is mainly based on digital innovation and telemedicine as a lever of health care advancement. Nevertheless, the actual relevance of an investment in innovative infrastructures always resides in the organization's ability to make the most from the asset acquired by fully adopting the innovation into its current operating procedures. Therefore, if healthcare organizations were unable to manage telemedicine infrastructures in their daily processes, there would be a serious risk that investments (financed by PNRR funds) would not create value for the community. This would represent both a failure for public management to meet the health system reform goals and a waste of public financial resources.

Accordingly, as presented in this chapter, the general operating model for telemedicine services could be suitable to support healthcare management to understand the processes (and related resources) needed for the provision of remote health care, and by also laying the foundations for the assessment of necessary changes to fully adopt the desired innovation (Solberg et al., 2020).

In this direction, this study firstly provides an operational definition of telemedicine, which is useful to encapsulate the subject under the sphere of medical acts that need specific inputs (staff, assets) and operating rules (structured flowcharts) so as to be run. Secondly, by referring remote healthcare services to the field of "HUB & SPOKE" models (Elrod & Fortenberry, 2017), the chapter defines the operational relationships between actors and technologies involved in the healthcare provision when patient and provider are not in the same place simultaneously. As a result of telemedicine information exchange between hub & spoke (healthcare organization and patient), modeling the operating flows allows readers to map activities and tasks that should be carried out by the different subjects involved in order to run the service.

Thus, starting from phases of the general operating model for telemedicine service delivery, it is possible to classify both physical and intellectual resources necessary to implement and deliver remote health care. This should be the first step for an operational upgrade of business structures, through which healthcare organizations strategically adapt themselves to an external environment and users' needs (Cavalieri et al., 2005; Bryson, 2015). Accordingly, this study might represent some support to healthcare managers involved in assessing investment decisions about specific telemedicine projects (Amatucci & Mele, 2011; Cavallo, 2008; Tarricone, 2004).

Finally, this research opens up room for discussion about the role of new digital technologies in involving patients' active participation in health care delivery, according to co-production schemes (Cepiku & Giordano, 2014). By entering into new experiences of their healthcare management, patients could undertake a transition from simple users to makers and shapers of health services (Cornwall and Gaventa, 2000; Renedo et al., 2015). Healthcare based on patient participation is expected to improve the performance (Bouckaert & Halligan, 2007) of existing public services (Osborne & Strokosch, 2013) by also enhancing their sustainability.

In conclusion, this chapter represents a first step toward representation of operational models that combine digital health technologies within clinical practice toward patient-centered healthcare. Its ultimate goal is fostering debate, both theo-retical and operational, about the appropriateness of healthcare strategies focused on best outcomes for patients, while respecting cost containment. Clearly, full val-idations of both the definition of telemedicine and the model proposed require empirical evidence about their reliability in actual operational contexts. There-fore, future research should focus on refinement of the model in order to analyze its effectiveness and its adaptability within the current processes of healthcare providers.

References

Afzal, M., Islam, S. R., Hussain, M., & Lee, S. (2020). Precision medicine informatics: Principles, prospects, and challenges. *IEEE Access, 8*, 13593–13612.

Alonso, S. G., de la Torre Díez, I., & Zapiraín, B. G. (2019). Predictive, personalized, preventive and participatory (4P) medicine applied to telemedicine and eHealth in the literature. *Journal of Medical Systems, 43*(5), 1–10.

Amatucci, F., & Mele, S. (2011). *I processi di acquisto di beni e servizi nelle aziende sanitarie: elementi di innovazione e modelli di accentramento.* Milan, Italy: EGEA.

Anderson, S., Nasr, L., & Rayburn, S. W. (2018). Transformative service research and service design: Synergistic effects in healthcare. *The Service Industries Journal, 38*(11–2), 99–113.

Banta, H. D., Behney, C. J., & Willems J. S. (1981). *Toward rational technology in medicine: Considerations for health policy* (Vol. 5, No. v–xiv, pp. 1–242). Springer Series Health Care Society.

Bäuerle, A., Teufel, M., Musche, V., Weismüller, B., Kohler, H., Hetkamp, M., Dörrie, N., Schweda, A., & Skoda, E.-M. (2020). Increased generalized anxiety, depression and distress during the COVID-19 pandemic: A cross-sectional study in Germany. *Journal of Public Health, 42*(4), 672–678. https://doi.org/10.1093/pubmed/fdaa106

Bellè, N. (2015). Performance-related pay and the crowding out of motivation in the public sector: A randomized field experiment. *Public Administration Review, 75*(2), 230–324.

Bergmo, T. S. (2015). How to measure costs and benefits of eHealth interventions: An overview of methods and frameworks. *Journal of Medical Internet Research, 17*(11), e254.

Bharadwaj, A., El Sawy, A. O., Pavlou, A. P., & Venkatraman, N. (2013). Digital business strategy: Toward a next generation of insights. *MIS Quarterly, 37*(2), 471–482.

Bick, A., Blandin, A., & Mertens, K. (2020). *Work from home after the COVID-19 outbreak.* CEPR Discussion Paper No. DP15000.

Binci, D., Palozzi, G., & Scafarto, F. (2021). Toward digital transformation in healthcare: A frame-work for remote monitoring adoption. *The TQM Journal.* Vol. ahead-of-print No. ahead-of-print. https://doi.org/10.1108/TQM-04-2021-0109

Black, J. T., Romano, P. S., Sadeghi, B., Auerbach, A. D., Ganiats, T. G., Greenfield, S., Kaplan, S., Ong, M. K., & The BEAT-HF Research Group. (2013). A remote monitoring and tele-phone nurse coaching intervention to reduce readmissions among patients with heart failure: Study protocol for the better effectiveness after transition-heart failure (BEAT-HF) randomized controlled trial. *Trials, 15*(1), 124.

Bouckaert, G., & Halligan, J. (2007). *Managing performance: Internaconal comparisons.* Rout-ledge.

Bradford, N., Caffery, L., & Smith, A. (2016). Telehealth services in rural and remote Australia: A systematic review of models of care and factors influencing success and sustainability. Retrieved July 25, 2022, from www.rrh.org.au/journal/article/3808

Bryson, J. M. (2015). *Strategic planning for public and nonprofit organization: A guide to strengthening and sustaining organizational achievement.* New York, USA: Wiley.

Burri, H., Heidbuchel, H., Jung, W., & Brugada, P. (2011). Remote monitoring: A cost or an investment? *Europeace, 13*(2), 44–48.

Carosi, G., Cauda, R., Pession, A., & Antonelli, G. (2021). La pandemia di COVID-19 in Italia. Harrison Principi di Medicina interna 20a edizione-2021. CEA-Casa Editrice Ambrosiana-Rev.

Cavaleri, E., & Ferraris Franceschi, R. (2005). *Economia Aziendale,* Vol. 1, *Attività aziendale e processi produttivi,* Giappichelli, Turin, Italy.

Cavallo, M. C. (2008). *Le tecnologie sanitarie e il loro ruolo nella tutela della salute: i dispositivi medici in una prospettiva Europea.* Milan, Italy: EGEA.

Cavallone, M., & Palumbo, R. (2020). Debunking the myth of industry 4.0 in health care: Insights from a systematic literature review. *The TQM Journal, 32*(4), 849–868.

Cepiku, D., & Giordano, F. (2014). Co-production in developing countries. Insights from the community health workers experiences. *Public Management Review, 16*(3), 317–340.

Cepiku, D., Giordano, F., Bovaird, T., & Loeffler, E. (2021). New development: Managing the Covid-19 pandemic—From a hospital-centred model of care to a community co-production approach. *Public Money and Management, 41*(1), 77–80. https://doi.org/10.1080/09540962.2020.1821445

Cornwall, A., & Gaventa, J. (2000). From users and choosers to makers and shapers repositioning participation in social policy1. *IDS Bulletin, 31*(4), 50–62.

Dávalos, M. E., French, M. T., Burdick, A. E., & Simmons, S. C. (2009). Economic evaluation of tele-medicine: Review of the literature and research guidelines for benefit–cost analysis. *Telemedicine Journal and E-Health, 15*(10), 933–948.

Demaerschalk, B. M., Miley, M. L., Kiernan, T. E. J., Bobrow, B. J., Corday, D. A., Wellik, K. E., & Koch, T. C. (2009). Stroke telemedicine. Elsevier. *Mayo Clinic Proceedings, 84*(1), 53–64.

Deming, W. E. (1994). *The new economics: For industry, government, education. MIT Center for Advanced Engineering Study* (2nd ed.). Cambridge: MIT Press.

Driessen, J., Bonhomme, A., Chang, W., Nace, D. A., Kavalieratos, D., Perera, S., & Handler, S. M. (2016). Nursing home provider perceptions of telemedicine for reducing potentially avoidable hospitalizations. *Journal of the American Medical Directors Association, 17*(6), 519–524.

du Toit, M., Malau-Aduli, B., Vangaveti, V., Sabesan, S., & Ray, R. A. (2017). Use of telehealth in the management of non-critical emergencies in rural or remote emergency departments: A systematic review. *Journal of Telemedicine and Telecare, 25*(1), 3–16.

Elrod, J. K., & Fortenberry, J. L. (2017). The hub-and-spoke organization design: An avenue for serving patients well. *BMC Health Services Research, 17*(1), 457.

European Commission. (2004). Libro bianco sui servizi di interesse generale. COM. 374. Eurpean Commision.

European Commission. (2008). Telemedicine for the benefit of patients, healthcare systems and society. COM (689). European Commision.

Farooq, A., Laato, S., Islam, A. N., & Isoaho, J. (2021). Understanding the impact of information sources on COVID-19 related preventive measures in Finland. *Technology in Society, 65,* 101573.

Ferreira, A., & Otley, D. (2009). The design and use of performance management systems: An extended framework for analysis. *Management Accounting Research, 20*(4), 263–282.

Fotheringham, A. S., & O'Kelly, M. E. (1989). *Spatial interaction models: Formulations and applications.* Norwell, MA: Kluwer.

Gabbrielli, F. L. G. M., Bertinato, L., De Filippis, G., Bonomini, M., & Cipolla, M. (2020). Interim provisions on telemedicine healthcare services during COVID-19 health emergency. *Version of April, 13*(2020), 1–32.

Gagnon, M.-P., Desmartis, M., Labrecque, M., Car, J., Pagliari, C., Pluye, P., Fremont, P., Gagnon, J., Tremblay, N., & Legare, F. (2012). Systematic review of factors influencing the adoption of information and communication technologies by healthcare professionals. *Journal of Medical Systems, 36*(1), 241–277.

Garshnek, V., Logan, J. S., & Hassell, L. H. (1997). The telemedicine frontier: Going the extra mile. *Space Policy, 13*(1), 37–46.

Green, S., & Vogt, H. (2016). Personalizing medicine: Disease prevention in silico and in socio. *HUMANA.MENTE Journal of Philosophical Studies, 90*(30), 105–145.

Griffiths, K. M., & Christensen, H. (2007). Internet-based mental health programs: A powerful tool in the rural medical kit. *Australian Journal of Rural Health, 15*(2), 81–87.

Hasan, A., & Paul, V. (2011). Telemonitoring in chronic heart failure. *European Heart Journal, 5*(32), 1457–1464.

Hess, D. C., Wang, S., Hamilton, W., Lee, S., Pardue, C., Waller, J. L., Gross, H., Fenwick, N., Hall, C., & Adams, R. (2005). REACH: Clinical feasibility of a rural telestroke network. *Stroke, 36*(9), 2018–2020.

Hood, L., & Friend, S. H. (2011). Predictive, personalized, preventive, participatory (P4) cancer medicine. *Nature Reviews Clinical Oncology, 8*(3), 184–187.

Huddleston, P., & Zimmermann, M. B. (2014). Stroke care using a hub and spoke model with telemedicine. *Critical Care Nursing Clinics, 26*(4), 469–475.

ISTAT - Italian National Statistical Institute. (2021). Conti economici Nazionali. Anni 2018–2020. Prodotto interno lordo e indebitamento netto delle Amministrazioni pubbliche. Retrieved November 04, 2022, from https://www.istat.it/it/files//2021/09/CS_Conti-economici-nazionali_2020.pdf

Italian Ministry of Health. (2014). Telemedicina–Linee di indirizzo nazionali. Retrieved July, 23, 2022, from http://www.salute.gov.it/imgs/C_17_pubblicazioni_2129_allegato.pdf

Italian Ministry of Health. (2020). Indicazioni Nazionali per l'erogazione di prestazioni in telemedicina. *Versione, 4*, 27. Italian Ministry of Health (Ed.), Italy.

Jung, C., & Padman, R. (2015). Disruptive digital innovation in healthcare delivery: The case for patient portals and online clinical consultations. In R. Agarwal, W. Selen, G. Roos, & R. Green (Eds.), *The handbook of service innovation* (pp. 297–318). London: Springer.

Kaplan, R. S., & Porter, M. E. (2011). How to solve the cost crisis in healthcare. *Harvard Business Review, 89*(9), 46–64.

Kaplan, R. S., & Norton, D. P. (2001). *The strategy-focused organization: How balanced scorecard companies thrive in the new business environment.* Watertown, Massachusetts, MA: Harvard Business School Press.

Kemm, J. Parry, J., & Palmer, S. (2004) *Health impact assessment.* Oxford, NY, USA: Oxford University Press. ISBN 978-0-19-852629-2.

Kieweg, P. H., Schöberl, S., & Palozzi, G. (2021). The role of communication in COVID-19 crisis management: Findings about information behavior of German and Italian young people. *International Journal of Business Research and Management (IJBRM), 12*(5), 263–288.

Kim, Y., Lee, H., Lee, M. K., Lee, H., & Jang, H. (2020). Development of a living lab for a mobile-based health program for Korean-Chinese working women in South Korea: Mixed methods study. *JMIR MHealth UHealth, 8*, e15359.

Kroenke, K., Theobald, D., Wu, J., Norton, K., Morrison, G., Carpenter, J., & Tu, W. (2010). Effect of telecare management on pain and depression in patients with cancer: A randomized trial. *JAMA, 304*(2), 163.

Kyle, E., Aitken, P., Elcock, M., & Barneveld, M. (2012). Use of telehealth for patients referred to a retrieval service: Timing, destination, mode of transport, escort level and patient care. *Journal of Telemedicine and Telecare, 18*(3), 147–150.

Mettler, T., & Pinto, R. (2018). Evolutionary paths and influencing factors towards digital maturity: An analysis of the status quo in Swiss hospitals. *Technological Forecasting and Social Change, 133*, 104–117.

Moffatt, J. J., & Eley, D. S. (2010). The reported benefits of telehealth for rural Australians. *Australian Health Review, 34*(3), 276–281.

Mueller, K. J., Potter, A. J., MacKinney, A. C., & Ward, M. M. (2014). Lessons from tele-emergency: Improving care quality and health outcomes by expanding support for rural care systems. *Health Affairs, 33*(2), 228–234.

OASI Report. (2018). *Osservatorio sulle Aziende e sul Sistema sanitario Italiano.* Retrieved July 24, 2022, from https://cergas.unibocconi.eu/sites/default/files/files/Capitolo-2-OASI-2018.pdf

OASI Report. (2021). *Osservatorio sulle Aziende e sul Sistema sanitario Italiano.* Retrieved July 24, 2022, from https://cergas.unibocconi.eu/observatories/oasi_/oasi-report-2021

OECD. Elderly population (indicator). (2019). Organisation for Economic Co-operation and Development (OECD, Ed.) Retrieved July 24, 2022, from https://data.oecd.org/pop/elderly-population.htm#indicator-chart. https://doi.org/10.1787/8d805ea1-en

OECD. (2021). Strengthening the frontline: How primary health care helps health systems adapt during the COVID-19 pandemic POLICY BRIEFS, Organisation for Economic Co-operation and Development (OECD, Ed.). Retrieved July 24, 2022, from https://read.oecd-ilibrary.org/view/?ref=1060_1060243-snyxeld1ii&title=Strengthening-the-frontline-How-primary-health-care-helps-health-systems-adapt-during-the-COVID-19-pandemic

O'Kelly, M. E., & Miller, H. J. (1994). The hub network design problem: A review and synthesis. *Journal of Transport Geography, 2*(1), 31–40.

Osborne, S. P., Radnor, Z., & Strokosch, K. (2016). Co-production and the co-creation of value in public services: A suitable case for treatment? *Public Management Review, 18*(5), 639–653.

Osborne, S. P. (2006). The new public governance? *Public Management Review, 8*(3), 377–387. https://doi.org/10.1080/14719030600853022

Osborne, S. P., & Strokosch, K. (2013). It takes two to Tango? Understanding the co-production of public services by integrating the services management and public administration perspectives. *British Journal of Management, 24*(S1), S31–S47. https://doi.org/10.1111/1467-8551.12010

Ostrom, E. (1996). Crossing the great divide; Co-production, synergy, and development. *World Development, 24*(6), 1073–1088.

Palozzi, G., Binci, D., & Appolloni, A. (2017). e-Health & co-production: critical drivers for health diseases management. In M. A. Pfannstiel, & C. Rasche (Eds.). *Service business model innovation in the healthcare and hospital management; Models, strategies, tools* (pp. 269–296). Cham: Springer Nature. https://doi.org/10.1007/978-3-319-46412-1

Palozzi, G., Chirico, A., Falivena, C., & Calò, L. (2018). How information availability changes healthcare chronicity management: Findings from a pilot case study. In *International Forum on Knowledge Asset Dynamics (IFKAD) Proceeding*, e-Book. ISBN 978-88-96687-11-6, ISSN 2280-787X

Palozzi, G., Chirico, A., & Gabbrielli, F. (2020a). Cost analysis of telemedicine implementation in the lens of healthcare sustainability: A review of the literature. In *EAI International Conference on Smart Cities within SmartCity 360° Summit* (pp. 451–469). Cham: Springer Publishing.

Palozzi, G., Schettini, I., & Chirico, A. (2020b). Enhancing the sustainable goal of access to healthcare: Findings from a literature review on telemedicine employment in rural areas. *Sustainability, 12*(8), 3318.

PNRR - Piano Nazionale di Ripresa e Resilienza. (2021). Italian Government, Rome, Palazzo Chigi, 25.

Porter, M. E. (1991). Towards a dynamic theory of strategy: Special issue. *Strategic Management Journal, 12*(51), 95–117.

Porter, M. E. (1997). Competitive strategy. *Measuring Business Excellence, 1*(2), 12–17.

Porter, M. E. (2008). Value-based health care delivery. *Annals of Surgery, 248*(4), 503–509.

Porter, M. E. (2010). What is value in health care? *The New England Journal of Medicine, 363*(26), 2477–2481.

Porter, M. E., & Teisberg, E. O. (2006). *Redefining health care: Creating value-based competition on results.* Boston, MA: HBSP.

Preston, J., Brown, F. W., & Hartley, B. (1992). Using telemedicine to improve health care in distant areas. *Psychiatric Services (Washington, DC), 43*(1), 25–32.

Quattrociocchi, L., Tibaldi, M., & Caputi, M. (2020). Invecchiamento attivo e condizioni di vita degli anziani in Italia. Italian national statistical institute—ISTAT, Italy.

Razmak, J., & Belanger, C. H. (2017). Connecting technology and human behaviours towards e-health adoption. *International Journal of Information Systems and Change Management, 9*(3), 169–192.

Renedo, A., Marston, C. A., Spyridonidis, D., & Barlow, J. (2015). Patient and public involvement in healthcare quality improvement: How organizations can help patients and professionals to collaborate. *Public Management Review, 17*(1), 17–34.

Rghioui, A., & Oumnad, A. (2018). Challenges and opportunities of Internet of Things in healthcare. *International Journal of Electrical and Computer Engineering, 8*(5), 2088–8708.

Roine, R., Ohinmaa, A., & Hailey, D. (2001). Assessing telemedicine: A systematic review of the literature. *Canadian Medical Association Journal (CMAJ), 165*(6), 765–771.

Rosenberg, C. N., Peele, P., Keyser, D., McAnallen, S., & Holder, D. (2012). Results from a patient-centered medical home pilot at UPMC health plan hold lessons for broader adoption of the model. *Health Affair, 31*(11), 2423–2433.

Sampietro Colom, L., Lach, K., Haro, I. E., Sroka, S., Cicchetti, A., Marchetti, M., Iacopino, V., Kidholm, K., Ølholm, A. M., Birk Olsen, M., Pasternack, I., Roine, R. P., Halmesmäki, E., Fure, B., Arentz Hansen, H., Frønsdal, K. B., Rosenmöller, M., Ribeiro, M., Garcia, E. V., Wild, C., Patera, N., Fischer, S., Kisser, A., Kahveci, R., Tutuncu, T., Yuksek, Y. N., Kucuk, E. O., Wasserfallen, J. B., Pinget, C., Kiivet, R. A., & Ulst, M. (Eds.). (2015). The AdHopHTA handbook: A handbook of hospital-based Health Technology Assessment (HB-HTA). Public deliverable, The AdHopHTA Project (FP7/2007-13 grant agreement nr 305018), Barcelona, Spain.

Sankaran, S., Luyten, K., Hansen, D., Dendale, P., & Coninx, K. (2018). Have you met your METs?—Enhancing patient motivation to achieve physical activity targets in cardiac tele-rehabilitation. In *Proceedings of the 32nd International BCS Human Computer Interaction Conference* (Vol. 32, pp. 1–12). Retrieved July 24, 2022, from https://doi.org/10.14236/ewic/HCI2018.48

Segrelles-Calvo, G., López-Padilla, D., Chiner, E., Fernandez-Fabrellas, E., & de Granda-Orive, J. I. (2017). Acceptance of telemedicine among respiratory healthcare professionals. *European Research in Telemedicine/la Recherche Européenne En Télémédecine, 6*(3–4), 147–155.

Shaw, S. L. (1993). Hub structures of major US passenger airlines. *Journal of Transport Geography, 1*(1), 47–58.

Skorin-Kapov, D., & Skorin-Kapov, J. (1995). On hub location models. *Journal of Computing and Information Technology, 3*(3), 183–192.

Solberg, E., Traavik, L. E., & Wong, S. I. (2020). Digital mindsets: Recognizing and leveraging individual beliefs for digital transformation. *California Management Review, 62*(4), 105–112.

Spano, A., & Aroni, A. (2018). Organizational performance in the Italian health care sector. In E. Borgonovi, E. Anessi-Pessina, & C. Bianchi (Eds.), *Outcome-based performance management in the public sector* (pp. 25–43). Cham, Switzerland: Springer International Publishing.

Stensland, J., Speedie, S. M., Ideker, M., House, J., & Thompson, T. (1999). The relative cost of outpatient telemedicine services. *Telemedicine Journal, 5*(3), 245–256.

Switzer, J. A., Demaerschalk, B. M., Xie, J., Fan, L., Villa, K. F., & Wu, E. Q. (2013). Cost-effectiveness of hub-and-spoke telestroke networks for the management of acute ischemic stroke from the hospitals' perspectives. *Circulation: Cardiovascular Quality and Outcomes, 6*(1), 18–26.

Tarricone, R. (2004). *Valutazioni economiche e management in sanità. Applicazioni ai programmi e tecnologie sanitarie* (Vol. 1). Milan, Italy: McGraw-Hill.

Taylor, M., Caffery, L. J., Scuffham, P. A., & Smith, A. C. (2018). Economic modelling of telehealth substitution of face-to-face specialist outpatient consultations for Queensland correctional facilities. *Australian Health Review, 42*(5), 522–528.

Terry, N. P. (2016). Will the Internet of Things transform healthcare? *Vand. J. Ent. & Tech l., 19*(2), 327–352.

Tresp, V., Marc Overhage, J., Bundschus, M., Rabizadeh, S., Fasching, P. A., & Yu, S. (2016). Going digital: A survey on digitalization and large-scale data analytics in healthcare. *Proceedings of the IEEE, 104*(11), 2180–2206.

Uphoff, M. E., & Krane, D. (1998). Hospital-based health technology assessment: Essential questions and an operational model. *Public Productivity and Management Review, 22*(1), 60–70.

Wang, K., Wong, E. L.-Y., Ho, K.-F., Cheung, A. W.-L., Yau, P. S.-Y., Dong, D., Wong, S. Y.-S., Yeoh, E.-K. (2021). Change of willingness to accept COVID-19 vaccine and reasons of vaccine hesitancy of working people at different waves of local epidemic in Hong Kong, China: Repeated cross-sectional surveys. *Vaccines, 9*(1), 62. https://doi.org/10.3390/vaccines9010062

World Health Organization. (1998). A health telematics policy in support of WHO's Health-For-All strategy for global health development: report of the WHO group consultation on health telematics, 11–16 December 1997, World Health Organizcation (WHO, Ed.), Geneva.

World Health Organization. (2021). Coronavirus disease (COVID-19) advice for the public. World Health Organizcation (WHO, Ed.). Retrieved July 23, 2022, from https://www.who.int/emergencies/diseases/novel-coronavirus-2019/advice-for-public

Yilmaz, S. K., Horn, B. P., Fore, C., & Bonham, C. A. (2019). An economic cost analysis of an expanding, multistate behavioural telehealth intervention. *Journal of telemedicine and telecare, 25*(6), 353–364.

Gabriele Palozzi is an Official at the Italian Ministry of Economy and Finance, and Aggregate Professor of Managerial Control both at the Open University San Raffaele of Rome and the University of Rome Tor Vergata, where he received his PhD in Public Management and Governance. His studies address the spheres of Managerial Accounting, Strategic Controlling, Performance Management and Spending Evaluation. Particularly, his research focuses on economic, social, and clinical joint impacts connected to digital transformation and new technologies in health care.

Francesco Ranalli is Full Professor of Accounting at the University of Rome Tor Vergata - Italy, Department of Management and Law. He is Head of the Department of Management and Law and the former Coordinator of the Ph.D. Course in Public Management & Governance for the University of Rome Tor Vergata. Author of several publications, his main research interests include Financial Reporting & Analysis, Control, Governance and Management both in the Public and Private sectors.

Integrated Care Models in Aged Care: The Role of Technology

Madhan Balasubramanian, Mark Brommeyer, Lucy Simmonds, and Angie Shafei

ABSTRACT

Health systems globally are struggling to respond to a rapidly ageing population and promote positive trajectories for healthy ageing. Integrated care models
provide an avenue towards care being delivered in a coordinated and structured
manner across different levels of care (primary, secondary and tertiary). Technology is vital in providing timely and effective integrated care for older people.
Emerging technologies can play a role both in aged care facilities, as well as
in-home services. This chapter discusses the role of technology in facilitating
or enhancing integrated care models in aged care.

1   Introduction

The rapidly ageing population presents a global crisis for health and aged care. By
2050, the world's population aged 60 years or more will nearly double, bringing
profound consequences to health systems. Multi and co-morbidity of chronic conditions are prevalent amongst older people, adversely affecting health outcomes

M. Balasubramanian (✉) · M. Brommeyer · L. Simmonds · A. Shafei
Health Care Management, College of Business, Government and Law, Flinders University, GPO
Box 2100, Adelaide, SA 5001, Australia
e-mail: madhan.balasubramanian@flinders.edu.au

M. Brommeyer
e-mail: mark.brommeyer@flinders.edu.au

L. Simmonds
e-mail: lucy.simmonds@flinders.edu.au

A. Shafei
e-mail: angie.abdelshafei@flinders.edu.au

and quality of life. Health systems are struggling to respond to these diverse challenges and promote positive trajectories for healthy ageing. Integrated care models offer viable solutions for implementing a complex spectrum of interventions for older people, to experience the best outcomes.

Integrated care focuses on services that extend the care continuum and are integrated across the different levels (primary, secondary and tertiary) and locations of care (hospitals, homes, clinics, etc.). Care provisions can extend to include both health, community and long-term care, thus, a wide range of service providers must work together in a coordinated and structured manner to effectively deliver integrated care. Using a person-centred approach, care must be designed based on the unique experiences, needs and preferences of older people. Technology is vital in providing timely and effective integrated care for older people. However, this area is yet to receive much attention. Emerging technologies can play a role both in aged care facilities, as well as in-home services.

In this chapter, we discuss the role of technology in facilitating or enhancing integrated care models in aged care. We first examine the relevance of population ageing across the globe, within the context of transition healthcare environments (demographic, epidemiologic and technology). Later, we discuss integrated care models, examining challenges and opportunities for improving aged care services. Digital technologies in aged care including major national strategies and solutions are then discussed. Finally, we provide recent and relevant examples from developing and developed countries, where technology has been effectively used in improving integrated care for older people, including telehealth, electronic health records, mobile technologies, use of sensors, big data and health data science solutions.

2 Ageing Populations and Transition Environments

Population ageing is a consistent demographic trend, and in many countries, both the number and proportion of older people aged 60 years and above are rapidly increasing. According to the United Nations report on "shifting demographics", older people currently outnumber children under the age of five years, and by 2050 older people will also outnumber adolescents and youth between the ages of 15–24 years (United Nations, 2019). Between 2015 and 2020, the proportion of older people over 60 years is set to double from 12 to 22 per cent (World Health Organization, 2021). By 2050, it is projected that nearly 2.1 billion people will be aged 60 years and over, and nearly 426 million will be aged 80 years or older (World Health Organization, 2021, 5–36). Today, older people comprise the world's fastest-growing age group (United Nations Department of Economic & Social Affairs, 2019, 5–36). All regions in the world are expected to see an increase in the number of older people, with the largest increase projected to occur in the Eastern and South Asian Region countries (312 million between 2019 and 2050) (United Nations Department of Economic & Social Affairs, 2019, 5–36). Further, the fastest increase in the number of older people is set to occur in North Africa and the West Asian Regions (226%), followed by Sub-Saharan Africa (218%) (United Nations Department of Economic & Social Affairs, 2019, 5–36). Comparatively, the proportion of the increase in older people is expected to be relatively small in Australia and New Zealand (84%), and in Europe and North America (48%), where the older people population is already higher than in other developing countries (United Nations Department of Economic & Social Affairs, 2019, 5–36).

The rapid increase in the older population groups can be attributed to increased life expectancy and declining mortality rates (Wahdan, 1996). Countries can be classified into five stages based on the demographic transition model: high stationary, early expanding, late expanding, low stationary and declining (Omran, 2005; Wahdan, 1996). At the earliest stage, we find both a high birth and death rate, contributing to the population growth being low. In the next stage, death rates start to decline but birth rates remain high, causing an expansion in population growth. In the later stage, we find the birth rate beginning to fall sharply, but the death rate also continues to fall leading to a late expanding stage of the population. As both the death rate and the birth rate continue to decline and fall to low levels, where they reach approximately each other the population growth becomes relatively stationary. A possible fifth stage, which some developed nations are beginning to experience is when the death rate becomes higher than the birth rate, suggesting a receding population growth.

Omran (2005) in his seminal work on the epidemiological transition suggested that a vast array of social, cultural, economic as well as epidemiological factors contribute to population change (Omran, 2005). In general, the shift from acute infectious and deficiency diseases to chronic non-communicable diseases is referred to as epidemiological transition. An ageing population has undoubtedly attributed to the rise in several chronic conditions such as cardiovascular disease, neoplasms, chronic respiratory disease, diabetes, neurological disorders, musculoskeletal disorders, sense organ disease and other non-communicable diseases (such as dental and craniofacial diseases) (Chang et al., 2019). Multimorbidity (co-occurrence of chronic conditions) is also more common among older people (Britt et al., 2008). For example in Australia, among older people aged 65+ years, nearly 60% had two or more chronic conditions (Australian Institute of Health and Welfare (AIHW), 2016b). Arthritis, back pain, cardiovascular disease and psychosocial problems were the more commonly reported co-occurring conditions (Australian Institute of Health and Welfare (AIHW), 2016a).

Disability Adjusted Life Years (DALYs) are used to quantify the number of healthy life years lost due to the presence of disease/disability (Hay et al., 2017). A large number of developed countries in the American and European Regions, as well as a few in the Western Pacific Region report low DALYs, compared with many developing countries in the South Asian and African Regions. Older people in developing countries appear to face a larger burden of disability/disease; health system response in these countries could be slow or limited, due to a lack of necessary resources or expertise. Nevertheless, many developing countries are facing a seismic demographic shift, with falling fertility rates, increasing life expectancy and gradual improvements in health care. It is projected that by 2050, over three-quarters of the world's older people will be living in the developing world (Shetty, 2012). Health professionals, as well as health systems in these countries, have not traditionally had to deal with ageing and the complex needs of older people (Shetty, 2012).

Rapid advancements in technology have also contributed to improvements in health care for older people. Innovations in consumer electronics, communication, home automation, big data and robotic solutions have enhanced care provision for older people (Pilotto et al., 2018). Information and communication technologies can include applications such as internet systems, virtual support groups, video conferencing, online computer services and electronic health records. Assistive technologies can include services that are designed to help the activities of daily living and safely of older people. Behavioural monitoring tools (sensors, wearables, warning systems), telehealth/telemedicine tools and smart home tools are types of assistive technologies designed to help older people. In addition, robotic systems can include technologies such as robots for supporting people with mobility or cognitive limitations.

3 Integrated Care Models

'Integrated Care' has often been limited in its definition and scope, and synonymously used with terms such as seamless care, coordinated care, care pathways, care continuum and interdisciplinary collaboration, among others. We adopt a health system-based definition proposed by the World Health Organization (see Fig. 1), which focuses on integrated health service delivery and thereby aligning health system functions as well as effective change management (World Health Organization, 2016, pp. 3–15).

Integrated care is a multifaceted concept. At least four types of integration have been identified: organisational, functional, service and clinical (World Health Organization, 2016, 3–15). Organisational integration could be argued as collectives and coordinated provider networks, brought together formally as mergers or corporate entities, or also as separate organisations brokered by a purchaser. Functional integration involves integration of office and non-clinical support, including systems such as electronic health records. Service integration involves integration of various health services at organisation level and using multidisciplinary teams. Clinical integration involves coherent delivery of care to patients within and across professions, using shared guidelines and protocols. Further, integration can also be considered as horizontal or vertical (World Health Organization, 2016, 3–15). In horizontal integration we are looking at activities at the same stage of the process of delivering services. In vertical integration, we are looking at activities at various stages and across different levels within the organisation under one management (including primary, secondary, tertiary care or general practice and community care).

Type of definition	Simple explanation	Definition
Process based definition	Understanding different components of integrated care	Integration is a coherent set of methods and models on the funding, administrative, organizational, service delivery and clinical levels designed to create connectivity, alignment, and collaboration within and between the cure and care sectors. The goal of these methods and models is to enhance quality of care and quality of life, consumer satisfaction and system efficiency for people by cutting across multiple services, providers and settings. Where the result of such multi-pronged efforts to promote integration leads to benefits for people, the outcome can be called integrated care.
User-led definition	Supports definition narrative and purpose of integrated care strategies at all levels of the system	My care is planned with people who work together to understand me and my carer(s), put me in control, coordinate and deliver services to achieve my best outcomesî
Health system based definition	Integrated health service delivery through alignment of all health system functions and change management	Integrated health services delivery is defined as an approach to strengthen people-centred health systems through the promotion of the comprehensive delivery of quality services across the life-course, designed according to the multidimensional needs of the population and the individual and delivered by a coordinated multidisciplinary team of providers working across settings and levels of care. It should be effectively managed to ensure optimal outcomes and the appropriate use of resources based on the best available evidence, with feedback loops to continuously improve performance and to tackle upstream causes of ill health and to promote well-being through intersectoral and multisectoral actions.

Fig. 1 Definitions of integrated care. *Source* World Health Organization (2016, pp. 3–4)

Integrated care is a key enabler for health ageing and essential to "prevent, slow or reverse declines in the physical and mental capacities of older people" (World Health Organization, 2019). Based on the WHO integrated care for older people guidelines, integrated care models need to be person centred, rather than being disease centred (Tavassoli et al., 2022). The WHO approach calls for greater integration of the health and social care workforce, including a coordinated person centred approach, through multidisciplinary engagement, interprofessional collaboration and teamwork (World Health Organization, 2019). Technology plays a vital role in integrated service provision and bringing health professionals to work more collaboratively as well as improve timely provision of care and health outcomes.

4   Digital Technologies in Aged Care Services

Digital technologies improve access to care and coordination, improve self-management, support decision making, assist monitoring, risk analysis and facilitate proactive interventions in a health care scenarios (Baltaxe et al., 2019). The use of digital technologies for aged care services is a growing area of research, with several new solutions being designed both for institutional usage (in hospitals, nursing homes and rehabilitation facilities) as well as mobile services and at-home monitoring and care provision (Baltaxe et al., 2019; Ienca et al., 2021). A few solutions are being purposefully designed to meet the needs and wishes of older people, named as 'gerontechnologies' (Ienca et al., 2021). For example, intelligent assistive technology (IAT) is of particular value to older people with dementia, or other age-related cognitive disability. Other technologies (such as telehealth, electronic health records) cater all population groups, including older people.

Digital transformation of community health and social services can also bring profound implications for integrated service provision for older cohorts (Rogelj et al., 2021). Solutions such as social support networks, and developing age friendly digital social environments can provide avenues for improved connectivity among health and social care workforce (Rogelj et al., 2021). We now offer a few case studies on integrated care models in aged care and explore the role of digital health.

5   Case Studies

The following sub-sections provide case studies on a few emerging technologies used to improve integrated care provision in aged care services. We first discuss on wearable sensor solutions, followed by telehealth and electronic health records.

5.1   Wearable Sensor Solutions in Aged Care

Wearable sensor technologies (wearables) can help older people retain independence living in their own home and enable monitoring for safety in assisted living and hospital environments. The goal of wearables is to improve older people's quality of life, support care and reduce load on health services by triggering an alert based on abnormal parameters. Wearables can promote independent living (e.g. by reducing the risk of falling), manage chronic disease (e.g. cardiac monitoring) and reduce risk of illness (e.g. implantable bladder sensors help reduce risk of infection) as detailed in the three brief case studies below.

Older people are at risk of falls, which frequently result in fractures and other serious injuries that restrict movement and may lead to reduced independence. Person-worn sensors enable movement recognition and location tracking to trigger alert messages if they are at risk of a fall (Bet et al., 2019). Fall sensors can also be used in assisted living and hospital environments to trigger alert messages to staff when risky movements occur. In this way, wearable sensors may offer advantages over bed and chair pressure alarm systems because they allow for monitoring of multiple risk activities. The AmbIGeM (Ambient Intelligent Geriatric Management system) is an example of a fall-risk detection wearable Bluetooth device (Visvanathan et al., 2022). The wearable contains accelerometer and gyroscope sensors (15 g) held in a pocket over the sternum of a cotton singlet worn by the older person. Staff are alerted to risk movements through a mobile app on their smartphone.

Cardiovascular disease, such as heart attack and atrial fibrillation, is common in older people. Wearable monitoring devices can detect arrhythmia and continuously monitor cardiac health status through electrocardiography (ECG) (Bayoumy et al., 2021). There is growing demand for cardiac wearables to assist clinicians in diagnosis, clinical decision-making, treatment and ongoing management of heart conditions in older people. Along with detecting risk in heart rhythms, cardiac wearables can call emergency services and assist in triaging the patient at the emergency department based on the severity of the patient's condition. Zio patch is an example of a wearable adhesive patch to monitor heart rhythm for a prolonged duration (Bayoumy et al., 2021).

Stroke patients suffering from urinary incontinence traditionally undergo a catheter insertion, which can result in a risk of infection. Providing an alternative to catheter insertion, implantable bladder sensors measure bladder urine volume and pressure (Dakurah et al., 2015). There is no risk of infection caused by traditional measures, such as catheters, improving the older person's quality of life.

There are currently mixed results in the clinical perspective of utility and evaluations of effectiveness in the emerging field of wearables for older people (Ferguson et al., 2020; Visvanathan et al., 2022). However, the potential for wearables to improve the safety, health and well-being of older people will likely see substantial future development and research until highly useful and effective wearables are a reality, enabling real-time physiological monitoring of older people to be integrated with electronic medical records.

5.2   Telehealth Technologies

Aged care consumers are often besieged with mobility issues as well as additional needs for specialist support. Demand for flexible, accessible and specialist services is rapidly increasing with the growth of aged care facilities (institutional and home based). Telehealth helps to connect healthcare providers through information technology, resulting in better access to care for aged care consumers. Telehealth services also minimise the need for travel, improve health outcomes, and caries an indirect impact toward reducing hospital admissions and waiting lists. Prior research has provided evidence that services such as telehealth contribute to improving the quality of care, by offering services that are timely and more accessible to a large group of populations (such as rural and remote, disadvantaged people) (Gentry et al., 2019; Haydon et al., 2021; Kaambwa et al., 2017).

Telehealth has several applications in aged care. A common telehealth service is a specialist consultation using telehealth services, rather than physical travel to meet a specialist. One case study of successful telehealth in aged care is Geri-Connect service, a medicare-funded model for geriatric medicine by Bendigo Health providing care in 58 residential aged care facilities in regional Victoria, Australia (Haydon et al., 2021). More than 1935 video consultations for over 1103 patients were conducted from 2017 to 2020. The model utilises an integrated service model involving a clinical nurse coordinator, geriatrician, general practitioners (GP) and including aged care workers and family members (Haydon et al., 2021). Residents are triaged by the clinical nurse coordinator and video consultations with the geriatricians resulting in care management plans that are taken to the GP. Success of the program was evident with additional insights on this service addressing a clinical need and, in some instances, more efficient than in-person consults. The service was reported to be clinically safe and effective, multidisciplinary, reducing polypharmacy, as well as reducing the need for patient travel to external facilities (Haydon et al., 2021). In addition, the service was patient-centred, well accepted by patients, comfortable, convenient, and also inclusive of aged care workers and family members (Haydon et al., 2021).

Another case study aiming to close gaps in service delivery transition between hospital and community, was an integrated response model for palliative care (Runacres et al., 2022). Using a videoconferencing platform, this included tertiary hospital outreach palliative care, integrated community care and residential care and community palliative care. Identified patients were virtually reviewed daily, assessed and family members invited to attend the clinical review and subsequent care planning sessions (Runacres et al., 2022). This collaboration using integrated care included education on prognosis and symptom assessments, education, and standardisation for medication, as well as team role clarification for staff and family members (Runacres et al., 2022). The proposed telehealth model was scalable with staff reporting more confidence in resident identification, as well an excellent management for symptoms and palliative care needs (Runacres et al., 2022). In addition, utilising this model enabled efficient patient reviews, maximum communication between the different services, goal clarification and treatment consensus (Runacres et al., 2022). Inclusion of family members and community palliative care in the virtual review enabled more inclusive discussions, better understanding and needs assessment, higher scope for family caregiver needs and bereavement support (Runacres et al., 2022).

Prior to the COVID pandemic, uptake of telehealth services was slow due to multiple factors, including patient and provider scepticism as well as multiple factors hindering scaling up such services including technology, patient safety, data confidentiality, legal issues, unclear health insurance coverages, among many others (Doraiswamy et al., 2021). With the COVID-19 pandemic in 2019, rapid global adoption was seen for use of telehealth with uptake increasing and several models of care being explored and implemented (Doraiswamy et al., 2021). Telehealth brings a significant impact towards improving access and outcomes of older people. Future research needs to focus on models of care and how telehealth services can be integrated within the care continuum including a range of providers, social and welfare personal as well as family members.

5.3 Electronic Health Records

The role of electronic health records (EHRs) in aged care services is increasing becoming more relevant (Bail et al., 2022; Fennelly et al., 2020). Widespread adoption of EHRs brings the potential to offer efficient and improved sharing of patient-related data across the aged care continuum (Bail et al., 2022). Care providers including GPs, specialists, pharmacists, allied health professionals, nurses, dentists and practice managers can access relevant patient-related information using EHRs. In Australia, the national EHR system is called My Health

Record, a safe and secure digital space to store, update and access relevant health information (Australian Digital Health Agency, 2022). Authorised personnel can instantly access patient information, improving care coordination and reducing risk of medical errors. In addition to patient information, EHR also provides various tools to practioners such as clinical decision support systems, predictive and prognostic tools, as well as integration to a range of additional health intelligence tools. The use of EHRs in real-time decision support systems brings the potential to both reduce costs as well as quality of patient care (Rothman et al., 2012).

While the applications of EHRs to aged care and improving integrated care services is becoming more relevant, only about 37.45 percent of aged care facilities in Australia had adopted an EHR system by 2013 (Jiang & Yu, 2015). It becomes increasingly important that appropriate information systems, including EHRs form part of accreditation standards for aged care facilities and service provision in the future so to enable the full potential of EHRs across the care spectrum for older adults.

6   COVID-19 and Post-COVID-19 Environments in Aged Care

Pandemic scenarios such as COVID-19 increases barriers to access and utilisation of health care services. Aged care is increasingly relevant; barriers can appear even more prominent with restrictions on health professional visits to aged care facilities, and limited scope of practice of available aged care staff (mostly nurses and aged care workers). A systematic review on the factors utilising access and service utilisation among older people during the COVID-19 pandemic identified mental health as a key challenge (Bastani et al., 2021). Digital health, including telehealth and improved information systems (EHRs) were also identified as key enablers to both facilitate integrated care provision as well as improving the quality of care (Bastani et al., 2021). This raises the importance of enhanced use of aged care workers as well as social and welfare personnel within the care continuum (Balasubramanian & Short, 2021a, 2021b). Policy interventions towards more sustainable and equitable care among older aged groups is vital in post-covid19 environments.

7   Conclusion

This chapter has provided an introduction to integrated care models in aged care, with a focus on the role of technology. Digital health provides several tools to foster collaborative practice and teamwork and enable an integrated health and social workforce.

References

Australian Digital Health Agency. (2022). *My health record in aged care*. Australian Digital Health Agency. Retrieved July 21, 2022, from https://www.myhealthrecord.gov.au/for-healthcare-pro fessionals/aged-care.

Australian Institute of Health and Welfare (AIHW). (2016a). Australian burden of disease study: Impact and causes of illness and death in Australia 2011. In *Australian burden of disease study series no. 3. Cat. no. BOD 4*. Canberra: Australian Institute of Health and Welfare (Ed.). Australian Burden of Disease Study Series no. 3. BOD 4.

Australian Institute of Health and Welfare. (2016b). Chapter 3: Chronic disease and comorbitites. In *Australia's health 2016. Australia's health series no. 15.Cat. no. AUS 199* (pp. 73–83). Canberra: AIHW.

Bail, K., Gibson, D., Acharya, P., Blackburn, J., Kaak, V., Kozlovskaia, M., Turner, M., & Redley, B. (2022). Using health information technology in residential aged care homes: An integrative review to identify service and quality outcomes. *International Journal of Medical Informatics, 165*(2022), 104824. https://doi.org/10.1016/j.ijmedinf.2022.104824

Balasubramanian, M., & Short, S. D. (2021a). The future health workforce: Integrated solutions and models of care. *International Journal of Environmental Research and Public Health, 18*(6), 1–4. https://doi.org/10.3390/ijerph18062849

Balasubramanian, M., & Short, S. D. (2021b). *A major revamp of health workforce planning and research infrastructure is necessary in Australia*. Pearls and Irritations. John Menadue's Public Policy Journal. Kingston ACT. Retrieved July 21, 2022, from https://johnmenadue.com/a-clear-revamp-of-health-workforce-planning-and-research-infrastructure-is-necessary-in-australia/

Baltaxe, E., Czypionka, T., Kraus, M., Reiss, M., Askildsen, J. E., Grenkovic, R., Lindén, T. S., Pitter, J. G., Rutten-van Molken, M., Solans, O., Stokes, J., Struckmann, V., Roca, J., & Cano, I. (2019). Digital health transformation of integrated care in Europe: Overarching analysis of 17 integrated care programs. *Journal of Medical Internet Research, 21*(9), e14956. https://doi.org/10.2196/14956

Bastani, P., Mohammadpour, M., Samadbeik, M., Bastani, M., Rossi-Fedele, G., & Balasubra-manian, M. (2021). Factors influencing access and utilization of health services among older people during the COVID–19 pandemic: A scoping review. *Archives of Public Health, 79*(1), 190. https://doi.org/10.1186/s13690-021-00719-9

Bayoumy, K., Gaber, M., Elshafeey, A., Mhaimeed, O., Dineen, E. H., Marvel, F. A., Martin, S. S., Muse, E. D., Turakhia, M. P., Tarakji, K. G., & Elshazly, M. B. (2021). Smart wearable devices in cardiovascular care: Where we are and how to move forward. *Nature Reviews Cardiology, 18*(8), 581–599. https://doi.org/10.1038/s41569-021-00522-7

Bet, P., Castro, P. C., & Ponti, M. A. (2019). Fall detection and fall risk assessment in older person using wearable sensors: A systematic review. *International Journal of Medical Informatics, 130*, 103946. https://doi.org/10.1016/j.ijmedinf.2019.08.006

Britt, H. C., Harrison, C. M., Miller, G. C., & Knox, S. A. (2008). Prevalence and patterns of multimorbidity in Australia. *Medical Journal of Australia, 189*(2), 72–77.

Chang, A. Y., Skirbekk, V. F., Tyrovolas, S., Kassebaum, N. J., & Dieleman, J. L. (2019). Measur-ing population ageing: An analysis of the Global Burden of Disease Study 2017. *The Lancet Public Health, 4*(3), e159–e167. https://doi.org/10.1016/S2468-2667(19)30019-2

Dakurah, M. N., Koo, C., Choi, W., & Joung, Y.-H. (2015). Implantable bladder sensors: A method-ological review. *International Neurourology Journal, 19*(3), 133–141. https://doi.org/10.5213/inj.2015.19.3.133

Doraiswamy, S., Jithesh, A., Mamtani, R., Abraham, A., & Cheema, S. (2021). Telehealth use in geriatrics care during the COVID-19 pandemic—a scoping review and evidence synthesis. *International Journal of Environmental Research and Public Health, 18*(4), 1755. https://doi.org/10.3390/ijerph18041755

Fennelly, O., Cunningham, C., Grogan, L., Cronin, H., O'Shea, C., Roche, M., Lawlor, F., & O'Hare, N. (2020). Successfully implementing a national electronic health record: A rapid umbrella review. *International Journal of Medical Informatics, 144*(July), 104281. https://doi.org/10.1016/j.ijmedinf.2020.104281

Ferguson, C., Inglis, S. C., Breen, P. P., Gargiulo, G. D., Byiers, V., Macdonald, P. S., & Hickman, L. D. (2020). Clinician perspectives on the design and application of wearable cardiac technologies for older adults: Qualitative study. *JMIR Aging, 3*(1), e17299. https://doi.org/10.2196/17299

Gentry, M. T., Lapid, M. I., & Rummans, T. A. (2019). Geriatric telepsychiatry: Systematic review and policy considerations. *The American Journal of Geriatric Psychiatry, 27*(2), 109–127. https://doi.org/10.1016/j.jagp.2018.10.009

Hay, S. I., Abajobir, A. A., Abate, K. H., Abbafati, C., Abbas, K. M., Abd-Allah, F., Abdulle, A. M., Abebo, T. A., Abera, S. F., Aboyans, V., Abu-Raddad, L. J., Ackerman, I. N., Adedeji, I. A., Adetokunboh, O., Afshin, A., Aggarwal, R., Agrawal, S., Agrawal, A., Kiadaliri, A. A., Ahmed, M. B., Aichour, A. N., Aichour, I., Aichour, M. T. E., Aiyar, S., Akinyemiju, T. F., Akseer, N., Al Lami, F. H., Alahdab, F., Al-Aly, Z., Alam, K., Alam, N., Alam, T., Alasfoor, D., Alene, K. A., Ali, R., Alizadeh-Navaei, R., Alkaabi, J. M., Alkerwi, A., Alla, F., Allebeck, P., Allen, C., Al-Maskari, F., Almazroa, M. A., Al-Raddadi, R., Geleijnse, J. M. (2017). Global, regional, and national disability-adjusted life-years (DALYs) for 333 diseases and injuries and healthy life expectancy (HALE) for 195 countries and territories, 1990-2016: A systematic analysis for the Global Burden of Disease Study 2016. *The Lancet, 390*(10100), 1260–1344https://doi.org/10.1016/S0140-6736(17)32130-X

Haydon, H. M., Caffery, L. J., Snoswell, C. L., Thomas, E. E., Taylor, M., Budge, M., Probert, J., & Smith, A. C. (2021). Optimising specialist geriatric medicine services by telehealth. *Journal of Telemedicine and Telecare, 27*(10), 674–679. https://doi.org/10.1177/1357633X211041859

Ienca, M., Schneble, C., Kressig, R. W., & Wangmo, T. (2021). Digital health interventions for healthy ageing: A qualitative user evaluation and ethical assessment. *BMC Geriatrics, 21*(1), 1–10. https://doi.org/10.1186/s12877-021-02338-z

Jiang, T., & Yu, P. (2015). The relationship between using electronic health records and meeting accreditation standards for client safety in residential aged care homes. *Studies in Health Technology and Informatics, 214*, 134–138.

Kaambwa, B., Ratcliffe, J., Shulver, W., Killington, M., Taylor, A., Crotty, M., Carati, C., Tieman, J., Wade, V., & Kidd, M. R. (2017). Investigating the preferences of older people for telehealth as a new model of health care service delivery: A discrete choice experiment. *Journal of Telemedicine and Telecare, 23*(2), 301–313. https://doi.org/10.1177/1357633X16637725

Omran, A. R. (2005). The epidemiologic transition: A theory of the epidemiology of population change, *83*(4), 731–757.

Pilotto, A., Boi, R., & Petermans, J. (2018). Technology in geriatrics. *Age and Ageing, 47*(6), 771–774. https://doi.org/10.1093/ageing/afy026

Rogelj, V., Salaj, A. T., & Bogataj, D. (2021). Digital transformation of community health and social services for ageing cohorts. *IFAC-PapersOnLine, 54*(13), 756–761. https://doi.org/10.1016/j.ifacol.2021.10.543

Rothman, B., Leonard, J. C., & Vigoda, M. M. (2012). Future of electronic health records: Implications for decision support. *Mount Sinai Journal of Medicine: A Journal of Translational and Personalized Medicine, 79*(6), 757–768. https://doi.org/10.1002/msj.21351

Runacres, F., Steele, P., Hudson, J., Bills, M., & Poon, P. (2022). We couldn't have managed without your team: A collaborative palliative care response to the COVID-19 pandemic in residential aged care. *Australasian Journal on Ageing, 41*(1), 147–152. https://doi.org/10.1111/ajag.13013

Shetty, P. (2012). Grey matter: Ageing in developing countries. *The Lancet, 379*(9823), 1285–1287. https://doi.org/10.1016/S0140-6736(12)60541-8

Tavassoli, N., de Souto Barreto, P., Berbon, C., Mathieu, C., de Kerimel, J., Lafont, C., Takeda, C., Carrie, I., Piau, A., Jouffrey, T., Andrieu, S., Nourhashemi, F., Beard, J. R., Soto Martin, M.

E., & Vellas, B. (2022). Implementation of the WHO integrated care for older people (ICOPE) programme in clinical practice: A prospective study. *The Lancet Healthy Longevity, 3*(6), e394–e404. https://doi.org/10.1016/S2666-7568(22)00097-6

United Nations Department of Economic and Social Affairs. (2019). World Population Ageing 2019. In *World Population Ageing 2019*. Retrieved July 21, 2022, from https://doi.org/10.1007/978-94-007-5204-7_6

United Nations. (2019). *Shifting demographics; UN75: Shaping our future together*. United Nations (UN), Retrieved July 21, 2022, from https://www.un.org/sites/un2.un.org/files/2019/10/un75_s hifting_demographics.pdf

Visvanathan, R., Ranasinghe, D. C., Lange, K., Wilson, A., Dollard, J., Boyle, E., Jones, K., Chesser, M., Ingram, K., Hoskins, S., Pham, C., Karnon, J., & Hill, K. D. (2022). Effectiveness of the wearable sensor-based ambient intelligent geriatric management (AmbIGeM) system in preventing falls in older people in hospitals. *The Journals of Gerontology: Series A, 77*(1), 155–163. https://doi.org/10.1093/gerona/glab174

Wahdan, M. (1996). The epidemiological transition. *Eastern Mediterranean Health Journal, 2*(1), 8–20.

World Health Organization. (2016). Integrated care models: An overview. *Health Services Delivery Programme* (pp. 1–31). World Health Organization (WHO, Ed.), Retrieved July 21, 2022, from http://www.euro.who.int/__data/assets/pdf_file/0005/322475/Integrated-care-models-ove rview.pdf, http://www.euro.who.int/__data/assets/pdf_file/0005/322475/Integrated-care-mod els-overview.pdf, http://www.euro.who.int/__data/assets/pdf_file/0005/322475/In

World Health Organization. (2019). *Integrated care for older people: Guidelines on community-level interventions to manage declines in intrinsic capacity*. World Health Organization (WHO, Ed.). https://doi.org/10.1007/978-3-319-96529-1_19

World Health Organization. (2021). *Ageing and health*. World Health Organization (WHO, Ed.): Factsheets. Retrieved July 21, 2022, from https://www.who.int/news-room/fact-sheets/detail/ageing-and-health

Madhan Balasubramanian is a Senior Lecturer in Health and Aged Care Management at the College of Business Government and Law, Flinders University. He was previously a Research Fellow at the Menzies Centre for Health Policy and Economics at the University of Sydney, and NHMRC Sidney Sax Research Fellow at the University of Sydney and Kings College London. He brings expertise in future health workforce, health services and public health, has published 50+ research articles, and won three nationally competitive Australian Government fellowships.

Mark Brommeyer has spent over thirty years in the health sector, with significant experience in digital health strategy, change, training and risk management across primary, secondary and tertiary care. Mark has provided healthcare consultancy, training and change management services in public and private health sectors in Australia, New Zealand, Malaysia, China, Singapore, Indonesia, England, Ireland and Wales. Mark is a Senior Lecturer in Health Care Management, Flinders University, where he has developed a Health Informatics course which he delivers in China, Singapore and Australia. Mark is currently undertaking his PhD research focusing on digital health competencies for health service managers.

Lucy Simmonds is Lecturer in Health Care Management, with particular expertise in Health Marketing. She has a Bachelor of Science in Genetics, and a PhD in Health Marketing and was previously a Postdoctoral Research Fellow in Behaviour and Practice Change at the South Australian Health and Medical Research Institute. She has professional experience in health marketing and communications, and has authored 13 peer reviewed articles.

Angie Shafei is Director of Healthcare Management Programs at Flinders University. Angie (MD, DBA) is a Clinical Pathologist, Pracademic, and an interdisciplinary researcher with a focus on innovation and transformation in health. She is a co-founder of a Technology start-up specialising in Medtech. Angie has over 25 years of experience in the medical education, and accreditation sectors in Australia, Singapore, China, North Africa and the Gulf. Angie's interests span the healthcare consumer's journey, patient-centred care, digital health and uses of emerging technology in improving the healthcare delivery including health apps, wearables, virtual reality, telehealth, and social media in health.

Exoskeletons—Human-Centred Solutions to Support Care Workers?

Riika Saurio, Satu Pekkarinen, Lea Hennala, and Helinä Melkas

ABSTRACT

Care work involves various physically strenuous stages. Tools of different kinds, such as cranes, can be used to facilitate the work, but if no suitable tool exists, the care worker's physical strength is used as an aid. This can easily lead to injuries, sick leaves and early exits from work life. Exoskeletons, a form of wearable robotics, can support care workers by reducing physical exertion and supporting posture and motion. They are being used in other fields, such as industry, with good results, but little is currently known about the use of exoskeletons to support care work. Integrating technology into care work is a question of mutual adjustments between technologies and various work practices. In this chapter, we examine—from the point of view of technology domestication—the implementation and use of exoskeletons in care services. We make use of a field study of user experiences with the Auxivo LiftSuit exoskeleton in elderly care that was conducted in two care homes in Finland. Both factors that support domestication and those that delay it are presented, resulting in new knowledge concerning the exoskeleton in question and the more general prerequisites for domestication of exoskeletons in care work. These findings may be utilised to develop future domestication processes, thus advancing human-centred service design in care services.

R. Saurio · S. Pekkarinen · L. Hennala · H. Melkas (✉)
Lappeenranta-Lahti University of Technology LUT, Mukkulankatu 19, 15210 Lahti, Finland
e-mail: helina.melkas@lut.fi

R. Saurio
e-mail: riika.saurio@lut.fi

S. Pekkarinen
e-mail: satu.pekkarinen@lut.fi

1   Introduction

Care work involves many kinds of physically strenuous stages. Physical work stages can be facilitated by various tools, like cranes; there is naturally no suitable tool for every stage of multi-faceted care work. The caregiver's physical strength is traditionally used as an aid, which can easily lead to injuries, sick leaves and early exits (Davis & Kotowski, 2015, pp. 754–792; Trydegård, 2012, pp. 119–129). In light of this, changes to Finland's population structure, especially regarding the dependency ratio, which is at its highest value in sixty years (Kalluinen, 2018, p. 1), have been worrying. An increased dependency ratio means, among other things, that the number of care workers decreases in proportion to the growing number of people who require care (United Nations, 2007, p. 104). The same phenomenon has been observed elsewhere in the world (Skirbekk et al., 2022, p. e332). Concerns have thus arisen regarding this growing shortage of care workers. In the current era of healthcare transformation, exoskeletons, a form of wearable robotics, have been introduced as a way to support care workers by reducing their physical exertion.

According to ASTM International (2021, p. 2), an exoskeleton is "a wearable device that augments, enables, assists, and/or enhances physical activity through mechanical interaction with the body." According to the same standard, an exoskeleton may include rigid or soft components, or both, and the physical activity may be static or dynamic. For this reason, exoskeletons can be classified as active or passive (de Looze et al., 2015, p. 671). Active exoskeletons use actuators, such as electric motors, that increase the human's power and reinforce their joints. Passive exoskeletons do not use actuators but instead use materials, such as springs, which store the energy harvested by human motion and then use that energy to support the user's posture or motion. Exoskeletons have been deployed in other fields, such as industry, with good results (de Looze et al., 2015, p. 671).

A review of the scientific literature reveals a research gap concerning the implementation of exoskeletons in care work; further research is needed to ensure that the related service design is human-centred. It is also necessary to clarify whether there are indeed exoskeletons that are suitable for care work and how they should be implemented. The implementation of exoskeletons could potentially prolong the careers of nurses and increase the number of active care work professionals in the future. However, the field of social and health care services is challenging and complex, and it is therefore necessary to think carefully about how to bring new tools to care work and precisely what tools are needed.

The aim of this research is to examine—from the point of view of technology domestication—the implementation and use of exoskeletons in the field of social and healthcare services. This is done with the help of a field study concerning user experiences with the Auxivo LiftSuit exoskeleton (referred to as "suit" or "device" hereafter) in elderly care that was conducted in two care homes in Finland. The research questions are: (1) How are exoskeletons implemented and used in the field of social and healthcare services? (2) What are the user experiences of exoskeletons in care work? and (3) What are the central prerequisites for domestication of exoskeletons in care work? This research makes several contributions. By examining implementation and use via a field study, both factors that support domestication and those that hinder it are highlighted, resulting in new knowledge concerning the exoskeleton in question as well as the general prerequisites for domestication of exoskeletons in care work. With the help of our findings, future domestication processes will likely be developed, leading to advances in human-centred service design in care services.

2   Background

This section discusses definitions and characteristics of robots in care and the concept, process, and dimensions of technology domestication. Four dimensions of technology domestication are evaluated in this research.

2.1   Robots in Care

Care robots are defined as partly or fully autonomous machines that perform care-related activities for people with physical or mental disabilities related to age or health restrictions (Goeldner et al., 2015, p. 115). Care robots may also assist care workers, for example, assistant nurses, in their daily tasks (Melkas et al., 2020, pp. 4–5; Tuisku et al., 2022, pp. 1–2), allowing more time to perform those tasks that require human touch (Bush, 2001, p. 256). Wu et al. (2012, p. 121) divided such robots into monitoring robots (to observe behaviour and health), assistive robots (to provide support to the individual or their caregiver in daily tasks) and socially assistive robots (to provide companionship).

Niemelä et al. (2021, pp. 12–13) classified robotic applications and services according to their use contexts and purposes, differentiating between robots created to (a) maintain the independence and participation of an older adult, (b) improve the efficiency and ergonomics of the care worker, (c) improve recreation and non-physical rehabilitation and therapy, (d) automate secondary tasks in care, (e) improve physical rehabilitation therapy and experience, (f) support manual work (e.g. in terms of precision or heavy lifting) and (g) support logistics and safety in hospitals. Examples of these robots are telepresence robots (e.g. Double and Giraff), medicine-dispensing robots (e.g. Evondos), robotic walking aids (e.g. Lea), robotic spoons (e.g. Gyenno), exoskeletons for the rehabilitation of the patient (e.g. Indego) or for supporting the care worker (e.g. Laevo, Auxivo), transportation robots for delivering meals and medicine (e.g. TUG), and social robots for therapy, entertainment, and communication (e.g. Paro, JustoCat, Zora, & Pepper; Niemelä et al., 2021, pp. 12–13).

In several studies, attitudes toward robots in care are found to be more negative than in many other occupational fields, including education, business and industry (European Commission, 2012, p. 4–5, 2015, p. 58; Taipale et al., 2015, p. 18). The general public's attitudes toward the use of robots in the care of older people were also examined in a media analysis that showed that opinions were mostly negative (Tuisku et al., 2019, pp. 61–63). These results may be explained by the fact that people consider it inhumane for a robot to take care of a person; the main concern was that robots would replace human-to-human contact and care. However, Broadbent et al. (2010, p. 608) found that participants could identify many benefits and applications for healthcare robots, including performing simple medical procedures and providing physical assistance. Turja et al. (2018, pp. 304–305) investigated the attitudes of Finnish healthcare workers toward the use of robots in welfare services and discovered that their views were generally negative. However, the healthcare workers did consider a robot to be acceptable for certain work tasks, such as heavy lifting. So, attitudes toward robots depend upon the specific robot and task in question. A lack of knowledge related to robots may lead to false impressions concerning robots' capabilities and the associated risks, thus leading to negative attitudes (Johansson-Pajala et al., 2019, pp. 220–223; Tuisku et al., 2019, p. 64). The provision of hands-on experience and promotion of increased awareness and education about what care robots can do are both necessary to moving away from preconceptions based on fiction and imaginary images of robots (Frennert et al., 2021, p. 322). Studies have indicated that prior exposure to robots—when people were given more knowledge about robots, were shown a robot, or were able to use one—positively affects attitudes toward them (Broadbent et al., 2010, p. 612; Johansson-Pajala et al., 2019, p. 222; Melkas et al., 2020, p. 5).

2.2   Technology Domestication

Technology domestication theory (Haddon, 2011, pp. 311–323; Sørensen, 2005, pp. 40–61; Silverstone & Haddon, 1996, pp. 44–74) describes the unlinear processes that occur between people and technologies when users "tame" technologies and integrate them into their everyday lives (Hargreaves et al., 2018, p. 129). The concept has its roots in the 1990s, when there was a holistic view of ICT use in homes (Haddon, 2006, p. 195) and in media studies (e.g. Silverstone et al., 2003 pp. 13–28, and Silverstone & Haddon, 1996, pp. 44–74; see also Hartmann, 2020, p. 47), but it has grown to include study of the adoption of specific technologies as well, such as cable TV (Haddon, 2011, pp. 316–317), mobile phones (Haddon, 2003, pp. 43–56) and cars (Sørensen, 2005, pp. 40–61; see also Haddon, 2006, pp. 1–9, 2011, pp. 311–323). The framework considers the processes that shape the adoption and use of ICTs; in so doing, it also asks what the technologies and services mean to people, how they experience them, and what roles these technologies come to play in their lives (Haddon, 2011, p. 312).

Domestication theory emerged in response to the classic idea of diffusion of innovations (Rogers, 1983), which views technologies as pregiven, unchanging entities that diffuse through society in a linear way, implying an extremely passive role regarding the user, who simply adapts what is offered to them, little by little, in one social stratum after another (Hargreaves et al., 2018, p. 129; Lehtonen, 2003,

p. 364). Innovation is not only a matter of production but one of consumption and use, which are essential components of the innovation process (Silverstone & Haddon, 1996, p. 44). Thus, regarding innovation processes, domestication represents the user side of innovation: domestication is anticipated in design, and design is completed in domestication (Silverstone & Haddon, 1996, p. 46). This is linked to an idea from the STS (science and technology studies) literature that views technologies as being "scripted" by technology designers, meaning that the technology itself gives hints about how technology will function and how it should be used. Technology also makes assumptions regarding users' needs and the related contexts (Akrich, 1992, pp. 208–209; Stokke, 2017, p. 3), with which users may align or dissent. Likewise, when technology is domesticated, users can follow or disregard these initial scripts. Users are not passive adaptors of technologies but rather give meaning to them, and technology addresses users in specific, targeted ways.

The domestication perspective highlights that technologies are not fixed entities; they acquire specific forms of use and meanings when they are adopted and embedded in a given locality (Ingeborgrud & Ryghaug, 2019, p. 510; Silverstone et al., 2003, pp. 13–28). This perspective does not only focus on how technologies are "accepted" through practical use but also on how people learn to use a new technology and, not least, on the symbolic values and meaning creation central to the adoption process. In the process of domestication, users make technology meaningful in their lives (Pols & Willems, 2011, p. 485). Technology domestication aims to open the "black boxes" in technology use and reveal the processes and practical, symbolic, and cognitive negotiations that occur when technology is integrated into use (Aune, 2002, p. 5). These processes include technology producers, users, managers and decision makers, and the technology itself. Through these processes, technology and people shape each other: the technology has an impact on users, for instance by changing their practices, and the users have an impact on the technology.

Technology domestication is not a one-off event but a process that includes the effort invested before acquisition to imagine how technology might find a place in people's lives (Haddon, 2006, p. 2). Domestication mainly focuses on three generic feature sets (Sørensen, 2005, p. 47):

(1) The construction of a set of practices related to an artefact. This might include the routines related to using the artefact as well as the establishment and development of institutions to support and regulate this use;
(2) The construction of the meaning of the artefact, including the role the artefact could eventually play in relation to the production of the identities of the actors involved and
(3) The cognitive processes related to learning the practices and meaning.

In other words, the practical dimension concerns the ways in which users integrate the technology into already existing routines and how they establish new routines through use; the symbolic dimension refers to the ways in which users attach meanings to a new piece of technology, including self-representation, by means of using the technology; and the cognitive dimension refers to how people learn to use new technologies. These three dimensions are overlapping. When people domesticate technology, they fit it into their routines, place it, give it meaning, and learn to use it, or they abandon it (Aune, 2002, p. 5). Thus, domestication theory addresses both questions of use and of nonuse with a holistic view of people's circumstances (Haddon, 2011, pp. 319–320).

Søraa et al. (2021, p. 8) suggested that the social dimension should also be added to the domestication theory and highlighted the social processes involved in technology domestication. In these processes, technology can be seen as an actor that impacts the interaction between people and is coproduced, not only by the individual but by a wide variety of actors (Søraa et al., 2021, p. 11). The social dimension is therefore included in this study.

Most prior domestication studies have concentrated on the micro level (individuals and households), so less attention has been given to life outside the home (Haddon, 2011, p. 315; Pierson, 2006, p. 206); however, some recent studies have also considered societal-level domestication (Morley, 2005, pp. 21–39; Sørensen, 2005, pp. 40–61; see also Haddon, 2011, pp. 311–323). In this study, we evaluate technology domestication in a specifically organisational and work environment context (see Peine & Herrman, 2012, pp. 1495–1512; Pierson, 2006, pp. 205–226), but this context also speaks to the suitability of exoskeletons in the care field more widely.

3   The Field Study

The basics of the field study are described in this section. We introduce the tested exoskeleton and explain the data collection and analysis.

3.1   The Tested Exoskeleton

Auxivo LiftSuit® (see Figs. 1 and 2) is a Swiss passive exoskeleton that supports the back when lifting objects below waist level or when working in a forward leaning position. Textile springs on the back store energy, which is released when used to support the user's movements. The support is activated and deactivated by the straps in the front. The suit comes in two basic sizes but is designed to further adapt to wearers of different sizes via an adjustment mechanism. The suit can be washed in the washing machine at 30 °C and wiped with disinfectants. Safety loops, that is, rubber bands that can attach to the straps of the adjustment mechanisms in order to avoid leaving them hanging, help to ensure safety during use (Auxivo AG, 2022).

Fig. 1. Auxivo
LiftSuit® (front).
Source Photo Riika Saurio

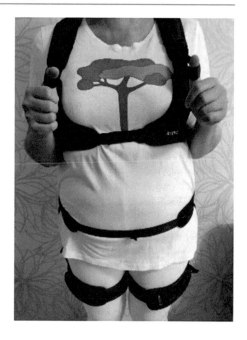

Fig. 2 Auxivo
LiftSuit® (back). *Source*
Photo Riika Saurio

3.2   Data Collection and Analysis

The research environment was a care home called Pohjola, which is located in and run by the city of Tampere, Finland. Pohjola offers round-the-clock housing services for older persons. Eight assistant nurses, recruited on a voluntary basis, took part in the field study. They were 19–61 years old, and their working experience in the care sector ranged from 1.5 to 40 years. The participants were divided into two groups, and each participant was able to use an Auxivo LiftSuit exoskeleton for three weeks (four assistant nurses at any given time).

This study uses qualitative data that were collected through pre-interviews and post-interviews as well as user diaries written during the trial. This research is part of the TUEKS project, "Exoskeletons and caregivers' changing daily work", supported by the Finnish Work Environment Fund (in addition to the qualitative data presented here, quantitative data were collected via physiological measurements by the Finnish Institute of Occupational Health). During the day of the pre-interviews, the participants received a comprehensive orientation and introduction to the use of the device from a researcher who also has a background in nursing. The number of participants was considered adequate for the nature of the research (see Turja et al., 2020, p. 13). The interview questions concerned expectations for and experiences of the use of the device, its experienced impacts on work, orientation needs, and other people's reactions toward use of the device. The user diary collected information on immediate experiences and the purposes and times of use.

The qualitative data were analysed with the help of content analysis and data categorisation. In the analysis, there were both inductive and deductive phases. After data transcription, the data were reduced into essential contents and then inductively coded using an interpretive approach that involved searching for recurrent themes and naming them. Subsequently, the themes were deductively categorised into the four dimensions of domestication theory (practical, symbolic, cognitive, and social). The findings, organised by dimension, are presented below. At a later stage, an implementation model for exoskeletons will be developed and piloted by the researchers. This model will utilise domestication theory and focus on what implementation requires from the nursing staff, organisation and managers.

4   Findings

The findings concerning practical, symbolic, cognitive and social domestication of the exoskeleton are presented in this section. Descriptive quotations are given where appropriate.

4.1   Practical Domestication of the Exoskeleton

When studying the practical dimension of domestication, we need to examine the ways in which users integrate the technology into already existing routines and establish new routines through use (Ingeborgrud & Ryghaug, 2019, p. 510), as well as the construction of a set of practices related to the artefact. This could mean the routines involved in using the artefact but also the establishment and development of institutions to support and regulate this use.

According to our field study results, the practical domestication-related issues— the ways in which users integrate the technology into already existing routines and create new routines through the technology use—were related to, for example, practicalities concerning work tasks and storage locations of the exoskeleton. The device was felt to be most practical for bed care activities, such as bed washing and changing diapers. During showering days, it was useful for helping the resident to the showering platform and doing the showering in the sauna facilities.

> For evening wash and posture shifting, and for assisting residents in wheelchairs to the toilet and from there to bed. And evening activities […] I used it when there was feeding and during mealtimes […] that's when I tried to wear it quite a lot.

The starting point for the trial was that the device could be used in all work tasks, and therefore, during the field study, use of the device did not necessitate any extra planning. However, once the most suitable tasks were identified during the field study, it was noted that proper planning would definitely be needed for regular use of the device. The participants wished that they could reserve the suit for a showering day, for instance.

> … About the planning, well, I didn't really plan it. I thought I'd wear it and let's see …

Practical issues considered to be challenging included tasks that had to be done in a squatting position (such as assisting during toileting), as the exoskeleton felt tight or compressing during those times, especially on the thighs and shoulders. During showering tasks, it felt sweaty. A few other details were also brought up:

> … the straps […] you always had to adjust those, and sometimes it happened that they got tangled in the edges of the bed. […] We work inside, and it can be hot sometimes. When you think that we would use it in the summer, it's really hot, sweaty.

Participants also mentioned that the device is not able to be used by diverse body types. On the other hand, one interviewee mentioned:

> It kept the posture perhaps a bit better. It makes you automatically straighten up, I had that feeling. So it helped in having a better posture, as you tend to stoop anyway, so that was a good thing.

Fig. 3 A handy place for storage. *Source* Photo Satu Pekkarinen

The participants thought that it was practical that the exoskeleton was unobtrusive; as a result, the residents did not pay much attention to it. The caregivers usually wore blue workwear, and they felt that the LiftSuit did not stand out.

As a prerequisite for use, it was necessary that the device be visible and available in the workplace, which ensured that care workers remembered to use it. A good place for storage was found to be the door stoppers on the doors, where the exoskeletons could hang freely (see Fig. 3). The interviewees mentioned that if exoskeletons were stored in lockers, for instance, their use would be less convenient. The participants also noted that the skills related to using the device had to be mastered before adjusting it to the user's specifications became an easy task.

Hygiene—how the exoskeleton would be washed or disinfected—was seen as a practical challenge that also affected the domestication process. The exoskeleton is washable, but could it be washed together with other laundry (e.g. residents' clothes)? Should it be washed separately, even in a separate washing machine? Could it be used by several nurses before it needed to be washed?

> … That it would be visible so that you would in general remember that [the exoskeleton] exists and we can use it … and of course, the hygiene; how it could be used by many of us and so forth …

4.2   Symbolic Domestication

The symbolic dimension of domestication refers to the ways in which users attach meanings to a new technology (Ingeborgrud & Ryghaug, 2019, p. 510). The construction of the meaning of an artefact, including the role that the artefact could eventually play in relation to the production of the identities of the actors involved, is examined in this section.

According to our results, the suit was typically considered by participants to be a normal or traditional work assistive device and had no specific connotations. However, some caregivers interestingly called it by Finnish male names: "Esko" and "Eki."

One of the participants experienced the use of the exoskeleton as an extra burden. When the participant could take the suit off, it was a relief. Another participant, who was over 50 years old, felt that the suit would be more suitable for younger care workers, as the skin and the body become less flexible as one ages, making the suit uncomfortable:

> … in the final stage I felt it was a bit burdensome to use it, it somehow felt a bit distressing to wear it [a laugh].

Some of the participants noted that simply bringing up nurses' need for help in their physically burdening work and showing that technology like this can be developed for them carries significant symbolic societal value. This is important in comparison with other fields of services and in relation to the service clients. The interviewees emphasised that, in general, there is great need in an ageing society to develop solutions and work practices that enable nurses to cope with their work.

> And it is also that the voice of the nurses comes out, nurses' wellbeing is considered […] There is also that aspect, in my view. A kind of societal call from there – that nurses also need something […] some help.

> … the principle is really good in that [work] is aimed to be developed with the help of technology, or with the help of anything, because this is so heavy work. […] I haven't, fortunately, had to see anymore the beds without wheels and how nurses carried them. We have come from there, which is pretty staggering; the development of ergonomics during the last decades.

4.3   Cognitive Domestication

The cognitive dimension of domestication is related to cognitive processes that concern the learning of practices and meaning. The cognitive dimension thus refers to how people learn to use new technologies (Ingeborgrud & Ryghaug, 2019, p. 510).

According to our results, after pre-adjusting the suit, taking it on and off was generally felt to be easy. Some of the participants had challenges in putting on the thigh parts because of difficulties related to finding the right strap. The plastic parts were also felt to be somewhat challenging, as they were slippery. Two participants expressed a wish for a rougher material or for a ball- or T-shaped strap for the activating straps. The suit itself was felt to be easy to use, but there were issues concerning comfort of use.

The most challenging issue was remembering to activate and de-activate the suit. One participant, for instance, completely forgot to activate it during a work task. Reminders and getting properly used to the suit will help to overcome this obstacle.

Well, it was easy to put it on. [...] But you have to remember to activate the suit before you do some task, it was a bit ... in the beginning I hardly remembered to take care of activating and did the work without it.

The orientation focused on the use of the device was given in a slideshow format, and it described the purpose of the suit and possible barriers to use. Instructions for putting on the suit were presented in a video. Each participant then received individual assistance in putting on the suit and taking it off. In addition, there was a lifting exercise in which the participants lifted a chair with and without activation of the suit. This exercise demonstrated the powerful support that could be expected from the device. Finally, the participants received an instruction manual in their native language and the phone number of a researcher they could call if they experienced any problems. These were seen as good practices by the participants.

It is a certain type of a device that you need ... that people understand what this is all about. And then, how it is used and why [...] I think that all these became clear. There was also enough written material and you had the videos [...] so I think that they were clear and I don't believe that you could have presented it in any better way.

The instructor's own nursing background was a nice addition, I think it showed that the instructor has a good perspective to the use. [The instructor] should always understand what kind of work we are doing here, and that should be the starting point for the instructor, whoever it is.

Considering cognitive domestication, practical issues were most appreciated during the orientation. The participants wished that there had also been a practical aspect to the orientation in real work circumstances during which the instructor could tell them when to activate and de-activate the suit. Furthermore, the participants would have liked to hear about situations in which they could benefit most from the suit, such as changing diapers when the resident is bedridden.

We should have tried it in practice right away, we don't lift chairs here [like during the orientation]. [...] I think that we should have gone to a resident, that would be really important. It would have given a feeling that I learn myself in practice and then I would perhaps have internalised it better ...

The three-week testing period was felt to be too short to truly domesticate the suit in care work. As work at the facility was organised into three shifts, some nurses ended up having few shifts during which they could use the suit. Some of the participants mentioned that it should be used for at least six weeks, or even two to three months, to allow for better acclimation and to make it a more natural part of the work. One participant emphasised that people's diversity affects the way they internalise new things, such as adjusting and using the exoskeleton.

Managers may end up having new tasks related to guidance and monitoring, for example.

> Normally these come via our managers, all these. [...] And then it should be clear where you are supposed to use them and how. Who is involved, is it for everyone or just for some part of us or ...? [...] Somehow I think that if you say that we will purchase this [device], you should be using it then. So that it is not left lolling somewhere. And the use should be monitored, too, at some level.

4.4   Social Domestication

Social domestication, which some scholars suggest should be added to the domestication theory (Søraa et al., 2021, p. 4, p. 11), highlights the social processes in technology domestication: how technology can enter into and become part of our social interactions. The social dimension of domestication investigates, for example, how humans relate to other humans when domesticating a technology, and it considers how technological domestication is not an individual process but one that relies on a wide variety of actors (Søraa et al., 2021, p. 4).

In social domestication, technology is seen as an actor impacting both the interaction between the end-user and the caregiver and that between other stakeholders (Goodall et al., 2019, p. 20; Søraa et al., 2021, p. 4).

Our results, as well as similar observations made by care workers during the field study, indicate that some of the residents did not pay any attention to the suit, while others showed interest in and asked questions about it. Both the workwear and the device were blue, so the suit did not stand out from the workers' clothing in any striking way. Some of the residents of the research site had memory diseases, and the participants wondered if this was the reason that these clients did not react to the suit at all. However, most of the family members of the residents did not pay particular attention to the suit, either, though some did ask about it.

> But I don't know of any wider positive ... [...] the residents were very positive about it, some did worry a little, yes, but it was the kind of general worrying that they may want to show as a kind of compassion towards nurses.

> [A laugh.] A resident had three visitors and I took a dinner tray to the room. And I had this uniform on, and no-one said anything about it. Normally [they would] ...

Within the work community, there was interest towards the suit, and other care workers were intrigued and curious to know about the benefits and user experiences. Care workers from other workplaces were also interested when they saw the suit:

> The colleagues asked these questions, yes, … that does it help? What does it feel like? And such things.

Overall, discussions were characterised by curiosity and a neutral attitude. The participants felt that management and the organisation were supportive towards the research because they had been committed to it from the very beginning.

5   Discussion

In this research, the implementation and use of exoskeletons in social and health care were examined with the help of a field study concerning user experiences with the Auxivo LiftSuit exoskeleton. Analysis of the qualitative data with the help of the four domestication dimensions—practical, symbolic, cognitive, and social—revealed that there is potential for the domestication of exoskeletons in care work environments, as the participants noted many benefits and relatively few obstacles. There are, however, factors related to each dimension that either support or hinder the domestication process. These should be taken into account when introducing exoskeletons into care work environments.

From the practical domestication viewpoint, the exoskeletons were felt to be appropriate for certain work tasks. Nursing work includes many kinds of tasks, and the exoskeleton was beneficial for tasks that require leaning forward; the nurses wished they could reserve the suit for showering days, when much of the work requires leaning forward. Squatting positions, on the other hand, caused the suit to feel tight and uncomfortable. Planning concerning the order of work tasks and increased knowledge about situations in which the suit is beneficial are thus still needed.

Supportive factors included the suit's ease of use after initial adjustments and the fact that it was relatively unobtrusive and light. This is related to both the practical and symbolic dimensions; the suit did not attract special attention and was seen as a neutral tool. It was generally socially accepted, which relates it in turn to the social dimension.

Factors related to learning were largely practical but were also related to the cognitive dimension. When introducing the suit to workers, it is important to clearly mention the benefits of the device. Lucid guidelines regarding which tasks the exoskeleton is suitable for are critical, and the device orientation should include a practical exercise related to daily tasks. The instructor should explain when to activate the support and when to de-activate it; both reminders and time will likely be needed to ensure that nurses remember to activate the suit before appropriate work tasks. Importantly, all participants were ready to use some kind of an exoskeleton at work if they would gain benefits from the use.

The participants felt that societal appreciation of care work would perhaps increase through the development of such devices, which could lead to the voices of the nurses gaining more prominence. These findings are related to both the symbolic and social dimensions. On the other hand, the length of the three-week trial period was felt to be too short, and the need for longer implementation periods was expressed. This should be taken into account in future research.

6 Conclusion

The exoskeleton that was utilised in this research is a relatively simple device as compared to, for example, various types of active exoskeletons developed for rehabilitation. Nonetheless, various factors that either support or hinder domestication were found in this research. Technology domestication theory may thus provide significant help in research on exoskeletons or other novel types of technology that are introduced in care work environments, especially as it tackles questions of use and of nonuse with a holistic view of people's circumstances (Haddon, 2011, pp. 319–320). This research also shows in a concrete way how the domestication dimensions overlap. The factors related to learning (the cognitive dimension), for example, turned out to be very practice-oriented (the practical dimension), and the neutral meanings (the symbolic domestication) of the exoskeleton supported its implementation in the care practices (the practical domestication).

Indeed, central prerequisites for domestication of exoskeletons in care work are likely to depend on several matters, such as the type of exoskeleton being used, the characteristics of the care work in question, the environment, the nurses' interests and competences, planning and organisation of the work, and even the health of the clients. This research paves the way for identification of the best practices for domestication—of the Auxivo LiftSuit, in particular—and thus for increasingly human-centred service design in care services.

Acknowledgements This research was supported by the Finnish Work Environment Fund ("Exoskeletons and caregivers' changing daily work"—TUEKS project).

References

Akrich, M. (1992). The de-scription of technical objects. In W. Bijker & J. Law (Eds.), *Shaping technology–building society: Studies in sociotechnical change* (pp. 205–244). Cambridge: MIT Press.

ASTM International. (2021). Standard terminology for exoskeletons and exosuits (ASTM F3323–21). ASTM International (Ed.), West Conshohocken, PA.

Aune, M. (2002). Users versus utilities: The domestication of an energy controlling technology. In A. Jamison & H. Rohracher (Eds.), *Technology studies & sustainable development* (pp. 383–406). Munich: Profil Verlag.

Auxivo, A.G. (2022). The auxivo liftsuit. Retrieved June 30, 2022, from https://www.auxivo.com/liftsuit

Broadbent, E., Kuo, I. H., Lee, Y. I., Rabindran, J., Kerse, N., Stafford, R., & MacDonald, B. A. (2010). Attitudes and reactions to a healthcare robot. *Telemedicine and e-Health, 16*(5), 608–613. https://doi.org/10.1089/tmj.2009.0171

Bush, E. (2001). The use of human touch to improve the well-being of older adults: A holistic nursing intervention. *Journal of Holistic Nursing, 19*(3), 256–270. https://doi.org/10.1177/089801010101900306

Davis, K. G., & Kotowski, S. E. (2015). Prevalence of musculoskeletal disorders for nurses in hospitals, long-term care facilities, and home health care: A comprehensive review. *Human Factors, 57*(5), 754–792. https://doi.org/10.1177/0018720815581933

De Looze, M., Bosch, T., Krause, F., Stadler, K. S., & O'Sullivan, L. W. (2015). Exoskeletons for industrial application and their potential effects on physical work load. *Ergonomics, 59*(5), 671–681. https://doi.org/10.1080/00140139.2015.1081988

European Commission. (2012). Special Eurobarometer 382: Public attitudes towards robots. Retrieved June 30, 2022, from https://ab.gov.tr/files/ardb/evt/Public_attitudes_toward_robots_2012.pdf.

European Commission. (2015). Special Eurobarometer 427: Autonomous systems. Retrieved June 30, 2022, from https://www.europarl.europa.eu/cmsdata/102681/Autonomos%20systems.pdf.

Frennert, S., Aminoff, H., & Östlund, B. (2021). Technological frames and care robots in eldercare. *International Journal of Social Robotics, 13*(2), 311–325. https://doi.org/10.1007/s12369-020-00641-0

Goeldner, M., Herstatt, C., & Tietze, F. (2015). The emergence of care robotics—a patent and publication analysis. *Technological Forecasting and Social Change, 92*(March), 115–131.

Goodall, G., Ciobanu, I., Broekx, R., Sørgaard, J., Anghelache, I., Anghelache-Tutulan, C., Diaconu, M., Mæland, S., Borve, T., Dagestad, A., Bormans, P., Custers, M., Losleben, K., Valadas, R., de Almeida, C. V., Matias, A., Marin, A., Taraldsen, K., Maetzler, W., … Serrano, J. A. (2019). The role of adaptive immersive technology in creating personalised environments for emotional connection and preservation of identity in dementia care. *International Journal on Advances in Life Sciences, 11*(1–2), 13–22.

Haddon, L. (2003). Domestication and mobile telephony. In J. Katz (Ed.), *Machines that become us: The social context of personal communication technology* (pp. 43–56). New Brunswick: Transaction Publishers.

Haddon, L. (2006). The contribution of domestication research in in-home computing and media consumption. *The Information Society, 22*(4), 1–9.

Haddon, L. (2011). Domestication analysis, objects of study, and the centrality of technologies in everyday life. *Canadian Journal of Communication, 36*(2), 311–323.

Hargreaves, T., Wilson, C., & Hauxwell-Baldwin, R. (2018). Learning to live in a smart home. *Building Research & Information, 46*(1), 127–139. https://doi.org/10.1080/09613218.2017.1286882

Hartmann, M. (2020). (The domestication of) Nordic domestication. *Nordic Journal of Media Studies, 2*(1), 47–57.

Ingeborgrud, L., & Ryghaug, M. (2019). The role of practical, cognitive and symbolic factors in the successful implementation of battery electric vehicles in Norway. *Transportation Research Part A: Policy and Practice, 130*(December), 507–516.

Johansson-Pajala, R.-M., Thommes, K., Hoppe, J. A., Tuisku, O., Hennala, L., Pekkarinen, S., Melkas, H., & Gustafsson, C. (2019). Improved knowledge changes the mindset: Older adults' perceptions of care robots. In: J. Zhou & G. Salvendy (Eds.), *Human aspects of IT for the aged population; Design for the elderly and technology acceptance: HCII 2019*. Lecture Notes in Computer Science (Vol. 11592, pp. 212–227). Cham: Springer Publishing.

Lehtonen, T.-K. (2003). The domestication of new technologies as a set of trials. *Journal of Consumer Culture, 3*(3), 363–385.

Kalluinen, J. (2018). Huoltosuhde on nyt korkeimmillaan 60 vuoteen–suunta on yhä ylöspäin (in Finnish). Retrieved June 30, 2022, from https://www.taloustaito.fi/tyo-elake/huoltosuhde-on-nyt-korkeimmillaan-60-vuoteen--suunta-on-yha-ylospain/.

Melkas, H., Hennala, L., Pekkarinen, S., & Kyrki, V. (2020). Impacts of robot implementation on care personnel and clients in elderly-care institutions. *International Journal of Medical Informatics, 134*(February), 104041. https://doi.org/10.1016/j.ijmedinf.2019.104041

Morley, D. (2005). What's "home" got to do with it? Contradictory dynamics in the domestication of technology and the dislocation of domesticity. In T. Berker, M. Hartmann, Y. Punie, & K. Ward (Eds.), *Domestication of media and technologies* (pp. 21–39). Maidenhead, Berkshire: Open University Press.

Niemelä, M., Heikkinen, S., Koistinen, P., Laakso, K., Melkas, H., & Kyrki, V. (Eds.), (2021). *Robots and the future of welfare services–A Finnish roadmap* (publication series CROSSOVER, 4/2021). Espoo: Aalto University. http://urn.fi/URN:ISBN:978-952-64-0323-6

Peine, A., & Herrmann, A. M. (2012). The sources of use knowledge: Towards integrating the dynamics of technology use and design in the articulation of societal challenges. *Technological Forecasting and Social Change, 79*(8), 1495–1512.

Pierson, J. (2006). Domestication at work in small businesses. In T. Berker, M. Hartmann, Y. Punie, & K. J. Ward (Eds.), *Domestication of media and technology* (pp. 205–226). Maidenhead, Berkshire: Open University Press.

Pols, J., & Willems, D. (2011). Innovation and evaluation: Taming and unleashing telecare technology. *Sociology of Health and Illness, 33*(3), 484–498.

Rogers, E. M. (1983). *Diffusion of innovations* (3rd ed.). London: Free Press.

Silverstone, R., & Haddon, L. (1996). Design and the domestication of information and communication technologies: Technical change and everyday life. In R. Mansell & R. Silverstone (Eds.), *Communication by design: The politics of information and communication technologies* (pp. 44–74). Oxford: Oxford University Press.

Silverstone, R., Hirsch, E., & Morley, D. (2003). Information and communication technologies and the moral economy of the household. In R. Silverstone & E. Hirsch (Eds.), *Consuming technologies: Media and information in domestic spaces* (pp. 13–28). London: Routledge.

Skirbekk, V., Dieleman, J., Stonawski, M., Fejkiel, K., Tyrovolas, S., & Chang, A. (2022). The health-adjusted dependency ratio as a new global measure of the burden of ageing: A population-based study. *The Lancet Healthy Longevity, 3*(5), e332–e338. https://doi.org/10.1016/S2666-7568(22)00075-7

Søraa, R. A., Nyvoll, P., Tøndel, G., Fosch-Villaronga, E., & Serrano, J. A. (2021). The social dimension of domesticating technology: Interactions between older adults, caregivers, and robots in the home. *Technological Forecasting and Social Change, 167*(June), 120678. https://doi.org/10.1016/j.techfore.2021.120678

Sørensen, K. H. (2005). Domestication: The enactment of technology. In T. Berker, M. Hartmann, Y. Punie, & K. J. Ward (Eds.), *Domestication of media and technologies* (pp. 40–61). Maidenhead, Berkshire: Open University Press.

Stokke, R. (2017). Maybe we should talk about it anyway: A qualitative study of understanding expectations and use of an established technology innovation in caring practices. *BMC Health Services Research, 17*. (article no. 657). https://doi.org/10.1186/s12913-017-2587-3.

Trydegård, G. B. (2012). Care work in changing welfare states: Nordic care workers' experiences. *European Journal of Ageing, 9*(2), 119–129. https://doi.org/10.1007/s10433-012-0219-7

Taipale, S., Luca, F. D., Sarrica, M., & Fortunati, L. (2015). Robot shift from industrial production to social reproduction. In J. Vincent, S. Taipale, B. Sapio, G. Lugano, & L. Fortunati (Eds.), *Social robots from a human perspective* (pp. 11–24). Heidelberg: Springer.

Tuisku, O., Pekkarinen, S., Hennala, L., & Melkas, H. (2019). Robots do not replace a nurse with a beating heart: The publicity around a robotic innovation in elderly care. *Information Technology & People, 32*(1), 47–67. https://doi.org/10.1108/ITP-06-2018-0277

Tuisku, O., Pekkarinen, S., Hennala, L., & Melkas, H. (2022). Decision-makers' attitudes toward the use of care robots in welfare services. *AI & Society*, 1–17. Ahead-of-print.https://doi.org/10.1007/s00146-022-01392-4

Turja, T., van Aerschot, L., Särkikoski, T., & Oksanen, A. (2018). Finnish healthcare professionals' attitudes towards robots: Reflections on a population sample. *Nursing Open, 5*(3), 300–309. https://doi.org/10.1002/nop2.138

Turja, T., Saurio, R., Katila, J., Hennala, L., Pekkarinen, S., & Melkas, H. (2020). Intention to use exoskeletons in geriatric care work: Need for ergonomic and social design. *Ergonomics in Design, 30*(2), 13–16. https://doi.org/10.1177/1064804620961577

United Nations. (2007). Dependency ratio. Retrieved July 2, 2022, from https://www.un.org/esa/sustdev/natlinfo/indicators/methodology_sheets/demographics/dependency_ratio.pdf.

Wu, Y., Fassert, C., & Rigaud, A. S. (2012). Designing robots for the elderly: Appearance issue and beyond. *Archives of Gerontology & Geriatrics, 54*(1), 121–126. https://doi.org/10.1016/j.archger.2011.02.003

Riika Saurio, MSc (Tech), RN, is a junior researcher at Lappeenranta-Lahti University of Technology LUT, School of Engineering Science, Finland. Her research areas include implementation and use of welfare technology and user involvement.

Satu Pekkarinen, PhD, innovation systems, is associate professor on socio technical transition in services at Lappeenranta-Lahti University of Technology LUT, School of Engineering Science, Finland. Her research interests are relationships between technology, services and users, use of care robots and other types of welfare technologies, and socio-technical transition in elderly care.

Lea Hennala, PhD, innovation systems, recently retired from a position as a senior researcher at Lappeenranta-Lahti University of Technology LUT, School of Engineering Science, Finland. Her research areas include implementation and use of care robots in elderly care, user involvement, and co-creation of service innovations in both public and private sectors.

Helinä Melkas, DSc (Tech) and Lic Soc Sc, is professor of industrial engineering and management, especially service innovations at Lappeenranta-Lahti University of Technology LUT, School of Engineering Science, Finland, and professor II at University of Agder, Centre for e-health, Norway. Her research focuses on digitalisation, welfare technology, gerontechnology, robotics, service innovation, and user involvement.

Inclusive Smart Textile Design for Healthy Ageing

Shan Wang, Kai Yang, and Yuanyuan Yin

ABSTRACT

Population ageing is a global phenomenon. This trend poses healthcare services, social care, and political challenges, yet implies a growing demand for ageing-related products and services. Smart textile technology has been increasingly applied in healthcare applications to support healthy ageing from many aspects. This research indicated the challenges for older people to stay in their own house in later life from the previous literature and reviewed smart home healthcare products and smart textiles for healthy ageing. We found that the current development of elderly textile products neglects the real needs of older people in healthcare products in the home environment from their perspectives. Thus, this research aims to discover the health and well-being needs of people aged 60+ living independently at home in the UK, especially during COVID-19. This research conducted interviews with 12 individuals and questionnaires with 43 individuals for questionnaires. Results highlighted the current unmet healthcare-related needs at home and participants' experiences and attitudes towards healthcare products. Finally, it indicated the potential opportunity for inclusive smart textile design for healthy ageing in the future.

S. Wang · K. Yang · Y. Yin (✉)
Winchester School of Art, University of Southampton, Park Avenue Winchester, Southampton SO23 8DL, UK
e-mail: Y.Yin@soton.ac.uk

S. Wang
e-mail: shan.wang@soton.ac.uk

K. Yang
e-mail: ky2e09@soton.ac.uk

1   Introduction

The population of the world is ageing. The WHO predicted that people aged over 60 will be nearly doubled from 12 to 22% between 2015 and 2050 (WHO, 2021, n.d.). Due to such a substantial demographic shift, many researchers have highlighted the importance of Healthy Ageing and are keen to contribute to the UKRI's Challenge mission to "ensure that people can enjoy at least five extra healthy, independent, years of life by 2035".

Smart textiles are textiles that can sense and respond to changes in their environment and adapt to them by the integration of functionalities in the textile structure (Libanori et al., 2022, 142–156). Examples include basic functions such as heating textiles that provide warmth to advanced health monitoring and disease treatments (Liu et al., 2020, 1–7). Smart textiles have great potential to transform healthcare products and services mainly due to four key advantages: (1) textiles are conformable to wear and familiar to users, (2) they enable unobtrusive and ubiquitous deployment of sensors and actuators in clothing and furnishings, (3) they provide a single platform to integrate multiple sensors for the users, and (4) they link with other technologies (e.g., digital healthcare and AI) to provide accurate health information, and alerts can be provided through real-time feedback to the users (Scataglini & Imbesi, 2021, 311–324; Brauner et al., 2017, 13–24). Smart textile has been applied in healthcare applications, for example, ECG T-shirts for early warning of cardiovascular disease, electrode garments for stroke rehabilitation, smart garments with sensors and wearable cameras to support people with memory loss (e.g., dementias), and smart socks for diabetic patients' health monitoring (Mokhlespour Esfahani & Nussbaum, 2019, 1–14).

Although the existing smart textiles studies are notable, few of them explored the healthcare needs of older people at home. Studies have highlighted that living at home in later life the elderly may face various health issues, such as accidental injuries, dementia, social isolation, loneliness, and depression (Smith & Smith, 2019, 1709–1730; Hatcher et al., 2019, 1–10). For example, falls at home and fall-related injuries in older people can result in serious health and social consequences (e.g., hospitalization and permanent disability). As a consequence, older people are more likely to have accidents and emergencies, visit their GP, have multiple long-term conditions, and more likely to have mental health conditions (Burns, 2001, 3–6). Therefore, this project aims to investigate the healthcare needs of people aged 60+ who live at home, explore challenges that they face when they use healthcare-related products, identify their unmet needs, and develop inclusive smart textiles design insights to address their needs.

2   Literature Review

Recent studies reveal that many older adults wish to stay in their own homes for a longer term in their later life, where they need caregivers or medical experts to attend to and monitor or assist them (Wagner et al., 2012, 28–34). It has been confirmed that older people are better to stay in their familiar environment even after their family structure changes (such as their partner died) (Hatcher et al., 2019, 1–10). The change from a familiar environment to an unfamiliar one can have an impact on the risk of mortality in later life (Feng et al., 2017, 9–19).

2.1 Challenges for Older People to Stay in Their Own House

Due to physical and psychological changes, living at home in later life may cause different challenges and difficulties. For example, from a physical aspect, challenges are caused by older people's eyesight and hearing deteriorated (Maharani et al., 2018, 575–581), gait and balance disorders (Cuevas-Trisan, 2019, 173–183), and chronic illnesses increased (You & Lee, 2006, 193–201). Also, falling has been highlighted as one of the biggest issues for older people to keep living at home (Lee et al., 2011, 76–79). Other challenges are home environment accessibility issues (Slaug et al., 2020, 156–174), furniture-related usability and accessibility issues (Jonsson, 2013, 49–73), chronic disease care issues (Maresova et al., 2019, 1–17), and other healthcare issues (Ohta et al., 2020, 126–139). From a psychological aspect, due to older people's reduced ability for cognitive problem-solving and social participation (Kim & Park, 2000, 153–168), they fear illness and feel social isolation (Smith & Smith, 2019, 1709–1730; Kemperman et al., 2019, 1), especially during the COVID-19 outbreak (Radwan et al., 2020, 1–6). Hence, it is essential to develop new tools and technologies to facilitate independence at home for supporting ageing in older adults (Ollevier et al., 2020, 1–12).

2.2 Mainstream Digital Technologies in Home Healthcare Products

Within the last decade, a variety of new healthcare concepts have been developed for supporting older people to stay as long as possible at home while being medically cared for and monitored. Electronic Assistive Technology (EAT) products and Ambient Assisted Living (AAL) technology have played important roles to improve the physical and mental well-being of older adults at home (Song & van der Cammen, 2019, 50–56). These technologies have been used in a range of healthcare-related products and services within the home environment, to assess older people's health conditions and prevent accidents at home (Song & van der Cammen, 2019, 50–56). For example, voice-controlled intelligent personal assistants to support ageing in place in terms of entertainment, companionship, control of the home, reminders, and emergency communication (O'Brien et al., 2020, 176–179), such as Amazon Alexa and Google Home (Ermolina & Tiberius, 2021, n.d.), and health-monitoring technology and wearable smart healthcare products, such as Smart Watch, Personal Alarm Devices, Falls Detection Devices, Activity Monitoring Devices, Wearable Technology, and Smart textile products (Lu et al., 2016,

850–869), are used to track older people's activities to provide real-time monitoring and detect emergencies (such as asthma attacks, heart attack, diabetes, and fall) by adding intelligent and wearable sensors (Patel, 2022, n.d.); and, Internet of Things devices, such as telehealth care (Syed et al., 2019, 136–151), consist of a network of sensors in the human body which exchanges data with a hub to track health. It can assist older people to manage and prevent chronic conditions (Whitley, 2021, n.d.) and assist remote healthcare providers to take care of their patients with the continuous transmission of physiological information (Syed et al., 2019, 136–151).

While these digital technologies in smart healthcare products and services have been widely used to support older people living alone in recent decades, especially during COVID-19 (Hamblin, 2022, pp. 41–58), issues of ageing-friendly healthcare product design and older people's receptiveness to using technology remain (Buyl et al., 2020, 1–15). For example, older people may forget to attach some medical or prevention devices, such as heart rate monitors or fall alarms. Therefore, it is important to continually explore new methods to develop innovative and ageing-friendly healthcare products and services to support older people, such as via smart textile technologies. Much literature highlighted the technological barriers of older people to using smart healthcare products (Wilson et al., 2021, 1–12), which gave opportunities to raise the idea of smart textiles of attaching diminutive instruments to a garment to monitor and assess vital signs of older people at home, such as heart rate, respiration rate, blood pressure, and body activities (Esfahani, 2021, 93–107). The study found that smart textiles are easier to use than other smart healthcare products because they integrate computer technologies and interaction surfaces into everyday items such as clothes, sofas, and beds, which are familiar to older people (Ziefle et al., 2016, 266–276), as they have integrated computer functionality into textiles, older people have less interaction with the technology.

2.3   Smart Textiles for Healthy Ageing

The concept of smart textile, also called smart interactive textile, represented new healthcare applications in the last decade (Schaar & Ziefle, 2011, 601–608), and it has been indicated to have reached maturity (Brauner et al., 2017, 13–24) and is becoming commercial (Heek et al., 2017, 1–20). Smart textiles have been used in combination with the integration of invisible sensors, actuators, and the development of a Wireless Body Area Network (WBAN) that will be able to assess a person's physiological state and body activities (Libanori et al., 2022, 142–156; Esfahani, 2021, 93–107). For example, interactive textiles integrate communication and sensor technologies into clothing for consistent and accurate monitoring of people's health; related research is smart textile shoes (Pham et al., 2017, 269–274), smart textile shirts (Romagnoli et al., 2014, 377–384), smart textile belts (Okss et al., 2017, n.d), smart textile jewellery for medical and wellness purposes

(Capalbo et al., 2019, 1–6), and smart textile wristwatches and fitness trackers (Capalbo et al., 2019, 1–6).

Previous literature also highlighted how smart textile technology intervenes in physical health, such as activity monitoring (Mokhlespour Esfahani & Nussbaum, 2019, 1–14), rehabilitation (Lorussi et al., 2012, 217–228), and gait analysis and falling (Wang et al., 2019, 1–20; Mokhlespour Esfahani & Nussbaum, 2019, 1–14). In terms of intervention in mental health, Gravina and Li (2019, 1–10) developed a smart cushion and proposed an approach to analysing activities from the user's sitting postures and upper limb gestures, therefore recognizing users' emotion-relevant activities. Effective emotion regulation is important to older people as it is crucial to both physiological and psychological well-being (DeSteno et al., 2013, 474–486).

Challenges of smart textile

Despite the operation potential of these miniaturized systems of smart textiles, the usability of many wearable devices can be problematic. For instance, attaching these devices to the skin, body, or garment may be challenging because it is visible to others, making some wearers feel vulnerable and compromising their privacy (Schaar & Ziefle, 2011, 601–608). Meanwhile, previous research is often technology-oriented to reduce the digital barriers of older people (Wilson et al., 2021, 1–12) but neglects the real needs of living independently at home from older people's perspective. Also, there is a scarcity of research that discovered the need for older people to use smart textiles and smart healthcare products at home.

Thus, this project aims to investigate the healthcare needs of people aged 60+ who live at home, explore challenges that they face when they use healthcare-related products, identify their unmet needs, and develop inclusive smart textiles design insights to address their needs.

3   Research Method

In order to achieve the research aim, semi-structured interviews and questionnaires have been employed in this study to explore the unmet healthcare-related needs of people aged 60+ at home, their experience with existing healthcare products and services, and their attitude and needs towards smart textiles in healthcare applications. More specifically, the interviews aimed to understand participants' perceptions of healthy aging, healthcare needs at home, experiences with health and well-being products and services, and attitudes toward smart healthcare technology. The interviews were designed into three parts: the first part focused on health situations, such as health conditions, medication, and daily activity limitations; the second part focused on lifestyle perception, such as happiness with retirement life and what's their thought on a healthy lifestyle; and the third part focused on the lifestyle needs, such as how to monitor their body and whether to use any healthcare-related product and their suggestions of how to improve health and well-being at home. The questionnaires were designed to examine the priority

Table 1 Interview participant's information. *Source* Author's own table (2022)

Participant	Age	Genger	Living alone?
1	72	Female	Yes
2	92	Female	No
3	78	Female	No
4	91	Female	Yes
5	74	Female	Yes
6	64	Male	No
7	62	Female	No
8	63	Female	No
S	75	Female	Yes
10	88	Female	Yes
11	86	Male	No
12	70	Male	No

of older people's healthcare needs at home, verify findings from interviews, and explore insights into the smart textile design to promote healthy ageing at home. Consistent metrics, numerical scales, Likert, and closed-ended and open-ended questions were designed in the questionnaires. The interviews and questionnaires were conducted from April to July 2021, which is around the COVID lockdown period. Participants were recruited from ageing organizations, such as Age UK and MHA; retirement homes community; and ageing research organizations. 12 older people were interviewed, and 43 valid questionnaires were collected. The interview sample's general information is presented in Table 1. Research ethics approval was applied for first-hand data collection through the University of Southampton ethics committee (Ethics/ERGO Number: 64221).

Thematic analysis was applied to analyse collected qualitative data to strive to identify patterns of themes in the interview data (Maguire & Delahunt, 2017, 3351–33514). The process of data analysis involves checking the data, creating initial codes, collating codes with supporting information, grouping codes into themes, reviewing, and revising themes, and producing the report. Statistical analysis was applied to analyse collected quantitative data to test hypotheses and make estimates about populations. Steps to analyse questionnaire data: (1) check and select important variables; (2) descriptive analysis (frequencies and crosstab); (3) test statistical significance level (chi-square) to investigate the relationship between different variables we were comparing; (4) write results in themes and produce the report. The thematic analysis was conducted using Microsoft Excel 2022 and the statistical analysis was conducted using SPSS V28. Key findings from the questionnaire are presented in Table 2. Findings from qualitative and quantitative data analysis are supporting each other to explain older people's needs at home and the reasons behind them.

Table 2 Summary of the key findings from the questionnaire. *Source* Author's own table (2022)

Age range	60−74 (56%)	75−84 (30%)	85+ (14%)	
Gender	Male (30%)	Female (70%)		
Whole sample age between 60 and 92, Mean = 73				

		Yes	**No**
Exercises is helpful		98%	2%
Have enough exercise everyday		19%	81%
Physical ability decreased	Male	31%	69%
	Female	13%	87%
Prefer outdoor activities	All	61%	40%
	Male (n = 13)	77%	23%
	Female (n = 30)	50%	50%
Played games on digital devices	All	49%	51%
	Male	23%	77%
	Female	60%	40%
	Easy to play	86%	14%
Have arthritis		63%	37%
Have hand arthritis		82%	18%
Easy to open bottle		40%	60%
Easy to perate small buttons on devices		85%	15%
Preferences of garment design			
Easy put on and take off		67%	33%
Without zip at back		58%	42%
Use elasticated waistband		60%	40%
Easy cleaned materials		93%	7%

[a] Across whether to have hand arthritis, the P-values for the preferences of garment design are <0.05

---

4   Key Findings

The following sessions present key research findings of this study from four perspectives: (1) older people have decreased physical exercise during COVID-19; (2) hand arthritis has a great impact on older people's daily activities; (3) increased engagement with technologies; and (4) older people's usage of health-related products at home.

4.1   Decreased Physical Exercise During COVID-19

Although most of the participants (98%, N = 43) agreed that doing exercises were helpful to health and well-being, 81% of the participants felt that they did not have enough exercise every day. This was mainly because most of them were advised to self-isolate at home during the COVID lockdown period. The lockdown had more impact on the male participants than on the females in their daily physical exercise. 31% (N = 13) of the male participants reported that they experienced a decrease in physical ability during COVID, and only 13% (N = 30) of the female participants agreed with this statement. This is possible because there were more male participants who preferred outdoor exercise (77%, N = 13) than female participants (50%, N = 30). In the same vein, some female participants mentioned that they preferred to do exercise at home, "I preferred to do my one at home even if we weren't in a lockdown" as she felt that indoor exercise was "more convenient (to do exercise indoors). I like to get up to do my exercises, have a shower and then I set for the day."

Several home-based exercises were discussed during the interviews, such as cycling, attending online exercise sessions, using a stretch band, climbing stairs, and gardening. However, home-based exercises may be a challenge for participants who had physical problems. For example, a few participants said they needed care support while doing home-based exercises, because of their reduced physical ability from knee surgery, back pain, mobility issues, or balance issues.

One participant aged 93 lives independently in a house by herself. She replaced her knee and had a foot problem around two years ago. She needed a home physio to assist her to do home exercises two times per week. She mentioned that she felt more confident walking with her physio. "My mobility is not as good as I would like it to be, so I was still paying the physio and hoped that it will improve. She takes me for a walk and then she comes, and I do exercise as it is a program of exercises. She is very good, and she changes her exercise. I've also had quite a bit of back ache and so she gave me some back exercises as well. I can walk reasonably well with her … I think with her I have the confidence that if I should fall or something then I have someone with me." However, due to COVID-19, she could not have physio service at home, therefore, her mobility decreased dramatically and had a negative impact on her other knee.

Therefore, it is worth exploring how smart textiles can be applied for home-based exercise, physiotherapy, and rehabilitation, so older people can have sufficient exercise at home independently. Also, it is necessary to consider gender differences and individual health conditions among older people in the design of smart textiles to promote home-based exercise.

4.2   Hand Arthritis Has a Big Impact on Older People's Daily Living

The research findings show that 63% (n = 43) of the participants reported that they had arthritis. Among them, 82% (n = 27) had hand arthritis. Based on the questionnaires, the participants with hand arthritics had challenges opening bottles and jars and felt difficult to press small buttons on devices, such as TV remotes. For example, one participant mentioned "I've also got to attach of arthritis as well in my hands. It does affect me when I'm knitting. I am trying to open the vitamin D bottle. But I can't get the grip with the thumb. I haven't had to go into neighbours (for help) yet, but sometimes I feel like hitting it with a hammer. I mean that will probably get worse and you know, I have to have help with opening jars, and stuff." There also emerged a need to improve gadgets designed to support older people with hand arthritis in their daily life. Some participants indicated although there were some existing gadgets on the market to assist with arthritis hand issues, they still had problems using these gadgets due to the limited flexibility of their fingers.

Keeping personal hygiene and doing home cleaning is another challenge for older people with hand arthritis. As it was difficult for them to use heavy cleaning facilities (such as vacuum cleaners) and ironing, they wanted easy-to-maintain materials for the home environment (such as cushions, bed sheets, and the surface of a sofa), clothes, and shoes. In addition, hand arthritis also has affected how older people dress up. The findings show that they needed garments designed with the features to put on and take off easily without zipping at the back using an elasticated waistband, no tightness getting over the head, and easily opened buttons on clothes. Participants also highlighted the need for easily cleaned materials in the home environment and clothing design.

Therefore, it is necessary to discover how smart textiles can be used to support older people with arthritis, especially hand arthritis, from home environment, product design, and garments design. It is important to consider older peoples' reduced hand functions (hand arthritis) in smart textile and wearable product design for easy-to-use, easy-to-wear, and easy-to-clean products in the future.

4.3 More Seniors Are Embracing Technology During COVID-19

The findings show that the participants had a positive attitude about the benefits of technologies to their day-to-day life and had an improved acceptance and adoption of technologies during COVID-19. All participants in this study were using digital devices, such as smartphones and tablets.

The findings also reflect the benefits of using technology among older people at home. Some of the participants highlighted that technology helped them to maintain a good relationship with their family and friends, and for physical activities. For example, during COVID-19, they joined community meetings with Zoom, communicated with others via video or audio calls through Facetime or WhatsApp, and sent Emails via iPad. Other participants joined online live physical activities to keep healthy during COVID-19, such as the Yoga video training course.

Furthermore, 49% (n = 43) of the participants indicated that they played digital games on digital devices such as iPad and tablets to keep their mental wellness. 86% (n = 21) of the digital game players felt easy to play games on digital devices. 83% of them agreed that they keep learning new skills that can improve mental well-being. Compared with the male and female participants, findings show there were more female digital game players (60%, n = 30) than male players (23%, n = 13), as the male participants preferred to spend their time reading, watching TV, and doing gardening rather than playing games.

It has been found that the younger older participant group (aged between 65 and 75 years older) felt more comfortable with new technology and believed smart textiles would help tremendously in medical and health services than the older groups (aged 75+ years old). One participant mentioned that the consistent monitoring function via smart textiles can contribute to health-date generation. Another participant mentioned the idea of embedding technology via smart textiles: "If we had something that was attached to us or even embedded that could monitor certain aspects of blood that would be revolutionary."

Meanwhile, some participants have shown some concerns about technology applications in their daily life. For instance, some participants worried that technology may overcontrol their life. If they rely on technology too much, they will not be independent and capable of daily activities in the future. And some aged 75+ participants felt uncomfortable with technology because of digital divide and privacy issues.

Therefore, during the smart textile products and service design and development process, we need to consider (1) the functionality of the product to meet older people's psychical and mental well-being needs, (2) the acceptive level of technology for older people, and (3) privacy and data protection-related concerns.

4.4 Weight Scale and Blood Pressure Monitor Are the Most Frequently Used Health-Related Products at Home

It has been found that weight scales were the most frequently used health-related product at home. 81% of the participants weighed themselves regularly to maintain a healthy weight, because weight is an important index of healthy ageing (Gill et al., 2015, 379–388). "I just jump on the scales every morning … I do weigh myself a lot. because I've always had a weight problem". The second popular health-related product used at home was blood pressure monitors. 63% of the participants have used it at home. However, some participants also indicated some problems while they were using a blood pressure monitor at home. For example, one participant mentioned that "… it tightens on the arm and then gives a reading. Then I normally do it four or five times because then I get different readings and then I average that …". Other popular healthcare products at home that have been found in this study include checking water drinking amount (26%), checking blood oxygen levels (23%), checking sleeping hours (16%), electric pad to relieve pain (12%), check blood glucose levels (9%), check daily standing hours (9%), pendant alarm (7%), and circulation booster (5%). Issues of these products were mainly about functionality and comfortableness. For example, one participant said "I got alarm thing. My children want me to have that. They feel happy that I have got that… but you can't press it accidentally (as the care line will call you). You can have it around your neck or your wrist. I like to put it on my wrist.

But I have knocked it accidentally sometimes" and another participant mentioned "I put it (pendant alarm) on the table, I didn't like it on my wrists because it kept falling …". Therefore, designing an ageing-friendly interface and user-centred design should be considered in smart textiles-related products or service designs for older people.

5 Discussion

Need to monitor older people's physical and mental well-being at home

Keeping physical and mental well-being is important for older people living independently at home. This research has found that older people believe that they did not have enough physical activities (such as walking times) during the COVID-19 lockdown period, which caused reduced mobility of some older people. This finding is consistent with some literature (Goethals et al., 2020, n. d.). Moreover, they suggested that older people could increase their daily activities at home by changing their lifestyle, physical activity habits, strengthening social connections, etc. The recommended physical exercise time was 150–300 min per week, such as for moderate-intensity aerobic physical activity and muscle strength training sessions at home. However, how to deliver these services to older people is not discussed yet. Yet there is a range of online videos for aerobics for older people; how to monitor their health situation and keep track of their daily activity tasks still needs further development. Smart textiles (e-textiles, or smart fabrics) technology can incorporate sensing functionality to monitor and support older people for a healthier lifestyle (Yang et al., 2019, 1–21). For example, the Chem–Phys patch, attached to garments, can monitor human physiological signals and sweat-lactate levels to encourage activities and maintain the functions of older people (Imani et al., 2016, 1–7). However, researchers have indicated the constraints of the smart textile, such as material, battery, integration, and interactive system (Yang et al., 2019, 1–21; Imani et al., 2016, 1–7).

Thus, it is necessary to develop smart textile technology in the home environment with smart healthcare products to monitor older people's daily activity to help them reach their daily activity goals.

Need user-centred and ageing-friendly design

The findings confirmed that hand arthritics had a great impact on older people's hand functions and limited their daily activities and instrumental activities of daily living (Proffitt et al., 2019, 1–10). Many product, service, and garment designs rely on older people's hands to manipulate controls, move, and exert force. For example, an automatic pill dispenser was designed to solve older people's medication management issues (Lima et al., 2021, 552–564). However, it needs a better ageing-friendly design to consider the user's hand flexibility, as older people had hand issues, and it was difficult to manage the small pills that were stuck in the pillboxes. Therefore, products, services, and garments need to be designed to meet the demands of older people's hand capabilities. Researchers at the University of

Cambridge developed ageing simulation gloves (2022, n.d.) as a means of gaining a better understanding of how limitations in hand movement can negatively impact the use of products and to build empathy for older individuals. These design theories can be used in exploring, designing, and developing user-centred smart textile products or smart textile interaction designs to meet the demands of older people's hand capabilities.

Moreover, this study found that older people had increased acceptance and adaption of technology in their daily life. This finding is consistent with Hamblin (2022, 41–58) who indicated that older people are getting more technology support to promote health, wellness, and communication during COVID-19 (Hamblin, 2022, 41–58). The local authority and social care departments had provided some support for using digital technology for older people during COVID-19 (Hamblin, 2022, 41–58), however, depended on older people's age range, gender, previous working environment, and their attitude towards life, the challenges of using technology among ageing group remain. Therefore, while designing a smart textile product, one needs to consider the complex design of the interface to make sure older people can easily adapt to it.

6   Conclusion

Smart textiles have been considered to be the key technology innovation to monitor, engage, entertain, and overall improve the safety and quality of life in the recent decade. Much research and resources have been invested in the development of smart textiles to support people's healthy lifestyles. However, in the home environment context, few of them explored the healthcare needs of older people. In addition, the implementation of smart healthcare products, including smart textiles, and the usability of many wearable devices are still problematic for older users.

This research found that despite older people's increasing acceptance of technology, there is still a need to improve smart healthcare products at home. Therefore, while designing smart healthcare products and using smart textiles, need to investigate older people's real needs, challenges, and motivations.

This research also indicated the need for daily exercise for older people. Smart textiles can be used in wearable garments designed to monitor older people's daily exercise goals, for example, shoe insole and wrist braces to track their daily activity data and monitor their health conditions, such as weight, heartbeat, and blood pressure. Moreover, health conditions and requirements are different for individuals, thus, smart textiles healthcare-related products need to provide personalized services for individuals. Moreover, it also needs to consider how to use an ageing-friendly interactive design to deliver those results to older people. To achieve this mission, it needs multidisciplinary research, engineers, designers, and relevant stakeholders to collaborate; meanwhile, it needs to involve older people in the design process to understand their attitudes towards smart textiles design ideas and experiences of using relevant interactive flatforms.

References

Brauner, P., van Heek, J., & Ziefle, M. (2017). Age, gender, and technology attitude as factors for acceptance of smart interactive textiles in home environments. In *Proceedings of the 3rd International Conference on Information and Communication Technologies for Ageing Well and E-health, ICT4Agingwell* (pp. 13–24). SCITEPRESS.

Burns, E. (2001). Older people in accident and emergency departments. *Age and Ageing, 30*(suppl_3), 3–6.

Buyl, R., Beogo, I., Fobelets, M., Deletroz, C., Van Landuyt, P., Dequanter, S., Gorus, E., Bourbonnais, A., Giguère, A., Lechasseur, K., & Gagnon, M. P. (2020). e-Health interventions for healthy aging: A systematic review. *Systematic Reviews, 9*(1), 1–15.

Capalbo, I., Penhaker, M., Peter, L., & Proto, A. (2019). Consumer perceptions on smart wearable devices for medical and wellness purposes. In *2019 IEEE technology & engineering management conference (TEMSCON), 12–14 June 2019* (pp. 1–6). Institute of Electrical and Electronics Engineers, Atlanta, GA, USA, IEEE Publishing.

Cuevas-Trisan, R. (2019). Balance problems and fall risks in the elderly. *Clinics in Geriatric Medicine, 35*(2), 173–183.

DeSteno, D., Gross, J. J., & Kubzansky, L. (2013). Affective science and health: The importance of emotion and emotion regulation. *Health Psychology, 32*(5), 474–486.

Ermolina, A., & Tiberius, V. (2021). Voice-controlled intelligent personal assistants in health care: International Delphi Study. *Journal of Medical Internet Research, 23*(4), e25312.

Esfahani. I. M. (2021). Smart textiles in healthcare: A summary of history, types, applications, challenges, and future trends. In *Nanosensors and nanodevices for smart multifunctional Textiles* (pp. 93–107). Netherlands: Elsevier Publishing

Feng, Z., Falkingham, J., Liu, X., & Vlachantoni, A. (2017). Changes in living arrangements and mortality among older people in China. *SSM-Population Health, 3*, 9–19.

Gill, L. E., Bartels, S. J., & Batsis, J. A. (2015). Weight management in older adults. *Current Obesity Reports, 4*(3), 379–388.

Goethals, L., Barth, N., Guyot, J., Hupin, D., Celarier, T., & Bongue, B. (2020). Impact of home quarantine on physical activity among older adults living at home during the COVID-19 pandemic: Qualitative interview study. *JMIR Aging, 3*(1), e19007.

Gravina, R., & Li, Q. (2019). Emotion-relevant activity recognition based on smart cushion using multi-sensor fusion. *Information Fusion, 48*, 1–10.

Hamblin, K. A. (2022). Technology in care systems: Displacing, reshaping, reinstating or degrading roles? *New Technology, Work and Employment, 37*(1), 41–58.

Hatcher, D., Chang, E., Schmied, V., & Garrido, S. (2019). Exploring the perspectives of older people on the concept of home. *Journal of Aging Research, 2019*, 1–10.

Heek, J. V., Brauner, P., & Ziefle, M. (2017, April). What is hip?–Classifying adopters and rejecters of interactive digital textiles in home environments. In *International conference on information and communication technologies for ageing well and e-health* (pp. 1–20). Cham: Springer Publishing.

Imani, S., Bandodkar, A. J., Mohan, A. M., Kumar, R., Yu, S., Wang, J., & Mercier, P. P. (2016). A wearable chemical–electrophysiological hybrid biosensing system for real-time health and fitness monitoring. *Nature Communications, 7*(1), 1–7.

Jonsson, O. (2013). Furniture for later life: Design based on older people's experiences of furniture in three housing forms, Doctoral dissertation, Department of Design Sciences, Faculty of Engineering, Lund University Publishing. Norway.

Kemperman, A., van den Berg, P., Weijs-Perrée, M., & Uijtdewillegen, K. (2019). Loneliness of older adults: Social network and the living environment. *International Journal of Environmental Research and Public Health, 16*(3), 406, 1–16.

Kim, K. T., & Park, B. G. (2000). Life satisfaction and social support network of the elderly living alone. *Journal of the Korea Gerontological Society, 20*(1), 153–168.

Lee, W. J., Cheng, Y. Y., Liu, J. Y., Yang, K. C., & Jeng, S. Y. (2011). Living alone as a red flag sign of falls among older people in rural Taiwan. *Journal of Clinical Gerontology and Geriatrics, 2*(3), 76–79.

Libanori, A., Chen, G., Zhao, X., Zhou, Y., & Chen, J. (2022). Smart textiles for personalized healthcare. *Nature Electronics, 5*(3), 142–156.

Lima, O., Terroso, M., Dias, N., Vilaça, J. L., & Matos, D. (2021). Development of the business model and user experience for a pill dispenser: A designer perspective. In *International conference on design and digital communication* (pp. 552–564). Cham: Springer Publishing.

Liu, M., Ward, T., Young, D., Matos, H., Wei, Y., Adams, J., & Yang, K. (2020). Electronic textiles based wearable electrotherapy for pain relief. *Sensors and Actuators A: Physical, 303,* 111701.1–7.

Lorussi, F., Galatolo, S., Bartalesi, R., & De Rossi, D. (2012). Modeling and characterization of extensible wearable textile-based electrogoniometers. *IEEE Sensors Journal, 13*(1), 217–228.

Lu, T. C., Fu, C. M., Ma, M. H. M., Fang, C. C., & Turner, A. M. (2016). Healthcare applications of smart watches. *Applied Clinical Informatics, 7*(03), 850–869.

Maguire, M., & Delahunt, B. (2017). Doing a thematic analysis: A practical, step-by-step guide for learning and teaching scholars. *All Ireland Journal of Higher Education, 9*(3), 3351–33514.

Maharani, A., Dawes, P., Nazroo, J., Tampubolon, G., Pendleton, N., & Sense-Cog WP1 Group. (2018). Visual and hearing impairments are associated with cognitive decline in older people. *Age and Ageing, 47*(4), 575–581.

Maresova, P., Javanmardi, E., Barakovic, S., Barakovic Husic, J., Tomsone, S., Krejcar, O., & Kuca, K. (2019). Consequences of chronic diseases and other limitations associated with old age–a scoping review. *BMC Public Health, 19*(1), 1–17.

Mokhlespour Esfahani, M. I., & Nussbaum, M. A. (2019). Classifying diverse physical activities using "Smart Garments". *Sensors, 19*(14), 3133, 1–14.

O'Brien, K., Liggett, A., Ramirez-Zohfeld, V., Sunkara, P., & Lindquist, L. A. (2020). Voice-controlled intelligent personal assistants to support aging in place. *Journal of the American Geriatrics Society, 68*(1), 176–179.

Ohta, R., Ryu, Y., Kitayuguchi, J., Gomi, T., & Katsube, T. (2020). Challenges and solutions in the continuity of home care for rural older people: A thematic analysis. *Home Health Care Services Quarterly, 39*(2), 126–139.

Okss, A., Katashev, A., Mantyla, J., & Coffeng, R. (2017). Smart textile garment for breathing volume monitoring. *Biomedical Engineering 2016, 20*(1) n.d.

Ollevier, A., Aguiar, G., Palomino, M., & Simpelaere, I. S. (2020). How can technology support ageing in place in healthy older adults? *A Systematic Review. Public Health Reviews, 41*(1), 1–12.

Patel, N. (2022). Internet of things in healthcare: applications, benefits, and challenges. Retrieved July 8, 2022, from https://www.peerbits.com/blog/internet-of-things-healthcare-applications-benefits-and-challenges.html

Pham, C., Diep, N. N., & Phuong, T. M. (2017, October). e-Shoes: Smart shoes for unobtrusive human activity recognition. In *2017 9th international conference on knowledge and systems engineering (KSE), 19–21 Oct. 2017* (pp. 269–274). Institute of Electrical and Electronics Engineers (IEEE). Hue, Vietnam.

Proffitt, R., Abraham, M., & Hughes, C. (2019). Experiences of individuals with arthritis who participate in quilting-related leisure activities. *International Journal of Therapy and Rehabilitation, 26*(10), 1–10.

Radwan, E., Radwan, A., & Radwan, W. (2020). Challenges facing older adults during the COVID-19 outbreak. *European Journal of Environment and Public Health, 5*(1), em0059, 1–6.

Romagnoli, M., Alis, R., Guillen, J., Basterra, J., Villacastin, J. P., & Guillen, S. (2014). A novel device based on smart textile to control heart's activity during exercise. *Australasian Physical & Engineering Sciences in Medicine, 37*(2), 377–384.

Scataglini, S., & Imbesi, S. (2021). Human-centered design smart clothing for ambient assisted living of elderly users: Considerations in the COVID-19 pandemic perspective. In *IoT in healthcare and ambient assisted living* (pp. 311–324). Singapore: Springer Publishing.

Schaar, A. K., & Ziefle, M. (2011, May). Smart clothing: Perceived benefits vs. perceived fears. In *2011 5th international conference on pervasive computing technologies for healthcare (PervasiveHealth) and workshops, 23–26 May 2011* (pp. 601–608). Institute of Electrical and Electronics Engineers (IEEE). Dublin, Ireland.

Slaug, B., Granbom, M., & Iwarsson, S. (2020). An aging population and an aging housing stock–housing accessibility problems in typical Swedish dwellings. *Journal of Aging and Environment, 34*(2), 156–174.

Smith, K. J., & Smith, C. (2019). Typologies of loneliness, living alone and social isolation, and their associations with physical and mental health. *Ageing & Society, 39*(8), 1709–1730.

Song, Y., & van der Cammen, T. J. (2019). Electronic assistive technology for community-dwelling solo-living older adults: A systematic review. *Maturitas, 125*, 50–56.

Syed, L., Jabeen, S., Manimala, S., & Alsaeedi, A. (2019). Smart healthcare framework for ambient assisted living using IoMT and big data analytics techniques. *Future Generation Computer Systems, 101*, 136–151.

University of Cambridge. (2022). Inclusive design toolkit, reach and dexterity. Retrieved June 30, 2022, from http://www.inclusivedesigntoolkit.com/UCdex/dex.html

Wagner, F., Basran, J., & Dal Bello-Haas, V. (2012). A review of monitoring technology for use with older adults. *Journal of Geriatric Physical Therapy, 35*(1), 28–34.

Wang, C., Kim, Y., Shin, H., & Min, S. D. (2019). Preliminary clinical application of textile insole sensor for hemiparetic gait pattern analysis. *Sensors, 19*(18), 3950, 1–20.

Whitley, M. (2021). 7 best innovative products for the elderly. Retrieved July 8, 2022, from https://www.aplaceformom.com/caregiver-resources/articles/cutting-edge-products-for-seniors

WHO. (2021). Ageing and health, World Health Organization. Retrieved June 24, 2022, from https://www.who.int/news-room/fact-sheets/detail/ageing-and-health#:~:text=Between%202015%20and%202050%2C%20the,%2D%20and%20middle%2Dincome%20countries

Wilson, J., Heinsch, M., Betts, D., Booth, D., & Kay-Lambkin, F. (2021). Barriers and facilitators to the use of e-health by older adults: A scoping review. *BMC Public Health, 21*(1), 1–12.

Yang, K., Isaia, B., Brown, L. J., & Beeby, S. (2019). E-textiles for healthy ageing. *Sensors, 19*(20), 4463, 1–21.

You, K. S., & Lee, H. (2006). The physical, mental, and emotional health of older people who are living alone or with relatives. *Archives of Psychiatric Nursing, 20*(4), 193–201.

Ziefle, M., Brauner, P., & Heek, J. V. (2016). Intentions to use smart textiles in AAL home environments: comparing younger and older adults. In *International conference on human aspects of IT for the aged population* (pp. 266–276). Cham: Springer.

Shan Wang is a Lecturer in Design Management at the Winchester School of Art, University of Southampton. She was awarded a scholarship from the University of Southampton and received her Ph.D. degree in 2020. Her research has concentrated on inclusive design for the ageing population, such as home environment, healthcare products, and services. She is also interested in UX experience, product and service development, branding design, and communication design.

Kai Yang received her Ph.D. degree from the University of Leeds, Leeds, U.K., in 2009. She is an Associate Professor at the Winchester School of Art, University of Southampton. She has over ten years of experience in e-textiles. Her work primarily focused on e-textile materials, manufacturing, and application development, such as healthcare and wearable technologies. She was awarded an EPSRC Innovation Fellowship in 2018. She has been PI on £3.5 M e-textile healthcare projects. She is also the Co-Founder of Smart Fabric Inks and the Founder of Etexsense.

Yuanyuan Yin is an Associate Professor at the Winchester School of Art, University of Southampton. Her research has been concentrated on promoting business performance through developing design and brand strategies, understanding customers and users, supporting design collaboration, and improving innovation in product design. In recent years, she focused on research in inclusive service design for the ageing population. She has received more than £1.3 M grants income from ESRC, the British Council, Confucius Institute Headquarters, and the University of Southampton.

Co-designing a Dementia Village: Transforming Dementia Care Through Service Design

Maria Taivalsaari Røhnebæk, Marit Engen, and Ane Bast

ABSTRACT

Dementia villages have gained attention as a promising new way of providing dementia care. The construction of dementia villages involves efforts to create more stimulating, healing and safe environments, and focuses on creating a homely atmosphere rather than one that is institutional and clinical. The concept originates from the Netherlands and is currently exported to various countries, which involves translations and adaptions when the concept is being implemented in diverse, new contexts. This chapter explores the role of service design in such translation processes, based on a study of creating a dementia village in a Norwegian municipality.

1 Introduction

With an ageing population comes public health challenges that are related to the increasing prevalence of dementia. This has various kinds of costs for individuals, families, communities and society at large, and addressing ways to tackle the increasing pressure on formal and informal dementia care is a top public health priority (WHO, 2017, pp. 10–12). There is a need for innovative solutions that

M. T. Røhnebæk (✉) · M. Engen · A. Bast
Inland Norway University of Applied Sciences, P.O. Box 400, 2418 Elverum, Norway
e-mail: maria.rohnebak@inn.no

M. Engen
e-mail: marit.engen@inn.no

A. Bast
e-mail: ane.bast@inn.no

can enhance the quality of dementia care while also ensuring cost efficiency and equal access to care services. This requires experimentation with new forms of treatments, technologies, physical surroundings, organisational structures and care philosophies.

Such experimentations take place, among others, in the context of dementia villages (Chrysikou et al., 2018, n.d.; Haeusermann, 2018, n.d.). Dementia villages can be described as hybrid living environments for persons with dementia diagnoses. The village concept mixes elements from a traditional home, created as townhouses in a small-scale community context, with elements from healthcare institutions. It can also be seen as mixing elements from health care with hospitality services and creating so-called 'hospitality healthscapes' (Suess & Mody, 2017, pp. 59–60).

The architectural and physical environment is just one element of the dementia village concept. The creation of such villages also implies the introduction of a new care philosophy, resonating with the principles of individualised and person-centred care (Chrysikou et al., 2018, n.d.). This implies changes in caring practices and managerial systems and structures, organisational culture, professional hierarchies and more.

The basic idea of dementia villages is to develop care services and surroundings that enable residents to continue living their life as before, but in a safe environment. The idea stems from the Hogeweyk in the Netherlands, which is presented as the first and 'original' dementia village. Its inception is said to spring out of a question among management in the previous Hogeweyk nursing home: 'Suppose we ourselves, or one of our loved ones, had to live here. How would we like to have it?' (Enninga, 2018, p. 142). A central answer was that the services should be more coordinated around living than care, and this formed the development of the new care philosophy that underpins the dementia village (Enninga, 2018, p. 142).

In this chapter, we explore how this new dementia care concept 'travels' to a new context: a Norwegian municipality. We suggest that the concept cannot be easily adopted; the 'travelling' involves translations and adaptations that can be analysed and understood through the lens of translation theory (Røvik, 2016, n.d.; Wæraas & Nielsen, 2016, n.d.). In our case, the project team uses service design methods to facilitate these translations, making the case a fruitful site for studying how service design may facilitate healthcare transformations (Koskela-Huotari et al., 2021, n.d.; Patricio et al., 2020, n.d.; Vink et al., 2019, n.d.).

The chapter is further structured as follows. We first account for the study's theoretical framework, the methodological approach and the data. We subsequently present findings from the case study, and we finally discuss how the case brings forward new insights into the connections between service design and healthcare transformations.

2 Theoretical Framework: Translation Theory

Translation theory initially springs from science and technology studies (STS), and the work of Callon (1984, n.d.) and Latour (1984, n.d.) on actor-network theory (ANT), and was later introduced to organisational studies (Czarniawska & Joerges, 1996, n.d.; Demers, 2007, n.d.).

Within organisational studies, translation theory is particularly associated with a research tradition labelled Scandinavian neo-institutionalism (SNIT) (Lundberg & Sataøen, 2019, n.d.; Wæraas & Nielsen, 2016, n.d.). The SNIT research tradition has theorised how broad reform ideas manifest and shape organisational practices in different policy and organisational contexts. The translation concept has been central for analysing the modification, editing and cultivation taking place when organisational concepts travel across contexts (Czarniawska & Joerges, 1996, n.d.; Sahlin-Andersson, 1996, n.d.).

Within this tradition, Røvik (2016, n.d.) argues that organisational translations entail processes of 'decontextualisation' and 'contextualisation'. Decontextualisation is the first critical phase of a translation and involves processes in which organisational practices are transformed into abstract representations (such as texts, images and models). These abstractions reduce the complexity of the actual practices, and the tacit knowledge embedded in the practices is sought to be made explicit. Thus, the practices are made into a 'concept', existing as abstract representations, which can be taken up and implemented in new organisational contexts. This implementation is, according to Røvik (2016, n.d.), the second critical stage of the translation process and is labelled contextualisation. Contextualising involves adapting a new concept to the recipient context. The level of complexity involved in the contextualisation processes is linked to the compatibility between new and existing practices and the degree of differences between the source and the recipient organisation. Moreover, Røvik (2016, pp. 296–298) argues that there are different 'rules' and 'modes' of translation. He differs between three translation modes: a reproducing mode (copy/replication), a modifying mode (additions and omissions) and a radical mode (alteration). These are analytical categories that can be used to analyse, contrast and compare different patterns of translations. We draw on this as a backdrop for our analysis.

While the SNIT research tradition has been influential in theorising the notion of translations in and across organisations, it tends to fall short in providing insights into how such translation processes actually unfold (Lundberg & Sataøen, 2019, p. 42). This requires empirical studies of everyday life in organisations, making ethnographic studies a suitable methodological approach. This resonates with an emerging research stream on institutional ethnography (Lundberg & Sataøen, 2019, n.d.), and reconnects translation theory in organisational studies with actor-network theory (ANT) (Wæraas & Nielsen, 2016, n.d.). Actor-network theory is anchored in ethnography (see, for instance, Latour, 2005, n.d.), and focuses not only on how translations involve power struggles and the building of alliances, but also sensemaking and interpretation of meaning (Cooren, 2001, n.d.; Czarniawska, 1997, n.d.; Czarniawska & Joerges, 1996, n.d.; Li, 2014, n.d.).

We draw on different aspects of translation theory in our study of how the dementia village concept travels from the Hogeweyk in the Netherlands to a Norwegian municipality. First, when analysing the process's planning and design stages, we find concepts and insights from translation theory within the SNIT tradition helpful. Specifically, we study the first stages of the contextualisation process in which the idea, or the dementia village concept, is adapted to the local context. Second, we take a preliminary look into how these adaptations are enacted through daily care practices when the village opens. Through participant observations in two different townhouses (four different wards), we study the translations taking place in the village's daily practices, resonating with translation research focusing on sensemaking and interpretations through practices.

3 Methodology

The Norwegian dementia village has a gross area of 18.000 m^2, with accommodations for 136 residents divided into 17 shared apartments and a single unit for 22 residents. In addition to the residential units, the village includes a grocery store; restaurant; bar; services, such as hairdresser, pedicure and gym; and spaces for activities and cultural meeting places, all of which surround the village's open square.

Translating the original Hogeweyk concept into the first Norwegian dementia village entails a set of interrelated and overlapping processes. When our research started, the formal decisions regarding architecture and physical surroundings were already set. Our study thus covers two main phases of translating and designing the village. The first phase addresses the planning and development of the new care concept and services, referred to as 'life in the village'. These events took place during 2018–2020, and service design methods were applied during this development process. The second phase concerns the processes of transforming these designed ideas into new service practices, occurring in the village's daily operations. This started in 2021 and should be considered as ongoing processes (due to the outbreak of the COVID-19 pandemic, all design activities were stopped in March 2020. The village opened and was operative from November 21, 2020, but due to the pandemic, it was operating as a temporary care facility. The new care concept was first introduced during the fall of 2021). These two phases of translation, although coupled, are presented separately when we portray the structure of our data collection in the next section.

3.1 Data Collection

The study is based on an ethnographic approach, but combines different strategies for data collection. Ethnography is largely associated with participant observation, but acknowledges that contemporary ethnographic fieldworks, especially in organisations, largely involve participant listening (Forsey, 2010, n.d.). Participant listening takes place through observations of formal and informal meetings and engagement in informal conversations. We have additionally conducted more formal and semi-structured interviews with key informants, and treat project documents as a central part of the data. Below is a brief description of the different forms of data collection.

The data from the first phase are based on the participation of around 38 formal and informal meetings, in which at least one researcher was present. Central observations from meetings were recorded with notes and subsequently shared with the research team (consisting of the three researchers authoring this chapter). Observation data are also based on participation in various design activities: (1) a half-day ideation workshop with 38 participants, (2) a half-day workshop on homeliness (with 22 participants), (3) an observation (by four researchers) of a 'design sprint' lasting for five full days and involving 20 participants working in four different groups and (4) an observation of 'staged' daily activities (grocery shopping). Finally, observations also involve a field visit to the 'original' dementia village in Hogeweyk (two researchers), together with the employees from the municipality and the project team. Furthermore, a total of 23 semi-structured interviews were conducted with different groups of informants, such as political and administrative leaders in the municipality, the project team, participants in the design sprint and healthcare professionals responsible for interviewing people with dementia. Finally, documents like minutes and summaries from the early insight work the project team conducted, the project teams' reflection notes and the political and administrative steering documents are included. These documents provide insights into the project's background and organisational and political contexts.

The second phase of translation focuses, as mentioned, on how the designed care concept and services are performed through daily care practices. These are ongoing processes, and our data is based on the first five months of operating the village (without COVID-19 restrictions) from January 2022. So far, observations of daily life in the village have been carried out in four different wards (10 days). The data also consist of observations conducted during the fall of 2021, of on-boarding and concept workshops for employees (4) and middle managers (5). These workshops focused on introducing the dementia village's care concept and evoking reflections concerning its implementation in daily care practices. Observations also include participation in various internal meetings. All observations were carried out with between one and three researchers present. In addition, semi-structured interviews were conducted with middle managers (6) and the head manager of the village, as well as with administrative employees in the municipality (3). Documents, such as workshop presentations and real-life cases used for reflections, are also included in the data.

3.2   Analysis

There are numerous options for how case study data can be analysed, synthesised and presented (Yin, 2009). Since this chapter is set in longitudinal case research that is still ongoing, the purpose is to mainly give a bird's-eye view of the project with a focus on the first phase and the application of service design methods. Moreover, we introduce theoretical resources that are relevant for analysing the processes, and provide some empirical illustrations of the theories' applicability. We follow what can be termed a narrative strategy for the sensemaking of process data (Langley, 1999, pp. 695–697). This is often used as a preliminary step in research based on eclectic data sets, and works as an important device for organising and structuring the data. Our case narrative not only provides a foundation for analysis and further theorisation in subsequent research, but also offers valuable insights into the key issues involved in the travelling, translation and design of innovative concepts in health care.

4   Case Study: Creating Life in the Village Through Service Design

In this section, we illuminate the processes of translating the Hogeweyk dementia village into a Norwegian context. As introduced, the Hogeweyk is known as the first village-type accommodation for patients with dementia that attempted to transform a traditional nursing home by replacing the clinical and institutional atmosphere with a more homely environment. It is located in Weesp, the Netherlands, and opened in 2009. It is a small community that now consists of 27 houses with six to seven residents in each, providing care for a total of 169 residents. The village has streets, courtyards and squares, and offers a diversity of facilities, such as a theatre, supermarket, café and club rooms that organise different activities. The Hogeweyk's vision is 'Living as usual' and encapsulates the village's care philosophy of combining care, living and well-being, thereby enabling an active life with freedom within a safe environment (Be Advice, 2022, n.d.). This implies no locked doors within the village and the residents are free to walk around and use the facilities as they wish. The Hogeweyk also has a large number of volunteers that enable services to support living an active life.

The Hogeweyk concept is founded on seven pillars: (1) favourable surroundings, (2) life's pleasures and meaning of life, (3) health, (4) lifestyle, (5) formal and informal networks, (6) organisation and (7) social inclusion and emancipation. These pillars constitute what the Hogeweyk describes as 'quality of life'. The Hogeweyk village and its care concept have spurred inspiration for developing similar care facilities around the world, such as in Denmark (Peoples et al., 2020, n.d.) and Germany (Haeusermann, 2018, n.d.). Next, we turn to the translation of the concept in a Norwegian context.

4.1   An In-House Design Process

The initiative to develop a dementia village in the municipality came from a group of local politicians (across parties) after a field trip to Hogeweyk. The journey was conducted to search for new ideas regarding how to improve dementia care, and the politicians and other people that became involved in the project were greatly inspired by the Hogeweyk concept. Yet, there was also an agreement across the informants that the model had to somehow be adapted to the municipality's local conditions. Hence, returning to the theory of translation introduced above, the project followed an explicit 'modifying' translation mode from the start (Røvik, 2016, n.d.). This implies that the involved actors made additions and omissions to the original concept. The following quote from one of the project team members interviewed in the first phase illustrates how this modifying mode was pursued as an explicit strategy: 'Pulling one concept from another place is scary. We need to take the philosophy but make it our own.'

The interviews and informal discussion captured throughout observations all point to a common understanding of how 'context matters', along with the fact that both societal aspects and geographical location leave imprints to consider in the development process. Most informants stated that they had to create their localised version of the original concept, but they had somewhat different perceptions of how to adapt the model and to what degree. Therefore, the question of how the model should be translated and which type of adjustments are to be made were a subject for discussion.

A service design approach was used to facilitate these translations with the aim of ensuring the involvement and engagement of various stakeholders in the community. Relevant stakeholders were local citizens, potential residents, family caretakers, public service managers, healthcare professionals, politicians, local businesses and special interest organisations. Hence, the translation process was based on co-creation principles underpinning service design methods (Schneider et al., 2010, pp. 38–39; Stickdorn et al., 2018, pp. 24–27).

The service design processes were mainly led by two members of the innovation and development unit in the municipality. They were not formally trained as service designers, but had extensive experience with process work and facilitating creative and innovative processes in different organisational contexts. They took service design courses and continuously experimented with elements from the service design toolbox. For the dementia village project, they also procured some support from a professional design firm, but this was only used for consultations and advice on how to organise the processes, which tools to use, how to adapt them, etc. As such, the service design process was mainly conducted in-house, based on available competencies in the municipality. Moreover, the design team not only made use of established service design methods, but they also adapted existing tools to the complexity of the dementia care context. Furthermore, the design process did not follow a fixed and predefined plan. The process evolved more organically, and the project team chose applicable methods and next steps based on considerations of the knowledge they acquired during the process and what they needed to know more about in order to proceed. The process was, in this way, adaptive·and based on gradually emerging insights.

By drawing on service design, the project team was also dedicated to taking a user-centred approach to the creation of 'life in the village', implying that the needs and outlooks of potential residents should guide the translation process. As expressed by a member of the project team, 'Then we know that we have a solid foundation [for the village]'. Due to the impediments related to involving people with cognitive impairments (Bast et al., 2021, n.d.; Sangiorgi et al., 2019, n.d.), the project team had to find creative ways to involve the users' voices in the design activities. They started off by conducting 'service safaris', i.e. visiting existing nursing homes to observe and gain insights into the current state of affairs in these facilities. They also carried out interviews with people suffering from dementia and their family caretakers, in addition to conducting group interviews with healthcare professionals. These data were analysed and eventually condensed into seven 'user insights', summarising the potential end users' wishes for the new care concept:

1. To have a nice home to live in.
2. To be part of the community, but not with too many people, with the option of peacefulness.
3. To be met with respect and dignity, feel well kept and to decide by themselves.
4. To get food in a safe and nice environment.
5. To have activities for the body and soul throughout the whole year, outdoors and inside, for everyone.
6. To be safe, especially at night.
7. To be useful in everyday life and keep the old life as much as possible.

These seven insights came to symbolise the user-centrism underpinning the entire design process. One of the in-house designers explained: 'What I have been very focused on is to construct the insights. They will be the foundation of the whole development. Everything else will just be as a supplement; we must base our further work on this.'

The seven insights did, indeed, form a central pivot point for the processes. As we will show, they were in various ways embedded in different design events that the project team arranged, as a constant reminder to everyone involved as to who they were designing for and what was important to them.

4.2   Main Design Events

Three main design events were conducted during the planning phase. Details of each event are presented next.

4.2.1   Ideation Workshop

The first workshop was conducted as an ideation workshop with different participants representing diverse sets of interests, like family caretakers, politicians, healthcare employees and representatives from special interest groups (such as senior centres and volunteers). The workshop's purpose was to involve a broad group of citizens within the municipality and collect their ideas and insights. The seven insights presented above were printed on posters and handouts, and the participants were encouraged to regularly consult the insights when working on ideas for life in the village. The workshop resulted in 255 ideas that the project development team subsequently processed and sorted into four priority areas:

1. 'Welcome'—the transition from home or nursing homes to the dementia village for both users and next of kin.
2. 'An army marches on its stomach'—food and dining experiences.
3. 'Volunteers'—volunteers as a stable resource for the village.
4. 'Activities for body and soul, all year in and out, for everyone'—organising activities.

4.2.2   Design Sprints

These four areas were used as input for the second design event: a sprint workshop that ran for 5 days over a three-week period with 20 participants. The participants were people with different competencies, experiences and interests, like employees from elderly/dementia care facilities, family caretakers, volunteers from the municipality, employees from the municipality administration (e.g. within procurement and digitalisation) and citizens with work experience outside of health care (e.g. hotel and business park). Four working groups were established, and each was assigned to one of the four priority areas (as listed above). The sprint was a version of the Google-Sprint (Knapp et al., 2016), yet it was adapted to fit the context, both regarding the organisation of tasks and how it was structured in time. For instance, according to the original sprint model, sprints should last for five intensive days in a row, but the project team spread the five days over three weeks, thereby making it easier for participants to take part as it required them to be away from their regular work. The first three days aimed at creating ideas through iterative processes and finally defining one main concept, leaving days four and five for making a prototype and testing it. The relevance of the seven insights was also highlighted in this event. They were printed in the method instructions for the four sprint groups and were available on posters in the room. Again, the participants were advised to consult the insights when developing ideas within their respective focus areas.

The design sprint resulted in the presentation of four main ideas developed as prototypes and then tested with users. Or rather, the testing took the form of a kind of deliberation of proposed ideas through dialogues with users and user representatives. The prototypes were presented as small roleplays with card boxes and drawings used for illustrations and the creation of small displays (for instance, a 'homely' set table). This set the stage for invitations to discuss various ideas. Each of the groups proposed solutions that included several ideas and suggestions, and the project team drew on different elements from across the groups when considering which ideas to follow up. There were essentially two main inputs from the design sprint which the project team strived to implement.

First, the activity group proposed that the village should hire a 'Minister of Culture'. This was proposed as an important measure for ensuring that the new care concept maintained its ambition to create more meaningful everyday lives by ensuring access to cultural and social activities. This idea was followed up on by creating a new position, and the vacancy was announced prior to opening the village. Even though the 'Minister of Culture' was not accepted as the formal title within the municipal system, it was used as the informal title of the person holding this position. The door sign even reads 'Minister of Culture', and the role is performed in line with the ideas proposed in the design sprint.

Second, all groups were somehow concerned with ideas connected to the use of new digital technology. The groups highlighted the potential for improving information flows and infrastructure for communication internally and externally through new digital tools. The groups' different ideas were brought together, and the IT department was invited to formulate a proposal for an integrative digital tool that could serve various purposes. For instance, it was envisioned that the system could enable registration and communication with volunteers, registration of information about residents and displaying of their 'profiles' in terms of interests, background and needs, which would also provide valuable information for the village employees. The IT department started the process of procuring a customised and integrative system, but this has not yet been fully developed and implemented. The development process has encountered several hindrances, among others, related to information security and privacy issues. This is still a work in progress, and the system is expected to be implemented in a more modified version compared to what was first envisioned.

4.2.3   Homeliness Workshops

The third design event took place in parallel to the ideation workshop and design sprint, and focused on sensemaking processes related to the idea of 'homeliness' in the context of the village. This was organised as four workshops with different groups of participants, such as healthcare employees, administrative staff, family carers and volunteer representatives (the number of participants in each workshop varied from 11 to 32). These workshops were important for the overall development of the new services because, as introduced, the creation of a 'homely' atmosphere rather than an institutional one lies at the core of the dementia village concept. However, there is no simple answer as to what constitutes the feeling of a home, and 'homeliness' may mean different things to different people.

In the Hogeweyk, this has been dealt with through the development and implementation of different 'lifestyles'. The notion of lifestyles is based on the idea that a population can be categorised into different groups adhering to similar social values that connect to certain lifestyles. Originally, the Hogeweyk was organised around seven different lifestyles reflected in the interior and furnishings of the village houses (Enninga, 2018, pp. 144–145). Even though the titles and numbers of lifestyles have been changing, the Hogeweyk village concept is still organised around different lifestyles. The webpage explaining the concept states, 'In the Hogeweyk you will find houses where people live together based on similar lifestyles' (Hogeweyk, 2022). Whether and how to adapt the notion of 'lifestyles' to the new dementia village in Norway was much debated and remained a matter of controversy in the design process. It was the area in which the translation elements of the design processes were most evident. One of the project team members explained for instance:

> 'We should of course take with us a lot from there [Hogeweyk] but we must adapt it. Especially these things with the lifestyles that we are dealing with a lot. I am very sceptical to that […] this segmentation; or I am perhaps more puzzled than sceptical. Is this how we want it? [...] First of all; I'm thinking are we all that different? […] There may be different units, and they may look differently, but does it need to be based on 'lifestyles'? '[quote from interview with member of the project team in the first phase].

Others asserted that the notion of lifestyle, in some sense, was vital to the project, and although it could be problematic, it also represented a path worth exploring:

> 'We should dare to look at this [lifestyles] in Norway as well, or in our municipality in this case. I think a key to success is whether we manage to do that [employ the lifestyles principles]. [...] This will evoke various problems to be considered, for instance related to the administration of admission of residents like I discussed. Is it feasible? How can we do it? These are things we need to work on. And I'm thinking that when I say the word homeliness, then people think about the colour of the wallpaper and the interiors, but it's more about the whole lifestyle' [quote from interview with member of the project team in the first phase).

As the quotes reveal, the issues of homeliness and lifestyles were a matter of continuous discussions and negotiations. They were also ingrained elements of the other design events because they connect processes such as welcoming, activities and dining. However, the homeliness workshops zoomed specifically in on the applicability of the notion of lifestyles for the village's organisation. More specifically, these workshops (4) explored which lifestyle categories could be relevant in the municipality, and what they could 'look like' in terms of interiors and the creation of different senses of homeliness.

The homeliness workshops were based on data from a market research company that the municipality hired to conduct a classification analysis of the population. This was an element in the exploration of the possibilities for developing a local version of the lifestyle concept. The company's method differentiates populations into a set of broad consumer categories and more comprehensive and fine-grained subcategories. These are meant to be 'building blocks' for developing targeted marketing strategies. When applied to the work with the dementia village, this method was used to gain an idea of what kinds of lifestyle categories could be relevant around which to organise the village. The company's analysis resulted in three main categories, and the homeliness workshops used different methods and strategies to interpret and make sense of these categories. They explored what this differentiation in lifestyle categories could imply in practical terms, conducted a small user journey mapping, created small narratives or personas related to the different lifestyle categories and tried to contemplate and visualise how the lifestyles denoted certain interior styles visualised through collages of pictures.

4.3   The Translated New Care Concept

In the end, what was the translated concept for the Norwegian dementia village? What was the role of the design methods applied to translate the concept to the new context? There are (at least) two ways of looking at this. First, the translated new care concept can be understood as the officially stated vision for the Norwegian dementia village (the concept in theory), and we may assess whether the various service design activities contributed to shaping this concept. Second, the translated new care concept can be understood as being manifest in the daily service practices of the new village (the concept in practice). As previously explained, these are ongoing processes that recently started, thus we have relatively limited data to fully answer the latter question, but we still aim to shed some light on both these questions in this final section.

4.3.1   The Translated Concept in Theory

After the different design events were completed, the project team sat down and attempted to draw together the essence from the insights, reflections and ideas that were produced through the design activities. How could this inform the overarching concept of the new village, and how would their concept connect to the original concept of the Hogeweyk? On the one hand, the project team members were concerned with how the seven user insights should form the foundation of their concept. On the other hand, they tried to relate their idea to the original Hogeweyk concept. As shown, this was based on seven pillars with 'quality of life' being an overarching theme. As one of the project team members stated, 'So, what are the relations between the seven pillars of Hogeweyk and our "insights"?'.

This formed a point of departure for the project team's explorations of their concept. Someone asked, for instance: 'Should we rewrite the insights into founding pillars?' Thus, in their discussions, the project team was going back and forth between their inspirational source from the Hogeweyk and the insights generated through their local design work. After several rounds of discussions, the team agreed that a flower could serve (at least temporarily) as a unifying metaphor and visualisation of the village's essence. The textual content for the flower was based on efforts to create even more condensed versions of the seven insights derived from the user interviews. The two simple words 'see me' were placed in the centre, and on five surrounding petals, it said 'a home', 'love for food', 'feeling safe', 'meaningful days' and 'unity and calmness'.

However, the discussions continued, and one of the team members eventually expressed concerns that their efforts to develop a formal concept for the village would just leave them with 'empty phrases'. What they needed, she argued, was 'an ideology that can guide how we will work'. Other team members followed up on this, suggesting that perhaps, 'We should, in fact, develop these pillars together with the employees …' Yet another continued, 'Perhaps we could make it a bit unfinished, and then they (the staff) can take part in specifying it further and in this way getting it (the concept) under their skin?' This also seems to be what the project team decided on in the end. When presenting the concept, for instance, in introductory training with recruited employees, they highlighted the seven insights from the user interviews as being the village's defining traits. Moreover, they constructed cases that could evoke reflections on how the idea of creating a home could be interpreted and enacted in practice. Thus, the project team did not promote a fixed and clearly stated concept for the village, but highlighted some key issues that could guide the new services. They kept the concept malleable and to be further shaped through the activities and daily practices in the village.

4.3.2   The Translated Concept in Practice

As we have shown, a certain foundation was set when the village opened for residents and staff. As the village opened and we could observe everyday life, we found that new practices emerged as the result of negotiations and compromises between different expectations of what constituted 'good care'. On the one hand, the village associates good care with a kind of organic and informal form of care that we find in a home or in a closely-knit community. This is juxtaposed with the bureaucratically regulated and institutionalised forms of care characterising traditional nursing homes in which the clinical and medical aspects of care tend to emphasise. The new care practices seem to emerge as compromises between these two juxtapositions. In the following, we illustrate how these compromises manifest in the village's everyday life.

The village's planning and design focused on creating a homely atmosphere for the residents, with spaces and structures for activation and socialisation. A central part of the design process was to flipside the idea that nursing homes constitute workplaces for providing professional care. Instead, the involved actors were encouraged to think of the village as primarily being a home for the residents where the healthcare staff are visitors. This is reflected in the architecture and design of the entire village. There are, for instance, no visible spaces or rooms for employees to take breaks or to do administrative or back-office work in the townhouses. However, while the staff are visitors in the sense that they are only temporarily present in the village, they are still there as employees and not guests. Moreover, when visiting, they are obliged to perform professional work in line with a series of demands and regulations in order to ensure quality and safety in various respects. These needs for providing adequate care were somewhat downplayed in the design activities of the planning phase, leading to some dilemmas surfacing once the village opened. For instance, in some wards, the staff found that they needed access to a separate and quiet space for doing administrative work such as documentation and reporting between shifts. A small extra sitting room, available in all wards, was adapted as a type of staff room with a small office corner. In this way, the staff could withdraw and do administrative work more efficiently, and they could do oral reporting between shifts while ensuring confidentiality. The solution can be seen as a compromise between the village's new thinking and the conventional demands of a healthcare institution.

Another kind of compromise can be found in the decisions regarding the healthcare employees' uniforms. During the design phase, it was extensively discussed whether or not the staff should wear traditional white uniforms. Some argued that the white uniforms would break with the aim to create a homely and non-institutional atmosphere, while others found that it was important to be able to easily identify the professional healthcare staff who could provide help and support when needed. In the end, they ended up with grey uniforms with a somewhat loose and informal style. In this way, they ensured that the professionals could be identified, but they were somewhat less visible than if they had been wearing white clothing. The decision to use grey uniforms also signalled a certain break with traditional healthcare institutions. The discussions regarding the uniforms bring attention to the multifaceted perceptions of what constitutes safety and good care. To some, a clinical and institutional atmosphere can be alienating and distant from what is associated as a safe and cosy home environment. To others, a clinical and institutional atmosphere can be associated with hygiene, structure and predictability, evoking a different sense of safety than the one associated with a home.

As previously shown, part of the concept of 'homeliness' in the Hogeweyk was solved through the notion of lifestyles, where people's similar interests and backgrounds were reflected in their living environments. In the Norwegian municipality, the idea of lifestyles was met with a certain resistance. This was partly due to practical and bureaucratic hindrances, but also because it was perceived as conflicting with ideas of egalitarianism, equality and 'sameness' that tend to be highlighted as dominant Norwegian societal values (see, for instance, Gullestad, 1992, n.d.). The municipality still explored the potential applicability of the lifestyle concept but struggled to find a way of operationalising it. It was difficult to distinguish between the three identified categories, and neither did they manage to implement administrative procedures for assessing residents in terms of 'lifestyle' categories when assigning appropriate groups to different houses.

In terms of physical space, the idea of lifestyles was also vaguely reflected in the different living units. All units have a similar basic style, but are decorated with different colours and interiors. This gives a more homely atmosphere compared to traditional institutions which tend to be more standardised. At the same time, the living units have a generic style and do not denote a clear 'lifestyle'. This allows for flexibility when it comes to assigning residents to the different units, and the somewhat controversial idea of group belonging based on the background is thus downplayed. Our preliminary observations and informal interviews with middle managers and employees in the village also point to the fact that the progression of the residents' diagnoses, and their levels of functioning both in terms of cognitive and physical impairments seem more important to consider than background and interests when assigning residents to the different houses.

As shown, the service practices in the dementia village are still unfolding, but the enacted concept may, at the present time, be seen as a hybrid between a health-care institution and a home, or a set of homes. It is also emerging as a compromise between the original model from the Netherlands and the traditional local nursing homes. Adaptations and compromises are also found when the dementia village concept has been introduced in other national contexts. During the establishment of the first dementia village in Germany, aspects of the concept were seen to conflict with local prerequisites (Haeusermann, 2018, p.154). Particularly, the notion of lifestyles was rejected altogether because it was seen as incompatible with societal values and principles in the national healthcare system. This does not imply that the shift towards new forms of care is rejected, but that the new care concepts need to be adapted to local conditions to be accepted.

5   Conclusion

This chapter accentuates the role of service design in providing space and methods for interpretations, sensemaking and reflexive practices in healthcare innovation and transformations. This aspect of service design, as a kind of facilitator for reflexivity and sensemaking, has been elaborated upon in the literature (see, for instance, Patrício et al., 2019, n.d.; Vink & Koskela-Huotari, 2021, n.d.). However, our research highlights the interlinkages between translation theory and service design as sensemaking. Translation theory offers tools to analyse the interpretations involved when ideas and innovations are disseminating and travelling across organisational contexts. These theoretical interlinkages have been scarcely addressed, and there is potential to further explore their interconnections. Organisational innovations and transformations, perhaps especially within health care, tend to come about when solutions scale or spread across organisations. This takes place through the active involvement of situated actors that contextualise new ideas through interpretations and sensemaking.

This dementia village example highlights the importance of translation processes that adapt innovations to the local context, reducing chances that innovation efforts are met with resistance and possibly destructive controversies. Our study indicates that service design can aid such translation processes by supporting the inclusion of various voices and perspectives in the sensemaking of new concepts. The dementia village example also indicates that making space for translations through sensemaking may be particularly important in contexts characterised by hybridity in which actors need to negotiate between conflicting demands and different sets of values.

References

Bast, A., Røhnebæk, M. T., & Engen, M. (2021). Co-creating dementia care: Manoeuvring fractured reflexivity in service design. *Journal of Service Theory and Practice, 31*(5), 665–690. https://doi.org/10.1108/JSTP-11-2020-0251

Be Advice. (2022). Living as usual for people with severe dementia. Retrieved July 13, 2022, from https://www.bethecareconcept.com/en/hogeweyk-dementia-village-hogeweyk-netherlands/.

Callon, M. (1984). Some elements of a sociology of translation: Domestication of the scallops and the fishermen of St Brieuc Bay. *The Sociological Review, 32*(1_suppl), 196–233. https://doi.org/10.1111/j.1467-954X.1984.tb00113.x.

Chrysikou, E., Tziraki, C., & Buhalis, D. (2018). Architectural hybrids for living across the lifespan: Lessons from dementia. *The Service Industries Journal, 38*(1–2), 4–26. https://doi.org/10.1080/02642069.2017.1365138

Cooren, F. (2001). Translation and articulation in the organization of coalitions: the Great Whale River case. *Communication Theory, 11*(2), 178–200. https://doi.org/10.1111/j.1468-2885.2001.tb00238.x.

Czarniawska, B. (1997). *A narrative approach to organization studies* (Vol. 43). Thousand Oaks, CA: Sage Publications.

Czarniawska, B., & Joerges, B. (1996). Travels of ideas. In B. Czarniawska & G. Sevón (Eds.), *Translating organizational change* (pp. 13–48). Berlin, New York: de Gruyter Studies in Organization.

Enninga, T. (2018). Armchair travelling the innovation journey: Building a narrative repertoire of the experiences of innovation project leaders. Ph.D. dissertation. Delft: Delft University of Technology.

Forsey, M. G. (2010). Ethnography as participant listening. *Ethnography, 11*(4), 558–572. https://doi.org/10.1177/1466138110372587.

Gullestad, M. (1992). The art of social relations: Essays on culture, social action and everyday life in modern Norway. Oslo: Scandinavian University Press.

Haeusermann. (2018). The dementia village: Between community and society. In F. Krause & J. Boldt (Eds.), Care *in healthcare: Reflections on theory and practice* (pp. 135–167). Cham (CH): Palgrave Macmillan. https://doi.org/10.1007/978-3-319-61291-1_8.

Hogeweyk. (2022). he Hogeweyk®-normal life for people living with severe dementia, Retrieved June 27, 2022, from https://hogeweyk.dementiavillage.com/#NaN.

Knapp, J., Zeratsky, J., & Kowitz, B. (2016). *Sprint: How to solve big problems and test new ideas in just five days.* London: Bantam Press.

Koskela-Huotari, K., Patrício, L., Zhang, J., Karpen, I. O., Sangiorgi, D., Anderson, L., & Bogicevic, V. (2021). Service system transformation through service design: Linking analytical dimensions and service design approaches. *Journal of Business Research, 136*(n.d.), 343–355. https://doi.org/10.1016/j.jbusres.2021.07.034.

Langley, A. (1999). Strategies for theorizing from process data. *The Academy of Management Review, 24*(4), 691–710. https://doi.org/10.2307/259349

Latour, B. (1984). The powers of association. *The Sociological Review, 32*(1_suppl), 264–280. https://doi.org/10.1111/j.1467-954X.1984.tb00115.x.

Latour, B. (2005). *Reassembling the social: An introduction to actor-network-theory.* Oxford: Oxford University Press.

Li, Z. (2014). Narrative rhetorics in scenario work: Sensemaking and translation. *Journal of Futures Studies, 18*(3), 77–94.

Lundberg, K. G., & Sataøen, H. L. (2019). *From translation of ideas to translocal relations: Shifting heuristics from Scandinavian Neo-Institutional Theory to institutional ethnography.* Institutional Ethnography in the Nordic Region (1st ed., pp. 39–50). London: Routledge.

Patrício, L., Grenha Teixeira, J., & Vink, J. (2019). A service design approach to healthcare innovation: From decision-making to sense-making and institutional change. *AMS Review, 9*(1), 115–120. https://doi.org/10.1007/s13162-019-00138-8.

Patricio, L., Sangiorgi, D., Mahr, D., Čaić, M., Kalantari, S., & Sundar, S. (2020). Leveraging service design for healthcare transformation: Toward people-centred, integrated, and technology-enabled healthcare systems. *Journal of Service Management, 31*(5), 889–909. https://doi.org/10.1108/JOSM-11-2019-0332.

Peoples, H., Pedersen, L. F., & Moestrup, L. (2020). Creating a meaningful everyday life: Perceptions of relatives of people with dementia and healthcare professionals in the context of a Danish dementia village. *Dementia, 19*(7), 2314–2331. https://doi.org/10.1177/1471301218820480

Røvik, K. A. (2016). Knowledge transfer as translation: Review and elements of an instrumental theory. *International Journal of Management Reviews, 18*(3), 290–310. https://doi.org/10.1111/ijmr.12097.

Sahlin-Andersson, K. (1996). Imitating by editing success. The construction of organizational fields and identities. In B. Czarniawska & G. Sevón (Eds.), *Translating organizational change* (pp. 69–92). Berlin, New York: de Gruyter Studies in Organization.

Sangiorgi, D., Farr, M., McAllister, S., Mulvale, G., Sneyd, M., Vink, J. E., & Warwick, L. (2019). Designing in highly contentious areas: Perspectives on a way forward for mental healthcare transformation. *The Design Journal, 22*(Suppl. 1), 309–330. https://doi.org/10.1080/14606925.2019.1595422.

Schneider, J., Stickdorn, M., Bisset, F., Andrews, K., & Lawrence, A. (2010). *This is service design thinking: Basics, tools, cases.* Amsterdam: BIS Publishers.

Stickdorn, M., Hormess, M. E., Lawrence, A., & Schneider, J. (2018). *This is service design doing: Applying service design thinking in the real world.* Sebastopol: O'Reilly Media, Incorporated.

Suess, C., & Mody, M. (2017). Hospitality healthscapes: A conjoint analysis approach to understanding patient responses to hotel-like hospital rooms. *International Journal of Hospitality Management, 61*(n.d.), 59–72. https://doi.org/10.1016/j.ijhm.2016.11.004.

Vink, J., Joly, M., Wetter-Edman, K., Tronvoll, B., & Edvardsson, B. (2019). Changing the rules of the game in healthcare through service design. In M. A. Pfannstiel, & C. Rasche (Eds.), *Service design and service thinking in healthcare and hospital management; theory, concepts, practice* (pp. 19–37). Cham: Springer Publishing. https://doi.org/10.1007/978-3-030-00749-2_2.

Vink, J., & Koskela-Huotari, K. (2021). Building reflexivity using service design methods. *Journal of Service Research, 25*(3), 371–389. https://doi.org/10.1177/10946705211035004

WHO. (2017). Global action plan on the public health response to dementia 2017–2025. Retrieved July 13, 2022, from https://www.who.int/publications/i/item/global-action-plan-on-the-public-health-response-to-dementia-2017---2025.

Wæraas, A., & Nielsen, J. A. (2016). Translation theory 'translated': Three perspectives on translation in organizational research. *International Journal of Management Reviews, 18*(3), 236–270. https://doi.org/10.1111/ijmr.12092.

Yin, R. K. (2009). *Case study research: design and methods* (4th ed., Vol. 5). Thousand Oaks, CA: Sage Publishing.

Maria Taivalsaari Røhnebæk is an Associate Professor at Inland School of Business and Social Sciences at the Inland Norway University of Applied Sciences. She holds a master's degree in Social Anthropology and a PhD in Technology, Innovation and Culture from the University of Oslo. Her research focuses on innovation, service design and digitalisation in public services, with emphasis on welfare, care and social services.

Marit Engen is an Associate Professor at Inland Norway University of Applied Sciences. Marit is working within the domains of service research, service innovation and employee-driven innovation. She is currently conducting empirical research on the opportunities and constraints of using service design in the development of services aimed at vulnerable groups. Her work has appeared in journals such as Public Management Review, Australian Journal of Public Adminis-tration, The Service Industries Journal, Journal of Service Theory and Practice, Journal of Service Management, Creativity and Innovation Management and EPA: Economy and Space.

Ane Bast is a PhD student at Inland School of Business and Social Sciences at the Inland Norway University of Applied Sciences (INN University). She holds a master's degree in innovation from INN University. Her research focuses on innovation, design and co-creation in public services.

Printed in the United States
by Baker & Taylor Publisher Services